KEN SCHULTZ'S

Fishing Encyclopedia

Worldwide Angling Guide

VOLUME 3

KEN SCHULTZ'S

Fishing Encyclopedia

Worldwide Angling Guide

Ken Schultz

IDG Books Worldwide, Inc.
An International Data Group Company
Foster City, CA • Chicago, IL • Indianapolis, IN • New York, NY • Southlake, TX

IDG Books Worldwide, Inc.
An International Data Group Company
919 E. Hillsdale Boulevard
Suite 400
Foster City, CA 94404

Copyright © 2000 by Ken Schultz

All rights reserved. No part of this book shall be reproduced, stored in a retrieval system, or transmitted by any means, electronic, mechanical, photocopying, recording, or otherwise, without written permission from the publisher. No patent liability is assumed with respect to the use of the information contained herein. Although every precaution has been taken in the preparation of this book, the publisher and author assume no responsibility for errors or omissions. Neither is any liability assumed for damages resulting from the use of the information contained herein.

Webster's New World is a registered trademark of Macmillan General Reference USA, Inc., a wholly owned subsidiary of IDG Books Worldwide, Inc.

The IDG Books Worldwide logo is a registered trademark under exclusive license to IDG Books Worldwide, Inc., from International Data Group, Inc.

For general information on books from IDG Books Worldwide's in the U.S., please call our Consumer Customer Service department at 800-762-2974. For reseller information, including discounts and premium sales, please call our Reseller Customer Service department at 800-434-3422.

For information on a multimedia version of this book, available from Tricom Intrtactive, Inc., please go to this Web site: intellipedia.com

To contact the author, please visit: www.kenshultz.com

Library of Congress Cataloging-in-Publication Data

This edition of *Ken Schultz's Fishing Encyclopedia,* which is published in 7 volumes, contains the entire contents of the work as previously published in a single volume: *Ken Schultz's Fishing Encyclopedia,* ISBN 9780028620572

This is Volume 3 of 7

Schultz, Ken, 1950–
Ken Shultz's fishing encyclopedia: worldwide angling guide/ Ken Schultz. — 1st ed.
p. cm.
ISBN 0-02-862057-7
Volume 3: ISBN 9781684427673 (hardcover) | ISBN 9781684427680 (paperback)

1. Fishing—Encyclopedias. 2. Fishes—Encyclopedias. I. Title.
SH411.S38 2000
799.1'03—dc21 99-033719
CIP

Manufactured in the United States of America

First Edition

Trademarks

All terms mentioned in this book that are known to be trademarks or service marks have been appropriately capitalized. IDG Books cannot attest to the accuracy of this information. Use of a term in this book should not be regarded as affecting the validity of any trademark or service mark.

Table of Contents

Introduction
vii

Acknowledgments
ix

Photo Credits
xix

Fishing Encyclopedia Entries

F
1

G
149

H
197

I
233

Appendix: Conversion Charts for Weights and Measures
275

Introduction

*"Ah, the gallant fisher's life! It is the best of any;
'Tis full of pleasure, void of strife, And 'tis beloved by many."*
—IZAAK WALTON

"All men are equal before fish."
—HERBERT HOOVER

WHILE PRODUCING THIS FISHING ENCYCLOPEDIA I SPOKE TO MANY HUNDREDS OF informed anglers. Nearly all of them thought the compilation of all things piscatorial was too overwhelming to contemplate because the angling universe is so enormous and diverse.

Certainly a modern fishing encyclopedia—if it truly provides a full field of knowledge—runs counter to the short and specialized tenets of today's journalism. Yet it is precisely because there is so much to the sport of fishing, plus an increasing profusion of specialized equipment and confusing terminology, that it was necessary to bring order and perspective to all of this in one definitive book.

Ken Schultz's Fishing Encyclopedia & Worldwide Angling Guide has been a long time in the making. I started thinking about it in 1991. Since work began in earnest in 1995, the project became even more expansive than expected, and indeed there were times when it was nearly overwhelming. As a result, the book (now a series of books) grew much bigger than originally planned, becoming 50 percent larger than any fishing encyclopedia that has heretofore been published.

As a result, however, this encyclopedia contains the equivalent of thirty standard-length books, meaning that there is ample space to devote to the species, equipment, techniques, locations, and ancillary matters that encompass the angling universe. Consider that nearly one-third of the encyclopedia series is comprised of the most comprehensive information on worldwide angling opportunities ever assembled. There is absolutely no place to find these details together; indeed, some elements of the *Worldwide Angling Guide* cannot be found anywhere else at all.

Likewise, the coverage of angling methods and equipment has never been addressed more comprehensively between the covers of any other book. In fact, *Ken Schultz's Fishing Encyclopedia* contains the most modern, illuminating, and extensive discourses on the basic elements of fishing tackle—baitcasting, big-game, conventional, flycasting, spinning, and spincasting—ever found in one place. Each of these entries undoubtedly contain more than all but the most scrupulous person will want to know.

Great lengths were also taken, however, to make sure that the less obvious subjects in the angling universe were included and reviewed in comprehensive fashion. For example, nowhere else is there a more extensive review of the principles, methods, and pros and cons of catch-and-release—perhaps the most important angling conservation development of the twentieth century.

Topics like fisheries management, angling-related travel, choosing guides and charter boats, and the care and preparation of fish for consumption, which are among many unglamorous subjects taken for granted elsewhere, receive complete explanation and review here. Likewise the otherwise oft-ignored subjects of ethics and etiquette—increasingly important issues as human pressures increase—are included.

Although there's an enormous amount of information in this series of books, every topic was approached with the intent to take nothing for granted and to present information in straightforward language. Angling is not like nuclear physics, and if it was half as complicated as some people try to make it, no one would enjoy it or have success. The extensive insertion of cross references is thus intended to direct you through a continuing stream of appropriate topics, so you can take any subject as far as you want to go. Some cross references appear within entry text next to topics that are more thoroughly reviewed elsewhere; many cross references appear at the end of entry text, either to direct you to the appropriate subject entry or to note related topics.

We've tried to make things easy to find and to place subjects where you're most likely to look for them, even if you're unsure of the proper terms or spelling. As an example, you'll find rainbow trout under the "T" entries (trout, rainbow) rather than under the "R" entries. Also, at the back of each book is a weights and measures conversion chart; this will be convenient for many readers since there's a liberal mix of metric and U.S. customary weights and measures throughout this book, just as there is at boat docks, fish camps, and tackle shops throughout the world.

Because the text is encyclopedic in format, however, it does not provide a full sense of the joy or spirit of sportfishing—the pleasure that makes it "beloved by many," as Izaak Walton said. Perhaps the accompanying photos help convey this. Photos and line art, incidentally, were planned and selected to reflect the broad, eclectic places and situations that so many anglers experience, as well as to reflect the great diversity of its participants. Angling is a very democratic recreation; as the quotation from President Hoover implies, the fish don't care who hooks them.

It is a special delight to publish this encyclopedia at the close of the twentieth century—a period with the most phenomenal sportfishing growth in the history of mankind—and at the advent of a new millennium. Knowing that the decades ahead will require proper stewardship of aquatic resources—something that anglers in particular have always demonstrated personal and financial support for—this text has been written and edited with sensitivity to conservation issues while also being realistic about the role that humans play as the highest predators and the diverse motivations they bring to angling.

In a sense, the sport of fishing is like a book with as many footnotes as main text. It is full of variables, especially individual skills, weather issues, peculiarities among species, habitat differences, and so forth. You may notice that the words "usually" and "generally" occur often in portions of the text. This isn't meant to be vague; it's because there are often no hard-and-fast rules in catching fish, no matter what you may have heard to the contrary. There are norms, but straying from norms is common for one reason or another, as any angler who has been humbled at a "hot" site at the "best" time of the season can attest.

While there is a wealth of reliable information here, a caveat is in order with regard to the contents of the *Worldwide Angling Guide*. Many of the countries profiled have not in the past provided, or do not currently provide, or may not in the future provide stable travel environments, especially to tourists of certain nationalities. Jungle fishing opportunities are especially among those that may present danger. Angola, Colombia, and Zambia come immediately to mind in this regard. Civil unrest can likewise make travel in certain places dangerous; recent troubles in Kenya, Indonesia, Russia, Uganda, and the Balkans serve as examples. The adventurous angler needs to use good judgment.

Things change the environmental order and aquatic resources, too. Yugoslavia hadn't been wrecked by bombs when that entry was written; Nicaragua and Honduras were leveled by Hurricane Georges right after those entries were written. Environmental changes sometimes radically alter the presence or availability of certain gamefish species, and in the more remote pockets of the world only native people and intrepid explorers are likely to know it.

On a final note, it is tempting to say, as marketers and publicists are wont to do, that this book contains everything an angler will ever need to know about fish and fishing. But new developments in fishing tackle will surely come along, changes in some habitats or in fish populations will alter the techniques and equipment used, and certainly natural changes will take place in some of the world's best angling spots. However, a lot of the fundamentals—the underlying principles of fish behavior, the function of basic equipment, and angling methodology—will be constant, making most of the information in this book relevant to the discerning angler even in years to come.

I expect to add to this body of knowledge in time, so if you think there's something that should have been included, if you have knowledge about fishing in a country that wasn't covered, or if you can suggest an improvement to any aspect of this book, please visit my website—www.kenschultz.com—and post a message about it.

Now, turn to any page and become absorbed.
—Ken Schultz

"If I fished only to capture fish, my fishing trips would have ended long ago."

—ZANE GREY

Acknowledgments

PRODUCING A BOOK OF THIS MAGNITUDE REQUIRED THE INVOLVEMENT OF A tremendous number of people and a great array of talents. This encyclopedia would not have gone beyond a mere suggestion, however, had it not been for the endorsement and encouragement of Natalie Chapman, a former publisher at Macmillan General Reference, now IDG Books Consumer Reference, whose confidence and vision made this book possible, and who gave me free rein to produce it as necessary. I'm also indebted to publisher Marie Butler-Knight, who took this project over in mid-stream, marshaled all the resources, and fervently shepherded the book to completion. Sincere appreciation is also extended to Renee Wilmeth and Kristi Hart, who directed the publisher's nitty-gritty editorial and production work with outstanding dedication and professionalism, plus a reassuring enthusiasm; to Pamela Benner, who paid excellent attention to details in the copyediting process and made good suggestions; and to many other directly involved personnel, particularly Beth Jordan, Faunette Johnston, and Jeanine Bucek.

This book could also not have been completed without the special assistance of my wife, Sandy, and my daughters, Alyson, Megan, and Kristen. They each helped in a variety of ways, especially by being patient. Sandy's assistance with a host of matters was very beneficial, and Kristen was particularly vital, pitching in for a second time during a desperate period with important research and writing assistance.

In order to make this encyclopedia truly comprehensive and of worldwide significance it was imperative to involve a host of contributors with expertise in technical fisheries matters, regional angling opportunities, and specialized sportfishing topics. I'm grateful for their participation and excellent contributions, the bulk of which made up the *Worldwide Angling Guide*. In particular, appreciation is extended to the incomparable Ed Migdalski, who provided technical scientific fisheries advice and vetted all of the fish art.

I'm also indebted to the late, and incomparable in his own right, A. J. McClane. His fishing encyclopedia of 1965 and 1974, though now outdated, was not only a phenomenal reference work, but a monumental achievement in an era before personal computers, electronic mail, fax machines, scanners, laser printers, and the various modern technology that made putting this book together far easier than it was in his time. Unlike me, he was unable to write and edit on a laptop computer in cars, planes, airports, hotel rooms, and other places, or receive electronically transmitted text. More significantly, McClane set a very high bar for what a real fishing encyclopedia ought to be, and provided a template for such a book for the twenty-first century. Without his accomplishment, it would have been much more difficult to plan and publish this book. (Aside to historians: four contributors to this project—Ed Migdalski, George Reiger, Jack Samson, and Bill Scifres—were also contributors to McClane's encyclopedia.)

Just as McClane, the contributors to this book, and the people at IDG Books Worldwide are the best in their fields, so is *Field & Stream* the largest and best fishing and hunting magazine in the world, and I've been privileged to be part of this publication continuously since 1973. I appreciate the confidence and opportunities provided me over that time by its editors. Those opportunities laid the groundwork for this encyclopedia. I'm especially grateful to Editor Slaton White and Managing Editor Mike Toth for allowing me leeway over the last several years that I've been working on this project.

Information, suggestions, encouragement, technical advice, reference paraphernalia, reviews and critiques, and assorted material assistance were received from so many individuals and organizations that some will likely be overlooked in these acknowledgments, for which I apologize.

I'm very grateful to the following individuals:

Blaine Anderson
John Anthon
Dick Ballard
Ron Ballanti
LaVerne Barnes
Cameron Baty
Susan Baumgartner
Gene Bay
Dick Bengraff
Virginia Benoit
Walt Boname
Toby Bradshaw
Eric Burnley
Cyril Calendini
Bill Chapman, Jr.
Jim Chapralis
Larry Columbo
David Cosby
Gary Dollahon
Lou Duarte
Todd DuPuis
Jack Erskine
Mike Fine
Paul Fuller
Riccardo Galigani
Ken Gangler

Acknowledgments

Guy Geffroy
Lois Gerber
Alessandro Giangio
Barry Gibson
Gary Giudice
Fred Golofaro
Jerry Gomber
George Gowen
Garry Gurke
Judy Hammond
Bill Hilts, Jr.
Bruce Holt
Dr. James Imai
Jimmy Kano
Nick Karas
Glenda Kelley
Gary King
Jason Klein
Bob Lang
Steen Larsen
Mike Leech
Bill Liston
Chun Liu
George Loechl
Paulo Loes
Frank Longino
Jim Matthews
John Mazurkewicz
Tom Melton
Paul Merzig
Ed Mesunas
Bill Miller
Gail Morchower

András Nagy
Andy Newman
Stuart Newman
Donald J. Orth
Tom Pagliaroli
Sheldon Pasternack
Dennis Phillips
Stanko Popovic
Norville Prosser
Jim Reist
Al Ristori
Milt Rosko
Gail Ross
Sharon Rushton
Pat Salimeno
Marty Salovin
Glenn Sapir
Christine Moore Serrao
Vin Sparano
Ron Speed, Sr.
Roy Stiner
Mick Thill
Roger Tucker
Jerry Valentine
Mike Walker
Ben Wechsler
Mark Weintz
Fenner Weller
Jim White
Anthony M. Williams
Dick Wood
Peter Yaskowski

I'm also grateful to the following companies and organizations (and specific people where noted in parenthesis):

American Sportfishing Association (Mike Hayden)
American Wire (Michael Shields)
Arkie Lures
The Atlantic Salmon Federation
Bay de Noc Lure Co.
Bead Tackle (Peter Renkert)
Bear Advertising (Dick Bear, Mark Malkin)
Big Jon (Jerry Livingstone)
Bullet Weights (Douglas Crumrine)
Bushnell Sports Optics (Barbara Mellman)
Cabela's Inc. (Tony Dolle)
Classic Fishing Products (Mike Richards)
C-Map USA (Pam Oldham)
Computrol, Inc.
Cossack Bait Products (Garry Shaw)
Cuba Specialty Mfg. Co. (Craig Osterhus, Dana Pickup)
Daiwa Corp.
Earie Dearie Lure Co. (Helen Galbincea)
EZE Lap Diamond (Donna Long)
Fin-Nor (Niels Stenhoj)
Flambeau Products Corp. (Jason Sauey)
Florida Keys and Key West Visitors Bureau
Flow-Rite of Tennessee (Don Zielinski)
Furuno
Future Fisherman Foundation
Garmin International (Steve Featherstone)
G. Loomis (Gary Loomis, Steve Rajeff)
Gudebrod
International Game Fish Association (Jim Brown)
Hudson River Foundation
Interphase Technologies
K-C Tackle (Raymond Packer)
L. L. Bean (Mary Rose MacKinnon)
L&S Bait Co. (Eric Bachnik)
Lowrance Electronics (Darrell Lowrance, Steve Schneider)
Luhr Jensen & Sons (Phil Jensen, Barry Ternahan)
Magellan Systems Corp. (Don Meyer)
Mann's Bait Co.
Marado Inc.
Old Town Canoe (Jim Kaiser)
O. Mustad & Sons USA (John DeVries)
National Freshwater Fishing Hall of Fame
Nomadic Expeditions (Denise Gogarty)
Normark Corp. (Ron Weber, Craig Weber)
The Orvis Company
Outdoor Technologies
Owner America Corp. (Kat Shitanishi)
Penn Fishing Tackle
Pradco (Joe Hughes, Bruce Stanton)
Scientific Anglers
Shakespeare Fishing Tackle (Mark Davis)
Sheldon's Inc.
Shimano American Corp.
Si-Tex Marine Electronics
Storm Lures (Sharon Andrews, John Storm)
Sufix USA, Inc.
Techsonics Industries
Len Thompson Lures (Richard Pallister)
Top Brass Tackle (Eric Cosby)
Tru-Turn Hooks (Wes Campbell)
Wisconsin Pharmacal
H. D. Wood Advertising
Worden's Lures
The Worth Co.
Wright & McGill Co. (George Large)
Yakima Bait Co. (Rob Phillips)
Zebco Corp. (Jenni Foster)

Gratitude is also due the following government agencies and government-funded programs (and the people noted in parenthesis), which provided research and reference materials, and, in some cases, other forms of assistance:

Alabama Cooperative Extension Service (Richard Wallace)
Alabama Department of Conservation and Natural Resources (Stan Cook)
Alabama Sea Grant Extension Program
Alaska Department of Fish and Game (Jon Lyman)
Alaska Sea Grant College Program (Kurt Byers)
Alberta Department of Environmental Protection

Acknowledgments

Arizona Game and Fish Department
Arkansas Cooperative Extension Program, Univ. of Arkansas (Nathan Stone)
Arkansas Game and Fish Commission (Keith Sutton)
Auburn University Marine Extension (Richard Wallace, William Hosking, Stephen Szedlmayer)
Brazil Embratur
British Columbia Ministry of Environment, Fisheries Branch
California Department of Fish and Game (A. Petrovich)
Canada Department of Fisheries and Oceans
Canadian Consul General
Cayman Islands Department of Tourism
Colorado Department of Natural Resources
Connecticut Department of Environmental Protection
Delaware Division of Fish and Wildlife
Florida Department of Environmental Protection, Marine Research Institute and Division of Marine Resources (Jim Lewis)
Florida Game and Freshwater Fish Commission, Division of Fisheries (Henry Cabbage)
Georgia Department of Natural Resources (Chris Martin)
Great Lakes Fishery Commission
Guam Department of Agriculture (Gerry Davis)
Hawaii Department of Land and Natural Resources, Division of Aquatic Resources
Idaho Department of Fish and Game (Jack Trueblood)
Illinois Department of Natural Resources
Indiana Department of Natural Resources (Jon Marshall)
International Center for Living Aquatic Resources Management/Food and Agriculture Organization of the United Nations
Iowa Department of Natural Resources (Steve Suman)
Kansas Department of Wildlife and Parks (Mike Miller)
Kentucky Department of Fish and Wildlife Resources (J. Beth Garland)
Louisiana Department of Wildlife and Fisheries
Louisiana Sea Grant College Program
Maine Department of Inland Fisheries and Wildlife (V. Paul Reynolds)
Manitoba Department of Natural Resources, Fisheries Branch (Carl Wall)
Maryland Department of Natural Resources (Eugene Deems, Jr.)
Maryland Sea Grant College Program (Jack Greer)
Massachusetts Division of Fisheries and Wildlife
Michigan Department of Natural Resources, Fisheries Division
Michigan Sea Grant College Program (Martha Walter)
Minnesota Department of Natural Resources (Tom Dickson)
Mississippi Department of Wildlife, Fisheries and Parks (Jim Walker)
Missouri Department of Conservation (John McPherson)
Montana Division of Fish, Wildlife, and Parks
Nevada Department of Conservation and Natural Resources
New Brunswick Department of Economic Development and Tourism
New Brunswick Department of Natural Resources, Fish and Wildlife Branch (Peter Cronin)
Newfoundland Department of Natural Resources
New Hampshire Fish and Game Department (Patricia Fleurie)
New Jersey Division of Fish, Game and Wildlife (Dave Chanda)
New Mexico Department of Game and Fish (Ruth Anderson)
New York Department of Environmental Conservation (Robert Brandt)
New York Sea Grant Program (David MacNeill, Mark Malchoff)
NOAA/Gray's Reef National Marine Sanctuary (Beth Kostka)
NOAA/National Marine Fisheries Service
NOAA/National Weather Service
North Carolina Division of Boating and Inland Fisheries (Fred Harris)
North Carolina Sea Grant
North Dakota Game and Fish Department (Terry Steinwand)
Nova Scotia Department of Fisheries (Murray Hill)
Nova Scotia Department of Lands and Forests (Barry Sabean)
Ohio Department of Natural Resources
Ohio Sea Grant College Program
Oklahoma Department of Wildlife Conservation (Nels Rodefeld)
Ontario Ministry of Economic Development, Trade & Tourism (Tom Boyd)
Ontario Ministry of Natural Resources
Oregon Department of Fish and Wildlife (Randy Henry)
Oregon Sea Grant (Pat Kight)
Parátur, State of Pará, Brazil
Pennsylvania Fish and Boat Commission
Portuguese National Tourist Office (Maria Joáo Ramires)
Prince Edward Island Department of Environmental Resources
Quebec Department of Recreation, Fish and Game
Rhode Island Division of Fish and Game
Rhode Island Sea Grant
Saskatchewan Department of Environment, Fish and Wildlife (Bruce Howard)

South Carolina Department of Natural Resources (Greg Lucas)
South Carolina Sea Grant Consortium (John Tibbetts)
South Dakota Department of Game, Fish and Parks
Spain Ministry of Commerce and Tourism
Tennessee Wildlife Resources Agency (Dave Woodward)
Texas Parks and Wildlife (Steve Lightfoot)
Tourism British Columbia
Tourism New Brunswick
Tourism Newfoundland and Labrador
Tourism Nova Scotia (Randy Brooks)
Tourism Prince Edward Island (Carol Horne)
Tourism Quebec (Siegfried Gagnon)
Tourism Saskatchewan (Gerard Makuch, Nadine Howard)
Travel Alberta (Peter Gregus)
Travel Manitoba (Dennis Maksymetz, Colette Fontaine, Gord Richardson)
University of Connecticut Sea Grant Marine Advisory Program (Nancy Balcom)
University of Delaware Sea Grant College Program
University of Florida Cooperative Extension Service
University of New Hampshire and University of Maine Sea Grant College Program
U.S. Fish and Wildlife Service
Utah Department of Natural Resources (Gerry Schlappe)
Vermont Department of Fish and Wildlife (John Hall)
Virginia Department of Game and Inland Fisheries (Mitchell Norman)
Washington Department of Fish and Wildlife (Nina Carter, James Chandler)
Washington Sea Grant Program (Kris Freeman)
West Virginia Division of Natural Resources (Hoy Murphy)
Wisconsin Department of Natural Resources (David Kunelius)
Woods Hole Oceanographic Institute (Tracey Crago)
Wyoming Game and Fish Department
Yukon Territory Department of Renewable Resources (Susan Thompson)

Finally, I'm also grateful to four student interns, whose early work compiling and organizing research materials was of much help—Kristen Schultz of Oberlin College, Alyson Schultz of Boston University, Mathew Kane of Hamilton College, and John Kuhner of Princeton University—and to Megan Schultz of Ithaca College, for website development and advice.

—Ken Schultz

About the Author, Artists, and Contributors

PRINCIPAL AUTHOR AND EDITOR

Ken Schultz has been a staff fishing writer and editor for *Field & Stream* since 1973. His feature articles and columns for that publication appear monthly, and he contributes to the magazine's nationally syndicated weekly radio show and to its website. Schultz is a frequent author of the outdoors column of the *New York Times*, and he previously was a syndicated newspaper columnist for Gannett. He has authored a dozen books on sportfishing and angling travel topics, has been a featured guest on CNBC, ESPN, and The Nashville Network, and appears regularly in assorted fishing segments for the Outdoor Life Network. A widely traveled angler, Schultz is a former holder of seven line-class world records and was inducted into the Fishing Hall of Fame in 1998. He lives in Forestburgh, New York.

THE ARTISTS

Steve T. Goione is a rising star in the world of fishing and boating art, working in mixed mediums to present his lifelong passion for angling in a dynamic and realistic style. Although he drew the distinctive pen-and-ink illustrations for this book as well as the cover, Goione is primarily a creator of fine art. From his studio in Toms River, New Jersey, he produces commissioned fishing scenes for private collections and limited-edition prints, and he has created original artwork for Sea World in Florida. Goione has also made a mark among boat builders and owners for commissioned renderings of big-game sportfishing craft, and he recently created original artwork for the latest products of Hatteras Yachts. A frequent guest artist on the big-game fishing tournament circuit, Goione appears at exclusive contests each year from Nantucket to Venezuela, and his work is regularly featured at fund-raising events for prominent conservation organizations.

David Kiphuth, whose renderings of fish appear in this book, has had a varied career in the field of art, having been a professional illustrator since 1969. His work has included portraiture, architectural renderings, maps, and book illustration. Kiphuth has created archaeological and scientific book and exhibit renderings for the Yale Peabody Museum, the Yale Department of Anthropology, and Yale University Press. He formerly maintained a studio and gallery in Branford, Connecticut, where he created and sold wildlife and nature art and animal portraits. Since 1989, he has been the staff illustrator for the *Gazette Newspapers* in Schenectady, New York. He lives in Saratoga Springs, New York.

THE CONTRIBUTORS

Brett Albanese of Virginia is a Ph.D candidate at the Department of Fisheries and Wildlife Sciences at Virginia Polytechnic Institute; he formerly worked at the Mississippi Museum of Natural Sciences.

Ken Allen of Maine is Associate Editor of *Maine Sportsman* and a prolific writer, photographer, newspaper columnist, book author, and guide.

Michael Babcock of Montana is Outdoors Editor of the *Great Falls Tribune*.

Ken Bailey of Alberta is Manager of Field Operations in central Alberta for Ducks Unlimited Canada; he is a prolific writer and President of the Outdoor Writers Association of Canada.

Dick Ballard of Missouri is President of Dick Ballard's Fishing Adventures and a foremost authority on Amazonian angling; he's sent anglers fishing around the world for 18 years, and established the first travel service for Bass Pro Shops.

Scott Bannerot of Pennsylvania and Florida has a Ph.D. in fisheries science and has worked in marine biological research and consulting; he is a photojournalist and a charter boat captain.

John A. Barnes of Bermuda is the Director of Agriculture and Fisheries for Bermuda; he authors a weekly fishing column in the Bermuda *Mid Ocean News*, and is an IGFA representative.

Rob Barraclough of Indonesia and England works in the oil industry and is a charter boat captain and freelance writer.

Carlos M. Barrantes of Costa Rica established the first two sportfishing camps in Costa Rica; he is an IGFA representative and was the first President of the Costa Rican Fishing Federation.

Cody Beers of Wyoming works for the Wyoming Game and Fish Department as Associate Editor of *Wyoming Wildlife* magazine and Editor of *Wyoming Wildlife News and Wild Times*; he is also a freelance writer and photographer.

Bob Berry of California is one of the world's top fish carvers and sculptors, and swept all divisions of the 1986 world championship of fish carving; he is a foremost competition judge, a former professional taxidermist, and author of the book *Fish Carving*.

Mike Bleech of Pennsylvania is a writer and photographer whose work has appeared in most major U.S. fishing and hunting magazines.

Larry Blomquist of Louisiana is Publisher of *Breakthrough*, the world's largest taxidermy trade magazine, and one of the top competition judges in North America; he is a retired award-winning taxidermist, and former President of the National Taxidermists Association.

Fred Bonner of North Carolina is Editor of *Carolina Adventure* magazine; he is also a syndicated newspaper columnist, fisheries biologist, and an IGFA representative.

Judith Bowman of New York has been a foremost sporting books dealer for over twenty years; she produces two sporting book catalogs a year, with special emphasis on fishing.

John Brownlee of Florida is Senior Editor of *Salt Water Sportsman* and a former charter boat captain; he has served on the South Atlantic Fishery Management Council, is former Chairman of the Florida Conservation Association, and is an IGFA representative.

Eric B. Burnley of Virginia is the author of *Surf Fishing the Atlantic Coast* and a radio show host; he is a charter boat captain and Regional Editor of both *Salt Water Sportsman* and *The Fisherman* magazines.

Erwin Bursik of South Africa is Publisher of *Ski-Boat* and *Flyfishing* magazines of Durban, a member of the executive board of the South African Deep Sea Angling Association, and an IGFA representative.

Mac Campbell of Great Britain works for *Angling Plus*, a match fishing magazine, and has previously worked for *Sea Angler*, *Trout Fisherman*, and *Angling Times*.

Jim Casada of South Carolina is the author of many books, including *Modern Fly Fishing*; he is Senior Editor of *Sporting Classics* magazine, and outdoor columnist for the Rock Hill *Herald* and Greensboro *News and Record*.

Göran Cederberg of Sweden has been Editor of several international fact-packed large-format angling books, including *The Complete Book of Sportfishing*; he contributes regularly to north-European publications and has been chief editor of a Swedish sportfishing magazine.

Matthew D. Chan of Virginia is a Ph.D candidate at the Department of Fisheries and Wildlife Sciences at Virginia Polytechnic Institute; he formerly worked as a fisheries biologist for the U.S. Army Corps of Engineers.

Dawn Charging of North Dakota is Outdoors Director for the North Dakota State Tourism Department; she is also a writer and photographer whose family owns a successful fishing resort on Lake Sakakawea.

Homer Circle of Florida has been Angling Editor of *Sports Afield* magazine for 34 years; the dean of American outdoor writers, he is the recipient of numerous media and achievement awards, a former member of the Arkansas Game & Fish Commission, and a renowned television and video host.

Barry Ord Clarke of Norway is a professional photographer and writer and the author of several books on fly fishing and fly tying; he contributes regularly to most European fishing magazines, and is fishing consultant to Norway's largest private sporting estate.

Soc Clay of Kentucky is an accomplished and prolific fishing writer and photographer whose work has appeared in every major outdoor periodical in North America.

Angelo Cuanang of California is a Pacific Regional Editor for *Salt Water Sportsman* and a freelance writer and photographer.

Paula J. Del Giudice of Nevada is Outdoor Columnist for the *Las Vegas Sun*; a freelance writer, photographer, and book author; and former President of the Nevada Wildlife Federation.

Arthur De Mello of Uganda is a representative for the IGFA in Uganda.

Hansjörg Dietiker of Switzerland is Editor of the Swiss Anglers Magazine *Petri-Heil*, and an IGFA representative.

Philippe Dolivet of France is the Chief Editor of the French fly fishing magazine *Plaisirs de la Pêche* and a professional photographer; he is a fly fishing instructor and competitor, an ichthyologist, and an IGFA representative.

Gary Edwards of Wyoming is a longtime fishing guide and a television show host; he is the former Editor and Publisher of *Salmon Fever* magazine, and a former fly rod world record holder.

D'arcy Egan of Ohio has been a sportswriter for *The Cleveland Plain Dealer* for over 20 years; he authored the book, *Guide to Ohio Fishing*, and is host of the American Outdoorsman Radio Network.

Bill Ensor of New Brunswick works for the Fish & Wildlife Branch of the New Brunswick Department of Natural Resources; he was formerly marketing manager of fishing and hunting for the New Brunswick Department of Tourism, and is a longtime fishing guide.

Jack Erskine of Australia is a foremost big-game tackle designer and technical innovator who has helped design many of the modern rods, reels, and drag systems in use today.

Stan Fagerstrom of Oregon is one of the world's best known trick and accuracy casters, and has been featured at sport shows worldwide for half a century; he is also a book, magazine, and newspaper writer.

Jan Fogt of Florida is Editor of *The Bahamas Sportfishing Guide* and was the founding editor of *Bahamas Blue Water Magazine*; she is a contributing editor for *Sport Fishing* and *Marlin* magazines, and is also a book author.

Frank Fry of the Yukon Territory has worked with the Yukon Territory's Department of Natural Resources on various fishing projects.

Mike Garzillo of New Hampshire has been a newspaper columnist for 24 years; he is a regular contributor to various publications and a former regional editor for *Outdoor Life*.

Alessandro Giangio of Italy writes for Italy's premier fishing magazine, *Pesca in Mare*, and has been published worldwide; he has authored five books, is owner and master instructor of the Fishbuster Trolling School and Sportfishing Travel, and has a charter boat in Huatulco, Mexico.

Jerry Gibbs of Vermont is Fishing Editor of *Outdoor Life*, where his career as a staff writer has spanned three decades and made him one of North America's most respected angling authors; he has written several books and has been inducted into the Fishing Hall of Fame.

Barry Gibson of Massachusetts is Editor of *Salt Water Sportsman* and a longtime Maine charter boat captain; he is a former member of the New England Fishery Management Council, and former advisor to the International Commission for the Conservation of Atlantic Tunas.

Jerry Gomber of New Jersey has over twenty-five years of experience in design, development, and marketing of fishing rods and reels; during that period he has been responsible for several successful product innovations.

George Gruenefeld of Quebec and Saskatchewan is Editor of *Canadian Outdoor Publications*; he has written for many magazines in Canada and the U.S., is a book author, and was formerly Outdoors Editor for the *Montreal Gazette*.

Chris Hanks of the Northwest Territories is an anthropologist, freelance writer, and author of the book *Fly Fishing in the Northwest Territories*.

Steve Harper of Kansas is the Outdoors Editor of the *Wichita Eagle* and author of the book *Kansas Day Trips*; in 1995 he was named Conservation Communicator of the Year by the Kansas Wildlife Federation.

Dan Heiner of Alaska is an advertising agency executive and former editor and writer for *Alaska Outdoors* magazine; he is the author of four books on Alaska fishing, including *Fly Fishing Alaska's Wild Rivers*.

Bob Hodge of Tennessee is the Outdoors Editor of the *Knoxville News-Sentinel*; he was named the state's Best Outdoor Writer for 1996-97 by the Tennessee Sportswriters Association.

Grant Hopkins of Ontario is the outdoor columnist for the *Ottawa Citizen*, a frequent contributor to *Ontario Out of Doors*, and retired from the Royal Canadian Air Force.

John Husar of Illinois is the longtime outdoors columnist and general sportswriter of the *Chicago Tribune* and co-host of a Chicago radio show; he has worked for newspapers in Kansas, Texas, and New Mexico, and has covered the last nine Olympics.

Jim Imai of California has a Ph.D in physics and is Professor of Physics at California State University, Dominguez Hills; he is a Consulting Physicist for the Daiwa Corporation, and a leading authority on the design and performance of fishing reels and rods.

James Kano of Ontario is the Marketing Director of Japan Communications in Toronto and Outdoor Coordinator for the Press and Tourism division of the Ontario government; his articles have appeared online and in newspapers, guide books, and magazines.

Nick Karas of New York is the retired outdoor columnist for (New York) *Newsday* and a charter boat captain and ichthyologist; he has written for many national magazines and authored a dozen books, including *The Striped Bass* and *Brook Trout*.

Lee Kernen of Wisconsin is the retired Director of Fisheries for the State of Wisconsin; he is also a writer, fishing guide, and fisheries consultant.

Ronnie Kovach of California is a radio and television show host, educator, magazine writer, guide, and author of five books, including *Bass Fishing in California*, *Trout Fishing in California*, and *Saltwater Fishing in California*.

Steen Larsen of Denmark is one of Europe's leading sportfishing writers and photographers; he is a book author and lecturer, and contributes widely to many European angling publications.

Dick Lewers of Australia is Technical Editor of *Encyclopaedia of Australian Fishing*, author of seven books on angling, a former IGFA representative, 35-year columnist for *Modern Fishing Magazine*, and past President of the Australian National Sportfishing Association.

Bill Loftus of Idaho is the Outdoors Editor of the *Lewiston Morning Tribune* and the author of two guidebooks to Idaho.

Maurice Loustau-LaLanne of Seychelles is the Principal Secretary in the Ministry of Tourism and Transport for the Seychelles, and an IGFA representative.

Carl. F. Luckey of Alabama is a writer specializing in antiques and collectibles; he has authored ten books, including his best-selling, 618-page work, *Old Fishing Lures and Tackle*.

Joe Macaluso of Louisiana is an award-winning outdoors sportswriter/editor for the *Baton Rouge Advocate*; his weekly fishing reports have appeared in Louisiana newspapers since 1976.

Rosanne Macfarlane of Prince Edward Island recently received her Masters degree in Biology at

Acadia University; she works for the Department of Fisheries and Environment.

Dennis Maksymetz of Manitoba is Manager of Tourism Marketing for the Industry, Trade and Tourism division of the Manitoba government.

Don Mann of Florida is a longtime contributor to *Florida Sportsman*, a record-holding big-game angler, and book author; his articles and photographs have appeared in many publications.

Al Marlowe of Colorado has written numerous articles for outdoor magazines; he authored a trail guide for the Flat Tops Wilderness area and a fly fishing guide for the Colorado River.

Peter B. Mathiesen of Missouri is Executive Editor and Producer of the *Field & Stream Radio Hour*; he is also a magazine writer, photographer, and video and television show producer.

John McCoy of West Virginia is Outdoors Editor for the *Charleston Daily Mail*, Regional Editor for *Field & Stream*, and a frequent contributor to regional and national magazines.

Tom Meade of Rhode Island writes about the outdoors for the *Providence Journal-Bulletin*; he is the author of *Essential Fly Fishing*, and writes for various magazines.

Ed Migdalski of Connecticut is the retired Director of Yale University's Outdoor Education and Club Sports Programs, retired Ichthyologist for the Yale Peabody Museum, and holder of the current world record for the largest strictly freshwater fish (pirarucu) ever caught on rod and reel.

Kent Mitchell of Georgia has covered outdoor sports for the *Atlanta Journal-Constitution* for three decades; he has received the Communicator of the Year Award from the Georgia Wildlife Federation, and has authored three books on martial arts.

Bill Monroe of Oregon has covered the outdoors for his state's largest daily newspaper, *The Oregonian*, for 18 years.

Gary W. Moore of Vermont is a freelance writer and photographer; he is former Commissioner of the Vermont Fish and Wildlife Department and former Chairman of the Vermont Water Resources Board.

Sam Mossman of New Zealand is Special Projects Editor for *New Zealand Fishing News* magazine; he is the author of three books and hundreds of magazine articles, and has held five world and numerous New Zealand fishing records.

Perry Munro of Nova Scotia is a writer and artist who contributes to *The Atlantic Salmon Journal* and various other magazines; he is also an outfitter, master guide, operator of Maple Mountain Lodge, and a Director of Trout Unlimited Canada.

Iain Nicolson of Angola is an IGFA representative and has a Ph.D. in molecular genetics; he and his family pioneered fishing for blue marlin in Angola and collectively established six world fishing records.

Chris Niskanen of Minnesota is the Outdoors Editor of the *St. Paul Pioneer Press*.

Donald J. Orth of Virginia is a Professor of Fisheries Science in the Department of Fisheries & Wildlife Sciences at Virginia Polytechnic Institute.

Tom Pagliaroli of New Jersey is an advertising agency executive, freelance writer, and photographer whose work has appeared in various regional and national publications.

Ali Pasiner of Turkey is an attorney, the author of two fishing books, and a consultant to the Turkish version of the *Encyclopaedia Britannica*; he is also a writer, editor, and representative of the IGFA.

C. Boyd Pfeiffer of Maryland is a longtime journalist and photographer, a regular columnist for many angling magazines, and the author of numerous books on fishing topics, the latest of which is *Fly Fishing Salt Water Basics*.

Larry Porter of Nebraska has been on the sports staff of the *Omaha World-Herald* for over three decades and their outdoors writer since 1990; he has been named Nebraska Sportswriter of the Year three times, and is a former professional tournament angler.

Steve Price of Texas is a longtime Senior Writer for *Bassmaster* magazine and contributor to a wide variety of national sporting magazines; he is an accomplished photographer and author of several books.

Gareth Purnell of England is Editor of Britain's leading angling magazine, *Improve Your Coarse Fishing*, and former News Editor of *Angling Times*; he has fished annually in the World Freshwater Angling Championships since 1993.

George Reiger of Virginia is Conservation Editor of *Field & Stream* and *Salt Water Sportsman* magazines and the most widely respected conservation writer in North America; he has been a staff writer for *Field & Stream* since 1972, is the author of seven books on angling and marine ecology, and the recipient of numerous honors and awards.

Tim Renken of Missouri has been the outdoors writer for the *St. Louis Post-Dispatch* since 1963; he previously worked for the Nebraska Game Commission.

Len Rich of Newfoundland is the author of two books and many outdoor magazine articles; he operates Awesome Lake Lodge in Labrador, is a former Hunting and Fishing Development Officer for Newfoundland and Labrador, and is a past representative of the Atlantic Salmon Federation.

Tom Richardson of Massachusetts is Managing Editor of *Salt Water Sportsman* magazine, as well as a freelance writer and photographer.

Al Ristori of New Jersey is Saltwater Fishing Editor of the *Newark Star-Ledger*, Regional Editor of *Salt Water Sportsman*, Conservation Editor of *The Fisherman* magazine, and the author of several books;

he is also a charter boat captain and has served on the Mid-Atlantic Fishery Management Council.

Jim Rizzuto of Hawaii is Hawaii Editor for *Salt Water Sportsman* and *Western Outdoors*, a longtime columnist for *West Hawaii Today* and *Hawaii Fishing News*, and the author of the books *Modern Hawaiian Gamefishing* and *Fishing Hawaii Style*.

Nels Rodefeld of Oklahoma is an avid angler and hunter who frequently covers Oklahoma's hunting and fishing scene.

Milt Rosko of New Jersey is a writer for *Big Game Fishing Journal* and various other publications and a longtime authority on saltwater sportfishing; he is a photographer, book author, magazine feature writer, and lecturer.

Terry Rudnick of Washington has been writing articles on Northwest fishing subjects for more than 25 years; he is the author of the book *Washington Fishing, the Complete Guide*, and co-author of *How to Catch Trophy Halibut*.

Bob Sampson, Jr. of Connecticut is a writer, photographer, science teacher, and fisheries biologist; his work has appeared in numerous national and regional magazines.

Jack Samson of New Mexico is the retired Editor-in-Chief of *Field & Stream* and a former Associated Press columnist; he is Saltwater Editor of *Fly Rod & Reel* magazine, author of twenty books, and the first angler to catch both Atlantic and Pacific sailfish and all five species of marlin on a fly.

Ray Sasser of Texas is the Outdoor Editor of *The Dallas Morning News* and a freelance contributor to various magazines; he has been writing about outdoor sports for over 25 years.

Carl Werner Schmidt-Luchs of Germany is a contributor to *Blinker*, the largest angling magazine in Europe; he is a photographer, writer, and author of a dozen angling books.

Kristen Schultz of Massachusetts is a writer who recently graduated from Oberlin College; she works for an engineering consulting firm.

Bill Scifres of Indiana has been the Outdoor Editor of the *Indianapolis Star* since 1953; he is a book author, freelance writer, and photographer.

Eric Sharp of Michigan is Outdoor Editor of *The Detroit News*, and was formerly Outdoor Editor of *The Miami Herald*.

Luis Sier of Argentina is a newspaper columnist, a former magazine publisher, and an outfitter who operates several Argentinian fishing camps.

Jeff Simpson of South Dakota is an information officer for the State of South Dakota, a book author and freelance magazine writer, and former project developer for Cowles Creative Publishing.

DeWayne Smith of Arizona is an information officer for the Maricopa County Parks and Recreation Department; he covered the outdoors for over 30 years for *The Phoenix Gazette*.

Ryan Smith of Virginia is a research assistant with the Department of Fisheries and Wildlife Sciences at Virginia Polytechnic Institute.

Michael Snook of Saskatchewan is a freelance writer, conservationist, outdoor educator, and television producer.

Frank Sousa of Massachusetts is a writer for the *Springfield Sunday Republican* and the *Union News*, Editor/Publisher of *Northeast Woods and Waters*, and a freelance writer and photographer.

Vin T. Sparano of New Jersey is Senior Field Editor and retired Editor-in-Chief of *Outdoor Life*, for whom he worked for over three decades; he is a former syndicated columnist for *Gannett Newspapers*, and the author/editor of fourteen books, including *The Complete Outdoors Encyclopedia*.

Vladimir Stakic of Yugoslavia is Deputy Editor-in-Chief of the Yugoslavian angling magazines *Ribolovacka Revija* and *Ribolovacke Novine*, a freelance writer, and the author of three books of short stories.

Bob Stearns of Florida has been the staff boating/saltwater fishing writer of *Field & Stream* for 20 years and is the Electronics Editor of *Salt Water Sportsman*; the author of two books, he is a renowned fly fishing and light tackle expert, and has held two fly rod world records for sailfish.

Larry Stone of Iowa has been a writer and photographer for over three decades, and writes about the outdoors for the *Des Moines Register*.

Keith Sutton of Arkansas is Editor of *Arkansas Wildlife magazine*, a conservation publication of the Arkansas Game & Fish Commission, and a prolific freelance writer and photographer.

Ferenc Szalay of Hungary is Editor-in-Chief of *Magyar Horgász*, Hungary's premier fishing magazine; he is also President of the Hungarian National Committee for Match Fishing and Executive Board member of the Federation Internationale de la Pêche Sportive en Eau Douce.

Allan Tarvid of Texas is a contributing editor for *Sport Fishing* magazine and has authored hundreds of articles on electronics for sporting and commercial fishing and emergency service use; he has been a fishing guide and search and rescue diver.

Rikk Taylor of British Columbia is Editor and Publisher of *British Columbia Sport Fishing* magazine.

Mick Thill of Illinois and England is one of the world's top professional match fishing anglers and the first and only person to medal in the open water and ice fishing World Freshwater Fishing Championships; he is also a prominent float designer, and coach of the U. S. World Championship fishing teams.

Albert A. W. Threadingham of Fiji is an IGFA

representative for the Fiji Islands and Governor of the Hawaiian International Billfish Association and the Pacific Ocean Research Foundation; he is a former world-record fish holder.

Raj Tilak of Maryland and India is co-author of the book *Game Fishes of India and Angling*, and author of more than 200 research publications; he is experienced in fisheries and wildlife management, with extensive knowledge of gamefishes and their ecology in India.

Anssi Uitti of Finland works for the Finnish outdoor magazine *Metsästys ja Kalastus*, and his articles have appeared in *Urheilukalastus* (Sportfishing) and *Perhokalastus* (Flyfishing) magazines.

Luis Umpierre of Puerto Rico is a physician, Editor of *Notipesca* (Fishing News), President of the Puerto Rico Sportfishing Association, and advisory member of the Caribbean Fishery Management Council.

Rudy Van Duijnhoven of Holland is a freelance photographer and author; his work appears monthly in *BEET-Sportvissers* magazine, and he is European Correspondent for Fly Fishing in *Salt Waters* magazine.

Carlo Vernocchi of Italy and Zanzibar introduced modern big-game fishing to the Zanzibar archipelago of Tanzania in 1992; he is an IGFA representative and charter boat captain.

Victor Villavicencio of Manila is a representative for the IGFA in the Philippines.

Tsutomu Wakabayashi of Japan is the General Manager of the Japan Game Fish Association; he has written for several Japanese fishing magazines, and is an IGFA representative.

Steve Waters of Florida is the outdoors writer for the *Fort Lauderdale Sun-Sentinel* and occasionally writes for national magazines; he was formerly a newspaper writer and video executive in New York.

Tom Wharton of Utah has been Outdoor Editor of the *Salt Lake Tribune* since 1976; he has co-authored five books, and is past President of the Outdoor Writers Association of America.

Jesse E. Williams of New Mexico is the retired Chief of Public Affairs for the New Mexico Department of Game and Fish, and a former Colorado wildlife manager and environmental education supervisor.

Juergen Willms of the Yukon Territory has worked with the Yukon Territory's Department of Natural Resources on various fishing projects.

Jorge Xifra of Paraguay operates El Pescador, a sportfishing outfitting service; he is a writer, television show host, IGFA representative, and holder of four world fishing records.

Photo Credits

ALL PHOTOGRAPHS BY KEN SCHULTZ EXCEPT FOR THE FOLLOWING:

Rob Barraclough 252, 253
Bob Berry 31
Ian Chapman/Mick Thill 92
Cabela's 120

Alessandro Giangio 271
Bruce Holt 206
Nick Karas 267
Steen Larsen 1, 5, 237

Mustad 221, 222
Penn Fishing Tackle 127
Milt Rosko 110, 112
Mick Thill 94, 142
Zebco 128

FAD
Acronym for Fish Attracting Device.
See: Fish Attractor.

FAEROE ISLANDS
See: Denmark.

FALKLAND ISLANDS
Located about 600 kilometers east of the southern tip of South America, the Falkland Islands lie in the South Atlantic Ocean and encompass more land than most island groups. There are about 200 islands in this self-governing British dependency, but East and West Falkland Islands cover most of the group's 16,000 total square kilometers and are separated by Falkland Sound. The Falklands are one of the most spectacular and remote places in the world.

The visitor may be surprised to find that these islands offer fishing for resident and sea-run brown trout. These trout were introduced to a few rivers here in the 1950s and acclimated well. Today they inhabit many rivers and streams, and some migrate to and from the sea. Several larger lakes exist on rivers with sea access, but it is uncertain whether they support trout fisheries.

The average sea trout in rivers weighs around 5 pounds, but much larger specimens exist here. A 22-pound sea trout was reportedly caught in the San Carlos River. The main rivers on East Falkland Island are the San Carlos, Malo, and Murrell; on West Falkland they include the Warrah and Chartres.

A trout is hooked on the Chartres River on West Falkland Island.

Freshwater fishing rights in the Falklands are privately owned. On West Falkland, a fishing lodge in the Port Howard settlement provides access to the Warrah and the Chartres Rivers, as well as smaller streams and brooks, with a 4-wheel-drive vehicle. On East Falkland, a road runs from the capital city of Stanley, which holds about half of the Falklands' 2,300 residents, across the northern part of the island to Port San Carlos. The road passes several small streams and estuaries, all of which hold trout but require access permission from local farmers. Near its end the road passes the San Carlos River, where local farmers offer bed-and-breakfast accommodations and fishing.

The trout fishing season here extends from September through April. Spring (September/October) and autumn (March/April) are best for river fishing.

Saltwater fishing is accessible to the public. Sea trout can be fished in saltwater along the open coast and especially outside the river mouths year-round. Along the coast, anglers also catch Falkland mullet, which can reach 20 pounds. These mullet, which are strong fighters, are primarily fished near the bottom with flies, bait, and lures. Near- and offshore fishing opportunities are unknown but could be minimal due to climate and wind.

The climate is often harsh, and summer temperatures are relatively cold; rain and high humidity are frequent. The islands are so windswept that the countryside is treeless. Despite this, the Falklands possess varied wildlife, including more than 200 species of birds, and several of these are rare outside the islands; the Falklands also host five species of penguins, as well as sea lions and seals, and the enormous elephant seal.

FALLFISH *Semotilus corporalis*.
Other names—windfish, silver chub.

The fallfish is a member of the Cyprinidae family, the largest family of freshwater fish, which also includes minnows *(see)* and carp *(see)*. Often confused with the creek chub *(see: chub, creek)*, the fallfish is the largest in its minnow clan, and is a common catch for anglers. Rather than the result of targeted effort, these landings are typically accidental, and there is little constituency for these fish from an angling standpoint. The fallfish is likewise seldom used as table fare, but it is important forage for larger fish.

Identification. The body of the fallfish is slender with a bluntly pointed head. There is a

Fallfish

Fallfish

single, long dorsal fin. On adults, the scales are arranged in a pattern of dark, triangular black bars. The mouth is terminal and has barbels—which are characteristic of cyprinids—that are sometimes hidden. Its coloring is olive on the back, silvery on the sides, and white on the belly. Breeding males have tubercles on the snout and a pinkish coloring. Juveniles have a dark black line along the sides. The fallfish can be distinguished from the creek chub *(Semotilus atromaculatus)* by the absence of a black spot at the base of the dorsal fin.

Size/Age. Fallfish may grow to 16 inches or more in length. In smaller streams, they are more likely to be smaller, averaging 10 to 15 inches. A common weight is 1 to 2 pounds. Fallfish have been known to live as long as 10 years.

Distribution. These fish are commonly found from eastern Canada into the James Bay drainage, and south on the east side of the Appalachian Mountains to Virginia.

Habitat. Fallfish inhabit the gravel- and rocky-bottomed areas of cold, clear streams, as well as the edges of lakes and ponds. In rivers and streams, adults prefer deeper, quieter waters, whereas juveniles often frequent swifter, shallower water.

Spawning behavior. The spawning season is from spring through summer, beginning in early May when the water warms. The male builds a pit-ridge nest out of small stones and pebbles in shallow areas or quiet pools over a clean gravel bottom. The nest can reach 6 feet in length and 3 feet in height. It can weigh up to 200 pounds, due to the volume of pebbles, and is the largest stone mound nest built by any fish. The male repeatedly spawns over one nest with several different females. Each female releases roughly 2,000 eggs. The eggs become adhesive after fertilization and are then covered by the parent with gravel. They hatch within 138 to 144 hours.

Food. Adult fallfish consume aquatic and terrestrial insects (such as mayflies, beetles, wasps, and ants), small crustaceans, small fish, and algae. Juveniles feed on zooplankton and phytoplankton.

FALSE CAST

An element of flycasting in which the fly line is cast forward and back without allowing line or fly to touch the water. It is achieved by making a new back cast as soon as the loop of a forward cast has rolled out and before it has a chance to fall on the water. Repeated false casting is done to dry out a fly for better flotation, or to lengthen or shorten the overall length of line being fished without disturbing the surface. When you are ready to stop false casting, simply stop the forward motion and lay the line down on the water.
See: Flycasting Tackle.

FAMILY
A group of closely related species *(see)*.

FAN CASTING
A method of fully covering the water in front of an angler by casting in an arcing pattern. Whether in a boat, fishing from shore, or wading, the angler starts casting with a lure or fly in one spot and makes successive casts clockwise or counterclockwise from the original starting point until the full range of water has been covered. If no strikes are received, casting may be repeated with a different lure or fly, or the angler can move and start anew from a different position, covering new water that has not been previously cast over. The objective is to systematically and thoroughly cover all likely fish-holding water.

FANWING
A type of dry fly *(see)* with matching wings that stand upright and are curved outward to help the fly fall gently on the water, hook down.

FATHOM
A common nautical measurement in the Imperial system, equaling 6 feet, or 1.83 meters.

FATHOMETER
Antiquated term for sonar.
See: Sonar.

FAUNA
The animal life of any particular area or of any particular time.

FEATHER
To use a thumb or fingers to apply light pressure on the line of a reel to help achieve accuracy when casting *(see)*.

FEATHERING
A manner of controlling line to help achieve accuracy during a cast with spinning, spincasting, and baitcasting tackle.

On a spinning reel, line can be feathered by placing the index finger of the rod-holding hand near the lip of the spool and allowing the line to brush against it. This slows line flow and shortens distance to help place a lure at a given target. The same effect can also be accomplished by allowing the outgoing line to brush against the palm or finger of the noncasting hand. On a spincasting reel, line can be feathered by using the thumb and forefinger of the noncasting hand to apply varying degrees of pressure to the outgoing line.

On a baitcasting reel, feathering is accomplished by applying pressure from the thumb of the rod-holding hand onto the revolving spool, rather than touching the outgoing line. This is a better means of obtaining accurate lure placement and is also necessary to help prevent a spool overrun, or backlash *(see)*.
See: Baitcasting Tackle; Casting; Spincasting Tackle; Spinning Tackle.

FEATHERS
A type of weighted trolling lure.
See: Trolling Lures, Saltwater.

FEATHERWING
A fly tied primarily with hackles instead of with fur (which is a hairwing).

FEDERAL AID IN SPORT FISH RESTORATION ACT
Established by Congress in 1950 and also known as the Dingell-Johnson Act, this legislation captured the funds from a manufacturer's excise tax on fishing rods, reels, creels, and artificial lures that had been established as a luxury tax during World War II. The law required a state match of 25 percent on project funding and was intended to provide capital for sport fishery restoration, management, or enhancement projects. It also protected anglers' license fees by prohibiting their diversion to other than approved purposes. It was, and still is, administered by the U.S. Fish and Wildlife Service in partnership with the states.

In 1984, the Wallop-Breaux Amendment of the Federal Aid in Sport Fish Restoration Act was passed and allowed for expansion of the tax base to include essentially all items of fishing tackle, electric (trolling) motors, and flasher-type sonar devices; plus motorboat fuel taxes and import duties on fishing tackle and boats. This amendment changed the program from a small but valuable source of funding for state fisheries agencies to a significant portion of their fisheries management budgets, and it broadened the constituency base within the angling and boating communities. In 1990, the act was expanded again by an additional increase in the federal excise tax on gasoline, and also by deposit of the federal tax on gasoline from small nonhighway engines into the program (although millions of dollars of boater-paid taxes have annually been diverted by Congress for federal deficit reduction).

Funds may be used for almost any type of sport fishery restoration, management, or enhancement projects; and the Wallop-Breaux Amendment mandated that each state spend at least 10 percent for boat access projects, and that each could use up to 10 percent of its apportionment for aquatic resource education. The required portion for boating improvements was increased to 12.5 percent in 1992.

An annual apportionment of these monies is made available to each state. Forty percent of this amount is based on the state's land and water area in relation to the total land and water area of the United States. Sixty percent of this amount is based on the number of paid sportfishing license holders in each state in relation to all the paid sportfishing license holders in the United States.

The funds in the Federal Aid in Sport Fish Restoration Program have come under frequent attack from Congress, particularly as a means to reduce the federal deficit and to support omnibus budget bills. Many anglers are unaware of the nature of this program or of the impact that it has had on fisheries management and the creation of fishing and boating opportunities in the United States.

The Federal Aid in Sport Fish Restoration Program, particularly through the Wallop-Breaux Amendment, was designed to bridge a growing gap between the needs of state fishery programs and the funding available. In other words, the state programs were (are) costing more to run than the user base could (or will) provide through license, stamp, and permit fees to run them. In addition, as state government budgets have tightened, general appropriations for conservation programs (including fisheries management) have declined. Not only has the program provided much-needed state funding, but it has been matched with state dollars that have partly come from increased license fees, and it has spurred increases in funding from nonfederal sources.

The Federal Aid in Sport Fish Restoration Program has been responsible for important programs and access projects in all states, and many hundreds of millions of "user-pay" dollars are annually channeled to the states for fisheries management, fish production and stocking, state university research activities, boat access improvements, and other undertakings. The program has specifically been responsible for:

- Acquisition of tens of thousands of acres for access
- Development of thousands of boating and fishing access sites
- Production of several billion fish for restoration or maintenance projects
- Work on habitat enhancement projects at over 2,000 stream sites
- Work on habitat enhancement projects at over 2,300 lakes and reservoirs

- Review of hundreds of thousands of public projects
- Technical assistance to hundreds of thousands of private landowners
- Surveys of thousands of fish populations
- Investigation of thousands of habitats
- Aquatic education courses to several million students

Funding has allowed states to seize fisheries enhancement opportunities that might otherwise have been missed, and to undertake large projects that might otherwise have been unfunded, such as hatchery construction or rehabilitation, or acquisition of important habitats. All of these efforts translate into more sport fishery conservation efforts and more angling opportunity.
See: Fisheries Management.

FELT SOLE
See: Waders.

FENDER
An object hung over a boat to cushion it from impacts with docks, piers, or other boats. In big-game fishing, large polyfenders are sometimes used as teasers (see) to attract marlin from the depths. These are spray painted to look like bait or other pelagic fish (like dolphin), rigged with a weighted trailing skirt, and towed on a weighted line (egg weights crimped to the line at the nose), which allows them to kick up a greater disturbance than conventional attractors.

FERRULE
The mating sections of a rod blank, which are joined to form a complete fishing rod. In the past, these sections were produced by cutting a rod blank and joining the sections with separate metal fittings or ferrules, which produced multipiece rods but hampered the action. The majority of rods today are joined with integral ferrules. The sections of multipiece rods are manufactured as separate blanks with ferrules integral to the blanks; if properly designed and manufactured, the ferrules allow the rod to perform as if it were a one-piece rod.

The receiving end is called the outside or female ferrule, and the other the inside or male ferrule. The outside ferrule is a bit larger so that the inside section slides into it. The joint is ground with a precision taper, and the friction fit is sufficient for a secure grip.

Many anglers lubricate this joint with beeswax both to increase the grip and to promote smoother assembly and disassembly. Do not apply wax excessively, or it will trap abrasive dirt particles; always wipe a ferrule before assembly. For disassembly, hold the rod firmly at both ferrules and turn each in opposite directions while gently pulling each away from the other.
See: Rod, Fishing.

FIBERGLASS ROD
A fishing rod that uses fiberglass material in the construction of the blank. The evolution of fiberglass proved the demise of steel rods (see) and eventually bamboo rods (see), although some limited fabrication of split-cane bamboo rods is still practiced by custom rod builders. Uniform quality of production was the key to the success of early fiberglass rods, and several processes evolved, using different types of fiberglass, particularly today E-glass (see) and S-glass (see).

Modern rods are primarily made of fiberglass material, especially those having lower cost and offering certain performance distinctions (durability and softer recovery); graphite material; and, increasingly, a blend of fiberglass and graphite.
See: Rod, Fishing.

FIELD DRESSING
A method of cleaning fish that involves the removal of the entrails, gills, and kidney.
See: Fish Preparation—Cleaning/Dressing.

FIGHTING BELT
See: Rod Belt.

FIGHTING BUTT
An extension to the base of a fly rod handle. Because fly reels sit at the base of most fishing rods, it is awkward, if not inhibiting, to fight strong fish by jamming the rod and reel into the angler's midsection. A fighting butt, which is from 2 to 6 inches long, improves leverage and places the reel and its handle far enough away from the angler's body to allow unimpeded cranking.

A fighting butt may be an integral part of a fly rod, and not removable, or it may be an optional extension of the reel seat, employed by removing the butt cap and inserting it into the portal at the base of the reel seat. An optional extension is useful on a rod that sees varied fishing activities, since the extension can be removed when the angler is casting for small fish. When a fighting butt is used, the rod-holding hand is placed at the top of the handle, or often above the handle on the blank, for fighting leverage. The end cap of the butt is usually rounded to ease its effect on the body, although a prolonged battle with a fish will leave a bruise on the body where the fighting butt has been jammed, unless something buffers it (like heavy clothes or a rod belt).

FIGHTING CHAIR
Also known as a fishing chair, this specialized chair

is used on sportfishing boats and is designed to give anglers an advantage when fighting large fish. Fighting chairs used for smaller species are usually free-standing, resting on four legs. These chairs have the advantage of mobility, since they can be placed wherever desired in the boat.

Larger fighting chairs are mounted atop fixed pedestals, and they turn on some sort of bearing so that the angler can keep the rod tip pointed toward the fish at all times. Pedestal chairs usually have footrests for leverage and have rod holders in the arms of the chair.

Rod gimbals are normally mounted on the front of a fighting chair and allow the angler to pump the fishing rod in a fore-and-aft motion for leverage and to gain line. These gimbals swing in one direction only and contain a receiver with locking mechanism to receive the rod butt.

See: Sportfishing Boat.

FIGHTING FISH
See: Playing Fish.

FIGHTING GRIP
The foregrip on the handle of a fishing rod *(see)*, located ahead of the reel and used by an angler for gripping when applying pressure to strong, deep, and hard-pulling fish.

FIGURE EIGHT
A motion made when a muskie, and sometimes a northern pike, follows a lure (especially a bucktail spinner) to the boat, in order to induce a strike. This is done from a standing position by keeping the lure a few inches from the rod tip, pointing the rod tip close to the water's surface, and quickly making a series of wide figure-eight motions to try to get the following fish excited enough to pounce on it. A figure eight works only occasionally, but it is better than removing the lure from the water and casting again quickly, especially for muskies.

FIJI ISLANDS
Fiji consists of about 332 islands, which vary in size from 10,000 square kilometers to tiny islets a few meters in circumference. One-third of these are inhabited, and they spread over thousands of square kilometers of ocean in the heart of the South Pacific. Although distant and exotic to many people, Fiji has become a crossroads of air and shipping services between North America, Australia, and New Zealand. Travelers and international vessels enter the country via the international airports at Nadi or Nausori, or the natural harbors at Suva and Lautoka—all located on the largest island, Viti Levu. The second largest island, Vanua Levu, is about 60 kilometers from Viti Levu, and together they constitute 85 percent of Fiji's landmass.

Fiji enjoys a tropical maritime climate without great extremes of heat or cold. It lies in the area occasionally traversed by tropical cyclones. They occur mostly between November and April, with greatest frequency around January and February. On the average, some 10 to 12 cyclones per decade affect some part of Fiji, and 2 to 3 do severe damage.

In all seasons the predominant winds over Fiji are the trade winds, blowing from the east to southeast. On the western and eastern sides of Viti Levu and Vanua Levu, however, daytime sea breezes blow in across the coast.

Temperatures at low elevations are usually fairly uniform. Because of the influence of the surrounding oceans, the changes from day to day and season to season are relatively small. Sunshine duration is relatively high in the northwestern area, especially in winter. Southeastern coastal areas and the high interior often experience persistent cloudy, humid weather.

Rainfall is highly variable. It is usually abundant in summer (particularly January)—especially over the large islands—but in winter and spring it is often deficient, particularly in the dry zone on the western and northern sides of the main islands. The dry season is from May through October, and the wet season from November through April. In the drier half-year, from May through October, the heaviest rainfall occurs on the windward (southeast) sides of the larger mountainous islands.

Some of the first attempts at gamefishing here were made from the old capital, Levuka, on Ovalau Island in 1918. These efforts were followed in later years by angling in the area between Ovalau, Wakaya (which has wild deer and where the German raider Baron von Luckner was captured during World War II), and Makogai Islands; Makogai was a leper colony and, with the eradication of that disease, is now a government station.

Tropical gamefish species are abundant in the waters around Fiji, and angling exists year-round

Although most fishing in the Fiji Islands is for big-game species, the shallow waters also provide diverse opportunities.

for some; billfish, tuna, dolphin, wahoo, barracuda, and narrowbarred mackerel are most prominent. World records have been established here for Pacific sailfish, dogtooth tuna, wahoo, kawakawa, and giant trevally. There are no long coastlines in Fiji to monitor fish migration; however, pelagic species, especially billfish, migrate through these waters, providing year-round fishing activity as they move through and back again.

Because of Fiji's geographic location, it is difficult to know whether the fish caught were migrating north or south, or visiting to feed in one particular area. Local anglers have made observations about this, drawn from trends in neighboring countries. It is known from participation in New Zealand tournaments that Fiji's winter months—June, July, and August—are likely to produce the best catches of striped marlin. Fiji appears to be too distant from other significant marlin species' territories, such as Cairns in Australia and Kona in Hawaii, to monitor or have knowledge of the movement of black or blue marlin through the Fiji Islands, as both species are taken almost year-round here.

Many very large specimens of blue marlin have been hooked and lost. The local records for marlin (all marlin are known to Fijians as *sakuvorowaqa*) are 447 kilograms for blue (caught in January 1997), 184.6 kilograms for black, and 133 kilograms for striped.

Pacific sailfish, known here as *sakulaca*, appear to be present throughout the year, with captures every month. The recent local best was a 77.11-kilogram fish, but an 85.72-kilogram line-class world record, which still stands, was caught in 1967.

Wahoo are Fiji's main species and usually appear in early May, but the length of the wahoo season has been erratic of late. They are best caught from May through July. A 63.8-kilogram specimen is the local record.

Tuna species include yellowfin, bigeye, dogtooth, skipjack, kawakawa, and Pacific bonito. Tuna are locally known as *yatu*, and island records for the larger species include a 111.5-kilogram yellowfin, a 74.3-kilogram dogtooth, and a 64.8-kilogram bigeye.

Yellowfin occur from November through March and migrate back through the island group from May through August, occurring in schools with skipjack and kawakawa. Large bigeye tuna are less available to anglers and are usually caught deep, on live bait, when the angler is pursuing yellowfin or marlin. Fish up to 20 kilograms are caught in schools, sometimes mixed with yellowfin. Dogtooth tuna are fished in deep water, using downriggers or drop lines along dropoffs and over seamounts, with dead or live bait.

Skipjack occur in large schools and are usually easily caught. Used as live or dead bait, they are occasionally cut into strips for trolling or to enhance plastic trolling lures. They are available in most months, with the middle of winter producing the largest specimens.

Kawakawa occur mainly around passages and in the large areas of lagoons, often in less than clear water, where they feed on herring, squid, and crustaceans. The best time is November through May. Bonito occur in schools and are sometimes mixed with skipjack, but are not recorded often.

Mahimahi (dolphin) are abundant in almost all months. The largest average approximately 19 kilograms. Known here as *ika narokaveisau*, these fish are caught to 26.76 kilograms and take almost all known baits and lures; many have been caught on Fiji's traditional *viavia* lure, fashioned from a plant. This has a shiny silver texture similar to onion flesh. It is rolled around the hook and trace, and cut to desired shape—Kona head or bullet-nosed, according to preference. This type of lure has caught many other species as well, although modern lure technology has caused a marked decline in its use.

Barracuda, in particular great barracuda and pickhandle barracuda, occur throughout the year. Some very large barracuda (called *ogo*) have been known to attack anglers and divers in Fiji, and some attacks have been fatal. The largest recorded great barracuda here was over 45 kilograms (100 pounds), and many have been taken over 23 kilograms. A 28.3-kilogram line-class world record was established in Fiji at Serua in 1988.

Narrowbarred mackerel, known as *walu*, are an important local species. This fish bears a high price in Fijian markets and is the basis of *kokoda*, the traditional raw fish delicacy of Fiji. Apart from being a prominent food source, mackerel are sought by anglers and occur here mainly from February through July, and weigh an average of 18 kilograms. From July through September, however, schools appear off the north coast of Vanua Levu, where it is believed they spawn, and some large specimens from this area have weighed more than 47 kilograms.

The most successful rig for this species is a specially designed and shaped lead weight created by an avid local angler. Aptly named after its designer, the Houng Lee rig consists of a short trace attached to the lead, and two hooks that are rather short but still in accordance with International Game Fish Association (IGFA) rules. A small baitfish, known locally as *salala* and similar to scad, is attached to the hook. The best speed for trolling this rig simulates the speed of the swimming rigged bait; the size of the bait determines the speed at which the bait swims. A rigged bait trolled at the correct speed looks so lifelike that a novice would mistake it for a live fish.

Many species of trevally are regularly caught in Fijian waters. Giant trevally to 68 kilograms have been landed here, although the most common size is from 13.5 to 23 kilograms, and all species are taken when casting from beach, pier, wharf, or boat. As with other pelagic species, trevally *(saqa)* school and hunt for herring *(daniva)*, which occur in great schools.

Also common are rainbow runners, which range

to 10 kilograms. Other species include Pacific crevalle jack and horse-eye jack. Permit have not been caught on rod and reel, although they are here in numbers. Also present but not generally caught by anglers are African pompano and a variety of small inshore species, some of which are used as whole trolling baits. Swordfish are caught commercially by longliners, although none have been recorded on rod and reel.

In freshwater, largemouth bass have been introduced into Vaturu Dam, the main water supply for Nadi. Sportfishing techniques have recorded these fish up to 2 kilograms.

FILLET BOARD
In a commercial sense, a fillet board is a narrow wooden or plastic board for cleaning and filleting small fish, usually with a spring clip at one end, that holds the fish in place while it is being dressed. A homemade fillet board or cleaning board often lacks the clip but is larger and wider. In saltwater, a fillet board may be constructed with a back and sides and lower dimensions that allow it to fit over the gunwale of a boat; the board is used for cutting up fish for chumming, chunking, or bait use, as well as for cleaning the catch.
See: Fish Preparation—Cleaning/Dressing.

FILLET KNIFE
See: Fish Preparation—Cleaning/Dressing.

FILLETING
Cutting the sides of a fish lengthwise, parallel to and free from the backbone, accompanied by removal of the rib cage.
See: Fish Preparation—Cleaning/Dressing.

FIN
An organ on different parts of a fish's body that may be used for propulsion, balance, and steering.
See: Anatomy; Fish.

FINDING FISH
Successful fishing is the result of many activities, the foremost of which is finding fish. The act of finding fish involves a combination of elements, including visual observation, intensive searching, an understanding of the habits of fish and their preferred habitat (which varies from species to species), and savvy and good judgment to realize how these elements relate to one another and how they can be taken advantage of.

Visual observation is one factor in selecting places to fish and in looking for signs that indicate the presence of fish (see: sight fishing). In a stream, trout may indicate their presence by rising to the

Learning to read the flow of rivers, such as this one in Labrador, will help keep you fishing in the most productive places.

surface to capture insects. In a lake, a school of bass chasing shad may force their prey to the surface, and the resulting commotion allows anglers to pinpoint a group of fish and perhaps readily intercept them. In saltwater, the frenzied activity of a distant group of birds (see) may indicate a school of bluefish that is ripping into bait. And on a grassy flat at low tide, the exposed tail of a bonefish or redfish that is scrounging the bottom may give away its presence to the stalking angler. In all these instances and in many others, the problem of locating a fish—which is just one element of the game of catching them—has been solved because of the activities of the quarry and the observance of the angler. Most of the time, however, fish are not readily found by observation, and anglers must search for them by other means.

It is important to realize that fish are not found everywhere in a given body of water; they inhabit specific places, primarily for food, cover, and temperature reasons. The extent to which they inhabit specific places or prefer certain habitat varies with the species and may be influenced by seasons, spawning, water conditions, and other factors. Clearly, many variables influence the location of fish.

For anglers, the question of where to fish—presumably in a place where the quarry is or will be—can become a big issue when the fishing location is new or unfamiliar. The answer, in the modern fishing era, is increasingly supplied by sophisticated electronic equipment. Some of this equipment has become important, if not almost indispensable, to many ardent anglers, satisfying their desire and need to learn more about the places they fish. Sonar devices and temperature-sensing units are chief among these and are truly instrumental in helping boat anglers unlock the secrets of the places they fish. Using sonar (see) to locate fish has become one of the foremost facets of fishing from boats in the modern era. But sonar does not tell you where to look for fish; it only tells you if they are where you are, and then it does not assure you that the fish you find are the species you want to find.

So you have to evaluate the place that you're fishing, observing water conditions to determine where fish may be and how to present lures or bait to them. This skill is referred to as "reading water" and can be practiced in all types of environments, especially in freshwater. It is sometimes easier in rivers than in stillwaters (ponds, lakes, reservoirs) because many elements are more obvious. For example, in current, any sizable obstruction (boulder, bridge footing, pier, etc.) creates a slack pocket where fish can lie without exerting much effort and watch for food; these are readily located. Stillwaters especially pose problems for many anglers, particularly in places that they do not know well, and for the obvious reason that the surface usually gives no indication of what is below.

Lakes, ponds, impoundments, bays, oceans, and other bodies of water are all quite different, so the type and the size of a body of water play a role in what you do and how you do it. The species available and/or desired is another consideration; obviously the more you know about fish behavior and habitat, the better. Gamefish are usually found in certain places for specific reasons, and the better you understand the relationship between their depth, cover, temperature, food needs, and other requirements, the better you are able to put the pieces of the underwater puzzle together while employing electronic equipment.

The pieces of that puzzle can be filled in by making preparations before you get on the water. You can get a head start (especially on unfamiliar water) by simply talking to those who know something about it. Visit local tackle shops (several if possible), and talk to the people there as you purchase bait, license, lures, etc. Talk to people at the launching ramp and marina. Ask specific questions and be observant. Look at the products being sold in the stores to see what the most popular lures and colors are.

Obtaining and studying charts and maps *(see: maps)*, particularly those with underwater contours and with depth and channel markings, can be a key factor. At the very least, they will familiarize you with the general layout of the place and its characteristics, but they also may detail some very specific structures (such as rock reefs, rips, shoals, flats, old roadbeds and culverts, sunken weeds, etc.) that may be important to fish. Such maps are not available for all waters, unfortunately, or the ones that are available may not be as detailed as you'd like. Even the best maps often fail to pinpoint certain underwater features that attract gamefish. Such features might include a nearshore trough that is created by wave action, or a slight pinnacle, mound, or hump that rises high enough off the lake or ocean floor to attract baitfish and thus predators, but not enough to be highlighted on a map. So don't let maps be the last word. In any event, you still have to put your boat in the water and wet a hook.

Picking a spot to fish and immediately wetting a hook, however, is often not such a good idea. Everyone wants to get fishing right away, but you are wise to do some cruising first, looking over the water with your electronics as you go. Sonar study is especially important, but at certain seasons a temperature evaluation may be equally so.

A typical freshwater lake scenario. To illustrate how an initial exploratory trip might be carried out, let's take a freshwater scenario and assume that you're on an unfamiliar lake. You leave the ramp or dock, and the first thing you do is check for surface water temperature. This is a matter of habit, like making the bed in the morning, and something that is more important at some times than at others. Spring is a season when evaluating surface water temperature is of utmost value.

If it is spring, you may want to seek the warmest locales on the lake first. Often that is along the north or northwest shores, where tributaries enter (especially after a warm rain), or in coves, bays, and sloughs. Many freshwater gamefish, and/or baitfish, spawn sometime in spring, often near shore or in and near tributaries; and water temperature is a triggering factor. By finding spots that have favorable temperatures, or temperatures warmer than other areas in the lake, you may locate either the places where fish are congregated or the places

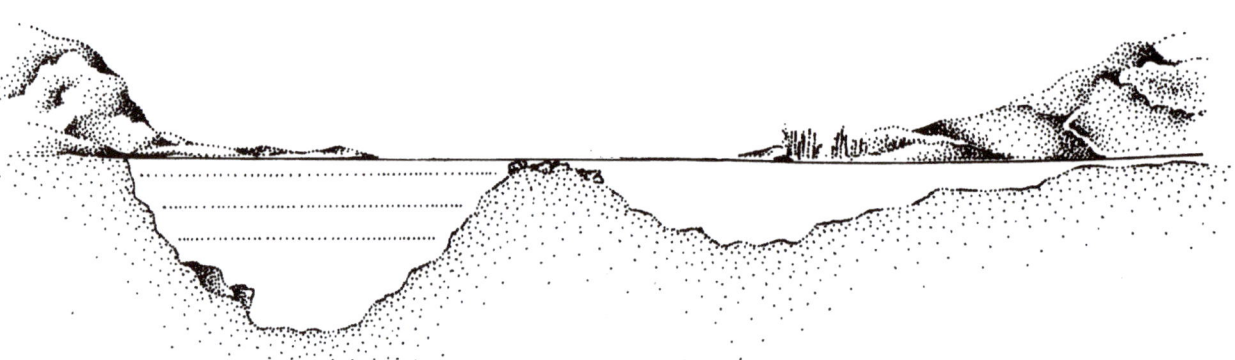

This cross-section view of a lake, with a tributary entering at far right, helps put into perspective the underwater characteristics that are not visible to the eye above water, though they are detectable with sonar.

where fish are most likely to be active.

As full-time guides and charter boat captains can attest, angling for inactive fish is very tough; obviously, fishing where they aren't is a waste of time. Therefore, monitoring a surface temperature gauge (available as a self-functioning unit or as an option with sonar instruments) in the spring is an important adjunct to the business of casting or trolling.

As you move out on the lake, you also watch your sonar instrument. That, again out of habit, was turned on right after you started the motor and will stay on until you stop fishing (unless it is a portable, battery-operated unit). For the moment, let's assume that you're trying to unlock the secrets of this lake in the summer. What you'll look for depends largely on the species of fish you intend to catch, but let's say you have an interest in all gamefish and thus need to consider all of the variables.

You could begin simply by looking for fish on the sonar unit. When you know your quarry well, you may be able to identify the species you see on sonar, but most of the time specific identification is uncertain. Knowledge of the habits and locales preferred by certain species of fish makes them easier to identify on sonar, but there is a lot of gray area here.

In some cases, the level at which concentrations of fish, especially large ones, are found is an important clue to the depth at which you should be fishing. This information is especially pertinent in midlake open-water situations, in trolling, and in seeking such species as trout, salmon, suspended walleye, and striped bass. In other cases, finding schools of bait and knowing their preferred depth can point you to the depth to fish. Looking for fish, then, is something that is often best accomplished while simultaneously learning the lake and looking for suitable places to cast or troll for targeted species.

Observe general depths and underwater contours as you move around the lake. In certain waters, such observations are one of the most interesting aspects of unlocking the secrets of a lake. People who seldom use sonar may have no idea how deep the water is in a chosen spot, meaning that they often fish less efficiently.

Attend to the slope of the shoreline, to the depth near shore, and also to the depth as you move away from shore, especially if there is rock, wood, or vegetative cover. This information can be gauged to some extent by visual observation of the land formation onshore. A gradual slope on land usually indicates a flat and gently sloping terrain under adjacent water, whereas a sharp slope onshore indicates a quick dropoff underwater. However, the particulars aren't as readily discerned without sonar. In the spring, certain species of fish, such as bass, might be more attracted to a shallower shoreline area (which would warm up faster) than to one that dropped off quickly. The reverse could be true later in the year, especially if the steep shoreline was protected from late-day sun.

If you will be fishing in open water (well away from shore), check not only for basic depth but for the presence of such features as shoals, submerged timber, and old creekbeds or channels. Many types of warmwater and coldwater fish are attracted to a shoal because of the proximity to deep water and the ability to find prey there. When you find a shoal (or hump, mound, or reef), glue your eyes to the sonar and motor all around it; watch the conformation on all sides, noting how quickly it drops off and whether bait or larger fish are hanging along the dropoff to deeper water. Scour the shoal with your underwater eyes first; don't just motor over it, but rather stop at the shallowest spot and start fishing. Use the sonar to learn about the shoal first; it takes only a few moments.

Sonar is also helpful in checking out timber and the tops of submerged trees—an important fishing location. When those trees are 30 or more feet below the surface, sonar allows you to stay in the right position. Clearly you need to study the sonar to know about the timber before fishing, as well as watch the sonar closely while fishing. You also should be looking for fish (striped or white bass, in particular). You might use marker buoys to define the edges, channels, and other key features.

One of your main tasks is to check out any points in the lake. A point is a place where the land juts out in the water away from the shore and where the bottom terrain underwater continues to taper down and off. Some points are very obvious, and others are subtle; some taper very gradually and extend (almost like a bar) a long way out into the lake, yet others end abruptly and drop quickly to deep water.

Points are important lake features for many species of fish, so you will use the sonar to do several things: look for fish in the immediate vicinity of well-defined points and on the breaklines (the distinguishable drops to greater depths), establish the contours of points in order to fish them most effectively, and look for less obvious points while otherwise fishing or cruising. Some of the best places to fish in many freshwater environments are points that are not readily detected by looking at the shore, but that are found by accident while fishing along a shoreline and watching sonar.

Vegetation is another important lake feature, especially for walleye, bass, pike, and muskies. It may consist of lily pads, cabbage weeds, milfoil, hyacinths, or other aquatic plants. Look over the vegetation carefully, with and without sonar, if you seek the aforementioned species.

If vegetation appears in shallow water and you're fishing for largemouth bass or pike, use sonar mostly to monitor depth while casting, since you can visually find the places that you should fish. But when the vegetation lies in deeper water, tapers from shallow to deeper water, and/or is submerged, the sonar is helpful for precise positioning and depth monitoring, and it becomes much more important to your fishing.

Initially, slowly cruise along the edges of the vegetation. Try to define its contour, establish the

Fisherman James Heddon, father of the casting plug, ran one of the largest apiaries in the United States, held six patents for beekeeping equipment, founded a newspaper, and was Mayor of Dowagiac, Michigan.

depth at which it ceases growing (which is the weedline and which often appears in 12 to 14 feet of water in northern lakes), look for clusters of isolated weeds or for open patches amidst thick weeds, and generally get to know what lies below.

Because fish are often close to the bottom in the weeds or are deep in the vegetation, you may not see fish on the sonar while scrutinizing the weed edges. However, it is possible to see fish amidst scattered weeds, and sometimes you will do so. Primarily, though, you're trying to establish an underwater picture of what you might see with your eyes if the weeds were on the surface. This picture will point you to the places (edge, irregular features, pockets, etc.) to concentrate your angling efforts.

As you use your electronic equipment to learn about this body of water, try to determine whether the bottom composition—soft as in sandy or hard as in rocky—in specific places is noteworthy; this information may be a clue that the species of fish you seek are in that area. The thermocline, which can be a summertime clue to locating certain fish, is identifiable on some high-quality sonar units.

Once you've spent a little time familiarizing yourself with this lake or with selected areas of it—you don't try to survey the whole lake at one shot—you can stop to fish. How you will do so depends, of course, on what species you seek, the time of year, and the depths or techniques involved. Suppose your sonar shows fish at 30 feet along the dropoff of a point. It won't pay to cast a crankbait into shallow water and crank it back; a better move would probably be slow- trolling with a bottom-bouncing sinker rig or with a lure behind a downrigger; another option is jigging.

You also might employ buoy markers, incidentally, to help identify the places checked on sonar and to act as reference points. These are typically used, for example, to mark the deep sides of shoals, the breaklines on either side of a long point, the location of a cluster of fish or a pile of brush or a road bridge, the meandering of a submerged weedline, or the course of a channel.

Observing features. Although the preceding scenario emphasized the use of electronics as an aid in exploring and learning about a body of water, much can be learned simply by observing the shoreline and surrounding topographical features. If the shore is sandy or rocky, the bottom of the body of water nearby will likely be similar. When the land declines steeply down to the water level, the lake there will drop off sharply into deep water, but where the shore slopes gradually, the lake near shore will do likewise. This is particularly true in man-made bodies of water and in times of high water.

As already noted, points are an important land form in fishing. Many points extend underwater well out into a lake before dropping off abruptly into deep water. This feature can attract both migratory and nonmigratory species of fish and can be worth exploring, although by looking strictly at

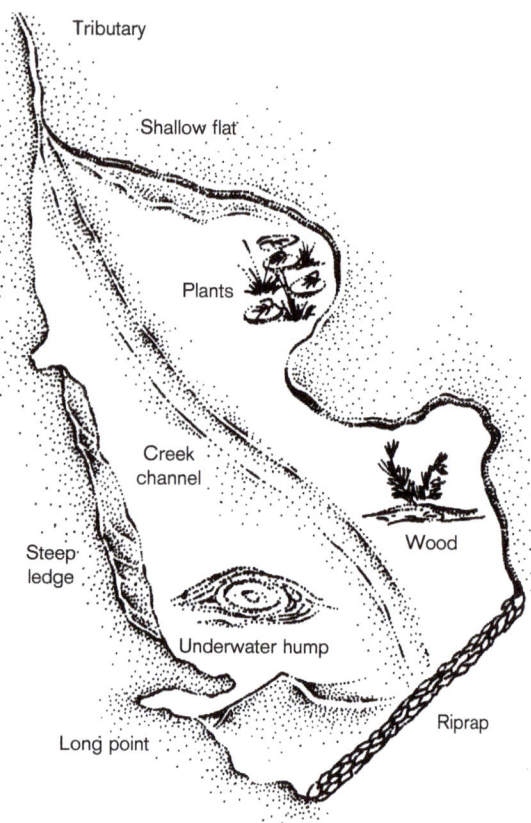

This simplified view of an impoundment depicts many different features that may be relevant to fishing efforts.

the water's surface you seldom have a clue that anything unusual is below and near the point.

Perhaps more obvious are such features as rock walls, fence posts, and roadbeds, which are typically found in bodies of water that have been artificially made or enlarged, and which extend from shore into the water and provide cover for some species of fish.

Even more obvious, of course, is vegetation, stumps, timber, docks, and the like, which provide cover and attract bait and smaller prey fish. Some species of fish are especially attracted to various forms of cover, and you should look for emerged and submerged cover, especially if it is near deep water, because it may hold the type of fish you seek. By judiciously fishing these objects (and in the case of vegetation, seeking the pockets and edges within), you can enhance your opportunities for catching fish.

Big water considerations. Many anglers enjoy fishing in streams, ponds, rivers, inlets, marshes, and small lakes because of their relatively small size, not only from an accessibility or boating standpoint, but because the options are narrower. A big body of water, with miles and miles of shoreline or a maze of islands, can be intimidating.

Big waters have abundant populations of major gamefish, in many cases species and sizes of fish unknown or rarely found in small waters. To enjoy these bounties, you must solve the problems posed by fishing big water and not be overwhelmed by them.

In big lakes and river systems, tributaries play a

critical role in gamefish behavior and therefore fishing success. This is especially true in the spring when many predator and prey species enter tributaries to spawn, or when they come into the near-shore areas influenced by tributaries because of the presence of food and more comfortable conditions.

Tributaries, whether they are major rivers, small streams, the outlet of upstream dams, etc., are the lifeblood of big water. In the spring, they bear the rain and the runoff from snowmelt that helps open up the lake, then the warm water that ultimately raises the temperature of the cold main lake. A warm rain is a blessing for a big body of water that is influenced by a major tributary, because the warmth will stimulate activity, feeding, and possibly spawning, though it sometimes takes two or three days for a heavy warm rain to have an impact on a big lake system. This phenomenon is most evident in large mid-South impoundments hosting stripers, white bass, black bass, and walleye.

However, the area where a tributary intersects a lake is an edge that attracts bait and major gamefish. Water that is a few degrees warmer than the main lake temperature flows into the lake and mixes with it, encouraging fish activity. A distinct mudline, the result of stained or muddy spring runoff, is often created around tributary mouths. On some waters, this mudline attracts gamefish because there is usually a thermal break here as well, with the inner edge being warmer and the mudline itself being attractive to bait and prey species.

Water temperature is certainly a key to gamefish behavior. In the Great Lakes, for example, early-season fishing primarily occurs in fairly shallow water close to shore. Trout and salmon seek warm water there, as do the alewife and smelt that they feed on. Sometimes the way to get action is to find the warmest water along the shore.

Elsewhere, however, the upper layer of water may warm up a bit on a mild, sunny spring day and act as an attracting edge, where fish may be caught very shallow. This is especially so for bass, for example, which will eventually make nests in warm shallow water, or for trout or salmon, which will be attracted to pockets of warm water or vertical separations of different-temperature water away from immediate tributary areas. Such areas may be in the vicinity of a warmwater discharge or may simply be the phenomenon of water movement and mixing. Nonetheless, surface temperature variants can be edges.

Perhaps the most extraordinary example of this phenomenon is that of the so-called thermal bar that exists in mid- to late spring on the Great Lakes, where there is a sharp surface distinction between temperatures offshore at a time when nearshore environs are relatively warm and theoretically in a temperature range that should attract trout and salmon. Nevertheless, colder offshore water on a distinct surface thermal break is the better place to be looking for fish, particularly salmon and steelhead.

Temperature remains a factor after spring for many fish species. Water stratification sends cold- and coolwater fish to deeper freshwater locales in the summer. Thus, when you fish open-water areas, you must know the preferred temperature of the species you seek, attempt to find out the depth at which this temperature is found, and try to relate this to prominent areas that would attract your quarry (such as long sloping underwater points, submerged creek channels, sharp dropoffs, and so forth).

The thermocline is usually a fairly narrow band of water, but it is found where temperature drops off sharply, often averaging a drop of .5° to 1°F degree every foot. Sometimes it is only 10 feet wide and 15 to 20 feet below the surface; usually it is a bit wider and begins deeper. To locate the thermocline, lower a thermometer on a rope or fishing line, checking it every 5 feet or so. Give the thermometer enough time at checked depths to register the proper reading.

Most lakes that stratify like this have a good deal of deep water. Shallow lakes don't stratify, since they become uniformly warm with too little variation from top to bottom. Fewer southern lakes stratify than northern ones; many lakes display the same patterns from year to year.

In lakes with clearly defined thermoclines, you can identify the thermocline on a good sonar instrument. Try to fish in and around the thermocline because it will have the best combination of food, oxygen, and temperature. But keep in mind the temperature preferences of the fish you seek, since the actual temperature of the thermocline will vary by locale and the fish may be just above or below it.

A thermocline usually lasts until the fall, or when there is a trend toward cool air temperatures. When the surface water cools off enough, a body of water mixes and the thermocline dissipates. This is often referred to as the "fall turnover."

Big waters are slow to warm up in the spring and slow to cool off in the fall. This fact means that small bodies of water may be better to fish in the earliest part of the season—until the larger waters warm up—and that big waters may sustain good fishing for a longer period of time in the fall.

Other places offering warmth are bays and coves, especially if they are shallow and contain the type of cover preferred by the species you seek. Bays are especially good places to fish in the spring on natural lakes that are not fed by major tributaries; bays may also be productive in sprawling man-made lakes that do have tributaries. Bays with a north and northwest exposure (or sections of a bay with such an exposure) get the most sun in the day. They also benefit from southerly winds, which stack warm surface water up on their shores. Thus, they tend to warm up fast and may attract certain species if the habitat is right.

Grass, weedbeds, and other forms of vegetation may also be important fishing areas of big lakes, but this habitat may not be readily observable or may not be found in all sectors of a lake. Bays, coves, islands, and shoals are usually good places to start the search for vegetation, which is as likely to be

 Mako shark (Isurus oxyrinchus) fossils have been dated to the Miocene epoch 25 million years ago; a prehistoric relative of that era, Isurus hastalis, may have reached 6 to 8 meters long.

submerged in moderate depth water as it is visible and close to shore.

A good tactic for anglers apprehensive about where to begin fishing is to approach big water as if it were several smaller bodies of water, and focus on one section at a time. Some anglers become familiar with big lakes by zeroing in on prominent points. Some fish use points as full-time domiciles because they offer frequent opportunities to ambush prey. Others migrate by them often, or they leave deep-water haunts temporarily to visit points for feeding.

When you are solving the mysteries of where to fish and what to look for in a big body of water, your knowledge of fish habits and seasonal habitat requirements will prove a great ally. In freshwater, for instance, if lake trout are your quarry, you should be looking for rocky shoals, reefs, and islands near deep water, since lakers come in from deeper water to such areas, feed, then leave. In contrast, open-water salmon don't orient much to underwater features; thus, when they aren't close to shore in spring or fall, you have to fish specific temperature zones (mostly in deep water) and aggressively search for them and for baitfish. Stripers, too, are often nomadic and follow schools of bait, although they do seek out impoundments, where the tops of submerged timber, old river channels, and other identifiable underwater terrain give them a place to find food. Largemouth bass and pike orient strongly toward various forms of cover, usually near shore, so they present different demands upon the angler. Draw upon your knowledge of a species when deciding where to go and what to do.

Also, think in terms of edges. Fish, like most animals, are attracted to some type of edge, whether one of structure or temperature. Think about the type of edge—for example, a long sloping underwater point, a reef or shoal, or even a rocky versus sandy bottom—that may appeal to your target species for reasons of comfort, security, or feeding.

A prominent edge lair might be a shoal or reef. Underwater mounds or islands, sandbars, and gravel bars are similar. These locations may be rocky or boulder-strewn, or they may be sandy with moderate weed growth; in any case, they attract small baitfish, which in turn attract predators. Often, there is deep water on one side.

How you fish such places is almost as important as the fact that you do fish them. When trolling the perimeter of weeds, sandbars, shoals, and so forth, for example, you might have a shallower running lure on the side of the boat nearest the edge, and your deepest running lure on the opposite side. If fishing two lures off the same gunwale, put a deep runner on the inside rod on a short- to medium-length line and a shallow runner on the outside position but on a longer length of line (it might get as deep as the other lure but be further back to avoid tangling and to aid in fish playing and hooksetting). Or, use a lure on a short line behind a downrigger and use a diving lure on a longer flatline.

The deep-water/shallow-water interface near islands can be similarly thought of as an edge, as can a sharply sloping shoreline. These are places to which bait migrates naturally, and logically they present feeding opportunities.

Current is also a factor. Locales where a strong current retards the movement of weak, crippled, or wounded fish, or brings bait washing by, are possible fishing spots. Back eddies, slicks, tidal rips, and current edges are more good spots. In rivers, where a secondary tributary meets a major flow is also a

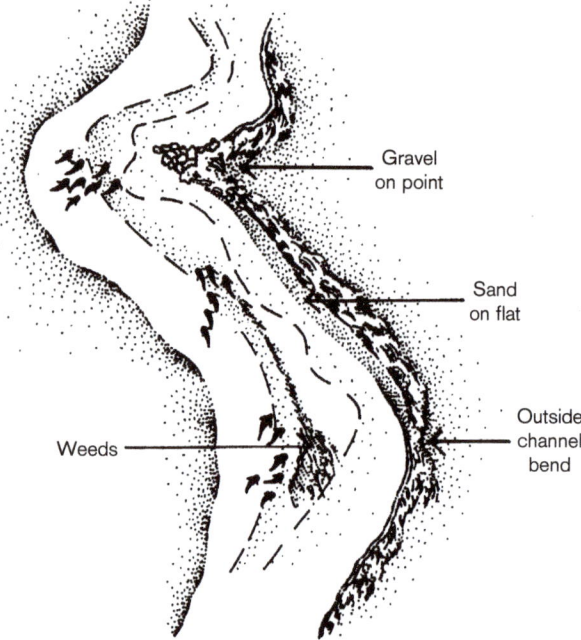

This compressed view depicts some of the common characteristics of a river.

promising intersection, especially in summer when the secondary tributary may be dumping cooler and more oxygenated water into the main flow.

Knowing which types of edges appeal to which species of fish makes a difference when fishing in current. For example, the inside bend of major tributaries is often a hotspot to troll or cast for stripers in the spring. Stripers like a point where water rushes by, so they hold on the inside bend of a channel and use this spot to ambush whatever comes around. Walleye are known for locating along an edge, particularly along a deep-water breakline. Walleye commonly move shallower in the evening to the fringes of a bar or a rock or gravel point that breaks sharply to deep water. One successful fishing tactic here is to use plugs that dive to 8 or 10 feet and troll from deep water to the point; then go along one side and work along the edge.

Some fish are known for congregating in or along the edges of vegetation. Weeds attract small baitfish and larger fish in the food chain, and they also offer protective cover. Working submerged weed lines, where the weeds end and the bottom begins to drop off to deeper water, is not only possible, but an especially effective fishing method.

Many fish use the edges of vegetative cover or other structures to hide and to ambush prey. They lurk in or by places where food is abundant and where they can lie relatively concealed to pounce on appropriate-size forage. Some anglers refer to such feeding stations as ambush points, and they like to be as close as possible to deep water, dropoffs, shelves, ledges, creekbeds, channels, and the like. Whether you angle for species that prefer the confines of cover or the vastness of open water, be aware of the subtle borders and margins of these habitats and seek and fish those places.

Much of the preceding information also applies to flowing water, especially large rivers. The reading of water is most obviously practiced by anglers who fish in smaller rivers and creeks, where some boating is done, but most fishing is by wading or angling from the bank. Current in rivers and creeks is a premier influence on where and how fish are situated, both for resting and for feeding purposes. Fish face flowing water, so lures must generally come downcurrent toward them in a natural manner.

In flowing water, the deeper places are the ones that often hold fish and are sought by anglers. Slow-moving water is a sign of depth. Water is deepest where the current comes against the bank; years of this action have gouged the bank and bottom, resulting in deeper water. Shallow water is found on the inside of a bend. In many places the bank is much steeper on the outside of a bend than on the inside, and this is another clue to the location of the deeper and shallower portions. This information is important not only for angling but also for navigating a boat or wading safely.

When current strikes an object, it may cause less turbulence in front of, or behind, that object. Fish may locate here because they don't have to work as hard to resist the flow and also because it may be a good place to find food. Boulders are the most common objects in currents, but small islands or shoals also exist; in high water, stumps and fallen trees are objects that can attract fish.

Saltwater tides and current. Many of the same factors that apply to finding fish in freshwater also apply in saltwater, one major difference being that saltwater involves a much broader expanse of water and not as many forms of cover. However, in saltwater, finding fish is influenced by tide *(see)*, current *(see)*, and weather *(see)*. The effect of weather can sometimes be greater than either tide or current. For example, murky water caused by severe storms stirring up the water in inshore areas can temporarily impact bottom fishing adversely.

Tides and current have a major impact not only on where fish may be found, but on whether they are likely to be feeding. There are exceptions, but many saltwater fish, particularly species inhabiting inshore areas, bays, and brackish water, are more active when the tide is moving than when it is slack. The effect of tide can be more pronounced in certain places

Shallow-draft boats and poling platforms are used to search Gulf Coast waters for redfish and seatrout.

than others, and underwater structures (like rips) or differing bottoms (like flats) may present good feeding opportunities when a tide is falling, rather than when it is rising. Tides act much like a river current in many places, especially in bays and estuary areas.

Currents are more pronounced in offshore waters, and fishing where main warmwater currents exist is important for certain species, although eddylike pockets of ocean currents may hold pelagic species.

Obviously, changes in tides affect much of the inshore, nearshore, estuary, and marsh environment. Jetties that might be good to fish just before and after a high tide are probably not worth fishing at the other end of the tide range. Some flats, mangrove islands, marshlands, and the like will be dry or nearly so on a low tide. And yet, in some instances (for example, when you are stalking bonefish), the low water is best because it makes the fish easier to spot. So the places that you fish in high water and low water may be greatly different. And this difference is more profound during a high or new moon.

Tide, current, and weather affect more than just your target species; they also affect the availability of bait and the behavior of different species, and these factors should be considered when deciding where to fish.

FINESSE BAIT

A bass fishing term for a small lure, especially a soft tube lure or light jig, used on light line for heavily pressured fish, especially in clear deep water. Finesse fishing is a term often used to refer to the use of light or ultralight tackle and appropriately sized lures.
See: Jig.

FINFISH

An alternative collective term for all species of fish, used to separate true fish from crustaceans and mollusks, which are collectively termed shellfish. The term is rarely used in reference to freshwater species but is commonly used to refer to saltwater and anadromous fish, particularly by fisheries managers.

FINGERLING

A young fish about 2 to 4 inches long.

FINLAND

A northern European country with strong ties to sportfishing, Finland is situated on the northern side of the Baltic Sea, northwest of Russia and east of Sweden and Norway. Renowned for its many lakes and ponds, Finland is called the "Land of a Thousand Lakes"; in actuality, there are more than 62,000 lakes here.

Comprising an area of 130,085 square miles, Finland spreads over 600 miles from south to north, and its geography is as varied as the country is long. Southern Finland is flat; the rivers flow slowly for short distances, and the lakes are typically shallow and warm. Hardwood like birch, aspen, and alder are present in the forests, although softwood, pine, and spruce are dominant. Central and eastern Finland have some longer rivers and extensive lake formations, the largest of which is the Saimaa lake system. Farther north are extensive spruce forests, low wetlands, and longer rivers. Near the Arctic Circle, the forests and the soil get drier, and pine is the dominant tree. Even farther north lies Lapland, the land of the reindeer, the dwarf birch, and the midnight sun. In general, Lapland is a country of smallish lakes, rivers, and brooks, although huge Lake Inarinjärvi breaks the rule.

Finland's lakes, combined with its numerous rivers and streams and more than 2,760 miles of Baltic shoreline, offer fine and varied opportunities for anglers. Trout are the most sought-after sportfish in Finland, and there's also great enthusiasm for salmon and charr; however, northern pike, European perch, zander, bream, and many lesser members of the carp family offer opportunities for good sport.

The Baltic Sea and Åland Islands

The northern Baltic Sea has an extremely low saline content and thus a peculiar saltwater fishery; one can catch many common freshwater fish in the brackish coastal waters of the Gulf of Bothnia and the Gulf of Finland. Northern pike and sea-run brown trout (sea trout) are at the top of the list, and some specialists troll for Atlantic salmon. In some areas of the Gulf of Bothnia it is even possible, and productive, to cast flies for big grayling in the sea. This is truly exotic fishing of a sort available almost nowhere else in the world.

Casting for sea-run browns is a Scandinavian specialty and a particularly popular form of sportfishing in Finland. Trolling for these fish is also popular, especially in the summer, when trout cruise in deeper water. A limited number of people cast flies for them.

The favored tackle for sea trout consists of a sturdy, but not too stiff, rod and a reel that can hold at least 100 yards of 10-pound nylon line. Long, slim spoons in sizes of $1/2$ to 1 ounce are the most popular bait, but minnow plugs and larger spinners also produce results.

Handmade Finnish minnow-spoons are a local specialty and were originally developed for this fishery, which is often practiced in very shallow water. They might not be readily available in Europe or North America, but they can be bought from most tackle dealers in the coastal towns of Finland. Several skilled local artisans here make fine minnow-spoons.

The best seasons for sea trout are early spring and late fall, when air and water temperatures chill and trout swim closer to shore, but some fish can be caught at any time of the year. A boat is almost essential for success, however. In larger towns professional guides are available to assist the visiting angler. These silvery fish are worth a lot of trouble; when fresh from the sea, they are almost always in top condition, and their average size lies around 3 pounds, with double-digit fish not a rarity. During the best seasons, especially in the fall, the weather may get rough, and the air temperature falls well under 0°C, so it is very important to dress accordingly and have a flotation aid of some sort; a flotation suit is best.

Northern pike can be caught along the entire coastline, but the most popular and productive fish-

A pike comes to hand in Baltic waters among Finland's Åland Islands.

ing is in the archipelago between the town of Turku and the Åland Islands. The latter is an autonomous province of Finland and can be reached from the mainland by boat or plane. The sportfishing in Åland is well organized, and several skilled professional fishing guides operate in the area. Pike can be caught almost year-round, but spring and fall offer the best opportunities for big fish. The sea trout fishing in Åland is also very good, and as the top seasons for both species overlap, it is possible to fish both species successfully during the same day.

Åland pike are rarely exceptionally large; the average fish is 5 to 10 pounds, but specimens up to 35 pounds are caught every year. Fishing methods include casting and trolling. Standard pike spoons work well in these waters, but there are local favorites. Anglers after truly large pike prefer trolling with enormous plugs, especially deep-diving versions. Excellent fly fishing for pike exists in the Åland Islands and has been gaining in popularity. Large streamers are the standard offerings.

The perch is a humble inhabitant of these waters; nevertheless, it is valued for its fine table quality. In Baltic waters these fish grow well, and 2-pounders are regularly caught. Spinning tackle, small spinners, and various jigs are effective.

Southern Region

The lakes of southern Finland are mostly shallow and warm. The most popular fish species in these waters are northern pike, pike-perch (zander), and European perch. Pike and perch are common everywhere. Zander inhabit many larger lakes and, although not great fighters, they are highly regarded for their tasty fillets. Trolling is the most popular way to catch zander, and minnow-type plugs are the preferred lures. The best time to fish for zander is July, and the average size is around 2 pounds.

Perch are the most common fish in Finnish lakes and ponds. This species is found practically everywhere and is caught year-round. It grows well in larger lakes, which produce bigger fish on average than those found in smaller waters. Many small ponds hold an enormous population of dwarfed perch. This is the standby, and most important, species for ice anglers. Ice fishing competitions are popular, and perch are normally the only qualified species.

Southern Finland offers many coarse fishing opportunities. The European bream and ide are the most sought-after species. Anglers typically use earthworms or bread as bait, but stream-dwelling ide also take small spinners and artificial flies. Roach are fairly common, but due to the severity of the winters, carp exist in only a few lakes and ponds in southern Finland.

Some southern rivers have runs of salmon and sea trout. One of these, the Vantaa, flows on the outskirts of Helsinki, but only the river Kymijoki near the town of Kotka is a true salmon river. This fishery is detailed later. Most trout streams in the south are small, but several streams and brooks, as well as some trout lakes within a one-hour drive from Helsinki, are available. Although they are not untamed wilderness waters, they do offer nice fishing near the capital. These waters mainly hold stocked rainbow and brown trout; some have brook trout, and the smallest brooks hold native wild brown trout.

Eastern and Central Regions

Looking over a map of eastern and central Finland, it is easy to see why these regions are popular among anglers: There seems to be more water than land. Some area lakes are large and deep. Lakes Pielinen and Saimaa in the east are good examples, and both are prominent for lake trolling.

Brown trout and Saimaa salmon, a landlocked form of the Atlantic salmon, are the most important species. The latter is a relic form that has inhabited these waters since the Ice Age. It was earlier found only in the lakes of the Saimaa watershed but has lately been introduced into many other lakes as well. The average fish is smaller than its sea cousins, but 10-pounders are caught every year; larger fish are caught occasionally. The average brown trout in these lakes is about the same size as the Saimaa.

The trout streams of eastern and central Finland are mostly short links, called rapids *(koski)*, between lakes. For many Finnish fly anglers, the rapids of central Finland are the true classic brown trout waters of the country. Although they are short—some only a hundred yards long—they offer fine fishing; the lakes constantly produce trout and grayling, which run into these rapids for feeding.

The water is often deep and fast flowing, so a pair of good felt-soled waders and a wading staff are a must for effective fishing. Many of these rapids are stocked regularly with catchable-size brown and rainbow trout, whereas others yield only native fish, and if any stocking is carried on it is done with fingerlings.

The rapids are exciting waters to fish, both with fly and spinning rods. The average trout caught weighs about 2 pounds, but 4- to 6-pounders are not rare. Smallish plugs are popular, but spinners and spoons produce, too. Fly anglers use streamers, nymphs, and dry flies. Caddisflies dominate during the high season (June through August), so their imitations are preferred, and they may be quite large, too. The larval and pupal imitations of caddisflies are deadly. High-floating deer-hair patterns are effective as well. A 9-foot, 5- to 7-weight rod with enough backbone for long casts and windy conditions is a good choice. Floating line covers most situations, but it is wise to have a sink-tip or a full-sink line for high-water conditions and the deepest pools.

There are hardly any no-kill areas here, but almost all rapids have a small limit—usually two or three trout a day—and a large minimum size for brown trout. Day tickets for the very best waters are usually limited, so it is advisable to book in advance.

Some of the best stream fishing for brown trout in eastern and central Finland occurs near the towns of Viitasaari, Rautalampi, and Heinåvesi.

Northeast Region

The northeastern corner of Finland, particularly the area around Kuusamo, includes vast spruce forests and several great rivers. The Kitka, Oulanka, and Kuusinki—Kuusamo's major rivers—all have their source in Finland and flow across the border into Russia. These are famous as world-class brown trout fisheries, and the World Fly Fishing Championships took place on these rivers in 1989.

The major attraction of these waters is the so-called Russian brown trout, which has a life cycle similar to that of Atlantic salmon. They spend their early life in the headwaters, then migrate downstream into several large lakes in Russia. There they feed on small fish, grow to very respectable size, and return (normally in midsummer) to the rivers to spawn.

These browns may not be numerous, but they are big. Specimens under 4 pounds are rare, and the average size is around 6 to 8 pounds. Trout up to 15 pounds are caught every year, occasionally even bigger ones. Russian browns are fished with various tackle. Plugs are reliable lures, but many locals use traditional Devon minnows successfully. Fly fishing is also popular. Streamers and special local trout flies that resemble smaller salmon flies are standbys, but even dry flies and nymphs take their share of large trout.

Although these three famous rivers are in a class of their own, many smaller streams and a variety of lakes in the area offer fine fishing for trout and grayling.

Lapland

Known as The Land of the Midnight Sun, Lapland is a prime place for anglers who enjoy solitude and wide-open space, and who don't mind blackflies and mosquitoes. An ample supply of bug repellent is a necessity when fishing here.

Except for salmon anglers, Lapland is not a place for those after trophy-size fish. This doesn't mean that one couldn't catch the trout of a lifetime, but most of the fishing is on smaller streams, and small lakes and brooks. Winters are tough, and trout grow slowly. A 2-pounder is a very good fish, except in the few stocked waters. Trout in smaller brooks are usually in the 10- to 12-inch class. They are nevertheless fine, wild fish and full of fighting spirit.

Grayling are an important gamefish in Lapland. They are present almost everywhere and grow well in all but the smallest streams. In bigger rivers they reach 2 pounds and more. The largest fly-caught grayling, those over 4 pounds, are usually taken in western Lapland, with the Låtåseno watershed on the top of the list. The salmon rivers of northeastern Lapland—the Teno and Nåätåmö—however, have enormous grayling populations, and the fish tend to be good sized.

The northernmost lakes and streams of Lapland hold arctic charr. These little jewels are highly prized by Finnish anglers. Charr are fished with flies and small artificial lures. Ice fishing is also popular, especially in the late "winter" months of April and May, when sun warms the angler.

Arctic charr are seldom big, usually under two pounds, but backpacking anglers are ready to walk miles through rough terrain for them. Some of the larger lakes have bigger charr, and trolling with downriggers is the way to get them. The most popular trolling water in Lapland is the vast Lake Inarinjårvi. In the 1980s this lake produced a charr of almost 20 pounds. Inarinjårvi also has brown trout, grayling, landlocked salmon, and even some stocked lake trout.

Most anglers visit Lapland for trout, charr, and salmon only, but for more broad-minded anglers there is good fishing for large whitefish, big pike, and perch.

Atlantic Salmon

Finnish salmon fishing has declined from its former glory, but significant improvements have been made in recent times. In Finland, an angler can't have an exclusive salmon beat, as occurs elsewhere. Fishing rights are not sold this way. Some fisheries might have rod limits, but day tickets are available for everyone on a first-come, first-served basis. Day tickets are available for all salmon rivers and are inexpensive given the quality of the fishery. Theoretically, it would be possible for a group of anglers to buy all-day tickets for a river with a rod limit and then have it all to themselves, but this rarely happens.

The most classic salmon river in Finland is the massive river Teno (Tana in Norway), which forms the northernmost border between Finland and Norway and flows to the Arctic Sea. This may very well be the greatest salmon river in the world. Harling *(see: backtrolling)* with flies, plugs, and spoons is the most popular fishing method, even though strict regulations make fishing from boats a bit difficult for the visiting angler nowadays. The same applies to spinning and baitcasting from shore. There are some very good places for the wading fly angler, however, and as the regulations treat fly fishing more freely, this method is recommended for visitors. The most popular place is by the swift rapids of Alaköngås.

The Teno is a wide river, where long double-handed rods are the norm. On the upper river (from the village of Karasjoki upstream), the stream is narrower and one can fish it effectively with a single-handed rod. Many traditional and modern salmon patterns are used on the Teno; this includes flies like the Green Highlander, Black Doctor, Thunder & Lightning, and a wide variety of hairwings. The same flies are used in harling, but they are tied very sparse and slim. Many popular Finnish salmon patterns have been devised on the banks of the Teno, and various plugs are popular there, too.

The salmon run normally starts in late June and continues through late August. Early in the season the run consists of smaller groups of large fish. Later, the river is filled with grilse. Teno salmon are big; the average size is about 20 pounds, and every year the river yields at least a fish or two in the 50-pound class. Teno also has a good stock of European grayling, and the river is a world-class grayling fishery, with specimens over 2 pounds common.

The only other Finnish salmon river flowing to the Arctic Sea is the Nåätämö, which is a genuine wilderness river, as there are no roads or people living nearby. The Nåätämö River rises from the northeastern corner of Lapland, flows across the border, and runs some 10 miles through Norway before it reaches the ocean.

To visit this site, one has to get to the small village of Sevettijärvi, situated on the northern shore of Lake Inarinjärvi. From this village one can trek to the Näätämö (about 6 miles) or hire a helicopter. Chopper pilots are locals, who can give good tips regarding the best fishing places and camping areas. On the upper river there is a fly-fishing-only area.

Näätämö salmon are, in general, smaller and less numerous than those of the Teno, but they are nevertheless well worth the effort. Näätämö also has a good stock of grayling, which are often large.

On the Baltic side are two notable salmon rivers: the river Tornionjoki, which forms a natural border between Finland and Sweden, and the river Kymijoki in the south.

Like Teno, the Tornionjoki is a huge watercourse. It is hundreds of miles long and boasts almost unlimited possibilities. Just a few years ago, Tornionjoki (also called Tornio) was a beautiful, free-flowing river, but there were practically no salmon in it. The closure of commercial netting in the river mouth and increased stocking efforts have brought salmon back, and today the river is almost as good as it was in the late 1940s. Harling with plugs and spoons is the most common fishing method, but some areas offer good possibilities for spinning and fly fishing from shore and by wading. The salmon run starts in mid-June, with July and August the best months. The average salmon is around 15 pounds. Accommodations are easy to find, boats are available in many places, and access is easy, as a road runs parallel to the river along the length of the main fork.

The Kymijoki, or Kymi, is the southernmost salmon river in Finland. It flows to the Gulf of Finland near the town of Kotka, about 100 miles east of Helsinki. Only a few sections are open to anglers, and some of them don't have rod limits. They can get fairly crowded when the run is in. At special areas, however, like the short Langinkoski rapids near the river mouth, the number of day tickets is limited. These rapids are seldom crowded, because the area is fly-fishing-only and a little more expensive than others. The Kymijoki is a beautiful place, and on its bank stands the former fishing lodge of Russian emperors, built in the late 1800s and today a museum.

There are two reasons for the popularity of this river: It is situated in a metropolitan area, and the salmon are especially large. Some seasons the average weight is well over 20 pounds, and every year the river produces some 40- to 50-pound fish. The salmon run starts in mid-July and continues through the fall. Sea-run browns arrive in larger numbers in October, and there is another smaller run in the spring. Trout are not plentiful, but their size is impressive; 6- to 10-pound fish are the norm, and some twice as large are caught occasionally. Day tickets for Kymijoki are reasonably priced.

Licenses and Regulations

Most fishing waters in Finland are privately owned; the Finnish Forest and Park Association administers state (national) fishing waters, the majority of which are in northern and eastern Finland. There are closed seasons for some species, particularly salmonids, and restrictions and regulations on private waters are often more severe than prescribed by national Fishing Acts.

Licensing requirements are complicated for the visitor to comprehend, and they vary considerably across the country. To practice sportfishing in Finland, other than angling with an ordinary baited hook or ice fishing, a visiting angler over 18 or under 65 years of age must pay a state fishing management fee, available in seven-day or calendar-year options. This is not a fishing license, and it can be obtained at banks or post offices on weekdays, as well as through a self-service payment machine or through home computer.

In addition to this, one must have the permission of whoever owns the fishing rights to each body of water, and/or one must purchase a daily permit or day ticket to access specific sites. The fee for this varies, and may depend on the manner of fishing (with lures or bait), the type of water, or the species present.

A newly enacted license is called a "Lure Fishing Fee," which government literature says "opens new opportunities for trolling, fly fishing, or fishing with other types of lures in addition to the lure fishing permits available from water owners, fishing corporations, etc. Paying a lure fishing fee entitles you to practice lure fishing within a single province, using one rod, reel, and lure."

Outfitters and fishing agents usually have these matters sorted out for clients, but visitors traveling on their own must seek permits from local fishing associations, hotels, holiday villages, and the like. Tourist offices may be able to provide information and direction, as will tackle suppliers and local fishing associations. Separate fee arrangements exist in the province of Åland, which has its own Fishing Act.

Finland has only about 5 million inhabitants, so there is plenty of water for everyone to fish. Angling tourism is developing, and many new fisheries are opening every year.

> "All Americans believe that they are born fishermen. For a man to admit a distaste for fishing would be like denouncing mother love and hating moonlight."
> —John Steinbeck, 1954

FINNING

A fish that is basking near the surface with dorsal and/or tail fins protruding from the water is said to be finning. This action is most often observed in saltwater, particularly with such large creatures as billfish and sharks. When fishing on the open ocean, big-game skippers often look for finning fish in order to intercept them and bring a trolled bait or lure in front of them.

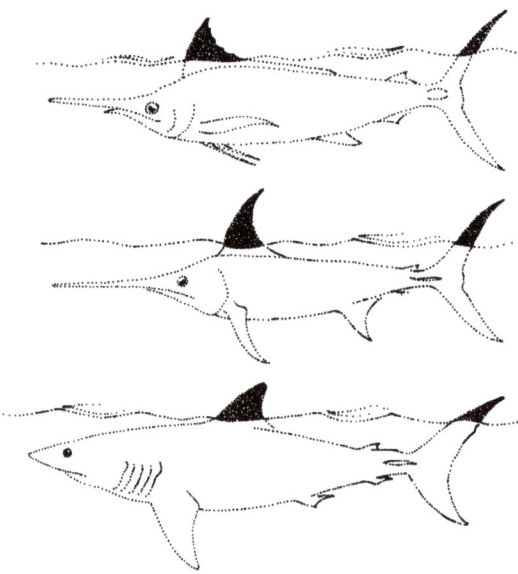

The exposed portions of the dorsal and tail fins of marlin (top), swordfish (middle), and shark (bottom) help distinguish them from each other when they are spotted finning on the surface.

Experienced anglers are able to identify marlin, swordfish, and sharks on the surface by the characteristics of the visible portions of their fins, as depicted in the accompanying illustration. The marlin's tail fin is rigid and pointed; its dorsal fin is folded into a groove and not extended unless excited. The swordfish's tail fin is rigid and pointed; its dorsal fin sickle shaped and rigid, and it cannot be folded into a groove. The shark's tail fin is flexible and rolls when moved; its dorsal fin is more rounded than pointed and stays fixed in position.

FIRST AID
Treatments and Preventions

Knowledge of basic first aid, as well as advanced aid for the treatment of such serious problems as burns, sprains, fractures, broken limbs, shock, poisoning, bleeding, and heart failure is certainly at least as useful in the field as at home. Nevertheless, it is beyond the scope of this book to thoroughly document and illustrate these issues. Instead, this section will be devoted to the first aid, or medical, issues that are most common to sportfishing activities and that are most likely to be encountered owing to the nature of angling and the places visited by anglers. This includes a discussion of preventions as well as treatments.

First aid situations include exposure to the sun, heat, cold, and wind; insect bites and stings; cuts, bruises, and punctures, including those of fish hooks; and waterborne ailments, such as giardia, dengue, and others. Seasickness *(see)*, an inner ear problem, is detailed separately.

Insect Bites and Stings

Anglers come into contact with creatures that bite or sting more often than most people who spend time outdoors. Some of these are aquatic insects that have food value to small fish and are not harmful to humans, but many are flying or crawling bugs that bite or sting and can be harmful or annoying to varying degrees. Bees, horseflies, deerflies, mosquitoes, blackflies, and no-see-ums are the common airborne pests; and ants, spiders, tarantulas, scorpions, and centipedes are among the common terrestrial pests. Encounters may occur from the tropics to the Arctic.

Many insects bite or sting and can cause itching, but few cause serious symptoms by themselves unless the person bitten or stung is allergic to them. However, some insects transmit diseases. For example, certain types of mosquitoes transmit malaria, dengue, yellow fever, and other diseases; certain types of ticks transmit spotted or Rocky Mountain fever or Lyme disease; and certain types of biting flies transmit tularemia or rabbit fever.

Occasionally, stinging or biting insects that have been feeding on or have been in contact with poisonous substances can transmit this poison when they sting or bite. People who have experienced serious reactions from previous insect bites should secure any possible immunization or have an antidote readily available to prevent more serious reactions from future insect bites and stings.

The stings of bees and the bites of many insects usually cause only local irritation and pain in the region stung or bitten. Moderate swelling and redness may occur, and some itching, burning, and pain may be present.

First aid includes:

The sting area should be inspected to determine whether the stinger is still in the body. If it is, remove it in order to prevent further injection of toxin. The stinger should be carefully scraped off the skin, rather than grasped with tweezers, so that toxin is not squeezed into the body.

Application of ice or ice water to the bite helps to slow absorption of toxin into the blood stream. A paste of baking soda and water can also be applied to the bite.

The victim should be observed for signs of an allergic reaction. For people who are allergic, maintain an open airway and get the victim to medical help as quickly as possible.

Prevention. Many insects are attracted to dark colors, so wearing light-colored clothing can be helpful. Covering exposed areas prevents many problems with flying insects, and tucking pant cuffs into socks or boots is good for keeping out ticks. Even with long-sleeved shirt, long pants, and a hat, there are still exposed areas, so using an insect repellent will probably be necessary.

Choice of insect repellent depends to some degree on the level of problem that has to be dealt with. Some anglers encounter situations with enormous concentrations of mosquitoes or heavy outbreaks of blackflies, and only the most potent repellents will do. Such repellents are also necessary in places where there are known disease problems associated with biting insects (malaria, dengue, encephalitis, etc.). The most effective insect repellents contain the chemical DEET, which has been subject to some health concerns, but which has proven safe when used according to label instructions. The use of products with DEET is recommended by the World Health Organization and the Center for Disease Control and Prevention when traveling to countries where insect-borne diseases are prevalent.

The concentrations of DEET vary within specific products, ranging up to 95 percent. Lotion products with the maximum concentration of DEET have proven to be most useful to anglers where mosquitoes and fly numbers are heavy. Products with lesser concentrations (typically under 30 percent) have shorter terms of effectiveness and are meant for use where infestation is light. Lotion, spray, and ointment products are available; lotions cost more but are viewed by many people as being more effective and longer lasting per application, especially when compared with sprays, unless a spray is applied to the hands and then rubbed on.

When using repellents, always follow the label instructions and keep the repellent away from your eyes and mouth. After application, wash the palms of your hands before touching other objects, especially food. Keep repellents off fishing equipment, plastics, and clothing. Be especially careful with children; repellents without DEET are best for them.

An alternative to repellent use is to wear a mesh jacket that can be sprayed with repellent, or wear a mesh headcover. The headcover may impair vision and is uncomfortable for many people, but it is effective.

Sun

Anglers are exposed to a lot of sun in all seasons of the year. Over time this exposure can lead to problems—melanoma and nonmelanoma skin cancer, immune suppression, cataracts, and premature skin aging—that require medical attention. This is more of a preventive issue than it is first aid treatment, although a sunburn does require minor first aid attention. Preventions are especially important today because skin cancer cases have grown dramatically in recent years.

Problems are caused by ultraviolet (UV) radiation, most of which is screened out by the ozone layer. UV radiation that penetrates the ozone layer also penetrates the surface of the skin. Factors that affect UV levels and degrees of exposure include the condition of the ozone layer (thinner is poor), time of day, time of year, latitude, altitude, and weather conditions.

Minimizing exposure. To protect your eyes, wear sunglasses (see) that block 99 to 100 percent of UV radiation. For the sake of reducing glare and improving your through-water vision when fishing, the sunglasses should also be polarized. Many anglers prefer sunglasses with side protection as well. In terms of eye care, the proper sunglasses reduce sun exposure that can lead to cataracts and other eye damage.

Wearing a hat, especially one with a wide brim, helps shield your face, ears, nose, and neck, which are vulnerable areas prone to sun overexposure. Exposed skin should be covered with clothing to protect it. Light, tightly woven clothing is best, and this includes long pants and long-sleeved shirts.

Skin that is directly or indirectly (like your face that is shielded by a hat) subject to UV radiation should be protected by sunscreen with at least a Sun Protection Factor (SPF) factor of 15, preferably one that guarantees "broad spectrum" protection. This blocks most harmful UV radiation. People with red or blonde hair, fair skin, and light eyes should consider sunscreens with a higher SPF factor, which goes up to 50. Sunscreen should be applied liberally, and as frequently as recommended by the manufacturer. Make sure to reapply it when you towel off perspiration or water. Apply especially well to the nose, ears, neck, wrist, and the back of the hands.

Bear in mind that the most recent medical research on sunscreens indicates that they alone do not prevent skin cancer. A combination of sunscreen use and wearing protective clothing and a wide-brimmed hat is recommended by dermatologists. Furthermore, prevention of overexposure to sun should start in childhood, since the greatest exposure to sun and potential damage is incurred by the age of 18.

Heat

Extreme heat can require first aid because of the reactions that some people incur. Medical problems resulting from heat exposure are less well known than those from cold exposure, but more deaths and injuries are caused by summer heat than are caused by all kinds of storms. Heat is actually only one part of the problem; high humidity increases heat stress.

Heat stroke. Heat stroke is a sudden onset of illness from exposure to the direct rays of the sun or from too high temperatures without exposure to the sun. Physical exertion and high humidity definitely contribute to the incidence of heat stroke.

The most important characteristic of heat stroke is the high body temperature caused by a disturbance in the body's heat-regulating mechanism. The affected person can no longer sweat, and this

 Coelacanths, which can manipulate their pectoral and pelvic fins independently like four-legged animals, are related to extinct species that scientists say are closest to amphibians, the earliest land animals.

causes a rise in body temperature. The elderly are very susceptible to heat stroke, as are alcoholics, obese persons, and those on medication.

The signs and symptoms of heat stroke include:

- The skin is flushed, very hot, and very dry; perspiration is usually absent.
- The pulse is usually strong and rapid, but it may become weak and rapid as the victim's condition worsens.
- The respirations are rapid and deep, followed by shallow breathing.
- The body temperature can reach 108°F.
- The victim rapidly becomes unconscious and may experience convulsions.

Care should be centered around lowering the body temperature as quickly as possible. Failure to do this will result in permanent brain damage or death. The care for heat stroke is as follows:

1. Maintain an open airway.
2. Move the victim to a cool environment.
3. Remove all clothing.
4. Wrap the victim in a cool, moist sheet and use a fan to cool the victim.
5. Immerse the victim in cool water if the preceding treatment is not feasible.
6. Use cool applications if neither of the previous treatments is feasible.
7. Transport the victim to the hospital as rapidly as possible, continuing cooling en route.

Heat exhaustion. Heat exhaustion is brought about by the loss of water and salt through sweating. This loss of fluid will cause mild shock.

This illness occurs most commonly in persons unaccustomed to hot weather, those who are overweight, and those who perspire excessively. The signs and symptoms of heat exhaustion include:

- The skin is pale and clammy.
- The skin shows evidence of profuse perspiration.
- Breathing is rapid and shallow.
- The pulse is rapid and weak.
- The victim may complain of nausea, weakness, dizziness, and/or headache.

First aid for heat exhaustion is as follows:

1. Move the victim to a cool and comfortable place, but do not allow chilling.
2. Try to cool the victim by fanning and/or wiping the face with a cool, wet cloth.
3. Loosen the victim's clothing.
4. If fainting seems likely, have the victim lie down with feet elevated 8 to 12 inches.
5. Treat the victim for shock.

Heat cramps. Heat cramps affect people who work in a hot environment and perspire. The perspiration causes a loss of salt from the body; if replacement is inadequate, the body will suffer from cramps.

Signs and symptoms of heat cramps include:

- The presence of profuse perspiration is evident.
- The victim complains of muscle cramps, painful spasms in the legs or abdomen.
- The victim may feel faint.

First aid for heat cramps is as follows:

1. Move the victim to a cool environment.
2. If the victim is conscious, give sips of cool salt and sugar water (1 teaspoon of salt plus as much sugar as the person can stand, per quart of water) or commercial electrolyte solution.

Prevention. The first rule for avoiding thermal shock is to slow down and don't try to do too much, especially in the first few days of exposure; this is especially important for anglers who visit hot (and humid) places when they are unaccustomed to these conditions. Stay in cool, shaded places during the worst part of the day if possible. A midday siesta may be a good idea for those who are older or whose physical condition is below par.

Proper clothing will help you stay as cool as possible. Light-colored garments that fit loosely and are light in weight are best; a hat, preferably one that shades all of your face and neck, is important. Sunglasses are also necessary, if only to save stress on your eyes. Using a sunscreen is important for avoiding burns; sunburns not only damage your skin but make your body work harder to dissipate heat.

In extreme heat and high humidity, it is essential to replenish fluids lost through perspiration. Do this with nonalcoholic drinks. Cold water, juices, and sports drinks with high glucose content are good choices. Pay more attention to drinking fluids than to eating.

Cold Weather

People who are exposed to the cold, whether on land, on the water, or in the water (falling overboard, capsizing, etc.), run the grave danger of becoming hypothermic. Conditions that may induce hypothermia include being on the ice in winter, being in a boat exposed to strong winds blowing across the water in spring, or being caught lightly clothed during a backcountry storm in the fall. Everyone should know what to do when someone falls into cold water, and this circumstance is covered under survival *(see)*. How to care for a victim of cold is discussed here. Prevention is mostly a matter of common sense, primarily wearing appropriate warm clothing and layering it, and covering your head and neck. Outerwear should be suitable for conditions and should keep out water and wind.

Hypothermia. Hypothermia is a general cooling of the entire body. The inner core of the body

---

In olden times, Scottish law required commercial fishermen to wear a gold earring, which would be used to pay for funeral expenses if they drowned and washed ashore.

is chilled so that the body cannot generate heat to stay warm. This condition can be produced by prolonged exposure to low air or water temperatures or to temperatures between 30° and 50°F with wind and rain. Also contributing to hypothermia are fatigue, hunger, and poor physical condition. Exposure begins when the body loses heat faster than it can be produced. When the body is chilled, it passes through several stages.

The initial response of a victim exposed to cold is to build a fire and to voluntarily exercise in order to stay warm. The fire can also signal rescuers if the victim is lost.

As the body tissues are cooled, the victim begins to shiver as a result of an involuntary adjustment by the body to preserve normal temperature in the vital organs. These responses drain the body's energy reserves.

The symptoms of hypothermia are:

- Cold reaches the brain and deprives the victim of judgment and reasoning powers.
- The victim experiences feelings of apathy, listlessness, indifference, and sleepiness.
- The victim does not realize what is happening.
- The victim loses muscle coordination.

Cooling becomes more rapid as the internal body temperature is lowered. Eventually hypothermia will result in a coma. The victim will have a very slow pulse and very slow respirations. If cooling continues, the victim will die.

The victim of hypothermia may not recognize the symptoms and may deny that medical attention is needed. Therefore, it is important to judge the symptoms rather than what the victim says. Even mild symptoms of hypothermia need immediate medical care.

First aid for a victim of hypothermia is as follows:

1. Get the victim out of the elements (wind, rain, snow, cold, etc.).
2. Remove all wet clothing.
3. Wrap the victim in blankets. Be certain the blankets are under, as well as over, the victim.
4. Maintain the victim's body heat by building a fire or placing heat packs, electric heating pads, hot water bottles, or even another rescuer in the blankets with the victim. Do not warm the victim too quickly.
5. If the victim is conscious, give warm liquids to drink.
6. If the victim is conscious, try to keep the victim awake.
7. CPR is indicated if the victim stops breathing and the heart stops beating.
8. Get medical assistance for the victim as soon as possible.
9. Remember to handle the victim gently. In extreme cases, rough handling may result in death.

Frostbite. Frostbite results from exposure to severe cold. It is more likely to occur when the wind is blowing, rapidly taking heat from the body. The nose, cheeks, ears, toes, and fingers are the body parts most frequently frostbitten. As a result of exposure to cold, the blood vessels constrict. Thus, the blood supply to the chilled parts decreases and the tissues do not get the warmth they need.

The signs and symptoms of frostbite are not always apparent to the victim. Since frostbite has a numbing effect, the victim may not be aware of it until told by someone.

The beginning stage of frostbite is called frostnip. The affected area will feel numb to the victim, and the skin becomes red, then white. Treatment consists of placing the hand over the frostnipped part, and placing frostnipped fingers in the armpit.

The second stage is called superficial frostbite. As exposure continues, the skin becomes white and waxy. The skin is firm to the touch, but underlying tissues are soft. The exposed surface becomes numb. Treatment requires removing the victim from the cold environment and applying a steady source of external warmth.

Do not rub the affected area. Cover it with a dry, sterile dressing (when dressing the foot or hand, pad between the toes and fingers). Splint the area if dealing with an extremity, and transport the victim to the hospital. As the area thaws, it may become a mottled blue color, and blisters will develop.

The most advanced stage is deep frostbite. If freezing is allowed to continue, all sensation is lost, and the skin becomes a "dead" white, yellow-white, or mottled blue-white. The skin is firm to the touch as are the underlying tissues. Areas affected with deep frostbite should be left frozen until the victim reaches a hospital. Dress, pad, and splint frostbitten extremities (when dressing the injury, pad between the fingers and toes), and transport the victim to a hospital.

If there is a delay in transport, rewarming may be done at the site. Place the affected part in a water bath of 100° to 105°F. Apply warm cloths to areas that cannot be submerged. An extreme amount of pain is associated with rewarming. Rewarming is complete when the area is warm and is red or blue in color, and remains so after removal from the bath. Do not rewarm if there is a possibility of refreezing.

General rules for treating frostbite are:

- Apply loose, soft, sterile dressings to affected area.
- Splint and elevate the extremity.
- Give the victim warm fluids containing sugar to drink if he or she does not have an altered level of consciousness.
- Do not rub, chafe, or manipulate frostbitten parts.
- Do not use hot water bottles or heat lamps.
- Do not place the victim near a stove or fire; excessive heat can cause further tissue damage.

- Do not allow the victim to smoke; nicotine constricts the blood vessels.
- Do not allow the victim to drink coffee, tea, or hot chocolate; these substances will cause the blood vessels to constrict.
- Do not allow the victim to walk if the feet are frostbitten.

Cuts and Punctures

Anglers are subject to minor cuts, lacerations, and skin punctures when fishing, mainly as a result of landing, unhooking, and cleaning fish, but also from the use of knives and hooks. Wounds produced by a sharp cutting edge are smooth without bruising or tearing. If such a wound is deep, large blood vessels and nerves may be severed, and bleeding may occur freely and be difficult to control. This not a common problem, but it is a possibility. Minor cuts are common in fishing, many caused by the sharp teeth of fish.

Puncture wounds are produced by pointed objects passing through the skin and damaging tissues in its path. The small number of blood vessels that are cut sometimes prevents free bleeding. The danger of infection in puncture wounds is high because of this poor drainage. There are two types of puncture wounds. A penetrating puncture wound causes injured tissues and blood vessels whether it is shallow or deep. This type is most common in the fingers, often occurring when the angler is fishing, and is caused by contact with hooks and the spiny fins of fish. A perforating puncture wound has an entrance and an exit wound. The object causing the injury passes through the body and out to create an exit wound, which in many cases is more serious than the entrance wound. This type of puncture wound is not common, except in some rare cases where a hook is deep and has to be pushed through skin.

Hook removal. When a hook becomes embedded in human flesh, the first consideration is whether it's safe to attempt removal. If the hook can be moved gently and doing so does not increase the pain, then the injury is most likely in a soft tissue area and hook removal can be attempted. Single hooks or a single point of a treble hook that is lodged in fleshy exposed skin are good candidates for removal.

If moving the hook gently causes greater pain, tingling, or numbness, it is likely near a tendon, bone, or nerve, and you should head to the nearest doctor's office. If more than one point of a treble hook is embedded in the skin, you should leave removal to a doctor as well, since removing one point may drive the other one deeper. A hook that is anywhere near the eye should be left to medical experts.

There are two ways to remove a hook in the field, the first being the push-through method. To do this, first cut the hook from the lure or line; then get a firm grip of the shank with a sturdy pair of

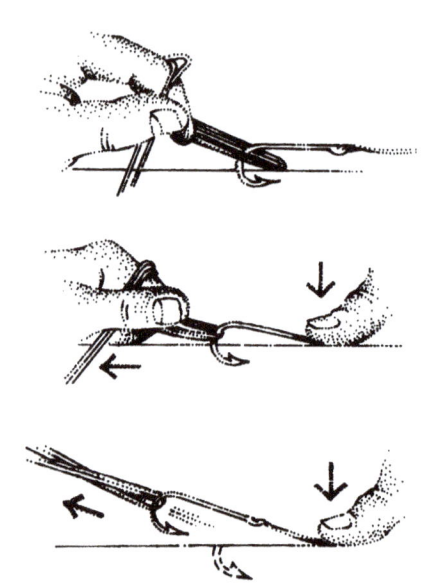

To use the line-pull method of fishhook removal, take a doubled length of strong line and run it behind the bend of the hook (top). Apply thumb pressure to the eye or lower shank of the hook, pressing it toward the skin (middle). Pull sharply backward on both ends of the doubled line.

pliers. Push the hook point forward, following its natural curve, until the barb is free of the skin. Cut off the barb with the cutting edge of the pliers; then back the hook out the way it went in.

The other way to remove a hook is the line-pull method. To do this, first cut the hook from the lure or fishing line; then take a 36-inch length of heavy line (20 pounds or greater) and double it to make an 18-inch piece. Run this behind the bend of the hook; use a thumb to apply pressure to the eye or the lower shank of the hook, pressing it toward the skin. This frees the barb from the soft tissue under the skin and provides a path for removing the hook.

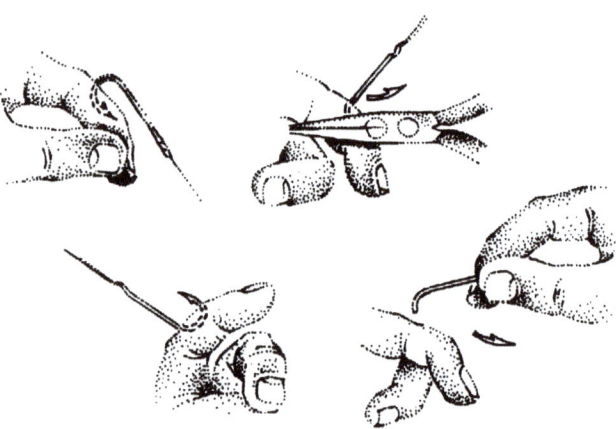

To use the pull-through method of removing a fishhook whose point is near the skin (left, top) or protruding through the skin (left, bottom), get a firm grip of the shank with a sturdy pair of pliers and push the hook point forward, following its natural curve, until the barb is free of the skin. Cut the barb off, then back the hook out the way it went in.

Grab both ends of the doubled line and pull sharply backward. If this doesn't work with one quick jerk backward, do not attempt it again.

When the hook is out, cleanse the wound. Soaking it in clean water is a good idea, and an antibiotic ointment should be applied under a bandage. If an infection occurs, see a doctor. A tetanus shot may be in order.

Waterborne Ailments

Traveling anglers should not overlook the fact that drinking water, and even just coming into contact with it (as in swimming or wading wet), can be harmful in some places.

Schistosomiasis, for example, is a tropical disease caused by a freshwater parasite *(see: diseases and parasites)* that enters the skin through direct contact with infected water. It is also known as bilharzia. Acute symptoms are flulike and include fever, chills, cough, diarrhea, weakness, and headache. It requires treatment by a doctor, and the prevention is staying out of water that may be infected.

More common for most people is giardiasis, known as giardia and "beaver fever," which can be contracted anywhere in the world and has been especially prevalent in Russia. There are several types of giardia and similar parasites; some of these are not killed by freezing or chlorination, and have been known to infiltrate public water supplies. Giardiasis results in chronic diarrhea and can lead to dehydration. Prescription medicines are used to treat it. The best preventive is to boil water for at least 3 minutes and then let it cool slowly; this also will purify water that might contain viral pollution.

Any water to be consumed should be boiled, since it is often unknown which water source may have the problem (even in the cool, clear waters of high-mountain country), and the problem is widespread. The alternative is to carry bottled water with you, an option not practical for backcountry-camping anglers. Some chemical water purifying treatments (which use iodine) will remove many but not all potentially harmful items in the water. The ones that have Environmental Protection Agency approval will remove nearly all the bad bacteria and parasites that might be encountered.

FISH

Usage 1 As a noun, the word "fish" is commonly used by anglers for both the singular and the plural form and is used in a generic sense without regard to species. Anglers might say, "Tuna are the strongest fish" or "We caught three fish this afternoon." It is uncommon for anglers to employ the word "fishes," although "fishes" is a required usage by scientists and in technical literature, especially when referring to two or more kinds or species. The compound word is also used similarly; the plural of catfish is "catfish," not "catfishes." However, scientists would say, "South America is home to many catfishes," distinguishing between species as opposed to overall numbers. This book generally uses the common form rather than the scientific.

Usage 2 As a noun, the word "fish" is used to refer to the flesh of a fish used as food.

Usage 3 As a verb, the word "fish," as in "He fishes every evening," is the act of catching, or trying to catch, fish. It has a general meaning with no explicit distinction between commercial or recreational action or, in the latter case, the techniques or equipment employed. The words "angle" and "sportfish" are often used interchangeably with the word "fish," although they refer solely to the recreational activity and the implied usage of sporting equipment.
See Angler; Angling; Sportfisherman; Sportfishing.

Defined

The term "fish" is applied to a class of animals that includes some 21,000 extremely diverse species. Fish can be roughly defined (and there are a few exceptions) as cold-blooded creatures that have backbones, live in water, and have gills. The gills enable fish to "breathe" underwater, without drawing oxygen from the atmosphere. This is the primary difference between fish and all other vertebrates. Although such vertebrates as whales and turtles live in water, they cannot breathe underwater. No other vertebrate but the fish is able to live without breathing air. One family of fish, the lungfish, is able to breathe air when mature, and actually loses its functional gills. Another family of fish, the tuna, is considered warm-blooded by many people, but the tuna is an exception.

Fish are divided into four groups: the hagfish, the lampreys, cartilaginous fish, and bony fish. The hagfish and lampreys lack jaws, and as such they form the group called jawless fish; the cartilaginous fish and the bony fish have jaws. The bony fish are by far the most common, making up over 95 percent of the world's fish species. Cartilaginous fish, including sharks, rays, and skate, are the second largest group, numbering some 700 species. There are 32 species of hagfish and 40 species of lamprey.

Overview

Body of the fish. The body of a fish is particularly adapted to aquatic life. The body is equipped with fins for the purpose of locomotion. Scales and mucous protect the body and keep it streamlined. The skeleton features a long backbone that can produce the side-to-side movements needed for forward propulsion in water. Since water is 800 times more dense than air, fish must be extremely strong to move in their environment. Fish respond to this condition by being mostly muscle. Thus, muscles make up 40 to 65 percent of a fish's body weight. Many fish have air or gas bladders (sometimes called swim bladders), which allow them to float at their desired depth. Fish also have gills, their underwater breathing apparatus, located in the head. Most fish have only one gill cover, although some, like sharks, have gill slits, some as many as seven. The gills are the most fragile part of the fish; anglers should avoid touching the gills on fish that they plan on releasing.

The limbs of fish come in the form of fins. A fin is a membrane that extends from the body of the fish, and is supported by spines or rays. Because the number of rays is usually constant within a species, a ray count is often used by scientists to determine the species of a fish. Each of the fins on a fish has a name. Since these names are used in almost all descriptions of fish, and are used in this encyclopedia, it is worthwhile to become familiar with the different fin names.

Moving from the head toward the tail, the first fins are the pectoral fins. The pectoral fins are used for balance and maneuvering in many species, and in a few are used for propulsion. Further down the underside of the fish are the pelvic fins, located beneath the belly and used for balance. On the back of the fish is the dorsal fin. Some fish have more than one dorsal fin; in this case the dorsal fins are numbered, with the fin closest to the head called the first dorsal fin. Behind the dorsal fin on the top part of the fish there is occasionally a smaller, fleshy fin called the adipose fin. Back on the underside of the fish, behind the pelvic fins and the anus, is the anal fin. The final fin, usually called the tail, is known scientifically as the caudal fin. The caudal fin is the most important fin for locomotion: By moving it from side to side, a fish is able to gather forward momentum.

The scales of a fish form the main protection for the body. Fish scales are kept for the entire life of a fish; as a fish grows, the scales get larger rather than growing anew. Scales are divided into several types. The majority of fish have ctenoid or cycloid scales. Ctenoid scales are serrated on one edge and feel rough when rubbed the wrong way (largemouth bass have such scales). Cycloid scales are entirely smooth, like the scales of trout. More rare types of fish have different types of scales: Sharks have more primitive placoid scales, which are spiny; sturgeon have ganoid scales, which form armor ridges along parts of the body. Some species, like catfish, have no scales at all. Fish scales can be used to determine the age of a fish. A fish scale will develop rings showing annual growth, much like the rings of a tree.

Many fish also have a covering of mucous which gives them a slimy feel. This covering helps streamline their body and prevent infections. The mucous covering will rub off onto a person's hands (this is the slimy substance that you can feel on your hands after handling a fish). Since the loss of mucous is detrimental to the fish, it is better to wet your hands before handling a fish which will be released to minimize the amount of mucous removed, being careful not to harm a fish by holding it too tightly *(see: catch-and-release)*.

The skeletal and muscular systems of fish work together to maximize swimming power. The serially repeated vertebrae and muscle structure work together to create the shimmering, undulating muscle movements that allow a fish to move forward quickly. This structure is particularly evident in a filleted fish, where the muscles show themselves in their interlocking pattern. The muscular nature of fish is the reason why fish make such good eating, and also is a factor in making fish a high-yield food source.

Bony fish have developed an organ called an air bladder, which acts as a kind of flotation device. A fish's body is naturally a bit more dense than water, but the air bladder, filled with gas, increases a fish's ability to float. Fish can change the depth at which they float by varying the amount of gas in their air bladder. This allows a fish to float at any depth it desires without expending any effort. Fish that do not have air bladders, such as sharks, must continually move in order to prevent sinking.

Like virtually all animals, fish need oxygen to survive. However, a fish can get all the oxygen it needs from water by use of its gills. Water entering through the mouth of the fish is forced over the gills, and oxygen is removed from the water by the gills. In order to breathe, fish must constantly have water passing over their gills. However, in order to get enough oxygen, certain fish must either move continually or live in water with a strong current.

Although most fish are referred to as cold-blooded creatures, this is mostly but not entirely true. Some species are called warm-blooded, yet they cannot sustain a constant body temperature as humans do. Instead, the body temperature of fish approximates that of its surrounding medium—water. Certain types of fish, such as tuna, by their constant vigorous propulsion through the water, sustain high muscular flexion that creates heat associated with rapid metabolism. Through built-in heat conservation measures, the fish is capable of maintaining a warmer body temperature than the medium that upholds it; for example, a bluefin tuna's fighting qualities are not impaired physically when it suddenly dives from surface waters where it was hooked down to the colder depths.

Fish Shapes

Fish shapes have also uniquely evolved to suit the needs of their aquatic life. The body shapes of fish fall into general categories: Some are narrow, with bodies that are taller than they are thin, like sunfish, largemouth bass, or angelfish. Some are flat, with bodies that are shorter than they are wide, like flounder. Some are torpedo-shaped, like tuna or mackerel. Some are tubular and snakelike, such as eels.

Shapes tend to be related to a fish's habits and habitats. Narrow-bodied fish are extremely maneuverable, and tend to live in reefs or densely weeded ponds where the ability to maneuver between rocks or plants is essential. Flatfish tend to live on the bottom, where their low profiles prevent recognition. Torpedo-shaped fish are built for speed and are found either in open water or in strong currents where less-streamlined fish would be swept away. Tubular fish often live in small crevices and areas that are inaccessible to other animals, rather than in wide-open ocean waters.

Fish Color

The amazing variety of colors that fish display clearly demonstrates the importance of color in the fish world. Most fish are colored for purposes of camouflage. When viewed from above, fish tend to be dark in order to blend in with the dark bottom of the water. When viewed from below, they look light in order to blend in with the sky (this is called countershading). Fish have developed a huge variety of colors and markings that allow them to escape detection in their own environments. Color is also used for mating purposes. Certain fish have special breeding colors, usually brighter than normal colors. Many reef fish have brilliant colors year-round. The wide variety of colors of reef fish helps to differentiate between the many species that live on the reef.

Fish Senses

An angler should understand the way a fish's senses work. Knowing what a fish is sensitive to helps an angler approach the fish without scaring it. Although some fish rely more on certain senses than on others, there are statements about senses that apply to all fish.

Fish hear very well. Sound travels five times faster in water than in air, and fish are quite sensitive to loud noise (which is why you should not tap on fishtank glass). Fish can be scared off by the noise from people banging around in a boat, loud talking, and motors. Although fish do not have external ears, they do have internal ears. These internal ears, set in the bones of the skull, hear very well. The role of sound in the lives of fish is not entirely understood, but many fish are known to be noisy; fish have been recorded grunting, croaking, grinding teeth, and vibrating muscles. The importance of these sounds is not yet fully known; but what is known for certain is that hearing is an important sense for fish.

A fish's sense of smell is often very good, but the importance of this sense varies widely among species and may be subordinate to other senses, especially vision. With olfactory nerves in their nostrils, fish can detect odors in water just as terrestrial animals can detect odors in air. Some fish use their sense of smell to find food, detect danger, and perhaps also to find their way to spawning areas. There is evidence that a salmon's keen sense of smell contributes to its ability to return to its birthplace. Certainly a salmon's sense of smell must be considered incredible: Salmon can detect one part per billion of odorous material in water. They may refuse to use fish ladders if the water contains the smell of human hands or bear paws. Salmon will panic if placed in a swimming pool with one drop of bear-scented water. With the apparent importance of smell to many fish, removing human scents from fishing tackle is something that anglers should consider, although the extent to which this is useful varies widely with species, and is considered important by some anglers and irrelevant by many others.

Sight varies in importance for fish. Most fish are nearsighted; although they can see well for short distances, their vision gets blurry past three feet or so. Some fish are exceptions to this rule; brown trout, for instance, have excellent vision. An important fact to realize about most fish is that they can see almost 360°; the only space they cannot see is a small patch directly behind them. Fish can also see color. In laboratory experiments, largemouth bass and trout have been able to identify red, green, blue, and yellow. Some fish have demonstrated preferences for certain colors, and red has long been considered a foremost attraction, although this is subject to a host of variables as well as disagreements among anglers.

The sense of taste does not seem to be as important to fish as other senses; taste buds are not as well developed, although there are exceptions, especially among bottom-scrounging fish. Some species, like catfish, use taste to find food and utilize this sense much more than other species of fish. Catfish even have taste buds on their barbels, and certain species have them on the underside of their body.

Fish have an additional sensory organ called the lateral line. Visible as a line running along the length of the body of many fish, the lateral line is used to detect low-frequency vibrations. It acts like both a hearing and a touch organ for fish, and it is used to determine the directions of currents, the proximity of objects, and even water temperature. The lateral line is sensitive to water vibrations and helps fish escape predators, locate prey, and stay in schools.

The senses of fish are more highly developed than most people realize; this is a chinook salmon.

Reproduction

Fish reproduce in many different ways. Most lay eggs, but some bear live young; most eggs are fertilized after they are released from the female's body, but some are fertilized inside the female's body. Since almost all gamefish are egg layers (sharks being the main exception), the reproductive habits of egg-laying fish are the most important to the angler. Mating, called spawning in egg-laying fish, usually occurs once a year at a particular time of year. Each species has its own spawning habits, which have a great influence on behavior. Some fish do not eat when they are in a spawning mode; others are voracious prior to spawning. Some migrate; some build visible nests, and others have no nests; some move to the deep water, and some move to shallow water. Once a site is chosen for spawning by fish, or the time is right, they begin to mate. Sometimes the mating is an elaborate ritual; sometimes it merely amounts to the female scattering the eggs and the male fertilizing them. After the eggs are fertilized, some fish guard and care for the eggs, and some do not. The eggs hatch fairly quickly, at times in as little as 24 hours, although the time is influenced by such factors as water temperature, turbidity, sunlight, salinity, and current. The young fish just out of the eggs are called fry. Fry are usually so much smaller than their parents that they are not recognizably similar. Fry live on microorganisms in the water until they are ready for larger food. In certain species, each spawning pair can produce thousands of fry, but only a few grow to adulthood. Most fall victim to predation; fry are eaten by many predators, including other fish and, in some species, their own parents.

Certain types of fish spawn in habitats other than their normal ones. Some fish that live in the ocean spawn in rivers, and some fish that live in rivers spawn in the sea. Fish that live in the ocean yet spawn in freshwater are called anadromous. The most prominent examples of such fish are salmon. Fish that live in freshwater and spawn in the sea are called catadromous. The most prominent examples of such fish are eels.

Fish Food and Feeding

Fish have evolved to fill almost every ecological niche. Many fish are strictly herbivores, eating only plant life. Many are purely plankton eaters. Most are carnivorous (in the sense of eating the flesh of other fish as well as crustaceans, mollusks, and insects) or at least piscivorus (eating fish), and some—like the great white shark or the piranha—are among the most feared predators in the world by humans, although their danger to humans is oversensationalized. Almost all species that are considered gamefish are predators because their eating habits and aggressive behavior lead them to strike bait or lures that essentially mimic some form of natural food. Many predaceous fish eat other fish, but they also eat insects, worms and other invertebrates, and other vertebrates. Some fish will eat almost anything that can fit in their mouths and is alive. Some fish are scavengers, and will consume dead fish or parts of fish. Many fish fill only specific niches and have very specific diets. As a result, knowing the natural food of a gamefish can be important for anglers.

Fish Growth

Growth in fish is affected by many factors; especially important are heredity, length of growing season, and food supply. Although each species can be expected to reach a predetermined size, the length of time required to reach this size is extremely variable. The growing season is the time during the year when a fish will actively feed and grow. Generally, fish living in northern latitudes and colder waters have a shorter growing season than fish living in southern latitudes and warmer waters. If all other growing factors remain the same, the fish with the longer growing season will reach a greater size over a given time period.

Additionally, a fish that has optimum food and space conditions will grow more rapidly than one that must compete more heavily for food and space. This in part explains why fish of the same species in the same latitude and growing seasons, but in different bodies of water, may have different rates of growth.

The Diversity of Fish

Fish are the most diverse class of vertebrates. There are more fish species than all other vertebrate species combined. Their sizes can vary from the Philippine gobies, no more than a third of an inch in length (the smallest of all vertebrates), to whale sharks that can reach 60 feet in length and can weigh 150,000 pounds. Fish live in almost every aquatic environment in the world, from lakes 14,000 feet above sea level to 36,000 feet beneath the ocean surface. Fish are found in desert pools that are over 100°F and in Antarctic waters that are only 28°F (water freezes at less than 32° there because of the salinity; the fish do not freeze because they have a special biological antifreeze in their bodies). Some fish can survive for entire summers out of water by hibernating; others can glide out of the water for several hundred feet; a few can produce their own electricity or their own light. Some can achieve speeds of 50 or 60 miles an hour, and some live immobile, parasitic lives. In terms of biological and habitat diversity, no group of animals can outdo fish.

See: Anatomy.

The Evolution of Fish

Ostracoderms. Fish are the most ancient group of vertebrates. Fossil records indicate that they first appeared in the Ordovician period, more than 400 million years ago. The earliest types were covered with several kinds of armor, from which the name "ostracoderms," or shell-skinned, is derived. The

Ostracoderms

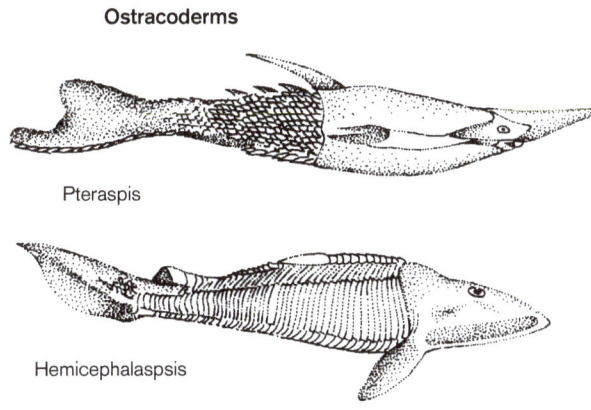

The extinct Ostracoderms are the oldest known fish. They were armor-plated; lacked a well-defined head; and had no scales, jaws, or paired fins.

oldest positive remains were found in rocks from Colorado and other western states. The nature of the sediments involved suggested that the ostracoderms lived in inland waters, supporting an early theory that vertebrates were of freshwater origin. Analyses of the habitats of early fossils by paleontologists, however, have led to the conclusion that, as a group, the invertebrates were originally marine.

Ostracoderms are now extinct. Their living relatives are the Agnatha, or Cyclostomes (hagfish and lampreys), which are the most primitive of the present-day fish. Generally eel-like in shape, cyclostomes lack a well-defined head and have no scales, jaws, or paired fins. Outwardly, in bodily outlines and in the presence of hard skeletal parts, the ostracoderms appear to be more remote from the cyclostomes; yet both are characterized by the absence of jaws and by the absence or weak development of paired fins. Other resemblances in structural features also exist with the two groups.

Placoderms. In the Devonian period of the geologic time scale, often called the "Age of Fish," the placoderms, or plate-skinned fish, were the most abundant forms. This group of fish, peculiar in structure, consists of several types now long distinct.

The various fossil groups have been assigned to many different positions in the classification system, and there is no complete agreement about their arrangement.

Chondrichthyes. In the evolutionary order, the ostracoderms and placoderms are followed by the sharks and their relatives, which extend to the era of modern types of jawed fish. Here the jaws are highly developed, and the fins and general body structure resemble a more familiar design. These types of higher fish forms are easily divided into two definite groups that may have evolved in a separate but parallel fashion from placoderm ancestors. They are the cartilaginous, jawed fish (sharks, skates, and rays) called Chondrichthyes, and the higher bony fish called Osteichthyes.

Bone is completely absent in the Chondrichthyes, and the internal skeleton is entirely cartilaginous. The principal advancements in these fish over earlier types are scales, paired fins, and well-developed jaws on a definite head. Some of their chief or distinguishing characteristics include five to seven pairs of gill clefts, all opening separately to the exterior; dorsal fin or fins and also fin spines, which, if present, are rigid yet not erectile; spiracles present or absent; skin covered with many placoid scales, or "dermal denticles"; and numerous teeth. In bottom-dwelling types of skates and rays, where the mouth is on the underside, water enters through a pair of spiracles on the top of the head and is expelled through the gill clefts, located on the underside of the head. In males, the pelvic fins bear projecting claspers that aid in internal fertilization. Development is oviparous (the eggs are laid before hatching), ovoviviparous (the eggs hatch and embryos develop within the mother but without placental attachment), or viviparous (born alive, embryos are attached to the uterine wall of the mother by a yolk-sac placenta).

Osteichthyes. The archaic fish that preceded the bony fish in the evolutionary scale were prominent in older geologic periods, but they diminished in later times. In contrast, the Osteichthyes, or the higher bony fish, became more abundant and more prominent and eventually dominated lakes and

Placoderms

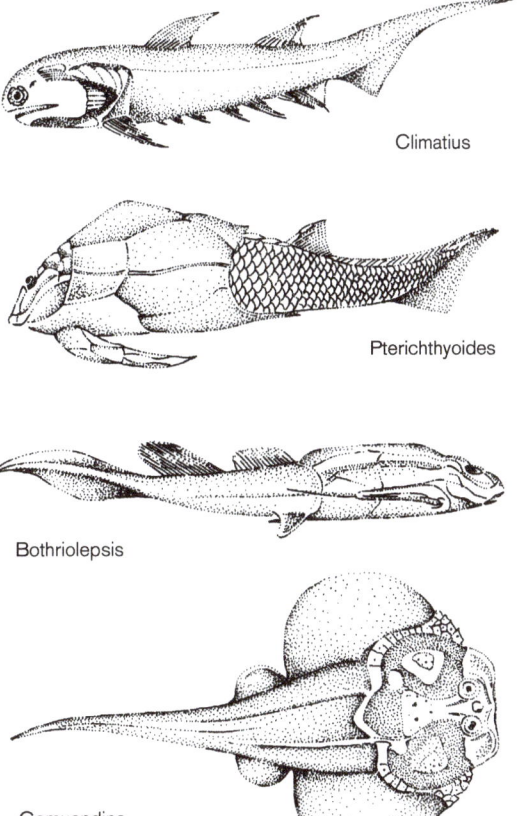

The extinct but once abundant Placoderms were plate-skinned fish.

streams. This group, at present, includes all freshwater fish and the great majority of marine types.

The chief characteristics of the bony fish are skeletons of bone; a single gill cover or operculum over the cavity containing the gills; fins strengthened by spines or soft rays; and scales that partially or completely cover the body, or which may be absent entirely. Today the bony fish far outnumber the cartilaginous fish. The most reliable estimates indicate that Osteichthyes include more than 20,000 species, in contrast to approximately 550 species for the Chondrichthyes.

FISH AMERICA FOUNDATION
Formed in 1983 for the purpose of assisting the enhancement of water quality and fish populations, the Fish America Foundation funds grass-roots projects in the United States and Canada. It helps create partnerships that involve industry, private citizens, foundations, and governments, and funds such hands-on fishery enhancement projects as shoreline restoration, plantings, artificial reef/habitat construction, fish rearing/stocking, and fishery education. It has supported over 450 such projects in 47 states and five provinces.

The Foundation especially works with angling and conservation groups to produce self-sustaining projects, most of which rely on volunteer manpower. All are funded only after receiving the endorsement of the appropriate governmental resource agency.

The Foundation is financed through the cooperative efforts of a coalition of sportfishing and boating manufacturers, and is unusual in that it has the ability to overcome the political and bureaucratic obstacles that often prevent small volunteer groups from receiving government assistance for conservation projects.

Fish America Foundation, 1033 North Fairfax Street, Suite 200, Alexandria, VA 22314; phone: 703-548-6338.

FISH AND WILDLIFE SERVICE
Founded in 1871 as part of the United States Commission of Fish and Fisheries, the U.S. Fish and Wildlife Service (USFWS) is the federal agency that is charged with managing and maintaining fish and wildlife and their habitats, with major responsibility for migratory birds, endangered species, certain marine mammals, and freshwater and anadromous fish.

The agency is part of the Department of the Interior, where it was placed in 1939 when it was called the Bureau of Fisheries. It became the Bureau of Sport Fisheries, and then the U.S. Fish and Wildlife Service in 1974. One of its primary responsibilities is managing the National Wildlife Refuge System, the world's largest and most diverse collection of lands set aside specifically for wildlife. Another is the conservation of over 800 species of migratory birds, the regulation of migratory bird hunting, and implementation of the North American Waterfowl Management Plan. Another is helping to save endangered species (more than 700 species are currently on the Interior Department's official "List of Endangered and Threatened Wildlife and Plants").

It is also charged with restoring nationally significant fisheries that have been depleted by overfishing, pollution, or other habitat damage. Major efforts are currently directed at lake trout in the upper Great Lakes, striped bass of the Chesapeake Bay region and the Gulf Coast; Atlantic salmon of New England; and the major salmonid species of the Pacific Northwest. As part of this program, nearly 80 national fish hatcheries produce some 60 species of fish, totaling over 200 million fish annually.

The Fish and Wildlife Service also enforces federal wildlife laws that protect endangered species, migratory birds, certain marine mammals, and fisheries. It undertakes activities designed to deter illegal trafficking in wildlife, and employs a nationwide network of special agents and inspectors who help enforce wildlife laws and treaty obligations.

Two federal laws administered by the Fish and Wildlife Service—the Federal Aid in Wildlife Restoration Act and the Federal Aid in Sport Fish Restoration Act (see)—have created some of the most successful programs in the history of fish and wildlife conservation. These programs provide federal grant money, which is derived from excise taxes on equipment and certain fuel sales, to support specific projects carried out by state fish and wildlife agencies.

The Fish and Wildlife Service is not involved with the management of strictly saltwater fish, which falls under the jurisdiction of respective state fish and wildlife agencies and the National Marine Fisheries Service (see), which is part of the Department of Commerce.

FISH ATTRACTING DEVICE
A man-made fish attractor, also known by the acronym FAD.
See: Fish Attractor.

FISH ATTRACTOR
Many fish are found close to structural objects of some kind, be they natural or man-made. The construction and planting of artificial habitat has become a very popular activity over the last few decades by groups and individuals as well as by state agencies, specifically to attract fish for angling. These structures, called attractors, provide shade, shelter, and food. They concentrate small plant and animal life that attracts the intermediate-size fish which larger fish prey upon. Thus, they may also concentrate sportfish and become good places to angle throughout the year, and especially in the summer.

Coelacanths are rare, living fossil fish that date to nearly 250 million years ago; once thought extinct, the first living specimen was found in 1938 off South Africa.

Freshwater

Through the planting of brushpiles in some lakes, ponds, and reservoirs that are largely devoid of cover, individual anglers have created habitat that attracts warmwater species and offers open-water angling opportunities. Channel catfish, bluegills, largemouth bass, and crappie are particularly concentrated by the existence of brush and automobile-tire attractors.

In some freshwater locales, large attractor structures planted by fisheries agencies or sports clubs are well marked and known to the general public. But many anglers plant their own. Private and commercial dock owners, for example, often plant brushpiles to provide fish habitat at arm's length. Some guides and avid anglers plant their own brushpiles to have "secret" fishing holes that often are very productive places. These are unmarked and located at sites known only to those who do the planting.

A pile of brush, attached to a block and located near a submerged stump along a sloping bottom, provides cover and food for different species of fish.

Types. Brush shelters are the oldest and most commonly used types of attractors. Virtually any type of woody brush can be used, but hardwoods resist decay longer than do softer pines. Discarded Christmas trees, for example, generally last only a few years, whereas scrub oak may be almost as resilient five years after being planted. A variety of brush shelter designs can be made, including crescents, pyramids or tepees, rings, and horizontal bundles. Those that are spread out generally prove more useful in shallow water, whereas taller structures are better in deeper water. However, providing variation within each attractor is probably the most important single characteristic for success. The most successful shelters usually contain areas of sparse, moderate, and thick brush cover, and use a variety of brush diameters.

Another successful shelter is an attractor made from bundled and weighted old automobile tires. Cement blocks or cement poured into a portion of the tire cavity is used for weight, and holes can be drilled into the tires to allow air to escape. Often, five or six tires are bundled together, although they can be piled at a site. Bundles may follow different patterns and bottom arrangements like brush shelters.

While brush and tires are the primary materials for attractors, some are made out of rubble, including broken bricks and cement blocks, slabs from demolition projects, and rocks. Large piles of rubble are not that efficient, since the major volume of rubble is covered by outer objects, but when it is spread out, more surface area is exposed. Another possible attractor is a stake bed. This is made from shafts of 1 × 2 lumber that is 4 to 6 feet long and which are driven into the lake bottom about 1 to 2 feet apart. In deep water where the stakes cannot be driven into the bottom, they are nailed to a 2 × 4 lumber frame. These cover an area that is a few feet wide and 4 to 6 feet long.

Planting. If you have a notion to create your own hotspot, check first to make sure that it is legal to do so. Planting brushpiles or any structural attractor is prohibited in some places. In some bodies of water, you must first check with the controlling agency (municipal water supply, Corps of Engineers, etc.); a permit may be required, and attractors may be prohibited from specific navigational channels where they might obstruct boat operation (especially in times of low water).

Shallow flat areas, large sandy bars, the backs of creeks, and ledges adjacent to dropoffs are popular sites for planting attractors. These usually are placed in locations that are devoid of structure or cover, as there is seldom a need to supplement existing cover with more. Some anglers place brushpiles a good distance away from a creek channel or breakline because they feel it is less likely to be spotted (on sonar) by other anglers.

Small trees and an accumulation of brush and limbs are the most favored attractors for individual planting. This is true for a few reasons. They're economical and readily available. They aren't as unsightly as other materials, in the event that low or clear water makes them visible. They pose less of an environmental concern.

Hardwood trees last longest and are preferable for durability. However, discarded Christmas trees (which are softwoods) are widely used because of their abundance, especially for crappie shelters. Trees can be planted singly or in clusters, which are usually better; they must be weighted and tied down. Cinder blocks work well for weights. Tying should be done with nylon rope or nylon-coated wire.

If the objective of planting a brushpile is to attract panfish, it's a good idea to spread out a lot of brush. But a room-size area of brush isn't necessary to attract bass. Placements of single trees or treetops or small amounts of brush can be just as effective for attracting good-size bass, and by placing a number of these in good places, you can create a host of private hotspots. The smaller groupings, incidentally, are also harder for other anglers to detect with their electronics.

In northern areas, brushpiles can be constructed on the ice and left to sink when the ice melts, although you can't be sure that they'll land exactly where or how you want them to unless they are heavily weighted so that they sink straight and don't glide. Elsewhere, you must put the brush or trees on a boat (pontoon boats can be good for this), bring them to the site, and then plant them. On lakes where the water level is lowered in the late fall or winter, you may be able to affix an attractor to a stump or rock that is exposed and that will be well covered by spring. Or you may be able to physically plant the brush on the bottom that you can walk or wade to, although this defeats the purpose of secretiveness.

Don't plant in places where navigation may be impeded or where motors may strike the structure. Attractors are usually planted 3 to 20 feet deep, but depth is relative to the situation. In water that usually stays turbid, 10 feet may be enough. If it is in the intermediate-clarity range, then 15 to 17 feet is about right. Clear, deep lakes may require deeper positioning, perhaps around 30 feet. Most brushpiles in reservoirs are planted on sloping banks and laying down, but in places with constant water levels they can be placed on a flat in a standing-up position with a super-heavy trunk weight and by slowly lowering them down with a rope.

On large bodies of water, you should use the sonar on your boat to precisely pinpoint the place to set the attractor, and use permanent landmarks as reference points to line you up when you want to return unerringly to the attractor without having to do a great deal of searching.

When you plant brushpiles, it is worthwhile to take the time to do it in a way that also aids future fishing efforts. Trimming bushy branches and stripping them of leaves may make it easier for your lures to avoid snagging. Also, planting the brush so that it lays at the right angle may be helpful. For instance, consider planting a small tree so that the trunk faces shore and the top lays down facing away from shore. Since you will usually cast to it from back to front, your lure works in the same direction as the limbs extend, which causes fewer hang-ups than if your lure runs against the grain.

Saltwater

In saltwater, attractors are much larger and more substantial in material. They are usually called artificial reefs (see), which result from the deliberate sinking of large vessels in strategic locations. There are also smaller attractors, commercially made fish attracting devices (FADs) that are placed in the water (free-floating or anchored) to help attract small baitfish and larger gamefish. The more extensive these are and the farther they extend into the water from the surface, the more they are likely to be effective and to attract diverse species. Less-substantive but portable and temporary attractors can be made by spreading newspapers, cardboard, old bed sheets tied to floats, and so on, over the surface to provide shady cover for baitfish. Even a drifting boat sometimes act as an attractor by providing shade that brings in baitfish.

Fishing

As for fishing attractor sites, jigs are a hands-down favorite lure. In saltwater, lead jigs with bucktail or plastic bodies, and heavy jigging spoons are the primary lures, but assorted bait or strips of fish can also be used depending on what you're fishing for. In freshwater, small light-wire jigs (the hook can be bent to work free when it is hung) are tops for crappie and other panfish around brushpiles in relatively shallow water, and live minnows and crickets fished on floats are also popular. Plastic worms, spinnerbaits, and crankbaits are top bass producers, but in deeper water, a jigging spoon is also effective and may catch white bass or stripers as well.

FISH BOX

A compartment for storing fish. On many larger boats, a fish box is integral to the interior layout of the boat and provides storage for fish that are to be kept and not released. Unlike a livewell, it is not meant for the containment of live fish or bait;

An insulated box, complete with crushed or cubed ice, keeps fish fresh. (Fish should be completely covered.)

the fish box is readily accessible and provides a compartment where fish can be stored off the floor of the boat and out of coolers that would take up cockpit space.

The fish box is located either beneath the cockpit sole of a boat or in a transom wall, and dimensions are dependent upon the size of the boat and the game to be pursued. It drains overboard either directly or through a macerator pump, but not into the bilge; this drainage system facilitates cleaning and permits the removal of blood and debris while fish are being stored. A fish box can also be a removable large ice chest or cooler. Fish that are kept in fish boxes should be iced down, especially in warm weather and on hot sunny days, to keep their temperatures low and to stay fresh.

See: Fish Box; Sportfishing Boat.

FISH CARVING

Fish carving is one of the fastest-growing areas of decorative carving. Fish are good subjects for wood reproduction in exacting detail, and an expertly carved and painted fish is often thought to be an outstanding taxidermy mount or fiberglass reproduction. In fact, the best fish carvers consider their art form far ahead of taxidermy, and the commissions received by the world's top fish carvers, which rival those of wildlife painters, reflect this judgment of fish carving as an art form.

Noted carver Bob Berry created this decorative 24-inch rainbow trout.

Although there are carvers who are masters of this art form and carve fish professionally, there are many home workshop carvers who replicate fish in wood for their personal enjoyment. Like all crafts or expressions of art, fish carving can encompass a wide range of styles and interpretation, from a simple folk-art style to the finest highly detailed and realistically painted contemporary wood sculptures that can be made. Competitions for carvers reflect the sophisticated level to which this art form has risen, and the competitions are held nationally in conjunction with taxidermy competitions. Many people who create wooden carvings of fish are, or once were, taxidermists; and some sculpt fish out of materials other than wood.

Individual carvers have personal preferences in the types of wood they use. The most commonly used woods are tupelo, jelutong, and basswood. Sugar pine, alder, and cedar are also used. Carvers who specialize in interpretive natural finish carvings prefer hardwoods with color, figure, and character to enhance their work.

The carving tools and supplies for fish carving are the same as those used for all other types of carving, and primarily consist of a few knives, chisels, and rasps. As carvers develop experience, their tools may become more sophisticated. Modern, high-speed, flexible-shaft machines that cost hundreds of dollars are used by some.

As fish carving has developed through the 1990s, specialized tools have been invented or designed especially for this type of work. The most commonly designed and altered tools are ones for making lifelike scales. These generally consist of wood burning tips, which are implements for pressing in scales or are rounded chisels that cut in and lift an edge of wood to resemble a scale. Since fish come in all sizes and shapes, their scales do also. Fish carvers are constantly trying to come up with a perfect tool for a particular fish scale pattern and size.

The actual carving of a fish from wood is sometimes the best part of the overall project. Not all wooden fish carvings are crafted entirely from a single piece of wood. Some carvers do a few or all of the fins separately, and may cut off and later reattach the top of the head to provide extensive inner mouth detail. The presentation of the fish on accurate habitat is often more tedious and intricate than creating the fish itself. Many of the best pieces blend the habitat in exquisite composition and design that complement and complete the carving of the fish. This is essential for submissions in competitions but certainly not necessary in the majority of fish carvings. Simply mounting the carved fish on a piece of driftwood that nicely complements the carving is often enough.

However, as fish carvers progress and strive for the best possible work they can do, they usually find that attaching a nicely carved and painted fish to a piece of driftwood is not satisfying enough. They become more observant of details and accuracy. The best carvers leave nothing to chance. They carve, texture, and paint every part of their piece in realistic detail. This level of craftsmanship generally happens only with carvers whose years of experience in combining carving and painting skills have developed into an artistic style that accurately depicts the carved fish and the entire setting.

Accuracy is something that the top carvers work hard at, and they use plenty of reference materials—from photos in magazines and books to their own photos of the actual subjects—to re-create the fish and the habitat properly. The painting of the piece, especially the fish, is an art form in itself; advanced carvers may employ dozens of steps in completing complicated projects.

Some of the most difficult parts of a carving that includes habitat are aquatic plants. Most, being leafy and delicate, pose major problems to the carver. Carving realistic rocks and driftwood can also be very time-consuming. Many smaller elements that are often included in a carving to set the theme—like a minnow or group of minnows, a snail, or a crayfish—can take as long as carving the fish itself.

The matter of water is always difficult for beginning carvers to overcome. The best carvings imply the water surface with floating plants such as lily pads. Splashes with jumping fish are quite difficult to imply. Although these elements can be conveyed through the use of cast resin or Plexiglas, and might be suitable to some people, this technique is generally not acceptable in fish carving competitions.

Fish carving is a good fit with the catch-and-release *(see)* fishing ethics commonly practiced today, and to some people it is preferable to a taxidermy mount or a fiberglass reproduction. An angler needs only a good photograph and a length measurement for a skilled carver to re-create a particular fish. A highly detailed, accurate depiction of the angler's fish is usually appreciated by everyone who sees it.

Recreating actual fish, however, is just one facet of fish carving. There are not many limits on a fish carver. An angler's fish of a lifetime, caught many years before, can be re-created; rare, endangered, protected, and world-record species can be depicted; many such carvings are done, in fact, with amazing accuracy for display in museum exhibits or nature centers. Scale can be easily adjusted; large fish can be miniaturized, and small fish enlarged.

Nor is the fish carver limited to species caught by anglers. Tropical reef fish are a favorite of many carvers. They are relatively small and have exceptional colors and patterns that can be a challenge to re-create accurately. Their coral reef habitat, with its extreme variety of life, offers limitless possibilities.

FISH CLEANING
See: Fish Preparation—Cleaning/Dressing.

FISH CULTURE
See: Hatchery.

FISH EGGS
See: Natural Bait.

FISHER
An archaic and non-gender-specific version of the word "fisherman," and one that may refer to an individual engaged in sportfishing, commercial fishing, or recreational fishing. Fisher is receiving increased current use in an attempt to employ politically correct terms; however, the word "angler" is used in this book not only because it isn't gender-specific, but because it cannot be confused with commercial fishing or non rod-and-reel recreational fishing.
See: Angler; Commercial Fisherman; Fisherman; Recreational Fisherman; Sportfisherman.

FISHERIES
All the activities involved in catching a group of species; the places where a group of species are caught. This term is used interchangeably with fishery *(see)*.

FISHERIES MANAGEMENT
Recent decades have seen an increase in the number of regulations pertaining to the sport of angling, in both freshwater and saltwater, for the purpose of managing fisheries resources. However, such regulation and management are not new. One of the earliest laws regulating the taking of fish was implemented in 1678 when Virginia banned the use of lights to attract fish.

In the eighteenth and nineteenth centuries in North America, several factors—an abundance of fish, a relatively small population of people, and unsophisticated means of harvesting fish for food or catching them for sport—meant that fisheries resources were seldom threatened. In time, some resources were adversely impacted, largely because of the alteration of the landscape through timber harvesting, and pollution caused by burgeoning industry and population concentrations. Anglers and hunters, who were the early conservationists and forerunners of today's environmentalists, clamored for regulations that would foster fish (and game) conservation, the establishment of public parks where natural resources could flourish, and the creation of government agencies to conduct resource management and research. Indeed, American fisheries research first began in 1871 at Woods Hole, Massachusetts, with the establishment of the United States Commission on Fish and Fisheries, and 10 states had established fisheries commissions prior to that year.

Eventually all states and the United States government became responsible for the oversight and management of fisheries resources. A similar situation evolved in Canada. In time, that management became not only an issue of doing what was best for the betterment or maintenance of fisheries resources, but also an issue of managing other natural resources and, perhaps most importantly, managing people and their divergent needs and interests.

Hundreds of years ago, European community leaders observed that when a resource was owned by the people, no one took responsibility for maintaining the resource. Human nature being what it is, each person tended to use the resource to the maximum extent. There was little incentive to conserve or invest in the resource because others would then benefit without contributing to the welfare of the resource. In the case of common (public) grazing areas in England, grass soon disappeared as citizens put more and more sheep on the land held in common. Everyone lost when "the commons" were overgrazed, and this situation became known as "the tragedy of the commons."

To prevent "the tragedy of the commons," most common property resources are held in trust and managed for the people by government agencies. Fish living in public waters are such a common property resource. In the United States, state and federal governments have the responsibility of managing the fish for the benefit of all citizens, including those who do not fish. In order for all to benefit from this renewable resource, the fish are supposed to be managed on the basis of scientific principles.

Managing public fishery resources is ultimately the responsibility of elected officials. Elected officials, however, have delegated much of that responsibility to resource agencies that employ people trained in the sciences of fishery biology, economics, and natural resource management. The National Marine Fisheries Service (NMFS) *(see)* is the federal government agency in the United States with primary responsibility for managing marine fish from 3 to 200 miles offshore. Coastal states are responsible for inshore waters and offshore waters out to 3 miles (9 miles on the Florida west coast and off Texas). State agencies are responsible for freshwater resources within their state.

In an idealistic and theoretical sense, the purpose of fishery management is to protect and maintain fish resources, but in a practical sense the purpose is to satisfy the desires and needs of people. Those desires and needs are varied but primarily include outdoor recreation and food. Therefore, this entails fishery (and water) management based on scientific principles to provide continued sustained utilization of those resources for maximum public benefit. It also entails dealing with social, political, and economic issues.

Biological Principles

Renewable resources like fish and shellfish are living things that replenish themselves naturally and can be harvested within limits on a continuing basis

Managing people, such as these on a Washington river, is a major element of modern fisheries management.

without eliminating them. The scientific principles behind this renewability are well known and provide the basis for fish and game management. To understand these principles, it is helpful to know that, in fish resource management, "species" refers to a group of similar organisms that can freely interbreed; a "population" is a group of individuals of the same species living in a certain area; "stock" means a harvested or managed unit of fish; and "fishery" encompasses all of the activities involved in catching a species of fish or group of species.

Survival

All animals produce more offspring than survive to adulthood as a kind of biological insurance against natural calamities. Actually, for a species to maintain itself, each pair of fish has to produce only two offspring that in turn survive to reproduce. However, most individual fish and shellfish produce tens of thousands to millions of eggs. Most of their eggs do not survive to become juveniles, and even fewer live to become adults. This extra production, together with the effects of harvesting fish, can result in surplus or sustainable production.

Surplus production. The theory of surplus production goes something like this: In an unfished, or unexploited, population, the biomass (total weight) of fish in a habitat will approach the carrying capacity (maximum amount that can live in an area) of the habitat. This population will have a lot of older, larger fish compared to a fished, or exploited, population. These older fish dominate the habitat, and their presence prevents all but a small percentage of the young fish produced each year from surviving to become old fish. When fishing begins (this includes recreational, commercial, and personal subsistence fishing), many large, older fish are removed. Removal of these older fish, as well as other fish, reduces the biomass below the carrying capacity and increases the survival chances for smaller, younger fish. Thus, the unfished population can be viewed as a relatively stable population with moderate production.

The fished population, on the other hand, is a dynamic population with a higher turnover of individuals as the older fish are replaced by younger, faster-growing fish. Some of this new production must be allowed to survive and reproduce to maintain the population. The remaining, or surplus, production is available for harvest.

Surplus production, however, is a complex biological process that is influenced by several factors, particularly carrying capacity and habitat loss. Carrying capacity can be thought of as the amount of fish an area of habitat will support. Habitat that historically supported a certain amount of fish is unlikely to support a lot more or a lot less unless conditions change. If the amount or quality of habitat is reduced, carrying capacity will likewise be reduced.

Human activity has obviously altered, and in some cases reduced, fish habitat. Water pollution, loss of wetlands and seagrasses, destruction of spawning areas, thermal changes, and changes in freshwater flows are some of the many factors that have led to habitat reduction. Unfortunately, fishery managers and anglers have had little influence on, or control over, habitat alterations. Fishery managers have to manage the fish populations that the habitat can support at the present time, not the fish populations that past habitat conditions supported.

Furthermore, carrying capacity changes as environmental conditions change from year to year. When environmental conditions are good in a given year, there is more suitable habitat and more young survive. When environmental conditions are poor in a given year, there is less suitable habitat and fewer young survive. The biological principles that cause surplus production are the natural methods that a species uses to increase the population when environmental conditions are favorable.

Harvesting

The basic goal of fishery biology is to estimate the amount of fish that can be safely removed, or harvested, while keeping the fish population healthy. That estimated amount is called total allowable catch, and it may be modified by political, economic, and social considerations. Overly conservative management can result in wasted fisheries production because of underharvesting, whereas too liberal or no management may result in overharvesting and severely reduced populations. Harvesting fish lowers the population below the carrying capacity of the environment. Continued harvest depends on the ability of the population to produce enough offspring to move toward the maximum carrying capacity. Variations in natural conditions can alter the carrying capacity, resulting in good years and bad years for survival of young.

Populations and Stocks

Ideally the various populations of a species would be the units that are managed. In freshwater environments, a population would be the entire group living in that body of water, and it is usually managed as a whole. Freshwater environments are relatively small in area and in volume when compared with the sea (even a large lake is small compared with the ocean), and they are essentially treated as closed systems. The number of species in freshwater is smaller than in saltwater, and their interrelationships are different.

It is rarely practical in saltwater to manage the population of a species as a unit. There, fishery biologists often refer to stocks rather than populations. For example, Spanish mackerel occur from Maine to the Yucatan Peninsula in Mexico. For purposes of management in the United States, Spanish mackerel are divided into two stocks. Fish from one stock migrate from Florida northward along the East Coast of the United States, and the others migrate from Florida into the Gulf of Mexico. The two stocks may represent one or several populations that make up the species. However, current knowledge about harvesting and migration patterns dictates that they be managed as two stocks. Sometimes more than one species is included in a stock because they are harvested together as though they were one species. In other cases, different species may be managed together for convenience.

Because so many saltwater species are targeted by commercial fishermen, and many are targeted by recreational anglers, management of stocks necessarily takes into account the efforts and results of both groups. In freshwater in the United States, commercial activity is very limited, especially for game species; thus fishery management efforts are primarily focused on the impacts of recreational anglers on populations, and on the impacts of habitat loss or change.

Management in Freshwater

(*Note:* Because there is overlap in principles and methodology, not all aspects of freshwater fisheries management have been discussed in the following section, and likewise in the saltwater management section. Readers are urged to review both sections for the most complete view of these issues.)

Freshwater fishery management in North America has had an interesting evolution in terms of angling interests and attitudes, and in terms of management activities.

Because fishery management (research, regulation, and resource manipulation) has always been geared to the needs and interests of people, it has had an erratic and sometimes conflicting development. For example, at the same time late in the nineteenth century that fishery research in the United States was started, fish culturists were eagerly importing, shipping, stocking, and tinkering with fish species in freshwaters all over North America.

Some of that turned out to be beneficial; some turned out to be disastrous.

Procuring fresh food has been, and continues to be, a strong reason for fishing in freshwater, but fishing purely for recreational fun has also become an increasingly important reason in itself. Other motivators, including the act of fishing as a means of enjoying the outdoor environment, also exist. Selective effort aimed at specific species—most of them at the top of the food chain—and the increasing embrace of catch-and-release *(see)* have been more recent influences on management. Thus, an evolution in attitudes, in addition to increasing demands and influences on natural resources, has resulted in changing and primarily reactionary management activities.

With commercial fishing largely nonexistent in freshwater, competition for the fish is strictly between recreational anglers. Commercial fishing is permitted only for those species and in those locations where there is little or no interference with the recreational fisheries (although in some waters there is competition with native treaty fishing). Thus, the major focus of management activities has been on preserving or enhancing habitat, sustaining or increasing fish populations, and managing angler activities. The objective is to produce abundant and diverse fish life and enhance fish populations so that they are accessible to anglers in desirable quantity, variety, and size range. Accomplishing this takes a knowledge of fisheries science and aquatic ecology, and an understanding of socioeconomic factors, including angler attitudes.

Optimum yield. Optimum yield is the harvest level for a species that achieves the greatest overall benefits, including economic, social, and biological considerations. This is different from the traditional biological concept of maximum sustainable yield, which is the largest average catch that can be taken continuously and which considers only the biology of the species and the production of protein.

The concept of optimum yield has long been used in freshwater fishery management, and it comprises the sometimes intangible factor of "quality." Angling quality includes considerations of species, sizes, and quantity of fish involved; situations in which they are found; and methods of capture. Optimum yield management requires establishing and maintaining ecological supplies of some species in order to sustain other desired species or merely to assure diversity of abundant life forms. It also requires establishing safety factors in the total allowable catch to moderate effects of unanticipated disasters and human errors.

Biology
In the broadest sense, fisheries management activities are predicated upon knowledge of the species, which requires extensive and time-consuming research. From the late nineteenth century until after World War II, research at all levels was probably the foremost activity of fishery scientists. Understanding the life history of a given species is the underpinning of biological efforts, and it includes knowledge of spawning habits and early development, age and growth, food and feeding, migration and movements, diseases and parasites, predators, subpopulations, and physiology and behavior.

Much is known about the biology of many primary freshwater species, while less is known about the biology of others. The biology of most of the species of interest to anglers is by now fairly well understood, and there has been a lot of research on the dynamics of predator-prey relationships. Nevertheless, the biology of some nontargeted species and some prey fish is less well understood, and an understanding of the dynamics between all species is still being explored.

Methods. Freshwater fisheries management involves a number of methods. These include: hatcheries and stocking of popular game species; establishment and enforcement of regulations to prevent overfishing; management and enhancement of streams, lakes, and reservoirs to stabilize populations; surveys to determine angler needs and wants; allocations to user groups, primarily for sport and recreational use and occasionally for industry, farming, and commercial purposes; and research to address specific fisheries management problems and issues.

Since fisheries management encompasses all action that protects, enhances, improves, or maintains fisheries and fishing areas, methods include such diverse activities as protection of a woods or forest serving as a buffer zone to prevent agricultural runoff; institution of unique slot limits or catch-and-release regulations; protection of certain species and sizes of fish; and creation of regulations limiting water use by some groups in order to protect the resource.

Hatcheries and Stocking
Early attempts at raising fish for food date to the Orient and early Roman times, but fish culture for sport purposes began in Europe prior to 1850. At that time, fish hatcheries could be found for a number of species, even though, at the same time, breeding and hatching trout in North America was still a novelty.

Hatcheries might seem to be the solution for all fishing problems, since stocked fish from hatcheries theoretically could be raised to fill every angler's needs and wishes. In the early days of stocking, that is how they were viewed, and there are still some anglers who feel that stocking is the absolute answer to population abundance problems, which it often is not.

Hatcheries and stocked fish can be expensive and are not always practical or possible. At one time, shad hatcheries abounded all along the East Coast, but their minimal replenishment of the species and high expense doomed them. There are very few hatcheries for saltwater species, although

 Bycatch is the term for the unwanted fish that are commercially netted along with targeted species; these fish often are dumped back dead into the sea. The ratio of bycatch to intended catch can be as high as 4 to 1.

Atlantic salmon are raised in this New Brunswick hatchery.

technical difficulties in raising marine species are beginning to be overcome; red drum, snook, and sea trout are among the species now being raised successfully.

Even in freshwater, the costs, food needs, possible cannibalism, and habitat requirements of different species make some difficult to raise. Muskellunge, for example, are very difficult to raise, since they tend to be cannibalistic; and satisfactory foods and (economical) feeding systems are still being developed. Trout, including rainbow, brown, and brook, are easier. They can be kept in large areas, exhibit little cannibalism, and eat food pellets. Trout also are easy to strip (remove the eggs and milt from spawning adults), fertilize, and produce from eggs. However, even the trout species differ in cost effectiveness. Rainbow are the easiest and cheapest (and thus most heavily stocked by most states); brown and brook trout are more difficult and costly.

The size of the fish stocked also determines the ultimate cost, and thus reflects the number of fish stockings that can be made with a given amount of money. The smallest fish, called fry, are less than finger length and are generally inexpensive to produce. Little time, money, manpower, or food is allotted to them, although their natural mortality is high when released.

Fingerlings, which are 3 to 5 inches long, or a finger's length, are more expensive but may still be economical with most species. The mortality will be less with these fish than with fry, but higher than with adult fish. The optimum size for stocking will vary with each species and situation, but usually fish 6 to 8 inches or longer will have low mortality if handled carefully. Obviously, larger fish are more expensive. Adult fish can be economical or expensive, depending upon the species. Rainbow trout are generally less expensive than muskies.

There are problems associated with rearing fish in hatcheries. Under the crowded conditions of a hatchery, cannibalism can cause large losses. The fish also become trained to feed on hatchery food and need time to make the transition to wild conditions. In addition, the opportunity for disease or fungus to develop is greater, and serious problems can be caused when diseased fish or fry are released in the wild. Another problem, though not a biological issue, is the fact that hatchery-raised fish seldom taste as good as their wild counterparts, especially if they are caught soon after release. Although hatchery managers have learned to control most of the biological problems, there are still occasions when things go wrong.

The majority of anglers prefer the stocking of adult fish, especially trout, since these fish can be readily and immediately caught. However, the costs are high. Stockings of smaller fish may be more cost-effective and may be accepted by the fishing community, especially if time and conditions for growth in the wild are provided.

In states, hatcheries and the numbers of fish stocked depend upon funding, which is largely derived from the revenues obtained from angling license fees or stamps. The federal government also operates fish hatcheries to restore certain major and indigenous fisheries or to mitigate the effects of federal water development projects. Some federal stockings are allocated to the states annually. Other federal-hatchery fish go to federally managed lands or to such interjurisdictional waters as the Great Lakes or the Columbia River. Many states have species-specific stamps in addition to the standard fishing license; these help pay for species-specific stocking and management programs.

It should be repeated that stocking has had some beneficial results and some notably harmful ones, and that it is still controversial in current times as a management method for certain situations. Many of the harmful results came early in the days of fish culture and fisheries management. The widespread and indiscriminate stocking of carp across North America, for example, which were imported from Europe, is generally regarded as the most disastrous hatchery-raising and stocking effort ever accomplished in freshwater. On the other hand, the raising and stocking of striped bass in freshwater impoundments, and the stocking of steelhead and salmon in the Great Lakes, have been extremely successful from the perspective of anglers. Stocking, however, especially of nonnative species, can be, and in some cases has been, harmful to other populations of fish and the cause of multiple changes in assorted aquatic resources.

Regulations

Many populations of popular game species in freshwater would be in danger of rapid depletion without regulations attempting to control their harvest. Fishing regulations cover a variety of issues but are most typically associated with size and creel limits. Size limits usually state the minimum legal size for specific species, the rationale being to prevent small fish from being kept and to allow fish to spawn at least once. Some biologists feel that this simple designation places too much emphasis and fishing pressure on larger fish. Slot limits, where anglers can keep fish only above and below a certain specified size, and catch-and-release areas have become popular in some waters for population management reasons and because of expressed angler interest.

Creel limits regulate the number of fish that can be taken daily. They are usually based on an aggregate number, although some specify limits for fish of a certain large size within that number. Possession limits are similar to creel limits but specify the number of fish that can be in one's possession. Possession limits are usually equivalent to a two- or three-day creel limit, and thus they prohibit anglers from repeatedly catching creel limits and storing them for future use. Creel limits attempt to distribute the catch among more people over a greater time period.

Slot limits allow harvesting of fish of only a certain size and prohibit the taking of fish smaller or larger than that size. Many biologists believe that this is a better way to limit catches, since it protects not only the smallest of the species but also requires release of trophy fish. These trophy fish can then theoretically be caught another day, and their return to the water helps to repopulate the species during spawning season and to maintain predator-prey balance.

Some regulations restrict catches on specific waters to only one large trophy fish, thus ensuring that many will be left to replenish the species. Some fishing camps or lodges or managers of privately controlled waters impose regulations that are more restrictive than government-imposed regulations. They realize that their continued success depends upon constant catches of fish and angler satisfaction.

Catch-and-release fishing is popular in certain areas and is a method utilized by some agencies to limit harvest. An increasing number of anglers practice partial or total catch-and-release on a voluntary basis, but catching any fish in any water that does not meet regulations for harvest requires release, so there are various forms that this concept can take. Specific total catch-and-release fishing by regulation is usually limited to certain waters, and this method requires the immediate release of every fish that is caught. Variations of this are "lure fishing only" or "fly fishing only" and other regulations in which certain types of equipment (lures but no bait or traditional flies only) are allowed. Some fly-fishing-only regulations are also accompanied by other regulations regarding equipment, particularly the use of barbless hooks, and some catch-and-release area regulations also prohibit the use of bait or barbed hooks.

Other regulations prescribe the fishing seasons for selected species. Usually the closed seasons are those in which the fish are spawning. This prevents too many from being taken and permits adequate replacement, although there is not uniform agreement among fisheries biologists as to the need for closed seasons; some states have them and others don't. For similar reasons, other regulations prohibit night fishing for some species, or establish off-limit areas on certain waters.

Regulations that prohibit the use of certain types of bait are enacted to prevent the entry of undesirable species into streams and lakes. Thus, a common regulation is one that prohibits the use of goldfish, carp, or species not bought from a bait shop. Other regulations unilaterally prohibit any use of baitfish. The reason for such prohibitions is that it is possible to adversely affect predator or prey species in a certain location by the deliberate or inadvertent release of these undesirable fish. Similarly, transferring game species from one body of water to another is prohibited by most agencies to protect existing populations of fish. The deliberate or inadvertent transferring of yellow perch, for example, to lakes and ponds with trout, has been detrimental to trout because the perch prey on the young trout and eventually overtake the trout.

(For more information about special regulations, see that section later in this entry.)

Habitat Management

Habitat management involves the protection, restoration, control, or enhancement of lakes, ponds, streams, rivers, and other habitat areas. In some cases, habitat management or improvement is accomplished with the help of fishing clubs, scout troops, community groups, and the like under the direction of state or federal fisheries personnel.

Stream improvements can be accomplished by building small dams to raise pool levels, reinforcing banks with rock or logs, and creating cover from log and brush cuttings. On lakes and ponds, the planting of structure such as weighted brushpiles and Christmas trees, cutting and chaining shoreline logs for cover, planting water weeds, and building small reefs to hold fish can improve fish habitat.

Artificial reefs are an important way to improve some fisheries and increase available fish. Reefs can be as simple as a Christmas tree weighted with concrete blocks or as complex as the sinking of large scrap freighters (largely a saltwater phenomenon) or the sinking of wired tires and concrete block and rubble. While artificial reefs connote a bottom structure, there are commercially available reefs that are anchored to the bottom but are mid-depth structures to attract fish.

Reefs are important in two different ways. Reef structure will hold, foster, and develop algae, weeds, invertebrates, crustaceans, and other flora and fauna, which are the bottom of the food chain and the basis of life for larger prey and predator species. The structure provides comfort, safety, and food. Also, reefs help to gather and hold fish. Fish species that seek structure will not stay in areas with plain flat bottoms. The presence of structure in these areas gathers those species and improves fishing.

In freshwater, the quality of the water is part of the habitat concerns, and the acidity of an environment is one water-quality issue that can have a large influence on fish. Water pH within certain narrow ranges close to a neutral pH of 7.0 is important for the maintenance of fish life. A pH of 7.2 to 8.3 is typical, a pH of 6.0 to 9.0 is acceptable, and a pH of 5.5 to 9.5 is generally tolerable. However, fish prefer neutral (pH 7.0) or slightly alkaline (up to pH 7.9) water. Acid rain, acid mine runoff, and acid industrial pollution make pH abnormally low and kill fish life. Some pH control is possible, either by using crushed limestone (alkaline) in affected streams and lakes or by releasing limestone slurry in careful doses to counteract any acid influx into the water. However, pH control is temporary, expensive, and needed most in those waters that naturally are least productive.

Another habitat concern, and one with many resource-user conflicts, is aquatic vegetation. Weeds or aquatic plants are important in most waters. They provide a basis for the food chain and protection for fish, and convert carbon dioxide to oxygen. However, uncontrolled vegetation growth can be bad, since some aquatic plants can choke waterways, make boat traffic impossible, and begin the eutrophication (overenrichment) process of small lakes and ponds. In some areas, artificially introduced plants such as hydrilla have become serious problems. There is no simple answer for aquatic plant control, although cutting, poisoning, uprooting, and introducing other species to eat or destroy the plants have all been tried, with varying results. In some cases, the eradication of certain aquatic plants has had major adverse impacts on fishing for certain species, especially bass.

Temperature is the most important factor affecting the species in a given body of water. All species have a range of preferred temperatures. Warm waters are best for the so-called warmwater species such as sunfish and bass; cold waters are best for coldwater species such as trout and salmon. Watershed protection will help maintain a cool temperature for trout streams. Temperature can be controlled in streams running from dam outlets by controlling the level of the outlet from a dam. High-level outlets, which take water from on or near the surface, result in downstream flows with higher water temperatures; low-level outlets, which take water from deeper levels, result in downstream flows with colder water temperatures. Since most dams are on fast-flowing streams, a low-level outlet for cold water is preferred for trout habitat. However, low outlets often result in water with little or no oxygen, and baffles leading from the outlet to the stream are often used to aerate and oxygenate the water.

Watershed maintenance involves everything from watershed protection to clearing of hazardous snags or obstructions. All waterways need a suitable buffer zone of forest land around them to protect them from rapid runoff; muddying of the water; and runoff of pesticides, herbicides, insecticides, and fertilizers from nearby agricultural areas; also necessary is adequate natural shoreline to protect against erosion. Good agricultural practices, control of urban development, and pollution control are vital components of watershed management.

Surveys

Management surveys provide information on the needs of anglers, the fish harvest, and the condition of fish populations. They can include angler surveys, biological surveys, and tagging surveys.

Angler surveys are conducted at points of access or on a roving basis. Access-point surveys are usually accomplished at dockside to compile information; roving surveys are done on the water. Fishing success, rate of catch, catch per unit of effort (hours, days, trips, etc.), number and size of catch, equipment used, locations fished, and similar information is recorded. This information can then be used to determine the need for creel or size limits, seasons, or stocking programs.

Biological surveys usually involve electrofishing (or electroshocking), poisoning, or netting. In shocking, waters are electrified with special equipment to temporarily incapacitate the fish, which can then be gathered for quantitative and qualitative data. This may be used to build a baseline

New York fisheries technicians sample a lake by netting.

of biological data trends, including information on the habitat and the food chain. Poisoning, using selective chemicals that pose little danger to humans, is generally reserved for very specific purposes. In addition to being used in surveys, poisoning may also be used to renovate or reclaim some bodies of water (usually small), killing all fish to permit restocking with other species more desirable or appropriate. Chemicals are also used in some control situations; the lampricide TFM, for example, is an effective, selective poison used to control sea lampreys.

The survey method of tagging involves placing a tag or mark on fish. Fish are marked through a clipped fin to obtain general information. However, this often does not provide data on fish growth (other than general data), since specific fish cannot be identified and measured without expensive tracking mechanisms *(see: tagging)*. Using various types of tags, placed in different locations on the body of the fish depending on the agency or the species of fish, allows biologists to obtain important information on growth rates, migrations and movements, species health, weight increases, and similar data when the fish are recaptured later. Comparing data taken at the time fish were released with similar data gained upon capture gives fisheries biologists important information.

Allocation

Water is basic to human life in a host of ways. Besides personal uses, it is necessary for manufacturing, trade (shipping lines), housing developments (thus increased prices for shoreline property), farming, and recreational interests. There is a constant demand for water from a variety of users, all vital in a way, but all in a way destructive to the natural waterway. The great amount of water needed for the production of aluminum might affect water usage in that area. Water utilized and released in chemical and steel production will pollute waterways if not monitored and treated. The damming of a stream for flow control or irrigation may deplete water flow downstream, affecting habitat and fisheries. A reservoir formed for recreation might be applauded by swimmers, water-skiers, sailors, boaters, and lake anglers but might ruin the favorite recreation of river canoeists, stream anglers, and whitewater rafters.

Constant water monitoring is required along with adequate controls to ensure that the quality remains high. When there are conflicting areas of water usage, a balance must be met to make sure that industry, farming, commercial, and recreational needs—including boating and many forms of fishing—are all treated fairly.

Since most freshwater commercial species such as trout and catfish are raised in ponds, and most freshwater commercial fishing is concentrated on species other than those sought by anglers, conflicts about fishing use, such as those experienced in saltwater between commercial fishermen and recreational anglers, seldom occur. Allocations based on economic issues with regard to freshwater fisheries usually focus on maintaining the fisheries or enhancing them to sustain or improve sportfishing participation, which is unarguably of significant economic importance, especially since it involves expenditures made for fishing and boating equipment, gasoline (for boats and for cars to reach the area), incidentals at convenience and grocery stores, lodging, dining, guide and charter boat services, boat rentals, and much more. Many billions of dollars are affected nationally by recreational angling, and economic considerations are among the factors affecting fisheries management.

Problems

In theory, fisheries management seeks to avoid problems through preventive measures, but in reality many of the practices of fisheries managers are in response to public needs or interests and in response to problems that develop with fisheries. Nevertheless, control measures and ongoing management can revitalize some fish habitats and fish populations, and such practices do prevent the occurrence of some problems or prevent existing problems from worsening.

Some common issues facing all fisheries managers include overharvesting, the depletion of genetic strains of fish, and loss of habitat. Habitat loss is by far the greatest danger, since it is generally out of the hands of anglers and fisheries biologists. Housing developments, shopping malls, industrial plants, human consumption, irrigation, loss of buffer zones, and natural disasters and environmental changes (like storms or changing weather patterns), and other factors can alter, reduce, or completely eliminate habitat areas or cause loss of natural waters.

Controlled size and creel limits and constant monitoring and surveys by fisheries biologists can prevent or curtail overharvesting. When it becomes a danger, emergency regulations usually allow for closure of an area, pending a more detailed survey and analysis.

Biologists can carefully control species so that hearty, viable strains are produced in hatcheries. A problem can develop when a hybrid is introduced in an area in which one of the parent species is still present. A dilution of genes or a loss of the original species can occur if the hybrid proves to be more adept in adapting to the environment, or if it proves to be a more dominant strain than the original stock.

Management in Saltwater

Marine fish have had a long history of importance for humans. This was always rooted in fish as a food source. Accounts of vast shoals of saltwater fish in the New World helped draw colonists, and fish were the first items exported. But even then,

Commercial fishing is often at odds with recreational fishing; this is a scene along the British Columbia coast.

fluctuations in abundance were noted, and catches were found to be variable. From the early days until the late nineteenth century, virtually all saltwater fishing was of the commercial, or fish-for-food, variety, and it was not until well into the twentieth century that fishing for recreation and food became a component of the utilization of marine resources.

Eventually, recreational angling would become a significant part of total marine fishing effort, although recreational anglers target a more limited number of fish species and do not target shellfish in volume. In time, recreational fishing evolved from being almost entirely a catch-and-keep endeavor to a more selective type of harvest, either by personal choice or by regulation. Some popularly sought saltwater species, like tarpon and bonefish, have negligible food value either to commercial fishermen or to recreational anglers and are primarily released by anglers. But such instances are in the minority. Nevertheless, when marine fishery resources are managed, both recreational and commercial uses and interests must be considered, even as the economic value of, and participation in, these activities change.

Stock assessment. Stock assessment encompasses all of the activities that fishery biologists undertake in evaluating the conditions or status of a stock. The result of this assessment is a report on the health of that stock and recommendations for maintaining or restoring it. These assessments often consist of two nearly separate activities. One is to learn as much as possible about the biology of the species in the stock. The other is to learn about the fishing activities for the stock. Historically, the demand for assessment has come after a stock is already declining. When the assessment begins, there may be little or no information on the biology of the species or the fishery. Meanwhile, there is pressure to complete some kind of assessment so that the stock can be managed. This leads to preliminary assessments that form the basis for initial management recommendations until more information is available.

Catch and effort. One of the simplest assessment methods requires almost no knowledge about the biology of the stock. However, good information about the fishery is required. In an assessment based on catch and effort, managers look at the history of landings for the stock and the effort expended to catch the stock. The key word here is effort. Data alone are not very useful for landings, the amount of fish caught and landed (kept) per year. Landings can fluctuate up and down for a variety of reasons. A trend of decreased landings may be a cause for concern, but the amount of effort made to catch the stock tells the real story.

Effort is calculated in various ways, including days or hours of fishing time. To account for effort, fishery biologists divide the yearly landings by the fishery effort; this gives the catch-per-unit effort. The catch-per-unit effort is directly related to the amount of fish in the stock. A decline in catch-per-unit effort usually indicates a decline in the stock.

A number of fisheries have followed a pattern in relation to the catch-per-unit effort. At the beginning of a new fishery, the catch-per-unit effort is high and the effort is low. As interest in the fishery grows, the effort increases, the catch increases, and the catch-per-unit effort usually levels off or declines. Finally, as more effort is applied, the catch declines and the catch-per-unit effort declines even more. A decline in both the catch and the catch-per-unit effort indicates that the stock is probably overfished. This means too much effort is being applied for the stock to maintain itself. Landings decline despite increasing effort. The obvious solution is to reduce the amount of fishing until the catch-per-unit effort returns to the earlier stages of the fishery.

This seems simple enough, but there are a number of reasons why assessments based on catch and effort aren't used or are not used more often. These include: insufficient landings data, insufficient effort data, and the use of new technology that makes it hard to compare the effort today with the effort of several years ago.

Adequate landings data are often available, but the effort data are usually missing, incomplete, or unusable. Another problem is that by the time there is a clear decline in catch-per-unit effort, stocks may be well overfished, even to the point of collapse.

If fishing effort is too high, the cause is usually too many boats in the fishery. Fishery managers call this overcapitalization, meaning that more money (capital) has been invested in boats than the fishery can support. Overcapitalization can also refer to the ability of fishermen to increase effort without increasing the number of boats. If no new boats are added to a fishery, but each boat doubles its fishing power through newer equipment or new technology, the resulting effort can be more effective and have the same result as doubling the number of boats.

Biology/spawning assessment. When little is known about the biology of a fish stock, one of the first questions asked is, At what age do the fish spawn? The second question is, What proportion of the fish caught are one year, two years, and three years old? If some of the fish spawn when they are two years old, and all spawn at age three, and most of the fish caught are two years old, then there is a danger that too many fish may be caught before they can spawn and replace themselves. This is called recruitment overfishing.

Harvesting some fish before they spawn does not automatically doom the stock, but the practice needs to be evaluated. Declining landings, greater effort to catch the same or smaller amounts of fish, or declines in average size of fish are all signs of possible problems. Determining the age of spawning and caught fish is one step toward management.

When fishermen appear to be catching fish before they have a chance to spawn and other signs of trouble exist in the fishery, the usual management response is to protect small fish. Protection most often takes the form of length limits or gear restrictions that favor the catch of larger fish. In commercial fishing, minimum limits on the mesh size of gillnets is a gear restriction that allows smaller fish to escape.

Unfortunately, protecting small fish does not necessarily address the larger problem of overfishing. Recruitment overfishing occurs when more fish are being removed than can replace themselves; even when the remaining small fish are protected, it can still occur because small fish produce fewer eggs than large fish.

Anglers sometimes suggest a closed fishing season during the period when a stock is spawning. This would seem logical, but marine biologists usually reject the idea. A fish caught before, during, or after the spawning season is still not available to spawn the next year. As a result, biologists prefer to focus more on protecting fish until they're old enough to spawn and then determining how many fish can be safely removed without harming the stock. Exceptions to this approach are cases where spawners gather in certain locations and are very vulnerable to being caught in unusually large numbers.

Other assessment information. Few fish stocks, if any, have been fully assessed. Fishery biologists and managers always wish they knew more about the fish and the fishermen. Full assessment would include some of the following information:

- The kinds of fishermen in the fishery (longliners, netters, recreational, etc.)
- Pounds of fish caught by each kind of fisherman over many years
- Fishing effort expended by each kind of fisherman over many years
- The age structure of the fish caught by each group of fishermen
- The ratio of males to females in the catch
- How the fish are marketed (preferred size, etc.)
- The value of fish to the different groups of fishermen
- The time and geographic area of best catches

Full biological information would include:

- The age structure of the stock
- The age at first spawning
- Fecundity (average number of eggs each age of fish can produce)
- Ratio of males to females in the stock
- Natural mortality (the rate at which fish die from natural causes)
- Fishing mortality (the rate at which fish die from being harvested)
- Growth rate of the fish
- Spawning behavior (time and place)
- Habitats of recently hatched fish (larvae), juveniles, and adults
- Migratory habits
- Food habits for all ages of fish in the stock

When the previous information is collected by examining the landings of fishermen, it is called fishery-dependent data. When the information is collected by biologists through their own sampling program, it is called fishery-independent data. Both methods contribute valuable information to the stock assessment.

Even in the best stock assessments, rarely is everything about a stock known. Assessments proceed with the assumption that the best available information (data) will be used. Fishermen often disagree with this assumption when they are adversely affected. Fishery managers respond that they are obligated to protect the stocks, and, in the case of federal fishery management, they are mandated by law to use the best available data.

The principle of best available data may create a conflict for fishermen. In the past, when managers have asked for more and better data from fishermen (primarily commercial fishermen), the result has usually been more regulations. From the fishermen's point of view, the data appear to have been used against them. From the managers' point of view, the data were used to ensure that the fishery could continue. When fishermen don't provide good data, then the fishery must be managed on the data available, which may be incomplete. This can result in overly restrictive management, which is wasteful, or in continued overfishing and declining catches. In either case, fishermen are the losers. It is in the long-term interest of fishermen to provide the best data possible.

Age, Growth, and Death

Any reliable information about the fishing process or the biology of the stock contributes to the stock assessment. Among the basic biological information that fishery biologists find most useful are the age structure of the stock and the relation between fish length and age. Once this is known, important characteristics of the stock, such as growth rate and death rate (mortality), can be determined. This information is used to create a picture of the stock that describes its current status.

Aging fish. Basic biological data are the foundation on which all assessments of fisheries resources are built. These include parameters such as the size and age composition of the population and catch (both landed and discarded), growth rates, and maturation. The most thorough and reliable assessments include age-specific estimates of stock biomass, mortality rates, and predictions of future stock conditions, for which knowledge of the size and age composition of the catch is essential. Rates of growth, mortality (due to natural causes and fishing), and reproduction can be calculated only if age-specific time vectors exist. Fish age is also a critical component of many biological and pathological processes.

Samples of fish for aging are collected from recreational anglers and commercial fishermen, as well as from the research activities of biologists or fisheries technicians. In saltwater, unbiased estimates of the age composition of a fish population are obtained by analyzing samples from surveys made by research vessels. These surveys are conducted several times each year in order to monitor the abundance of the species and to follow the seasonal progression of growth and maturation. Samples are also collected from commercial and recreational fisheries in order to estimate the age composition of the fish that are removed from the population. These samples are collected both from the docks (the landed portion of the catch) and directly from fishing vessels (to estimate the age composition of the discarded portion of the catch). Many fish may be aged in the course of a year; the Fishery Biology Investigation staff of the Woods Hole Oceanographic Institute, for example, ages up to 30,000 fish per year.

Age and length data are then utilized in models that allow assessment scientists to estimate the biomass of fish populations and to examine the potential effects of continuing removals from those populations. The choice of an age determination method for a given species involves deciding on an appropriate aging structure (scales, otoliths, vertebrae, spines, etc.) and processing method (impressions, thin sections, etc.) for that structure. The next step is validation, in which the marks used to age fish are verified to occur once per year and at approximately the same time each year. Common validation techniques include direct methods, such as tag/recapture studies and marking with chemicals; and indirect techniques, such as back-calculation, marginal increment analysis, edge progression analysis, length-frequency/year-class progression analysis, radiometric/isotope analysis, and elemental analysis.

To age a fish, one must identify the annual growth marks (annuli) on the structure chosen. You cannot tell the age of a fish by looking at it. There are too many differences between species and within a species. In temperate waters, fish growth is fast during the summer months when water temperatures are warm, and slow during the cold winter months. A year of growth is defined as one summer zone plus one winter zone. These zones are identified on scales as areas of wide (summer) and narrow (winter) circulus spacing.

Otoliths provide the most definitive biological information, including history, spawning, and environmental influences, plus age and growth. Otoliths are the layered stonelike buildups of calcium carbonate in the fish's inner ear, and are

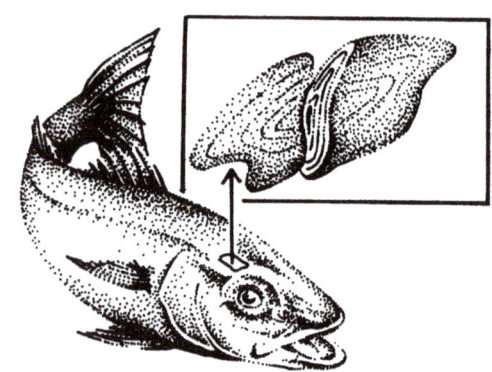

The age and environmental history of fish can be documented by examining a cross section of the otolith (inset).

also called ear stones. On otoliths, the zones of growth are identified as alternating opaque and translucent bands when viewed microscopically. Once it is established that each zone, or ring, truly represents a year, then the age of a fish can be determined.

After the fish have been aged, the length and weight are compared to the age of the fish. This results in a length-at-age key in which the age of a fish can be estimated from its length. Also, by looking at the change in length and weight from a one-year-old fish to a two-year-old fish etc., the growth rate can be estimated. The more fish that are aged, the better the picture of the stock. However, in the case of long-lived fish, growth usually slows in the older fish, and past a certain point the age cannot be readily assumed by the length. In these cases, it is better to age strictly on analysis of the bony parts rather than by length.

When enough fish have been aged, either directly or indirectly, a picture (catch curve) of the age structure of the stock may be drawn. The age structure of a stock is like an historic picture, revealing something about the current status as well as the past. Usually that picture will reveal that younger fish are more numerous and that there are fewer fish at each subsequent age owing to various causes. If younger fish are not being caught in proportion to their abundance, the reason may be that they are not as abundant in the same areas as the older fish, or they may not be caught by the fishing gear, or they may be caught but released. A fish that is readily harvested in a fishery during the first year is referred to as a recruit. Younger fish that are not being caught in proportion to their abundance are termed "not fully recruited" to the fishery, and those that are being caught in proportion to their abundance are considered to be "fully recruited."

A fishery assessment using the abundance of each age group is based on the portion of the stock that is fully recruited to the fishery. It would be desirable to know more about the unrecruited stock between the time of egg fertilization and the age of recruitment, but for many species there is little that management can do that would affect this part of the population. For other species, management could affect water quality, the amount of suitable habitat, or even the death rate to promote greater survival of young fish before they reach harvestable size (are recruited to the fishery).

Mortality and spawning potential. In order to determine the amount of fish that can be safely harvested from a stock, biologists must first determine how many fish in a stock can die (mortality) and still allow the stock to maintain itself. If 1,000 fish are alive at the beginning of the year and 200 fish die, then the annual mortality rate is 20 percent and the survival rate is 80 percent. Each year some fish die whether they're harvested or not. The rate at which fish die from natural causes is called natural mortality, and the rate at which they die from fishing (both commercial and recreational) is called fishing mortality.

Several methods are used to determine each mortality rate. For example, fishing mortality can be estimated from a tagging study. After many fish from a stock are tagged, the percentage of tagged fish that are caught and reported is an estimate of the fishing mortality. Natural mortality is then calculated by subtracting fishing mortality from total mortality. Sometimes there is no available estimate of fishing mortality for a stock. However, fishery biologists may have a good idea of what the natural mortality might be from studying other similar stocks. In this case, natural mortalities (or a range of possible natural mortalities) can be subtracted from total mortality to get fishing mortality (or a range of possible fishing mortalities).

Biologists often attempt to define a rate of fishing mortality that, when added to the natural mortality, will lead to the rebuilding of a stock or the maintenance of a stock at some agreed-upon level. The level being used in many coastal fishery management plans is based on the spawning potential ratio, which incorporates the principle that enough fish have to survive to spawn and replenish the stock at a sustainable level.

Spawning potential ratio is the number of eggs that could be produced by an average recruit over its lifetime when the stock is fished, divided by the number of eggs that could be produced by an average recruit over its lifetime when the stock is unfished. In other words, spawning potential ratio compares the spawning ability of a stock in the fished condition to the stock's spawning ability in the unfished condition.

As an example, imagine that in a fished population 10 fish survive the first two years of life and are now large enough to get caught. Four are caught before they spawn (no eggs produced), 3 others are caught after they spawn once (some eggs produced), and the last 3 live to spawn three times (many eggs produced) before dying of old age. During their lifetime, the 10 fish produced 1 million eggs, and the average egg production was 100,000.

Now take an unfished population in which 10 fish also survive for two years as before. Three die from natural causes after spawning (some eggs produced), and the other 7 spawn three times (very many eggs produced) before dying of old age. During their lifetime, these 10 fish produced 5 million eggs, and the average egg production was 500,000.

The spawning potential ratio is then the 100,000 eggs produced by the average fished recruit divided by the 500,000 eggs produced by the average unfished recruit, and is equal to 20 percent. Spawning potential ratio can also be calculated using the biomass (weight) of the entire adult stock, the biomass of mature females in the stock, or the biomass of the eggs they produce.

In a perfect world, fishery biologists would know what the appropriate spawning potential ratio should be for every harvested stock, based on the biology of that stock. Generally, not enough is known about managed stocks to be so precise. However, studies show that some stocks (depending on the species of fish) can maintain themselves if the spawning stock biomass per recruit can be kept at 20 to 35 percent (or more) of what it was in the unfished stock. Lower values of spawning potential ratio may lead to severe stock declines. If the spawning potential ratio is below the level considered necessary to sustain the stock, then fishing mortality needs to be reduced.

Growth overfishing. Growth overfishing occurs when the bulk of the harvest is made up of small fish that could have been significantly larger if they had survived to an older age. The issue here is that the fishery can produce more weight if the fish are harvested at a larger size. The question biologists must answer is how much bigger or older should the fish get before they are harvested.

Typically most fish grow rapidly in the first few years and grow more slowly in later years. One approach to getting the most out of a stock of fish would be to harvest them near the point where the growth rate begins to level off. However, this approach is too simple because all the while the fish are growing, their numbers are decreasing from mortality.

There are two opposing forces at work in a stock

> From the duplicate name file: You say you're going yellowtail fishing? Is that for the flatfish (yellowtail flounder), the snapper (yellowtail snapper), or the jack (California yellowtail)?

of fish. Growth increases the weight of fish, whereas mortality reduces the number of fish. Biologists can calculate the harvest (also called yield) that can be expected from different combinations of harvest rates and the age of the fish when they are first captured.

Another type of overfishing occurs when commercial fishermen catch fish before they reach their maximum price per pound. The idea here is that the catch will have a higher value if the harvest is delayed when a premium is paid for larger fish.

Management aimed at growth overfishing has more to do with getting the most benefit out of a stock than ensuring the renewability of the stock. This may be a legitimate goal for fishery management as long as recruitment overfishing is not a problem.

Virtual population analysis. At times, fishery biologists have more information available than what is provided by the snapshot of the age structure. Sometimes the number of fish caught from a single year class (the group of fish born in the same year) is known for each year that the year class is fished. Using the number caught each year from a year class and the mortality rate, the size of the year class can be reconstructed. The reconstructed year class can then be tested with different rates of fishing mortality to see what the effects might be, or the information can be used in other calculations, such as determining the spawning stock biomass.

Indices. Fishery biologists sometimes employ an index to help assess the general state of a stock. The index is an indirect measure of the stock and is taken the same way at the same time over many years. The index can be compared with the catch in the fishery or other data to see if there is a relationship between the index and the health of the fishery.

One of the better known fishery indices is the juvenile striped bass index. Since the 1950s, biologists have sampled streams surrounding Chesapeake Bay where striped bass spawn and have counted the number of recently hatched fish caught with standardized methods. The index closely follows the decline in the striped bass fishery with a three-year lag (striped bass do not appear in the fishery until they are three years old). An increase in the index is assumed to indicate improvements in the stock. Other indices use number of eggs, number of larval fish, or actual counts of fish through aerial, underwater, or acoustic (fish finder) surveys.

When an index is based on the early life history of a fish, it must be remembered that many things can happen to the fish before it is large enough to harvest. Despite some drawbacks, indices are usually easy to understand and can be useful indicators of changes in a fish stock.

Bycatch. Bycatch is all the animals that are caught but not used during the act of fishing. In the sense of catching untargeted species, it can be applied to recreational fishing but is seldom a factor there. Almost all commercial fisheries have an associated bycatch. When the bycatch includes endangered species or protected mammals, then regulations are made to reduce or eliminate the bycatch as required by federal laws. When the bycatch includes species that are targeted by other fishermen, the bycatch may be included in the overall quota for that species; in this case, the bycatch is simply a part of the total allowable catch for that species.

A more difficult problem with bycatch occurs when the bycatch contains undersized fish of economically desirable species. The undersized fish may be of the same species that the fishermen are targeting but have no economic value at the smaller size. Alternatively, the undersized fish can be the target species for other fisheries when they reach a harvestable size. In these cases, the effects of the bycatch on the stocks are often unknown. However, it is generally accepted that catching large amounts of a stock before it is old enough to spawn or before it has economic value is wasteful and possibly harmful to the stock. Fishery managers try to account for bycatch in their stock assessment because bycatch may be an important cause of mortality.

The bycatch of species that have no current economic value presents problems that traditionally have not been addressed by fishery managers but that can have serious implications to the food chain.

Since each species has a role in the community, the removal of an important food item (such as prey species) through bycatch could adversely affect other species (predators) that eat the item. However, predators often eat a variety of food items. Reduction in the numbers of a single prey species may lead to an increase in another prey species that the predator will readily consume, although bycatch of prey species may lead also to the reduction in numbers of multiple prey species. In moving down the food chain (big fish eat little fish, which eat smaller fish, etc.), the link between prey species in the bycatch and important predator species gets weaker and the relations less clear.

Understanding all of the relations among predator and prey species may be impossible. However, it is generally thought that less bycatch, rather than more bycatch, is more desirable for maintaining a balance among the various species in a community. Furthermore, the waste of bycatch by commercial fishermen is often viewed negatively by the public, and it may present a problem that exceeds biological issues.

Allocation. When the harvest of a stock is restricted by management, the different groups of fishermen using that stock often find themselves in conflict. The conflict occurs because each user group realizes it could harvest more fish if the other group didn't exist or if the other group were restricted even further. These disagreements occur among different kinds of commercial fishermen or between commercial fishermen and recreational anglers.

The decision as to how much each group gets to

Mosquitoes are a common accompaniment to anglers; only females are blood-suckers, and many require a blood meal before they can lay their eggs.

harvest is called allocation. From a strictly biological viewpoint, there is no fair or unfair allocation. It doesn't make any difference who catches the fish as long as the total allowable catch is not exceeded.

Allocation is a political, social, and economic decision usually made by elected or appointed officials, particularly the latter. In federal fishery management, the decision is made by regional fishery management councils (combination of managers and appointees). Similar boards or commissions are often responsible at the state level.

Allocation decisions are often made on the basis of historical catches. If Group A normally caught 60 percent of the landings and Group B 40 percent, then the fish are allocated on that basis. Disputes often arise over the accuracy of historical records, particularly when poorly documented fisheries are involved, and particularly as the amount and economic value of recreational fishing increases.

The determination of total allowable catch and the allocation decisions have not always been separated as described, and have often been tilted excessively to commercial fishing interests on the basis of prior activities or industrial economic concerns. Theoretically, fishery biologists determine the total allowable catch based on the scientific information available, but in reality many decisions are not made that way. In theory, the biological decision would not be modified by other considerations, but the regulations and allocations to achieve the target catch in fact often have been.

Critics charge that greed, not science, has dominated marine harvest allocation decisions in the past and continues to do so. And even though marine fishery resources still support substantial fishing by commercial and recreational interests, and provide important food resources to the fishing and nonfishing public, most of the major fish stocks have fallen to levels far below even the poor times. Many species have been heavily exploited, primarily by domestic and foreign commercial fishermen; and as popular or easily accessible fish stocks have been depleted, the focus has shifted to other, formerly less favorable, species. Management, despite its principles and capabilities, and in spite of the methodology previously outlined, cannot overcome human greed over a resource held in common.

Government management structure and federal law. The National Marine Fisheries Service (NMFS) is part of the National Oceanographic and Atmospheric Administration (NOAA), which in turn is part of the United States Department of Commerce. The NMFS is the federal agency with primary responsibility for managing marine fish from 3 to 200 miles offshore. Coastal states are responsible for inshore waters and offshore waters out to 3 miles (9 miles on the Florida west coast and off Texas).

The legislation that directs how NMFS manages the nation's fisheries is the Magnuson Fishery Conservation and Management Act, also known as the Magnuson Act. The Magnuson Act created eight regional fishery management councils to advise NMFS on fisheries management issues. The voting members of the councils include a representative from each state fishery management agency, a mandatory appointee from each state, at-large appointees from any of the states in the region, and the regional director of NMFS. The councils produce fishery management plans (FMPs), with public input, that describe the nature and problems of a fishery along with regulatory recommendations to conserve the fishery; in other words, they define overfishing and spell out steps to prevent or correct overfishing. After approval by the Secretary of Commerce, regulations that implement management measures in the FMP become federal law and are enforced by NMFS.

Although some recreational anglers are aware of this process, the majority are not, and are ill-informed about this federal legislation, the councils, and the management plans. It is imperative that coastal anglers become involved, attend public hearings, review management plans, and voice their opinions, in order to be part of the process of determining how marine fishery resources are both managed and allocated.

Special Regulations, Trends, and Funding

Special regulations. Fisheries scientists define special fishing regulations as those that differ considerably from the regulations that apply more broadly, usually across a state or province. This is a generic definition that can apply at any point in time. The regulations that were standard, or conventional, in 1990 were at one time considered special regulations, and the so-called special regulations that apply today will no doubt be conventional at some future time.

Initially, special regulations were meant to let fish have enough spawning opportunities to continue self-perpetuating populations and to protect fish with high growth potential so they could attain larger size. These regulations were not very effective and were generally very liberal until the latter half of the twentieth century when angler numbers and effectiveness increased substantially and at the same time the quality of many habitats began to deteriorate. Special regulations came into much wider use in recent decades; they have been effective in some cases and ineffective in others, and many anglers inappropriately view them as a panacea for reversing declining fisheries.

Special regulations, or regulations that are particular for certain species or locations, proliferate today. They may be used to maintain or protect a unique, threatened, or endangered fishery; to reserve a fishery for specific angler activities; to permit harvest of underutilized or highly productive populations; to improve or maintain fishing quality; and for other reasons. Sometimes these regulations are not clearly understood or clearly defined, and confusion exists.

Special regulations can be appropriate tools

for fishery management if based upon scientific principle, but they are often set in place as a result of socioeconomic considerations. Improper use of special regulations by fishery managers can result in negative angler perceptions, continued decline of fishing quality, loss of managerial credibility, and unrealistic angler expectations.

The American Fisheries Society, an organization mainly comprising accredited fishery professionals, in a position statement on special regulations, urges anglers and scientists to consider the following:

- Development of realistic and attainable goals and measurable objectives for a fishery. The fishery manager should ensure that the goals of a special regulation are compatible with broader, ecological management objectives. The goals of the regulation should be clearly defined and well-stated so they are easily understood by anglers. The regulation should include quantitative objectives that can be measured within a specified time frame, allowing for proper assessment of the regulation.
- Involvement of the angling public in all phases of planning, development, and implementation of a special regulation to help ensure public acceptance, support, compliance, and effective enforcement once the regulation is in place. The rationale for the regulation should be communicated to peers, associates, enforcement officials, and the public. Effective communication among all user groups minimizes conflict arising as a result of different expectations. Social conflicts stemming from different definitions of angling quality may be minimized if well-defined goals are developed and agreed on early in the process.
- Assessment that includes recognizing fiscal and temporal constraints. Evaluation techniques should be peer-reviewed to anticipate and minimize possible shortcomings, which reduce the credibility of the resource agency and its fishery managers. Natural fluctuations often influence population parameters for a short time and, consequently, short-term studies could indicate that a regulation was a success or failure when observed changes were actually a result of natural fluctuations. Replicates or use of reference waters may prove invaluable in accounting for natural fluctuations during an evaluation period. Additionally, lack of angler compliance could result in regulation failure even if biological considerations were correct.
- Recognition of unforeseen problems that arise during implementation and evaluation of special regulations to further the understanding of site-specific special regulations. For instance, special regulations may concentrate fishing pressure on particular waters or on certain segments of a fish population, or the value of catch-and-release regulation may be negated by high hooking or handling mortality. Compensatory responses such as reduced growth rates or increased natural mortality may produce unanticipated results. Angler behavior may change and also confound the evaluation process. For example, the increasing popularity of voluntary catch-and-release on a reference water could confound evaluation of a nearby special regulation. Angler use may initially decrease when a special, more restrictive regulation is applied. Several years of increasing use may then follow as anglers become accustomed to the new regulation.
- Communication of evaluation results to the public and to the professional community through news media, agency reports, peer-reviewed publications, and appropriate public and professional presentations. Successes and failures of a particular special regulation or modifications of the proposed special regulation must be reported because they can provide valuable guidance to other fishery managers. Agencies should strive to make the best use of special regulations as a fishery management tool. Well-developed goals and objectives, public participation in the process, adequate evaluation, and ongoing communication will contribute to successful use of special fishing regulations in fisheries management. To meet the challenge of appropriate use of special regulations, fisheries professionals must make a deliberate, planned effort to create long-term changes for the benefit of fisheries resources and user groups.

Trends in management and regulations. Making predictions about future management activities, the state of fishing in the future, and regulations that will exist to manage resources and people, is risky and foolish. However, in the near term, based on current and evolving attitudes and regulations, it is not so risky to suggest that some of the special regulations existing today will be even more prominent in the future, and that more restrictions will be placed on recreational anglers in both freshwater and saltwater, especially the former.

In those places where fishing seasons are identifiable, they will likely be extended, offering more opportunity; in general, however, limits will become more restrictive, probably with decreased bag limits and increased size limits. Bag limits may incorporate multiple species rather than apply on a species-by-species basis. In other words, a limit of five fish per day may be imposed regardless of species, or with restrictions on how many of the five may be of a certain species or size. This limitation already exists in the Great Lakes and in some Canadian waters, and may spread further in both freshwater and saltwater.

More restrictions on the equipment used by anglers could be imposed. Barbless hooks, and hooks that will rust or decompose more quickly, may be mandated in certain situations. The province of Manitoba was first (in 1990) to prohibit the use of barbed hooks, and more provisions mandating the use of barbless hooks are likely to be implemented. There may be further attempts to reduce the use of lead in terminal fishing tackle (lead weight for fishing has been banned in England for some time), and a greater interest in the environmental effects of some types of lures, especially soft plastics, which could eventually lead to attempts to control their use. Chemicals or substances that give (or are perceived to give) anglers an unfair advantage could be regulated. The use of nets and gaffs, or the type used, may come under more scrutiny and regulation. The number of rods used by anglers could be decreased. Throughout Canada, anglers are allowed to use one rod or line at a time in open water, but in the United States anglers are allowed to use two rods in most places and more in some others (ice fishing regulations may vary). If the number of rods or lines is not regulated, then the number of hooks used on a rod or line could be decreased.

In the future, more places in freshwater will probably be designated as trophy or complete catch-and-release waters, with correspondingly restrictive regulations. Some waters will likely be specifically managed for extensive harvest, such as designated panfish lakes. And more attention will be paid to the harvest of wild versus hatchery fish, especially in salmonid species, and to identifying and protecting wild fish.

In time, people may need to take an aquatic education course in order to receive a sportfishing license, similar in some respects to the hunter safety training course mandatory for all new hunters. Aquatic or fishery education courses are required in some European countries. Such courses might review the basics of aquatic ecology, fisheries management principles, local and regional regulations, ethics and etiquette, safety and first aid, and, of course, angling methods and equipment.

No courses, regulations, restrictions, or laws will protect or enhance resources without adequate enforcement. If a substantial number of anglers do not believe in and support the evolving ethics required to protect and maintain fishery resources, and if the number of law enforcement personnel is inadequate, then any new or special regulations will be problematic and likely ineffective. Furthermore, the usefulness or need for these regulations may be affected by factors such as the impact on fishery resources by an increasing or decreasing number of anglers, and increased demands on all natural resources because of population growth.

Funding. Most recreational fisheries management activities are funded by user taxes and fees. Hence the funding comes either directly or indirectly from those who use the resource.

The primary avenue of funding is license fees and special-use stamps. Usually license revenue provides funding for general fisheries management and for operation of a state fisheries department (or in cooperation with hunting licenses in a combined department). Special-use stamp revenues are allocated to specific programs or activities. In some instances, general fisheries management (and law enforcement) is partially subsidized from the general fund of state tax coffers, but this avenue is an uncertain and politically risky one that does not assure consistent levels of funding. However, one state, Missouri, funds conservation programs, including fisheries management programs, from a percentage of the revenue received from annual state sales taxes.

Additional money for fisheries management and conservation comes to the states from the Federal Aid in Sport Fish Restoration Act *(see)*, which levies an excise tax on the sale of certain fishing and boating equipment and motorboat fuel. These funds are apportioned to the states based on a formula weighted 40 percent on the basis of land and water area, including coastal and Great lakes waters; and 60 percent on the basis of paid fishing-license holders. No state receives less than 1 percent of the available money nor more than 5 percent. Approximately 6 percent of the funds are utilized for administration, and over 100 million dollars is annually available for use by the states.

The funds may be utilized for sportfish restoration and enhancement activities, including lake construction, motorboat access, fisheries management and research, and aquatic resource education. This highly effective program is administered by the federal government.

See: Catch-and-Release; Ecology; Regulations.

FISHERIES MANAGEMENT COUNCIL

Also known simply as a council, and as a Regional Fisheries Management Council, this is a group established by the Fishery Conservation and Management Act to develop fishery policy for managing those species most often found in federal waters.

See: Fishery Conservation and Management Act; Fisheries Management.

FISHERMAN

A person who catches, or tries to catch, fish. "Fisherman" has a general meaning with no explicit distinction between commercial or recreational action or, in the latter case, between the methods, techniques, or equipment employed. The words "angler" and "sportfisherman" are often used interchangeably with the word "fishing," although they refer solely to the recreational activity and the implied usage of sporting equipment. Thus, a person who sets a net in saltwater and one who uses a trotline in freshwater are both fishermen. The former is commercial fishing and the latter recreational fishing, but neither

A 30-foot basking shark weighing 6,580 pounds, taken off Monterey, California, had a liver weighing 1,800 pounds, 60 percent of which was oil.

is an angler or sportfisherman. However, the words "angler," "sportfisherman," or "fisherman" could describe a person using a rod and reel to catch fish for personal use.

Although "fisherman" has a masculine gender, it is used in a generic sense throughout the recreational and fisheries management communities, the sportfishing equipment industries, and the boat and motor manufacturing industries to imply females as well as males. That generic usage occasionally appears in this book (although preference is given to the word "angler") because of its overwhelming idiomatic dominance, and also because the alternative, "fisher," which is an archaic although non-gender-specific version of "fisherman," may also refer to an individual engaged in commercial or recreational activity.

See: Angler; Commercial Fisherman; Recreational Fisherman; Sportfisherman.

FISHERY

In a biological sense, all the activities involved in catching a species of fish or group of species; the place where a species or group of species is caught. In common usage by the general public, fishery also refers to fishing opportunity or species availability in either a recreational or a commercial sense, as in "the fishery for coho salmon does not commence until the annual migration run." This term is used interchangeably with fisheries.

FISHERY BIOLOGIST

An individual trained in the biological study of fisheries and who manages fisheries resources. This term is distinct from "ichthyologist," a person who studies fish, but practically synonymous with "fishery manager" and "fishery scientist." A fishery biologist undertakes all of the activities necessary to manage fisheries. Those activities include learning the biology and life history of fish (and also usually other aquatic organisms), gathering data, analyzing data, offering management options, and evaluating the status of the fishery, all of which are natural resource issues. A fishery biologist must deal with relevant social, economic, and political issues, none of which have to do with biological matters, but all of which have a great impact on effective fisheries management.

See: Fisheries Management.

FISHERY CONSERVATION AND MANAGEMENT ACT

Also known as the Magnuson Act, or the Magnuson-Stevens Fisheries Conservation and Management Act, this federal legislation directs how the National Marine Fisheries Service (NMFS) manages the nation's marine fisheries. This act empowered the federal government to regulate fishing from 3 nautical miles offshore (9 miles off the Florida Gulf Coast, Texas, and Puerto Rico) out to 200 nautical miles. This area is sometimes referred to as federal waters or the Exclusive Economic Zone. A main purpose of the act was to eliminate foreign commercial fishing while developing the United States commercial fishing industry.

This act created eight regional fishery management councils to advise NMFS on fisheries management issues. The voting members of the councils include a representative from each state fishery management agency, a mandatory appointee from each state, at-large appointees from any of the states in the region, and the regional director of NMFS. The councils produce fishery management plans (FMPs), with public input, that describe the nature and problems of a fishery and give regulatory recommendations to conserve the fishery; in other words, they define overfishing and spell out steps to prevent or correct overfishing. After approval by the Secretary of Commerce, regulations that implement management measures in the FMP become federal law and are enforced by NMFS.

In 1996, reauthorization of this act included an amendment that also required councils to identify all essential fish habitats including "those waters and substrate necessary for fish for spawning, feeding, or growth to maturity." Known as the Sustainable Fisheries Act, it is especially significant because it mandates not only the management of the harvest of commercial species, but also their environment. This act is thus a new legislative approach to environmental management.

See: Fisheries Management.

FISHFINDER

See: Sonar.

FISHFINDER RIG

A bottom fishing bait rig used in surf fishing (see).

FISHFLIES

See: Dobsonflies, Fishflies, and Alderflies.

FISH HATCHERY

See: Fisheries Management; Hatchery.

FISHHOOK

See: Hook.

FISHING

The act of catching, or trying to catch, fish. The word "fishing" has a general meaning with no explicit distinction between commercial or recreational action or, in the latter case, the methods, techniques, or equipment employed. The words "angling" and "sportfishing" are often used interchangeably with the word "fishing," although they refer solely to the recreational activity and the implied usage of sporting equipment. Thus, a person who sets a net in saltwater and one who uses a trotline in freshwater are both fishing. The former is commercial fishing and the latter recreational fishing, but neither is angling or sportfishing. However, the words "angling," "sportfishing," or "fishing" could describe a person using a rod and reel to catch fish for personal use.

See: Angler; Angling; Commercial Fisherman; Fisherman; Recreational Fisherman; Sportfisherman; Sportfishing.

FISHING CHAIR
See: Fighting Chair.

FISHING GUIDE

A person hired to take people fishing, usually by boat, sometimes on foot, in freshwater and saltwater. A guide is distinguished from the captain of a charter boat *(see)* by the size of the boat used and the number of people involved. Guides usually take one or two people fishing rather than a group. Although charter boat captains are commonly referred to as guides, charter boats are larger, capable of taking a group of people, and normally used on waters that require the comfort and security of a big vessel.

The types, abilities, and services of fishing guides vary as greatly as the species of fish, the conditions of fishing, and the nature of human beings. A guide may be associated with a fishing camp, lodge, or marina, or may be unaffiliated with any business. A guide may fish one body of water exclusively or many bodies of water; the guide may keep a boat on a trailer for mobility, starting each day wherever necessary, or the guide may keep a boat at a certain dock or marina and start each day from the same location. A mountain-country guide may use a canoe, jonboat, or inflatable that is hauled atop a truck and driven to whatever location is necessary. A guide may also accompany river, bank, or beach anglers by walking, wading, and fishing from shore or in the water. The possibilities are as broad as the fishing options.

The majority of fishing guides are found in freshwater by virtue of the number of opportunities, the differences in species and habits, and fewer charter boats (except in the Great Lakes). The craft that a freshwater guide uses includes canoes, jonboats, bass boats, walleye boats, and multipurpose craft, most accommodating two people in addition to the guide, and a few large enough to contain a third angler.

When a guide takes people for hire on navigable water under the jurisdiction of the Coast Guard, the guide must be certified by that agency and pass a rigorous examination to receive the mandatory

Guiding activities vary as widely as angling opportunities; these guided anglers are mooching for salmon in British Columbia.

captain's license. Even if that person operates a boat only on a bay, nearshore flats, or tidal river, and even if the person is called a "fishing guide," a captain's license is still required.

In all other cases, a guide is usually not required to have a captain's license, and the level of training, certification, and licensing varies greatly. In a few states, people who want to call themselves guides and hire out their services can do so without any formal process. In some states, the only requirement for being a guide is paying a fee to the appropriate government agency. In many Third World countries, there is usually no requirement for guiding, unless imposed by a lodge operator or outfitter. There, as well as in some North American locations, so-called guides are really boat drivers (although a boat driver with local waterway knowledge is important in many places).

Many states and Canadian provinces have a formal program established for guide certification. These vary but may include taking a written test(s) on fishing knowledge, game laws, water safety, and boating safety; demonstrating some level of in-field proficiency (this is rare); and completing basic first aid and cardiopulmonary resuscitation (CPR) courses.

Formal training and government certification does not in itself make a person a good fishing guide. Many guides have been around boats, the water, and fishing all or most of their lives, and they don't need a government endorsement to be competent. On the other hand, plenty of people have become state certified to guide but are nevertheless not proficient at finding and catching fish. And no amount of training will help someone who just isn't good with people.

One thing that is especially worth remembering is that in many cases there is a lot of responsibility, above and beyond catching fish, involved in a day of guiding. Traveling at high speeds in relatively small open boats (like bass boats and flats boats) can pose a risk if something goes wrong, such as snapping a steering cable (unusual) or striking some hidden obstruction (much more likely). A cold body of water can be life-threatening if you get tossed into it as the result of an accident. Some places present dangers like alligators, crocodiles, piranhas, and snakes. Exposure to storms and high winds, getting stuck with a hook, and injury from a thrashing fish tethered to a multihooked lure are other possibilities. There is a practical necessity for cautious behavior and attention to everything that is going on. A reckless and careless individual should not be a guide.

Guides are most often hired by the day but may be hired for longer periods, a common practice at fishing lodges or camps. Fishing guide work is seasonal in many locations, year-round in a few; many fishing guides also work as hunting, rafting, hiking, and/or camping guides. Some guides provide a shore lunch service; this is especially common in northern lodges and camps and is a very pleasant experience, although one that can take a good chunk of fishing time out of the day.

Guides who do wilderness trips may be responsible for more than just fishing, especially if camping, canoeing, and portaging are involved. Guides who strictly take people fishing generally work 8 hours but may work 10 or 12, usually starting early in the day, although hours and times of day vary. In midsummer in some places, it is common to fish with a guide for several hours in the morning, break for midday when the sun is scorching, and resume in late afternoon. In places with limited runs of seasonally available fish, guides may have an 8-hour trip starting at dawn and then take another party on a 3- or 4-hour pre-dark trip as well.

Usually guides are reserved in advance for specific dates, with a deposit, and during peak seasons they may be fully booked in advance. In places where guides are numerous, it may be possible to hire a guide on the spur of the moment for a day (through a lodge, hotel, or booking service). Hiring a guide is generally an elective activity, although in some places (parts of Canada especially) the law mandates that a nonresident angler be accompanied by a guide; this is mostly a government employment issue rather than a practical matter or one of demonstrated necessity. Some lodges or camps require guide use as policy or as part of the total package they provide, and anglers are assigned a guide rather than being given the option of selecting one, although repeat clients may be given the option of reserving a specific guide.

General Issues

The benefits of a guide. Hiring a guide doesn't brand you as someone who cannot catch fish on your own or who is deficient as an angler. Even if you have your own boat, or have plenty of fishing experience, there are times when you can benefit from using a guide. For some methods of fishing, or for species that you are unfamiliar with, or for locations that are tricky and foreign to you, a guide is an especially good idea.

It may, for example, be your intent to fish on your own for a week at a certain place. Hiring a guide for the first day of your week, learning the water, understanding the current conditions from the guide's perspective, seeing what the guide does, and more will improve the time spent on your own. Having the benefit of the guide's expertise for a day could save you a week of futility or at least a few days of blundering around figuring things out on your own. This is especially true if you don't fish that often or if you are completely new to that place and fishing.

Perhaps you need a guide because of tricky waters. Some places have dangerous sandbars, swift channels that have to be traversed, or other special conditions that not every person is able to handle equally well alone. In some northern Canada locations, for example, you have to use a guide because the waters are loaded with shallow rock reefs that will eat an outboard's lower unit or a boat hull, not to mention maybe putting you in a dangerous situation; the guide knows how to navigate here and has the responsibility that you may not want.

And, of course, in the most common scenario, a guide is someone that you can learn from. You're thinking of buying a certain type of boat? What better way to get acquainted with that model than to actually use it while fishing with a guide who has one? If you want to learn fly fishing for a particular species, then fish with a guide who specializes in this and tell the guide that you're there for instruction and education as much as, if not more than, fish-catching. Many guides are really good at teaching—about the body of water, about technique, about the habits of a certain species, etc. Unless they think that you're there to steal their spots, they'll explain the hows and whys to you, and the day not only will be a learning experience but also will produce fish as a bonus.

Although hiring a guide may be expensive on a

A river guide rows a drift boat for steelhead anglers in Oregon.

per trip outing (with fees for two people in a boat costing from $150 to $450 a day, depending on guide, season, type of fishing, location, etc.), guide fees may be economical if you are otherwise limited in the number of times that you're able to go fishing. If, for example, you have a boat but can use it only 10 times per season for fishing, you might find that the cost of equipment, fuel, amortization, insurance, dockage, repair, gas, and other items is annually greater than if you hired a guide 10 times, especially if you pool the cost with someone else— not to mention that using your own boat means finding and catching your own fish instead of being with a professional who does it day in and day out.

If you really do want to do your own thing, then hiring a guide(s), like hiring a charter boat, is a terrific way of learning about boats, fishing methods, equipment, locations, and other issues, and is a practical prelude to going off solo. Many people have plunged deeply into some facet of sportfishing (and boat and equipment ownership) after having hired a few guides and have acquired a yen to do it all themselves (some becoming guides as a result).

Selecting. What makes a good guide? Ability to interact well with clients is foremost. That is closely followed by knowledge of the waters and fishing experience but also includes boat-handling ability and willingness to work to achieve success.

Naturally, a guide with a few years of experience, either on that particular water or on other waters, is preferred over someone who is guiding for the first time as a summer job. Someone who is inexperienced on that water will probably be fine if the person has had significant guiding background elsewhere or if you are otherwise assured of the person's guiding skill. Although there is no substitute for experience, a lot can be said for hustle and effort when combined with fishing acumen, and many young guides make up for their shorter guiding experience by having good judgment, willingness to experiment and adapt, and energetic effort. If you are especially interested in learning about a certain type of fishing, try to find a guide who specializes in that type. More guides today focus on light-tackle and fly fishing, for example, or on certain species.

In some places, you need a guide less to show you what to do than to get you to the right places. In distant waters, the concern you should have is not just one of being able to navigate properly in tricky places, but one of knowing where to fish when the obvious spots aren't producing.

The more traveling and fishing experiences that you have, the better you'll be able to satisfy yourself when hiring a guide. Some guides advertise in various media, exhibit at shows, and have brochures or information available. Some do little if any of this. Word-of-mouth referral is the number one factor in hiring guides, as it is in selecting fishing lodges. People who are satisfied with guides they've used are good sources of information. If you are considering a particular guide but have no recommendations, then ask the guide you're considering for references and follow up by speaking to those references.

While word-of-mouth is helpful, it isn't essential. Clearly you have to first learn of the existence of a guide from some source. That process includes reading articles, attending sport shows, looking at advertisements and television shows, attending lectures, etc. If possible, try to visit a guide at a sport show, lecture hall, or other location. Speaking face to face is the best way to get direct answers to specific questions and also to see if you connect with this person and could establish a rapport in a day (or more) together on the water. This is also a prime opportunity to go beyond obvious questions and into details.

Articles in newspapers and magazines reflect the experiences of someone who has been there. Seldom are articles published about bad guides or locations. Sportswriters who review angling destinations and fish with guides focus on the positive. One of the drawbacks of most newspaper or magazine articles is that they place too much emphasis on exceptional catches and outstanding days. A result can be that a reader's expectations are easily raised too high. This is even more acute with television fishing shows; most people fail to realize that 23 minutes of constant video fishing action may have taken one or two weeks to actually experience and film. Seldom do all those TV lunkers fall cast after cast in real life, although it seems like they do on the tube. Every guide should have that kind of success on a daily basis! So, consider the reliability of these sources of information, and look through them with a careful eye to search for the details that are most important to you.

When you talk to a guide, find out if the person guides full- or part-time. Some part-time guides are excellent, but there is no substitute for being on the water daily. This is more critical in some types of fishing than others, and guides who fish every day usually don't have to spend much time on each outing figuring things out, especially when conditions change frequently and when pursuing species that move a lot.

Most guides that are booked in advance require a deposit, which is customarily refunded if you have to cancel. Inquire about cancellation policies and payment procedures, extra costs (bait or unusual gas consumption), etc. If you have special medical concerns, or any ailments or disabilities, you should discuss them. This is not as obvious an issue as it seems. You may, for example, have to get down to a boat from a high dock at low tide; if you are weak-legged that may prove too difficult or dangerous. Or, you may need to cross a few miles of potentially rough water in a small boat to get to the sacred fishing grounds; the pounding of the boat on rough water could aggravate a back condition. Often the guide can work around these issues, but you should bring them up.

Communication. Although many guided fishing trips go well and many first-time clients become repeat clients (in fact, repeat business is the backbone of a guide's success), some guided trips do not go as well as people would like. Changing weather and water conditions often cause this, and a conscientious guide will let you know if you should expect a problem. A good guide will cancel a trip if conditions are unsafe or if the fishing has been so poor that the guide knows you'll be wasting your time. It is much better for a guide to be honest and upfront about things and reschedule you at another time than to take your money in the face of a hopeless situation (which the guide may recognize but you probably won't).

Often, however, dissatisfactions with a guide or a day of guided fishing have to do with the client's failure to communicate. You have to tell your guide right at the beginning of the day, or maybe even when you book a trip, what you want and what you are particularly interested in. Most guides are very accommodating. In some cases, you must let a guide know in advance about your interests so that the guide can be prepared (with the right tackle, required bait, and so forth) ahead of time and not have to waste potentially important early fishing time.

If you have a particular interest in mind, as many experienced anglers do (this might include how far you travel by boat during the day, how long you stay in a certain place, whether you would prefer to have an in-boat lunch instead of a shore lunch, etc.), let your guide know. If you don't care for a certain kind of fishing or situation (like traveling a great distance for remote fishing only to be bunched with a group of other boats in the same place), tell your guide. But you'll get much further if you do this in a pleasant rather than confrontational manner or by barking like a general. You may be a big shot on the home front, and you are paying for the guide's services, but most guides are independent types who will tolerate a jerk for only so long.

Communication problems may occur with guides in foreign countries, especially when there is a language barrier. The client has to be the one to try to overcome this. Many native guides are very willing to please but don't always understand what the client wants, particularly regarding the fishing method (casting versus trolling, for example) and location selection. If you will be departing a camp or houseboat in the morning for a day of fishing, it's wise to construct your own plan before you leave and discuss it with someone at the base camp who can relay your interests and desires to the guide; if you don't do this, at least find out ahead of time what the guide is planning on doing so that you know what to expect during the day. Otherwise, you may think or assume that the guide understands you and then find yourself taken to some place you didn't want to go to (perhaps the same area that you fished the day before) and doing something that you didn't want to do. When this happens, typically the client gets mad and starts shouting, the guide doesn't understand the problem but knows the client is unhappy, and things deteriorate.

Many non-English-speaking guides try to learn to speak the client's language, but there is no guarantee that a passing acquaintance with English will lessen communication problems. Smart traveling anglers try to compile a list of key words and phrases in the local language (mostly Spanish, and Portuguese in Brazil) so that they can convey, however crudely, what they want (such as, "Can we move closer to shore," "I'd like to fish shallower," "Let's move to another spot," etc.). When there is a language barrier, it does not pay to get mad at the guide. Better to try to involve the guide in the pursuit, politely show the guide what to do (such as handling and releasing the fish more carefully), and give sincere praise or thanks where due. Treat the guide fairly and like an equal. The guide will be happier with you and will try much harder, even if you're unable to speak in complete sentences to each other.

When you can communicate with your guide, by all means ask plenty of questions; guides are used to this, although they do get tired of the same questions over and over again. A guide who is sullen and uncommunicative is not much fun to be with, but the person may make up for this by producing a great fishing experience. Many native guides in northern Canada have been criticized for monosyllabic responses, for a lack of communication and effort, and for ignoring the wishes of clients, but this is not a universal occurrence. Cultural differences and other issues are at play here, so you may need to dig into your motivational grab bag to get somewhere. On the other hand, some guides are truly unique and interesting characters but spend more time gabbing, telling jokes, and entertaining than working to produce fish. Storytelling is nice, but not if it's the sum result of a day mostly spent sitting on a hole waiting for something to happen. Obviously the ideal guide is someone interesting and perhaps entertaining to be with, yet one who really knows fishing and works at it to produce good results.

Fishing Issues

When in Rome. From the guide's perspective, the ideal client is someone who is a decent person to be with, a reasonably able angler, a person who can follow instructions, and someone who knows that fishing is not magic. Many clients do not understand that at times no one catches fish, or that even the best efforts can fail to produce, or that the lack of production is due to the inabilities of the angler rather than the guide. It is not always the guide's fault when you don't have a successful day; the fact that most inexperienced anglers do not understand this, or expect that paying a guide ensures success, is very frustrating to a guide.

You don't have to be a world-traveled angler to impress a guide. In fact, you shouldn't try to impress a guide with your knowledge and experience. If you're good, the guide will know soon enough. Many guides are shocked and pleased to find clients who can tie their own knots and unhook their own fish, and will let clients do so if they wish. Most people who talk a good line can't produce, and a guide finds this out fast. In fact, many guides recognize that the clients dressed in the latest brand-name outdoor wear are more fashion savvy than fishing savvy.

No matter what your level of experience, until you've developed a rapport with a guide, yield to the guide's direction and ways. In many types of fishing, there is a bit of a knack to doing certain things (hooking a bait, for example, or jigging method, or retrieval technique), and the guide would not do a certain thing unless the guide thought it was best. After all, the primary object is catching fish, and whether or not you catch fish is often the yardstick for measuring a day's success. A good guide wants to produce results and wants to do what will best accomplish that. Yield to the guide's discretion when reasonable; the guide should know best and, most of the time, does know best. That doesn't mean that some technique or lure or approach that you have in mind isn't worth trying or suggesting. Some experienced anglers know things that some guides have yet to learn, and you might teach the guide something (but don't do it by insulting the guide) that will benefit both of you.

Guides, however, are often frustrated by anglers who don't pay attention to what they are told and who do things their way rather than the guide's way. Some anglers have just enough fishing experience to think they know a lot, and these people are among the worst offenders because they already have developed habits and methods, whereas inexperienced anglers have not. Many guides say that greater success is achieved by children and women with little or no fishing experience, rather than by men with considerable experience, because the former follow instructions and pay better attention. There's a lesson here.

In instances where there is a knack to setting the hook, or a preferred method of doing so for a particular species and the way it strikes (like steelhead and salmon), many guides say that they have problems with people who are avid bass anglers. These anglers have a tendency to reel down and rear back ferociously on the hookset, sometimes ripping the hooks out of fish. So, listen to the guide, and if the guide says that you just have to lift up and keep a tight line, then do it that way.

Does the guide fish? This is an important issue to inquire about. In most types of guided fishing, the guide does not fish unless invited to by the client or unless the guide has to show the client how to do something. In some types of fishing, especially bass fishing, it is common for a guide to fish as much as or more than the client. Bass guides who have fully equipped bass boats and strictly cast lures are particularly likely to do this. Such guides run their boats from the bow and usually get first presentations at most cover; inevitably they catch a lot of fish during a good day. In effect, the clients are subsidizing the guide's fishing habit. A guide should fish only if there is prior agreement. If you have strong feelings about a guide fishing, then you should discuss the issue beforehand. But be forewarned that you are likely to meet resistance from bass guides, since this practice has become common.

In some cases, having several lures in the water will maximize your opportunities, and the lure or tactic that the guide is using may prove best. However, while the guide might show you this technique or strategy, the real object of a day of guided fishing is to get the client(s) to catch fish. In muskie fishing, for example, where the opportunities to catch fish are few and far between, a desirable outcome is not one in which a guide fishes and catches a muskie while the clients do not. If you merely wanted to see a muskie you could go to an aquarium. However, if the action on a given day or at a certain time/place is plentiful, then letting the guide fish is generous and appropriate, as long as boat handling and other chores are not neglected.

Hooksetting and rod handling. Although hooksetting and rod handling are more of an issue when you are fishing on charter boats than when fishing with a guide, on some guided fishing occasions the guide still hooks a fish and hands the rod to a client or takes a rod out of a holder, sets the hook, and then hands the client the rod. The reason that the guide does this is to ensure that the fish is well-hooked and to increase the chances of it being landed. For most people, especially in freshwater, such an action is not a problem. However, a few anglers will not take a rod and fight a fish if someone else has first set the hook and then attempted to hand over the rod. They feel that it's unfair and that the person who set the hook should play the fish. If one person sets the hook and then hands the rod to someone else, and the fish turns out to be a world-record candidate, that action, according to International Game Fish Association (IGFA) rules, would be judged unfair and would disqualify the catch from record consideration, much to the consternation of the person who caught the would-have-been record fish. Most big-game anglers, and many light-tackle saltwater anglers, are familiar with this rule but the majority of anglers are not.

If you have any concerns or interests in regard to establishing a record *(see)* catch, then no one else should touch your rod. If you feel strongly that having someone set the hook and hand you a rod is unfair, then you should make your feelings known to the guide or discuss it with the guide before the moment of truth arrives. There is, after all, something to be said for feeling the strike and setting the hook by yourself, since that is one of the intrinsically appealing aspects of sportfishing.

> The first of the 10 plagues of Egypt, described in The Bible's book of Exodus, may be one of the earliest recorded instances of a red tide (" . . . and all the waters that were in the river were turned to blood. And the fish that were in the river died; and the river stank. . . . ").

If you need instruction on the proper manner of setting the hook for the species being pursued or the method being employed, the guide should be able to instruct you; most guides are patient while you are trying to get the technique right. After all, it's your fishing trip.

If you have no qualms about being handed a rod, no concerns about records (the chances of catching a record fish are usually slim), and no deep feelings about setting the hook yourself, then these concerns are a nonissue. Most guides simply want their customers to catch fish, and since the guides are on the water every day, they are on top of their game while most of the customers are not. The majority of anglers, especially in freshwater, don't have any problem with taking a rod that someone has handed them, but most of them also don't understand all of the ramifications.

The best-time dilemma. The best times (or those perceived to be the best) are usually booked first by anglers-in-the-know, many of whom are repeat clients. How honestly a guide deals with this issue will tell you a lot about how the person conducts business. Ideally, any time in a given season will be a good time to visit; in a few cases this may be true but usually it is not. The best guides will tell you that this is so, and they will squarely lay out your options and explain to you how things differ at nonprime times. They will also tell you that conditions may not be the same from year to year on given dates and that weather (cold, excessive rain, excessive heat, storms) and other forces beyond their control can affect your success, even at those times that are usually reliable.

It is entirely possible to be somewhere at what is ordinarily the "best" time, with one of the best guides in the business, yet have terrible fishing. Experienced anglers know this happens. But many people who visit good fishing spots are not skillful or experienced anglers and do not understand this point.

Tackle and other gear. Although charter boats supply all customary fishing equipment unless specialized angling is preferred, a guide may or may not furnish equipment. For some types of specialized fishing (drifting egg sacks or pulling plugs for big salmon and steelhead, for example, or drifting with bait for striped bass), the fishing outfits and all terminal rigging will be supplied by the guide. Some guides, like those who fish on saltwater flats, provide tackle but invite you to bring your own if you choose; they'll check your equipment to see if it's suitable for the anticipated action. Some guides do not provide any fishing equipment other than bait or terminal rigs, and they expect you to bring your own; this is true for most bass fishing guides. Guides at distant locations (the Canadian wilderness, the South American interior, etc.) rarely have any tackle for you, although a lodge may supply some loaner equipment or sell lures and terminal items. Here, you usually are expected to bring whatever you'll need, and the guide provides no tackle (and may not have any in the boat either).

Naturally, guides who do not provide equipment should charge less than those who do. You should inquire about the equipment issue beforehand; when you are bringing tackle, ask the guide for recommendations. The majority of people who fish with a guide are relatively inexperienced, or at least unaccustomed to the style of fishing or the species pursued by the guide in that location. Many guides thus use fairly heavy tackle to compensate for their customers' lack of experience. An experienced angler who is skilled at light-tackle use will probably be disappointed most of the time when using the standard gear supplied by a guide, because it is in the medium to heavy range for durability. However, some guides specialize in certain techniques or species, and they cater to anglers with these interests or abilities, so they will have the corresponding tackle and their gear will be high quality.

Anglers who fish with guides are expected to bring their own food, beverages, and personal comfort items (sunglasses, sunscreen, foul weather gear, etc.). Anglers are expected to wear appropriate footwear for some types of boats; nonscuff boating shoes or sneakers are good for most situations, although in cold locations and in the far north a pair of warm waterproof boots may be necessary. Where a license is required, it is usually the client's responsibility to obtain it, but a good guide will check for one or assist in obtaining one if necessary. Sometimes guides are able to obtain licenses in advance for clients who are arriving too late to get the licenses themselves, or guides may get licenses required by bordering states/provinces, for which guides should be reimbursed.

It's a good idea to bring extra food, drink, or treats to share with the guide. The matter of beverage is left to personal discretion, but it is poor form for a guide to consume any alcoholic beverage while on the water, and clients shouldn't offer any. Some lodges and outfitters prohibit the consumption of alcohol by guides and request that anglers not give or offer any to their guides, either on the water or as a gratuity. Generally it is a good policy for anglers not to consume any alcohol while fishing for obvious practical reasons *(see: safety)*. Water and juice are the best cold beverages, especially under hot conditions.

Tipping. Tipping a guide is customary, and the tip, of course, varies depending upon the activities, the effort the guide has made, and whether any exceptionally good (or bad) things have happened. The customary cash tip for a guide is usually $15–20 per person per day for most fishing ($30 to $40 for a pair of anglers); a lesser tip might be in order if you have had major problems and more if the day is truly spectacular or extra services are rendered. Some guides will clean fish that are kept, but others do not; those that do, deserve something extra for this service. If you catch a record or contest-winning fish with a guide, then a suitable bonus is appropriate.

Sometimes anglers give tips in the form of merchandise, including fishing tackle, in lieu of, or in addition to, a cash tip. In distant locations where good equipment is costly or hard to obtain, fishing tackle (reel, tackle box, spools of line, etc.) may be especially appreciated by the guide for personal use or for its trading value. In poor countries, clothing items in addition to the cash tip are very welcome; you'd be surprised how much a T-shirt with a fish design on it is appreciated.

In distant places, however, you should check with the outfitter or lodge manager to see if it is appropriate to give a guide fishing equipment. In some Mexican bass lakes, for example, lodge managers discourage this, fearing that such tackle will wind up being used by someone for commercial fishing, and thus have a negative impact on the resource.
See: Fishing Lodge.

FISHING LICENSE
See: Regulations.

FISHING LODGE

A loosely used term that applies to facilities of various quality levels that cater to anglers (sometimes hunters and other recreationists) and that are either on or close to desirable angling waters. A lodge may provide only accommodations, food, and proximity to fishing spots; or it may also provide guides, boats, instruction, dockage, launch ramp, equipment, or some combination thereof. Accommodations may range from deluxe five-star resort quality with matching cuisine to a spartan main house with tent-frame cabins and family-style dining. Fishing lodges are sometimes referred to as camps, although camp usually signifies a facility with humble, if not rugged, accommodations, perhaps even of a temporary or tent nature. Lodges may house just a handful of people at one time or 50 to 60. Some popular lodges in the Pacific Northwest can accommodate more than that.

Fishing lodges exist in remote as well as readily accessible locations. They advertise in various media, exhibit at shows, and may be represented by booking agents and outfitters who specialize in outdoor travel. The better ones are usually booked well in advance, especially during peak fishing times. Most operate seasonally, although some are open year-round and others for a very limited time because of weather and water conditions; far-northern Canadian lodges have only a six-week season.

Selecting. Many lodges are too remote for people to visit personally before booking a stay, and since there are so many lodges, most with attractive brochures and rather generous claims, it can be difficult to select one that meets your interests, abilities, and budget.

The ideal setting, such as this one in coastal British Columbia, is remote and beautiful.

The more traveling and fishing experiences that you have, the better you'll be able to satisfy yourself when selecting a fishing lodge. Astute lodge owners and their representatives make this chore a little easier by anticipating the kinds of things that you might want to know about and by providing you with those particulars in their literature to help you make a decision.

That decision-making starts with how you learn about a prospective lodge in the first place. Word-of-mouth referral is the number one factor in getting people to a fishing lodge that they've never visited before. The recommendation of satisfied customers, especially if they are serious anglers, is important, and you should talk to anyone that you know who has been to a lodge that you're interested in.

While word-of-mouth is helpful, it isn't essential. Clearly you first have to learn of the lodge's existence from some source. That process includes reading articles, attending sport shows, looking at advertisements and television shows, attending slide lectures, checking direct mailings, soliciting booking agents, and so forth.

If you can visit a lodge owner at a sport show, you should do so. Shows include many exhibits by lodges and outfitters whose booths are usually manned by owners and/or their families and employees. Speaking with these people is the best possible way to get direct answers to specific questions. This is a prime opportunity to go beyond obvious questions (When is the best time to visit? or What lures should I bring?) to the most intricate matters (Are there reefs and shoals in the lake? If so, how deep are they and do you need sonar to locate them? Do they hold walleye throughout the summer?). Answers to such specifics will help an ardent angler make up his or her mind as well as plan ahead. Sometimes, booths are manned by people who are filling in for the lodge owner, and who cannot answer the most detailed angling questions;

Many fishing lodges are known for good food; this is the dining area of a lodge in Pará, Brazil.

that doesn't mean the place is unsuitable, but you will have to dig deeper for information.

Articles in newspapers and magazines reflect the experiences of someone who has been there. Seldom are articles published about bad lodges. Be aware, however, that sportswriters who review angling destinations focus on the positive and may omit negative comments about places that are otherwise commendable. The sportswriters usually receive red carpet treatment, visit at the best times, and are hosted to some extent by the lodge, so it is easy to accentuate the positive and bypass some of the things that are not as notable.

Not all of the things that interest or concern you will be mentioned in any article, and reading a very positive article doesn't prevent you from asking probing questions. In fact, it ought to help focus your questions. Photographs accompanying an article may be helpful in establishing the setting and the kind of place it is, but often the photos are too few or of people holding fish and little is seen of the other aspects of the lodge, the locale, or the body of water.

Keep in mind that most newspaper and magazine articles place too much emphasis on exceptional catches and outstanding days. They fail to note that every day was not fabulous and did not produce a monstrous fish, or that only one behemoth was caught all week even though there were 15 people at the lodge, or that it took a particularly skillful angler to really do well. A glowing account may raise readers' expectations too high, and when people do not attain the same level of achievement, they feel that the author of the article lied or that some special circumstances were at work. They're disappointed when they do not experience what the author experienced. This problem is even more acute with television fishing shows; most people fail to realize that 23 minutes of constant video fishing action may have taken one or two weeks to actually experience and film. Seldom do all of those TV lunkers fall cast after cast in real life, although it seems like they do on the tube.

It's important to note that the skill level of the angler who wrote an encouraging article about a good fishing locale may be quite different from the skill level of most other anglers. Of course, some readers will be better anglers and may find even better fishing than the author described, but many readers will be much less proficient and may be inadvertently set up for disappointment. Make sure that you ask the lodge staff whether you can expect to have the same kind of experience or whether you need special skill levels to do so.

One of the first things you'll do is look over the lodge's literature, usually a brochure, obtained from the lodge or its agent. This will range from a black-and-white photocopy to a glossy color folder. Be wary of the former and of literature that appears to have been hastily slapped together; that may reflect on the rest of the operation as well. Don't be too expectant based on the photos either. In the best brochures, the boats, rooms, facilities, and scenes seldom look as impressive in person as they do when the photographs were taken from the best possible angle, in the best possible light, with a telephoto or wide angle lens, and under the best of circumstances. Some lodges also offer videotapes, which give you a better feel for the type of water, boats, and facilities, as well as the area in general. Many also have Web sites, and the same issues apply to these as to literature.

Many lodge brochures and Web sites give good details about accommodations, food, and services but are less specific about actual fishing information, which is described in general and glowing terms, although there are certainly exceptions. Ardent anglers usually want as many particulars as possible about the fishing (boats, angling styles, equipment needs, etc.). If the lodge has guides, the brochure or other information may say that the guides will help you achieve success, but that may not be enough if success depends on casting extremely accurately but you cannot, or having the proper equipment for a technique but you don't. Lodges that are really fishing-oriented put together a seasonally detailed description of angling activity.

Most brochures and Web sites depict large fish, especially camp-record fish, but sometimes these are very old photos of fish taken years ago. What have you done lately? is a good question to ask. Be wary of photos that show strings or piles of dead fish; lodges that appeal to meat hogs tend to emphasize that aspect more than others. Many people aren't pleased to be at a place where the major interest of the staff and guests is in poundage and full coolers.

Look for a commitment to resource conservation and to the continuation of quality fishing. Far more lodges and outfitters are interested in advocating this today than in the past, because the clientele has matured into one that recognizes the value of sportsmanship and conservation. A lodge whose policy allows keeping only one trophy fish of a particular species, or total catch-and-release other than for a shore lunch meal, is one that is not attracting the meat hog element and is interested in having quality angling for the future. This kind of lodge plans to be around in the future rather than trying to make a quick buck, and it will be a place worth returning to.

Speaking to someone who has been to the lodge or the waters in question is an excellent idea, and some places encourage this and will gladly supply a few references. If a lodge doesn't volunteer this, ask. Certainly a lodge is only going to refer you to someone who has had a positive experience, but in speaking to such a person you can learn some valuable things. Among other questions, ask what the angler would do differently if he or she were to return (a different time of the season, different gear, things they wouldn't do, etc.). Ask for a guide, cabin, or room recommendation.

Here are some other topics to consider:

Distance to fishing grounds. Here's a subject many people don't inquire about. Great Bear and Great Slave Lakes in the Northwest Territories are excellent examples because they have good fishing, but much of it takes place considerable distances from the lodges. It is not uncommon to boat daily between one and two hours each way to get to the favored spots on these huge lakes. A lot of potential fishing time is spent riding. Maybe the time is worth it if you're assured of catching a big lake trout; but since such assurances cannot realistically be made, you may find the long boat rides unappealing.

Long boat rides may be worth taking once during a week's stay, especially if you can pick the right day. When it's calm, the ride can be quite nice, but when the wind picks up and you have to venture in rough open water for a great distance in a small boat with aluminum seats, little or no rump padding, and no back support, it can be uncomfortable (and wet) for many, and intolerable for those with back problems.

The distance issue is also relative to getting to the boats. Find out how far it is from the lodge to the boats, and how rugged the walk is.

How rigorous will the activities be? Some distant fishing adventures require getting in and out of high-sided boats and airplanes, assisting with portages, toting gear, trekking through rugged terrain, and so forth. They may entail enduring cold weather, extreme heat and humidity, exposure to biting insects, encounters with dangerous animals (bears especially), or exposure to other dangers. The personal safety and medical implications here seem quite obvious. Some lodges and outfitters will properly detail the nature of things and forewarn clients. But this is not always the case. When the client asks, "Why didn't you tell me?", the response may be, "You didn't ask." So ask.

The guides. A guide can make or break a trip. Not all guides are good, not all guides have been guiding very long, and in some places anyone can hang out a "guide shingle." What makes a good guide? Ability to interact well with clients is foremost. That is closely followed by knowledge of the waters and fishing experience but also includes boat handling ability and willingness to work to achieve success.

Everyone wants to get the lodge's top guide, which is impossible. It is reasonable to ask how many guides there are, how many years they have guided on the waters you will be fishing, if some specialize in certain techniques (fly fishing, trolling, etc.), and other questions. Better to be with someone who has a few years of experience on that water than with someone who is guiding for the first time as a summer job. Someone who is inexperienced on that water might be fine, however, if the person has had guiding experience elsewhere, or if the lodge owner assures you that the person is skillful. The concern here is not just being able to navigate properly in tricky places, but knowing where to fish when the obvious spots aren't producing. If you are especially interested in learning about fishing techniques, ask if you can be placed with a guide who is able and willing to communicate and show you how things are done.

Boats, motors, PFDs. Although this maxim is not carved in stone, it's generally better to be at a place where the motors and perhaps the boats are replaced fairly often. Most lodges replace their motors on a two-year cycle, sometimes annually. Motors are the lifeblood of many remote fishing experiences, and they have to work like a clock. In many places they are put through their paces all season, being run a lot and also abused, so it's a good investment for a lodge to change them frequently.

Boats don't need replacing as frequently, but it is not reassuring to arrive at a lodge where the boats are obviously old and battered. But if they are functional and, most importantly, don't leak, it may not matter. On the White River in Arkansas, a lot of older flat-bottomed boats are in guide use, but these are specialized craft and well cared for, so a newer boat is not always a necessity.

Safety equipment is a necessity, however, and personal flotation devices (PFDs) are the foremost concern. Some lodges don't put PFDs in the boats or may supply inadequate ones (a 200-pound angler isn't well served with a medium adult vest or a skimpy Type I orange neck-wrapper). Ask what they have. A top-quality lodge should have Type III upright flotation PFDs. You may want to bring your own. There is no harm in asking about the age of any lodge's boats and motors and about the availability of PFDs. Your life could depend on them.

Clothing and gear needs. Most lodges will advise clients what to bring; some provide more detailed and specific advice than others. Foul weather gear is always important but often underappreciated by novice travelers, who may not know what good rain gear and truly nasty weather are. Remember to ask whether you'll need waders and whether they should be lightweight models or the heavier (and bulky to pack) neoprene versions. In some places, you may need to bring a survival suit or snowmobile suit.

Specific advice about tackle needs (fly rod length and fly line size, for example) is never unwelcome. Experienced anglers can give themselves latitude, but the inexperienced need very explicit instructions. A lodge that will provide you with these details is one that is looking out for your best interests in all aspects of the experience.

The best-time dilemma. The best times (or those perceived to be the best) are usually booked first by anglers-in-the-know, many of whom are repeat clients. How honestly a lodge owner or agent deals with this issue will tell you a lot about how he or she conducts business. Ideally, any time of a given season will be a good time to visit, and in a few cases this may be true, but usually it is not. The best lodge operators will tell you that this is so, and they will squarely lay out your options and explain to you how things differ at nonprime times. They will also tell you that conditions may not be the same from year to year on given dates and that weather (cold, excessive rain, excessive heat, storms) and other forces beyond their control can affect your success.

It is entirely possible to visit at what is ordinarily the "best" time, yet the fishing is terrible. Experienced anglers know this happens. But a lot of people who visit good fishing spots are not skillful or experienced anglers and do not understand this point. Many lodges don't warn people about this, perhaps because they fear losing a prospective customer, but it's better to be forewarned than to learn after the fact when disappointment and frustration have set in.

Of course, there are other concerns regarding the selection of a fishing lodge, including deposit, cancellation, and final payment policies; extra costs (such as fly-out trips); travel routing (including overnight stays); special food concerns; language barriers, particularly with guides; availability and cost (usually high) of tackle at the lodge; and so forth. Ask.

The agent route. Some booking agents represent fishing lodges all over the world. If they have visited the places that they represent, they can give you a first-hand evaluation or direct you to another place within your means, interests, and abilities. They should be able to refer you to people who have been there if they have not. They probably know the best air routes to take and what to advise in terms of scheduling. It should not cost any more to use an agent, whose fee is derived from a percentage of the overall package cost, than to make the booking yourself.
See: Charter Boat; Guide.

FISHING PRESSURE

The amount of fishing effort generated is called fishing pressure. Effort is the time, expressed in number of people, boats, hours, days, and other units of measurement, as well as some combination of these, that is applied to one species or group of species. Biologists calculate effort for management purposes, especially through surveys or through landings *(see)* that have been reported. Anglers broadly refer to the number and frequency of people fishing as fishing pressure.

Excessive sportfishing pressure or effort in freshwater and saltwater may not reduce populations but may result in more difficult angling and a lower success rate. When combined with harvesting for personal or commercial purposes, the result may be overfishing *(see)*.

In freshwater, the more popular species of fish, and those at the top of the food chain, are especially likely to be subject to heavy, and perhaps excessive, fishing pressure. In saltwater, some species (such as tarpon) are only targeted by anglers, and the effect of fishing pressure varies. Many saltwater fish are sought by commercial as well as recreational interests, and fishing pressure combines effort and landings. A different level of harvest is achieved and may result in overfishing.
See: Fisheries Management.

FISHING REGULATIONS
See: Regulations.

FISHING TACKLE
See: Tackle.

FISHKILL

The die-off of fish, usually in numbers. Fishkills may occur as the result of chemical pollution, especially from pesticides in agricultural runoff, but most often happen as a result of insufficient oxygen in the water.

A winter fishkill occurs when ice and snow cut off the transfer of oxygen from the air to the water; the oxygen in the water gets used up, and fish die. This does not happen if there is enough oxygen in the water to last throughout the winter until the ice and snow melt.

A summer fishkill usually occurs when inadequate amounts of oxygen exist in the water during extended periods of hot, calm, and cloudy days. Warm summer water temperatures, high demands for oxygen, and days with no sunlight or wind to mix the surface water may lead to oxygen demands exceeding oxygen production. When this happens, distressed fish may be seen as they rise to the surface and gasp for oxygen, and dead fish may be seen floating on the surface.

FISH LADDER
See: Fishway.

FISH POISONING
See: Ciguatera.

FISH PREPARATION—CARE

There are no apologies here for killing and keeping *some* fish to eat. Indeed, surveys reveal that one of the primary purposes of sportfishing—and a chief benefit—is getting fish for the table, especially fresh fish. This includes numerous species that are not available in supermarkets or fish markets, species that are available only seasonally, and species that command very high prices commercially.

Many species of fish that are classified by state agencies as gamefish *(see)* cannot legally be sold in the United States, meaning that to enjoy them you have to catch them, or someone else has to catch them and share with you. If species classified as gamefish are available in markets, they have probably been imported from distant places where they can legally be sold, or they have been raised through aquaculture. Connoisseurs who know the difference will affirm that most species of farm-raised fish are not fully comparable to the same species from the wild.

Most species of freshwater fish taken from the wild cannot be sold. Even trout offered by the finest restaurants is not from the wild; those restaurant fish are raised in hatcheries, and although they seem good to many patrons, they rarely compare favorably in appearance or taste to a wild, native trout.

Eating the fish that you or friends and family catch is nearly as satisfying as catching a fish on a lure of your own making. In a world where most of the flesh from living creatures comes to us in sanitized pressure-wrapped packaging, having been killed and prepared by others, catching, cleaning, and eating your own fish is a direct reminder of the connection and dependence that human beings have always had upon these creatures. Of course, fish have a high nutritional value and, if properly cared for, are delicious when prepared in many different ways.

The key to enjoying fish isn't necessarily having a good recipe or using a certain method of preparation. Once the fish is in the kitchen, you can increase or decrease its palatability, but to enjoy its fullest taste and nutrition, you must give it proper attention from the moment you catch it until the moment you prepare it for the table. The advantage that anglers have over people who buy commercially caught fish is that anglers get their food as fresh as it can possibly be found, and they alone control its preparations and treatment. The foundation for enjoying fish and for having good-tasting fish is the treatment that this product receives after it is caught, the care that is given to transporting it from where it is caught to where it will be stored or consumed, and the storage that it receives between cleaning and preparing for consumption. The end results will be only as good as you want them to be, and as good as you make them.

There may be no other food that loses its freshness as quickly as fish. The flesh of a fish does not improve with aging, so it is literally true that the best time to eat a fish is immediately after it has been caught. Such a gastronomic utopia can be realized on big boats with galleys, in locations where a shore lunch is possible, and in situations when you are camping on or near the water or can head to the house immediately after catching a fish. Most of the time, however, eating a fish soon after catching it is not possible or feasible, or happens only occasionally.

Therefore, to avoid spoilage and to keep fish as fresh as possible, you should begin caring for it as soon as you've finished taking photos and congratulating yourself on your accomplishment. Unfortunately, many anglers, after devoting a lot of energy, time, and perhaps money to sportfishing, take fair to poor care of their catch, because of either ignorance, expedience, or lack of planning. Their fish may lose freshness even before it gets to the place of cleaning or storage. You can tell when a fish has lost its freshness because it looks dried and shriveled, it smells, the eyes are glossy, the skin is bleached, the flesh is soft, and so on. Fish that exhibit these conditions may be edible, but the manner of handling has contributed to some loss of freshness and therefore tastiness. Incidentally, a fish exhibiting these conditions is not necessarily unfit for consumption; the fish is simply not as fresh as it could be for maximum benefit. Many people take minimal care of their fish, yet still find them delicious. Clearly, some people are not as discriminating as others, and the purpose of the following information is to make you more discriminating so that you enjoy the fullest benefit and taste from your catch.

There are three main aspects to proper care: what you do after catching, what you do after cleaning, and how the fish is transported if more than just a short period of time is involved. Each

Start out with plenty of ice to help keep your catch in great shape.

of these is important and is linked to the others. It does no good to properly care for a fish until you get it home and then store it improperly for later consumption. On the other hand, if you've let a fish become stale in the hours after catching it, it will not improve in flavor no matter how well you later wrap and store it.

Many anglers recognize that fish are good to eat, but strangely enough they do not equate taste with proper handling. They, their spouses, or friends may spend more time looking up a recipe for the fish than caring for it in the first place.

Spoilage Facts

Changes take place in a fish after it is caught because of its biological composition and its environment. These changes begin when a fish is hooked, and they continue after it dies.

When a fish is hooked, it is engaged in a struggle for its life. It gets energy for this struggle from the glycogen in its muscles. (Glycogen is the animal kingdom's version of starch.) The longer the fish struggles, the more it depletes its energy reserve. This depletion can cause physiological changes. The fish's flesh may lose some of its natural sweetness, and metabolic products that can affect its flavor and texture begin to accumulate. These changes begin even before the fish is landed. Thus, a fish that will be used for food should be landed quickly.

As soon as a fish dies, an irreversible spoilage process begins. This process occurs through the activity of enzymes and bacteria. Enzymes that normally regulate a fish's metabolism can work unchecked after it dies. Digestive enzymes may begin to digest the fish itself, causing belly burn or softening of the flesh around the gut. This is especially likely if a fish is caught while feeding, since its digestive enzymes will already be active. Other enzymes in fish muscle can also begin to affect the flavor and texture of the fillet. Enzymes work rapidly at warm temperatures.

Fish are also subject to bacterial degradation after death. Natural barriers that protect fish while they are alive break down when they die. Bacteria from the environment and the gut can grow and multiply in fish tissue. This activity diminishes fish quality and eventually causes spoilage. Bacteria also grow rapidly at warm temperatures.

Finally, the highly unsaturated fat in fish is also affected by oxygen in the air. Oxygen reacts with this fat to produce the odors and flavors associated with rancidity. Fat oxidation can be a serious problem if the fish is to be frozen or stored for very long. This is one reason why fattier fish (like bluefish) do not remain in good condition during frozen storage as long as leaner fish (like flounder).

After the Catch

Preparations for taking care of your catch should really begin before you head to the water. In other words, before you go fishing, give some thought to whether you want to keep any of the catch and then to how you will store and transport it to maintain maximum freshness. If you catch a fish that you want to keep and have to ask "Now what?" you haven't planned properly. If you catch a fish you want to keep and you just toss it aside in the boat until you head for home, shame on you.

Let's say you've caught a good fish and it's been unhooked. Where are you going to put it? On the floor of the boat? On the pier? In a tub or bag? That's what a lot of people do, and this is okay if the weather is very cold, if the sun isn't shining on it, if it will be there for only a short time, or if you don't particularly care what it will taste like.

The worst thing you can do is pay no attention to fish you've just caught. Leaving fish exposed to air and sun for a long time is undesirable, as is leaving fish undressed overnight. Unaerated livewells, livewells filled with warm water, and stringers that are overcrowded or trolled or hung in warm surface water do not enhance the edibility of fish. Yet that's what so many people do with their catch. Not surprisingly, the result is a reduction in quality and taste of the catch.

Ideally you should clean or dress fish immediately after they've been caught (see: fish preparation—cleaning/dressing) and then put them on ice. But that isn't always practical. Maybe you can't clean fish at the place where you catch them (this is seldom the case in saltwater but is often the case

Keeping her crappie alive in the water in a wire basket has helped ensure that this angler will have fine eating.

Fish Preparation—Care

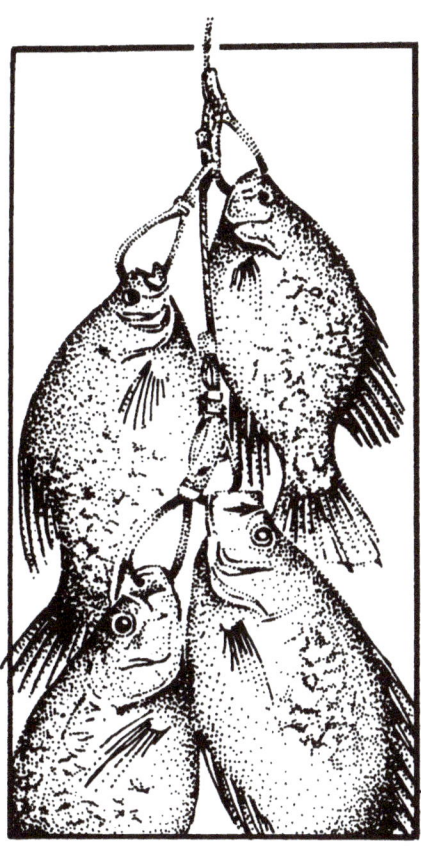

A stringer should be used only to retain fish that will be kept for consumption; the clip-on style, depicted here, is best for small fish and prevents overcrowding.

in freshwater). Or you simply don't want to stop fishing to do so. Or you don't have ice or a knife with you. Do, however, clean and dress the fish as soon as possible. If you've planned ahead, you have a cooler or ice chest and ice to keep the fish cool.

Air and water temperatures are partial keys to good fish care. The warmer the air and temperature, the harder it is to keep fish alive and/or fresh until you are ready to clean and store them, and the sooner you need to begin preparations. Although some angling takes place in conditions that allow freshly caught fish to stay cool naturally, these situations are usually the exception. Do whatever you can to keep fish protected from heat and warmth. At the very least, that may mean putting them in the shade, stopping fishing after a reasonable length of time to clean them, covering them with a wet cloth, or taking care to keep them alive in a protected, cool environment.

Containing fish alive. Many boats are equipped with a livewell *(see)*, which can be used for keeping small- to medium-size fish alive. Livewells work better for some species than for others. Freshwater bass, for example, are fairly easy to keep alive in a well, whereas most species of trout are not, unless the water is cold and well aerated.

A good livewell will not only aerate the water and provide plenty of oxygen, but also circulate the water to keep the temperature down and bring in fresh outside water. Livewells in saltwater boats are usually meant for bait storage but can accommodate some species of saltwater fish. Larger livewells are necessary for long fish and species that grow large, and are usually not practical for most small- to medium-size fishing boats. If you have a livewell, however, and can keep the water temperature down, this is a desirable way to store fish until you can get to the dock (or home in the case of trailered boats) and clean them. If fish die while they are in the livewell, remove them and place them on ice. Many livewells are not large, so watch out for overcrowding, particularly with large specimens.

People without livewells, which include those who fish from shore or from small boats, need some other method of retaining fish. One way to keep fish alive without a livewell is to use a wire or net mesh basket. This collapsible basket is commonly used for panfish and is hung over the side of the boat in the water. Fish need to have enough room to move around in the basket, so it can't handle larger fish and great numbers. Be sure to pull the basket out of the water when moving, and don't keep the fish out of the water long when you do move.

A stringer or rope is the most common way to contain whole fish until you can bring them home or to the landing site—and it is one of the poorest methods of retention. The fish inevitably become stressed and bruised while on a stringer, especially if they get dragged around a lot or taken in and out of the boat often. For fish, a stringer or rope is usually a means of dying slowly. Nevertheless, using a stringer is better than just laying fish on the floor of the boat, exposed to sun and dirt. And some species, such as panfish and catfish, do better on a stringer than other species.

If you must string fish, make sure they are allowed to breathe so they stay alive. A metal or plastic clip stringer is better than a rope stringer for small fish because it doesn't crowd them, but rope

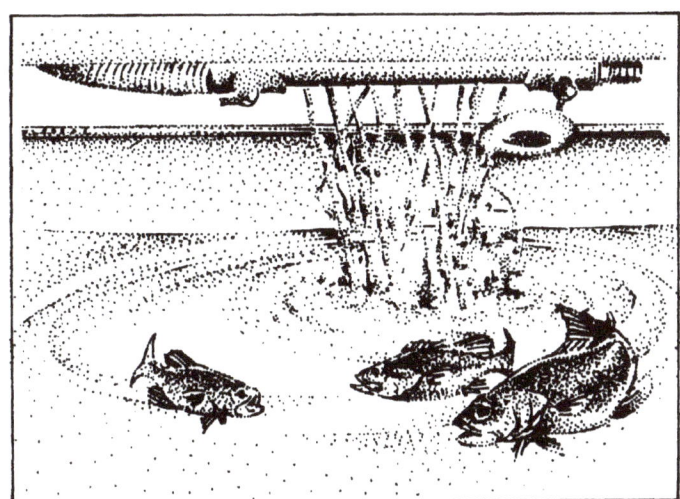

In a livewell, shown here in an interior view, the water streaming in from above is a significant help with aeration.

From the northernmost sportfish file: Arctic charr have been reported at 82' 34" degrees North on Ellesmere Island, about 497 miles south of the North Pole.

is better for large and lively fish. Don't run a rope stringer through the gill. Put it through the lower jaw (and in the case of big fish or weak stringers, put it through both jaws). Try to keep the stringer away from gasoline in the water or any other substance that might affect the flavor of the fish. Take the stringer out of the water when the boat is underway at full speed, and avoid leaving it out of the water for a long time. If you're going a long distance, stop for a minute and put the stringer back in the water or put the fish in a pail of water while you move. The more time that fish spend out of the water, the worse it is for them.

Whether the stringer is in the water or on the boat, keep it in a shaded locale. And always make sure that it is fastened to some solid object. Many anglers have lost their stringer when it slipped or pulled off an unsecured spot. Recognize that stringers can attract other creatures. In coastal waters a string of fish trailing from the belt of waders may bring in interested sharks. Snapping turtles, snakes, and even alligators in freshwater have found stringers of fish attractive, although this is not a regular occurrence.

If a fish dies on a stringer or in a basket, dress it and put it on ice or in a cool, shaded spot. Although this is not possible or practical on some occasions, be aware that once a fish dies its flesh starts to deteriorate, and deterioration happens more rapidly in the water than out of it.

Killing. There is merit to killing some fish immediately, even if you have the option of keeping them alive. On the other hand, some fish are better if kept alive. Fish that die slowly, struggling and bruising themselves in the process, won't taste as good as they might if they were simply dispatched with a couple of quick blows to the top of the head and stored temporarily in an appropriate environment. Still other fish are pretty hardy; if you have the option, for example, of keeping them alive in cool water rather than dead under a cloth on the floor of the boat, opting for alive may enhance the food value. You have to make this decision based on the circumstances. The bruises that fish receive, or the discoloration that results from the way they are stored or from their contact with other fish, is more likely to be an aesthetic default rather than one affecting edibility. If appearance matters to you (and it may to some family members or for the sake of artistic presentation in a recipe), then keep dead fish separated from each other and out of contact with objects.

If ice is available, the best option is to kill the fish after you've caught it, field dress it quickly, and then put it on ice. However, cleaning a fish on the water may not be legal in some places; in certain freshwater lakes, this practice is prohibited and may result in a fine. In this situation, you can still dispatch the fish and ice it down, and then clean it later at a fish cleaning station or at home. Killing a fish immediately after catching it and then cleaning it, even if legal, is not always practical. In the midst of promising activity, few anglers want to stop to deal with a fish they've caught when more or larger fish await. If that is the case, stop to take care of the catch as soon as you have a break in the action.

The actual act of killing a fish is a delicate subject in this modern era of heightened sensibilities, and one that is rarely addressed in most books and educational literature on fishing. Few, if any, laws address the manner or timeliness of killing a sport-caught fish, nor would it be reasonable or practical to have such laws. Similarly, there are no laws regarding the killing of the hundreds of millions of fish (and shellfish) that are taken by commercial fishermen every year.

From a practical standpoint, as already stated, killing a fish soon after capture may be best for the preservation of the meat if proper storing and chilling are available. That in itself should be reason enough to dispatch a fish as soon as the decision is made to keep it. This also seems reasonable from a humane standpoint, the purpose being to prevent death through a slow and presumably painful process.

Two questions must be raised: Is it inhumane to let fish die slowly, say by bleeding, by stringing or by placing in a basket or well; and what is the best method of dispatching a fish? The answer to the first question is best left to the sensibility of the individual angler, especially since the question of pain and suffering in fish is one that is prone to anthropomorphic assertions and there is practically no scientific information on the extent to which fish experience pain.

Some people feel that putting a live fish on ice, which slows the metabolism and produces numbing, is the most innocuous way to let a fish die, and many people do so. (Do, however, put the ice under, around, and on top if you can rather than just laying the fish on ice.) Many anglers allow a fish to die of its own accord, with or without ice, although others dispatch it with a quick blow or series of blows to the top of the head and just behind the eyes with a club—referred to as a priest (as in dispensing last rites) by some anglers. Striking a fish may or may not kill a fish immediately, but it does stop the fish from thrashing and flopping. The

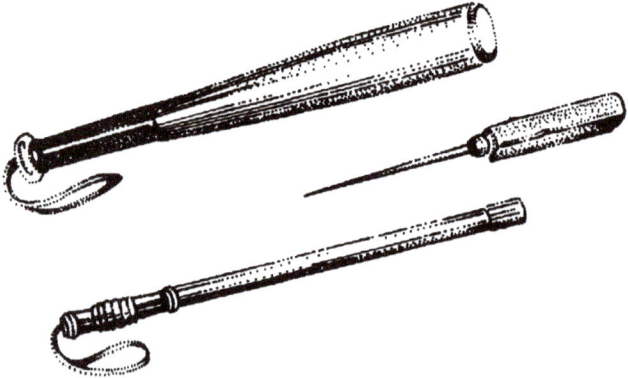

To dispatch a fish quickly and humanely, use a heavy club (top) in saltwater or a lighter club (bottom) in freshwater, or use a pick.

cessation of activity prevents the flesh from being damaged and ensures better and more attractive table fare. It also has advantages for your fishing gear and the cleanup. If you do crack a fish on the head, be careful not to hit yourself in the process; strike the fish in the right spot so that you accomplish your objective without ruining the meat.

Another method of killing a fish is pithing. A small pick is inserted into the back of the head from the top, scrambling the brain. Pithing is fairly easy to accomplish for some species and for small fish, but not for others, especially if they are lively and large.

In fact, some large species are customarily killed in ways that seem odd to those who don't know better or who are accustomed to catching only small fish. Huge Pacific halibut are a good example. These monsters can do a great deal of damage if brought alive into a boat, even though they have already been mortally impaled with a flying gaff. Their powerful and still beating tail could literally rip a boat apart. Therefore, big specimens are shot.

Many anglers dispatch fish just before cleaning or dressing them while the fish are alive, though seldom lively. Before using a knife or skinning tool, these anglers either pith the fish with a pick or knife blade, rap them on the head, or, in the case of some small species, snap their heads to sever the spinal cord.

Storing with and without ice. Once fish are dead, the flavor and texture of the flesh will start to deteriorate without proper care. As previously noted, deterioration is caused by many factors, chief among them being the presence of spoilage bacteria, blood, and normal digestive fluids. Thorough evisceration and cleaning will help remove these problems, combined with immediate icing to lower the temperature of the fish. Obviously it is important to slow down the natural deterioration that takes place. The factor that is easiest and the most important to control is temperature, and that can be handled with ice.

But what if you don't have ice? Avoid placing whole dead fish in a plastic bag unless they are in an unsealed bag in an ice-filled cooler; without air circulation, fish or fillets placed in a nonporous bag and kept outside will deteriorate quickly. On the other hand, if you fillet the fish immediately, place the rinsed fillets in a bag (sealable is okay now) and then place the bag on ice. If you have a paper towel or napkins, place the rinsed fillets on the paper towels and then put both towel and fish in the bag so that the towel can absorb moisture. Try to keep the fillets or the fish from soaking in water. Wicker creels, once a mainstay of stream and wading anglers, are less commonly used today, although they do provide reasonable air circulation. Layered with moss or grass or ferns, wicker creels are adequate for short-term storage (a few hours) of small fish and are preferable to canvas bags or other nonporous retainers.

If no conventional containers are available, you can improvise. A burlap bag, a mesh fruit or potato sack, wet newspapers or towels, or other objects that would allow fish to cool and allow air to circulate can be employed. Where necessary, you should rinse or clean them first. Keep the wrapping moist and shaded. If you add grasses, ferns, or other natural growth to the holding device to help air circulation, make sure that they are not aromatic; otherwise, the fish may develop that flavor.

If you have to hike to your fishing place, you may not have the luxury of bringing a cooler with ice. Consider taking a small amount of ice in a clean burlap bag. Put the bag in the shade (or bury it in moist sand if you are surf fishing) to keep the ice from melting for as long as possible. When ice is not available, use table salt and a burlap or similar type bag. When you catch a fish, eviscerate it and wash it. Rub about one tablespoon of salt for each pound of fish into the cavity, and then lightly salt the skin. Put the fish and enough wet seaweed to surround it into the bag. Keep the bag in the shade or bury it in moist sand. If you are at a suitable place, like the beach while surf fishing, and no container is available, bury the fish in moist sand near the waterline. To avoid losing your fish, mark the location carefully and watch the tide.

If you're not keeping fish alive, dispatch them right away and place them in an ice-packed food or beverage cooler for later cleaning. Separate the fish from food and beverages by placing the latter in bags. You can leave undressed fish on ice all day and clean them at the end of the day without sacrificing freshness or taste. Plan for this by obtaining ice before going fishing. For short-term storage, cube ice is better than block ice because you can cover fish fully with it, touching all parts. The best, however, is crushed, chipped, or shaved ice; unfortunately it's seldom conveniently available. Notice that a good fish market or supermarket always displays its fish and shellfish on crushed or chipped ice with good drainage. That's the best you can do.

When anglers talk about icing down fish, they often say they are putting fish "on ice." What is really best, though, is putting fish *in the ice*. To quickly cool the entire fish, including the core, use a cooler to surround the fish with ice cubes or crushed or flaked ice. If the fish have been eviscerated, store them in the ice with the belly facing down so that meltwater does not accumulate in the cavity.

Pounds of Ice Required to Chill and Store Fish at an Ambient Temperature of 80°F

Fish Weight (in lbs.)	Hours on Ice			
	6	12	18	24
10	4.1	8.3	9.5	10.7
20	6.8	12.9	14.8	16.6
30	9.3	17.1	19.6	22
40	11.8	21.1	24.1	27
50	14.2	25	28.4	31.9
60	16.7	28.8	32.7	36.5

Periodically drain the water from your cooler (or tub or fish box or whatever you hold the fish in) to eliminate standing water; dead fish are stored better on ice than in water, even if that water is ice cold. This is because the flesh becomes soft in water, and once softened it is very unappealing. Be especially careful to keep fillets out of water and keep the cooler top tightly closed when not in use; open and close it quickly just as you would a freezer door in warm weather.

If you have any doubts about the necessity or benefits of icing down fish, take a page from commercial fishermen. If their fish spoil, they don't make money. So commercially caught fish are processed immediately. They are usually dressed and placed on ice as soon as possible after they come onboard. In some cases, they are flash frozen.

If you're really fastidious about fish care, then you need to pay even closer attention to icing and to temperature control. Ideally, try to keep the internal temperature of fresh, unfrozen fish as close as possible to 32°F (the temperature of melting ice). The best way to do this is to pack fish in ice. Ice cools fish from the outside, and it can take considerable time for the center of a large fish to reach 32°. Make an effort to store fish on ice as soon as possible for complete and rapid cooling.

Placed in contact with the fish, the melting ice cools it, washes bacteria from its surface, and keeps it from drying out. Crushed or flaked ice is best because a greater amount of ice surface is contacting the fish and maximum cooling can occur. Large pieces of ice can also crush, tear, or bruise fish more easily than smaller pieces. Large pieces of ice, however, are better than no ice at all. If possible, break or crush large cubes or blocks before using them. Food technologists differ as to how much ice is necessary to maintain fish properly, but the general recommendation is 1 pound of ice to 3 pounds of fish for several hours. But it's better to have more ice than not enough. The preceding table, prepared by Michigan Sea Grant, makes a more generous recommendation, and puts the storage-on-ice question into perspective for longer periods.

Pack fish in ice made from clean, potable water if at all possible. Commercial ice and ice made at home work equally well. Use saltwater ice only if it is clean. The freezing point of saltwater is lower than 32°F. Although saltwater ice will cool fish faster, it can also stick to the skin and cause surface discoloration. Therefore, it's best to use saltwater ice in a slush or slurry. Chilled seawater, or slush, is a mixture of seawater and crushed or flaked ice. Making chilled seawater requires clean seawater, ice, and an insulated bucket, cooler, or tank. Partially fill the container with ice and add clean seawater. A mixture of 8 pounds of ice to 1 gallon of seawater makes a good slush. More ice may be needed on very warm days.

Wintertime—care on the ice. Speaking of freezing, how you care for fish caught on the ice in winter is a different story. Most anglers, because the air is cold and the lake frozen, simply drop their fish on the ice or snow and leave them there until it's time to go home. Naturally the fish freeze. If the fish are transported inside a heated vehicle, they warm up on the way home. Or they warm up later at home when it's time to clean them. If they are going to be consumed immediately or within a few days, this thawing may be fine, but it may not be fine if the fish (or fillets) are to be refrozen for longer-term storage. And in any event, the rapid change in temperature advances spoilage, so you would be wise to avoid premature thawing, especially since fish caught from cold winter waters have such firm and delicious meat. Although fish should not be frozen more than once, fish that have been frozen and then thawed and smoked can be frozen again.

The best way to keep fish caught on open ice is to make an ice-water tub in the area you're fishing. A little effort on your part is required. Chip out an area of ice that is large enough (maybe 2 by 3 feet) to hold a reasonable number of fish, poke a small hole in the bottom with a spud, and let the tub fill with water. Then put freshly caught fish in the tub, where they will remain alive until it's time to go home. Make sure the fish can't escape through the bottom—and they will if the ice is thin and you've made your initial hole too large and it has increased in size during the day. To avoid this problem, you can locate the tub near your fishing hole and chip a narrow channel from the fishing hole to the tub to import water. Or you could use a chain saw to nick a sliver at the bottom of the tub. The tub works well when the temperature is relatively mild, but when the temperature is less than 20° and/or the wind is blowing, the tub may freeze up.

An alternative is to bring a cooler with you, fill it with cold water, and put your fish in that, although the lack of aeration may cause the fish to expire after a while. You could always put your catch directly in the cooler with some shaved ice collected from around your fishing holes. If there is snow on the ice, you might be able to use that for insulation around a bucket, and place the fish in the bucket with a cover over the top.

Remember that the size of the fish affects whether it freezes or not. A 10-pound lake trout will not freeze as readily as a 10-inch perch; the former might be just fine if covered with snow. If you fish in a heated shanty, the fish may stay cold but not freeze if you keep them in a pail or bucket placed on the ice in a corner of the shanty. If you leave them on the ice, they will probably freeze. If the shanty is really toasty, make sure that the temperature of the fish does not rise significantly—unless the temperature is rising because you're putting the fish in the skillet, in which case the eating is as good as it ever gets.

Bleeding and Eviscerating

To ensure the quality of fresh fish, the commercial fishing industry bleeds and eviscerates (guts) many

---

In 1991, as a demonstration, U.S. National Long Distance Casting Champion "Big Lou" McEachern cast a 5 1/4-ounce weight 750 feet over the roof of the Houston Astrodome.

species. These practices enhance the appearance, shelf life, and overall quality of some commercially important fish. Although the beneficial effects of bleeding are still undocumented for many species, it is reasonable to assume that anglers can also use this technique to maximize the quality of the fish they catch. You will have to decide whether this practice makes a difference. Some anglers bleed their fish all the time, some never do, and some bleed only certain species (like bluefish and tuna).

Removing the blood from fish does, however, retard deterioration in several ways. It decreases the cooling time, since the fish loses heat from bleeding. It also gets rid of waste products and removes oxygen; rancidity, caused by the oxidation of fats in fish flesh, is an important consideration if fatty fish are to be stored for several months. Fish that have been bled also tend to have lighter colored fillets with fewer bruises, blood spots, and other defects.

Before bleeding a fish, you may want to stun it to make the fish easier to handle. If you do not kill it, more blood will flow out if the heart keeps pumping, although not killing it may run contrary to your views on humanely dispatching the fish, as noted earlier in this section.

To bleed a fish, make a tail and/or throat cut or eviscerate the fish. Make a tail cut about an inch from the caudal or tail fin, across the caudal peduncle. Slice across the tail until the knife touches bone. To ensure maximum bleeding in some species, such as dogfish, cut the tail completely off just behind the anal fins. However, the tail portion of the fillet may spoil faster when the entire tail is removed unless the fish is kept clean and iced down quickly. On some species, cutting the tail may not produce significant or quick bleeding, but it will serve to keep a lively fish from flapping, since the muscles and tendons connected to the tail will be severed.

The throat cut minimizes the risk of bacterial contamination to the edible part of the fish. Make a single cut, severing the main artery that runs from the gills to the heart. Do this by slicing through the flesh just behind the gill cover. Make sure the cut is ahead of the heart, which must be undamaged if it is to continue pumping blood. Eviscerating, or gutting, a live fish will cause significant bleeding through the internal organs and intestinal cavity. For large fish that have a lot of blood to circulate, it may be best to let the heart pump all the blood out and then shortly afterward eviscerate.

The fish should be bled for 10 to 20 minutes. Bleeding will be more effective if you immerse the fish in clean water or seawater after making the cut. The water you use should be as clean and as cold as possible. Use a bucket, cooler, or tub, and change the water in the bleeding container frequently. If containers are not available, hang the bleeding fish over the side of the boat in a mesh bag. If this method is not practical, the fish can be bled without a container. Pour water over it from time to time to remove the blood before it coagulates.

Eviscerate a fish as soon as possible after it has been bled or after you catch it. Keep the entrails intact if possible when eviscerating. The stomach and intestines contain enzymes and bacteria that can contaminate the edible part of the fish and accelerate spoilage, so try not to puncture them. Bile from the gall bladder will also taint any part of the fish it touches, and it is very difficult to wash away. Rinse the cavity to remove blood, slime, and bits of viscera, and rinse the exterior as well.

Keep your work area clean and avoid contaminating other fish with eviscerated matter. Wash your work area and knives after each eviscerating operation. Finally, do not allow your fish to become tainted by coming into contact with oily or dirty areas of a boat, workstation, or dock.

After Cleaning

Once you've cleaned the fish (see the following section), they must be stored properly, most likely in a refrigerator or freezer. If you're traveling and many days from reaching home, this storage may be a cooler. Obviously your catch will at times exceed what can be consumed in one sitting; then you will want to store the extra fish for later consumption, perhaps when the season is past. The length of time that you plan on storing the fish determines the type of storage.

Cold storage. How long fish will stay fresh in cold (unfrozen) storage once they've been cleaned will depend not only on storage temperature but on the fish and how you've treated them. Some delicate species, like stream and river trout, do not lend themselves to many days of cold storing, even under the best of conditions. Bluefish, with their strong flavor and oily texture, do not keep well for more than a day after cleaning. Lean fish, however, may keep well for several days. And some fish can be kept for up to a week if they are ultrachilled. It is possible to keep fish that are whole but eviscerated in good condition for up to five days if they are kept on crushed ice that is drained regularly and in

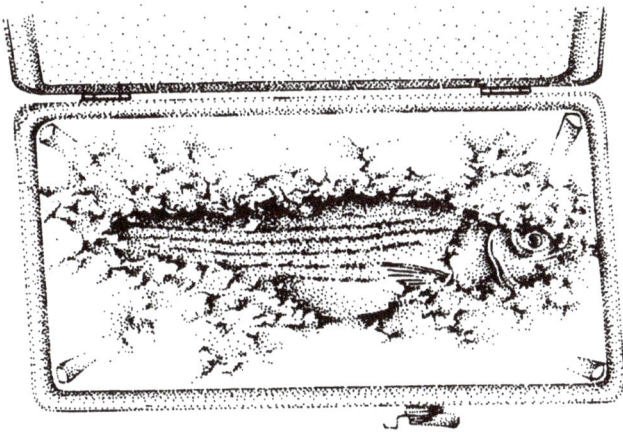

The best method of keeping fish in top condition is to put them on crushed ice in a cooler.

a container that is seldom opened.

Obviously the colder the storage temperature, the longer you can hold fish. Thirty-four degrees is better than 50°F. If fish are kept in an iced cooler for a long period, the ice should be checked every few hours, and the drain should be opened every time that the cooler is checked to release any liquid. Avoid opening the cooler any more often or longer than necessary; make sure that the lid fits snugly. You may have to tilt the cooler to drain it completely; if it is clogged, push something long and thin into the drain hole to unclog it.

If you have to hold fish for a long time, they can be ultrachilled by using a 20:1 mixture of crushed ice (chipped ice will work if you can't find crushed ice) and coarse salt. Spread half of the mixture on the bottom of the cooler. Place the fish, enveloped securely in a plastic wrap, on the mixture and then cover with the other half. This should bring the temperature down below 32°, making it cooler than a refrigerator but not as cold as a freezer.

If you plan to store dressed fish, steaks, or fillets in the refrigerator for several days, temperature control is critical. Because many home refrigerators operate at 40°F or higher, fish can spoil fairly rapidly. It's good to pack dressed fish on ice in the refrigerator. Seal fillets or steaks in plastic bags or containers and then cover them with ice in trays or pans. The vegetable bins in the lower part of the refrigerator make convenient containers. Empty the meltwater regularly and add more ice as necessary. Fillets take up less room in the refrigerator or freezer and cool more quickly. If the fillets will be used right away, prepare them as soon as possible. If, however, you plan to use fresh fillets several days later, and if you have room to refrigerate the whole fish, wait and cut the fillets just before they're needed.

For fish that will be consumed immediately, rinse thoroughly in cold water and pat dry with paper towels. Put a double layer of paper towel on the bottom of a plate or tray and place small fish, fillets, or chunks of fish on the towel and then cover tightly; plastic wrap is the first covering choice, aluminum foil second. Make sure the wrapping is tight and holds. Uncovered fish can dehydrate quickly and lose flavor even if you're going to cook them in a few hours. For large pieces of fish or whole fish, rinse and pat dry, wrap tightly in plastic wrap, and wrap tightly in freezer paper. Take the fish out of the wrapping only when you are ready to prepare it for consumption; don't leave it lying out on the kitchen counter for a long period of time.

Frozen storage. Before detailing the methods of home-freezing of fish, it is worth reiterating that if fish have been poorly handled before freezing, it will not be possible through freezing to get good results. Freezing only protects the quality of the fish at the time it was frozen. Airtight packaging and proper temperatures are critical to achieving this protection, however, and it is important to understand what happens when you freeze fish.

Although freezing prevents the growth of microorganisms, it only slows down the enzymatic and chemical reactions that cause flavor, color, and texture deterioration. As the temperature is lowered, these reactions occur more slowly; thus, frozen foods, including fish, should be stored at the lowest possible temperatures, and preferably in the coldest part of a freezer. Rapid freezing at the outset is very important for good long-term storage. Home freezers are primarily designed for storage, not for rapid freezing. A home freezer can properly freeze 1 to 2 pounds per cubic foot in 24 hours.

Don't overload the freezer. Fish will freeze faster if uncrowded, so don't bunch together pieces or whole fish or pans of fish when you first place them in the freezer. For the fastest freeze, place packages in direct contact with the freezer floor or walls until they are frozen. If the packages take more than 5 to 6 hours to freeze, they are too large. Store packages at a temperature of 0°F or colder, where the temperature doesn't fluctuate. The farther away from the freezer door, the more stable the temperature.

Properly packaged fish can be kept for a long time, although how long varies with the type of fish and with the method of freezing. Frozen fish

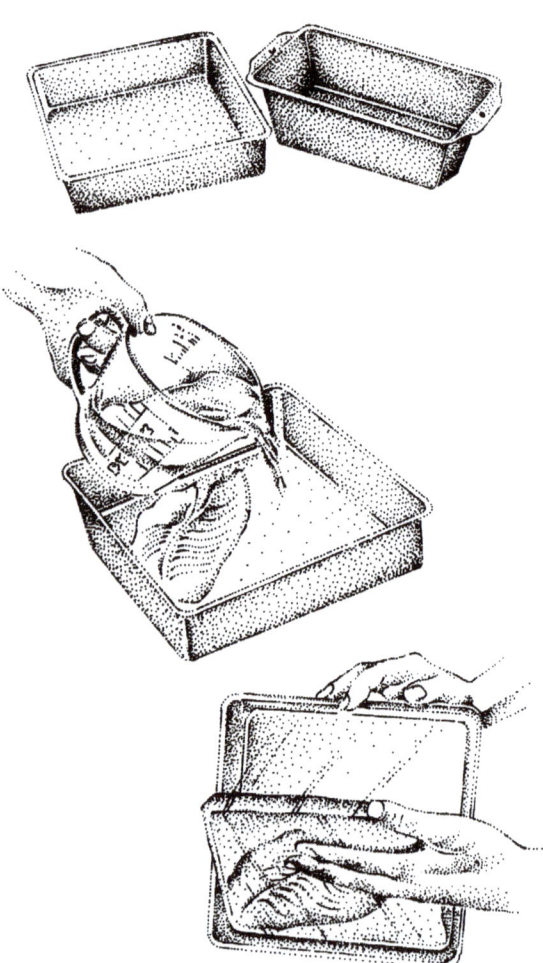

Place small fish and fillets in a pan, and cover them with water; after freezing, remove the block.

can generally be kept for up to one year, but this is merely a guideline for shelf life in a freezer rather than an indication of whether the fish will still be appetizing after such a long period. It is probably a very generous advisement, except for frozen smoked fish, which can last more than a year, and even longer if vacuum-sealed. If your freezer allows for really low temperature, you may be able to freeze fish longer than someone whose freezer temperature is barely below 32°F. Thus, if you have a separate freezer, it is better to store fish in that than in the freezer compartment of your refrigerator, which is subject to frequent opening and closing.

Large fish typically last a little longer than small fish, and whole fish last a little longer than steaks or fillets because they retain more moisture. Oily fish are best thawed and consumed within one to two months after initial freezing, and lean fish in three to six months. These are general guidelines, however; you can keep some fish, especially lean species, for longer periods, especially if frozen in blocks of ice. Taste varies among individuals, but seafood technologists advise that the best flavor in frozen fish is enjoyed in the first two months.

Regardless of these time frames, it's wise to eat fish as soon as possible. By labeling and dating packages, you can consume stored fish on a rotational calendar basis, using the older fish first.

Many of the undesirable flavor and color changes in fish are caused by oxidation of the unsaturated fats, oils, and color pigments in fish. This is a chemical reaction that cannot be stopped once started. Oily fish, like salmon and bluefish, are highly susceptible to oxidation. However, airtight packaging, especially if it is accomplished on a freshly caught fish, can help prevent oxidation, more so for some fish than for others.

Another benefit of airtight packaging is the prevention of water evaporation from the flesh of fish during freezing. When water evaporates from food, it causes the food to become dry and tough; this effect is called freezer burn. Freezer burn promotes oxidation and is always accompanied by substandard flavor, color, and odor. By packaging and freezing properly, you can entirely eliminate freezer burn.

If space is at a premium in your freezer and/or you'll be eating newly caught fish very soon, then you can simply double- or even triple-wrap small fish, steaks, and fillets using plastic wrap, aluminum foil, and/or freezer paper. Plastic or cling wrap should be used first for prewrapping, and it should be tight to the flesh of the fish; two wraps may be a good idea, folding and pressing the wraps against the skin to remove air. Over this, you can use an outer wrap to help protect the fish in the freezer. The delicatessen wrap, in which the ends of foil or freezer paper are brought over the fish to meet one another and then are folded together several times, ensures a reasonably good final seal over the initial plastic wrapping. This method is suitable only for short-term freezing, however, since it is very difficult without Cryovac sealing to eliminate all air. As best as possible, eliminate air pockets, which contain oxygen and space for moisture to be withdrawn from the flesh. Do not use plastic bags, and use freezer wrap only as an outer protective wrap over an inner wrap.

A larger fish that is drawn or dressed is more difficult to wrap and to protect from oxidation. It should be dipped in water, placed temporarily in an unsealed plastic bag, and frozen as is. Once frozen, take the fish out of the bag and dip it in cold water, then put it back in the bag and return it to the freezer. You might repeat this a few times to form a thick glaze over the entire fish, and check it every few weeks to reglaze.

For longer freezing, and for best overall results, freeze fish in a block of ice; the ice seals out air and preserves the quality of the product.

This method is especially recommended for fillets and for small, whole dressed fish. Trays, pans, cut-down beverage cartons or gallon jugs, plastic food storage containers, and similar items all make good storage containers for frozen fish as long as the containers are washed thoroughly and

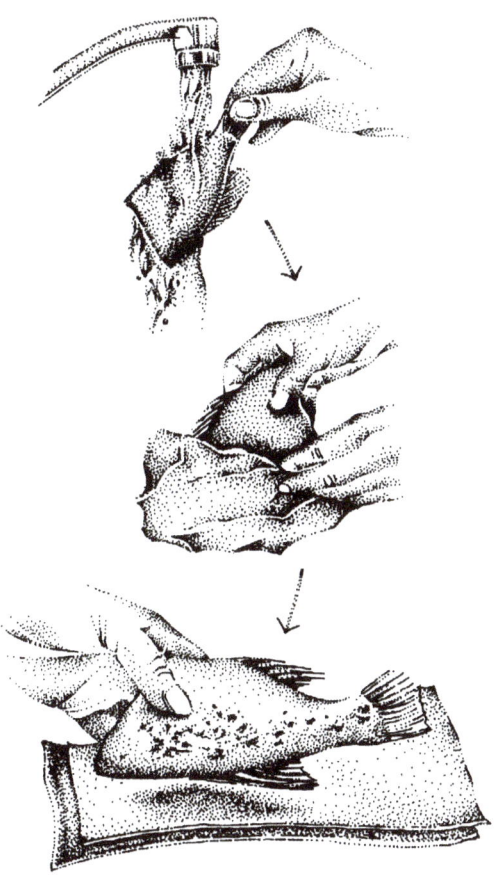

One way to freeze fish is to dip them in water (top), place them in a plastic bag (middle), and then put them in the freezer, where they will freeze with a glaze coating. Dip and reglaze a few times before covering in freezer wrap or foil (bottom).

are deep enough to hold the fish and a covering of water. Make sure that the containers bear no odor from previous usage, and fill them with ice water, leaving room at the top for expansion. Be wary of using chlorinated tap water, although you can use good-quality untreated well water from the faucet or bottled spring water.

After the fish have frozen, remove the block from the container; wrap it with aluminum foil or freezer paper; label the contents for species, portion, and date of storage; and then put the block back in the freezer. If you leave the frozen fish in the container, it may be good to add a little more water on the top of the block.

Smaller fish can also be glazed before wrapping for longer storage. Glazing builds up a thin layer of ice around the fish. To glaze, freeze the fish in a plastic bag. After it is frozen, remove it from the bag, dip it in ice water, return it to the bag, and place the bag back in the freezer. Repeat several times; the glaze can be as thick as a quarter of an inch. The plastic bag protects the glaze from evaporation and prevents wet pieces from freezing together or from freezing onto the shelf or other objects. An ice glaze will evaporate in the freezer, so you may need to renew it in a month. Cover the glazed fish tightly with plastic wrap and then foil.

Be sure to pack fish in large enough quantities for a single meal, whether for yourself or your family and friends; if you place freezer wrapping paper between the frozen fish or fillets, they will be easier to separate and thaw. Fish that are frozen separately will defrost more quickly than fish frozen together. Also, label each package by writing on the outside with an indelible marker, crayon, or grease marker (or put a piece of masking tape on the package and label that). Label the package with the date, type of fish, and number of servings or pieces. You can also keep a log that lists the contents of the freezer and possibly the section of the freezer where particular packages are stored. The purpose of the log is to help you locate packages quickly, so that the rest of the freezer contents don't warm up.

Thawing. How you thaw fish is important to their quality as table fare. The poorest choice is using hot water; never thaw fish in warm or hot water. Also poor is thawing the fish at room temperature, which hastens surface spoilage. The best option is to thaw fish gradually over an extended period. Japanese sushi chefs—known for their delicate, fresh, and finely prepared fish—use a controlled method of raising the temperature gradually over an extended period to thaw the fish and retain maximum taste and texture. This method is seldom possible in the home, but if you plan a day or two ahead of time, you can thaw a meal of frozen fish somewhat gradually in the refrigerator. A 24-hour period should be enough for smaller fish, pieces, and fillets that are separated; large fish can take longer.

Most people do not plan this far ahead and like to speed up the process. Some accelerate the thawing process via a microwave oven; microwaves have excellent thawing capability for most foods but require careful attention where fish are concerned. Whole fish, or pieces of fish, do not have uniform thickness, so a thinner section will defrost faster and may actually cook a little when thawed quickly in a microwave. If this happens, which it can easily, you would defeat all of your previous efforts to ensure a good-tasting fish.

Frozen fish or pieces that are not in a block of ice can be placed in a sealed (watertight) plastic food storage bag and then placed in a bowl of cold water to accelerate thawing. Fish stored in a block of ice can be defrosted fairly quickly if necessary by holding the block under cold running water or by immersing the block in a bowl of cold water until the block melts enough to separate the fish. Then pat the fish dry with paper towels, line a plate with fresh paper towels, cover the plate with plastic wrap, and put it in the refrigerator. In both methods, try to keep the fish out of stale melted water while defrosting, don't let it contact warm or hot water, and finish the thawing while the fish is covered in the refrigerator.

When thawing vacuum-sealed fish, open them immediately after thawing to allow air to enter the package. To help avoid botulism, never leave smoked or kippered fish in a tightly wrapped or vacuum package after it has thawed.

Storing for Transportation

Sometimes you must transport fish a considerable distance or for a long period of time before you can permanently store them. Examples of this situation would be while driving, boating, or flying back from a distant location. Refer to the earlier discussion of cold storage methods for information on keeping fish in good condition during transportation. Ultra- or superchilling, as described, is one method. Get a large supply of crushed ice, or if that is not available, get cubed ice; you will need a lot of ice, especially if the weather is warm. If dry ice is available, and your

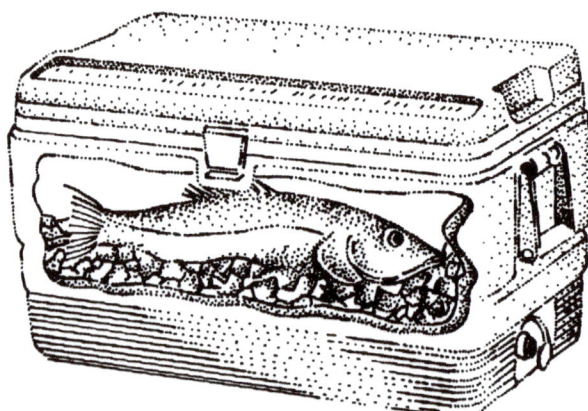

For long-term transportation, place fish on crushed ice in a cooler and open the vent to let water escape, so that the fish doesn't lie in the water. Add more ice as necessary.

cooler is large enough, place the dry ice in the cooler surrounded by crushed or cubed ice. If you can't get dry ice but can get regular ice in block form, put the block ice in a cooler surrounded by crushed or cubed ice with the fish mixed in.

Don't let the fish lie in melted water, which usually has blood and bacteria in it. Keep the drain open if weather and conditions permit, or periodically open the drain and let out accumulated water. This is not possible in a cooler transported by air carrier, since the cooler is out of your control for a long time; so proper packing is essential. If the cooler is transported in a vehicle, position the cooler so that it is accessible and can be drained. If the fish cooler is buried amid luggage and gear, you won't want to make the effort to get to it and drain it.

If you're transporting fish by air, as checked luggage, be advised that some carriers may not allow the shipment of a container with dry ice or may require notification that it contains dry ice. A noncrushable heavy-duty cooler is the best container for shipping; the lid should be completely secured with duct tape. Write the word perishable on the tape in several spots; a kindly baggage handler might put it in the shade if it has to sit on the tarmac, or might give it other considerations that will help.

At some remote camps and lodges, your fish can be frozen and then packed and shipped. The fish are usually shipped in a well-packed cardboard box. Unfortunately, the cardboard box isn't as good as a cooler. If the shipped fish is delayed in transit, the frozen contents could begin thawing and you may have to prepare and consume the fish at once upon reaching your final destination. In a worst-case scenario, the fish could be lost altogether, or misrouted for several days, and thus spoiled. If the fish haven't been frozen but have been packed in ice well, then a delayed trip may not adversely affect them as long as the ice holds up. If the ice does not hold up, the fish may spoil. How far you have to travel, whether an overnight stay is involved, and how much faith you have in the air carrier are factors in deciding whether or not to freeze.

If you are a traveling angler, especially one visiting the far north, you may have an overnight stay between leaving the fishing site and flying home. If this is the case, you'll need to make storage arrangements. If the outfitter or expediter doesn't make arrangements for you (they usually do), you'll have to fend for yourself. The situation may be difficult if you arrive late and leave early and haven't planned for this in advance. Many people no longer bring back fish from distant locations because of the hassle, the extra baggage charge, the possibility of spoilage, and the preference for catch-and-release, so storage arrangements may not be a concern. Also, some fishing places do not permit anglers to take fish home; thus storage is not even a consideration.

When you do transport fish, you must follow appropriate laws. The laws may require you to leave on the skin, or a patch of skin, for identification purposes; or to keep the fish whole after evisceration (to determine legal size); or to apply a tag to it until it reaches its permanent storage; or to identify the contents on the outside; or to follow some other procedures established by state and provincial authorities. Do not assume that following the laws of your home state or province will suffice when transporting fish from other places. And remember that it is your responsibility to find out what the law is.
See: Regulations.

FISH PREPARATION—CLEANING/DRESSING

Preparing a fish for the table or for storage is usually referred to as cleaning or dressing. It is not a difficult chore. Those with plenty of experience can do it quickly and in difficult circumstances. The native guides of northern Canada fillet big fish on the blade of a paddle before starting a shore lunch. Experienced anglers have been known to clean fish atop rocks and boulders when no suitable place was available. Some anglers are adept at cleaning small fish right in their hands. But cleaning can be a difficult chore for those who don't know what to do or who find the job distasteful.

Once the fish is killed, it becomes a food product. It can eventually be as appetizing and aesthetically pleasing as any well-wrapped, sanitized, store-bought food item if you treat it right.

For many people, even those who love to eat fish, the job of cleaning them is a distasteful or repulsive one because of the sight, smell, and feel of the dead fish and its body parts. This problem can be overcome if you have fresh air, running water, and a clean workstation to minimize exposure to the objectionable elements. If you like to eat fish, then keep in mind that cleaning them is the price you pay for having good table fare; so you might as well learn to clean the fish properly and safely, plus as enjoyably as possible. Think about how good the fish are going to taste later on.

A dislike for the cleaning process, or pure ineptitude, can result in unattractive table fare or, worse, the wastage of potentially fine food. If you can't learn to clean fish properly, then you probably shouldn't keep them in the first place, or you better find someone who can do it for you. Learning to clean fish simply takes a knowledge of what to do (either by watching someone else or following written instructions), the right tools, and a willingness to practice and be patient. Patience is necessary because cleaning fish can be exasperating when you're learning, and it helps to go slowly, despite the fact that the natural inclination is to hurry up and get it over with.

First Steps
Knives. If you've tried to clean fish and found it difficult, you're probably using the wrong knife or a dull knife or you're unfamiliar with using a

> From the muddled names file: Don't confuse the California sheephead, a member of the wrasse family, with the sheepshead, which is a member of the porgy family and also a common term for freshwater drum.

Fish Preparation—Cleaning/Dressing

Guides prepare salmon at a fish-cleaning station, where there is proper disposal of entrails.

knife *(see)*. Not everyone is adept at using a knife for things other than buttering bread and cutting a morsel of steak. That's why some people don't have a clue about carving a roasted bird. Such simple things as how you hold the knife, whether you cut in one direction instead of another, and when to use finesse instead of force, are aspects of knife wielding that you become familiar with only after you've used a knife often and for different tasks. So if you're a stranger to knives, your first fish-cleaning efforts are likely to be disappointing.

A dull knife defeats nearly all fish-cleaning efforts, whereas a sharp knife helps you do a professional job. A sharp knife keeps you from hacking away at a fish and losing meat or making it unattractive. Some people think you can have a fish-cleaning knife that's too sharp, but this is untrue. Although extremely sharp knives can cause people to make mistakes, the real problem is that they are not using the knife properly or are rushing. If you're cleaning a lot of fish, or filleting big fish with many large bones, you may have to stop during the process and resharpen the blade.

Despite the fact that someone who is experienced at fish cleaning can make do in a pinch with almost any blade if it's sharp, the perfect knife for all fish-cleaning tasks does not exist. A thin 6-inch blade is universally popular, especially for filleting most freshwater fish. A longer blade, in the 9-inch range, is necessary for larger fish, particularly many saltwater species. A small knife with a 3- to 4-inch blade is fine for dressing most small panfish and trout. You do not have to spend a fortune on knives for cleaning fish, but you should have the right one for the job.

Although a 6-inch blade does work when you're eviscerating (gutting) small fish, you don't have enough control over it unless you're especially careful; you have more control over a shorter blade. With the shorter blade, you are less likely to poke the blade too deeply into the stomach or to cut through the belly too far. A pocket knife with a narrow and pointed blade is adequate for the simple act of field dressing; it's portable and easily accessible.

For filleting fish, you need a blade that is slightly flexible and thin and that tapers to a sharp point at the tip. Many good filleting models sweep up slightly at the tip as well. The length is a function of the size of the fish. A filleting knife is slightly different than the knives found in most kitchens. The blade should be long enough to cut both the belly and the back with the same stroke; if the blade is just a bit short for that, you can cut the belly first and then the back and rib cage section before sweeping through the tail area (see the discussion of filleting, later in this section). On larger fish it may be more difficult to cut through the tough rib cage with a light knife, although if you fillet without slicing the rib cage, such a knife will be fine.

Additionally, a broad heavy-duty blade may be needed for steaking fish, since you're cutting through the backbone. You can easily dull a regular fillet knife by trying to saw through a thick backbone unless you get lucky and happen to find the spot between vertebrae. A large inflexible knife with a less tapered point, or a cleaver if you have one, makes a neat instant steak.

If you have a regular fish-cleaning station, keep your cleaning tools and a knife sharpener handy. If you clean in different places, bring your tools along so you can do the job right. A knife sharpener *(see)*, whether it's whetstone, steel, or ceramic, is a necessity for putting an edge back on your knife. The more fish you do at one sitting and the tougher their skin, bones, and scales, the quicker the knife seems to lose an edge. A knife that is hard to sharpen quickly will be a hindrance when you're filleting more than one or two fish. Blades made of soft steel will sharpen quickly, although they may lose their edge a little faster than hard steel knives. A thin knife with a tapered rather than a beveled edge will cut best, so try to hold the blade at a low angle when you sharpen it.

Electric knives are popular with some anglers, especially older ones whose grasp and dexterity isn't as firm as it used to be. These knives are particularly useful when filleting or cleaning a lot of fish, and many public fish-cleaning stations provide electrical outlets for them.

Location. There's little doubt that the best time to clean a fish is as soon as possible after catching it, or before leaving the water to head for home, especially if it will be a while before you get the

Fish Preparation—Cleaning/Dressing

A striped bass is cleaned at dockside, where remains discarded in the water become food for crabs.

catch to your final destination for cleaning *(see: fish preparation—care)*. If you're going to clean the fish on the water or on the shore, make sure that it's legal to do so and find out the extent to which it is legal (for example, you may be able to eviscerate the fish but not fillet it, or you may have to leave the skin intact).

On saltwater, you can generally clean fish on your boat, perhaps while headed back to port of it's not a rough ride, or just before you finish fishing for the day. Many large boaters improvise a removable wooden work board for fish cleaning, perhaps one that fits over the gunwale or sits in a rod holder. Such a board should have back and side stops to keep fish from sliding off, and should be large enough for the usual size of fish. Cleanup on the boat is easy, provided you have a washdown hose or at least a bucket and scrub brush. The offal gets flipped overboard and winds up feeding gulls, crabs, eels, and other scavengers.

Many marinas, launching sites, camps, and other public places have fish-cleaning stations or houses (in warm areas a screened site helps keep the bees and flies away). Some have waist-high aluminum tables with backstops for the cleaning chores; these are good for cleanup and don't absorb refuse, but they can be very slippery and tough on knife blades. Others have a wooden table, which is less slippery and easier on knives but not as clean for the less fastidious angler. If you have and can put a clean board down on an aluminum fish-cleaning table, you should be in good shape.

A board, incidentally, is useful for cleaning all fish anywhere, and you can often improvise. Some anglers like to use a commercially made board with a large spring clip at the head; the clip holds the head or tail of the fish in place. Some anglers use a board with a large nail driven into it at an angle. The head of a fish (via the gill and mouth) is placed over the nail to keep the fish in place while working on the body.

Most public facilities have a water supply at the fish-cleaning station for rinsing fish and also have electrical outlets. Some have a central pit for disposal of offal, and others grind the remains for appropriate disposal (disposal is a big benefit because it's one less thing you have to do at home). If you can use these facilities, you should do so; after cleaning your fish at a public facility, be sure to store them properly and keep them iced before heading home.

If a public fish-cleaning facility isn't available to you, it's best to do the cleaning outside, especially if you'll be scraping the scales off the fish. Dry scales may fly all over the place, and they can be a nuisance indoors, not to mention an obstruction in the kitchen drain. If you have to scale fish inside, then wet the fish thoroughly to moisten the scales and remove them under running cold water. This will minimize scale dispersion, but it will clog the sink strainer (which you did remember to put in the sink, right?).

When cleaning outside, make sure you cover the surface of the work area; cleanup will be a lot easier. You can put a clean board over the location, covering it with multiple sheets of newspaper; the paper is also good for small fish that are cleaned indoors on a countertop. Newspaper grabs the fish well and helps hold it in place, as well as soaks up moisture. When you're working on newspapers, periodically bundle up the soiled paper and fish remains and put them in the garbage. This gives you a clean surface to work on and avoids a large pile of repulsive refuse at the end. Keep the cleaned fish off the newspaper to avoid picking up ink or sticking to the paper.

If you have no source of running water, fill a deep bowl or clean bucket with ice cold water for rinsing the fish. Two such bowls are better, because one can be used for rinsing and the other for a final clean-water bath. In the ideal scenario, you have a helper who rinses the fish thoroughly after you clean them and then places them on paper towels. If you are working solo, you can put the fish aside after you clean them and rinse them afterward, but waste matter, especially blood, will harden and be much more difficult to rinse off even a short time later, especially if it's on the flesh instead of the skin. If you're doing all this fun work alone, you have two choices: You can stop and rinse each fish after you've cleaned it, which many people don't want to do because their hands are constantly getting dirty and then wet, or you can place the fish in a bowl of water (ice cold is best) and rinse them all

Fish Preparation—Cleaning/Dressing

at once after you're finished. Putting chunks of fish and fillets in water for long periods is not desirable, especially if the water is not super cold.

A final reminder: Wherever people congregate for fish cleaning, flies and bees seem to follow. If young children are around, watch out for bees that may have congregated in the garbage container where fish carcasses are disposed.

Methods

How you clean a fish depends on the size of the fish and what will be done with the end product. Small fish, for example, are seldom stuffed and baked but are often pan-fried. Very large fish are hard to cook evenly throughout, so steaking them, or the thickest parts of the body, is a good idea. Scaled fish that will be presented whole need to be eviscerated and the scales removed. Fish that will be filleted do not need to be eviscerated, and so on. In broadest terms, the complexity of cleaning is determined by the degree to which skin, bones, and scales must be removed. Novices attempting their first cleaning job may find it helpful to review the anatomy *(see)* of a fish, especially to become familiar with the basic skeleton. Knowing the layout of the skeleton is helpful when you are cutting through and removing bones, many of which are small and pliable; it also acquaints you with the names and location of fins.

Since fish cleaning involves the use of sharp knives, you obviously should be very careful when handling knives, especially when you're cleaning fish in cold weather and when your hands are cold. Gloves made of a high-tech material that resists knife piercing and slicing are available; they also give you a good grip on the fish and protect your hands from spiny fins, sharp gill covers or gill edges, and teeth. If you will be doing a lot of fish cleaning, you should consider using a pair. Holding fish properly and working at a moderate and careful pace will prevent a sore mishap. Finally, be careful if others are helping you clean the fish; they should not reach into the work area when the fish cleaner is cutting.

Field Dressing. The cleaning of small fish, such as stream trout and panfish, is referred to as field dressing. In field dressing, freshly caught fish are killed soon after their capture, eviscerated, and the bodies spread in well-ventilated wicker creels lined with grass to facilitate cooling. Field dressing requires the removal of the entrails, gills, and kidney. It is sometimes also referred to as gutting, although gutting usually refers to larger fish and basically implies the removal of just the intestines.

Field dressing small trout and salmon, head intact. Small trout and salmon are the simplest fish to field dress. They don't have to be scaled, and, once eviscerated and cleaned, they are ready for cooking. After you have learned to field dress a fish and have practiced a few times, field dressing takes only 30 seconds.

To field dress a small trout or salmon, begin behind the lower jaw by sticking the tip of your knife through the tissue that connects the lower

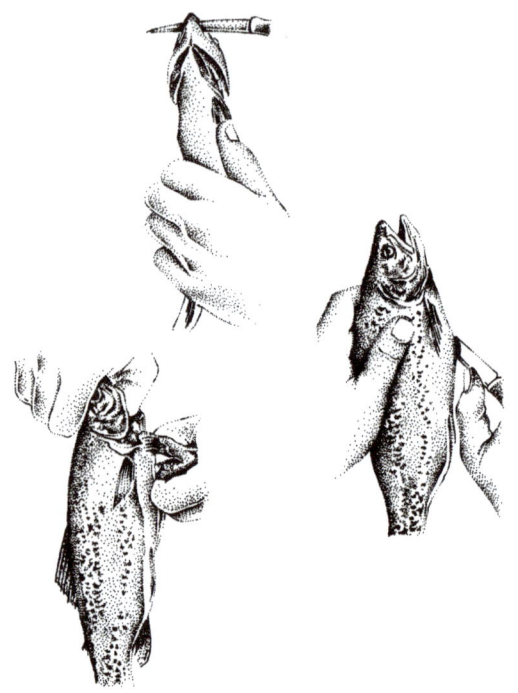

To eviscerate a small whole trout with head intact: slice the lower jaw away from the gill membrane (top); insert the knife blade into the anal vent and slice up to the gills without puncturing the intestine (middle); then place your thumb into the throat and pull down to remove the gills and entrails (bottom). Clean the body cavity thoroughly. This process can be done in the field with a small sharp knife.

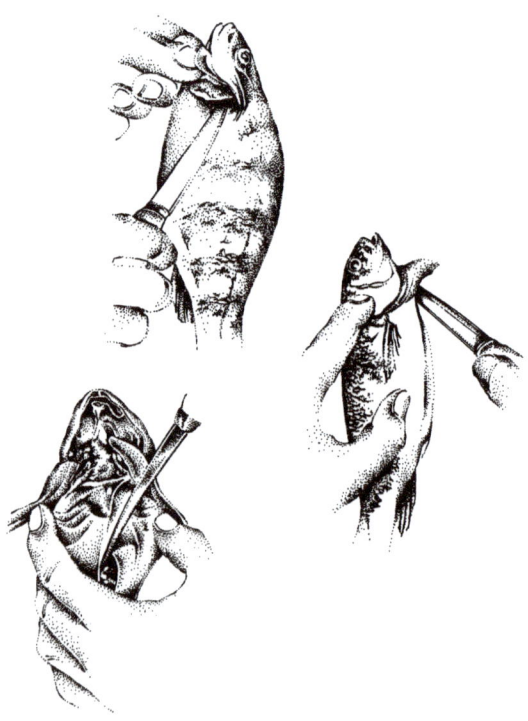

To eviscerate a small whole perch with head intact: slice the gills from the throat (top); insert the knife blade into the anal vent and, without puncturing the intestines, slice up to the gills (middle); remove gills and entrails, and scrape out the bloodline (bottom). Clean the body cavity thoroughly.

Fish Preparation—Cleaning/Dressing

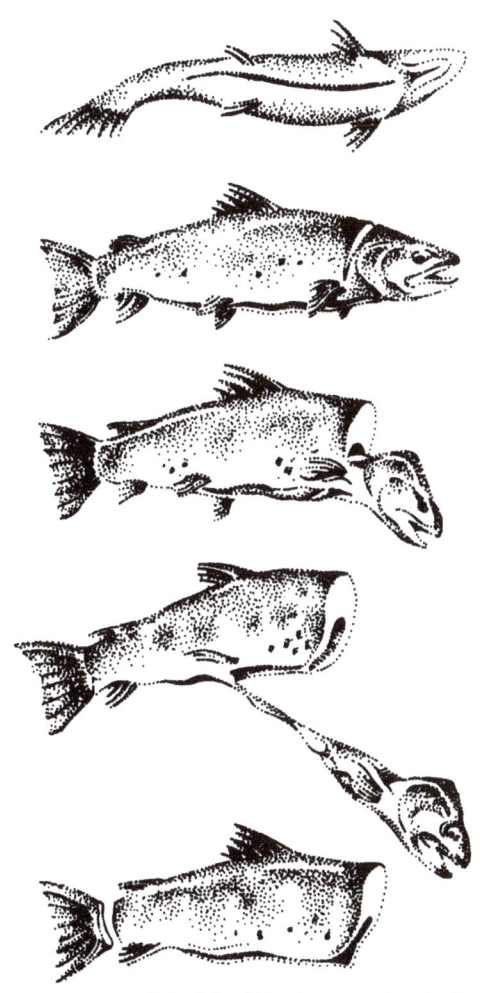

To eviscerate a whole fish while also removing the head: insert the knife blade into the anal vent and, without puncturing the intestines, slice up past the pelvic fins to a spot between the gill covers; cut downward behind the head and through the backbone; pull the head away from the body to remove both the head and the entrails. Clean the body cavity thoroughly. Cutting off the tail is optional.

jaw to the gills and slitting this tablike section free. This is actually the tongue that is being freed. Then insert the point of the knife into the vent (the anal opening); slit through the skin and up the center of the fish's belly in a straight line to the gills, stopping before you get to the V-shaped spot behind the jaw.

Try not to puncture the intestines as you make the slit. Put the knife down and hold the fish by the head with one hand. With the other hand, grab the tongue and pull down on it toward the tail; this will free the gills and the entrails. Remove the kidney, which is the bloodline along the backbone, with your fingers or a knife or spoon; then rinse the cavity with cold water and dry it with a paper towel or napkin.

Field dressing small trout and salmon, head removed. This procedure is one to follow when you don't want to leave the head on the fish (and are not restricted by laws). The process begins by inserting the point of the knife into the vent (the anal opening) and then slitting through the skin and up the center of the fish's belly in a straight line to the gills, stopping before you get to the V-shaped spot behind the jaw. Try not to puncture the intestines as you make the slit. Place the fish belly down and make a cut behind the head down through the backbone until it is severed, stopping after severing it and without cutting the head entirely free. Put the knife down, hold the body in one hand, and with the other hand grasp the head and pull it away from the body. This will remove the entrails and the head. Cut off the tail if you wish; then remove the kidney by the backbone, rinse, and pat dry.

Field dressing other fish. Most small to medium fish can be field dressed by following the previous directions, with some minor changes. Species like bluegills or perch, for example, must be scaled first. Do not field dress and then attempt to scale the fish. Also, be aware that the belly skin of some fish is tougher than others and requires more careful slitting. The belly skin of a trout is soft and easy to cut with a sharp knife; the belly skin of a yellow perch is tougher. Field dressing some fish (including perch) requires the additional step of cutting away the gill connections in order to remove the entrails and gills in one motion. To do this, pull up on the gill covering and slice under the gill to free it from the body; do this for each gill; then slit the tongue and the belly, and remove everything in one pull.

Of course, for any fish you can simply cut off the head, slit the belly from the anal opening on up, and then grab the entrails and remove them. The disad-

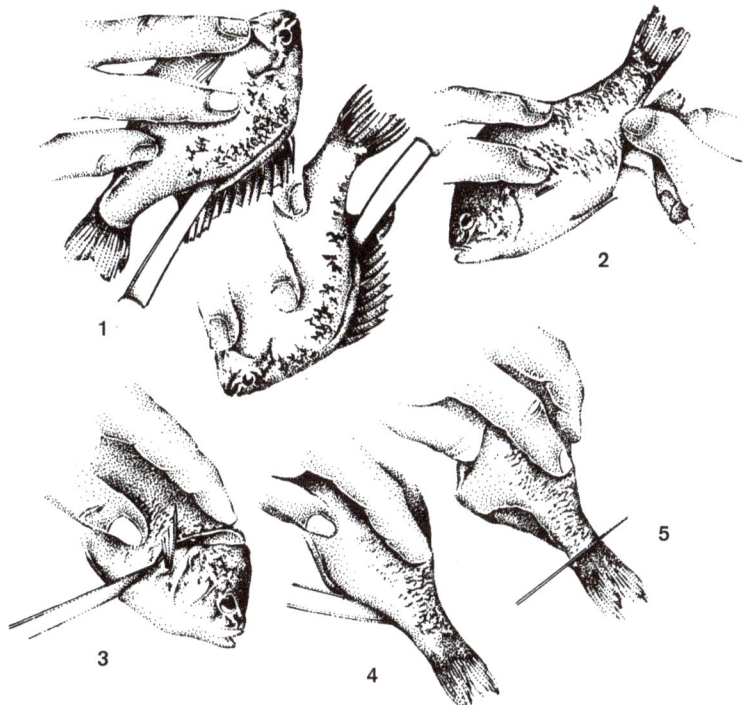

To pan dress a small whole panfish with skin and ribs intact: cut the top of the fish along both sides of the dorsal fin (1) and remove the fin; cut along both sides of the anal fin and remove it (2); cut off the head at an acute angle (3) and remove it; slice along the belly to the anal vent (4); as an option, cut off the tail (5). Clean the body cavity thoroughly.

Fish Preparation—Cleaning/Dressing

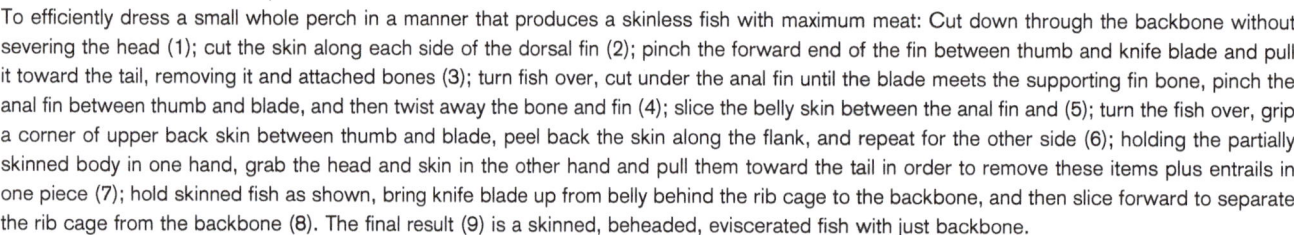

To efficiently dress a small whole perch in a manner that produces a skinless fish with maximum meat: Cut down through the backbone without severing the head (1); cut the skin along each side of the dorsal fin (2); pinch the forward end of the fin between thumb and knife blade and pull it toward the tail, removing it and attached bones (3); turn fish over, cut under the anal fin until the blade meets the supporting fin bone, pinch the anal fin between thumb and blade, and then twist away the bone and fin (4); slice the belly skin between the anal fin and (5); turn the fish over, grip a corner of upper back skin between thumb and blade, peel back the skin along the flank, and repeat for the other side (6); holding the partially skinned body in one hand, grab the head and skin in the other hand and pull them toward the tail in order to remove these items plus entrails in one piece (7); hold skinned fish as shown, bring knife blade up from belly behind the rib cage to the backbone, and then slice forward to separate the rib cage from the backbone (8). The final result (9) is a skinned, beheaded, eviscerated fish with just backbone.

vantages of this method are that it is usually messier than the other methods, requires more scraping and pulling to remove the contents of the cavity, and some of the innards contact the flesh (an action you should try to avoid). After cleaning a fish this way, make sure you rinse it immediately and thoroughly.

Pan Dressing. Small fish that are unsuitable for filleting or that are to be cooked whole by various methods can be prepared in a manner called pan dressing. The standard and most common method leaves the skin and ribs intact, but a more involved method allows for their removal. Both methods remove the head, entrails, and fin bones. Small fish should be pan dressed with a narrow knife having a short blade and a pointed edge, as opposed to a standard fillet knife having a longer, flexible blade.

Pan dressing, skin and ribs intact. Start by laying a scaled fish on one side and slicing along the dorsal fin on both sides. Then pull out the fin. Do the same thing for the anal fin. Do not cut these fins flat because you'll leave bones in the meat.

Cut off the head as close to the gill cover as possible, angling the knife over the top of the head to maximize the amount of meat. Slit the belly and remove the entrails; cut off the tail if desired and then rinse quickly in ice-cold water and pat dry.

Pan dressing, skin and ribs removed. Start by laying a fish with scales intact belly down on a cutting board. Make a cut over the top of the head and close to the gills, and continue cutting down through the backbone without completely severing the head. Slice the skin along each side of the dorsal fin from the head to the tail, making the slice as shallow as possible. Grasp the dorsal fin between your thumb and the fat part of the knife blade and pull it free; this will remove the dorsal fin bones. Turn the fish around and slice along both sides of the anal fin; pull the fin free to remove the anal fin bones. Now make a shallow slice from where the anal fin was to the tail. Turn the fish over again, and position the knife blade under the upper fold of skin near the back; pinching that fold between the knife blade and your thumb, peel the skin halfway down the body. Repeat on the opposite side. Then grab the

Fish Preparation—Cleaning/Dressing

partially skinned carcass in your left hand and the head and skin in your right hand, and pull both apart; this will liberate the head, skin, and entrails in one piece. Finally, hold the skinned carcass belly up, and slice off the rib cage by cutting from behind the first rib down to and then along the backbone. Rinse quickly in ice cold water and pat dry.

This method produces a fish with only the backbone, which easily parts from the meat after cooking. It also saves more meat than filleting.

Scaling. Removing the scales on a fish is referred to as scaling. You do not need to remove the scales on a fish if it will be filleted with the skin removed or if it is from a species that has no scales (bullhead) or has extremely small scales (small trout). Species that have large, loose scales and that will not be skinned should be scaled before field dressing. If you do not do this, and even if you have no intention of eating the skin, loose scales will almost certainly find their way into the food, which is unpleasant and shows carelessness.

Scaling can be performed on fish that have been eviscerated, but this is more difficult and could lead to tearing of the meat and an incomplete job. Scaling, therefore, is best accomplished on a whole fish, in the round, that can be scraped and pulled freely while still intact.

Scale removal can be accomplished with various devices. A knife blade is commonly used and is effective, provided you're careful and can handle the knife skillfully enough to avoid slicing into the

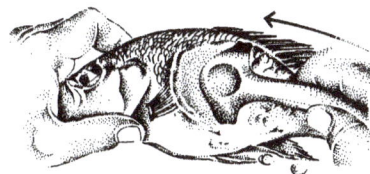

When scaling, run tool from tail toward head.

skin. Using a knife for scaling will dull the blade, however. Many anglers like to use scaling tools, usually called scalers, which have serrated edges; others prefer a thin-metal spoon for scaling small surface areas. The spoon can also be handy for scraping the bloodline out of the cavity.

Always scale against the grain, moving from the tail of the fish toward the head. Working against the grain can be a messy process, sending scales everywhere, but you can minimize the mess by wetting the surface of the fish before scaling, or scaling under the running water of a faucet. If you have a hose with a high-pressure nozzle and you're working outside on fish that have been kept wet, you can scale them quickly by holding them about 6 inches from the high-pressure water stream; it's effective, but it sends scales flying. The hosing method works better for loose-scaled species like bluegills and crappie than for tight-scaled species like yellow perch or walleye. In general, the longer a fish has been left dry and out of water, the harder the scaling process. If you have to scale in a kitchen, you can immerse the fish in a sink of cold water and ice, pin the fish against the bottom of the sink, and scale it. The scales stay in the water and should be caught in the strainer when the sink is drained.

Filleting. Generally the quickest method of cleaning fish is to fillet them. Filleting means cutting the sides of a fish lengthwise parallel to and free from the backbone, accompanied by removal of the rib cage. A fillet is typically a boneless piece of fish, and it may or may not have the skin removed. When correctly done, filleting causes little loss of meat, is accomplished easily with the proper instrument, and, most important, removes all the rib cage bones that anguish many reluctant fish-eaters. The word "fillet" is properly pronounced "fill-lay," not "fill-it."

Basic filleting, version 1. Place the fish on one side, and make an angled cut behind the pectoral fin down to the backbone, being careful not to sever the backbone. Reverse the direction of the blade so that it is facing the tail and lying flat on the

Basic Filleting, Version 1

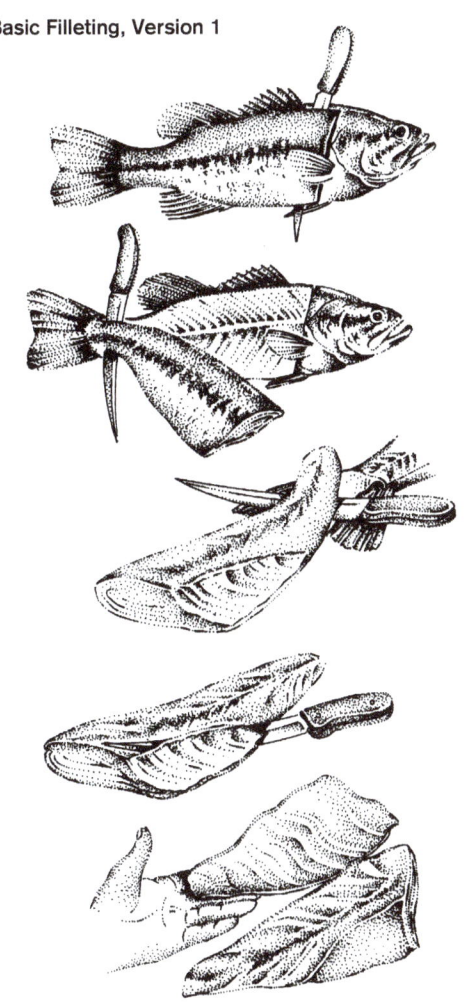

This is the most popular method of filleting. The same process is followed for both sides, with slicing the rib cage away from the fillet being the final step.

backbone, and slice back toward the tail along the backbone. A smooth cut, rather than a stop-and-go sawing motion, is best. If the fish has been scaled, cut through the skin at the tail.

If the skin is to be removed in the filleting process, do not cut through the tail but slice to the end without severing, and flop the meat backward.

If the fish has a thin skin that is easy to slice through, make sure you leave plenty of it attached to the caudal peduncle so that it grabs there and makes the skinning process easier. Angle your knife through the meat to the skin; then slice along the skin, separating the meat while exerting pressure on the skin with your free hand. If you accidentally cut through the tail, freeing the fillet from the carcass, you will find that removing the skin is a little more difficult. In this case, press the thumbnail of your free hand on the tail of the fillet (or use a fork), and cut between the skin and meat with your knife hand. You can use a sawing motion here and aid the effort by pulling on the tail of the fillet in the opposite direction of the cut.

Now, with either scaled or skinned fillet, cut behind the rib cage, slicing the whole section away. Use the same procedure for the other side of the fish. Rinse fillets quickly in cold water and pat dry. This filleting technique can be used on many fish, except those with additional Y-shaped bones. They require a few more steps (see the later section on filleting to remove extra bones).

Basic filleting, version 2. Place the fish on one side, and make an angled cut behind the pectoral fin down to the backbone, being careful not to sever the backbone. Slice the skin along the backbone from the head toward the tail, running the knife along the top of the rib cage but not cutting through it. Push the knife through the flesh at a point opposite the anal vent, and continue cutting, running the knife along the backbone until the blade slices the flesh away at the tail. A smooth cut, rather than a stop-and-go sawing motion, is best.

Lift the top of the fillet up to expose the rib cage; with smooth, measured strokes, flesh the meat away from the ribs, skimming the bones to procure as much meat as possible. Slice the fillet away from the carcass at the stomach. Turn the fish over and repeat on the opposite side, concluding with two boneless fillets with skin attached. If you have previously descaled the fish, the job is complete except for rinsing and patting dry. If not, you can remove the skin by pressing a fork or the thumbnail of your free hand on the tail of the fillet; cut between the skin and the meat with your knife hand. You can use a sawing motion here and aid the effort by pulling on the tail of the fillet in the opposite direction of the cut.

The second version is generally used less often than the first, but it has some benefits. It does not dull the knife as quickly since there is no cutting through rib bones. It produces slightly more meat than the first version, and it is better for use on larger fish. Large fish would be those for which the blade of the knife was not long enough to reach the top of the back and the bottom of the belly. For really large fish and those with thick bones, you may need a bigger, sturdier knife; it must, of course, be sharp. It's easy to lose meat on large fish when filleting if you don't do the job right. A heavy-duty blade will easily cut through the rib cage so that you don't have to hack at the fish; this is a big consideration if you're using the first filleting version. If you don't have a larger knife, you can still fillet with a smaller one by using version two and slicing in small sections while folding back the side of the fish to allow deeper penetration and continued slicing. To cut off the skin with a smaller knife, cut the skinned fillet in half lengthwise and then take off the skin as previously described.

If you make a mistake when filleting, try to correct the error rather than continuing with the mistake. The biggest problem when filleting, especially when the fish are small and you're using a sharp

Basic Filleting, Version 2

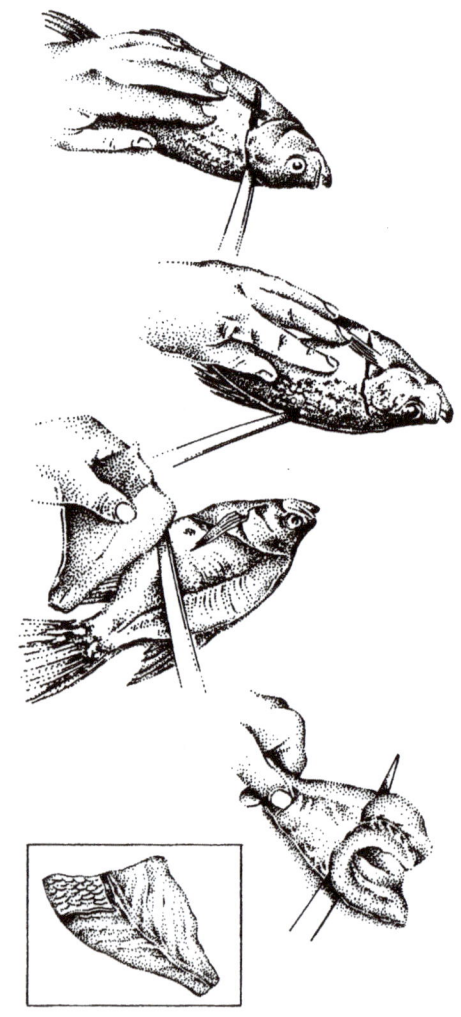

This is a good method of filleting; it requires a sharp knife and produces the maximum meat. The same process is followed for both sides. Leaving a patch of skin on a fillet (inset) may be necessary for legal identification purposes.

Fish Preparation—Cleaning/Dressing

knife, is inadvertently cutting through the backbone. If this happens, withdraw the knife and come back at another angle until you strike the backbone; then lay the blade down and make the stroke along the backbone. Another common mistake is cutting through the skin when you're trying to remove the skin from the fillet. If this happens, go to the head of the fillet, angle the blade through the flesh to the skin, and then start skinning from that direction.

Butterfly filleting. If you keep the skin attached to the sides of the fish while filleting and leave them joined at the belly, you can achieve a double fillet. This has some panache from a presentation standpoint. This method is used for smoking or planking fish, as well as for baking when stuffed. The skin helps hold in the juices for baking.

To butterfly a fish, first scale it if the species or your presentation demands it (planked fish do not need to be scaled since the meat is flaked away), and then cut off the head. With the belly away from you and the tail to the left, run the knife along the backbone, slicing through the rib bones and continuing through the tail, taking care not to cut through the skin at the belly. Turn the fish over and around so the tail is to the right and the belly is away from you; this time work from the tail toward the ribs, slicing the meat through the tail and then close to the backbone, continuing through the ribs and again taking care not to cut through the skin at the belly. Remove the entrails and backbone, and lay the double fillet skin-side down and open. Trim away whatever remains of the rib bones; then rinse in cold water and pat dry.

Filleting to remove extra bones. Some fish have more than the usual number of bones, and these cannot be removed through standard one-cut filleting. Such species include pike, pickerel, and muskellunge, all of which have additional intermuscular, or floating, Y-shaped bones. To deal with this, you can fillet the fish as previously described in version 1 and remove the skin. The Y bones are located on the fleshy back portion of the fillet above the ribs and run lengthwise to a point equal with

Butterfly Filleting

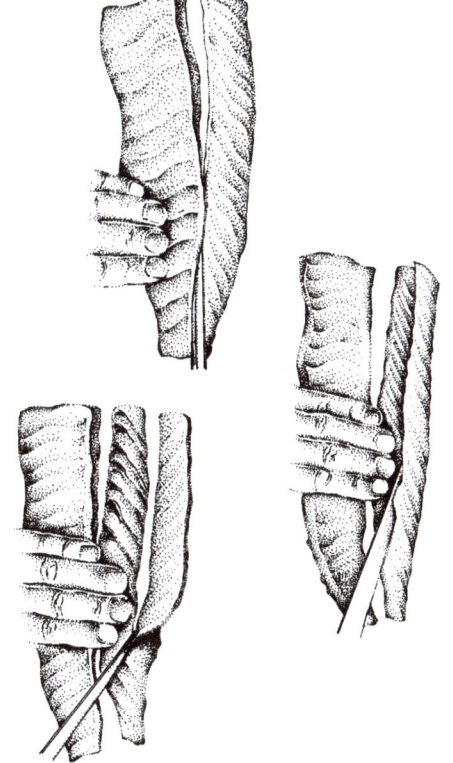

To create a butterfly fillet, first cut off the head (1); with the tail to the left and the belly up, slice along the backbone, cutting through the rib bones and continuing through the tail without cutting through the belly skin (2). Turn the fish over so that the tail is to the right and the belly is up, and cut from the tail toward the ribs (3), slicing the meat through the tail and then close to the backbone, continuing through the ribs, again not cutting through the belly skin. Remove entrails and backbone, and trim away whatever remains of the rib bones (not shown), creating a double fillet (4).

To remove Y-shaped bones from a skinless fillet of pike, pickerel, and muskellunge, locate these bones just above the midsection of the fillet and cut through the flesh beneath them all the way to the tail (top). Run the knife blade along the upper edge of the Y bones (middle), scraping gently against the bones and slicing down and away to the tail (bottom). Discard the middle piece, leaving two boneless segments.

Fish Preparation—Cleaning/Dressing

the ventral opening. Locate the lower edge of the Y bones just above the midsection of the fillet, and cut through the flesh beneath them all the way to the tail. Then guide the knife blade along the upper edge of the Y bones, scraping gently against the bones and slicing down and away to the tail. The upper and lower portions will be free of bones and can be rinsed in cold water and patted dry.

Some meat is obviously lost in this process, but a safer and more enjoyable fillet results. If you use the bony fillet for fish stock, and use a fine strainer, the bony strip does not have to be wasted. An alternative is to leave the strip of Y bones in the fillet, cut the skinless fillet into chunks, and run the chunks through a food grinder with fine blades, after which you can create patties or a fish loaf.

Filleting flatfish. Flatfish such as flounder are among the most popular of inshore saltwater species. Although they have a different body shape from most other fish, they are not difficult to clean, especially if you use a sharp knife with a long, slightly flexible blade.

To fillet a flounder, slice the meat across the body just behind the head and down to the backbone; then slice the length of the fish from head to tail, scraping the blade along the backbone. Continue this cut down to the other side of the fish, lifting the fillet up as necessary and slicing the entire fillet free. Lay the fillet skin down, and remove the skin by pressing a fork or the thumbnail of your free hand on the tail of the fillet; cut between the skin and the meat with your knife hand. You can use a sawing motion here and aid the effort by pulling on the tail of the fillet in the opposite direction of the cut.

Steaking. Steaking fish for frying or broiling is a good way to handle large specimens. To steak a fish, scale and eviscerate it first; then make a slice on both sides of the fins and pull them free. If the fish is firm or partly frozen, and you have a good cleaver, cut off the head and tail and make the steaks from three-fourths to one-inch thick, starting from the head and working toward the tail. You may find it easier to leave on the head and steak the fish from the tail toward the head, grasping the fish by the head. Trim the belly fat and any obvious bones from the steak; then rinse each steak quickly

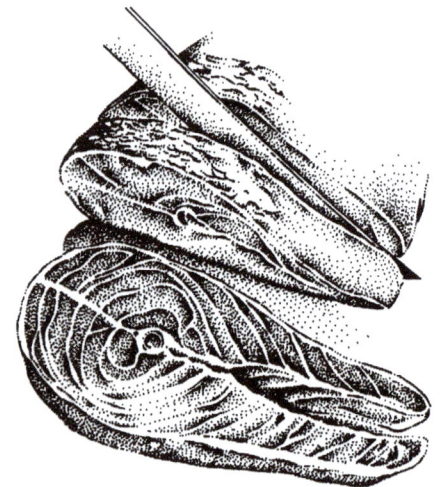

Steaks are created from a beheaded, eviscerated carcass by making equal-diameter cuts across the body and through the backbone.

To fillet a flatfish, cut across the body just behind the head and down to the backbone (1) and then slice the length of the fish from head to tail, scraping the blade along the backbone (2). Continue this cut down to the other side of the fish, lifting up the fillet as necessary (3) and slicing the entire fillet free (4). Remove skin if desired.

in cold water and pat dry. When you get to the tail section where no more steaks are available, fillet it.

A fillet knife won't do an adequate job of steaking fish. Steaks should be neatly cut, not ragged and hacked. Use a butcher's knife or a cleaver for steaking. Don't use a serrated knife or one that is likely to grind the backbone; fine pieces of ground backbone may get in or on the steaks. Fish that are very cold or partially frozen will steak better than those that are soft and fleshy, so if your knife isn't super sharp or you're making do with a less rugged

Fish Preparation—Cleaning/Dressing

blade, it might be good to chill or partly freeze the fish before steaking.

Skinning. Most fish skinning takes place during the filleting process, with the skin being separated from the flesh as a next-to-last step. However, some people like to have a whole fish without the skin and certain fish—like dolphin, for example—do not yield their skin very well when their sides have been cut away from the whole body. If you think that the skin may leave an objectionable flavor in the flesh, remove it; removing the skin also helps spices or sauces penetrate the flesh better. If the fish is slimy (some freshwater species have more abundant and more offensive-smelling mucous than others), the skin should be removed. Wiping with a cloth doesn't seem to remove slime unless you have a lot of clean cloths available. You can try placing the fish in a solution of one part vinegar and three parts water to help remove the mucous. You can also rub the fish with generous amounts of salt and then rinse with cold water.

Small fish can be skinned by following the procedure described earlier for pan dressing, with skin and ribs removed. Large whole fish can be skinned by making three shallow cuts: along the back and past the dorsal fin from just behind the head to just ahead of the tail; diagonally across the body, meeting with the forward end of the dorsal cut; and along the belly from the end of the diagonal cut past the anal fin to the tail. At the cut corner behind the head, pry up a small strip of skin with the knife; then grab this with your fingers or a pair of pliers and peel the skin back. Repeat this on the other side, and finish the fish by any method you choose.

If you have already eviscerated a fish but want to keep it whole without the skin, then cut the skin around the tail and head (behind the pectoral fins)

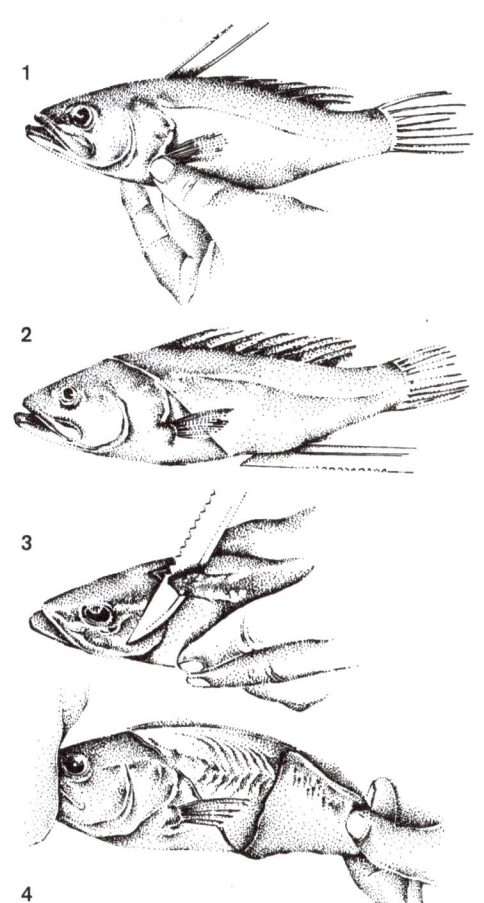

To skin a large whole fish, make shallow cuts along the back and past the dorsal fin from just behind the head to just ahead of the tail (1). Then cut diagonally across the body, meeting with the forward end of the dorsal cut (2), and cut along the belly from the end of the diagonal cut past the anal fin to the tail. At the intersected cuts behind the head, pry up a small strip of skin with the knife (3); grab this strip with your fingers or a pair of pliers and peel back the skin (4).

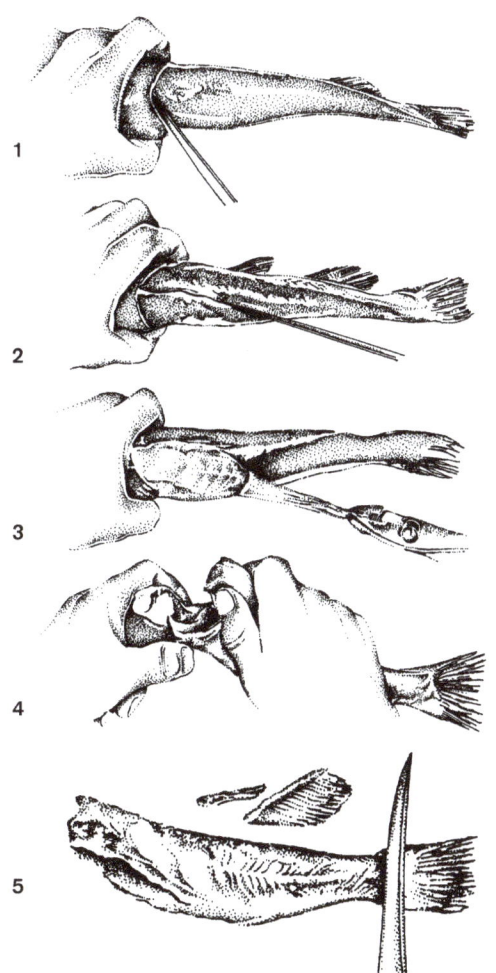

To skin and eviscerate bullheads and small catfish, hold them carefully at the head with your fingers pinning the sharp pectoral fins; make a shallow cut of the skin around the entire head of the fish (1) and also along the backbone from the dorsal fin to the adipose fin (2). With pliers, grab the skin at the back and pull it to the tail (3); repeat on the other side. Holding the fish as shown, bend the head down to break the backbone (4), and then pull the head away from the fish toward the tail, removing skin and entrails in the process. Cut off the tail and rinse the fish.

and along the back. Pry up a small strip of skin at the tail, grip this with pliers, and peel back the skin while holding the tail firmly.

Skinning small catfish. Bullheads and small catfish pose cleaning problems for many anglers, yet these fish can be dressed easily with proper treatment. They have a tough skin that is thin and slippery, and it cannot be removed like other fish. To skin and eviscerate bullheads and small catfish, make a thin slice on the top of the fish from behind the adipose fin up to the dorsal fin, and continue with a vertical cut from the dorsal fin down to the backbone. Put the knife aside, grab the head with one hand and the body with the other, and bend the head down to break the backbone. Hold the body portion firmly, with your finger over the broken backbone, and pull the head away from the fish toward the tail, removing skin and entrails in the process. Cut off the tail and rinse the fish.

With larger catfish, it's best to slice the perimeters of the skin. Hold the head firmly. Slice completely around the fish behind the pectoral fin. Slice along the top of the fish and around both sides of the adipose fin; then slice along the belly and around both sides of the pectoral fin. Use a pair of snub-nose pliers to grasp the skin near the pectoral fin, and pull back firmly toward the tail to remove it. Repeat on the other side. Sever the head and tail and remove the entrails. You can now fillet the fish, keep it as is, or steak it.

Trimming for Health and Taste Reasons

Some fish contain a dark lateral line that has a different flavor than the rest of the meat. If you fillet these fish and remove the skin, you can slice away this dark flesh (which is not detectable by taste, incidentally).

Many fisheries agencies advocate trimming away the fatty parts from fish, as well as removing the skin to reduce the intake of certain environmental contaminants. We are not talking about the taste or the flavor of fish flesh here. This is about the hidden and tasteless elements with such foreboding names as mirex, PCBs, dioxin, and chlordane. These contaminants have a long residual life in the aquatic environment and work their way through the food chain into the flesh of food and sportfish.

A high percentage of contaminants is found in the fatty portion of fish, so the best policy is to trim away the fatty area of the back, belly, and lateral line. A study that evaluated untrimmed brown trout fillets versus trimmed fillets found that trimming resulted in an average reduction of 62 percent in fat content and 45 percent in contaminants.

Researchers note that cooking trimmed fillets in a way that allows the remaining fat to drain out and away from the flesh will further reduce levels of contaminants. Some studies suggest that baking or broiling on a rack will result in further reduction in fats and the contaminants stored in them, although the exact percentage varies.

Depending on where you fish and what you keep for consumption, you can lessen potential health risks simply by carefully cleaning your catch.

Market Definitions

Although the terms used in this book are generally understood by anglers, supermarkets and fish markets may use slightly different terms. Here's a partial guide to the common terms used there.

Whole fish. An unprocessed fish exactly as it comes from the water, complete with head, scales, skin, and entrails. Another common term is "in the round." Whole fish are usually found at dockside.

Drawn fish. A fish with only the entrails removed. It may need to be descaled or filleted, or to have the head cut off, etc.

Dressed fish. A fish that has been descaled and eviscerated, with the head, tail, and fins removed. "Whole dressed" means that the head and tail are left on.

Steaks and fillets. Generally the same as the meaning used by anglers, although stores may offer different cuts of steak depending on the size of the fish and the location that the steak came from.

See: Regulations.

FISH SCALER

A tool for removing the scales from a fish.
See: Fish Preparation—Cleaning/Dressing.

FISH SCENT

See: Scents.

FISH SHELTER

See: Fish Attractor.

FISHWAY

A man-made passageway that allows fish to move around a dam in a river system or to migrate into a

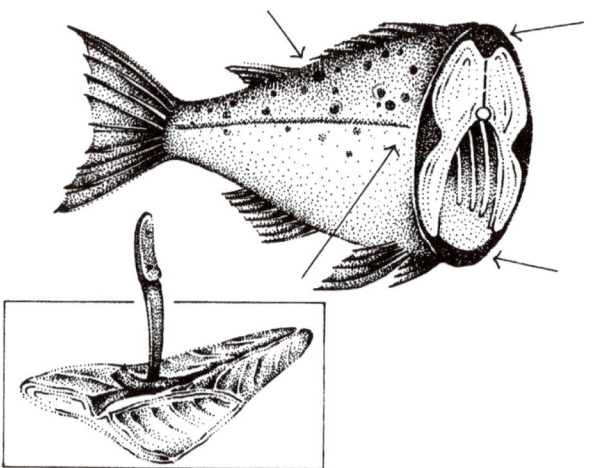

To remove fatty flesh that may contain contaminants, trim the flesh from the back and belly and also along the lateral lines (inset); then remove the skin.

This fishway for salmon and steelhead is a series of stepped pools leading to a fish hatchery.

fish hatchery. Also called fish ladders, fishways are primarily used by migratory (anadromous) species to continue natural migrations in a river system. Fishways have been constructed to help rebuild or reintroduce fish stocks that have suffered from the construction of dams; a dam may prevent the upstream movement of fish to natural spawning areas, and the downstream movement of out-migrating adults or juvenile fish. Fishways are also located below fish hatcheries so that fish can move into hatchery facilities.

Fishways are permanent fish passage devices. Ladderlike fishways are passive flume-type structures that are inclined and equipped with a series of baffles or weirs, which interrupt the flow of water and create ascending pools. They reduce water velocity so fish can navigate up them in a ladderlike progression at their own pace, just as they would negotiate natural rapids. One such style, the Denil, is suited to small to medium rivers having relatively consistent flows, is designed to pass small populations of fish, and is limited by large water depths. Another, the vertical slot, is suited to medium to large rivers having dramatic flow fluctuation, is designed to pass large populations of fish, and has a moderate slope.

Another fishway is the mechanical lift, or elevator, which is used at high hydroelectric dams. Here, attraction flows draw fish into a pool area equipped with a large hopper. At fixed intervals, a gate is used to crowd fish into a confined area. The fish are collected in the hopper and lifted to an exit channel at the top of the dam, from which they swim out into the river.

Incorporated into most fishways or ladders are facilities that allow for counting and identifying fish; in some places they include public viewing rooms with glass sidewalls.

FIZZING
See: Puncturing; Catch-and-Release.

FLARE
A bright light used as a distress signal, usually pyrotechnic; also the outward curvature of the topside of a boat.

FLASHER
(1) A type of sonar with a flashing light that indicates depth on a circular dial.
See: Sonar.

(2) A type of attractor used in trolling to get the attention of deep fish.
See: Dodger/Flasher.

FLAT
A long, level, and shallow part of a body of water adjacent to deeper water and/or channels. In freshwater, flats exist in rivers, lakes, and reservoirs and along tidal rivers; and in saltwater, flats are found in bays, estuaries, and marshes, as well as atop reefs and atolls and around islands. Some expansive shallow areas along a mainland coast or beach may also be considered flats.

The bottom composition of a flat may be mud, sand, gravel, rock, grass, or a combination of sand and aquatic vegetation. In many cases, flats having hard bottoms and shallow depths are suitable for wading, and may have enough water to float shallow-draft fishing boats, some of which are called flats boats *(see)*.

Flats, and the edges of flats, provide feeding opportunity for various species of fish as the fish move on and off them, migrate through them, and reside in them for varying periods. Flats with grass or other vegetation are among the best for fishing, since they offer cover for some species and food for smaller and larger fish alike. Mud and sand flats are not as productive, although those with cover, such as flooded bushes or stumps (in an impoundment, for example), may be used by such object-oriented fish as largemouth bass. The term "flats fishing" is usually specific to saltwater and to wading/poling/sight fishing activities, especially for tarpon, bonefish, permit, redfish, and seatrout. Angling for these species is discussed under their respective entries.
See: Sight Fishing.

FLATFISH

The term "flatfish" broadly refers to a group of more than 500 species of unique, compressed fish that have developed special features for living on the bottom, the most interesting of which is that both eyes are on one side of the head. They are capable of excellent camouflaging and are widespread, ranging from cold, boreal habitats to warm, tropical environments. The flatfish group includes among the world's most important commercial, recreational, and food fish, such as sole, flounder, halibut, dab, plaice, and turbot—names that often apply to species in different families.

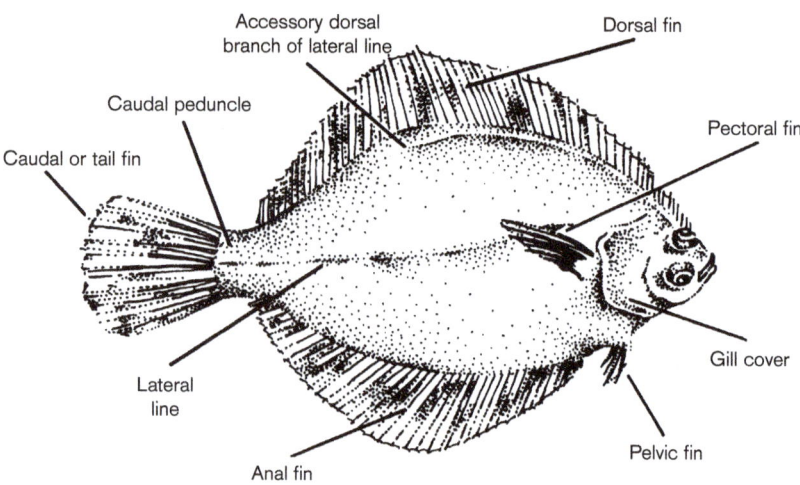

External Characteristics of Flatfish

Characteristics

Flatfish represent an unusual form of piscine engineering; as mentioned, they are unique in that the skull is asymmetrical with both eyes on the same side of the head. Nonflatfish species are typically streamlined, possess intricately carved fins and tail, and are adorned with neat, symmetrical coloration. Flatfish, however, look more like a squashed footballs or a large decaying leaves. Whereas one side of their body appears translucent or milky white, depending on the species, the other is a mottled assembly of muddy browns, reds, whites, and greens, which aids in camouflaging. The simple fins make an even fringe around the body, and a loosely shaped tail seems to have been tacked on. Oddest of all are the two beady eyes perched much too close together on the flatfish's brown side, adding the pièce de résistance to an already grotesque appearance.

Flatfish actually begin life like symmetrical fish, with an eye on each side of the head. A few days after hatching, their bodies flatten, one eye begins to migrate, and soon both eyes are close together on one side. At this time, the flatfish begins to swim and lies on its blind side. If the right eye migrates to the left side, the flatfish is left-eyed (sinistral). If the left eye migrates to the right side, the fish is right-eyed (dextral). Flatfish spend the rest of their lives on or near the bottom with the eyed side facing up.

In general, flatfish have a highly compressed body, which gives rise to the name "flatfish." Their dorsal and anal fins are usually long, the adults do not have a swim bladder, and they can change the color of their skin as well as the intensity of its coloration. This last trait of most flatfish takes advantage of their existence on the bottom, allowing them to match their background or sometimes bury themselves in the sediment and lie in wait for unsuspecting prey. If, for instance, a dark, pebbly patterned flounder settles on a light-colored, sandy bottom, the fish's skin will rapidly shift to a sand color, usually in less than a minute.

The lack of pigmentation on a flatfish's blind side has a purpose, too. Although this white half often rests against the bottom, where complex designs would be of no value, the absence of markings aids the fish when it swims high in the water (which some species do more often than others). Because of light reflecting off the surface, any flatfish predator looking upward sees a uniform whitish cast in that uppermost region; a flatfish passing through this light will be well concealed.

Flatfish also have a wide range in maximum size. Both Atlantic halibut and Pacific halibut have been reported to reach 700 pounds, although the largest specimens caught by anglers weighed 255 pounds and 459 pounds respectively. The smallest is probably the pygmy tonguefish *(Symphurus parvus),* which reaches its maximum size at 3 inches.

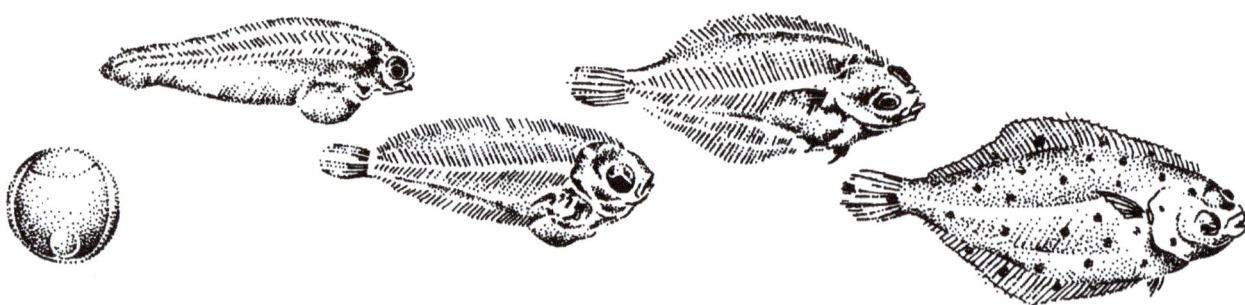

The amazing transformation of flatfish begins after the egg develops into a symmetrical fish with an eye on each side of the head. A few days after the fish hatches, the body flattens, one eye migrates to the opposite side of the body so that both eyes lie close together, and the flatfish begins to swim and lie on its blind side.

The Eye Development of a Right-Eyed Flatfish

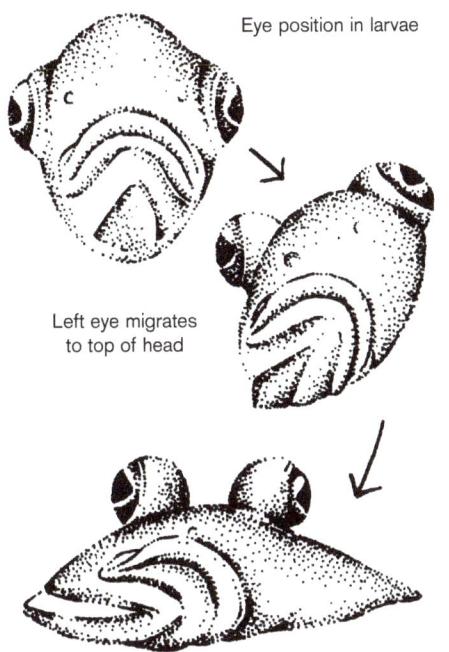

Eye position in larvae

Left eye migrates to top of head

Both eyes on right side

Flatfish resemble a fly carpet or a flying saucer as they ripple and glide through the water. The smaller inshore species found over sandy bottoms, especially flounder, glide to the bottom, flip sand over their backs, and become almost invisible except for their protruding eyes. When a small fish or other prey is spotted, they squirt water from the underside gill and quickly propel themselves outward in pursuit. As a result of their tendency to bury and camouflage themselves, flatfish are often tough for divers to spot with an untrained eye.

Flatfish make delicious eating. They have firm, white delicate flesh that adapts well to a variety of preparation methods. Because many flatfish are found in shallow estuaries and bays, however, they, and other bottom-dwelling species, are particularly susceptible to pollutants, especially those that gather in bottom sediments. As a result, in some locations, they may be covered by consumption advisories.

Classification

Flatfish as a whole are in the order Pleuronectiformes (sometimes called Heterosomata). Worldwide there are more than 500 (estimates say 520) species of flatfish, in six or seven families. Flatfish include flounder, sole, turbot, halibut, sanddabs, plaice, and tonguefish. These names do not indicate that a fish belongs to a specific family; for example, species referred to as sole occur in the Bothidae, Pleuronectidae, and Soleidae families. Flatfish found in North American waters fall in two broad categories; one includes the families Bothidae and Pleuronectidae, and the other includes the families Cynoglossidae and Soleidae.

The Bothidae is a very large family that contains more than 200 species. This family is called the left-eyed flounder because the eyes and dark color typically are on the left side. In some fish, like the California halibut *(see: halibut, California),* however, the eyes can be on the left side or the right side. Bothidae family members are closely related to those in the Pleuronectidae family.

The Pleuronectidae family is composed of right-eyed flounder, with the eyes and dark color usually on the right side. This family includes about 100 species, many of which are found along the North American coast. One, the starry flounder, regularly has the eyes on either the left or right side of the head. The Pacific halibut occasionally breaks the rule and is left-eyed.

The Cynoglossidae family comprises roughly 100 species of tonguefish. Their eyes are on the left side, and the dorsal and anal fins are joined to the pointed caudal fin. Cynoglossidae species are closely related to Soleidae (sole); the latter includes species with the eyes on the right side and a distinct caudal fin that is not pointed. True sole are members of the Soleidae family, but the word "sole" has been widely used to refer to some flatfish that actually belong to other families, such as petrale sole.

True sole are right-eyed flatfish. Species referred to as sole in North America are rarely seen by the recreational angler but are more common in cold European waters, where they are taken by both commercial and recreational anglers. In the Gulf of Mexico, sole are frequently caught in commercial or bait trawls. The lined sole *(Archinus lineatus),* is sometimes sold in aquarium stores as "freshwater flounder" because of its ability to tolerate freshwater or saltwater. The European sole *(Solea solea)* has been heavily marketed, and the term "fillet of sole," which was once specific to the European sole, is now applied to many other sole and indeed to many nonsole flatfish.

In North America, flatfish range along almost every coastline. Prominent or significant along the Pacific coast are the giant Pacific halibut, California halibut, Pacific sanddab, longfin sanddab, starry flounder, and petrale sole. Prominent or significant along the Atlantic and Gulf coasts are winter, summer, southern, windowpane, and gulf flounder, plus the endangered Atlantic halibut.

Some flatfish live along the continental shelf and slope, whereas others come into shoal and inshore waters, and are found in bays and estuaries. A good deal of diversity exists among the species, and some are even tolerant of brackish water. Along the northern Gulf of Mexico, for example, the southern flounder is found in waters of lesser average depth than the waters favored by the gulf flounder, and the southern flounder frequently occurs in low-salinity environs or even in freshwater. The gulf flounder rarely enters waters of reduced salinities, and it is usually caught outside Mobile Bay.

For specific species information, *See Brill;*

Halibut, Atlantic; Halibut, California; Halibut, Pacific; Flounder, Gulf; Flounder, Southern; Flounder, Starry; Flounder, Summer; Flounder, Windowpane; Flounder, Winter; Plaice, American; Plaice, European; Sanddab, Longfin; Sanddab, Pacific; Sole; Sole, Gray; Sole, Petrale; Turbot.

Angling

Although many anglers do not consider flatfish, especially the smaller varieties, as glamorous as red drum, bluefish, or striped bass, some flatfish do take artificial lures and most are game fighters. Fishing for flatties, as the shallower inshore flatfish are commonly known, does have its advantages. For instance, flatfish do not school, so they are found over a wide area; this is conducive to drifting with the tide and/or wind over bay and estuary flats, for example. Also, many species are easily caught in shallow, protected areas that are accessible in small boats. In temperate and warm waters, certain species are caught year-round, including times when other more glamorous sportfish are unavailable.

Angling techniques for these fish are noted in some species entries and are generally discussed in greater detail under other entries. For more information see: Drift Fishing; Inshore Fishing.

FLATHEADS

Dusky Flathead *Platycephalus fuscus.*
   Other names—estuary flathead, black flathead, mud flathead, lizard.
Sand Flathead *Platycephalus bassensis.*
   Other names—slimy flathead, southern sand flathead, bay flathead.

Members of the Platycephalidae family, flathead species number about 55 throughout marine and brackish Indo-Pacific waters. Of the many species found in Australian waters, the dusky flathead and the sand flathead are the two most highly regarded by anglers for their table qualities. There is a valuable commercial market for each species, the dusky flathead being taken by gillnets from estuaries and coastal bays, and the sand flathead from trawlers netting open coastal waters. There is a small, inshore, recreational fishery for a third species, the tiger flathead *(Neoplatycephalus richardsoni),* which is a target for anglers in Tasmania, Victoria, and New South Wales.

Identification. As the name implies, the flathead has a depressed or flattened head and a moderately elongate and moderately depressed body with a truncated to slightly convex tail. The eyes are set on top of the head, which carries two large preopercular spines. Pectoral fins are large. Its body colors are variable, from sandy to dark brown, and are influenced to a degree by the bottom upon which the flathead lies. There is a distinct black spot on the upper lobe of the tail of the dusky flathead, and one or two dark spots on the lower lobe of the sandy flathead's tail. Spinous and dorsal fins are separate.

Size. Dusky flathead can grow to at least 15 kilograms (an Australian record is 7.72 kilograms), and sandy flathead to at least 3 kilograms (the Australian record is 2.58 kilograms).

Distribution. Dusky flathead occur along the East Coast of Australia from Cairns in Queensland to the Gippsland Lakes in eastern Victoria. Sandy flathead range from northern New South Wales along the southern coastline to just north of Perth in Western Australia.

Habitat. The dusky flathead inhabits sheltered estuaries, bays, and inlets, and can range well into river systems, frequently being taken in freshwater reaches by lure anglers chasing the Australian bass. The sandy flathead also inhabits estuaries and bays but is more often taken from coastal waters over sandy bottoms. Both species are bottom dwellers living mainly over sandy, gravel, or mud bottoms, and in seagrass beds.

Life history/Behavior. Dusky flathead spawn during the warmer months (September through March) but at different times, depending on their geographic location. Sandy flathead spawn from August through October. Fecundity details are not known. Both species tend to be solitary.

In winter, they tend to spread upstream or move into deeper water off the coast. In summer, they gather in the lower parts of estuaries and along ocean beaches, where spawning occurs.

Food and feeding habits. Flatheads are carnivores and live on small fish (e.g., whiting, mullet), crustaceans (e.g., prawns, crabs), worms, squid, and octopuses. To capture these, they lie in ambush, concealed in the sand or mud with only their eyes protruding. Any of these are used for bait, as are, among others, cut baits of tuna, bonito, and whole pilchards.

Angling. The most popular angling method is bottom fishing while drifting in a boat. Shore, jetty, and beach fishing are also practiced. Boats rods are used, but handlines are common because they allow the angler to better feel the relatively timid bite of the flathead. Line strengths range from 3 kilograms to 7 kilograms, and hook sizes vary from 3/0 to 7/0. Ganged rigs—constructed by joining three, four, or more hooks, eye to bend, and baited with cut fish or whole pilchards—are especially popular. Live baits are favored over dead baits.

Movement of the bait across the bottom is very important for attracting the fish's attention. Jigging (known as yo-yoing in Australia) has a high priority as a handline method because it tempts the fish to leave its ambush position and take the bait in a more positive manner. Flatheads are sluggish fighters when taken on bait; when lures are used, their behavior is much more aggressive and challenging.

This fish will respond quickly to a lure fished close to the bottom. Small to medium diving minnow-type lures that have a lively action at a

---

The scientific names for fish are in Greek and Latin; the meaning for Pognias cromis, or black drum, is "bearded grunter," and the meaning of Mugil cephalus, or black mullet, is sucking helmet-head.

slow retrieve rate, soft plastics, spinners, and spoons are all used. Soft plastics should be allowed to sink, then bounced along the bottom to disturb the sand and attract the fish. Fly fishing is also effective, using No. 7 or 8 sinking lines and streamer flies; best results are had when fishing over sandy bottoms in water up to 2 meters deep.

Hooked flathead have a bad habit of fighting sluggishly to the side of the boat, then getting energized when about to be netted, which enables many to escape. When handling the fish, anglers should exercise care to avoid a painful wound from the preopercular spines.

FLATLINING

Trolling a lure or bait on an unweighted fishing line is known as flatlining. This is a popular technique for angling in relatively shallow water (1 to 25 feet), because the depth achieved is primarily dependent on the weight or diving ability of the object being trolled. Flatlines are used in freshwater and saltwater angling for a variety of species, and often in conjunction with planer boards or sideplaners.

Running a flatline is the simplest kind of trolling. Flatlines are set straight out behind the boat; there are no heavy sinkers, downrigger weights, diving planers, or other devices that influence the depth attained by the lure. Flatlines are sometimes referred to as high lines, usually when trolled in conjunction with some type of deep-diving lure. Anyone with a rod, reel, line, and lure can run a flatline. Most people who do some trolling in the course of their fishing run a flatline, usually for hours on end without regard to technique.

The keys to flatline trolling productivity are the length of line and how you maneuver the boat to position the lures or bait. Generally, in freshwater the clearer the water, the shallower the fish, the spookier the fish, and the more boat activity there is, the longer the line you need. Long lines are particularly important in inland, clear-water trout and salmon fishing, where it is not uncommon to troll lures 200 to 300 feet behind the boat. Long lines have also become more common in Great Lakes walleye trolling because of the increasing water clarity. If you're used to casting 50 or 60 feet to catch fish, trolling distances of 200 to 300 feet seem outlandish. They're not.

Trolling a line for seemingly endless hours is boring, unimaginative, and unproductive. You have to alter the lure's path regularly by turning, by steering in an S-shaped pattern or other irregular way, or by altering the speed of the boat. These changes enhance your presentation by altering the speed and action of the lure and making it appear less "mechanical."

In making a flatline trolling presentation, you must consider where the fish are and how to get your lures close without alarming them. Fish in shallow water near shore, or close to the surface in open water, characteristically move out of the boat's path because they are especially wary, perhaps even nervous. With few exceptions, you can't motor through the shallows and expect fish to stay around or to be receptive to your offerings. This is one reason why you seldom see fish in less than 15 feet of water on sonar: Fish swim off to one side of the boat as it approaches and thus are well outside the cone angle of the sonar's transducer.

After the boat has passed, the fish may continue to swim away, they may stay where they are once they have moved, or they may return to their original location. If your lure is trailing directly behind a straight-moving boat, the fish in the first two instances may never see your lure. If your line is too

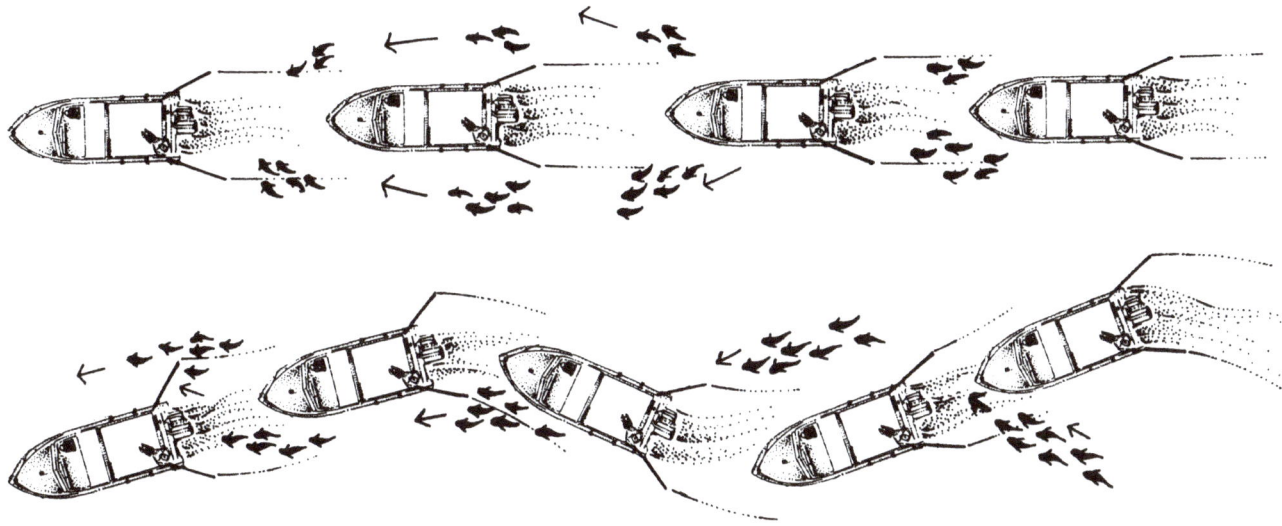

When using a long line (200 to 300 feet) in flatline trolling, you may intercept fish that move off and then return after the boat has passed by (top, right to left). It is often more productive to vary your course by making moderate or exaggerated S-turns, which allow lures to pass fish you might have missed otherwise (bottom, right to left).

short, fish in the third instance may not see it if they are slow to return to their position, or they may see it but associate it with the boat. This illustrates why a lure should be fished on a long line for some types of fish and how proper boat maneuvering can bring lures into the range of fish that may not have been in the boat's path or that may have moved out of it.

A lot of shallow-holding fish can be caught by trolling, particularly in the spring, when fish are most likely to be shallow. Correct line placement, lure presentation, and boat control are critical for shallow flatline trolling success. The true test of shallow flatline trolling is to make your presentations in tight areas. Near shore, around reefs or shoals or islands, along grass lines and weed edges, and so forth, are hard places to troll effectively because maneuverability is limited. Consider, for example, a lakeshore that drops off fairly sharply and has boulders or stumps submerged just under the surface. If you bring your boat too close to shore, your motor may hit these structures. You could try using an electric motor and steering around them, but this doesn't always work; and if the wind or current isn't favorable, you would go nowhere. The only way to deal with this problem when flatline trolling is to sweep in and out from shore and plan strategic approaches to points, sandbars, islands, shoals, channels, and the like. You may have to troll by these structures more than once and from different directions to cover the location effectively.

Flatline trolling is not just for shallow-water fishing, however; many anglers flatline both large and small deep-running plugs. When fishing deep water, though, you must know how your lures dive with various lengths and strengths of line, and you must pay attention to the depth beneath you and to the lures behind you while trolling. This applies equally to trolling weighted lures and medium- or deep-diving plugs. Learn to evaluate the depth that your trolled lures or bait actually attain to avoid haphazard flatlining and sporadic success.

When flatlining, either place lures or bait on a direct path behind the boat or place them to the side of the boat via sideplaners or outriggers (see). Those that are set off to the side are connected via releases (see) to the line that is towing the sideplaner or extended along the outrigger. Those that are run directly behind the boat are often not placed in any release, so the line extends directly from the rod tip to the trailing lure or bait. For some situations, this latter method may be adequate; adjusting the position of the rod is important for avoiding tangles or getting lures deeper in the water. Tangles are more likely when the line rides high and when it is windy.

The higher the rod tip, the more the lure or bait tends to ride toward the surface; if you want it to get deeper, you may need to position the rod tip closer to the water (by angling it to the side of the gunwales). To get the lines lower or to aid in setting the hook upon a strike, you can use a release clip that is attached to a low position on the transom of the boat. One way to do this is by securing a release to a stern cleat or to a transom eye bolt; after the lure or bait is placed the appropriate distance back, the fishing line is secured in the release, and the line from rod tip to release is tightened.

Another way to accomplish the same thing is to

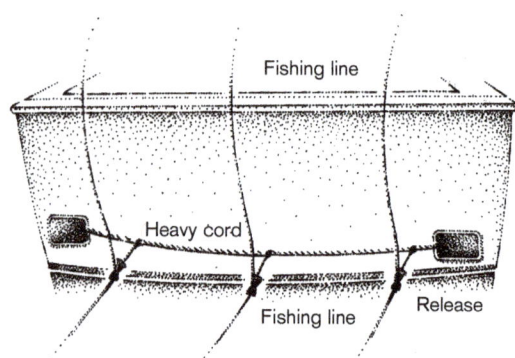

To increase hooksetting effectiveness when flatlining, attach fishing line to a release that is fixed to the transom of the boat.

run a heavy-strength fishing line, parachute cord, or other thin but strong line across the outside of the transom of an inboard boat. The line can be high and extend from one transom eye bolt to the other, or it can be lower by running through the scuppers. In the latter, connect the line to one stern cleat on the inside gunwale; run it out the scupper, across the outside of the transom, through the other scupper; and connect it to the stern cleat on the other inside gunwale. Leave some slack in the line for retrieval. Connect two or three releases to the outside lines, and you're ready to put trolling lines in them.
See: Planer Boards; Sideplaners; Trolling.

FLATS BOAT

A flats boat is not a flat boat. It's a shallow-draft fishing-only boat that was originally designed for use on saltwater flats, where the method of angling entailed poling in shin-deep water for shallow and often spooky fish, and where it was necessary to have a boat that drew little water, provided a stable standing and casting platform, was easy to pole, and was tough enough to cross long stretches of not-so-flat open sea in order to reach the flats. The concept of a boat that could do these things, provide plenty of storage, speed to the good spots, and not be a bear to ride in bad water has been evolving since the late 1960s. In some ways, the flats boat is analogous to a high-performance bass boat, which is also intended for the specific activity of casting and which includes high-speed travel and some contact with rough water in the mix.

Known originally as a flats skiff or flats boat, and originating in the Florida Keys, these 16- to 20-foot fishing vessels have become popular outside of Florida in many coastal locations, and have a small following in freshwater, partly with anglers who occasionally fish inshore in saltwater and want a boat for both. Thus, they are not a flat hull, but a modified-V hull with sharp water entry.

Owing to design and construction materials, flats boats sit high in the water. They are light, draw only a small amount of water, and have plenty of beam. Although at casual glance a flats boat looks somewhat like a bass boat, most flats boats actually have higher freeboard, which is flared to help deflect spray and keep the interior dry when running in rough water (though there are limits to how much can be deflected). The hull is also a little more V-shaped, which contributes to a gentler ride.

Flats boats draw roughly 6 to 12 inches of water depending on the particular boat, and this gets them into the skinny water of flats, bays, marshes, and the like, where not only bonefish and redfish prowl, but also sea trout, striped bass, and in some places largemouth bass and snook. Flats boats intended for the skinniest of water differ from those intended for general bay and shoreline fishing in more open and sometimes rougher water.

Although a flats boat is one that can float in mere inches of water, it also must be able to ride as comfortably as possible in the sometimes rough stretches of water between the various flats. It takes a lot of V in the hull to produce a good ride in a stiff chop, and the greater the V, the greater the draft. It's possible to make a 17-footer that rides like a dream at 30 mph in 3-foot seas, but unfortunately that same boat could not be poled in much less than 18 inches of water.

The first flats boats drew 13 to 14 inches, which was too much for many flats situations. But builders learned that by reducing the V to a modified form with between 12 and 14 degrees of deadrise at the transom, getting rid of as much weight as possible via lightweight hull materials (like Kevlar and/or carbon fiber composites), using a lighter and lower-horsepower engine, and leaving unnecessary junk ashore, that same boat would float in an honest 9 or 10 inches instead of 13 or 14. By adding a set of hydraulic trim tabs to the transom, they got back a lot of the soft (and drier) ride that can otherwise only be provided by a lot more V in the hull.

Nowadays if you're really serious about skinny water flats fishing, the issue is the number of inches in draft. However, not all flats boats are used in the shallowest water, and since different situations require different draft capabilities, flats boats have evolved up and down to meet specific conditions.

Bonefishing in thin water is what drove the creation of the genuine flats boat, and many flats boats today are still targeted directly at this activity. Decades ago, bonefish flats were reached with 16-foot flat-bottom wood skiffs powered by a 10- to 15-hp outboard. This produced a long, slow, and wet ride between flats, but the boats floated in 6 or 7 inches of water. Today's modified-V-hulled

A typical flats boat is poled across Florida Keys shallows.

boats get to the next flat much faster, smoother, and dryer, but if the boat draws too much water it is not truly a bonefish boat. You can catch bonefish (and redfish) by using boats that draw 13 to 14 inches of water, mostly by parking the boat and wading whenever the water is too shallow, though a soupy bottom precludes wading. And of course you can't follow or intercept moving fish as well on foot as you can in a boat. So the right boat is critical for several reasons.

If you're serious about flats fishing for bonefish, skip any boat that draws over 10 inches. Also, consider length, hull weight, and horsepower. Less total weight translates directly into easier poling. Wide boats are harder to pole; a long skinny boat pushes a lot easier than a short, beamy craft. Consistently successful bonefishing calls for precise boat maneuverability, even (especially) on windy days, so you will really appreciate a boat that is easy to pole.

Hull noise is a major factor in flats fishing. Bonefish, permit, redfish, snook, and sometimes tarpon are all affected by noise. There is a huge difference among hulls when it comes to noise. Boats with large reverse chines, which are downturned for a dryer ride, make noise in even the slightest ripple, and most of the time this noise alerts a bonefish long before you're within casting range. Manufacturers are working on making these boats stealthier, and some boats are much better at being quiet. Many anglers who have otherwise reasonably quiet hulls even refuse to have spray rails added to them because of the extra noise the rails make on the flats.

Some boats that are inherently noisy can become a lot less so by poling them from the bow. Aluminum hulls, especially jonboats, certainly fall into this category, but poling could be difficult with wide hulls.

No one boat can do it all. The quiet poling in super-thin water so essential to bonefish anglers is not critical in other flats boat applications, nor is the minimal draft. A 12-inch draft is not too much for chasing striped bass or bluefish on deeper northern flats, for example. You can get by with 14 inches in that environment and at the same time have a bigger boat to make the ride across miles of open water a lot easier. Plus you'll often fish in open water and/or around tide rips, where shallow draft is not an issue. Most anglers in this situation opt for an 18- to 20-footer, with 130 hp or more to get the desired cruising speed. Such a rig is big and heavy by southern flats standards, and it will pole like a dump truck, but mostly you'll be using the pushpole to control your drift with wind and tide. You could use the same rig for flats tarpon fishing, although the loss of pushpole mobility would be a little irksome.

At the other end of this spectrum are the super-thin flats where redfish shimmy into water so shallow that every inch of draft counts. A boat that draws 10 inches can be way too much here, although it can be used very successfully on the deeper flats and around the edges of the really thin stuff whenever the fish are found there.

A number of somewhat specialized boats have evolved for this fishery; these are not specifically flats boats in the high-tech modern sense, but they have a similar principle. For many years, the "scooter" was very popular in Texas because it drew only a few inches and planed like a jet boat. The original version was extremely plain, like a sled with handle bars built to carry one angler and powered by 10 hp or less. From a distance, it looked just like an old Cushman motor scooter, hence the name. The more modern versions are bigger, can carry two or three anglers, and have much larger engines. But they still can get into rather skinny water, even if they're not really popular elsewhere on large bodies of open water for obvious reasons.

Others who want that super-shallow capability turn to durable, thick-aluminum 15- to 17-foot jonboats. Versions with a shallow V that starts in the bow and runs almost to the transom ride far better than completely flat-hulled types, although they draw perhaps an inch more of water. A 16-footer that weighs about 250 pounds reaches 30 mph with a 25-hp engine and two anglers aboard, and it poles almost as easily as a canoe in just 5 inches of water. Some anglers custom-outfit these rigs very economically, with flooring and carpet as well as reinforced-top fore and aft deck coolers for mini-platforms.

Because casting is the only object with flats boats, and because they are geared for light tackle and especially fly tackle use, manufactured versions have a lot of fore and aft deck space. These decks are open and flush casting platforms with ample storage underneath, no pedestal seats, and no cluttering accessories. The large deck area, coupled with a wide beam, makes for living-room-like stability, and even when you get into one of these boats from a dock you'll notice how they don't lean to one side. Some newer flats boats, especially those intended for northern-water use, have a beam up to 8 feet, although most others fall into the 6- to 7-foot range. A wider beam makes for even more stability but a tougher boat to pole; those who would not be poling, either primarily drifting or using an electric motor, and those fishing in more open and thus rougher water, might opt for a boat with greater beam.

As noted, poling is the standard means of moving these boats along the shallows, and most flats boats are equipped with a transom poling platform, a feature relatively unique to this type of fishing boat and its signature characteristic. From the elevated high-above-the-outboard-motor transom platform, you gain the near and distant visibility advantage that extra height affords, and by using an 18-foot fiberglass or graphite pushpole, you can maneuver the boat appropriately to follow a contour, drift properly over a flat, or move to intercept a feeding fish, all while keeping a good lookout. This platform is also useful for sitting and casting, and it can be used in conjunction with a remote-controlled transom-mount electric motor. Many saltwater anglers are averse to using electric motors on flats boats, however, because of the added equipment, the battery needs (unless you run it off the main engine battery and use a recharge system), and the opinion that the motor noise may scare shallow clear-water fish.

Another characteristic of flat boats is the capacity to store plenty of fishing rods. Wide gunwales permit storage of six or more racks per side, with some allowing for full-length storage and having enclosed tip protectors. Livewells are featured on these boats as well, and most sport a center console and three-person bench seat arrangement; the center console on some is spartan, but the placement allows anglers who tangle with big or tough fish on light tackle to quickly run around the boat as necessary when fighting it.

Unlike bass boats, conventional flats boats aren't carpeted; they do have nonskid surfaces, but anglers need to wear shoes or sneakers with boat soles that grip well. In a flats boat, anglers spend most of the time standing and looking or casting; the only time they sit is when moving quickly to and from fishing areas or when stopping to eat lunch. However, some flats boats are equipped with a bow casting platform that elevates the angler 15 to 20 inches above the deck and that can double as a seat, and a few are outfitted with a thigh-high railing to lean against in rough water.

Flats boats are light enough for towing, and many are kept on fitted or customized boat trailers for mobility.

There are options to using flats boats in shallow-water fishing. Some bass boats, especially lighter ones, and some flat-bottom aluminum boats, draw little water. If you can access the necessary fishing areas without having to cross rough-and-tumble water, and if you can get by without flat and uncluttered casting platforms, these may do well. The absence of a poling platform will affect visibility but not necessarily maneuverability.

Certainly canoes offer shallow-water access, but they do not have the stability or casting advantages of other fishing craft. However, there are some places where fish go that even shallow-draft flats boats cannot. Filling this void are some canoelike fiberglass boats, with a pointed bow and square stern for a small outboard, that draw even less water than flats boats, are pretty stable, are far lighter (making them easier to maneuver with a pushpole or electric motor), and are much less expensive. These backwater boats are compromises of a sort for shallow-water use, but compromise is a factor in every fishing boat.
See: Boat; Trailer.

FLATS FISHING
See: Flat; Flats Boat; Sight Fishing.

FLIP CAST
See: Casting

FLIPPING
Flipping is a fairly simple, controlled short-casting technique used in close quarters for presenting a moderately heavy jig or plastic worm in a short, quiet, accurate manner to cover that cannot be properly worked by a lure cast from a long distance away. Some form of flipping has been around for years and was called dabbling or pitching until the marketing wizards latched onto this term. Flipping is a premier close-to-cover fishing technique almost exclusively used by bass anglers standing up in a boat. The basic principle of flipping, however, can be useful when fishing for other species and when wading, fishing from shore, or fishing from a float tube. It is best when there is thick cover, when the water is turbid, and when a jig or weighted worm is used, but flipping can be employed at times with other lures and in other circumstances.

The main purposes, however, are making a quiet presentation in close quarters for largemouth bass and putting the lure in places where other lures cannot be reached with conventional casts. To understand, imagine that you're looking at a bank with a sharply sloping shoreline. Within half a foot of the bank are some bushes, the bases of which may be in 2 feet of water. Any plug pitched at such a target will land directly in front of it and will be on its way without getting very near the fish. A worm might do the trick, but the first cast would have to be extremely accurate; most likely the worm will fall too far in front of the bush to entice the bass to come out. The advantage of flipping is that you can position your boat 15 to 18 feet from the bush and use a long rod to swing a jig or worm so

This thick fallen cover on Missouri's Truman Lake could not be fished properly by casting from afar.

that it lands in the most opportune place without smashing down noisily on the water's surface. Flipping is a surefire way of getting a lure literally in front of a bass in such thick cover as brush, standing timber and stumps, logjams or debris-filled flotsam, heavy lily pad and vegetation clusters, steep craggy ledges, docks, and boathouses.

The tackle required is a long rod, heavy line, and a jig or worm. The rod should be between 7 and 8 feet long, with a long, straight handle. It must be stout because bass are often violently jerked out of heavy cover on a short length of line; and the bigger the bass, the greater the stress and the greater the degree of difficulty. Flipping rods are one-piece, with an upper section that telescopes down into the handle for easy transportation and storage. Most flipping is done with baitcasting tackle, but some anglers prefer spinning gear. The same rod features, however, are applicable. Flipping takes a toll on arm muscles if done for a long period of time; because of this, a graphite rod, weighing considerably less than fiberglass, is desirable.

The reel used on a flipping rod can be the same that you use for other bass fishing applications, but it is best if the reel has a narrow spool (line capacity is not a factor) and is light. It should also have a clear sideplate (no knobs sticking out on which to catch line). A reel that allows one-handed operation is preferable. A so-called flipping feature, which allows the line to be stripped out without having to disengage and re-engage the free spool, makes a difference in convenience when flipping, since you often have to strip off more line but don't have to take time to crank the handle to engage the gears.

When flipping, many anglers use 25- to 30-pound-test nylon monofilament line because it takes a lot of effort to get it to stretch, abrades less, and is suitable for muscling big fish out of thick cover. You can use lighter line, however, although you have to be sensible. Braided and fused super lines, with their high strength and low diameter, are good candidates for flipping. Their low stretch improves strike detection, but because of the close sudden struggles that characterize flipping, you'll have to be careful that you don't overload your rod.

Black or brown jigs, primarily in $1/2$-ounce sizes, but also a little lighter and a little heavier, are the most popular flipping bait. These should have fiber weedguards when used in all but rocky ledge areas and should sport a "living rubber" type of skirt and a large hook. They are adorned with all manner of enticements, including worms, curl-tail grubs, pork strips, and the like, but black or brown pork chunks are the most popular.

You can also flip a plastic worm. Use a 7- to 8-inch worm on a 5/0 hook and a heavy ($3/8$- or $1/2$-ounce) slip sinker that is pegged to prevent it from sliding up the line. This seems to get hung up less frequently than a jig, and when you have a strike, you can hesitate for the slightest moment to get a firm hookset. Try a worm with a paddle or beaver tail when flipping, although curl tails work also if they aren't so sinewy that they grab onto every limb.

To flip properly, remember that the goal is to make a pinpoint bait presentation to a particular object within 10 to 20 feet of the boat and to do so in a quiet, splash-free manner. Seldom are you able to flip while sitting down; this is a technique that requires stand-up work, occasionally with two anglers close together in the bow of a boat (as when working every nook and cranny of a stump- and blowdown-filled stretch of shoreline). To begin flipping, let out about 7 to 8 feet of line from rod tip to lure; the rule of thumb is to let out about an amount equal to the length of the rod. Strip line off the reel until your free hand and rod hand are fully extended away from each other; this will give you 5 to 7 feet of line in your free hand. If you have a $7^1/2$-foot rod, you're now able to reach a target about 20 feet away.

To flip your bait out, hold the flipping rod at about a 45-degree angle and pull on the line with your left hand to get the bait moving backward. Now drop the rod tip, and start bringing it up to move the lure forward. Practice so you can speed the lure forward to its target with just a slight flexing of your wrist. Let the extra line you're holding in your left hand slide out through the rod guides. Move your left hand forward as the line flows out. Do it right, and the practice plug should go out in a low trajectory and land accurately and softly on its

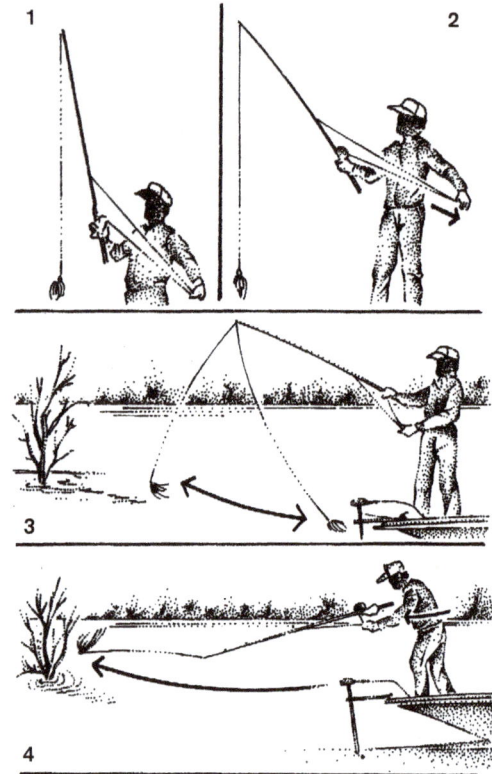

To flip, let out about 7 to 9 feet of line from rod tip to lure; strip line off the reel and hold it in your left hand (1). Point the rod tip up and out, and swing the jig forward (2). The bait will come back toward you; when it reaches the top of its pendulum-like swing, direct it toward the target (3). Lower the rod tip, and let line flow through your free hand; extend your rod arm if necessary to reach the target, and keep the line in your hand (4).

intended target. Extend your rod arm if necessary to reach the target, although you're too far away if you have to do this.

Do not hold onto the line in your hand once it reaches the target. As a flip cast is completed, let your left hand move forward as the extra line you've been holding in it slides out through the guides. It's natural and easy to make this movement. You should wind up with your left hand up close to the rod and just in front of the reel. At that point, position your thumb and the forefinger of the left hand on top of the rod. The other three fingers of the left hand should go under the rod. Make sure the line coming from the reel runs under your thumb and over the forefinger of your left hand. Having the line in this position lets your thumb and forefinger feel every little bump as the lure you're using works through cover. Having your left hand out there also permits you to grip the rod in two hands at the strike, making for a stronger, more solid hookset. Then you may play the fish in the conventional manner, with one hand on the reel handle and the other on the rod handle, and work it out of the cover.

An angler who holds the line in the left hand away from the rod is likely to struggle when a strike occurs, especially if it's from a big fish. There isn't time to grab the tackle conventionally, so you strip the free line back, jerk the rod tip up sharply, and hope you have hook penetration but can yank the fish out, all in the same motion. It doesn't always happen, and a lot of good-size fish are lost this way. Even when holding the rod with both hands, you have to work fast and try to muscle the fish through the cover as best as possible. At times you'll hook a small fish and yank it out of the cover, but when you hook a big bass while flipping, you'll have an excitingly fast and furious bulldog scrap.

When you retrieve the lure to move it to another spot, lower the rod tip and point it toward the lure; grab the line between the reel and the first guide with your free hand and strip it back while lifting up on your rod (similar to the hauling technique used by fly casters). Swing the lure out and back, and send it forward again to the next object.

When the lure is in the water, you may jig it up and down or crawl it along after it has fallen freely to the bottom. Climb it up, over, and through all of the cover. Closely watch the line for the slightest movement, and be attentive to the softest strike. Don't keep it in any one place long, and try to nudge it through cover instead of ripping it.

Practice is every bit as important in learning how to flip as it is in developing mastery of any casting technique. Even so, you'll see anglers trying to flip who obviously don't know how to go about it. An hour of practice on dry land would ease their problems and make them far more effective when the chance to fish comes along.

FLOAT

A lightweight surface-floating device attached to fishing line for indicating a subsurface bite or strike by a fish, primarily on some form of bait and occasionally on an ultralightweight jig or fly. Technically a float is the most prominent form of bite indicator (see) or strike indicator (see) although it is not actually referred to as either of these. In North America such a device is primarily called a bobber, sometimes a cork, and occasionally a float, but it is only known as a float in Europe, where such devices originated hundreds of years ago. Modern floats are primarily made of balsa wood or hollow plastic.

Modern float designs, rigging, fishing tactics, and control techniques are part of a highly effective fishing system that is an art form and a science in the hands of diligent anglers. Float fishing methods have evolved in recent years and have expanded opportunities to catch many species of fish, especially in freshwater lakes and rivers.

Until recently, floats and float fishing had changed little from their first recorded existence in the fourteenth century until the first modern-era reel development in the mid-nineteenth century. This development allowed anglers to make bigger

An assortment of balsa floats for varied types of fishing.

floats that could be cast farther and also to control their floats at greatly increased distances to reach fish that had previously been out of range before with just a pole. Progress remained stagnant again until spinning reels became popular in the mid-twentieth century and caused casting distance to advance again. In recent decades, floats and float fishing have also benefited from high-tech rods, reels, and lines that have dramatically extended distances, depths, and current speeds.

Thinner, stronger nylon, combined with long-distance casting spools on spinning reels and ultralightweight rods, permits a perfect natural bait presentation in many situations. You can, for example, cast a 13-inch float nearly 80 yards from the bank and place a baited hook or jig 20 to 40 feet deep to unsuspecting walleye, catfish, or trout; cast a $1^{1}/_{2}$-inch float to panfish in 12 inches of clear water 30 yards away; and tempt catfish or stripers with a live shad just off snaggy, rocky bottom in powerful flowing water below a dam.

A range of float designs can be bought or made, allowing you to literally fish anywhere at any time and to precisely and naturally present a hooked bait as the fish would expect it to behave and, in most cases, with the fish unaware that you are anywhere near.

There are three major styles of float fishing: fishing with a pole on stillwater and slow-flowing water, fishing with a rod and reel on stillwater, and fishing with a rod and reel on flowing water. Each of these styles employs specific float designs, balancing patterns, casting techniques, and control techniques.

Some Basics

Presenting a hooked bait naturally is an important concept in all types of fishing and especially when using floats. Many species of fish, particularly those that live in stillwater environments, inhale their food most of the time; this begins when they are tiny and start inhaling zooplankton for food. Many fish—most panfish, for example—feed this way their entire lives. Thus, when they suck in a bait that is attached to a float, they are acutely aware that something is very wrong if the bait doesn't move readily when they inhale it.

Anglers should remember that fish have different feeding states. For a small portion of their time they are aggressive, for a larger portion they are neutral, and for the greatest amount of time they are negative; some people estimate that the respective percentages for these behaviors are 10, 30, and 60. Whatever the percentage might be, these behaviors vary according to many factors, especially weather changes and fishing pressure.

When fish are in an aggressive mood, they will attack and consume a bait even if something is wrong with it. But they are especially likely to immediately reject a suspicious bait if they are in a neutral or negative mood. As a result, anglers have to use methods and equipment that will not alarm even the wariest fish.

A major factor in making an unalarming presentation is the float. In places where fish are not very astute or when fishing for aggressive species, a float that has a lot of buoyancy (such as the round bobber that is very common in North America) may be used with success often enough to overlook its deficiencies. However, such buoyancy acts as a drag on hooked bait and is a dead giveaway to light-biting fish. So it's better to fish with a float that is designed to avoid alerting fish and is still sensitive enough to alert the angler to a bite.

Using highly specialized tackle and the most delicately balanced floats, a match angler fishes the 1992 World Championships at the River Erne in Northern Ireland.

Correct float selection is dependent upon knowing the depth of the water at the fishing place. In a boat, depth is readily determined by using sonar; without sonar, and for shore fishing, it is necessary to use some type of weight attached to the line (called a plummet in Europe) to plumb the depth. Determining depth in this manner is known as plumbing. This activity also is meant to determine the composition of the bottom (mud, gravel, weeds, etc.), the location of stumps or other snags, and changes in depth so that the angler can create a mental picture of the area and visualize where the fish might be.

A major factor in float usage is balancing the float properly. This balancing is also known as shotting, since small split shot or a jig, or a combination of both, is added in just the right amount and placed so that only a minimum amount of the float tip is above the surface and visible to the angler depending on the circumstances. It is always best to have the least possible weight to get the float in a balanced position.

When casting modern floats, always lob the float upward slowly and smoothly. Never snatch it or cast it quickly, which causes tangles. When a float starts to lose momentum, feather the line as it comes off the spool; this pulls the float back so that the baited hook passes over the float before it hits the water.

Float Fishing with a Pole

Float fishing with a pole on stillwater and slow-flowing water is the oldest and simplest way to fish, and it is ideal for children or beginners of any age. Perhaps the earliest illustration of any type of angling is a hieroglyphic from about 2000 B.C. that depicts an Egyptian angler with a pole catching a fish. The use of a float with a pole was known to be practiced in the late 1300s, if not before.

Anglers learned by trial and error in the hundreds of years following the fourteenth century that it was vital to use the smallest possible float that was carefully balanced by lead shot. These floats were made from crow, goose, swan, or porcupine quills (cork bodies were used when extra weight was needed and pear-shaped cork floats were used for pike), and with proper balancing only a fraction of the quill's air chamber was above the surface. This was vital, since it gave the float an almost neutral buoyancy and meant that the most discriminating fish, or even a tiny specimen, could suck the bait into its mouth and simultaneously pull the float under, signaling the angler to set the hook.

This is exactly how the most famous angling writer of all time, Izaak Walton, fished his beloved River Lea, and his book *The Compleat Angler,* written in 1653, described how he used this technique to hook that river's famous, nervous, and difficult-to-catch roach. Even earlier, in 1496, the first English language essay to teach the art of angling, *A Treatyse of Fysshynge with an Angle* by Dame

Juliana Berners, illustrated an angler using a 16-foot pole to catch a fish from a river. While Berners graciously credited several earlier angling writers with teaching the fundamentals, both she and Walton noted that the golden rule was always to use the smallest float possible for the conditions and to carefully balance it with lead split shot.

Poles. There are actually two styles of poles: one-piece or telescopic versions that are 9 to 20 feet long, and multipiece (or take-apart) poles that are 18 to 60 feet long. These are both useful in any type or speed of water, but since they do not have a reel, the distance from the angler and the depth of water that can be fished are limited to the length of the pole. Longer poles have the advantage of allowing anglers to reach out to distant locations (such as a weedbed) from a bank or boat and carefully lower a float and bait into small pockets that would be impossible to cast into (or to cast into delicately) with a rod and reel. As a rule, the length of the line from the tip of the pole to the hook should always be shorter than the pole; use 12 feet of line, for example, for a 14-foot pole, and 18 feet of line for a 20-foot pole.

The main tackle component in pole fishing for the average angler is a 10- to 14-foot-long pole, which may be as simple and inexpensive as a cane pole; fiberglass or graphite poles, however, though more expensive, are deadly for anglers who are serious about catching more and bigger panfish.

Floats. For pole fishing in shallow water from 6 inches to 4 feet deep, mini-floats (called a mini shy bite by some) in several sizes from 1 inch to $2^1/_2$ inches long are perfect and are not likely to scare fish when they are presented in the water because of their smaller shape and lesser splash. These floats are easy to make or find in stores. In essence to make one, take a 1- to 2-inch piece of a thin dried tree branch ($^1/_8$-inch to $^3/_{16}$-inch thick), varnish it, and paint one end with a highly visible color (often red). In use, this is balanced with one or two small split shot. Such an all-balsa float is available in many sizes from stores; it is capable of being fished with up to four BB-size shot (one shot weighs about $^1/_{64}$ ounce).

For pole fishing in intermediate and deep water from 4 to 18 feet, a simple crow or porcupine quill float, or a balsa-bodied float on a thin dowel stem (called a shy bite by some and about 7 inches long in several sizes), is extremely sensitive and deadly for all panfish, catfish, and small carp. Because these floats have longer stems, they are more stable in the wind. Even the wariest old crappie, perch, or bluegill can easily suck these floats under when they are balanced to sit just $^1/_2$ inch or less above the surface.

Both of these styles are attached to the line and held in place by two silicone sleeves (which are first slipped onto the line before it is tied to the hook), one at each end, which allows the angler to interchange floats if the conditions or the location changes. Each time the float is changed, however, it has to be balanced either by adding or subtracting split shot. These floats are especially deadly for crappie fishing with small minnows.

Since these floats are attached to the line and held in place by silicone tubes at each end of the float, only the length of the pole limits the depths that can be fished.

Multipiece pole use. Multipiece, or take-apart, poles are used by professional tournament anglers in major match fishing events, including national and world championship events, and exist in lengths from 18 to over 60 feet long. These poles allow the angler to fish any depth of water, from as shallow as 8 inches to the length of the pole minus 24 inches from pole tip to float. For example, to catch crappie 2 feet deep and 30 feet away from your position under a dock or trees, simply place the float rig precisely where you want it. With just 6 inches of line between the float and pole, you can place or push the float into tight places.

To land fish with a multipiece pole, you push the pole behind yourself until the section where the pole is joined (about 5 or 6 feet) is reached and then take the sections apart to land the fish. After rebaiting, the pole is put together again and the float rig is placed anew.

These are very expensive graphite poles, however, and not necessary in normal angling situations; only when there are lots of anglers and spectators do these poles become important. There is also an entire range of pole floats that are specially designed for use with the long take-apart poles; these, too are very expensive and much more fragile than other

Pole Floats

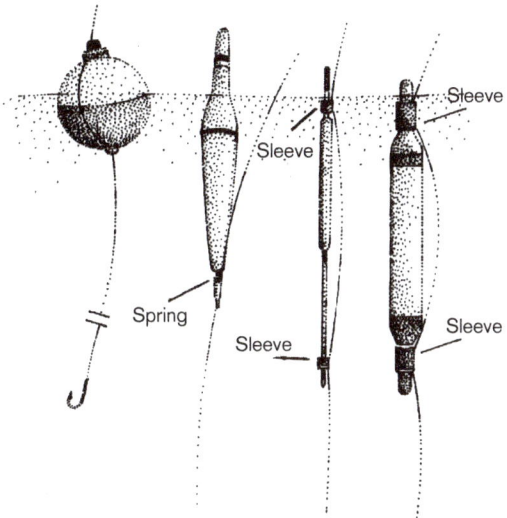

Shown are common floats used with poles. The two versions on the left typify highly buoyant floats that are not sensitive enough to depict light bites and the action of small fish; the two floats on the left, if balanced with the proper amount of weight, are very sensitive and able to indicate lift bites and the immediate bite of even small fish.

English centrepin reels used for float fishing.

floats, and are not necessary unless competing in bank-fishing events where the presence of competitors and spectators makes the fish much more difficult to catch.

Float Fishing with Rod and Reel

The techniques and float designs for float fishing with a rod and reel on stillwater and flowing water are completely opposite to each other and were developed in England in the 1850s. Anglers learned to drift floats in Nottingham by carefully controlling the float with the rod tip, so that the baited hook moved at the same speed as the slower flowing water near the bottom, where most fish feed. The improvement of the smooth-running centrepin reel (a single-action two-handled reel that is also called a float reel and features a large-diameter arbor) in England was the main contributor to this advancement.

About the same time around the major steel town of Sheffield, where there were slow-flowing rivers and drains (canals) and some 2,220 angling clubs, intense fishing pressure made it very difficult to catch fish close to the angler, especially in big competitions. Anglers were forced to find several ways to cast their floats across the drains and rivers in order to reach the wary, nervous fish that were scared off by the vibrations and movement of anglers, spectators, and people strolling the river banks. This method of float fishing was called the original Sheffield style and also known as Fine and Far Off, and today is known as waggler fishing.

Flowing water principle. In flowing water with a rod and reel, it's necessary to fish a controlled float that is connected to the fishing line on the top and bottom of the float, whether of a fixed or slip variety. When fishing a float in flowing water, the angler must be stationary in order to find the correct float speed that catches fish at that moment (this means anchoring when fishing from a boat). The reason is that stream flows vary from top to bottom and, even though floats are used on the surface, the baits are fished on or near the bottom. On a straight section of a trout stream that is 4 feet deep, for example, the flow just off the bottom will be approximately 20 to 25 percent slower than the surface speed. On a river that is over 20 feet deep, there will be very little current near the bottom, even if the surface speed is swift. These variations mandate that a float be controlled with the rod top and that the angler be stationary.

Even if you know the exact speed just off bottom, the fish may want the hookbait faster or slower. These factors can and do change every day, and learning them is part of the mystery and magic that continuously challenge anglers.

Floats on flowing water. The type of float used varies with the flow speed. Among fixed floats shown in the illustration above, the classic bulblike Avon style (A), for example, is used for medium flows, whereas a more buoyant float (B) is needed for fast and more turbulent water, where bait must be dragged along the bottom without being pulled under easily. These and other fixed floats stay on the line at a preselected position, usually being held in place by silicone sleeves at both the top and the bottom of the float.

Floats for Flowing Water

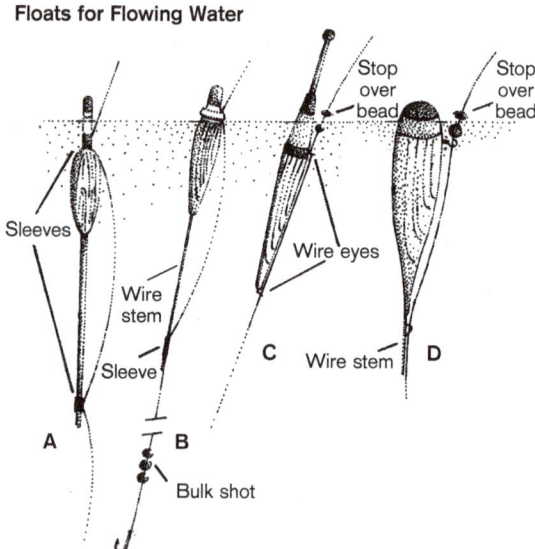

Shown are common balsa floats used in flowing water. The two on the left are fixed in place with silicone sleeves, with one being used in medium-speed flows (A) and the other in faster flows because of greater buoyancy (B). The two on the right are slip floats (C and D), in which line passes through wire arms, with a stop knot used for positioning.

There are two eyes on all flowing water slip floats—on the top and the bottom of the float. These floats slide on the line, with depth setting controlled by attaching a stop to the line. Smaller-bodied versions (C) are good all-around floats for any species when using small- to medium-size bait; larger and more buoyant versions (D) are good for big bait and big fish. A float stop and a bead must be used for both of these.

The simplest and often the best weight placement for balancing in flowing water is a bulk pattern. Place all the shot together a few inches in front of the hook if you want the bait to be just above, or just on, the bottom; or place the shot 18 inches from the hook if the bait is to be dragged along the bottom. In smooth-flowing water, shot can be spread out evenly from float to hook. In Europe this is called the equidistant or shirt button shotting pattern. There are many other ways to place shot, these being the most basic.

Stillwater principle. An important element of fishing a float with a rod and reel in stillwater is to cast a relatively long distance (in some places close

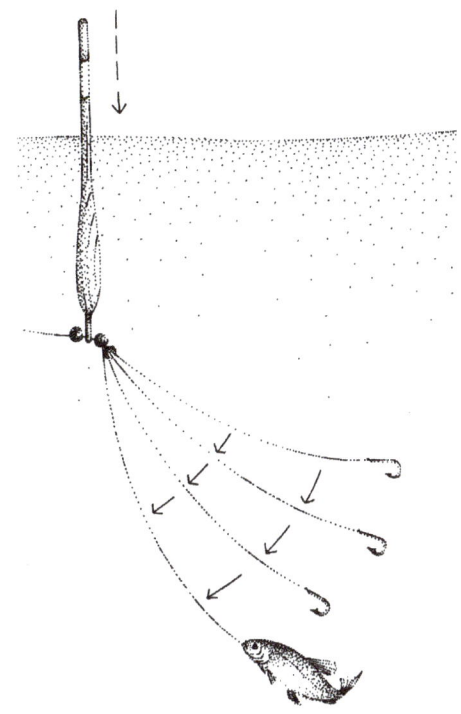

When a fixed float is cast in stillwater, the baited hook drifts down as depicted and the tip of the float settles down in the water. However, if a fish takes the baited hook while it is falling and before it reaches a vertical position, the tip of the float remains high in the water. This is a subtle but sure indication of a bite, and reason for the angler to set the hook.

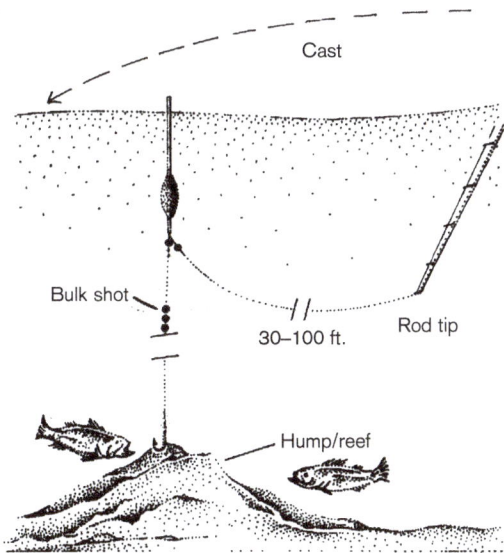

To bury the line so that wind and wave action don't move the float and baited hook away from a given position, cast beyond the target fishing area, place the rod tip under the surface, retrieve some line to get the float and bait where you want it (in this case over a hump or reef), then let the float settle on the surface. Keep the rod tip in the water so the line to the float remains submerged.

to the far bank) with floats that are attached only at their bottom (called waggler style in Europe), then push the rod top as deeply under the water as possible, and wind in quickly. This sinks the line and prevents the wind from affecting the float. If anglers will do this, they can master float fishing in windy and wavy conditions. This is the general method that was originally developed in Sheffield.

Floats on stillwater. The floats that have been developed for fishing with rod and reel in stillwater are called wagglers in Europe; they are used for fishing at any distance and at any depth, and may be used as slip or fixed versions. They are attached to the line only at the bottom, and because of their aerodynamic shape (bulbous at the bottom and long-stemmed at the top) they cast very well, infinitely better than any round type of float (such as a bobber).

When such floats are correctly balanced in the water, their shape is hydrodynamic, meaning that they slide through the water (with less drag than a round-shaped float) when a fish bites. When using these floats, you can catch fish as your bait falls through the water—fishing on the drop—and see bites if the fish moves up in the water as it takes the bait.

Generally the float settles in the water after the hookbait has fully dropped into position; when a fish takes the hookbait, the float lifts up in the water, indicating a strike. This is known as a lift bite. The angler sets the hook upon observing this, and since the float folds over when the hook is set (because the float is attached at the bottom only), the angler gets a better hookset. Always strike sideways with the tip near the surface, and after the fish is felt, lift the rod back up to normal playing position.

There are small and low-profiled balsa-bodied wagglers for casting to shallow water along the bank or up to 30 yards away, with larger models for windy conditions or longer casts. Deep fishing or very windy conditions require long peacock quills, some with and without a balsa body, to present the hookbait correctly on most windy days. Some of these models are up to 13 inches long.

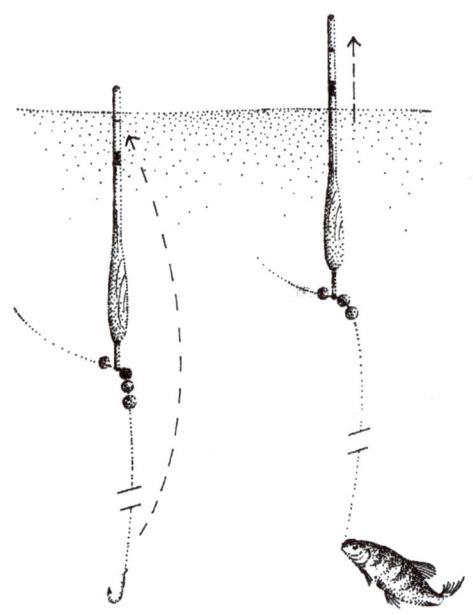

When a fixed float is balanced and positioned properly, the tip of the float is just below the surface (left). When a fish takes the baited hook and moves down, the float disappears, which is very obvious; but when the fish takes and moves upward, it is less obvious because the tip of the float moves up (right). This latter scenario is known as a lift bite, because the action of the fish lifts the float.

Stillwater Fixed Floats

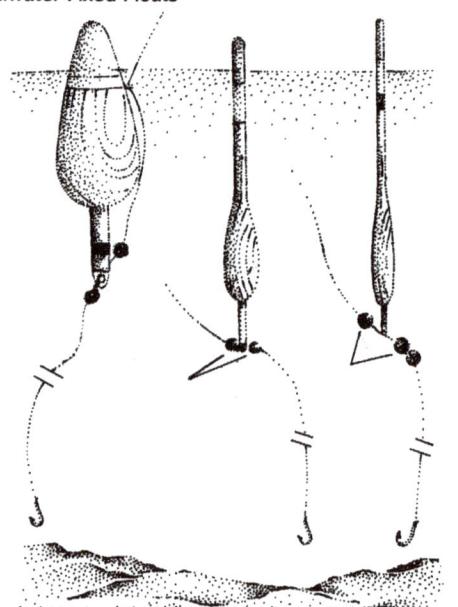

Shown are common fixed floats used for making distant casts when fishing in lakes and ponds. Although not drawn to scale here, they depict how split shot is used to fix various floats at given positions. The length of line below the float determines the level of the baited hook.

As a general guide for balancing, fixed wagglers should have at least 60 percent of the total lead shot positioned to lock the float in place, with the rest of it being drop shot (lower and closer to the hook or jig head). For slip wagglers, start with a bulk pattern, and for a rest shot place two smaller shot 4 feet from the bulk shot, which helps minimize tangles.

FLOATANT
Dressing applied to a fly to help it repel water and float.
See: Fly.

FLOATING/DIVING PLUG
See: Plug.

FLOATING LINE
The fly line that is designed to float on the surface of the water.
See: Flycasting Tackle.

FLOATING LURE
See: Plug; Surface Lure.

FLOATING/SINKING LINE
A fly line with a floating body and a sinking tip section, also called a sink-tip or sinking-tip line.
See: Flycasting Tackle.

FLOAT TUBES
Also known as belly boats, kick boats, personal inflatables, and U-tubes, the diverse category of fishing (and boating) accessories known under the generic umbrella of float tubes includes a broadening and evolving type of equipment used by anglers primarily to access ponds, small lakes, protected sections of bigger waters, secluded waters, and small to moderate streams and rivers. This new equipment is manually propelled, mostly inflatable, and is loosely called watercraft but is not actually recognized as boats in the formal sense, as in requiring state registration and meeting industry safety certification. However, the more complex and sophisticated models, and those that can be fitted with motors, may be recognized as boats and fall under established watercraft guidelines.

Float tubes for fishing purposes have been increasing in popularity since the 1980s, starting with inflatable inner tubes wrapped in a cover with seating support and propelled by fins or other devices. These evolved as alternatives to conventional boats and have matured into designs that feature high-placed seating and rowing.

Most float tubes have expediency as their primary virtue. They are light and easily stowed in a small car or a closet. They can be packed into a remote location and then inflated. They are quiet, relatively unobtrusive, and inexpensive in comparison with most conventional boat options, although comparably priced with canoes.

Float tubes are not only easy to transport, but also provide transportation. In rivers, tubes allow anglers to float downstream to fish selected places, rather than walking along trails or over often rocky and slippery river bottoms. In lakes, they allow anglers to drift along shorelines while casting, fishing farther from shore than they might if restricted to casting from shore. Tubes also make access and passage simpler; portaging—past swift water, over obstructions, or to nearby or connected bodies of water—is pretty easy. They even provide some security for waders in case they slip; anglers can wade conventionally while ensconced in tubes, knowing that they won't fall in and get wet because the tube will cushion the effects of a misstep.

Float tubes have their drawbacks, of course. Although some anglers use them in big lakes and quick waters, they aren't meant for places that can get rough, or where current or wind can overcome the power of foot propulsion. They can be effective under appropriate conditions for fishing, but they cannot cover ground in the timely and effective way that a small boat equipped with an electric motor can. Nevertheless, for anglers who don't have a boat and boating-related accessories, they provide a good way of reaching otherwise unreachable spots, and they invite a simple, different, and pleasurable experience attuned to a slower, more thorough pace of fishing.

The general scenario for fishing out of these devices is that an angler floats on or in a tube, wearing chest-high waders and a pair of fins on his or her feet. The waders are usually neoprene, but lighter materials work in warm waters at appropriate seasons. The float tube is propelled backward by leg power, which theoretically frees the angler's hands for casting and allows for constant positioning adjustments.

Float tube types. The first inflatable float tubes adapted for fishing were oval, like a donut with a hole. The oval shape, which created a lot of drag in the water and was hard to get in and out of with fins on, is now outdated, yielding to versions with the entry end open and the opposite end squared or pointed. Most of these have what is called a U shape, but some have a wedge or V shape for cutting through the wind and waves better. Remember that anglers in float tubes propel themselves backward and face the opposite direction of movement.

Early oval float tubes, which were commonly called belly boats, were essentially inner tubes covered with canvas or nylon cloth. Newer tubes have an open end that permits easy entry and exit, and better models have a stabilizer to keep the open end from collapsing on itself. The open ends also help propulsion by allowing operators to raise their legs more horizontally for increased thrust and to raise

A float tube angler lands a hefty rainbow trout.

legs to pass over obstructions, which is especially useful in current.

Whereas oval float tubes had one interior tube, U-shaped versions have separate arm and back bladders, which raise the level of the angler. The lower the angler sits, the less visibility and the harder it is to cast with certain tackle, so sitting higher is desirable if it does not adversely affect stability. The tubes or bladders are inflated by mouth (tough for many to do), foot pump, or compressor.

The better float tubes have a high back support, adjustable seat, an apron or lightweight basket for catching fly line or laying objects while rigging, and a lot of watertight zippered pockets for gear storage.

Float tubes are sometimes a bit awkward to maneuver and turn. With the angler's legs hanging down, they tend to get caught in weeds, brush, and logs, and to bump on rocks and other objects. They also don't provide a lot of thrust, and operators struggle to buck strong current, heavy wind, and wave action. They should always be worn with a PFD *(see)*.

Kick boats/pontoon tubes. Pontoon-style float tubes have evolved from the desire to make self-propelled watercraft more maneuverable and raise the angler to a higher, or at least an adjustable, position. These craft are primarily called kick boats, and the majority feature two inflatable pontoons, pointed at the ends, bridged by a frame with a seat. Some feature noninflatable molded hard-plastic pontoons. These were primarily set up for kicking with the feet, but many so-called kick boats now have oars and perhaps should be called row tubes.

These craft take longer to assemble than conventional float tubes, weigh two to three times as much in total, and cost more, but they are versatile, easier to maneuver, and faster. They have improved thrust when used with oars, and because so little of the angler is actually in the water, they offer more control. They also allow a little more gear to be carried than what a float tube allows, and they keep more of the anglers body out of the water. Some models can be disassembled and toted as a backpack.

Accessories. A good pair of swim fins is as important to using float tubes or kick boats as the boats themselves. Some anglers use paddle pushers in lieu of fins; these are devices that strap around the boot heel and have a paddle that allows you to go forward by moving your legs as if you were walking. Swim fins are preferred, however, because they provide quicker movement from point to point if your leg muscles are in good shape. You must move backward in fins virtually all the time to get anywhere, and they are tough to walk in on land or on a murky lake bottom. For beginners, paddling and traveling backward is a bit like walking backward.

Popular fins for tubes and kick boats are shorter than fins used for swimming and diving, and should have more rigidity. It's best if they float and also have a lanyard so that they can be readily retrieved if they fall off.

Many options are available for float tubes and kick boats today, especially with the increasing popularity of the latter. Most are involved with boating rather than fishing, and if you get too loaded up with the options, you might wonder why you didn't get a canoe or a jonboat in the first place.

Remember that tackle selection with many float tubes has to be a little conservative. You generally have only one rod with you, and you can't take a full tackle box of equipment, though with a fishing vest or suitable storage compartments on the float tube, you can still bring a fair amount along. Always be attuned to safety with these devices, and wear some type of PFD. Inflatable PFDs are a lightweight option.
See: Boat.

FLOOD TIDE
Incoming, or rising, tide.
See: Tides.

FLORIDA
Florida is justifiably called a sportfishing mecca. Millions make angling pilgrimages to the Sunshine State each year, many of them in search of the fish of their dreams, especially big largemouth bass, bonefish, tarpon, and sailfish. But these are just the most storied species. With tens of thousands of fish-filled inland waters, and 1,350 miles of coastline bounding the Atlantic Ocean and the Gulf of Mexico, the abundance of Florida's angling opportunities is rivaled only by their diversity.

The fabled St. Johns River, which empties into the Atlantic at Jacksonville, holds everything from largemouth bass and stripers to shad and seatrout. In the shadow of the space center at Cape Canaveral, anglers consistently catch huge red drum. Palm Beach, where the warm north-flowing waters of the Gulf Stream come closest to the United States, provides anglers with the chance to catch and release double-digit numbers of sailfish in a single day.

The Florida Keys, at the extreme tip of the peninsula, are perhaps the most hallowed destination in the state, offering saltwater aficionados everything from bonefish to blue marlin. The state's most remote waters are within Everglades National Park, home to a vast array of wading birds as well as snook, redfish, tarpon, and seatrout. Those four species are also found along the Gulf Coast. In the Panhandle, the seatrout is king, but anglers also target cobia in nearshore waters, and snapper and grouper on wrecks and artificial reefs. And so it goes, with ample interest for such other Florida saltwater species as barracuda, sharks, swordfish, spearfish, wahoo, white marlin, dolphin, amberjack, blackfin tuna, yellowfin tuna, bluefish, little tunny, flounder, permit, pompano, sheepshead, king mackerel, Spanish mackerel, and cero mackerel.

In freshwater, Florida is synonymous with big largemouth bass because of the year-round growing season and abundance of food. Lake Okeechobee, Lake Kissimmee, and Lake Seminole are among the best bass waters in the country, but the chances of catching a trophy are just as good in any number of Florida's ponds, lakes, and canals. In addition to largemouth and peacock bass, Florida also has white bass, sunshine bass, bluegills, black crappie (also known as speckled perch, or specks), redear sunfish (aka shellcrackers), spotted sunfish, warmouth, catfish, bullhead, chain pickerel, gar, bowfin, oscars, and tilapia.

Saltwater
Florida Keys. The Keys consist of 42 islands, connected by bridges, that stretch 100 miles from Key Largo to Key West, the southernmost point in the continental United States. Unlike other parts of Florida, the Keys have severely limited development, which contributes to the area's exceptional inshore and offshore fishery.

The flats on both the Atlantic Ocean and Florida Bay sides of the Keys are best known for big, silvery bonefish. Islamorada, the self-proclaimed Sportfishing Capital of the World, is the most popular bonefish destination. It is ideally located for running north to the flats of Key Largo or south to the flats of Marathon.

Keys bonefish can top 15 pounds but typically run 7 to 9 pounds. They can be caught year-round, but the best fishing is usually in late spring and

The bass are always in the grass at Lake Okeechobee.

early fall, when water temperatures are neither too cold nor too hot. During the summer, bonefish are on the flats early in the morning, when temperatures are relatively cool; then they seek the comfort of deep water before returning to the flats late in the afternoon. In winter, bonefishing is best a few days after a cold front, when the water has had a chance to warm.

Also known as the gray ghost of the flats, bonefish come onto the shallow flats to feed, rooting in the grassy bottom for crabs, shrimp, and other crustaceans. Anglers most commonly pursue them with light spinning tackle (6- to 12-pound line) and live shrimp, crabs, or jigs. Bonefish also are a favorite of fly anglers, who pursue these fish with 8- and 9-weight outfits. Extremely wary, bonefish will flee at the slightest hint of danger, such as a boat, or a cast that comes too close.

An effective way to catch bonefish is to anchor or stake a boat on the edge of a flat, put out pieces of shrimp as chum, then cast out a live shrimp and wait for a bonefish to swim through and eat it. Most experienced anglers prefer to sight-cast for bonefish. Typically, the angler stands at the bow of a flats skiff, which can float in just a few inches of water, while a guide or friend propels the boat forward with a pushpole from a poling platform at the stern of the boat. They scan the flat for signs of bonefish: shaky or nervous water, caused as the bonefish swim against the current; muds, created by bonefish as they root up the bottom; bonefish themselves, which most often appear as dark shadows; and tailing bonefish, who give themselves away in shallow water when their tails break the surface as they feed.

Casts must be on the mark, neither too close nor too far; too close and the bonefish will spook, too far and the bonefish will never find the bait, lure, or fly. A successful cast will result in an electrifying run, which is the event bonefish anglers live for, with the bonefish ripping out 100 or more yards of line as it streaks across the flat.

In addition to bonefish, Keys flats also have tarpon and permit. Tarpon fishing is best in the spring, when the fish migrate north through the Keys. From early March to late June, tarpon and tarpon anglers position themselves all along the flats, as well as at bridges.

As with bonefish, fishing for tarpon is most exciting when sight-casting. The spring migration finds tarpon on flats throughout the Keys, and the chance to hook a 150-pound fish in 3 feet of water is enough to make a veteran tarpon angler's legs shake. Fly fishing with a 12-weight outfit is effective, as is the use of 20- or 30-pound spinning tackle and live shrimp, crabs, and baitfish such as pilchards. Tarpon are most commonly found around openings in banks (raised areas on the flats), where they ambush baitfish as they are swept through the openings by the tide.

Tarpon also concentrate around bridges. Among the best bridges in the Keys are the Seven Mile Bridge and Bahia Honda Bridge, south of Marathon. Tarpon also frequent the channels that run through the bridges and in Key West Harbor. The standard technique is to anchor a boat and fish a live bait under a cork float. Mullet, pinfish, and crabs are the most popular bait.

Permit is the third member of the flats grand slam and usually the hardest of the three species to catch. Warier than bonefish, permit run a lot bigger, averaging 15 to 20 pounds and sometimes exceeding 40 pounds. These larger relatives of the pompano frequent many of the same flats as bonefish, but typically at high tide, when the water is deep enough to accommodate their wide, platter-like bodies. Permit also inhabit holes, channels, and rockpiles, with Key West and the Content Keys ranking among the best permit spots. A live crab is by far the best bait for permit. Tackle is the same as that used for bonefish.

Another common, but overlooked, Florida Keys flats inhabitant is the barracuda. These sharp-toothed predators take live bait, lures, and flies with gusto and produce sizzling runs when hooked. A variety of sharks—including bull, blacktip, bonnet-

One of Florida's top saltwater draws is fishing the Keys' flats, as here near Islamorada.

head, hammerhead, lemon, and nurse species—also cruise the flats.

From Marathon, located in about the middle of the Keys, to Key West, anglers have ready access to Florida Bay and the Gulf of Mexico. Some of the best fishing is on shallow wrecks for cobia, permit, jacks, sharks, grouper, and snapper.

The Keys' inshore fishing is rivaled only by its offshore fishing. From one end of the Keys to the other, anglers encounter amberjack, blue marlin, sailfish, dolphin, wahoo, cobia, king mackerel, snapper, grouper, and blackfin tuna as the fish migrate through the area.

Winter is prime time for sailfish, blackfin tuna, and king mackerel. Sailfish show up in November as they seek warm waters, and usually stay until late spring. Fishing is often best in December and January. Trolling lures, live bait, and dead bait is productive. When sailfish are especially abundant, many anglers run offshore and look for sailfish chasing bait or swimming down-sea. Then they use 12- to 20-pound spinning tackle to cast live bait in front of the fish. Catches of 10 or more sailfish in a day are not uncommon under those conditions.

Blackfin tuna are staples of the Keys in winter and early spring, especially around offshore humps, where the ocean bottom rises significantly and attracts huge concentrations of bait and fish. Blackfins, which range from 15 to 40 pounds, will hit trolled lures and bait, but live pilchards are preferred. Typically, charter boats will go offshore with 500 to 1,000 of the little baitfish. Upon arriving at a hump, two or more lines baited with live pilchards are put out, then the mate starts chumming by throwing handfuls of pilchards into the water, attracting the tuna.

Yellowfin tuna run much bigger than blackfins—50 to 150 pounds—but aren't nearly as abundant or easy to target. Key West has the best run of yellowfin, with ideal fishing typically in December.

The Keys get both Atlantic and gulf king mackerel as the fish head south for the winter. Kingfish, as they are known, are found along the edge of the coral reefs that run the length of the Keys. Some of the best fishing is south of Key West, where boats catch kings up to 40 or more pounds. The most common technique is to slow-troll with live or dead bait. Some anglers prefer to anchor their boats and, as with blackfin tuna, chum with live pilchards. When the kingfish show up—they'll often skyrocket behind the boat—they can be caught on everything from live bait to jigs to flies.

By March, amberjack begin concentrating at the humps as they prepare to spawn, and remain there through May. These hard-fighting fish can easily top 50 pounds. Anglers typically fish a live bait near the bottom in 200 or more feet. Thirty- to 50-pound tackle is needed to wrestle an amberjack to the surface.

One of the most popular species in the Keys, dolphin generally make their appearance in April and remain abundant for much of the summer. These colorful, acrobatic fish often travel in schools anywhere from 10 to 30 miles offshore. Depending on their size, they can be caught on everything from fly tackle or light (8-pound) spinning tackle to 30-pound conventional outfits. Schoolie dolphin run anywhere from 5 to 10 pounds, with the size of the school ranging from a few fish to more than 100. Gaffer dolphin, which are big enough to require the use of a gaff to get them in the boat, run up to 20 pounds. Fish bigger than that are known as slammers, and they can top 70 pounds. Typically, the bigger fish are farther offshore.

Most anglers locate dolphin around floating debris and weedlines or under frigate birds. The weeds and debris attract baitfish, which attract the dolphin. Frigate birds will follow dolphin in the hopes of picking up scraps when the fish feed.

Trolling dead ballyhoo or squid is the most common tactic for catching dolphin. When there are no signs of dolphin, blind trolling can produce fish in the middle of nowhere. When weeds, debris, or birds are located, trolling in the area often produces dolphin. Many anglers employ a run-and-gun technique, cruising in their boats until they come across dolphin. Then they cast jigs, live bait, or chunks of bait to the fish.

Blue marlin show up soon after the dolphin arrive and often are found in the same places. One of the best spots in all of Florida is The Wall, 19 miles south of Key West, where the ocean bottom drops off sharply. The fish range from 100 pounds to more than 500 pounds.

The coral reefs provide excellent fishing for a variety of snapper and grouper year-round, with the best fishing from spring to fall. Most anglers target yellowtail snapper, which run up to 5 pounds, and mutton snapper, which can top 20 pounds. The favored method is to fish dead bait on the bottom. Heavy chumming can bring yellowtail to the surface, where they can be landed on small jigs, dead bait, live bait, and flies.

Florida Bay/Ten Thousand Islands. In addition to great fishing, the southern end of Florida's mainland offers anglers an opportunity to experience Florida the way it was before hordes of people and condos arrived. This is true wilderness, and more than one angler has spent the night after getting lost in the maze of mangrove islands scattered throughout the vast area.

Much of Florida Bay is contained within the 1.5-million-acre Everglades National Park, which was created in 1947. Access is via boat from the Keys, but a favorite jumping-off point is Flamingo, an isolated outpost at the tip of the mainland. In addition to boat ramps, Flamingo has a marina with food, fuel, bait, tackle, rental boats, canoes, and a motel. Once you leave the dock, you're on your own. You have a choice of fishing out front in Florida Bay or heading north into what is known as the backcountry.

The backcountry features a tangle of mangrove islands separated by rivers, creeks, and rivulets. Anglers who venture here must remember the precise route they took if they plan to return to the dock the same day.

To successfully fish the backcountry, one must think of Florida Bay as a shallow body of water that simply floods and drains. When the water is high, fish forage for shrimp and crabs on the flats. When the level is low, they are forced to feed in deeper water, such as channels. At the edge of a channel intersecting the flats, predators ambush smaller fish carried from the shallows by the falling tide. That's where anglers can ambush the predators—primarily snook, seatrout, baby tarpon, and redfish, but also croaker, jack crevalle, ladyfish, mangrove snapper, catfish, and pinfish. The best fishing is during the spring and fall, when temperatures are tolerable for both fish and anglers. Spinning rods spooled with 8- to 20-pound line, and 8-weight fly-rod outfits, can handle just about everything an angler will encounter.

Whitewater Bay, near Flamingo, is one of the largest backcountry bodies of water. It has sea trout, redfish, jacks, snook, and tarpon. The fish typically aren't as large as those found in Florida Bay, but in the Whitewater area, Lake Ingraham, East Cape Canal, and other sheltered waters offer good fishing and protection from wind, even when it's blowing 15 to 20 mph.

Everglades National Park possesses several no-motor areas, such as the West Lake and Bear Lake canoe trails, where only hand-propelled vessels are allowed. Few anglers have the desire or stamina to paddle a canoe or row a boat into the remote interior of the park, which results in excellent fishing for seatrout, snook, redfish, black drum, snapper, jacks, and baby tarpon. Go far enough north and you can catch snook and largemouth bass on consecutive casts.

Given the challenges of navigating the interior of the park, it's no surprise that most anglers who depart from Flamingo fish out front around the channels, grassflats, and mangrove islands in Florida Bay.

Seatrout inhabit the grassbeds, where the standard tactic is to fish a live shrimp under a foam bobber, known as a popping cork. The bobber suspends the shrimp just over the grass and is jerked hard to gain a trout's attention. Flies and jigs also catch trout.

Redfish are commonly found on the flats near the islands in Florida Bay as well as in Snake Bight and Garfield Bight, two popular spots east of Flamingo. Fishing is typically best during a rising or falling tide, early or late in the day.

Although redfish can be caught by a variety of methods, the most exciting way is to creep up on tailing fish on the flats and cast with a fly rod or a light spinning rod. Redfish favor weedless spoons as well as jigs and live shrimp and mullet.

Snook frequent the same areas but prefer the mangrove shorelines, where they can ambush baitfish swept past by the tides. Flies, topwater plugs, jigs, live pilchards, mullet, and shrimp are all favorites of these hard-fighting fish. Tarpon, which can be seen rolling on the surface in channels and around mangrove islands, will hit the same offerings.

The large tripod markers that border Everglades National Park are helpful reference points on a run to the Flamingo area. During the fall and winter they also provide a focal point for schools of cobia ranging from 30 to 80 pounds. A brief stop at each marker is sufficient to discern whether cobia are present. If the cobia are home, hook a live grunt on a light or medium plug rod and troll it slowly past the marker.

Moving around the southwest tip of Florida, anglers encounter several rivers—Shark, Lostmans, Chatham, and Lopez—that offer good angling for snook, redfish, seatrout, and tarpon, especially at the mouths.

The Ten Thousand Islands are at the western end of Everglades National Park and are just as remote. Access is best from Everglades City and Chokoloskee Island, with the option of fishing the backcountry, the mangrove islands out front, or the Gulf of Mexico.

Most people primarily fish the rivers and bays of the backcountry for snook and redfish. Fishing around the islands out front produces snook, reds, seatrout, and Spanish mackerel, and sheepshead are commonly caught in the channels. The wrecks and artificial reefs in the Gulf of Mexico hold snook, cobia, and permit.

Pavilion Key and Rabbit Key, south of Chokoloskee, are among the more popular islands. Armed with flies, plugs, and live bait, one can work around the oyster bars for redfish, over the grassflats for seatrout, and along the shorelines for snook. From either island, it's a short hop to the gulf, where some anglers have created their own artificial reefs to attract fish. Anglers must watch their sonar closely, because the location of those reefs is seldom divulged.

East Coast

The majority of Florida's population lives on its eastern coast, from Jacksonville to Miami. Despite a population in the millions, sportfishing can be surprisingly good and is often excellent.

The Intracoastal Waterway, which runs the length of the state, offers much of the best inshore fishing along the coast for species such as snook, seatrout, and redfish. Offshore anglers target resident species such as snapper and grouper, as well as migratory species, including king mackerel, sailfish, tuna, and dolphin.

The St. Mary's River is the border between northeastern Florida and southeastern Georgia. St. Mary's Inlet, where the river empties into

 From the confusion file: Dorado refers to a prized South American river fish and also to the prized saltwater species known as dolphin, which in turn is a word used for porpoises, which are actually mammals.

the Atlantic Ocean at Fernandina Beach, offers good fishing for seatrout, redfish, and sheepshead. Striped bass are usually in the river in late winter.

The north-flowing St. Johns River meets the Atlantic at Jacksonville. The brackish waters of the river and the numerous tidal creeks that join it are home to redfish, seatrout, and flounder. At the mouth of the river and along the beaches there are sheepshead, whiting, and black drum. Winter is the prime season to catch striped bass at the mouth of the St. Johns, with morning and late afternoon best. Crankbaits, jigs, and live eels are the favorite baits. During the summer, stripers run up the St. Johns to spawn. Shad run up the river in winter.

Grouper can be found offshore, along with dolphin, wahoo, sailfish, and blue marlin, but the king mackerel is the lord of offshore species. Kingfish, as they are also known, migrate through the area starting in May and running through the summer. Trolling or drifting with live or dead bait and 20- to 30-pound tackle is the preferred strategy to take kings, which can range from 5-pound "snakes" early in the season to 50-pound "smokers" when the migration is at its peak.

St. Augustine is the oldest city in the country. No doubt its first settlers took advantage of the bluefish, Spanish mackerel, cobia, flounder, whiting, and pompano that still patrol the city's beaches, and the redfish and seatrout that swim in its inshore waters. A 50-mile, or longer, run to the Gulf Stream puts anglers in dolphin territory. Fifteen miles to the south is Matanzas Pass, which harbors redfish, tarpon, flounder, and sheepshead. Whiting and pompano lurk in the surf.

The Halifax River in Daytona Beach is home to redfish and sheepshead. Trout and snook show up in early spring. The river can be fished from a boat or from any numbers of piers. South of Daytona is Ponce de Leon Inlet. Flounder hang out near the inlet during winter. Seatrout and redfish start biting as the water warms. Sheepshead, mangrove snapper, and black drum also visit the inlet. In spring and summer, anglers run offshore in search of blue marlin and kingfish.

At Ponce Inlet, the Indian River begins to trickle south. Stretching all the way to Stuart, the Indian River is a fish factory. Name an inshore species, and chances are that the river has it; but the area here is best known for snook, redfish, seatrout, and tarpon.

The Mosquito Lagoon, part of the Indian River just north of the Kennedy Space Center, offers the best fishing for big redfish in Florida. The 20-mile-long lagoon is bordered by mangroves and features acres of grassbeds and clear, shallow water. Redfish inhabit the lagoon all year, but the best fishing is in fall and early spring, when water temperatures are neither too hot nor too cold. Seatrout also frequent the flats at those times.

Anglers in shallow-draft boats can sight-cast to schools containing a hundred or more reds. The biggest redfish run from 30 to 50 pounds. The standard offering is a weedless spoon or a live crab fished with an 8- to 20-pound spinning outfit. Fly fishing with an 8- to 10-weight outfit is also popular.

The Indian River broadens as it flows past Titusville and Cocoa. Anglers fish the flats from boats or shore, or by wading for snook, redfish, and "gator" seatrout weighing 8 or more pounds. The big trout are on the flats during warm weather, and in the holes and channels bordering the flats when the water cools. Seatrout hit flies, live shrimp, and jigs tipped with shrimp.

Canaveral National Seashore offers good surf fishing in a beautiful locale. Pompano, a favorite of beach anglers and gourmet cooks, bite best in winter, along with bluefish and whiting. In spring, cobia, Spanish mackerel, and even king mackerel come close enough to be caught from the beach.

Offshore anglers go out of Port Canaveral. Close to shore, there's bluefish and flounder in the winter, and snook, Spanish mackerel, and cobia in the spring. In May, anglers head for the Gulf Stream in search of dolphin and blue marlin.

Sebastian Inlet offers great fishing from boats, jetties, bridges, and beaches. Doormat flounder and bluefish bite during winter, then Spanish mackerel and cobia move in. Snook fishing picks up in early spring and remains excellent through early fall. Ladyfish, Spanish mackerel, king mackerel, jacks, and redfish are caught in and around the inlet.

At Fort Pierce Inlet, anglers enjoy similar fishing. They catch snook, redfish, tarpon, seatrout, and snapper on the inside, and pompano and bluefish in the surf. Cobia migrate along the beaches starting in early spring, when grouper and snapper begin congregating on reefs—both inshore and offshore. Sailfishing can be outstanding during the winter and early spring, especially when these fish are in close balling bait. At those times, it's not unusual to catch 10 or more sailfish in a day.

The Indian River meets up with the St. Lucie River in Stuart. Fishing on the flats inside St. Lucie Inlet is excellent for snook, redfish, trout, and tarpon, as there's usually plenty of baitfish to keep the predators around. The flats can be fished from a boat or by wading. An 8-weight fly rod or an 8-pound spinning outfit with a live shrimp, mullet, pilchards, or a baitfish imitation will catch whatever is on the flats. Stuart is the heart of Sailfish Alley, the stretch from Palm Beach to Fort Pierce where the Gulf Stream comes within a few miles of shore. Closer to shore there are bluefish, Spanish mackerel, and cobia. Bluefish and Spanish mackerel hammer silver spoons. Cobia prefer live bait such as pinfish and blue runners.

Jupiter Inlet is a favorite of snook anglers, especially during late spring, summer, and early fall. That's when snook concentrate at inlets as they prepare to spawn. Fifteen- to 30-pound snook are caught in the inlet itself, as well as along the beaches to the north and south. Diehard snook

The first adhesive stamp to depict a fish was issued in Newfoundland in 1865 and featured an Atlantic cod.

anglers typically go out with 500 to 1,000 baitfish (pilchards, croaker, or herring) and attract the snook by live chumming. When the snook show up, anglers toss out live bait on light spinning outfits, or cast flies. The Intracoastal Waterway offers shelter in windy weather, as well as the opportunity to catch snook, seatrout, jacks, and ladyfish. Surf anglers catch bluefish, Spanish mackerel, pompano, and jacks from beaches north and south of the inlet.

Lake Worth Inlet, at the north end of Palm Beach, harbors huge permit, African pompano, and jacks, which anglers catch by bouncing a jig off the rocky bottom. Inside the inlet, in Lake Worth, are 30-pound tarpon and snook as well as jacks and ladyfish. Anglers catch tarpon by drifting from a boat with live shrimp. The snook prefer live sand perch and pilchards, and are fished from boats and bridges.

Offshore reefs have a variety of snapper, including yellowtail, mangroves, and muttons, as well as opportunistic barracuda. King mackerel patrol the edges of the reefs, and sailfish are just outside in 100 to 200 feet of water. Drifting with live bait or slow-trolling with dead or live bait—most commonly ballyhoo and mullet—produces both species. Wahoo lurk in 100 to 500 feet. Dolphin fishing is best in spring and summer, and anglers routinely run up to 30 miles offshore to encounter a school.

There are four inlets between Palm Beach and Miami: Boynton Beach, Boca Raton, Hillsboro in Pompano Beach, and Port Everglades in Fort Lauderdale. Fishing opportunities are about the same at all four. Natural coral reefs as well as an abundance of artificial reefs in 40 to 400 feet provide consistent fishing for snapper and grouper, as well as for pelagic species.

Thanks to catch-and-release efforts, sailfish are a year-round species, but the best fishing is from November through April. King mackerel migrate through in fall and spring, with the biggest fish—20 or more pounds—typically showing up in early spring. Cobia migrating through the area swim along the beaches. Amberjack up to 50 pounds move onto artificial reefs in 200 to 250 feet in spring to spawn. Dolphin generally appear in March, along with blackfin tuna.

In summer, little tunny show up in force. When nothing else is biting, anglers will target this hard-fighting species, known locally as bonito. A popular technique is to anchor near a wreck in 100 or so feet and chum heavily with either live or dead bait. When the bonito show up on the surface behind the boat, they can be caught on bait, jigs, plugs, and flies. Fishing picks up with the cooler temperatures of fall. Mutton snapper spawn on reefs and wrecks, and kingfish start to head south. Spanish mackerel, which are caught from boats, beaches, and piers, show up in force a little while later, followed by sailfish and pompano.

Inshore opportunities center around snook and tarpon. Snook congregate at inlets in spring and summer. After spawning, they move back inshore, into canals off the Intracoastal Waterway. Snook lurk around bridge pilings and docks, waiting for unsuspecting baitfish to swim past. Most anglers use live bait, but deep-diving plugs trolled parallel to bridges, and jigs bounced along the bottom, are both top-notch snook producers.

Tarpon move inshore during winter in search of warm water. One of the best tarpon spots is near the power plant in Port Everglades, where water used to cool the plant's electricity-generating turbines is discharged into a canal. When cold fronts hit South Florida, tarpon flock to the area. The fish, which range from 50 to 150 pounds, eat live shrimp and mullet either slow-trolled or drifted up and down the canals.

Other tarpon hotspots include the two inlets that serve the Miami area, Haulover Inlet and Government Cut. Both inlets have significant runs of shrimp during the winter. Tarpon that routinely top 100 pounds wait at the inlets for the floating feast, which occurs from December through March. The best fishing is usually at night, when the shrimp run. Fishing for tarpon is as easy as drifting or slow-trolling a live shrimp on a 20-pound conventional outfit in and around the inlets. When shrimp aren't running, live mullet and live crabs will catch fish.

Like neighboring cities to the north, Miami has natural and artificial reefs that offer good fishing for bottom dwellers. Sailfish, kingfish, dolphin, pompano, Spanish mackerel, amberjack, and wahoo also are pursued by offshore anglers. Unlike its neighbors, Miami offers excellent flats fishing in Biscayne Bay, which extends from downtown Miami to the upper end of the Florida Keys.

The upper reaches of the bay hold snook, tarpon, jacks, and barracuda. During winter, seatrout frequent the bay's grassflats. South of Key Biscayne, but within sight of the Miami skyline, bay anglers catch bonefish. The farther away from Miami one goes, the better the fishing. South Biscayne Bay is known for its big bonefish, in the 10- to 12-pound class, and also has permit and tarpon. Most of the flats fishing is done within Biscayne National Park on both bay and ocean flats. Tarpon tend to hang out in the channels and on the edges of the ocean flats. Fishing techniques are the same as those employed in the Keys.

West Coast

Although it is bordered by the Gulf of Mexico, Florida's west coast is best known for its inshore fishing opportunities, primarily for snook, tarpon, redfish, and seatrout. Most of the effort is concentrated around mangrove islands, beaches, flats, and river mouths.

At the southern end of the coast, Marco Island and Naples feature bays, passes, and acres of mangroves, which are home to the aforementioned species, as well as to jacks and sharks. Tarpon migrate up the coast starting in early spring, making for exciting fishing off the beach. Live pinfish or crabs are fished from the surf or from boats.

Snook fishing turns on in late spring. The fish move out of the backcountry during the summer as they prepare to spawn. Angling is best in the passes and along the beaches using live bait or baitfish-imitating lures. Bridges and docks also are snook hangouts, with the best bite typically at night.

Other species that visit the area include sheepshead, Spanish mackerel, whiting, and pompano. The best fishing is in late winter and early spring. Cobia head north a little later. Gulf reefs and wrecks attract king mackerel, grouper, snapper, amberjack, and barracuda.

The Fort Myers area offers outstanding inshore fishing. There, the Caloosahatchee, Peace, and Myakka Rivers empty into a relatively small area, creating a prolific aquatic environment.

The Peace joins with the Myakka to form Charlotte Harbor, which—along with nearby Pine Island Sound—has an abundance of redfish, seatrout, small tarpon, and snook. Most anglers browse around the mangrove shorelines and grassy flats.

Charlotte Harbor feeds into the gulf at Boca Grande, which has a storied tarpon fishery. From mid-April to mid-July, Boca Grande Pass might hold 20,000 or more tarpon. At times, it seems almost as many boats are in the pass fishing for them. Traditional tarpon anglers use only live bait, such as crabs, squirrelfish, pinfish, and pilchards, fishing them at the bottom of the holes in the pass where the tarpon gather. Jigs work especially well. The rigs consist of a circle hook with a plastic grub. A round lead weight is attached to the hook with a tiewrap. The jig is fished just off the bottom from a drifting boat. When a tarpon hits, the weight breaks free.

Nearshore and offshore species in this region include cobia—which migrate along the gulf edge of barrier islands—sheepshead, sharks, permit, king mackerel, and grouper.

Sarasota Bay is a broad, shallow body of water separating Sarasota from Longboat Key and the gulf. With its grassy flats and mangrove-lined eastern shore, Sarasota Bay offers ideal habitat for snook, redfish, and seatrout. The passes at the north and south ends of Longboat Key are good spots for migrating Spanish mackerel in spring.

Tampa Bay is the next major fishery up the coast, and a heavily fished one given the number of anglers in Tampa and St. Petersburg. Despite the crowds, there is good fishing for seatrout, redfish, snook, and snapper along the shorelines of the bay and on the grassflats. Tarpon, cobia, and Spanish mackerel enter the bay in the spring. Grouper, pompano, and Spanish mackerel also hang around the islands at the mouth of Tampa Bay. The most popular offshore species is king mackerel.

Homosassa Bay is a late-spring hotspot for tarpon in excess of 150 pounds. It's the place fly anglers go in hope of landing a world-record fish. Beginning in May, the clear waters of Homosassa's flats attract large schools of tarpon, which often go through the prespawn ritual of daisy-chaining. When daisy-chaining, an angler, perched at the bow of a flats skiff, picks out a fish and delivers the bait, lure, or fly just ahead of the swimming tarpon. The island-studded waters where the Homosassa River flows into Homosassa Bay have excellent angling for redfish during the spring.

The Cedar Keys, a collection of islands where Florida begins to bend to the west, is perhaps best known for its seatrout. Fishing peaks during the fall but is good through the spring. Most anglers fish the grassbeds with live shrimp or shrimp-tipped jigs. Redfish also are abundant amidst the islands. Cobia move through the area in the spring. Seatrout and redfish are the predominant species up the coast at the mouths of the Suwannee and Steinhatchee Rivers, in the heart of the state's Big Bend region.

Panhandle

Florida's Panhandle is the long, narrow stretch at the northwest end of the state, bordered by the Gulf of Mexico. The shimmering blue waters of the gulf offer everything from red snapper to blue marlin; cobia cruise the nearshore waters, and a number of broad, shallow bays provide outstanding inshore angling, most notably for seatrout.

Starting at the easternmost end of the Panhandle, in what's known as the Big Bend region, is Apalachee Bay. In April, seatrout and redfish move out of the rivers and onto the lush grassflats of the bay. Initially, the trout stay close to shore as they prepare to spawn, spreading throughout the bay over the course of the summer. Redfish frequent rock-strewn areas along the shore. Both species hit live shrimp, jigs, and jigs tipped with shrimp.

To the west is Apalachicola Bay, which is perhaps most famous for its oysters. Protected by barrier islands, the bay's scattered grassbeds attract trout, while redfish lurk around oyster bars. Each spring, hordes of Spanish mackerel and pompano gather at the passes linking the bay with the gulf.

The next major body of water is St. Joseph Bay, which is best known for its scallops. Redfish and seatrout are abundant on the bay's expansive grassbeds. Up the coast in Panama City is St. Andrew Bay. Scattered grassbeds there hold trout and redfish, as do the grassbeds in the bays, coves, and lagoons around Pensacola.

April is when cobia move into the area, coming up from the south and migrating to the west along the Panhandle's barrier beaches through July. The standard strategy is to cruise the shallow waters just off the beach in a boat, preferably one with a tower, and look for the dark bodies of the cobia against the sandy bottom. When cobia are spotted, the boat is moved ahead of the fish. Then jigs or live bait (pinfish and eels work well) are cast in front of the cobia, which can exceed 100 pounds. Cobia also hang out by channel markers, buoys, artificial reefs, and wrecks.

About a month after the cobia arrive, king mackerel show up in the surf and feast on schools of baitfish, as do big schools of roving jack crevalle. The kings are caught by trolling feathers and dead bait. Live baiting also works.

In June and July, big schools of tarpon move into the area. Most anglers concentrate on the areas in and around passes, bouncing heavy leadhead jigs on the bottom.

Snapper and grouper are caught on wrecks and artificial reefs anywhere from 1 to 20 miles offshore. Farther out, along the 100-fathom curve, anglers catch blue marlin, white marlin, and sailfish.

Freshwater
Florida has excellent fishing for crappie, bluegills, and other panfish, but the largemouth bass is the undisputed favorite of freshwater anglers. Surveys have documented that nearly 80 percent of anglers prefer to fish for bass, while the remainder prefer crappie and bream.

A relative newcomer to the freshwater scene is the peacock bass, which has become a favorite of many former bass diehards. The feisty, colorful peacock is a South American native that was stocked by the state in urban canals in the Miami area in the mid-1980s. The fish, which cannot tolerate water temperatures below 60°F, have taken eagerly to South Florida.

The Everglades
The Everglades used to stretch from Lake Okeechobee to the southern end of the Florida mainland. Agriculture, roads, and homes have hemmed in the northern portion of the 'Glades, but the fishing remains quite good.

Most angling occurs in the flood-control canals that crisscross the Everglades. Although the canals are home to a variety of panfish—including oscars, a South American native that was accidentally introduced—most boaters target largemouth bass.

The edges of canals and cuts leading to the shallow flats of the Everglades are the favored areas to pursue bass. Anglers slow-troll shiners along the canal banks, which typically are lined with sawgrass, cattails, water hyacinths, lily pads, and hydrilla; work topwater plugs along the edge; or flip plastic worms and crawdads in the vegetation. The majority of the bass are under a pound, but the 'Glades does have a fair number of trophy fish, although not many over 10 pounds.

The Everglades can be accessed from three main roads: U.S. Highway 27, which runs north-south through the 'Glades; Interstate 75, also known as Alligator Alley, which runs east-west through the middle of the Everglades; and U.S. Highway 41, also known as the Tamiami Trail, which runs east-west through the southern part of the Everglades, just north of Everglades National Park. Most of the canals are connected, so it is possible to run from one end of the Everglades to the other.

The canals on both sides of Interstate 75 are popular with bass anglers, who have a choice of boat ramps along the highway. East of U.S. 27 is Sawgrass Recreation Park, which has two popular canals, one that runs north along the highway and one that runs east. West of U.S. 27 and south of Sawgrass is Everglades Holiday Park, a hub for canals that run north, west, and south. Some of the best bass fishing is in the L67A Canal, which runs from Holiday Park to the Tamiami Trail.

Bass fishing is at its best in winter and spring. Late winter is particularly productive, when water levels in the Everglades are at their lowest. When the water gets low on the flats, the fish are forced into the canals, and anglers have a field day. During those times, it's possible to catch a hundred or more fish on just about any lure you choose.

Lake Okeechobee
Lake Okeechobee is the crown jewel of bass waters in a state known for its bass fishing. The Big O comprises more than 450,000 acres, most of it shallow and filled with a variety of vegetation.

Due to expansive habitat and an abundance of baitfish, Okeechobee's bass grow big. Anglers come to the Big O from all over North America with the hope of catching a 10-pounder, the magic number for the species. Many of them hit that jackpot. Others are content to catch and release 30 or more 2- to 4-pound bass a day.

The biggest bass are usually caught during the winter and early spring, when the fish move into the shallows to spawn and countless anglers ply the waters with live shiners. In season, anglers commonly catch 7-pounders, and 10-pounders are a regular occurrence. Summer features lots of 2- to 3-pound bass, but the midday heat makes fishing early in the morning or late in the after-noon best.

In addition to large live shiners, bass anglers most often use plastic worms, crawdads, jerkbaits, weedless spoons, spinnerbaits, lipless crankbaits, and topwater plugs. Flipping worms and crawdads amidst the peppergrass, eelgrass, hydrilla, and bulrushes produces fish year-round and is a standard tactic. Weedless spoons and spinnerbaits are favored in spring and summer, when the bass are in the grass at first light, feeding on shad. Burning a crankbait over a submerged bed of hydrilla is a favorite tactic.

Where to fish is often determined by the wind direction and strength. Some areas of the lake can become unfishable because the water gets too dirty for the fish or too rough for boaters to safely navigate. At times the wind has blown parts of the lake dry, leaving anglers and their boats stranded in the muck. Optimal fishing location depends on water levels as well. When the lake is low, some fishing holes dry up, whereas others are crammed with fish. As the water level rises, new areas open and bass quickly move in. Some of these changes are

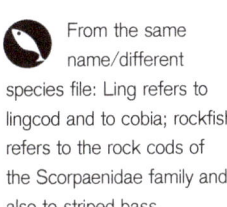

From the same name/different species file: Ling refers to lingcod and to cobia; rockfish refers to the rock cods of the Scorpaenidae family and also to striped bass.

subtle. A certain stretch of bulrushes might harbor lots of bass at a certain water level. A few days of rain can send those fish elsewhere and leave anglers scratching their heads, wondering why the fish are no longer biting. Likewise, a few windy days can shut down fishing at one location and turn it on at another spot 20 miles away.

Following are descriptions of some traditionally productive bass spots on the Big O.

Pahokee Rocks is a good area in the summer. Anglers favor crankbaits and Carolina-rigged plastic worms.

The rim canal, which encircles most of the lake, was created when a dike was built to prevent flooding. It offers protection from the wind and decent fishing for bluegills and speckled perch. Bass fishing is best around the cuts leading to the main lake.

Pelican Bay can be especially good in the winter. Focus on the back of the bay if the water is clean there but the surrounding water is dirty. Use plastic worms, jerkbaits, and spinnerbaits.

Bay Bottom encompasses the area from Belle Glade to Grassy Island and is one of the best winter spots for bass, as the fish come to the area to spawn. Flip plastic worms and crawfish in the peppergrass and eelgrass. Use spinnerbaits if it's windy.

Buzzard Roost can be good as long as the water is clean. If the wind is strong and out of the north, the area tends to get muddy and this makes fishing difficult.

At Ritta Island, fish the cattails on the inside using live shiners or hard jerkbaits.

East Wall/West Wall are two popular areas that get fished hard. In the fall, fish outside the joint grass and cattail edges with live shiners, or flip plastic crawfish and worms. As the fish move inside to spawn, move with them.

Coot Bay is a good shiner spot in the fall.

The Shoal is the area from Uncle Joe's Cut to almost the North Shore. It features a wall of cattails, bulrushes, and patches of grass. Fish the outside early in the fall, before the water gets muddy. When winter cold fronts sweep in, go inside and fish the clean, protected waters of Moonshine Bay, the Monkey Box, Fisheating Bay, and the North Shore.

Indian Prairie Canal is a good winter spot. Fish both sides of the canal on out to the North Shore. Use plastic jerkbaits or spinnerbaits, or pitch/flip plastic worms.

Cody's Cove to Indian Prairie Canal is a good place to use shiners, plastic jerkbaits, and white or chartreuse spinnerbaits. During winter, flip plastic worms on the inside and outside.

The Kissimmee River, which links Okeechobee to Lake Kissimmee, is best when bass are schooling. Chrome lipless crankbaits are the preferred lure.

Kings Bar is good when using live shiners, plastic jerkbaits, or plastic worms around the hydrilla, cattails, and bulrushes on the outside and just on the inside. Do the same when the fish move inside to spawn.

Little Grassy Island is good when bass move inside to spawn during the winter. Use spinnerbaits, plastic jerkbaits, and plastic worms.

Okeechobee also has a phenomenal crappie fishery, with an estimated 10 million of these tasty panfish, which often exceed 2 pounds. The best fishing is in winter, when crappie, known as speckled perch, bed in shallow, nearshore areas. Live minnows fished on cane poles and crappie jigs fished on light spinning outfits are the top producers. In the spring, bluegills and shellcrackers start spawning in shallow areas and under overhanging tree limbs in the rim canal. Live crickets, live worms, and small spinnerbaits are the top offerings.

Lake Kissimmee

Lake Kissimmee is located in about the dead center of Florida. It contains good numbers of big bass, crappie, bluegills, and shellcrackers. Most of the fishing is done around vegetation, primarily hydrilla, reeds, water hyacinths, and lily pads.

During winter and spring, anglers catch a fair number of bass from 7 to 10 pounds. Live shiners are popular with bass anglers, who slow-troll these baitfish along the edges of grassbeds. Whenever a bass bites, probe the area more thoroughly. Flipping plastic worms and crawdads in the vegetation is also a popular technique. The bass bite begins to slow during the summer but picks up again in mid-October.

Winter is prime time for crappie, which take live minnows best. Spring and early summer are the seasons to catch plenty of bedding bluegills and shellcrackers using live worms.

Ocala National Forest

Some of the biggest bass in the state used to be caught in the small lakes scattered throughout Ocala National Forest. The fishing pressure took its toll, and now big bass are a rarity. In addition, many of the lakes are crystal clear, making it difficult to fool a wary largemouth. Some of the best fishing is with live shiners at Lake Kerr, the largest lake in the forest.

St. Johns River

The St. Johns gets its start in Central Florida and flows northward, dumping into several lakes before winding its way to Jacksonville.

The best bass fishing begins in the lower middle portion of the 250-mile-long river, between Lake Harney and Lake Monroe in Sanford. During late winter and early spring, shad migrate down here to spawn. Most anglers either troll or fly-fish for shad, which run 3 to 5 pounds. When the shad run ends, the focus is on largemouth bass, although the river also offers excellent fishing for bluegills. Most anglers target the creeks that feed into the St. Johns.

The river goes from a relative trickle to the

broad, shallow expanse of Lake George, on the eastern side of Ocala National Forest. The lake has largemouth bass, striped bass, bluegills, crappie, and shellcrackers. The bass fishing is best in spring and fall, with live shiners, spinnerbaits, and plastic worms the favorite bait. Lake George has an average depth of 5 feet and little structure, so most of the bass fishing occurs in and around beds of eelgrass along the edges of the lake.

Flowing out of Lake George, the St. Johns begins to broaden and is influenced by tidal flow; this is where the bass fishing really gets good. The stretch between the lake and Palatka is the self-proclaimed "Bass Capital of the World."

Fishing is good in the main river, and innumerous creeks and lakes connected to the river. Boat docks and pilings often hold big bass in the river and in Lake Crescent. Boaters can lock through the Cross Florida Barge Canal to gain access to Rodman Reservoir. (Rodman also has access ramps.) This man-made lake has lots of hydrilla and hyacinths, and plenty of bass tournaments. In spring, anglers fish for spawning bass in the shallow creeks that feed into Rodman. On a good day, it's not unusual to catch 40 to 50 largemouths, and Rodman does produce 10-pounders; live shiners are the top bait. Striped bass run into Rodman in the spring, and there is good fishing for bluegills and shellcrackers from early spring through late summer.

Lake Seminole

Lake Seminole forms part of the border between Florida and Georgia in the Panhandle region. The lake was created in 1947 when a dam was built where the Chattahoochee and Flint Rivers meet. The Florida portion of the lake extends north along the Chattahoochee to Alabama. The Flint portion runs northeast and is entirely in Georgia.

The lake has an average depth of less than 10 feet and features lots of standing timber, more than 250 islands, and loads of sloughs and creeks. Fishing is good for sunshine bass and striped bass. Sunshines, which are hatchery-raised hybrid striped bass, average 5 to 6 pounds. Pure-strain stripers average 10 to 12 pounds. Seminole also has crappie, bluegills, channel catfish, and shellcrackers, but most anglers seek largemouth bass.

Much of the bass fishing centers around vegetation, primarily hydrilla. Flipping plastic worms and crawdads in and around the vegetation yields good fish in winter. Spring is the best season, as the bass move into the shallows and creeks and start bedding. Shiners, spinnerbaits, and plastic worms all work well. In the summer, when the bass start schooling, the topwater fishing is at its best.

FLOTATION DEVICE
See: Personal Flotation Device.

FLOUNDER
A group of bottom fish with compressed bodies, flounder are also known as flatfish *(see)*. Another marked characteristic is that both eyes are on one side of the head.
See: Flounder, Gulf; Flounder, Southern; Flounder, Starry; Flounder, Summer; Flounder, Windowpane; Flounder, Winter.

FLOUNDER, GULF *Paralichthys albigutta.*
Other names—flounder; Spanish: *lenguado tres ojos.*

The gulf flounder is a member of the Bothidae

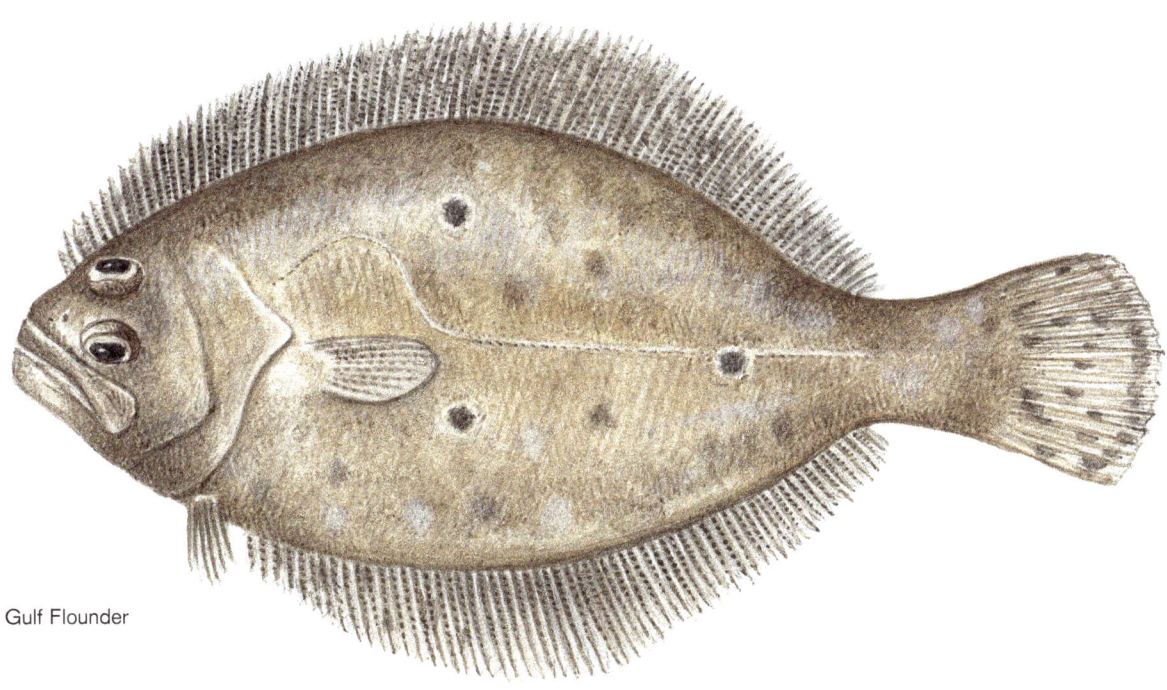

Gulf Flounder

family of left-eyed flounder and is an excellent table fish. It is one of the smaller fish in a large group of important sport and commercial flounder. Because of its size, the gulf flounder is of minor economic significance, and it is mixed in commercial and sport catches with summer flounder *(see: flounder, summer)* and southern flounder *(see: flounder, southern)*.

Identification. The gulf flounder has the familiar olive brown background of its relatives, the summer and southern flounder, but it has three characteristic ocellated spots forming a triangle on its eye side. One spot is above the lateral line, one below, and one on the middle, although these spots can become obscure in larger fish. Numerous white spots are scattered over the body and fins (*albigutta* means white-spotted), and the caudal fin is in the shape of a wedge, with the tip in the middle. This species has 53 to 63 anal rays, which is fewer than the 63 to 73 found on the southern flounder. Like other flatfish *(see)*, the gulf flounder can change color dramatically to match the bottom.

Size/Age. The average fish is under 2 pounds and between 6 and 10 inches long, although it is capable of growing to 15 inches. It is believed to live for at least three years. The all-tackle world-record fish is a 5-pounder, caught in Florida.

Distribution. The gulf flounder generally occurs in the same range as the southern flounder; it is common from Cape Lookout, North Carolina, to Corpus Christi, Texas, including southern Florida and the Bahamas.

Habitat. Gulf flounder inhabit sand, coral rubble, and seagrass areas near shore. They often range into tidal reefs and are occasionally found around nearshore rocky reefs. They commonly favor depths of up to 60 feet.

Spawning. Spawning season is in the winter offshore.

Food. The gulf flounder feeds on crustaceans and small fish.

FLOUNDER, SOUTHERN
Paralichthys lethostigma.
Other names—flatfish, flounder, halibut, mud flounder, plie, southern fluke; Spanish: *lenguado de Floride.*

The southern flounder is thought to be the largest Gulf of Mexico flatfish. A member of the Bothidae family of left-eyed flounder, it is a highly desired food fish, and a considerable amount is harvested by trawlers.

Identification. The southern flounder resembles the summer flounder *(see: flounder, summer)* in appearance.

Its coloring is light to dark olive brown, and it is marked with diffused dark blotches and spots, instead of distinct ocelli (spots ringed with distinct lighter areas). These spots often disappear in large fish. The underside is white, the simple fins make an even fringe around the body, and its beady eyes are located extremely close together. It can be distinguished from the summer flounder by having fewer gill rakers and by the presence of distinct spots. It is also similar to the gulf flounder *(see: flounder, gulf)*, which has no distinct ocelli.

Size/Age. Mature individuals grow to 36 inches and more than 12 pounds. The average size is 12 to 24 inches and 2 to 3 pounds. The all-tackle record is 20 pounds, 9 ounces. Southern flounder can live up to 20 years in the Gulf of Mexico.

Distribution. The southern flounder can be found from North Carolina to northern Mexico, although it is not present in southern Florida.

Habitat. As an estuarine-dependent bottom fish, the southern flounder commonly inhabits inshore channels, bay mouths, estuaries, and sometimes freshwater. It is tolerant of a wide range of temperatures (50° to 90°F) and is often found in waters where salinities fluctuate from 0 to 20 parts per thousand. No other flounder of the eastern United States is regularly encountered in this type of environment. Anglers regularly catch this fish inshore from bridges and jetties.

Spawning behavior. Southern flounder spawn in offshore waters. In the northern Gulf of Mexico, they move out of bays and estuaries in the fall; this occurs quickly if there is an abrupt cold snap, but it happens more slowly if there is gradual cooling. Spawning occurs afterward, in late fall and early winter. Females typically release several hundred thousand eggs, which hatch and migrate into the estuaries and change from upright swimmers into left-eyed bottom dwellers.

Food and feeding habits. The southern flounder feeds partly by burying itself in the sand and waiting to ambush its prey. Small flounder consume shrimp and other small crustaceans, whereas larger flounder eat blue crabs, shrimp, and fish such as anchovies, mullet, menhaden, Atlantic croaker, and pinfish.
See: Flatfish.

Southern Flounder

FLOUNDER, STARRY *Platichthys stellatus.*
Other names—rough jacket, great flounder,

California flounder, diamond back, emerywheel, emery flounder, grindstone, sandpaper flounder; Japanese: *numagarei*.

The starry flounder is a smaller and less-common member of the Pacific coast Pleuronectidae family of right-eyed flounder. Flounder and other flatfish *(see)* are known for their unique appearance, having both eyes on either the left or right side of the head, although the starry flounder can be either left-eyed or right-eyed.

It is a popular sportfish because of its willingness to bite and its strong fighting qualities. Although the starry flounder has tasty flesh, it is important mainly as a sportfish, having only moderate commercial value. Processing is difficult due to its rough skin, and it must be deep-skinned to remove its unappealing, dark fat layer.

Identification. The starry flounder belongs to the right-eyed family of flatfish, but, as noted, it can also be left-eyed. Its head is pointed, and it has a small mouth. The anal spine is strong. The caudal fin is square or slightly rounded. Its coloring is olive to dark brown or almost black on the upper side, and creamy white on the blind side. The unpaired fins, its outstanding feature, are white to yellow to orange with black bars. There are patches of rough, shiny, starlike scales scattered over the eyed side of the body, which give rise to its name.

Size. The average size is 12 to 14 inches, although it can grow to 3 feet and 20 pounds. Females grow faster than males and attain larger sizes.

Distribution. The starry flounder ranges from central California to Alaska, and south from the Bering Sea to Japan and Korea. This is one of the most numerous fish of central Northern California backwaters, particularly San Francisco Bay.

Habitat. It is usually found near shore over mud, sand, or gravel bottoms. Often entering brackish or freshwater, the starry flounder is most abundant in

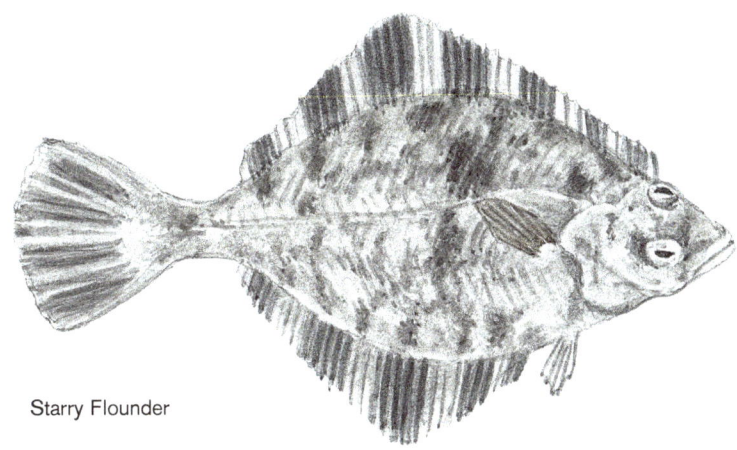
Starry Flounder

shallow water but can be found in depths of at least 900 feet. Juveniles are often intertidal.

Spawning behavior. Spawning occurs in late winter and early spring in California waters less than 25 fathoms deep.

Food. Adult starry flounder consume a variety of items, including crabs, clams, shrimp, and sand dollars. Large individuals also eat some fish, such as sardines, sanddabs, and surfperch.

Angling. Starry flounder are caught throughout the year in California but are more frequently taken from December through March. They accept a variety of natural baits, including chunks of sardines, clams, shrimp, squid, and worms.

Angling techniques are generally discussed in greater detail under other entries. For more information, *see: Drift Fishing; Inshore Fishing.*

FLOUNDER, SUMMER *Paralichthys dentatus.*
Other names—fluke, northern fluke, flounder; Dutch: *zomervogel;* French: *cardeau d'été.*

Summer Flounder

The summer flounder, most commonly called fluke, is a member of the Bothidae family of flatfish (see), or left-eyed flounder. Like other flatfish, the summer flounder undergoes a unique maturation from egg to adult flounder in which one eye migrates to the opposite side of the head. It is the most northerly and perhaps abundant of the three bothid species, as well as the largest and most prized flatfish caught in the mid-Atlantic region of the United States.

Fishing for summer flounder off jetties and bridges is a mainstay of Mid-Atlantic coastal sportfishing and a prominent commercial catch, primarily taken by otter trawl. Anglers in the Mid-Atlantic harvest a significant proportion of the total catch, usually about 40 percent, and in some years the recreational take has exceeded the commercial take.

Although not a powerful fighter, this species provides spirited and often dependable action. The meat is firm, white, and delicately flavored, and although some complain about the many bones (as with all flounder) and a dryness of the meat, proper filleting and moisture-retaining cooking methods can eliminate those issues.

Identification. The body is wide and somewhat flattened, rimmed by long dorsal and anal fins. Its mouth is large and well equipped with teeth. The eyes are on the left side of the body, and close together. The teeth are well developed on the right side of the jaw. Its background coloring is usually gray, brown, or olive, but it adjusts to the environment to keep the fish hidden by camouflage. There are also many eyespots that change color. The blind side is white and relatively featureless. The dorsal fin has 85 to 94 rays; the anal fin has 60 to 63 rays. There are only 5 or 6 gill rakers on the upper limb of the first arch and 11 to 21 on the lower limb.

In addition to their different color patterns, the three species of bothids can be distinguished by the number of gill rakers, anal fin rays, and lateral-line scales they possess. Summer flounder have the most eyespots, gulf flounder (see: flounder, gulf) have several eyespots, and southern flounder (see: flounder, southern) lack conspicuous spots.

Size. The average summer flounder weighs 2 to 5 pounds, the latter being about 23 inches long. It is capable of growing to 35 inches in length but rarely does, and the all-tackle world record is a 22-pound, 7-ounce fish caught at Montauk, New York. Historical data indicate that female summer flounder may live up to 20 years, but males rarely exceed 7 years of age. Growth rates differ appreciably between the sexes; females attain weights up to 26 pounds.

Distribution. The summer flounder occurs in the western Atlantic from Maine to South Carolina and possibly to northeast Florida, and is most abundant from Cape Cod to North Carolina.

Habitat. A bottom-dwelling fish, the summer flounder prefers sandy or muddy bottoms and is common in the summer months in bays, harbors, estuaries, canals, creeks, and along shorelines, as well as in the vicinity of piers and bridges or near patches of eelgrass or other vegetation. It typically prefers relatively shallow waters and depths of up to 100 feet during warmer months, then moves offshore in winter to deeper, cooler water of 150 to 500 feet.

Life history/Behavior. Sexually maturity is reached at age 3. Spawning takes place during the fall and winter while the fish are moving offshore into deeper water or when they reach their winter location. The eggs, which float near the surface, hatch in three to four days, producing larvae shaped more like conventional fish than flatfish. Water currents carry newly hatched flounder into the estuaries and sounds, where they undergo a transformation in shape and become bottom dwellers.

Food and feeding habits. Adults are largely piscivorous and highly predatory, feeding actively in midwater as well as on the bottom. Extremely fast swimmers, they often chase baitfish at the surface, which is not characteristic of most other flatfish. Fluke also bury themselves quickly, using undulating movements of their fins to throw sand or silt on their backs. The eyes remain uncovered and watch carefully for dinner prospects. Fluke are known to eat what is available, including shrimp, crabs, menhaden, anchovies, silversides, sand launce, killifish, weakfish, hake, and other flounder.

Angling. Although fluke can be caught from shore, fishing is usually best from a boat in 8 feet or more of water during the summer. This is especially true when water temperatures climb above 75°F, because the fish seek the cooler depths.

Commonly used baits are minnows, shrimp, and squid; artificial lures that imitate these items are also effective. A line is generally rigged with two leaders on a vertical spreader so that one hook is fished on or near the bottom, while the second is held about 1 foot off the bottom. If an artificial lure is used in combination with bait, it is attached to the upper leader so it stays off the bottom and

A summer flounder from Barnegat Bay, New Jersey.

can move realistically in the current. A sinker of sufficient size must be used so the line stays on the bottom even when there is a strong tidal flow.

Unless flounder are known to be in a certain area, it is usually best to drift for them, thereby covering a large area. Likely spots to try include places with rough or irregular bottoms, in or near inlets, and around pilings, wrecks, and jetties. Food is abundant in these locations. If you are fishing in one spot, it helps to jig the line up and down so the bait does not lie motionless on the bottom, as fluke (and other flatfish) are often attracted by movement.

Other aspects of angling for flounder are discussed in greater detail under other entries. For more information, *see: Drift Fishing; Inshore Fishing.*

FLOUNDER, WINDOWPANE
Scophthalmus aquosus.
Other names—sand flounder.

The windowpane flounder is a small, thin-bodied, left-eyed flounder that is seldom encountered by anglers but is noted for its sweet-tasting flesh. Like other flatfish *(see),* the windowpane flounder undergoes a unique maturation from egg to adult flounder in which one eye migrates to the opposite side of the head.

The commercial catch of windowpane flounder, primarily via otter trawl, increased in the mid-1980s as a result of an expansion of the fishery offshore, as well as the targeting of this species as an alternative to other depleted flatfish stocks. Like many other flatfish, it is considered overexploited.

Identification. The windowpane is a roundish flounder with a pale-white or translucent blind side, which gives rise to its name. It has many dark brown spots on the body and fins, and its lateral line is strongly arched to the front.

Size. It grows to 18 inches and in some areas is common to 16 inches, but many that are encountered by anglers are less than 11 inches and too small to keep for eating.

Distribution. This species ranges along the northwest Atlantic continental shelf from the Gulf of St. Lawrence to northern Florida.

Habitat. The windowpane flounder is found from shore out to roughly 150 feet of water, and occasionally deeper.

Spawning. Sexual maturity occurs between ages 3 and 4. Spawning occurs from late spring through autumn, peaking in July and August on Georges Bank, and in September in southern New England.

FLOUNDER, WINTER
Pseudopleuronectes americanus.
Other names—flounder, lemon sole, sole, blackback, blueback, black flounder, dab, mud dab, flatfish, Georges Bank flounder; French: *plie rouge;* Italian: *sogliola limanda;* Spanish: *mendo limon.*

One of the most common and well-known flounder of shallow Atlantic coastal waters, the winter flounder belongs to the Pleuronectidae family of flatfish *(see).* It is a right-eyed flatfish, with both eyes on the right side of its body, and gets its name because it retreats to cold, deep water in the summer and reappears in shallower water close to shore in the winter; its relative, the summer flounder *(see: flounder, summer),* does the opposite.

The winter flounder is an important food and commercial species, and a thick, meaty specimen. The meat is firm, white, and delicately flavored, and although some complain about the many bones (as with all flounder), proper filleting methods can eliminate this problem.

Identification. The body is oval and flat with a tiny mouth. Color varies from reddish brown to dark brown with small black spots. The underside is whitish and occasionally brown, tinged with blue around the edges. The caudal fin is slightly

Winter Flounder

A winter flounder from Shark River, New Jersey.

rounded. The winter flounder differs from the similar yellowtail flounder *(see: flounder, yellowtail)*, in its straight lateral line, no arch over the pectoral fin, thicker body, and widely spaced eyes.

Size. Most winter flounder weigh between 1 and $1^{1}/_{2}$ pounds and average less than a foot in length, although they are capable of growing to 8 pounds and 2 feet. The all-tackle world record is 7 pounds. Larger fish are sometimes called "sea flounder" to distinguish them from the smaller bay fish.

Distribution. Winter flounder are mostly inshore fish common in estuaries and the coastal area from Chesapeake Bay north to the Gulf of St. Lawrence. Stragglers occur south to Georgia and north to Labrador.

Habitat. Winter flounder are found inshore in estuaries and coastal ocean areas. In the Mid-Atlantic they stay inshore from January through April. Smaller fish occur in shallower water, although larger fish will enter water only a foot deep. They are range anywhere from well up into the high-tide mark to depths of at least 400 feet. Preferring sand-mud bottoms, they are also found over sand, clay, or fine gravel, and on hard bottom offshore.

Life history/Behavior. Spawning occurs in shallow water over sandy bottoms from January through May. Winter flounder eggs stick together and sink to the bottom, where they hatch in roughly 16 days, depending on water temperature. These fish move from deep water toward shallow water during the fall, and offshore again in the spring.

Food and feeding habits. When on a soft bottom, the winter flounder will lie buried up to its eyes, waiting to attack prey. Because of its small mouth, its diet includes only smaller food like marine worms, small crustaceans, and small, shelled animals like clams and snails.

Angling. Although these fish are caught in midwinter, they are more concentrated in late winter and early spring, and because anglers are more comfortable at that time, fishing activity for this species tends to pick up in March and April. Many anglers chum for winter flounder in order to concentrate them. They will often use a horizontal spreader when fishing two leaders on one line. This lets both baits rest on the bottom where the fish feed. Enough weight should be used to keep the baits on the bottom, and No. 8 or smaller hooks work well for these small-mouthed fish. Winter flounder do not bite particularly hard, and it's necessary to be aware of the light pressure on the line of a nibbling fish. If you are fishing in one spot, it helps to lightly move the line up and down so the bait does not lie motionless on the bottom for a long period, as these fish are often attracted by movement.

Other aspects of angling for flounder are discussed in greater detail under other entries. For more information, *see: Drift Fishing; Inshore Fishing.*

FLOUNDER, WITCH
Glyptocephalus cynoglossus.
Other names—gray sole, craig fluke, witch; Dutch: *witje;* French: *plie cynoglosse;* Icelandic: *anglúra;* Italian: *passera linguadi cane;* Norwegian: *mareflydre;* Spanish: *mendo falsó lenguado.*

The witch flounder, commonly called gray sole, is a moderate-size deep-water right-eyed flounder that is seldom encountered by anglers. It is of some commercial significance, however, and is mainly caught by otter trawl. Formerly, the commercial catch of witch flounder was a byproduct of shrimp trawling, but concerted targeting of this species by long-range fleets as an alternative to other depleted flatfish stocks has resulted in overexploitation. Like other flatfish *(see),* the witch flounder undergoes a unique maturation from egg to adult flounder as one eye migrates to the opposite side of the head.

Identification. The witch flounder is generally uniform brownish on its eyed side, sometimes with obscure darker bars. Its mouth is small and its lateral line straight, and it has large mucous pits on its blind side.

Size. Witch flounder attain lengths up to 31 inches and weights of approximately $4^{1}/_{2}$ pounds, although they are usually less than 25 inches long.

Distribution. The witch flounder ranges in the eastern Atlantic from northern Norway to northern Spain, and in the western Atlantic from the Gulf of St. Lawrence and Grand Banks to Cape Hatteras, North Carolina. It is common throughout the Gulf of Maine and also occurs in deeper areas on and adjacent to Georges Bank and along the shelf edge.

Habitat. Witch flounder appear to be sedentary, preferring moderately deep to deep areas and muddy bottoms. In the western Atlantic few fish are taken shallower than 90 feet by commercial fishermen, and most are caught between 360 and 900 feet. They range much deeper, however.

Spawning. Spawning occurs in late spring and summer.

Food. This deep-water dweller feeds on crustaceans and brittle stars.

FLOUNDER, YELLOWTAIL
Pleuronectes ferrugineus.
Other names—yellowtail, mud dab, rusty dab, sand dab; Finnish: *ruostekampela;* French: *limande à queue jaune.*

The yellowtail flounder is a small, right-eyed flounder that is seldom encountered by anglers. It has been an important component of commercial fishing, mainly caught by otter trawl. The commercial catch of yellowtail flounder has declined drastically in the 1980s and 1990s, and this species is greatly overexploited. Like other flatfish *(see)*, it undergoes a unique maturation from egg to adult flounder in which one eye migrates to the opposite side of the head.

Identification. The yellowtail flounder is generally uniformly brownish on its eyed side, with many rusty spots of various sizes. Its mouth is small and lateral line arched toward the front. The blind side has yellow at the edges of the fins and the caudal peduncle.

Size. This species can attain lengths to $18^{1}/_{2}$ inches and weights up to 1 kilogram, but high rates of fishing mortality have greatly reduced the average size and age, leaving fewer larger and older specimens.

Distribution. Yellowtail flounder range from Labrador to Chesapeake Bay. Commercially important concentrations have historically been found on Georges Bank, off Cape Cod, and in southern New England.

Habitat. This fish appears to be relatively sedentary, although seasonal movements have been documented. It is generally caught by commercial trawlers at depths between 120 and 240 feet, over sandy and muddy bottoms.

Spawning. Spawning occurs during spring and summer, peaking in May.

Food. The yellowtail flounder feeds on worms, amphipods, shrimp, crustaceans, and occasionally small fish.

FLUKE
A common name for summer flounder *(see: flounder, summer).*

FLUOROCARBON
Fluorocarbon is the name given to line produced from polyvinylidene fluoride, a nylon alloy that was created in the 1960s and that has seen increasing use in fishing line, particularly in fly and saltwater fishing.

A monofilament line, dry fluorocarbon looks virtually the same to the human eye as dry conventional nylon monofilament, but in water the material has a refractive index—the degree to which light is bent while passing through—that is considerably less than nylon mono and closer to that of water, meaning that it is technically less visible. Decreased visibility in a line should mean that it is less alarming to fish, resulting in more strikes in clear and shallow-water fishing, assuming all other things are equal s(no drag, etc.).

Fluorocarbon also has very high abrasion resistance, does not get weaker through water absorption, and is said to be impervious to ultraviolet light. These characteristics contribute to a very durable line. The lack of water absorption is an important and distinguishing characteristic. Most conventional nylon monofilaments have between 10 and 15 percent water absorption and are weaker in a wet state; fluorocarbon line does not change characteristics, so its breaking strength is the same when wet as when dry.

The combined attributes of abrasion resistance, strength, and decreased visibility offer anglers the advantage to drop down in tippet *(see)* or leader *(see)* size without sacrificing performance. Furthermore, fluorocarbon lines have a super slick finish on them, and as a result they do not pick up little bits of matter on their surface. This means that they produce less friction when going through the rod guides and thus cast better, although the average angler is unlikely to notice much difference, especially if using just a leader length of this material.

Since fluorocarbon is more dense than conventional nylon monofilament, it sinks faster, which can be an advantage or disadvantage depending on the type of fishing being done.

Fluorocarbon is expensive line, largely due to a complicated manufacturing process. And it is also a stiff line, which is why it was first available in short spools and used as tippet material and for shock leaders and not spooled fully onto a fishing reel. Some manufacturers have produced larger spools for filling up an entire reel. Originally available in high strengths, it is now manufactured in a full range of strengths/diameters and to International Game Fish Association (IGFA) record specifications.

See: Line.

FLY
(1) A natural aquatic or terrestrial insect, especially one that is consumed by fish.

See: Aquatic Insects; Caddisflies; Dobsonflies; Dragonflies and Damselflies; Mayflies; Midges; Stoneflies; Terrestrial Insects.

(2) In a generic sense, a fly is a type of extremely

A fly box with assorted Atlantic salmon flies.

lightweight lure, also known as an artificial fly (to distinguish it from a natural fly, which is rarely used by anglers), that is cast with a fly line and fly rod. Some flies are more imitative in appearance of natural insects than any other lure. Other flies are highly imitative of baitfish, crustaceans, and various small, natural, noninsect foods. Still others are more suggestive than imitative, meant as attractors rather than deceivers.

All of the objects considered "flies" by anglers have in common the fact that they are light enough to be presented with flycasting tackle (see) and too light to be effectively cast with other types of tackle without the addition of weight (and then not as effectively). Thus, whatever a fly is meant to represent, it is carried to its destination by the act of casting a fly line, which is connected to a leader (see), which is attached to the fly. This is the principle of fly fishing.

For the purpose of adhering to fishing regulations and for record keeping (world records are kept separately for fish caught by fly fishing), the definition of a fly and of fly fishing may be broader than the previous description. For example, some objects used with flycasting tackle are of such weight or design that they cannot be false cast but may actually be lobbed or stripped out with flycasting tackle. This may fit a very liberal definition of a fly, of fly fishing, or of casting, but it does not conform to the conventional and traditional perception of a fly as a lightweight object and of fly fishing as the use of a fly line in the repetitive casting and delivery of a lightweight object.

Types. An extremely wide array of flies is employed in fly fishing for diverse species in all areas of freshwater and saltwater. Flies range from less than $1/8$-inch long up to 10 inches long. Unlike many other lures, flies are entirely handmade, being tied on a single or double hook (seldom the latter) from a variety of natural and synthetic materials. They can generally be categorized as floating or sinking flies, and specifically typed as dry flies, wet flies, nymphs, streamers, and bugs.

Floating flies sit on the surface of the water and are made with materials that are buoyant. They include dry flies and bugs, and imitate a host of foods, including natural insects, frogs, mice or lemmings, snakes, and other creatures. Floating flies can be fished in many ways, but overall they are less effective than sinking flies, especially in cool or cold water.

Sinking flies are fished below the surface and are made with materials that absorb water or are more dense than water. They include wet flies, nymphs, and streamers, and also imitate many foods, including natural insects, small fish, crustaceans, worms, eels, leeches, and fish eggs. Sinking flies are likewise fished in many ways but are more productive overall because gamefish feed more often below the surface.

As with any lure used to entice fish, a fly's effectiveness depends on its overall appearance—size, shape, and color—plus its action. Since many flies are created to imitate specific food (especially insects), size and shape are nearly always important. Color is important in some cases and not in others, although it is seldom completely irrelevant and depends on the circumstances and species sought; it is more likely to be important in attractor flies than in imitative flies. Odor, which is an element for some lures, is often not a factor in fly usage, although the materials used for some flies can retain or absorb scents and may be imprinted with scent by the angler to help appeal to certain fish species.

A fly box with western-U.S. shad flies.

Using scent on a fly, however, prohibits any fish caught on it from receiving official world-record certification. Action is largely dependent upon the angler and the design of the fly. Flies do not have any action on their own and must be manipulated to move, although this movement is enhanced in some flies (such as those with feather, hair, or rubber legs).

Patterns. With the exception of bugs, the basic and standard fly has these components: a hook, which includes a point that may or may not be barbed, an eye that may be straight or turned up or down, and a shank that may be straight, curved, keeled, or humped; a head; a body, which is the main section along the shank of the hook and which may have ribs; and a tail. It may also have wings, hackle, a thorax, and sometimes legs.

The particular appearance of a fly—in essence the parts that make up its likeness, the way they are incorporated onto the fly hook, and the colors—not only characterize it by type, but also constitute a pattern, and make a given fly distinguishable from others. There are literally thousands, perhaps tens of thousands, of patterns. This can be confusing and intimidating, and it is impossible for even the most astute fly angler to recognize all of them. The fact that many fly anglers tie flies (comparatively few users of nonfly lures make their own lures) in large part contributes to this proliferation of patterns. A beginning fly angler is best advised to seek counsel at a local fly tackle shop for the recommended fly patterns and sizes for a specific area at a given time.

Fly patterns are named for myriad reasons, most often for their creator, a specific place, and the object they imitate. Dozens of flies are among the most well-known patterns, but there are many specific patterns for various species of fish. The most patterns exist for trout species, because of the long prominence of trout as an angling quarry and the long history of fly fishing for trout; as long ago as 1676, Izaak Walton's *The Compleat Angler* listed 65 fly patterns for trout. There are also a lot of patterns for Atlantic salmon. Patterns for Pacific salmon and steelhead are different than those for Atlantic salmon and trout. Saltwater patterns are entirely different than freshwater patterns.

The myriad of fly patterns is not unlike the existence of many specific nonfly lures for freshwater and saltwater fishing, and specifically for such species as bass, walleye, stripers, etc. Like those products, certain flies have crossover application. Small trout flies are equally effective on panfish, for example, and many saltwater streamers are also effective on northern pike and lake trout.

The huge proliferation of patterns, some of which are barely distinguishable from each other, would seem to suggest that a fly angler, especially one seeking trout in streams, needs hundreds of different patterns to be able to use the right fly that will catch fish at a given time. It is true that many fish, stream trout in particular, can at times be very selective about feeding and about what artificial flies they will take because of its resemblance to their currently preferred food; this makes matching the hatch, whether there is in fact a hatch or merely just a predominance of a certain food item, advantageous if not essential.

However, it is also true that fish take flies that merely suggest food rather than duplicate it, and there are many patterns that are close enough to food duplications to be effective. In truth, even the best flies that imitate specific insects are not clones of those insects. And in any case, the best fly cannot be effective if it is not properly presented and/or retrieved. Therefore, the best course of action is to focus on the type of fly that most closely represents the food that fish are feeding on, and to fish it properly.

Dry Flies

Dry flies are relatively diminutive objects that float on the surface and represent aquatic or terrestrial insects found on the surface of streams, rivers, ponds, and lakes. Most dry flies imitate specific insects, especially mayflies *(see)* and caddisflies *(see)*, which is important, as is their size and profile. They are notable for stiff hackle (water-repellent bird feather wound around the hook) and tail feathers, and also for the use of deer hair, all of which are tied on a lightweight (light wire) hook to float the fly. Many dry flies also have wings, and there are also some that don't have hackle. Depending on the pattern, the materials used, and the way they are tied, dry flies may ride very high on the surface or may rest low in the surface film; they may be bushy and high-profiled, or very sparsely hackled and more diminutive. They are tied on a wide range of hook sizes, with different waters and seasons affecting the appropriate size choice.

Since natural insects float on the water subject to surface current or to movement via a breeze, dry fly imitations must be light enough to do likewise, although they are restrained by attachment to a fine tippet *(see)*, leader, and floating fly line, which may cause drag and may unnaturally move or restrain the fly. Like natural insects, dry flies are generally allowed to drift on the surface subject to whatever natural current or wind influences exist, but to avoid drag the presentation may require in-air or on-water line mending *(see)*.

Less often, some deliberate movement of a dry fly by the angler may be appropriate. This would occur if the natural insect being imitated moved about, such as an adult depositing eggs, which is well imitated by dapping *(see)*. As a means of attracting fish, gliding or skating a dry fly is a technique used for Atlantic salmon and occasionally trout, often with a long-hackled fly referred to as a skater.

In flowing water, dry flies are primarily fished by casting upstream and allowing the flies to float downstream in a natural manner. The line should

Dry Flies

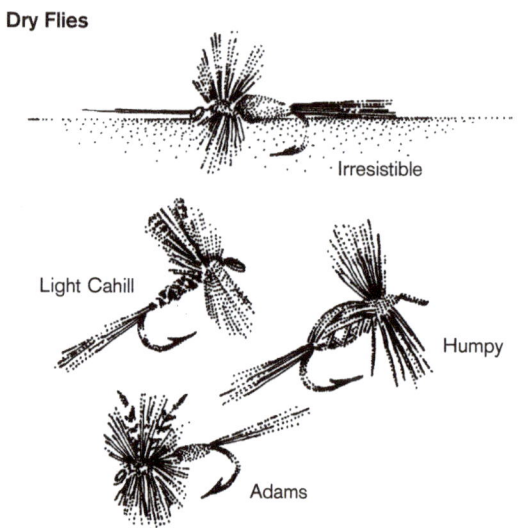

not be cast directly over the fish, or over the area to be worked with a fly, in order to avoid spooking the fish; the best manner of presentation is to cast up- and across-stream, floating the fly down. Seldom are dry flies fished by casting directly downstream, because this limits the length of the drift owing to the line that can be dispatched and is almost certain to create drag.

Watch the fly as it floats on the surface so that you know when a fish takes it and so you can react quickly. When a fish rises to a dry fly, it may do so in a violent and splashy manner, which is obvious and exciting, or in a nearly imperceptible dimpling manner, which can be missed if you're not paying attention. In either case, however, do not react with a violent hooksetting motion, which many new fly anglers do; this is likely to pull the fly away from the fish or to break it off if the fish has already hooked itself. Simply react with a moderate flick of the wrist to raise the tip of the rod (keeping the line pinched to the handle with your finger).

Dry flies may become waterlogged after long use and especially after catching fish. When they start losing their buoyancy, some air drying by repetitive false casting, if conditions permit, may temporarily restore floating characteristics, but more likely the fly will need floatant, or dressing, to help it repel water. Silicone and paraffin dressings can be applied to a dry fly to help it float. Some anglers prefer sprays and liquid dips because they keep the hands from getting wet and sticky, but they don't last as long as pastes. If the fly has absorbed a lot of moisture, press it with a cloth to remove the moisture and clean it; then apply dressing to it.

As noted, the patterns and sizes of dry flies vary greatly, and it takes experience to make a selection at any given time and place. A well-rounded dry fly collection should have a representative assortment of fly types. The following patterns are among those that widely work well: Adams, Blue Dun, Brown Bivisible, Dark Cahill, Gray Wulff, Green Drake, Hendrickson, Humpy, Irresistible, Light Cahill, Muddler Minnow (dressed to float), Quill Gordon, some type of hopper, and brown and gray midges.

Wet Flies

Wet flies are very much like dries, although they sink upon entering the water. They primarily represent subsurface forms of aquatic insects that are naturally found in freshwater environs when they are swimming, laying eggs, emerging to head toward the surface, or merely spent and drifting; to a lesser extent, they may also represent a drowned terrestrial insect or small fish.

Wet flies have the following characteristics: the

Parts of a (Wet) Fly

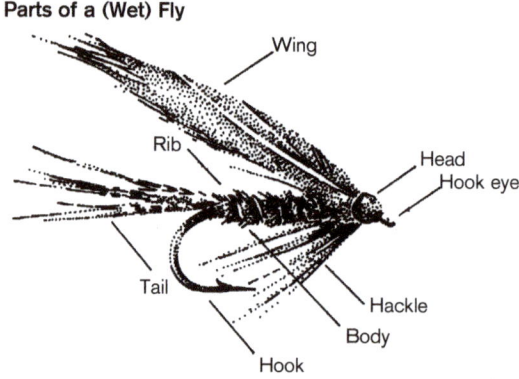

wings are tied to lie backward from the head; the body (often tinsel or chenille) is dense to help sink the fly; there may or may not be a tail; and a lesser amount of hackle at the head, also tied back, is present than on most dry flies. Unlike dries, the hackle on wet flies is soft, being derived from soft and water-absorbing bird feathers.

Wet flies are tied on a narrower range of hook sizes (mostly No. 6 to 18) than dry flies, and the hooks are heavier than those for dries to help with sinking. Often a bit of fine lead wire is wrapped on the shank under the body to also help the fly sink, or over the body as ribbing, which has both an appearance and sinking value. Wet flies may be imitative in appearance, or they may be brightly dressed attractors that don't bear close resemblance to natural insects.

Wet flies are unaffected by wind or surface current, but obviously they move with subsurface current; the connecting leader and fly line are affected by current on and below the surface, which may cause drag and unnaturally move or restrain what should be a free-drifting fly. Like natural insects, wet flies are generally allowed to drift in the water subject to whatever natural current exists, but to avoid drag the presentation may require line mending.

In flowing water, wet flies are primarily used by an angler who is above the fish's position, with the angler casting across-stream or across and downstream and allowing the fly to drift down to the (suspected) position of the fish. In this manner the line, leader, and angler are upstream of the fish. They

Wet Flies

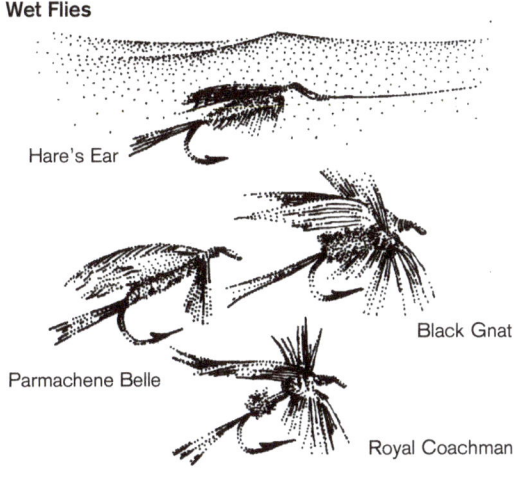

Hare's Ear
Black Gnat
Parmachene Belle
Royal Coachman

may be retrieved across the flow as well as drifted naturally, and are often employed in tandem, with a second fly as a dropper or with several wet flies (this is usually close to the surface). Depending on the circumstances, especially water depth, a wet fly may be fished with a floating line (fly just under the surface), a sink-tip line (fly at middepths), or a full-sinking line (fly at greater depths).

In ponds or lakes, a wet fly is generally used with a sink-tip or full-sink line and is fished with a stripping retrieve of the fly line, the speed of which varies according to whatever the fly is supposed to imitate. Wet flies that are attractors are generally fished at a quick pace.

The strike of a fish on a wet fly is typically felt rather than seen. The reaction by the angler should be to quickly pull on the fly line in the line-gathering hand, removing any slack, then pinch the line to the handle with the rod-holding hand, and flick the wrist upward to raise the rod tip.

There are many patterns of wet flies to employ. Sparsely tied and drab-colored wets are often preferred for trout fishing, but gaudy patterns have a good following in fishing for bass, panfish, salmon, steelhead, and brook trout. A wet fly collection should have a representative assortment of fly types. The following are widely known and popular patterns: Black Gnat, Blue Dun, Brown Hackle, Coachman, Dark Cahill, Hare's Ear, Ginger Quill, Gray Hackle, Light Cahill, March Brown, Parmachene Belle, Quill Gordon, and Royal Coachman. Numbers 10 to 16 are most common, with No. 12 being an all-around favorite.

Nymphs

Nymphs are also sinking flies, often more diminutive than wet flies and tied more precisely with wing cases and thorax to represent the larval stage of aquatic insects, including mayfly *(see)*, caddisfly *(see)*, and stonefly *(see)* nymphs. They are also tied to represent such noninsect foods as leeches, scuds, snails, worms, and the like. This covers a lot of food forms; thus, many artificial nymphs are nearly exact imitations of naturals, either the bottom-dwelling larval and pupal stages or the surface-emerging form, and many are more suggestive than imitative.

Natural nymphs, which are the immature stage of aquatic insects, have a long life in the water and are a major, if not the foremost, insect food source for stream-dwelling fish, especially trout. Thus, assorted nymph flies or nymphlike flies are an essential part of the freshwater angler's repertoire. They are generally dull or drab in color, and many have a thorax, which is material tied to form a hump at the shoulders to represent the undeveloped wings of cased larva.

The body is made from many materials, often fur, and many patterns have soft, sparse, leglike hackles under the head or neck. The materials used help determine whether a nymph sinks or swims (a few are meant to be fished low in the surface film to imitate an emerger) and how quickly it sinks. Various weights are incorporated into nymph patterns to affect sink rate, including wire that is wound onto the shank before the body material is applied, and lead or metal head beads.

Nymph flies run a wide gamut in dressing, from very sparse on the smallest nymphs to bushy and thick-bodied large patterns. They are tied on a wide range of hook sizes, with different waters and seasons affecting the appropriate size choice. Although a common size for nymphs would be in the No. 6 to 10 range, they run to both extremes, and extremely small nymphs (No. 22 and 24) may be used on heavily pressured, shallow small streams. Nymph size is often important in successful fishing, especially on trout streams, and especially when fish are feeding selectively.

All types of fly lines are used to fish nymphs, and choice depends on type of nymph, current flow, depth, and length of drift. Small nymphs, for example, are often fished on a floating line in small shallow waters, using a tiny split shot a short distance ahead of the fly to get it down quickly for what is usually a short drift. As a rule, floating and slow-sinking lines are used in all shallow waters,

Nymphs

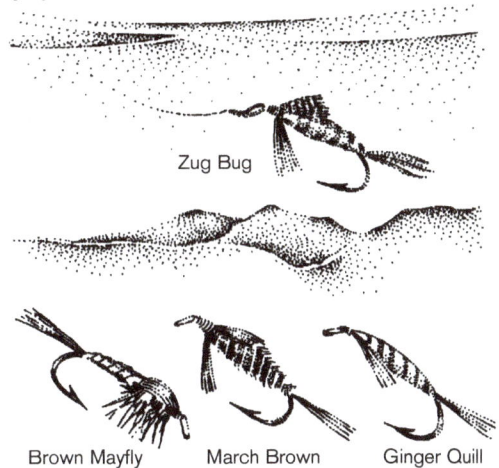

Zug Bug
Brown Mayfly
March Brown
Ginger Quill

sink-tip lines in intermediate depths in streams, and full-sinking lines with a fast sink rate in all deep waters.

In moving waters, a nymph is cast upstream or up and across stream with a floating line, with the fly sinking and drifting down with the current for a relatively short drift, or it is cast slightly up and across stream with a sink-tip or full-sink fly line to maintain contact with the nymph either when drifting it downstream or when swimming it. A strike indicator, which may be as simple as a swatch of deer hair, or a colorful adhesive patch, is often used on the leader to help show leader movement when a fly has been taken by a fish in moving water, so the angler can react quickly to a strike.

Often, and especially in small streams, nymph-fishing anglers hold the rod tip high to help maintain a desirable fly drift and keep more of the fly line off the water to minimize drag. In ponds or lakes, a nymph is generally used with a sink-tip or full-sink line, allowed to sink to a desired level, and fished with a generally slow stripping retrieve of the fly line.

As with other fly types, there are many nymph patterns. A nymph collection should have a representative assortment, and the following are widely known and popular patterns: Caddis Nymph, Dark Olive, Ginger Quill, Gray Nymph, Hare's Ear Nymph, Leadwing Coachman, Light Cahill, March Brown, Mayfly Nymph, Montana Nymph, Quill Gordon, Stonefly Nymph, and Zug Bug.

Streamers

As a group, streamers are primarily meant to represent specific or generic baitfish as well as such assorted prey as leeches, worms, eels, etc. They are popular in freshwater, especially in large rivers and in lakes and ponds, and are the foremost type of fly used in saltwater. Although streamers catch trout, they are not a large part of the stream trout angler's repertoire, but they are a factor in stillwater trout

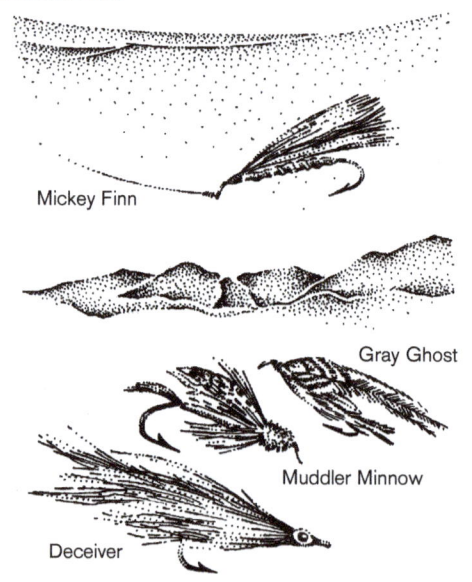

Streamer Flies

Mickey Finn

Gray Ghost

Muddler Minnow

Deceiver

fishing. For presentations to large predatory fish, including pike, muskies, lake trout, striped bass, and many saltwater species, especially pelagic species, streamers are the main offering when using flycasting tackle. This somewhat catchall category is sometimes subcategorized as streamers and bucktails.

Bucktails (also known as hairwings) feature hair or other fur, whereas streamers primarily feature feathers. However, other materials, like Mylar, are also used, and some streamers feature a very creative use of both natural and synthetic materials. Obviously streamers incorporate a lot of designs. They are characteristically all tied on long-shanked hooks, however, and are nearly always fished below the surface, although some may be treated with floatant on occasion to fish on the surface and look like struggling surface prey.

Since these flies cover a wide variety of possible forage, many are not exact imitations of specific prey and are dressed rather colorfully as attractors. Many are suggestive in appearance, and a lesser number are strictly imitative. Some are dressed on two hooks in tandem (which are often used for trolling), and many, especially those for big fish and saltwater use, are tied on larger hooks than those used for the most commonly dry flies, wet flies, or nymphs.

Streamers are fished on all line types in a manner that is similar to some aspects of wet fly and nymph fishing; choice is dependent on the type of water and depth to be fished, the circumstances, etc. Sink-tip lines are especially useful for streamers that are fished at moderate depths; full-sink lines are used for deep-water work; and floating lines are used for shallow fishing, where flies are weighted enough to get them beneath the surface a short distance.

These flies are only occasionally fished on a dead, natural drift (and usually when cast directly upstream in a river), and they have to be manipulated with the fly line and/or rod tip, usually by stripping in fly line to swim the fly. The speed of retrieval varies with the behavior of individual species; some require a slow pull-pause movement, whereas for others (often many saltwater fish) the streamer cannot be stripped too fast.

In current, a streamer is normally cast across the current and fished downstream in a combination of drifting and twitching until it reaches the full downstream extension of line, and then it is strip-retrieved back to the angler. It is sideways to the current when moving downstream, which may suggest an imperiled fish or other food; when it darts upstream, it may simulate the action of mobile prey. In open water situations, it is dispatched a full casting distance away or near a breaking fish, allowed to sink to the desired level, and then erratically strip-retrieved.

The size of the streamer and its silhouette are most important, because there are many patterns (and many unnamed creations) available. A collection of representative streamers for various fishing would include the following: Black Ghost, Black-

Nosed Dace, Clouser Minnow, Deceiver, Gray Ghost, Mickey Finn, Nine-Three, Silver Doctor, White-and-Red, and Yellow-and-Red, plus assorted colors of Marabous (black, white, yellow), Muddler Minnows (especially brown), and Marabou Muddlers. Woolly Worms, Woolly Buggers, and Zonkers (which are considered streamers by some people but not by others) are great flies that belong in this assortment, and there are many others that are equally effective in specific waters, especially items tied for saltwater use.

Bugs

It is arguable whether the lures known as fly fishing bugs are in fact flies or a separate category of fly

Bugs

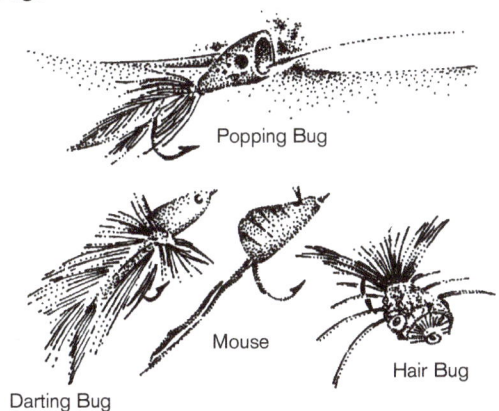

fishing lure. They are included here for simplicity in the sense that all items that are cast with flycasting tackle are generically called flies (although many do not imitate insects and are not fished like them). This is just one of many aspects of sportfishing that is rife with confusing and sometimes misleading terminology.

In any event, bugs include poppers and so-called bass bugs, and are also known as topwater bugs; they look nothing like other artificial flies or like natural insects. They are made from cork, balsa, cedar, deer hair or buoyant hair from other animals, and some synthetic materials, and are tied on a variety of hook sizes, with larger ones for bigger fish being created on single No. 6 to 2/0 hooks, and smaller ones (for panfish) being tied on appropriately sized hooks.

The range of natural foods that these items imitate includes frogs, rodents, and baitfish that would be found actively swimming or struggling to survive on the surface in freshwater, and primarily struggling or active surface baitfish in saltwater. Bugs are fished on the surface, probably 90 percent of the time with a floating fly line, although a sink-tip line may be employed with some diving and swimming bugs to help pull them briefly under the surface during retrieval.

Poppers are hard- or solid-bodied items made from cork, balsa, or cedar. They usually have some hackle or bucktail at the back of the lure to camouflage the hook or provide extra movement in the water, and they are fished in a popping or chugging manner, being jerked to surge forward and make a commotion that attracts fish through both noise and movement. The way a popper sits in the water, as well as the contoured design of its head or face, governs the action and degree of commotion that it makes, and there are many styles. Small versions, usually worked slowly, are preferred for panfish; larger ones, fished at various speeds, are intended for largemouth and smallmouth bass, northern pike, striped bass, and other saltwater fish.

Bass bugs have a hair body that is creatively tied and shaped or trimmed into a host of forms, the most familiar ones being mice- and froglike. Some incorporate a loop of monofilament line as a weedguard, and all are fished slowly. Because they are soft-bodied lures, bass bugs are less likely to be quickly rejected by striking fish.

Other Flies

There are other "flies" used in fly fishing that don't quite fit into categorical peg holes. These include many steelhead and salmon flies, some of which are quasi-streamers; most egg flies, which are simple and bright imitations of fish eggs and are made from yarn; foam-bodied spiders; Mylar-bodied fish imitations; and others. Innovative fly tyers have produced many fish-catching flies that defy categorization.

One of the benefits of tying flies is the ability to match food and create flies as necessary when you're out in the field.

Materials and tools used in fly tying.

Fly Tying

From a definitive standpoint, fly tying is the hand manufacture of an artificial fly by winding thread around a hook and attaching assorted materials to the hook with the thread. The attachments are known as dressing, which traditionally meant bird feathers, animal hairs, and metallic tinsel, but which today includes a wide range of natural and synthetic materials.

Although all types of flies for all kinds of fly fishing activities are available commercially, many anglers tie their own flies and consider this an important component of their total fly fishing involvement. They derive a lot of pleasure from catching fish on flies that they create, and they view tying as an interesting and challenging hobby that has direct tangible benefits to their angling. They can stockpile flies in the off-season or in other spare time, make creations or variations on standard patterns that are not otherwise readily available, and even tie flies at the fishing site if they need a size or pattern that they do not have. In the long run, fly tying can have an economic benefit; most of the cost of buying commercially tied flies is due to hand labor, so, in terms of materials, homemade flies can cost very little per fly.

Even a beginning fly tyer can produce flies that will catch fish, although, like many other activities, this hobby can be taken to very involved levels and does require knowledge of proper technique. Reaching an advanced level of fly craftsmanship, especially the ability to create specialty flies with some synthetic materials, takes most people years of development. There is good reason for fly tying to be considered an art form, and for the most exquisite flies to be works of art.

Fly tying is one element of sportfishing in which visual and hands-on instruction is immensely valuable, and a beginning fly tyer should receive guidance, if not instruction, from an experienced tyer to get a proper start. Many groups or individuals hold fly tying classes during winter months, and participating in these is probably the best way to get started in this hobby. You will learn to tie patterns that will have local relevance, so that you can successfully use what you create. Getting guidance from experienced tyers will also help you develop an understanding of what materials to use, how to assess the quality of materials, and how to work with the materials to dress the fly; not the least of your knowledge will be a greater understanding of aquatic and terrestrial insects and other natural fish foods.

There are many books, and some videos, available that teach fly tying, and these are also valuable sources. Fly tying instruction books should have step-by-step illustrations and clear photos that demonstrate every element of the tying process. They should also have good color photos of fly patterns. A good video may be even better for illustrating tying steps and the final look of the fly, although when you're learning to tie by following video instruction, it is annoying to have to keep rewinding a VCR to watch the tying steps (whereas a book is laid out in front of you). Since it takes a lot of photos and space to show the fly tying process for each of the various types of flies, and since that could not be adequately addressed in this book, you should check other information sources for a full and illustrated discourse on the techniques of fly tying.

However, a few general points about fly tying should be noted. It will cost less than a few hundred dollars to get well outfitted with the basic materials for fly tying. From a hardware standpoint, you'll need a vise for firmly holding the fly, hackle pliers for grasping the fine feather ends, sharp needle-point scissors for cutting and trimming, a bobbin to hold the spool of thread, a whip finishing tool for terminating the thread wraps, a single-edge razor blade for cutting and trimming, and a dubbing needle (bodkin) for separating materials and other tasks. Tying thread and head cement will round out the items that will be used time after time. After that, the basic components include the proper style and size of hook and the various components that will be used to dress the fly.

The vise is the most important tool and is more than just a clamp. A good vise should have a wide range of jaw adjustment, because it needs to firmly hold the hook at its bend without deforming it yet still accept a range of hook thicknesses as appropriate for the size of flies being tied; interchangeable vise jaws may be necessary in order to hold both the thinnest and the thickest hooks. There are, incidentally, folding models that are meant for travel and for use along the stream, as well as portable fly tying kits.

A bright lamp, preferably one that swivels to different positions, will be important for use at the fly tying location, and some people will benefit greatly from a magnifying glass on a stand or one that is attached to a band that rests on the head and slips over the eyes.

If you are getting started in fly tying on your own, begin by tying a few streamer patterns, even if it's unlikely that you'll have much need for them. Streamers are easiest to tie, and working on them will help you acquire the fundamentals.

See: Fly Fishing; Flycasting Tackle; Lure.

FLY BOOK

A flexible pouch, also known as a fly wallet, for storing artificial flies, especially streamers, when angling; a fly book is easily stowed in a fishing vest or jacket.

FLY BOX

A light, compact storage device for artificial flies. Fly boxes are made from various plastics and from metal, are rigid, and are sized to fit the pockets of a fishing vest or jacket. Some plastic versions are transparent to allow viewing of their contents. Some are compartmented for loose fly storage, but these allow accidental loss of multiple flies for a variety of reasons; better fly boxes have a means of retaining hooks, such as clips or foam lining, and are also deep and roomy enough to keep the flies from being flattened. Many fly boxes have two-sided interior storage, and they can be opened and laid flat for accessing the top and bottom; such boxes must have some means of retaining flies, or they will be scattered out of the box when it is opened.

Smaller boxes are meant for storing smaller flies, including dries, wets, and nymphs, but some boxes will take larger flies, including streamers, which are also often kept in a fly book or fly wallet *(see)*.

Care should be taken to keep moisture out of fly boxes, because the moisture can lead to rusty hooks. Air drying a used fly on a fleece patch before putting it back into a box is a good idea.

FLYCASTING TACKLE

Flycasting tackle is a special-purpose type of fishing equipment characterized by the use of a heavy and relatively thick line to cast a light, and in many cases nearly weightless, object that is generically referred to as a fly. This tackle is distinct from all other types of tackle, in which a weighty object carries a light and usually thin line (primarily nylon monofilament) when it is cast or when the reel is placed into freespool mode.

This is special-purpose equipment partly because the essential fly line cannot be cast with other tackle. It is also special because most of the objects cast with this equipment in the past, and many of them today—especially in trout fishing—are virtually weightless flies. However, with advancements in rods and lines, some of the "flies"

The payoff for matching flycasting gear properly and delivering the right fly is a good bow in the rod.

that have evolved in the modern era are extremely large and not-so-weightless objects, in effect greatly expanding the concept of an artificial fly. Thus, it is no longer entirely accurate to say that flycasting strictly involves the casting of weightless objects; huge streamers cast by offshore fly anglers, for example, are far from dainty.

The use of flycasting tackle—which is known as fly fishing—is also distinct in that line does not have to be fully retrieved and spooled onto the fly reel in order to recast the fly. In many situations, this feature allows for quick, repetitive presentations. Other forms of tackle don't permit this, or permit it only in special situations, since the object cast must be fully retrieved before it can be recast. Also, because of the light nature of most flies and the terminal tackle used (leader and tippet), presentations with flycasting tackle are usually subtle, and flies can be presented unobtrusively.

Although flycasting tackle has become more popular in recent years and has greatly widened its application, it is much less popular than spincasting tackle *(see)* in freshwater, spinning tackle *(see)* and baitcasting tackle *(see)* in freshwater and saltwater, and conventional tackle in saltwater.

Some dedicated fly anglers are snobbish about the artistry of fly fishing, but on a practical level the advantage of using flycasting tackle is the ability to make quiet presentations and repetitive casts without retrieving the line, as previously noted, and also to use featherweight artificial flies that in many cases are highly representative of natural forage both in appearance and in movement. A dry fly drifted on the surface of a trout stream, for example, can look and move with the current exactly like a natural insect, which is the primary food of trout, more so than a lure can. If the fish are selectively consuming insects, the fly angler has a far better chance of finding (or creating) an imitation to present naturally than the nonfly angler. Thus, in some circumstances, using a fly is the best way to

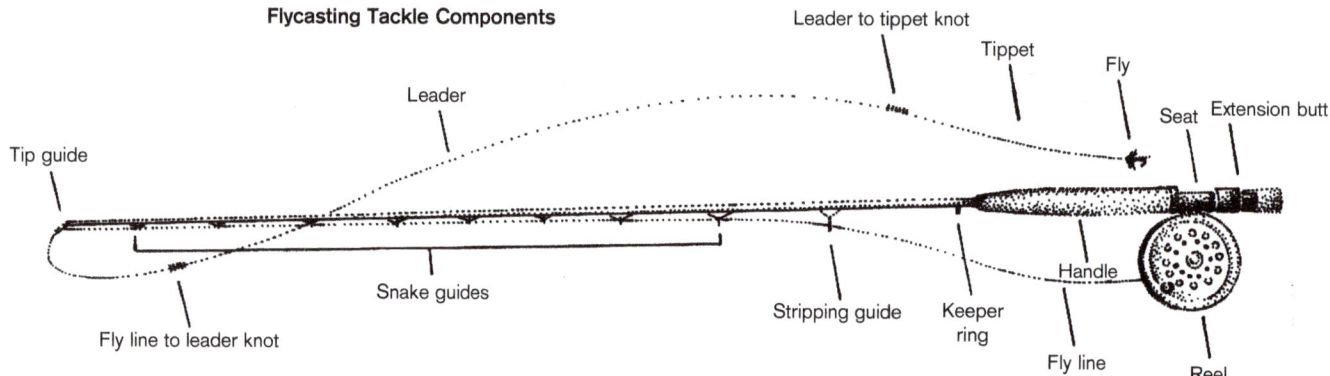

Flycasting Tackle Components

imitate natural forage and fool a fish, and flycasting tackle is necessary to make the proper presentation.

Although it isn't necessarily an advantage, the act of casting a fly line arguably has graceful beauty and symmetry, and many practitioners enjoy and appreciate fly casting as a developed skill. Many fly anglers feel that there is also a measure of special skill in selecting flies (matching the hatch), knowing where to cast, and controlling the line and the presentation, and they feel that these skills make angling with fly tackle stand out from other types of fishing and thus mean that fly fishing is more demanding. However, it is not necessarily more demanding, and this attitude fosters the unfortunate notion that fly fishing is difficult.

Some aspects of fly fishing do have the myth or the appearance—usually wrongly—of being more exacting and requiring exceptional levels of skill. The fact that a number of avid trout fly anglers—who as a group make up the majority of people who fish with flycasting gear—speak about flies and hatches in Latin terminology and with the precision of a single-minded scientist does not help demystify the sport. No matter what tackle anglers use, they all have the same objective of putting their lures or bait in the right place in a manner conducive to getting their quarry to strike, and the skills and complexities in each discipline can be equally challenging. In fly fishing, the methodology is different, but not entirely more complex or more demanding than other forms of fishing.

The art of casting a fly line is, however, a little more taxing to perfect, especially in the learning period, and some would-be fly anglers view this as a disadvantage. No one picks up a flycasting outfit for the first time, makes one or two practice casts, and is instantly fly fishing successfully, as can happen with spinning and spincasting tackle; it requires practice to learn to use fly tackle in even a basic way (no one picks up a baitcasting outfit for the first time either and immediately starts casting like a veteran). Flycasting isn't terribly difficult with the right instruction, but the fact that many schools exist to teach people how to cast with fly rods, whereas hardly any exist to teach other types of casting, is a telling indication. So, too, is the plethora of books, videos, and instructional materials on methods of casting.

Among the real but not insurmountable disadvantages to using flycasting tackle is the fact that it can be more of a problem than using other tackle in windy conditions and in tight quarters, and it has limited casting range for the average user (meaning that you may have to get closer to many fish to reach them with a cast). Fly fishing is also generally an inefficient means of angling deep in open waters, although it can be done.

It is worth noting that little trolling is done with flycasting tackle, and even less fishing with natural bait. Natural baits are mostly too heavy or impractical to cast or use with this equipment, and purists do not consider trolling an acceptable method of fly fishing; trolling is not allowed in flycasting competitions or in recognition of world-record fish caught with fly tackle. This doesn't mean that fly tackle can't or shouldn't be used in such a manner. Some trolling with fly tackle is done for trout and salmon in the spring when these fish are shallow, and also in some other circumstances. Nevertheless, flycasting gear, unlike other forms of tackle, is by tradition and preference almost entirely dedicated to actively casting with some type of fly.

Today, the boundaries between applications for flycasting tackle have blurred because of improvements in reels, rods, lines, and flies. Like other equipment, flycasting tackle has become very specialized (tackle and methods for trout are greatly different than for bass, general saltwater use, tarpon, or billfish), and some of it is much more expensive than other types of fishing equipment. It has become more prominent in saltwater in recent years, especially for pursuing tarpon, bonefish, permit, redfish, striped bass, bluefish, little tunny (false albacore), and sailfish.

There are five main components to flycasting tackle: reel, rod, line, leader, and fly. The last two are discussed in more detail elsewhere, and since the line is unique to this type of equipment and to the method of fishing, it's appropriate to review this component first.

Line

Fly line is critical to the presentation of flies and must be matched to the rod that is used. It is vital to have the right weight of line to bring out the action of the rod, so it's important to understand the fundamental design of fly lines as well as the various classifications and types for different applications. This process is complicated by the wide variety of fly lines now available, so selecting a fly line can be confusing.

Design and construction. Fly lines were once made of braided horsehair, braided silk, horsehair and silk, enamel-finished silk, and oiled silk. The latter was used into the middle of the twentieth century and required frequent cleaning and dressing, daily drying (being wound onto a line drier), and occasional refinishing. This gave way to nylon fly lines, which were more elastic than silk and not subject to rotting, but cracked easily. After nylon was developed, a succession of technological advances resulted in a revolution in synthetic materials, manufacturing processes, and designs. That lead to the sophisticated products of today, and it expanded fly fishing from what was primarily the use of dry flies and floating lines for trout and salmon in streams and rivers to a much wider activity.

The modern fly line is essentially an amalgamation of a coating and a core. It is a relatively thick product because of these elements, but the coating is necessary to give the line weight and allow it to be cast. Castability is the first and most critical performance characteristic of a fly line.

The core of the fly line is a braided synthetic that determines its tensile strength and stretch and that influences its stiffness. Individual fly lines are designed to be stronger than the heaviest tippet that the product will be used with, so their breaking strength ranges from approximately 20 pounds (lightweight freshwater lines) to over 40 pounds (heavy saltwater lines). The thickness or diameter of a fly line is not correlated to its strength as it is with conventional nylon monofilament line used with other tackle.

The amount of stretch is ideally controlled to achieve the proper medium between having a lot of memory (developing a set from a position in which the line has been placed for a long time), which hinders casting and fishing, and being so soft that the line is difficult to control. Braiding inherently contributes to flexibility and greater castability, which is generally advantageous, but the amount of braiding for the core synthetic may be more or less developed to adhere to the application of the type of line.

For specialty lines used in extreme conditions, the limpness or stiffness of the core can be manipulated to make products conducive to extreme conditions. Since heat can relax line, for example, a line primarily used in heated conditions must have enough stiffness to maintain its castability. On the other hand, since coldness can stiffen a line, a line used in cold conditions must have enough flexibility to maintain its castability. Unfortunately you can't have both properties in the same fly line to satisfy the extremes, and the coating is also a factor in this property.

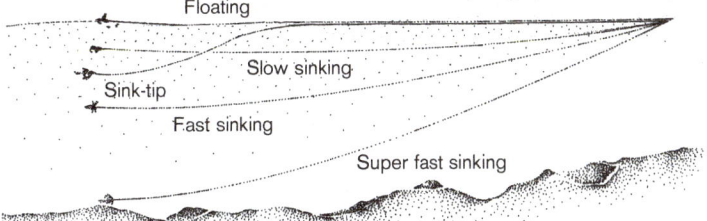

Fly Line Types

The coating of fly line is a modern plastic, mainly polyvinyl chloride, and it provides most of the weight needed to load the fly rod for casting and provides some of its flexibility, plus color, shape, and density for specific applications. It also contains ultraviolet inhibitors to make lines last and maintain their color and, in some products, may contain impregnated lubrication to resist rod guide friction. Its construction and properties make it a durable item that can last several years with little maintenance.

Density. Density determines whether the line floats or sinks, and it is a characteristic determined by the material in the coating and its construction. Essentially there are floating, sinking, and floating/sinking lines.

A floating line (designated by the letter F in labeling) is for surface or near-surface fishing and is often the first line possessed by a fly angler, particularly a trout angler who uses dry flies and nymphs in shallow water. A floating line is easiest to cast, to pick up off the water, and to fish, which is especially important for someone new to this activity.

A sinking line (signified by S) is used only for fishing below the surface. Sinking lines are also known as full-sink lines and are classified according to the speed at which they sink, which is known as sink rate and varies from roughly 1 inch per second (ips) to 10 inches per second; the slowest sinkers were known as intermediate (I) lines, a designation no longer used by some manufacturers.

Sinking line use is based upon fishing conditions; a slow-sinking line, for instance, might be used in shallow, gently flowing water, and a fast-sinking line might be necessary to fish near the bottom in a deep, swift-flowing river. Which sinking line to use is based on the depth to be fished and how fast you need to get to and maintain that level. Full-sinking lines can be used for fishing in depths to 30 feet, and they are used for trolling as well as casting.

Floating/sinking (F/S) lines possess a floating body and a sinking tip section and are commonly called sink-tip or sinking-tip lines. They are typically used as a second line on a spare fly reel spool to provide the option of easily changing while on the water. The length of the sinking tip varies, usually being from 10 to 30 feet; like full-sinking lines, these lines also vary in sink rate from slow to very fast.

A floating/sinking line allows you to get a fly

below the surface but also keep enough of the line on the surface to see it and mend it for a drag-free drift. Sink-tip lines are easier to cast and fish than full-sinking lines, and are especially useful for fishing from 2 to 10 feet below the surface with wet flies, nymphs, streamers, and other subsurface flies. Very fast sink-tip lines keep a fly deeper during a retrieve or drift.

Most sinking lines are dark colored, and most floating lines are light colored. Dark green and white have traditionally been favorite line colors, but floating lines in yellow, orange, lime green, and fluorescent colors are available, mostly as a visibility aid for casting and fishing control, and having no bearing on casting performance and usually no adverse effect on fishing success.

Shape/taper. Shape, which is also referred to as taper, conforms to the diameter of the fly line throughout its length and determines how energy is transmitted and dissipated during casting. There are basically four shapes: level, double, weight-forward, and shooting.

A level line (signified by the letter *L*) is the same weight and diameter throughout, and essentially has no taper to it. This is the least expensive fly line, but it is more difficult than others to cast and control in the water, and does not afford distance advantages or presentation delicacy. It is adequate for simplified fishing activities, including roll casts and short casts of 20 to 40 feet.

A double taper (*DT*) line has the same taper at both ends and a section of level line in the middle, and it is used primarily in short- to medium-range casting. Although this shape and its large level midsection is not conducive to casts beyond 50 or 60 feet, it is excellent for roll casting and for making a delicate presentation of a light fly. It has greater life than the following fly line shapes, because the ends can be swapped when the front taper wears out.

A weight-forward (*WF*) line is tapered only at the fishing end. It is designed to fish well at short, medium, and long distances. It is not good for long roll casts but is especially beneficial for standard distance casting since it sports a lighter and smaller-diameter back section that moves with less friction through the rod guides. This also makes it generally beneficial for casting large flies, bugs, and poppers.

A shooting (*ST*) line, which is also known as a shooting head (*SH*), is a 30-foot length of tapered fly line, similar to the head of a weight-forward line. It has a 12-foot tapered end followed by an 18-foot-long level section with a factory-installed loop at the end, which is attached to a long (100-foot) thin-diameter running line. The running line is often 20- to 30-pound nylon monofilament, but it may also be a thin-diameter (.029-inch) plastic-coated shooting line, and the combination results in maximum distance casting and smooth flow through the rod guides. This fly line is used often in big-water fishing and for casting at distances from 70 feet up to about the maximum of 120 (for the best casters); it is difficult to cast and not a line for the novice to start out with.

There are also specialty tapers that are variations of the weight-forward style, usually with different proportions to the overall length of the head or to the sections of the taper. The number of these has grown in recent years, with designs for such specific applications as bonefishing, striped bass fishing, steelhead fishing, and more. Of longer existence has been bass bug and saltwater tapers, which have a specially designed weight-forward portion and short front taper and short belly that facilitates turning over large and wind-resistant flies and popping bugs. Another style is the rocket taper, which has a long front taper that shoots well and allows finer presentations.

A leader *(see)* is always attached to the forward (fishing) end of the fly line. The leader makes the transition from the large and thick-diameter fly line to the fly. It is tapered from a greater strength and diameter at its connection to the fly line to a finer diameter and lighter strength at its connection to the fly, sometimes using a tippet *(see)* to bridge the end of the leader and the fly. The tapered leader is usually about the length of the rod, but this varies with conditions and may be longer or shorter; tapering helps extend the fly to the end of the overall line and to turn the fly over and make a quiet presentation.

Weight and line codes. Fly lines vary in length according to type of line and are commonly about 85 to 90 feet long; they may vary in overall length from 75 to 100 feet, with the exception of short shooting heads. The portion devoted to the head and the running line varies, but it is the grain weight of the first 30 feet of the line that determines its classification, according to a standard system in which lines are measured in weights from 60 to over 800 grains and translated into line weight or size, which is interrelated with the rods that are designed to properly cast such a class of line.

Line weights range from 1 to 15 in designation, the higher numbers being heavier and more difficult for the average person to cast. Line weights from 3 to 8 cover most freshwater needs, and from 7 to 12 most saltwater needs. The heaviest lines are used for casting huge flies with muscle rods

Fly Line Tapers

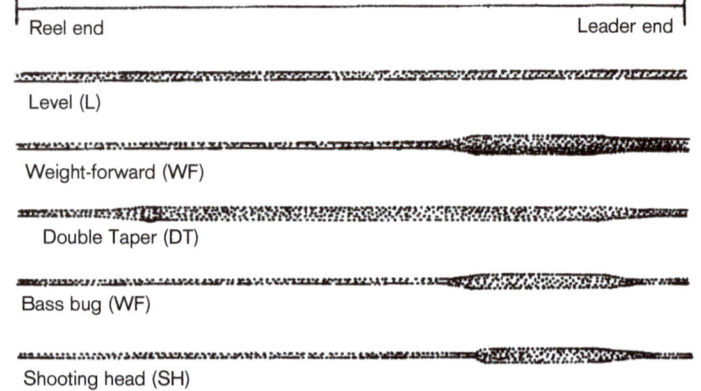

and handling big-game pelagic species, and the lightest lines are used on ultralight rods for minute flies and small-fish angling. Sizes 5 through 8 are most popular nationally, with 6 the most common because of its versatility in freshwater trout fishing.

Fly lines are labeled according to size, function, and taper, all of which must be married to do the job required for the fishing circumstances. To determine the classification and features of a fly line, read the line code of letters and numbers on the outer packaging. A product labeled DT5F, for example, is a double-taper 5-weight floating line. A product labeled WF8S is a weight-forward size 8 sinking line.

In addition to matching up with the right rod, a particular fly line also matches up with the size and weight of the fly to be used, as well as the conditions (open water and wind being more demanding than sheltered environs). Flies that are very air resistant or that are heavily weighted require greater line sizes, as do windy conditions.

Backing. With the exception of the smallest reels that accommodate the lightest line weights, the nonfishing end of fly line is attached to backing, which is a line that helps fill up the spool and stands in reserve to aid in playing large fish. Without backing it would take more turns of the handle to retrieve line onto the spool, and the line would be stored in small coils, which is harder to stretch out and may inhibit casting by having the line flap against the guides when cast. Backing promotes line storage in large coils, which are more easily straightened for easier use.

Backing also provides a reserve for those instances when a large fish takes a fly and heads to the next county. In most freshwater fishing and some saltwater fishing, the angler seldom gets to the backing on the reel when playing a fish, but when you need it, you'd better have it.

The size of the reel spool in conjunction with the length of the fly line determines how much backing is suitable; in turn, the size of fish that might be encountered and its fighting abilities determine how large a reel and overall capacity (fly line plus backing) is appropriate. Braided Dacron and braided or fused microfilament line, which have very low stretch, are the best products for backing because they wind on easily with less chance of binding than nylon monofilament line; 20-pound strength is standard for use with fly lines up to about the 7-weight class, and 30- or 40-pound strength is used with heavier fly lines. As a rule for the heavier lines, keep in mind the breaking strength of the fly line itself and don't undercut it. Smaller reels require only about 50 yards of lighter backing. The amount of backing necessary on larger reels used for bigger fish is in the 150- to 200-yard range, although greater backing is required for big-game species. Thin-diameter high-tech lines allow for the use of 50- and 60-pound backing line with the diameter of a conventional 20-pound line, and high-tech 30-pound backing with the diameter of conventional 15-pound line means that a much greater amount can also be employed (for more on standard lines, see: line).

Reels

Fly reels have long been described as storage devices for fly line that had little or no function in casting or playing fish; this is because they were, until recent decades, mostly used for relatively small fish in freshwater. With the application of flycasting tackle for very large and strong fish in all environments, reels have evolved into much sturdier products with more functional retrieval and fish-playing characteristics, in addition to being a way to store fly line and backing.

Although some type of reel used for catching fish can be first ascribed to the Chinese around the middle of the twelfth century, the earliest written account of fishing reels appeared in England in 1651 in *The Art of Angling,* a book by Thomas Barker; Izaak Walton even mentioned a "wheel" on a salmon fishing rod in *The Compleat Angler* two years later, and it can be assumed that these developments started an evolution in fishing rods or poles, not the least of which included the creation of guides for the passage of line. By the mid-nineteenth century in Europe, a revolving spool reel called a centrepin was widely used for varied fishing activities, although it had an inert and relatively wide spool and two-handled cranking. This was the forerunner of the fly reel.

Centrepin reels were revolving spool reels, and in appearance they were not unlike the earliest

Flycasting reels are basically simple line-storage devices, although some have more advanced drag-control features.

forerunners of baitcasting reels. Still in specialized use today in Europe for coarse fishing with floats *(see)*, centrepins are also known as float reels, have a 3- to 4-inch overall diameter, and feature a simple flanged spool on a single axle. They were greatly improved in Nottingham, England, in the midnineteenth century by the incorporation of a smooth, free-spinning spool, and the new found sensitivity revolutionized fishing for coarse species.

In the 1870s, several modifications by a number of craftsmen, including Charles Orvis, the founder of that prominent tackle purveyor and creator of the first perforated spool fly reel (1874), made these bulky and heavy reels more suitable for fly fishing and the lighter split cane bamboo casting rods that were being crafted. This included a narrow spool, single-handle cranking, lighter weight, and perforated spools to aid line drying and prevent line rot (the lines of that era required drying after each use). Reels made of aluminum first appeared during the 1870s and became prominent by the end of the century.

It was in the latter decades of that century that fly reels were mounted underneath a fly rod and in-line with it, as well as below the rod grip. The reels of that era are not much different than the simplest fly reels of today, yet these revolving spool products have diversified in many ways, especially in terms of materials, drag, retrieval speed, and features conducive to special and more demanding applications.

One thing that is unchanged, however, and that distinguishes flycasting tackle from many other forms of tackle (except spinning), is that the reel is always situated under the rod and below the handle grip. This placement counterbalances the weight of the rod (which is often relatively long), has a natural and comfortable feel, and reduces arm fatigue from repetitive casting.

Fly reels today are used in freshwater and saltwater, although more commonly in the former primarily by virtue of the greater number of freshwater anglers and the easier use (shorter casting and smaller fish) in those environs. They range from very light small-profile models matched with the lightest line weights in freshwater to large-profile saltwater heavyweights that have a lot of line capacity and drag mechanisms that help pressure the strongest fish. Size is important in terms of capacity to handle large fish, and for matching up with the rod and line being used. Lighter lines used for smaller fish don't need large reels, but heavier lines, which have a larger diameter and which are likely to be used for stronger and bigger fish, obviously require a large reel.

Unlike other reels, a fly reel has no casting or line- dispensing function owing to the different principle involved in flycasting. It holds line, of course, which is pulled out by hand to become available for the actual casting exercise; it retrieves line for storage but not for the act of manipulating a fly; and it provides a variable degree of drag to pressure a strong fish when it pulls line from the reel.

Types

Although fly reels may be referred to as trout reels, salmon reels, saltwater reels, and the like, such type-casting is more a function of a reel's line capacity and features than basic operation. Fly reels are most appropriately identified as being single-action, multiplying action, or automatic, categorizations that are all related to line recovery.

Single-action. A single-action fly reel is a spool inside a frame with the handle built on the spool. Each turn of the handle causes one turn of the spool, which means that there is a 1:1 ratio in line retrieval. This is also referred to as direct drive. About 90 percent of fly reels in use are of this type, and most of these are fairly lightweight models. When matched to the appropriate line weight for

Single-Action Fly Reel Parts

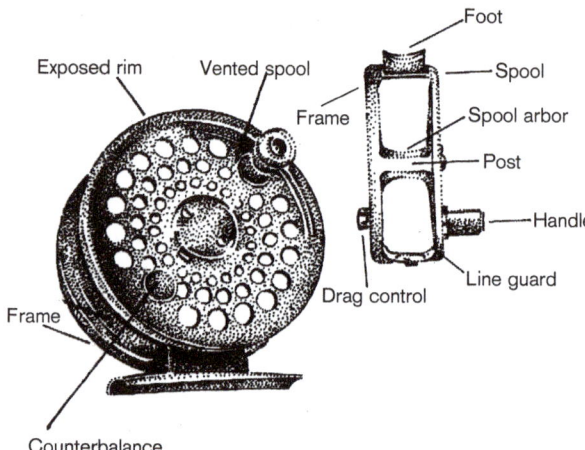

the species sought, single-action reels have plenty of line and backing capacity. A single-action reel has few moving parts and often minimal features, so it is simple and reliable, although models range widely in price due to materials and components.

It is easy to change line quickly on a single-action reel by carrying an extra spool filled with different line. This is most common for freshwater anglers and lets you adapt with one reel to fish throughout the water column. However, in heavier products used for big fish, a second reel might be better than an extra spool; if something goes wrong with the primary reel, having an extra spool won't help.

Multiplying action. A multiplying-action fly reel is similar in design to a single-action reel but sports internal gearing that causes one revolution of the handle to turn the spool more than one time, which is how other categories of reels, such as spinning, spincasting, and baitcasting, operate. Thus, in a multiplying-action fly reel with a 2:1 ratio, the spool revolves two full times for each full revolution of the handle. This gearing makes the multiplying-action fly reel more expensive than an otherwise comparable single-action reel, and it is used in situations where rapid recovery of fairly long lengths of line is important to keep up with a fast-moving fish (it is used by some steelhead, salmon, and big-game saltwater anglers). This type of fly reel has come in and out of popularity over the years and is currently fading because of the greater usage of large-arbor spools on single-action reels.

Automatic. An automatic fly reel doesn't have manual line retrieval by turning a handle, like single- and multiplying-action reels. It automatically winds line when a trigger is depressed, which releases tension in a prewound spring. That tension is built up when line is stripped off the reel. This is a fairly heavy reel with limited line capacity and without an extra spool option. Such reels are not used in saltwater and are primarily devoted to close-quarters freshwater fishing where quick pickup of loose line is desirable, and for smaller species that will not take a lot of line when fighting. Used mainly for panfish and small trout, they are also a viable fly tackle option for someone who has the use of only one hand or has limited use of both hands.

Features/Components

The key elements of a reel in use include smooth operation, durability, and—in the case of reels used for strong fish—good drag performance. Although most fly reels are fairly simple in construction and have fewer parts than other types of reels, they do have features that play important functional roles and deserve attention when comparing models. The more often that a reel is used, and the more demanding the fishing, the more important these various features become.

Frame. All fly reels have a foot that is attached to the frame or housing and that holds the reel in the rod handle. The frame itself varies in materials, and it includes the rear plate and the pillars or posts that cover the outer rim. The spool rests within this. Most better frames are made from machined or anodized aluminum and also have a line guard or guide that prevents line wear. On better products, the spool-to-frame tolerances are very precise; on poorer ones there may be some gap between these, which can allow line to slip between the two or increase the chance of getting dirt or sand in the reel (this is more true of older reels than newer ones).

Some frames may be of open or full design, and vented or solid. A full frame provides structural strength for reels made of less expensive materials and requires that line from the spool be directed through the frame before it can be run through the rod guides. Open frames make line changing and rigging easier, and in better reels that are machined from strong materials they do not sacrifice strength. A vented frame (perforated with holes of varying sizes and shapes on the sideplate) is preferred for stylistic as well as practical reasons, and venting exists on spools as well. This originated as a means of helping to dry out older lines, which were subject

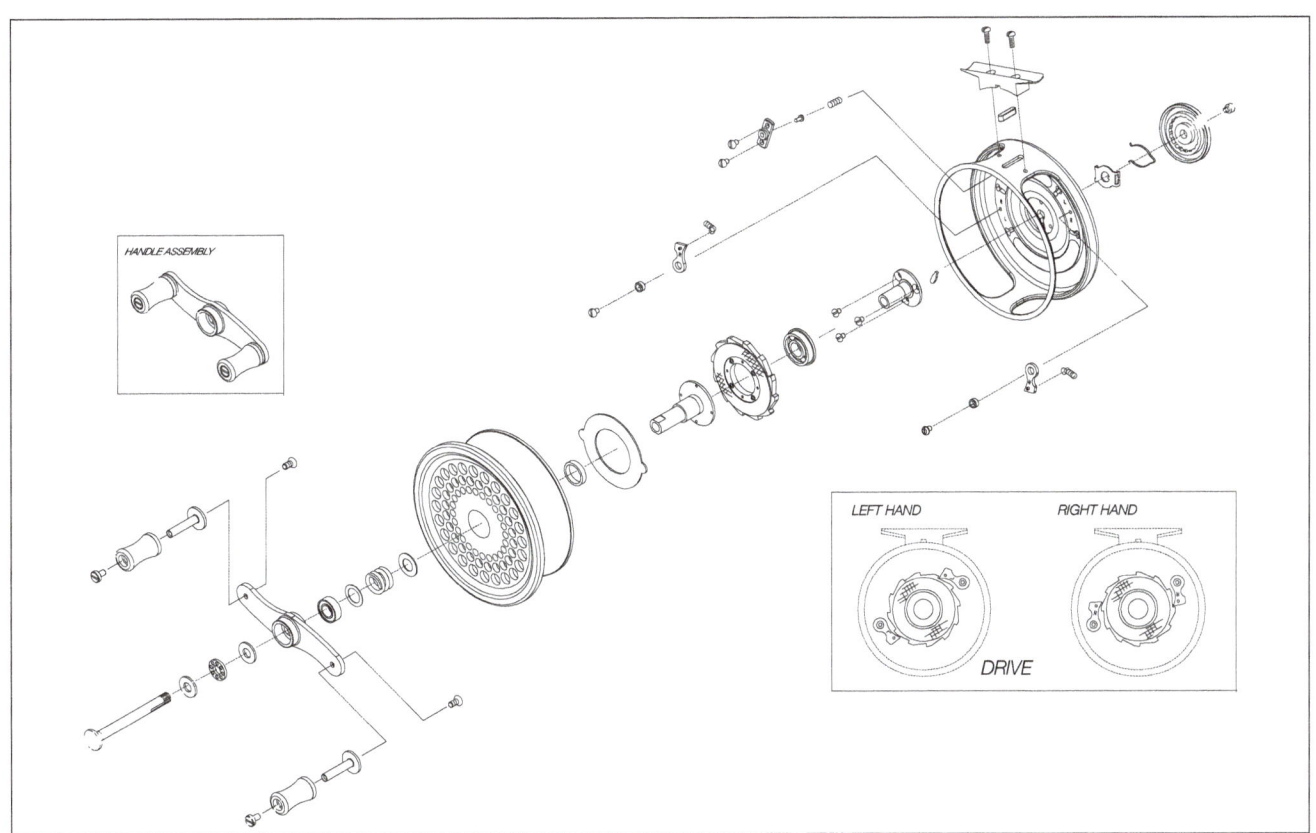

All of the parts of a heavy-duty Penn International saltwater flycasting reel are shown here; this product features a high-tech friction drag, a convertible drive, and an anti-reverse system that prevents the handle from turning backward when a fish strips off line.

to rotting; it exists today more for classic appearance but also to aid in rinsing with freshwater, which is important for reels used in marine environments. These holes also reduce weight, which appeals to many anglers who compare relative reel weights, although nearly anyone would be hard-pressed to detect the difference of an ounce or two in loaded reels.

Spool. Fly reel spools in general are deep and narrow, which facilitates line leveling during retrieve, although the angler still needs to guide the line with a finger of the rod-holding hand to prevent center-spool buildup. Newer designs incorporate a large arbor for greater line retrieval per turn of the handle without sacrificing capacity. Larger arbor reels are becoming popular and may be the standard of the future on better fly reels. To be of most advantage, they should also be part of a reel with a larger outside diameter than is conventional, in order to maintain necessary capacity. Line recovery is the main benefit here, and large arbor spools recover significantly more line than conventional arbor spools; they also have benefits for outward flowing line (slower speed and fewer turns), drag (shorter duration of application and less tension at greater line lengths), and line memory (less of it).

The handle knob is built on the edge of the spool, and it comes in many lengths and styles, as do knobs for other types of reels, indicating that there is little agreement among anglers about what is best for comfort or performance. Some anglers prefer a handle knob that is fairly short and round to keep loose line coils from wrapping on it when a fish takes and streaks off with line. Others like a large knob that is easy to grab and hold, especially when fighting big fish and when your fingers are wet or cold. A handle should be easy to release (when a fish streaks off), and many anglers prefer not to have a handle with an indentation so that they can let go of it in a heartbeat when they have to. Comfort is especially important in larger reels used for big fish, since a lot of winding is likely to be done; thin and/or short handles are generally not favored for this use, even though they're less likely to catch loose fly line.

Many fly reel spools have an exposed or overlapping rim flange, known as a palming rim, which allows the angler to apply extra, judicious tension on the spool with the fingertips or palm when a fish is taking line (too much pressure will snap the tippet) or, more important, when pumping a large fish during a battle. Some anglers using light tippets will set their drag light and use pressure on the spool rim as their primary control measure.

One-piece machined spools are found on better reels, and top models also have a counterbalanced design and turn easily on ball bearings. Balancing prevents spool wobbling, which occurs on unbalanced reels when a strong fish takes line and makes the spool spin at a furious pace, since the handle is on one side of the spool and there is nothing on the other. (A screw, with the head placed on the inside, can be bolted to the spool opposite the handle to help provide balance in older reels.)

Removing the spool of this heavy-duty Martin fly reel reveals a large surface area of Teflon and stainless steel drag discs.

Most spools are also vented with many holes, in some cases of varying sizes, and such reels are sometimes called ventilated spool reels. As noted before with vented frames, this has benefits for cleaning and weight.

Drag. Internally, the activation of a spring-loaded switch on the face of the spool allows the spool to be removed, and this reveals a simple brake or click drag that has one or two pawls engaging a gear. The simplest reels should have a drag that allows for enough adjustment so that when line is pulled off the reel quickly it doesn't cause a line overrun and tangling. These pawls cause an audible clicking sound that differs when line is being dispensed or retrieved (some can be used in a silent mode, which is not preferred by guides, who use the sound of the reel to help them determine what the fish is doing).

A lot of fly reels have a compression drag system that utilizes one or more washers (called discs by some) to press against the spool, which is similar to the drag system employed by other types of reels. When an external drag adjustment knob is turned, it puts tension on a friction washer, which applies pressure to the spool to slow it down. There may or may not be a metal drag washer in the system, which presses upon the friction washer, and the material that has long been favored for the friction washer is cork. The drags of some reels employ metal and friction washers via an adjustable caliper-type system that uses friction washers like dual braking pads to apply pressure to the spool. Some reels use O rings in a caliper-like system instead of disclike friction washers. In all cases, the rings or washers that are made of friction material compress with pressure, and in hard use there is a lot of heat built up within the drag system.

As with all other types of reels, the better drags are obviously those that operate smoothly over a wide range of adjustments with good braking systems, and heavier-duty models have various drag washer materials.

Cork is preferred by many fly reel manufacturers as fly reel drag washer material; it is durable, compressible, and light, and has been used for a long time. Cork is a high-service item, however, and can become distorted as well as wear down; when it gets wet, it can be jerky or inconsistent. Anglers who wade have a high tendency to get water in their reels, and wet reels also happen to those who fish from boats, even if only from incidental exposure. An interesting note here is that cork is not used as a friction drag washer material in most other types of reels.

Some top fly reel manufacturers are now using carbon-fiber drag materials, which are prominent in big-game reels. Carbon fiber has a natural slipperiness for smooth operation, but great friction properties. On big-game reels it is installed dry, but on some fly reels it is installed greased. The woven carbon fiber compresses slightly, and that little bit of give contributes to excellent drag range. Just as important, the carbon fiber doesn't change characteristics when it heats up, and doesn't build up friction as it heats up. This is very important during demanding fishing situations and battles with large, long-running, and hard-fighting fish (billfish, tuna, tarpon, etc.), and it is explained in more detail in the entry on big-game tackle *(see)*.

Heat buildup and the ability of a reel (and drag washers) to dissipate heat are important factors, especially for a reel that will be used on strong fish capable of quickly taking a lot of line off a reel. Also a factor is the initial startup of a drag and how easily it can overcome inertia (if it does not, the tippet will break). Many drag washers do not dissipate heat well and/or do not overcome inertia easily, and this is what causes inconsistent drag performance. In saltwater fly fishing, and fly fishing in rivers for salmon and steelhead, this inconsistency of performance is of greatest concern.

How easily the drag can be adjusted and how accessible the adjustment mechanism is, are other important design elements to consider. The adjustment knob, usually a small wheel, should be convenient and easy to grip when your hands are wet or cold. It should turn easily but not so readily that tension can be accidentally changed, and there should be a wide range of adjustment (preferably at least a 360-degree rotation). Too much range, however, such as several full turns of the knob, is just as bad as too little range; some knobs also have click stops to help identify the adjustment positioning.

As with other reel types, you should release drag tension at the end of the fishing day (or trip) in order to enhance the condition of the washer and keep the material from developing a set. This is less important with carbon-fiber drag washers than with other materials. The general principles of using and setting drag are covered in greater detail under that entry *(see: drag)*.

Anti-reverse. Some fly reels have an anti-reverse design, meaning that the spool turns but the handle does not when line is pulled from the reel, depending on the tension placed on the adjustment mechanism. The internal gearing of this adds considerably to their price, but anti-reverse fly reels are favored by some, who would like to avoid the knuckle or fingertip bashing that a furiously spinning spool can inflict when a strong fish streaks away with the fly.

Convertible retrieve. Another feature of some reels is ready convertibility to right- or left-hand retrieve. Fly reels by tradition are commonly set to retrieve right-handed, and many older reels were designed only for this operation (similar to conventional and baitcasting reels). But this seems more suited to left-handed anglers, since they can hold the rod in their dominant hand and retrieve with their subordinate hand. Thus, some right-handed anglers prefer left-hand cranking and right-handed rod holding, and convertibility (with some internal reconfiguring) is important to them, especially if they'll tangle with large fish that require a lot of pumping and reeling. If the reel is not convertible, they have to hold and fight the fish with their subordinate hand and turn the reel handle with their dominant hand, which also means that the rod is changed from dominant hand when casting to subordinate hand when playing a fish (this is actually what the majority of baitcasting tackle users also do).

Some anglers feel that such convertibility is detrimental for playing really big and tough fish, and they advocate using the dominant hand to turn the reel handle. However, anyone who has used spinning tackle, which is always held in the dominant hand while the reel handle is turned by the subordinate hand, can attest that this is easy to master and preferable. Turning a small handle, such as that of a fly reel, with the subordinate hand is something that anyone can quickly adapt to; working the rod properly to fight a strong fish is much better done with the dominant hand, not only to pump and fight the fish, but also to react to its maneuvers, especially when it is near the boat.

Quality issues. Although many fly reels are suitable for the average range of fishing conditions that anglers encounter, some stand out from others under stress, abuse, frequent use, and most demanding situations. That is when the value of better-quality items becomes apparent. One indication of better quality is a finely machined and finished frame and spool. An anodized finish, or other corrosion-resistant finish, is common to the better reels and any that are to be used in saltwater, and top reels are made of aluminum and stainless steel. Other quality matters include a smooth drag system and easy drag startup, a good range of drag adjustment, and a strong and smooth handle knob. These all add up to durability and top performance for demanding fishing. However, many fly reels are used in routine fishing for generally small or medium-size fish, and they do not require the best drag features or the top materials. As noted previously, most fly reels are used in freshwater, and many times the angler does not get into the backing on the reel.

Rods

Fly rods have developed over the ages in conjunction with other types of tackle and with changes and developments in both reels and lines. For centuries,

> A nine-year-old British Columbia boy hatched rainbow trout in the water tank of a toilet; he put eggs into a container with holes in it, and they got fresh water with every flush.

fishing was accomplished with what was actually a pole *(see)* rather than a rod, and these were mere wooden implements to which braided horsehair line was attached without a reel or line guides. Rod development with an eye toward casting technically had its modern genesis in the midseventeenth century when the first reel or "winch" was used with a pole, and these simple wooden implements were first fitted with guides for the passage of line. Different woods were used for the upper and lower sections, and many different materials were used in rod construction for the following two centuries.

In 1846 Samuel Phillippe, a master gunsmith and violin maker from Easton, Pennsylvania, built the first four-strip split bamboo cane rod and shortly after, the first six-strip rod. These were forerunners in a golden century of fishing rod development in which many famous craftsmen created exquisite bamboo fly rods, and especially the finest functional bamboo fly rods from the 1930s into the 1950s. However, with supplies of the world's best cane from China unavailable in the 1950s at the same time that nylon monofilament line, spinning reels, and fiberglass rods came into prominence, bamboo fly rods were nudged toward antiquity, and they were virtually fully displaced in ensuing decades when manufacturers improved high-quality fiberglass rod production and when high-tech graphite fibers emerged.

Although the old cane rods were long revered by anglers, few would argue that even the finest could match the functionality of the best graphite fly rods of today. Like other types of fishing rods, modern fly rods are vastly superior to what existed in the past, and indeed just two decades ago.

Because fly fishing requires the casting of a special type of line to carry and present a lightweight fly, the rods used have a particular and characteristic role. In situations where the reel is primarily a device for storing and retrieving line, the rod is actually more important than the reel because it is matched to the weight and design of the line and is essential to delivering the fly. The rod stores and transfers energy necessary to cast the heavy fly line; its length, taper, and action are specifically designed for this activity, meaning that other types of rods cannot properly cast a fly line and, conversely, a fly rod and fly line cannot properly cast a heavy lure or weighted bait.

Because they must be matched with a correct fly line weight for best operation, all fly rods today are identified on their shaft by the manufacturer as to the weight of line that they are designed for; some can accommodate two line weights. As with fly lines, weights range from 1 to 15, with 5 through 8 most common. Lengths are normally from 7 to 10 feet, although some shorter models for ultralight fishing exist, as do longer two-handed rods to 17 feet for specialty fishing (mainly big-river salmon casting and including so-called Spey models). Most fly rods are of two-piece configuration, but some long models have more pieces, as do travel models; excellent four-piece travel rods are available from many fly rod manufacturers today and are preferred by experienced traveling fly anglers.

As with spinning tackle, a fly reel mounts under the axis of a fly rod so that the reel sits under the handle instead of on top of it; this is in part because they are both theoretically geared more to casting functions than to fish-fighting functions. This doesn't mean that they do not fight fish well if properly designed, just that casting is generally the greatest attribute of the majority of fly rods (the models designed for big-game fish are designed less for casting and more for subduing fish).

Unlike other tackle, fly rod reel seats are positioned at the very end of the rod below the cork grip. There is a butt cap at the end of the rod just below the reel seat, and this sometimes has or incorporates a fighting or extension butt, which is used for additional leverage and keeps the reel away from the body for easier use when fighting large and strong fish. Unlike many other types of rods, fly rods all have a keeper ring, or wire hook keeper, on the shaft just above the grip, which is used to store the fly hook when the outfit is rigged but not in use.

Most fly rod guides are also different from those of other rods, with the exception of the lowest guide, called the stripping guide, which is a low-friction round ring model. There may be two or three round guides on some fly rods; like the lower guides on other rod types, they gather the outflowing line and funnel it down to run along the rod. The remaining guides of a fly rod are called snake guides; these light wire guides are nearly friction-free and aid the passage of the thick fly line during casting and retrieval.

Most fly rods today are made from graphite or a graphite composite, and few are manufactured of fiberglass. The lighter, more sensitive, and more powerful graphite is far better for picking up line, loading the rod, and propelling it through the air than other materials; and with various grades of graphite available in rods, there are models that can fit all budget ranges.

Fly anglers learn casting basics at a Colorado ranch before heading to the water.

Unlike fly reels, fly rods have many characteristics similar to those of other rods, and these are more fully detailed elsewhere *(see: rod, fishing).*

Using Flycasting Tackle

Matching and selecting. A balanced system is necessary to cast properly with fly tackle, and

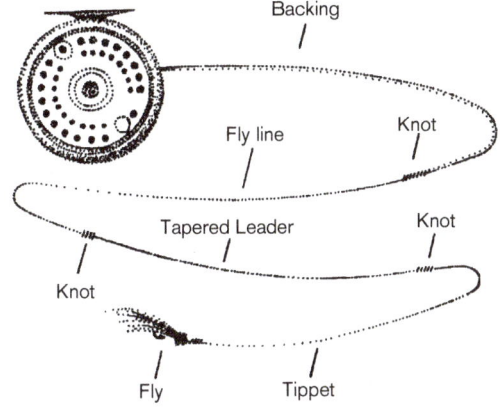

Reel-to-Fly Elements

matching the rod and line weight is the key element. Casting power comes from the relationship of the fly line to the rod. When fly line is picked up from the water, the rod receives enough weight to flex fully; this is called loading the rod and it sends the fly line backward. With a properly timed cast of a loaded rod, the flexed rod straightens out and then drives the fly line forward. With a mismatched outfit, this process is just about impossible. Therefore, to cast properly you need a balanced system.

The line, rod, and reel also have to be suited for the type of flies to be cast and the demands of the circumstances or species to be caught. It is often hard for a beginning fly angler to determine what outfit to start with (when you're trying to judge a rod for the first time, you have to cast it to really evaluate the item), and this is where the advice and assistance of knowledgeable personnel at a good fishing tackle shop (especially one that caters to fly anglers and has a lot of fly tackle) can be of great help.

Some general observations can be made, however. First, a weight-forward floating 6- or 7-weight line (WF6F or WF7F) and an 8-foot 6- or 7-weight rod are the standard equipment that most anglers, especially freshwater fly anglers, learn with. A double taper line is marginally better for easier short-distance casting but won't be as useful for fishing purposes. Whether you have a reel with a small amount of backing or one that can handle a lot of backing will depend on the ultimate fishing application.

Line weights are to a large degree related to the size of the fly or flies that will be used. There is a definite progression from the smallest flies for the lightest rods to the biggest and most wind-resistant objects for the heaviest lines. The in-between lines can handle a reasonable range of small to large flies, and that's where the taper of the fly line and the action of the rod also have a considerable influence.

Trout are the main quarry of flycasters, and they are mostly caught on 3- to 8-weight outfits. These outfits are also suitable for panfish, and the reel backing necessary ranges from 50 to 100 yards, the latter being very generous for most activities. The lightest categories are best for small waters, tiny flies, and delicate presentations, and the reels used here need only a minimal amount of backing, if any. The heavier categories are better for bigger waters, angling in open and windier conditions, using sinking lines in addition to floating lines, and casting longer distances with heavier flies.

Such freshwater species as bass, northern pike, and striped bass are usually caught on 7- to 9-weight outfits. These handle still larger and more wind-resistant flies, but the matching reels do not need a lot of backing, because these species, especially bass and pike, don't usually take great amounts of line. The same weight outfits with more backing are appropriate for big steelhead and salmon in rivers.

In saltwater, for lighter flats species and for inshore and small species, usage runs to 9- and 10-weight outfits with 200 yards of backing. Heavier usage for the likes of tarpon, sharks, and offshore species requires 11- to 15-weight tackle and perhaps 300 yards of backing.

The following list suggests tackle choices for species that are commonly caught by anglers.

Filling and rigging. The fly reel has to be filled appropriately with backing, then fly line and leader, and should be filled so that the business end of the fly line is just below the full spool level. Filling it properly helps reduce coiling and lessens the memory of the fly line on the spool. Technically the process is attaching one end of the backing to the spool of the reel, filling an appropriate amount on the reel, attaching it to the fly line, and then winding the full fly line onto the reel. The sticking point in this is getting the right amount of backing so that the reel is neither underfilled nor overfilled.

Since backing lines vary in diameter, it's hard to do the most logical thing and measure out the manufacturer's suggested backing length and then put it on the reel. You can estimate what seems right, but this often goes awry. The most precise way to fill the reel for the first time is to do it backward, working in an open field or on a large lawn.

Wrap the business end of the fly line around the spool arbor gently so that it gets a bite, and then reel it fully onto the reel, leveling it carefully as you fill it up. Then attach the backing firmly to the exposed end of fly line (use a Uni Knot) and wind the backing on, leveling it until the reel reaches a nearly full level. Cut the backing from the filler spool. Tie the backing to a solid object, and walk off with the reel, allowing the entire line to lie stretched out on the ground. When all the line is off the reel, walk back to where the line is tied and connect the end of the line to the reel arbor. Wind

Common Tackle

Fish	First Line	Second Line	Leader
Trout in streams	WF6F	WF6F/S (medium sink)	9-ft, 5x
Trout in lakes	WF6S (medium)	WF6S (fast sink)	9-ft, 4x
Panfish	WF6F	WF6F/S (medium sink)	7.5-ft, 4x
Bass	WF8F (bug)	WF8F/S (medium sink)	7.5-ft, 0x
Northern pike	WF9F (bug)	WF9S (medium sink)	7.5-ft, 0x
Steelhead	WF9F	WF9F/S (fast sink)	9-ft, 0x
Salmon	WF9F	WF9F/S (medium sink)	9-ft, 0x
Bonefish	WF8F (salt)	WF8F/S (slow sink)	9-ft, 10-lb
Snook, redfish	WF8F (salt)	WF8S (medium sink)	9-ft, 10-lb
Stripers, bluefish	WF10F (salt)	WF10S (medium sink)	9-ft, 12-lb
Tarpon	WF12F (salt)	WF12S (medium sink)	9-ft, 16-lb

all of the backing and then the fly line onto the reel, leveling it as it fills. Attach a leader to the fly line, and you're ready to rig the rod.

To rig the rod for casting, secure the foot of the reel in the rod's reel seat so that the line guide faces forward; then strip off the leader and a few feet of the fly line. Double the first foot of the fly line, and pass the doubled line through the stripping and snake guides, pulling the leader out once the doubled line is through. Now you're ready to practice casting.

Straightening leader/line. Both the leader and the fly line may develop a set when they have been left in the spooled position for a while. This can produce coils that may adversely affect how the lines lie in or on the water and how they turn over when cast. The set can be removed from the fly line by stretching it; attach the line to a solid object or have a companion hold it at least a normal casting distance away, pull on the fly line for about half a minute, and then release it. To straighten the leader, have someone hold the end of the fly line taut or attach it to a firm object; work from the butt of the leader toward the tip, holding the lower area of the leader in one hand and stroking the tight section repeatedly with your other hand until it warms to the touch. Repeat this as you work down the leader to the tip. These actions should not be necessary if you've just put the line on the reel or have been using the line and reel regularly.

Holding rod and reel. To cast, hold the rod with a comfortable relaxed grip in which the thumb rests atop the handle and the other fingers curl around it, with the knuckle of the forefinger at about the same level on the handle as the thumb. This is quite similar to how you would hold a screwdriver. Don't wrap your thumb around the handle on top of your index finger, and don't hold the handle in a tight vise grip, both of which cause fatigue. Some casting instructors recommend a grip with the forefinger extended along the top of the rod and the thumb along the side; this can offer good control, but it is not a strong grip for most people, especially with heavier tackle.

If you're retrieving line with the other hand, you can keep holding the rod this way to play a fish, but if you use your casting hand to turn the reel handle, you will have to switch the rod from your casting hand to your other hand to play a fish off the reel.

Holding line for casting/retrieving. Both the casting and noncasting hands play a role in hold-

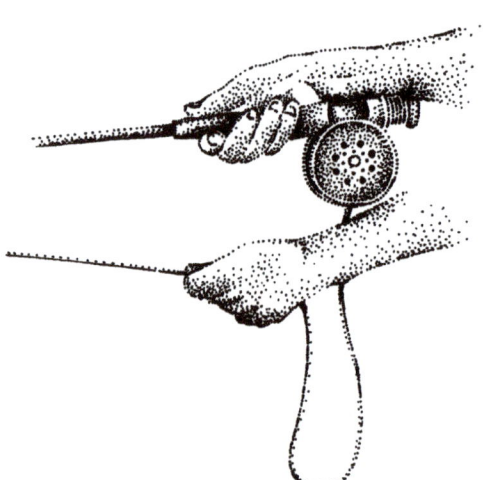

The correct grip of a fly rod is with the thumb on top of the handle in line with the reel, and with the other fingers wrapped around the side. The hand should be relaxed for most casting. The left hand grips the line for some casts, especially when hauling and shooting the line.

To gather line and lay it evenly on the reel, hold the line as shown, using the pinky to distribute the line from side to side on the spool. This is done whenever you have to spool up loose line, and especially to retrieve loose line quickly to play a just-hooked fish from the reel.

ing the fly line at different times, and line control is an important element of casting, retrieving, and playing a fish.

Small fish in freshwater are often played without using the reel. To do this, as well as to keep the line under control when you have to set the hook, the line should be caught beneath a finger on the rod hand and pulled over the finger and through the guides by the left hand. Fish can be controlled by the pressure from this finger on the line. If the fish starts taking line, lessen finger pressure; when the fish comes toward you, strip the line in with your left hand, letting the extra line fall into the water or onto the ground or floor of the boat. Pin the line firmly against the handle when landing the fish and also when setting the hook. Letting the line fall into the water can lead to tangling, however; tangling will be a problem if the fish runs off and takes line from you, and it can interfere with playing or landing the fish.

Figure-Eight Line Gathering

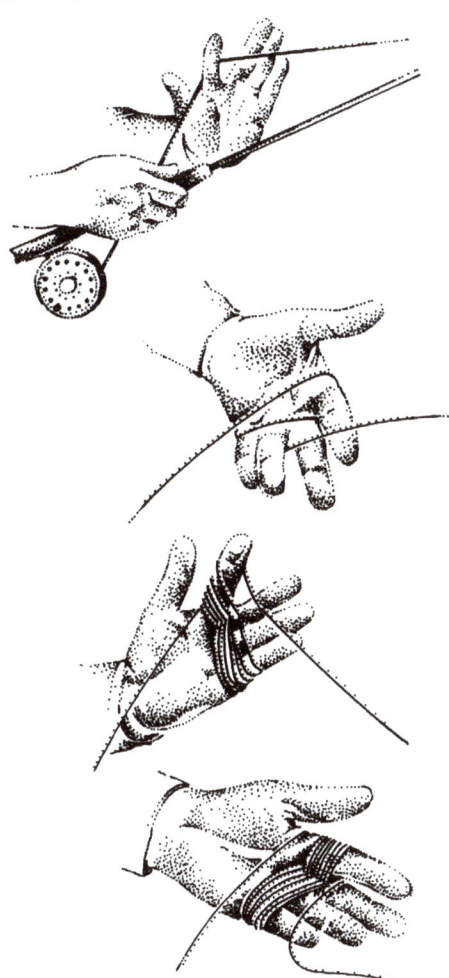

To gather line, drape it under the thumb, over the forefinger, and under the other three fingers; tilt your hand down and drape the line behind the last two fingers and between the second and third fingers to form a figure-eight pattern. Work the line toward your palm by wiggling your fingers, then repeat.

The line should also be under the same finger control for retrieving a fly, which is done with a stripping motion. When a large fish is hooked, the line stays pinned to the handle by the forefinger so that the hookset can be made; the finger is kept in position, but tension is relaxed to allow the fish to take line if necessary. At this time, any loose line should be quickly reeled onto the spool, so that the fish is played from the reel. Do not leave line lying about when playing a large fish; loose line can wrap on an object and be snagged when a big fish wants to run, causing the tippet or leader to snap. To gather slack line, keep the forefinger on the line, use your free hand to drape slack nearest to the reel over your pinky, and use the pinky to gather and direct untangled line onto the spool as you turn the handle with your other hand. When fighting a fish off the reel, you still have to use your pinky to level the line on the spool.

Fly line is often held in small loops in the noncasting hand and is freed during false casting to lengthen the amount of line that is cast. Holding it in the hand is more likely to avoid tangling than letting it fall free to the ground or water, but it is not tangle-proof. These loops are gathered on the noncasting hand when line is stripped and retrieved.

To hold moderate amounts of line, try wrapping it in a figure-eight manner over the fingers of your noncasting hand. This is best done when fishing in freshwater for small species of fish, because you don't want line wrapped around your hand when a big fish might strike and suddenly pull on your tied-up fingers. However, this is a very effective way to gather line in small-stream fishing situations, and it allows the line to spiral off the fingers during a cast without tangling and without jamming in the stripping guide.

To use figure-eight line gathering: Drape a section of line under the thumb, over the forefinger, and under the other three fingers; then tilt the hand downward and drape it behind the last two fingers and between the second and third fingers to form a figure-eight pattern. Work the line toward your palm by wiggling your fingers, and then repeat the steps. To release the line, point your fingertips toward the stripping guide on the forward cast and let it spiral off, which will shoot it easily through the guides.

Casting Technique

Casting with fly rod and fly line has the aura of being difficult, but it needn't be. It does require an adroit combination of coordinated wrist and forearm movement, however, but brute strength isn't necessary, nor is a lot of wrist action or quick, whippy rod movements. Flycasting is different from other types of casting because the line is cast instead of the lure and because two hands are used in the process, one for rod control and the other for line control. There are two primary casts: the overhead and the roll, with the former predominating.

Basic Flycasting

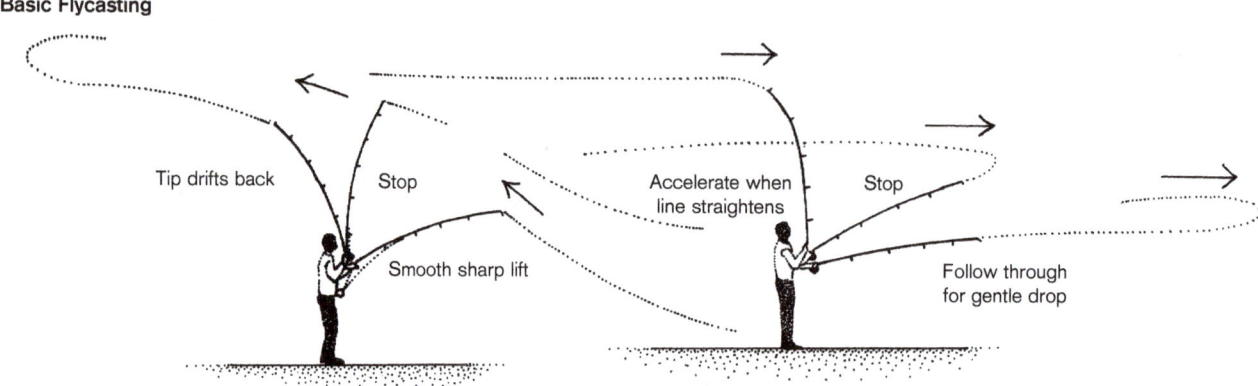

Back cast | Forward cast

Hauling is a maneuver used in overhead casting to accelerate the line.

Overhead cast. The overhead cast is the basic cast in fly fishing. It has both forward and backward movements, with a brief pause in between, and starts with picking line up from the water. A good back cast is dependent on picking the line up off the water properly and is important for presenting the fly ahead of you, so all of the elements of this cast are interrelated.

This is the basic overhead flycasting process, assuming that you are facing right and casting to the right: Beginning with the fly line and leader fully extended straight out in front of you and the rod in an approximate 3 o'clock position (if viewed from the side with the rod pointed to the right), raise the rod decisively to the 12 o'clock position and flick your wrist sharply, allowing the rod to go no further than an 11 o'clock position. This action brings the fly line and leader off the water and sends it in the air behind you. Pause for an instant to let the line straighten out, and, just as it does, bring the rod forward to the 1 o'clock position. A tight loop should unfurl. As the line straightens and the fly reaches its destination, follow through by lowering the rod tip. The forward casting movement is akin to hammering a nail into the wall, and the right timing is needed to load the rod properly for optimum forward impetus. Realize that the clock positions mentioned are guidelines for casting, but not absolutes, and that the quality of the rod and length of line cast have a bearing on exact positions and variances in timing.

Since this cast starts with the action of raising the rod, which picks up the line in front of you and starts it into the air, it is important to get the initial element right. This is best done with a somewhat slow and deliberate motion rather than a quick, snapping one. Using your left hand to pull down on the fly line, which is known as a single haul, helps.

Unlike casting with other types of tackle, most flycasting is not a series of one-shot casts. It is often necessary to move the fly line and fly through the air in a series of continuous motions to get out the right amount of line to place the fly correctly. This is called false casting, and it means making two, three, or sometimes four backward and forward casting motions without allowing line or fly to touch the water before laying down the line and fly. This is also used to dry surface flies out so that they float better.

The overhead cast is used for all distances, although as the distance to be cast increases, many anglers tend to push at the end of the forward cast, or wait too long for line to unfurl on the back cast. Shooting tapers and weight-forward lines help achieve distance, as does employing coils of line in one hand for quick release or using the single- or double-haul technique.

Beginning flycasters should practice on a closely cropped lawn with targets and then move to practicing on the water, instead of trying to learn while actually fishing. Beginners, and anglers having casting trouble, should make short-distance casts and watch the line unfurl behind them to get the timing between the end of the backward motion and the beginning of the forward motion right, and to see if they are managing to get tight loops in the unfurling line. If you hear a snapping or cracking sound when casting, the forward cast was started too soon; this rarely happens when you start the back cast because the line is in front of you and you can see it readily. Watch behind you to help develop timing and rhythm.

Getting in-air line loops under control is important to good casting and also for dealing with certain situations. The size or width of the loop is determined by the length of the casting stroke and the movement of the rod tip. If the tip of the rod moves in a wide arc due to a long powerful stroke, the line will have a wide, or deep, loop, and the line will fall on the water with a lot of slack in it. This may be desirable in some situations, such as when you need to have a long natural drift in flowing water. A short stroke produces a tight, or narrow, loop, which has less air resistance and thus is better for distance and accurate fly placement. Generally, a tight loop is preferable for fishing, and it is especially desirable when casting into the wind.

If you are a new caster, it is important to keep your arm movements to a minimum, relying on wrist and forearm action when casting; do not lift your elbow up high or raise your arm so that the

Double Haul Casting

In a double haul, the nonrod hand provides speed both to the pickup and forward momentum of the fly line. On the back cast, use this hand to grip the line (1), then briskly pull the line as you raise the rod (2). The line hand drifts back up toward the reel (3) as it yields some line and as the line straightens on the back cast. On the forward cast, the line hand, now closer to the reel, briefly comes forward with the rod and then briskly pulls the line (4), which speeds up the outflow (5). Release the line from your noncasting hand and allow extra fly line to shoot out the rod guides (6) to gain distance.

rod hand winds up over your head. If your arm moves a lot, casting will suffer. Try to perfect a motion that is more akin to hammering a nail than to tossing a ball.

Hauling. Hauling is a means of accelerating the line to load the rod and is used to help pick the line off the water for the back cast or to shoot out a greater length of it in the forward cast. Doing either one of these alone is a single haul, and doing both in the same casting sequence is known as a double haul. In a double haul cast, the angler uses the nonrod hand to give some speed to both the pickup and the forward momentum of the fly line. It is a technique that takes practice to master because the motions have to be blended properly together.

Assuming that you cast with the right hand and hold fly line in your left, you would accomplish this as follows: Hold the line firmly in your left hand ahead of and close to the reel; at the same instant that you raise the rod to lift line off the water for an overhead cast, pull sharply on the line in your left hand, bringing it down toward your left hip. As the line rises into the air on the back cast, raise your left hand and release some of the line to extend the backward length of the fly line in the air; as the line straightens out behind you, grab the line near the reel with your left hand and, at the same time as your right hand begins to power the rod forward, pull sharply down on the line in your left hand. As the rod comes forward, release the line in your hand to shoot it through the guides and extend the casting distance.

To get greater amounts of line out, which is called shooting the line, you can strip 10 to 12 feet of it off the reel onto the ground (beware of line-catching obstructions) and send it "shooting" through the rod guides by properly hauling it. This is preferable to using a series of tiring false casts to extend the length of line being cast.

Inexperienced flycasters should not attempt hauling until they have mastered a fluid basic overhead casting motion with tight loops. Start with the single haul, especially for lifting line off the water, and begin with modest amounts of line to master the motion.

Roll cast. The roll cast is a very practical cast for making fly presentations at a distance of 40 to 50 feet and also as a means of laying out line to pick it up for a standard overhead cast. It is often used as a standard means of manipulating a line and presenting a fly when there is no room behind you to make a back cast for overhead casting. A roll cast has no back casting motion per se, and the line is not lifted off the water into the air as in an overhead cast.

To roll cast: Raise the rod tip up steadily but not too quickly until it is just past a vertical position (generally when the rod gets past your ear) and at a point where there is a curved bow of line extending from the rod tip behind you; then bring the rod sharply forward and downward in a nail-hammering motion. The last action brings the line rolling toward you with leader and fly following, then rolls it over, and lays it all out straightaway. When you bring up the rod to execute this cast, cant it slightly

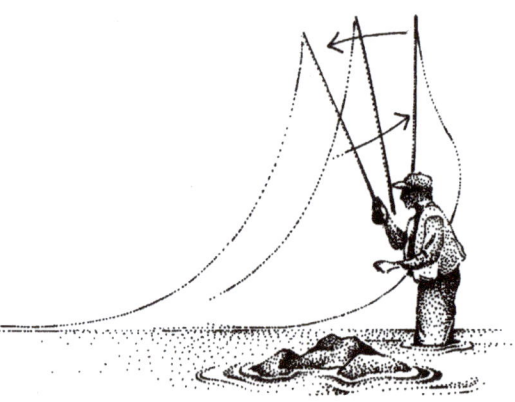

The critical elements of roll casting are smoothly bringing the rod tip up to just past a vertical position, keeping the fly line to the far side of the rod, and punching the rod sharply forward.

outward; the line coming from the rod tip must be to the outside of the tip, not between the tip and your body.

You can also use the roll cast to straighten out line that is crumpled in front of you, or otherwise lying awkwardly, and lift it smoothly off the water. Make a relaxed roll cast to get the line straight ahead of you, and then immediately lift it off the water to execute an overhead cast.

Roll casting is easiest with floating and slow-sinking lines and with sink-tip lines that are not too deep. A distance of 20 to 30 feet is easiest to roll cast.

Specialty casts. The fly line, leader, and fly can be manipulated during or after the cast. Manipulation during the cast is called an in-air mend; after the cast, it is an on-water mend. In-air mends include an S cast, curve cast, reach cast, and pile cast *(see: mending)*. The technique of mending fly line is used in flowing water to aid the natural drift of a fly, and it is something not done with other types of fishing line or tackle.

The same motion that is used for overhead flycasting can be adapted to sidearm casting with a bit of practice, although not many anglers are very accomplished with it. In close quarters and wind, the best way to get a fly to a target is to turn your body directly away from the target, cast in the opposite direction, and use what would ordinarily be the back cast to lay the fly down.

Problems/solutions. Casting problems essentially result from bad habits and poor technique, which underscores the importance of learning fundamentals. Some of the common difficulties experienced by flycasters are briefly noted here, along with ways to deal with them.

A wind knot is an overhand knot that is usually found in the leader and most often results from overacceleration of the rod; a smooth stroke helps eliminate this and also prevents the fly from hitting the rod or hooking the line.

Hitting the water on the back cast is a result of a low back cast, caused by overextending the back-ward casting stroke, which drives the line down, or is the result of slow line speed; the solution is to cast with a stiff wrist, stop the back cast in a high position, and keep the rod tip from drifting back.

Piling up line, leader, and fly at the end of the cast is caused by a wide loop, which results from an overextended casting arc; shorten the casting stroke, and stop the rod abruptly to get a tighter loop and extended line.

Slapping the water with the fly, leader, and fly line is caused by lowering the rod tip at the end of the forward casting motion; keep a short stroke, and aim the cast higher so that the line and fly settle gently.

Failure to get even a short amount of line out and moving fluidly is often the first problem a beginning caster has and is due to mismatched tackle, letting line slip out during the casting stroke, or waving the rod through a wide instead of narrow arc. Using properly matched tackle and keeping a firm grip on the line will solve this issue. Proper technique requires using only your wrist and forearm to move the rod in a narrow path to create tight loops, which will allow the line to cast smoothly.

See: Baitcasting Tackle; Casting; Knots, Fishing; Line; Reel, Fishing; Rod, Fishing; Spincasting Tackle; Spinning Tackle.

FLY DRESSING

The materials that, when tied on a hook, form the appearance, or pattern, of an artificial fly.
See: Fly.

FLY FISHING

In the broadest sense, fly fishing is angling with flycasting tackle *(see)*. One of the oldest forms of angling, fly fishing is most commonly associated with casting lightweight objects via a heavy line,

Fly fishing for pike has become popular lately; this angler found a good fish where a tributary emptied into a Saskatchewan lake.

An angler and friend fish for trout at Moose Lake, British Columbia.

which therefore distinguishes it from all other forms of angling in which weighted objects carry lightweight line. There are exceptions to this, because not all lightweight objects are actually cast with flycasting tackle (they may be trolled or dapped, for example), and some of the objects used are bulky if not weighty (such as saltwater streamers).

To traditionalists, fly fishing strictly connotes the physical act of casting with a fly rod to present conventional flies that imitate natural insects; this narrow view is derived from English sporting traditions for stream trout and salmon. Since the 1960s, however, increased knowledge of fish and fishing techniques, enormously better equipment, and expanded angling interests have led to a much wider view of the scope of fly fishing. Today an extremely wide array of lightweight natural food imitations are employed in fly fishing for diverse species in all areas of freshwater and saltwater.

Avid and overzealous fly anglers often attest that fishing with flycasting tackle is more fun, more productive, or more challenging than fishing with other types of equipment or methods. Such broad testimonials, however, do a disservice to other types of fishing, which, in fact, are far more popular with the majority of anglers and clearly provide high levels of fun, productivity, and challenge. They also ignore the fact that using flycasting tackle is one of many ways to sportfish and that it, like the others, has particular advantages and disadvantages.

While the tackle and technique components of fly fishing are discussed in detail elsewhere, it is helpful to understand the principles and underpinnings of fly fishing, since it differs in a significant way from other forms of fishing and because misconceptions still persist about it to this day.

In general terms, more fly fishing is done in freshwater than in saltwater, although the bounds of saltwater fly fishing have been greatly expanded since the 1980s. Most fly fishing in freshwater is done for trout in streams, but fly fishing for panfish, largemouth and smallmouth bass, northern pike, salmon in streams, and some trout in still-waters has devotees. Other freshwater species can be caught on flycasting tackle, but many of them, for various reasons, are seldom pursued with this equipment. In saltwater, most fly fishing occurs in inshore environs and tidal rivers and estuaries for striped bass, bonefish, tarpon, bluefish, redfish, seatrout, snook, and mackerel, plus some other species. Pelagic fish, especially sailfish and smaller marlin, are caught with specialized techniques in offshore environs. With all of these fish, except for trout in streams and Atlantic salmon, fly fishing as a method constitutes a minority of fishing effort overall.

Principle. With the exception of fishing with live or dead natural bait, every type of fishing is an effort to entice fish to strike an object that is meant to represent food. Some of those objects closely resemble food in the way that they swim or are retrieved, some by virtue of their physical appearance, and some by both. Today, plastic, wood, and other materials are fashioned into objects that very closely represent food consumed by various predatory fish; many plastic worms, for example, are nearly indistinguishable from a natural earthworm. Before there were food imitations made from metal, wood, rubber, plastic, or other synthetics, anglers used artificial flies—small hooks dressed with fur and feathers to imitate an aquatic or terrestrial insect. These were used for catching fish, such as trout, that feed on insects. Thus, fly fishing as a method of angling is derived from the creation and use of featherweight artificial flies.

As already noted, an artificial fly today may imitate various types of food, from an insect to a crustacean to baitfish, in appearance as well as in the way it is fished. In some instances, it does this better than other objects that also represent natural food. The fly is carried to its destination by the casting of heavy line that is connected to a leader, which in turn is attached to the fly.

To the uninitiated angler, the mechanics of casting an artificial fly and a large weighty fly line appear difficult. In fact, many aspects of fly fishing can seem complicated if you read one of the many advanced books that are devoted to fly fishing and if you review the thousands of fly patterns and involved esoterica of the activity. In truth, casting an artificial fly is no more, and no less, complicated than other types of fishing, all of which can be taken to extreme levels of involvement by those who desire.

The casting hurdle, however, is a large one to overcome, because if you can't get your offering to the fish, you're completely lost. Despite what many proponents of fly fishing say, it is not simple to learn flycasting, but it is not exceedingly difficult either; flycasting invokes a different principle than casting with spinning, spincasting, or baitcasting tackle, and is a little more involved (which is why fly fishing schools spend a lot of time on casting instruction). Once this is overcome, however, the fact that fly fishing is fun and effective in many situations becomes apparent. For some anglers, it will be the only way that they choose to fish; for others, it will be one of the many ways that they choose to fish. Like all types of fishing, fly fishing can be enjoyed by anyone, with no gender limitations and few physical ones.

Pros and cons. Besides the casting difference, there are some things that are possible in fly fishing that aren't possible when using other fishing tackle. Precise placement of small flies, for example, is not possible with other tackle choices without the use of casting aids. Likewise, when using flies it's possible to precisely match many food items, especially insects, that some fish eat; this ability can be essential when they are exclusively consuming specific insects. Natural movements and actions of insects are also easily imitated through proper manipulation of the tackle. Furthermore, the ease and quickness of making repeat presentations, especially when using a floating line—since it usually isn't necessary to retrieve all of the line to recast—is often a benefit that is unmatched with other tackle, not to mention that the art of flycasting in itself can be an enjoyable activity. In addition, fly fishing offers a complete package of natural imitation and selectivity, which makes many practitioners more observant in the outdoors.

On the downside, although there are quick, deep-sinking fly lines, fly fishing is often an inefficient method of angling for fish in deep water, especially in large bodies of water and in really turbulent flows. This applies to fish that cruise deep midlevel water as well as those that reside on the bottom. The difficulty is not that you can't get deep enough but that you need time to do so, and also more time to retrieve the line, and these are problems when you're drifting or when there is current.

Also, casting in open environs, such as flats and big rivers, when the wind is blowing hard, is a problem for many anglers, and it hampers their effectiveness; other types of tackle handle this common situation better for the average angler. Likewise, achieving significant distance is difficult with flycasting tackle for all but the most proficient casters, although distance is not a necessity in many angling situations.

See: Dry Fly; Flycasting Tackle; Nymph; Streamer Fly; Wet Fly.

FLYING BRIDGE

A helm station located on top of the salon area of an offshore sportfishing boat (see). These raised helm or steering areas, also known as flybridges, give the captain a clear view of both the cockpit and the water all around the boat. The flying bridge is usually accessed via either a ladder or steps leading up from the cockpit.

FLYINGFISH

Other names—French: *exocet*; Spanish: *volador*.

Flyingfish are members of the Exocoetidae family and are closely related to halfbeaks and balao (see: halfbeaks and balao) and needlefish (see). They have normal-length jaws, unlike these other species; the fins are soft rayed and spineless; and the lateral line is extremely low, following the outline of the belly. The dorsal and anal fins are set far back on the body. The pectoral fins of flyingfish are greatly expanded, forming winglike structures. The round eggs are generally equipped with tufts of long filaments that help to anchor the eggs in seaweeds.

These fish travel in schools and are abundant in warm seas. They are important food fish for pelagic species, especially billfish, and may be used as rigged trolling bait for marlins, dolphin, and other big-game fish encountered in blue water. On occasion at night, and attracted by light, a flyingfish may leap into a boat, sometimes striking an occupant, which is a startling occurrence and one that

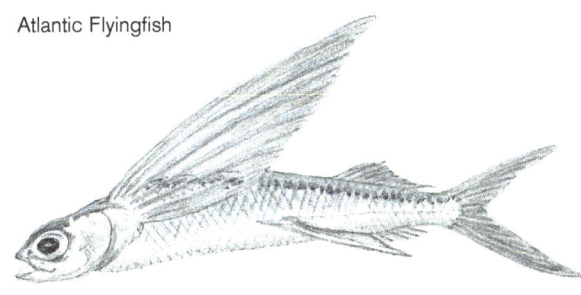

Atlantic Flyingfish

may provide a live flyingfish for use as bait.

Frozen packs of flyingfish are found at some marinas and tackle shops, and defrosted specimens are used for offshore fishing in some places, notably the Florida Keys. The rigged flyingfish is worked away from a slow-moving boat via a kite, and the rod to which the bait is attached is worked by hand to repeatedly lift the flyingfish out of the water as if it were naturally flying.

Flyingfish are readily observed in offshore environs when they suddenly burst through the water's surface and glide for a short distance before re-entering the water. When a flyingfish takes to the air, it comes from below at top speed, which has been clocked at up to 35 mph, and bursts into the air. As soon as it is out of the water—not before—it expands its broad, spineless pectoral fins and, in some species, its pelvic fins. These are held out stiffly, serving only as gliding membranes. They are not vibrated or flapped to help in flying. Last to leave the water is the tail, and the long lower lobe is vibrated rapidly to give additional momentum. As the fish's speed decreases to 20 or 25 mph, it begins to drop back toward the water tail first. As soon as the long lower lobe of the caudal or tail fin enters the water, it is again vibrated rapidly (about 50 times per second), which sometimes gives the fish enough speed to send it airborne again. A succession of these short flights may carry the fish for more than a quarter of a mile.

None of the flights lasts long, usually less than 30 seconds each and often much less for short bursts. Occasionally a flyingfish comes out on the crest of high waves so that its glide starts 15 or more feet above the trough. As a rule, however, flyingfish skim just above the surface of the sea. The young of most flyingfish have long filaments, sometimes longer than the body, trailing from the lower jaw. These are lost as the fish matures.

The reason for flight remains speculative to most observers, although it is presumed to be related to some survival need. Flyingfish feed on small fish and crustaceans, and they spawn in the open ocean around floating weeds and debris.

The largest of all North American flyingfish is the California flyingfish (*Cypselurus californicus*), which may be 1½ feet long. It is found only off the coasts of Southern California and Baja California. It is one of several species of flyingfish that are caught commercially for food. They are also used as bait, especially in trolling for big game. It is one of the "four-winged" flyingfish, because the pelvic as well as the pectoral fins are large and winglike.

The common Atlantic flyingfish (*C. heterurus*; also *C. melanurus*), found in warm waters throughout the Atlantic, is two-winged, with a black band extending through the wings. It averages less than 10 inches in length, rarely larger.

Other common species of warm Atlantic and Caribbean waters are the margined flying-fish (*C. cyanopterus*), the bandwing flyingfish (*C. exsiliens*), and the short-winged flyingfish (*Parexocoetus mesogaster*), the latter ranging through all warm seas and noted for shorter wings than found in most species.

The smallwing flyingfish (*Oxyporhamphus micropterus*), which is cosmopolitan in warm seas, also has very short wings, and its glides are never of long duration. Its wings are no longer, in fact, than those of some halfbeaks, and the lower jaw of the young fish is as long as the jaw of halfbeaks.

Another widely distributed genus is *Exocoetus*. About 22 species are found off the Atlantic and Pacific coasts of North America.

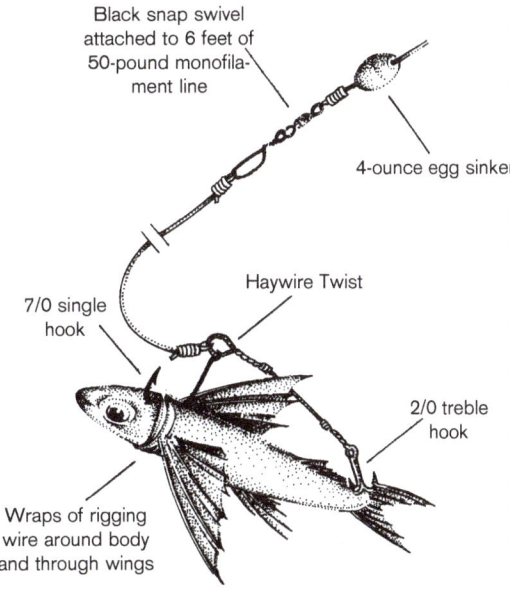

A flyingfish rigged as shown is used underneath a fishing kite.

FLYING GAFF
A type of gaff used for large fish.
See: Gaff; Landing Fish.

FLY LEADER
The line connecting fly line and artificial fly, with or without a tippet.
See: Flycasting Tackle; Leader.

FLY LINE
A line of relatively thick diameter with a coating and a core that is essential to casting a fly, because it

is the weight of the line that delivers the fly. There are floating, sinking, and floating/sinking fly lines, and various shapes or tapers.
See: Flycasting Tackle.

FLY REEL
See: Flycasting Tackle.

FLY ROD
See: Flycasting Tackle.

FLYRODDER
A person who fishes with flycasting tackle *(see)*.

FLYRODDING
Fishing with flycasting tackle *(see)*.

FLY TYING
The hand manufacture of an artificial fly by winding thread around a hook and attaching assorted materials to the hook with the thread.
See: Fly.

FLY WALLET
A flexible pouch, also known as a fly book, for storing artificial flies, especially streamers, when angling; a fly wallet is easily stowed in a fishing vest or jacket.

FOLLOWING SEA
Waves coming toward the stern of a boat and going in the direction in which the boat is headed.
See: Waves.

FOOD CHAIN
The progressive, linear passage of food energy from plants to plant-eating animals to carnivorous predators as organisms feed on each other. In a food chain, also called a pyramid, each member uses the member immediately before it on the chain as a food source.

Organisms are not limited to only one source of food but may feed on several sources and on other like members (for example, sharks and tuna both eat herring, but sharks will also eat tuna), so there is an interconnected sequence or cycle of organisms through which nutrients move in an ecosystem, which is called a food web.

Humans are the top predators in the overall food chain. The majority of the fish species pursued by anglers, and especially the most popular ones, are among the top predators in their respective aquatic food chains.

FORAGE FISH
Prey or food species of predatory fish.

FORCEPS
Surgical gripping tool used for removing hooks from small-mouthed fish.

FORK LENGTH
The length of a fish as measured from the tip of the snout to the fork in the tail.
See: Measuring Fish; Regulations.

FORWARD CAST
The forward motion of the rod and line in flycasting.
See: Flycasting Tackle.

FORWARD TAPER LINE
A weight-forward fly line.
See: Flycasting Tackle.

FOUL HOOK
To hook a fish accidentally in some part of its body other than its mouth. Foul hooking is not uncommon when using lures with multiple hooks, when there is an abundance of frenzied fish activity, and when certain aggressive species strike at a lure to stun it rather than initially consume it. Sometimes foul hooking occurs when a fish is properly hooked in the mouth by one set of hooks from a multihooked lure and, in its struggles, also becomes hooked on the outside of the body, usually around the head, by another hook from the same lure; the hook that was in the mouth may or may not remain there, but when it does not, the fish is actually foul-hooked when landed.

The inadvertent foul hooking of a fish is distinguished from snagging *(see)*, which is deliberately hooking a fish in any part of its body. This is illegal in many places, although legal in some for certain species (including paddlefish).

In many places, a fish that is foul-hooked when caught must legally be released. Foul-hooked fish are ineligible for world-record consideration. In waters where illegal snagging (usually of salmon and trout) is likely, there are also regulations regarding the size (hook gap) of a hook that may be used.
See: Regulations; Snagging.

FRANCE
With 58 million inhabitants and a landmass of 551,602 square kilometers, France is the largest country in western Europe, and has one of the widest varieties of landforms and geological features in the region.

Including estuaries and islands, the country

has 5,533 kilometers of coastline. This is deeply irrigated by many rivers, and abuts the North Sea, the British Channel, the Atlantic Ocean, and the Mediterranean Sea, offering opportunities for such popular species as tuna, European bass, cod, and pollock, and an assortment of bottom dwellers.

As a result of its terrain and diversity, France has an extraordinary amount of freshwater and thus a great deal of opportunity for diverse species. This includes 123,894 kilometers of salmonid rivers and streams (without tributaries), 65,710 hectares of trout lakes, 100,403 kilometers of cyprinid streams, and 131,353 hectares of coarse-fish lakes and ponds.

Combined with a diversity of climates—from Alpine to continental and oceanic to Mediterranean—France has much to interest anglers.

Freshwater

Although freshwater resources in France, as elsewhere, are either public, which means belonging to the state, or private, which means belonging to landowners, water and fishery management is handled by resident landowners, or by the fishing and water protection associations to which they commit the charge of managing their lots.

The Superior Fishing Council, a national government management agency, is in charge of technical and scientific follow-up as required by the fishing associations. The council is directly related to the Ministry of Environment, whose role is advisory and scientific rather than executive. It collects the piscicultural tax (national yearly sportfishing license) and is in charge of water and fishery policy across the country, which is divided into 22 regions and 96 departments.

French national law assigns the property of the bottom of a waterway to residents, with the water itself being free. No one is allowed to fish on community lots without giving access to one's own lots. Thus, fishing rights belong to the state on navigable public waters, and to the riparian owner (a fishing association or local authority) on private waters. Trout and salmon rights are nearly always privately held, but visitors can obtain permits by checking with the local fishing club or tackle shop. There are closed seasons for some species, as well as regulations pertaining to methods and tackle.

Today people involved in fishing tourism are becoming more aware of the value of wild salmonid streams. In France, many fly fishing circuits, or sections of river, have been established, and these are often also regulated for no-kill (catch-and-release and flies only with barbless hooks). Fly fishing in France has been steadily growing, and practitioners now number about 60,000. Because the large cities are far from the natural and protected fishing sites, anglers often fish on stretches full of trout that are kept exclusively for fly fishing. In France, more than a hundred sites (fly-fishing-only reservoirs or fisheries) are accessible 12 months a year for a price varying from 100 to 400 French Francs, according to the services offered.

Most French fishing takes place in rivers and streams. Which species a river shelters depends on whether it flows toward the Mediterranean Sea, the Atlantic Ocean, or the English Channel. Shad, sea-run brown trout, European eels, and Atlantic salmon are the most common migrants.

The sea-run brown trout is the most popular freshwater fish in France. In some coastal rivers of Normandy, the biggest specimens can weigh up to 10 kilograms.

Even within species, characteristics vary according which body of water a particular river flows into. The Mediterranean strain of the French sea-run brown, called a zebra trout, has golden tones and many color variations. This fish is covered with small black spots and is the only example in the world of a sea-run brown trout strain with dark vertical stripes on the sides. The sea-run brown found in French rivers that flow to the Atlantic has a much more motley appearance, with large red, blue, or black spots, depending on which rivers it inhabits. Atlantic-strain browns can stay in the sea for a while without being considered a true sea-run brown trout. In that case, they have a silvery coat.

Although it is often overlooked by traveling anglers, coarse fishing is highly developed in France, and native anglers have become so sophisticated in coarse fishing techniques that they have garnered numerous world titles and individual championships. Heavy fishing pressure via club and organized match fishing, and many years of catch-and-release for coarse species, have greatly educated the targeted fish (mostly roach and bream), and made it necessary to use ultrafinesse methods for catching them. Small specialized floats, balanced carefully so that all bites can be detected, are necessary, as are long poles to place and control tackle in areas that are carefully chummed. A method developed near Roubaix on the France-Belgium border, and called *roubaisienne,* which requires the use of take-apart poles from 2 to 12 meters in length for this fishing, is heavily practiced.

Major Rivers

The Rhine system. The Rhine River has a total length of 1,300 kilometers, from its source in Switzerland to its estuary in the Netherlands. It is still an Alpine river in spite of its 190-kilometer-long border with Germany.

The Rhine offers excellent sportfishing opportunities. European grayling are found in some areas, and a few salmon and sea-run brown trout migrate up the Rhine due to the restoration of natural strains (through salmon farms and smolt overflow).

The best sportfishing sites are above Strasbourg, the seat of the European Parliament. The main tributaries of the Rhine are the Moselle, the Meurthe, and the Sarre, which are salmonid streams in their upper parts. The Haute-Moselle and its tributaries

> From the same name/different species file: Beluga is used to refer to the white whale and also to the beluga sturgeon; kingfish refers to the king mackerel and also to whiting.

A pole fisherman angles on the Rhine River.

are known for salmonid sportfishing.

The Rhône system. The Rhône River is 812 kilometers long, from its source in Switzerland to its delta in the Mediterranean Sea. It crosses almost 20 French departments, and all of the main streams from the Alps and the Jura flow into it along its left bank. The tributaries and subtributaries of these streams represent almost 50 percent of the French sportfishing circuits.

The native species in these waters are brown trout, European grayling, and arctic charr in high-mountain lakes. Rainbow trout, brook trout, lake trout, and huchen have also been introduced in many areas.

The best fishing streams are in the upper part of the Rhône after it leaves Lake Geneva. These include its direct tributaries, the Fier, the Arve, the Valserine, the Ain (both the upper and lower stream), the Isere, and the Durance; the sub-tributaries, the Verdon, the Ubaye, the Doubs, and the Loue; and the tributaries and sub-tributaries of the Saône River, which joins the Rhône in Lyon.

Some of the Rhône's numerous backwaters and oxbows are rich in such predatory species as northern pike, zander (also called pike-perch), perch, and especially largemouth bass. The biggest bass reach 3 to 4 kilograms, but there is no management of this species, and all methods of capture are allowed. This practice threatens a fish that is highly popular with anglers.

Almost 30 percent of France's freshwater anglers, especially its fly anglers, live in the regions of Rhône-Alpes, Franche-Comté, and Provence-Alpes-Côte d'Azur. The well-established fly fishing areas are the Franco-Swiss Doubs in Goumois, the Loue around Ornans (Doubs), the lower Ain around Priay (Jura), and the upper Ain around Champagnole (Jura). The hub of this region is the city of Lyon and its surroundings, which house many fly fishing clubs. Anglers from around the world have fished such Franche-Comté streams as the Loue, Doubs, or Dessoubre.

Sportfishing represents a real culture in these regions, and age-old fly-tying traditions remain. The Maison Devaux in Champagnole, for example, on the banks of the Ain River, still makes unique artificial flies of the "forward tying" style created by Aimé Devaux, one of the most famous French anglers. The largest part of the production is now subcontracted to Thailand, but the spirit lingers.

The Garonne system. The Garonne River has a total length of 647 kilometers, from its source in Spain to its estuary in common with the Dordogne River below Bordeaux. It receives most of the streams flowing down the Pyrenees, the Cevennes, and the Massif Central.

Several of the most beautiful rivers in France—the Tarn, the Ariège, the Lot, and the Dordogne—flow into the right bank of the Garonne, and are notable in their own right. The Tarn is famous for its gorges, which are popular tourist sites; its tributaries, which include the Tarnon, the Jonte, and the Dourbie, provide good trout fishing. The Lot and its tributaries—the Colagne, the Truyère, the Bès, and the Cère—and the Ariège and its tributaries—the Hers and Vicdessos—are worthy trout streams.

Between the towns of Beaulieu and Argentat, the Dordogne is well known for numerous big trout and European grayling. Located downstream from several hydroelectric dams, it is one of the best tailwater fisheries in France. The Dordogne and its tributary the Vézère are part of a plan for reintroducing Atlantic salmon, but this has not been very successful so far. In the lower Dordogne, an important upstream migration of shad occurs in May, and this provides good sportfishing.

The Garonne itself is mainly a coarse fish river, but it offers great fly fishing sport downstream of Agen for mullet, which are locally called "freshwater bonefish."

The Meuse system. The Meuse River runs 950 kilometers, from its source in Burgundy to 15 kilometers south of Rotterdam in the Netherlands. In France, it is mainly a whitefish river. The Semoy, which is a good salmonid stream in Belgium, flows into it and can produce Atlantic salmon.

The Loire system. The Loire is the only one of six major rivers in France that flows entirely within the country. Its total length is 1,012 kilometers, from its source in the Ardeche Mountains to Nantes, where it flows into the Atlantic. Although many salmon used to run up the Loire, numerous dams currently prevent them from migrating upriver.

The main salmonid tributaries of the Loire are the Allier, which was formerly a natural spawning ground for salmon and is now an interesting fly fishing stream for trout and grayling; and the Sioule, Allagnon, Vienne, Gartempe, Thaurion, and Creuse. Most of the Loire's right-bank tributaries, such as the Mayenne, Loir, and Sarthe, cross intensive farming areas and provide anglers with very few fishing opportunities. An exception to this is the Huisne, a tributary of the Sarthe, which is the closest European grayling stream to Paris (150 kilometers distant). Fishing in its downstream sector is possible until around Christmas.

The Seine system. The Seine River is 1,776 kilometers long, from its source in Burgundy to its estuary at Le Havre. This is the most famous river in France because it runs through Paris.

The Haute-Seine is a beautiful trout river in the first 50 kilometers downstream from its source, and is well known for its massive green drake hatch in early June. Nice European grayling exist here as well.

The major sportfishing tributaries upstream from Paris are the Aube and the Haute-Marne, which have trout and grayling. Below Paris the Oise flows into the Seine, and there are several interesting tributaries at its headwaters near the Belgian border.

Chalk streams that originate in Normandy also flow into the Seine and are renowned for their numerous brown trout. In the mid-twentieth century, the Andelle, the Risle, the Avre, and the Epte were famous streams that could be compared to the best chalk streams in southern England. Today the majority of the best circuits on those waters are private and not accessible to the public, but a few possibilities to seduce wild brown trout still exist in the Risle or the Avre.

Normandy is noteworthy, however, for numerous streams in its coastal milk-farming region. The Touques, which joins the Channel in Deauville, is a small stream (a maximum of 30 meters wide), but it has one of the best populations of sea-run brown trout in Europe. Every year more than 1,500 of these fish are caught by anglers, and the total stock is estimated at around 4,000 to 5,000 fish. Most anglers use plugs, but in the fall, fishing is with flies only.

La Touques is undergoing a vast improvement in quality. Sections for fly-fishing-only and for catch-and-release exist along its 100-kilometer length. Nonmigrant brown trout also frequent these waters, as do Atlantic salmon and rainbow trout. North of the Seine estuary and near the Belgian border, other coastal chalk streams like the Bresle, Canche, and Authie support sea-run salmonids.

The Adour system. The Adour is a significant coastal river with a total length of 335 kilometers, from its source in the Hautes Pyrénées to its estuary in the Basque country downstream of Bayonne. The major streams from the Pyrenees flow into the Adour; these streams used to be famous for Atlantic salmon and are now well known for trout fishing.

The Gaves are among the best wild brown trout streams in France. The Gave d'Oloron, Gave de Pau, Gave d'Aspe, and Gave d'Ossau are excellent trout streams; trophy specimens weighing more than 5 kilograms may flourish in the deepest part of the river. Flies and lures work best, although local anglers fish for food by using various natural baits.

Boasting fish averaging 10 kilograms, the Gaves used to be among the best European Atlantic salmon streams. Today, because of commercial and/or illegal net fishing in the river mouth, wild Pyrenees Atlantic salmon populations have decreased dramatically. Nevertheless, a sportfishing tradition once existed on the Gave; the famous Salmon Fishing World Championship took place every year in Navarrenx on the Gave d'Oloron, and a double-handed fly-rod tradition using local fly patterns still exists.

Brittany

Brittany (La Bretagne), the Celtic part of France, is the only region of the country in which good Atlantic salmon populations and reliable fishing for this species still exist. Brittany consists of four departments and benefits from a dense hydrographic network made up of rather short coastal streams, similar to those in Wales and Ireland. Most of them contain migratory Atlantic salmon and sea trout.

There are numerous rivers along Brittany's 1,100 kilometers of coast. The significant ones from east to west on the Channel side include the Trieux (Atlantic salmon and brown trout), the Léguer (Atlantic salmon, sea-run trout, and brown trout), and the Dossen (brown trout). On the Atlantic side the major rivers are the Elorn (the best Atlantic salmon stream in France); the Aulne (at 140 kilometers the longest trout stream in Brittany and also the second best Atlantic salmon stream in France); the Goyen (brown trout, Atlantic salmon, and sea trout); the Odet (flowing through Quimper, the cultural capital of Brittany, and supporting both Atlantic salmon and brown trout); the Laïta and its two tributaries, the Elle and the Isole; and the Blavet and its tributary, the Scorff.

Since the late 1970s these coastal streams have been intensively protected against industrial and agricultural pollution. Although significant water quality problems exist elsewhere in the country, Brittany remains the only part of France with healthy stocks of Atlantic salmon. Ironically, billions of French Francs have been spent for other watersheds like the Loire and the Adour, with few noteworthy results.

The best time for Atlantic salmon fishing is during the fall run from mid-September through the end of October. Atlantic salmon in Brittany are small, with spring salmon having an average weight of 4 to 6 kilograms. Grilse are becoming more numerous each year, with frequent sea lice–fresh fish weighing 1 to 3 kilograms. Fall-run Atlantics weigh from 5 to 7 kilograms and are subject to fly fishing only.

The best months for trout fishing in Brittany are May, June, and September. Drennec Lake, at the headwaters of the Elorn in Parc d'Armorique, offers great sport for rainbow and brown trout. The lake has 110 hectares of pure and clean water surrounded by the picturesque Arree Mountains. Also within that park is Saint-Michel Lake (or Brennilis), which has 550 hectares of pure water in a landscape similar to that of Scotland. Rainbow and brown trout thrive there, and the lake is especially good for northern pike, which enable first-class sportfishing with fly rods and large streamers. With the help of a local guide, one may be able to catch pike up to 10 kilograms.

Although the most common fishing technique combines spinning tackle and worms, Brittany also has an established tradition of wet-fly fishing for brown trout and Atlantic salmon. In the last century in Brittany, peasants fly-fished with long rods made from ash, and flies made from materials found on the birds in their poultry yards and on animals killed by hunting. The traditional wet fly from Brittany is made up of a body in wild boar flock ribbed with copper wire, a collarette in gray-dotted rooster feather, and a wing in peahen feather fiber.

Saltwater

The extensive French ocean coast offers many opportunities for anglers. In France, saltwater fishing is unrestricted, free of charge, and accessible to everyone. The favored methods are surf fishing, lure casting with spinning tackle, and bottom fishing from beaches, piers, and jetties. Trolling from a boat can be very effective for large gamefish species like tuna, and for smaller ones like European bass and mackerel. Anglers also benefit from thousands of hectares of oyster parks, estuaries, beaches, and rocky coasts. Net fishing is free on the coastal fringe for amateur (not commercial) fishermen. Fishing for crustaceans and shellfish is common on the French coasts.

The most common species pursued by anglers is the European bass, a close relative of the American striped bass; pollack; pollock or coalfish; Atlantic mackerel; needlefish; royal sea bream; various mullet (thinlip, thicklip, striped, and golden); spotted bass; Atlantic cod; conger eels; turbot; and burbot.

Despite massive use of its sea resources, France offers excellent fishing opportunities along the coasts of Normandy and Brittany, and also along the Languedoc coast on the Mediterranean, where there is a blue-water fishing tradition for pelagic species, including tuna. Along the northern Brittany coast excellent fishing possibilities for European bass abound, whether one uses spinning or fly casting tackle.

Saltwater gamefish are not managed in France, where the sea is still considered as an endless food resource. Legal capture sizes for some saltwater species have been introduced, but they are extremely low and allow the legal sacrifice of very young fish. To protect fish of high economic value, like European bass, actions on behalf of the breeding and growth areas of juvenile fish have to be taken, especially in the estuaries, but this has not yet occurred. Some coasts are more protected than others and are less in demand by commercial dragnetters.

The first set of stamps to depict fish in color was issued in Mozambique in 1951; it included 24 stamps depicting tropical western Indian Ocean species.

FREEBOARD

The vertical distance from the gunwale on a boat to the waterline.

FREELINE

To remove all resistance from a line and let a live bait—or sometimes a fish that has just taken a live or dead bait—swim freely without the pull of a weight or float or without resistance from the drag on a reel. This is accomplished by putting the reel in freespool (see) or by using a drag-bypass feature on some reels (called a baitrunner).

FRENCH POLYNESIA

French Polynesia consists of five main island groups—the Marquesas, Gambier, Austral, and Society Islands, and the Tuamotu Archipelago—spread over a vast portion of the eastern-central South Pacific between Pitcairn Island to the southeast and the Cook Islands to the west. The more than 130 islands here exhibit the complete range of island types possessing a volcanically derived geological origin: towering sharp peaks plummeting steeply into the surrounding sea; older, more weathered islands that have subsided enough to be surrounded by coral-walled lagoons; and low-lying coral atolls, where the central landmass has subsided beneath the sea surface, leaving only a ring of reefs and tiny islets that was once the outer lagoon rim exposed. The land area of these islands totals only 3,543 square kilometers but encompasses 5,030,000 square kilometers of the South Pacific Ocean by virtue of the 200-nautical-mile Exclusive Economic Zone.

The entire area is administered as a French Territory, a process initiated in 1842. The official languages are French and Tahitian, although most formal and business communication is in French. Marquesan and Tuamotun dialects are also spoken, and English is used to some extent, particularly in the tourist-related businesses. The population is approximately 213,000, centered mostly in Tahiti and the Society Islands.

The economy is heavily subsidized by the French. The advantages to visiting anglers are regular air service and at least some degree of tourist accommodation throughout much of the territory. Nevertheless, the number of visitors is a small fraction of the annual number that visit, for example, Hawaii. An even smaller number venture beyond the Society Islands. Thus, sportfishing tourism is nearly completely undeveloped everywhere outside the Societies, and not strongly developed there.

As in other Pacific island areas, however, fishing plays a definite role in the culture and everyday life of the natives. The relative prosperity of the local economy compared to that of some poorer independent Pacific nations results in more modern boats and equipment, all of which are ingeniously applied to traditional fisheries.

Small skiffs, propelled by powerful inboard/outboard engines and equipped with bow-steering stations, are used to harpoon mahimahi (dolphin); troll for tuna, wahoo, and other pelagic species; fish outer reef slopes for deep-water snapper and grouper; employ traditional drop-stone fishing near reef and lagoon passes; and troll cane poles armed with pearl oyster shell lures to catch skipjack tuna. Larger "bonito boats," which are fast 35- to 40-foot locally constructed flying-bridge fishing boats usually powered by single turbocharged diesels, are pervasive throughout much of the territory. They speed from school to school of surface-feeding skipjack tuna and troll the same pearl oyster shell lures to commercially cane-pole their catch. On the islands experiencing the highest tourist flow, some of these vessels have been converted to part- and full-time sportfishing.

Ciguatera (see) poisoning can be a problem at various locations throughout the territory, and local knowledge should be consulted before consuming any reef-associated fish species.

Marquesas Islands

The Marquesas comprise 10 islands characterized by steep, rugged peaks, jungle valleys, and no significant fringing reefs or lagoons. They form a loose, elongated group oriented over a 300-kilometer northwest to southeast diagonal located 1,400 kilometers northeast of Tahiti. Six are inhabited, and the total population is only 10,000. Tourist accommodations of some kind can be found on each of the inhabited islands, but boat chartering arrangements for sportfishing have to be made with local commercial and subsistence-oriented fishing vessels or tourist dive boats.

The Marquesas are the only French Polynesian island group located squarely in the productive Pacific equatorial upwelling zone. Although the Marquesas are an eastern outlier in terms of inshore fish colonization, with only 350 estimated species, the level of biological production in the surrounding ocean is high. Asian longliners, licensed by the French, continue to record significant catches in this area. Due to the lack of sportfishing data, an indication of available offshore resources has been derived from commercial fishing records. Local anglers are knowledgeable about species targeted closer to shore and near several charted and uncharted seamounts in the area.

Surface-feeding schools of Pacific little tunny, skipjack, and yellowfin tuna (to 40 pounds), often mixed, are pervasive throughout the Marquesas year-round. Larger yellowfin tuna and bigeye tuna are also present. Although seldom targeted, blue marlin are seen and caught year-round. Sailfish are landed on occasion, more often here than in the Society Islands. Large wahoo are particularly abundant from May through September.

Canal Haava, the narrow channel between the islands of Hiva Oa and Tahuata, is a consistent producer of sizable (50- to 60-pound-class) wahoo at this time. Mahimahi in a variety of sizes are inconsistently available through the year. Japanese longline efforts indicate that shortbill spearfish are relatively numerous around the Marquesas. Two tagged blue marlin were recaptured in 1997 near the Marquesas (one tagged off of Kailua-Kona, Hawaii, the other off the tip of Baja, Mexico).

Since Marquesan shorelines frequently fall off abruptly to deeper water, large inshore and pelagic fish are frequently caught in bays and close to shore. Giant trevally, Pacific little tunny, and yellowfin tuna to at least 40 pounds are caught on a regular basis, for example, as they chase bait into the shallows of Taiohae Bay at Nuku Hiva. Motu Iti—a small, rocky pinnacle guarding the eastern mouth of Anaho Bay at Nuku Hiva—consistently holds wahoo close to its outer wall only a few meters from shore. Sharks are numerous, more so in some areas than others.

Inshore trolling, casting, and bottom fishing produce a mixed bag, including bluefin and giant trevally and other jacks, plus queenfish, jobfish, red snapper, emperors, and a variety of small grouper species. Deeper on the outer reef slopes and seamounts, local anglers target red snapper, emperors, deep-water snapper (including queen snapper and similar species, and jobfish), and grouper (white-margined grouper, occasional giant grouper, and others).

In general, most fish populations in the immediate vicinity of the Marquesas remain very lightly exploited due to the small demands of the local population. Offshore longlining operations can be expected to have some influence on sport-catch rates of billfish and other species, but there are no data because virtually no sportfishing is done here, offshore or otherwise. Anglers who journey here can be assured of wetting a line where few have come before them.

Tuamotu Archipelago

The Tuamotu Archipelago is composed entirely of low-lying coral atolls, a complete contrast to the Marquesas 660 kilometers to the north. There are 78 atolls here, only 45 of which are inhabited by a total of 14,000 people. They stretch in a northwest-southeast arc, 600 kilometers wide and 1,200 kilometers long, between the Marquesas and Tahiti. They comprise the world's largest group of coral atolls.

Lying between 1° and 23° south latitude, the Tuamotus are outside the equatorial upwelling zone but more within the main belt of estimated Indo-Pacific fish species colonization. This creates two more sharp differences between the Tuamotu Archipelago and the Marquesas: crystal clear water (the underwater visibility on the outer reefs is routinely unlimited) due to sharply reduced phytoplankton density and lack of runoff from land, and nearly double the number of inshore fish species.

Although the details vary from atoll to atoll within the archipelago, most feature sizable enclosed lagoons that communicate to varying degrees with the open sea, often in the form of deep, high-current passes that become focal points for feeding pelagic and inshore fish as they flush tremendous volumes of water out of the lagoon. Large lagoons with ample exchange are often entered by schooling pelagic species normally encountered outside the reef, such as smaller tuna and rainbow runners. They also provide habitat for a large number of inshore species. The outer reef slope is typically steep, plummeting away to great depths, often in the form of sizable sections of near-vertical coral walls patrolled by many larger predator fish. Lack of land, freshwater, and fertile soil has kept human populations historically low, which has helped preserve the pristine natural environment of this island group.

As in the Marquesas, sportfishing here is almost entirely undeveloped, although scattered airstrips and accommodations throughout the archipelago make access possible. Rangiroa, the largest of the group with a 1,020-square-kilometer lagoon, is the most developed, but despite numerous hotels has no dedicated charter fishing boat. Fishing trips on local vessels can be arranged, similar to the routine in the Marquesas.

Offshore fishing can be productive for skipjack and yellowfin tuna, wahoo, and mahimahi. Surface-feeding schools do not appear at quite the frequency seen in the Marquesas, although they are still numerous, particularly in the vicinity of atoll passes on the outgoing tide. Blue marlin are more abundant between November and March but are caught year-round by local anglers in the course of pursuing other species. It is rare to catch a sailfish.

In addition to blue-water species, fishing along the outer reef slope or around the passes of Tuamotun atolls can result in the capture of a wide variety of fish, including various trevally (giant, golden, bluefin, bigeye, and yellow-spotted), dogtooth tuna, barracuda, African pompano, rainbow runners, red snapper and several smaller snapper, and a number of colorful grouper (commonly coral trout, marbled grouper, and peacock grouper). Humphead wrasses that may weigh up to 175 pounds can be baited with crabs or small fish. Deep-water species of snapper and grouper inhabit the greater depths of the reef slope.

Many of these fish are caught inside the lagoon. Spawning aggregations of marbled grouper make periodic mass journeys in and out of lagoon passes on certain moon phases and at specific times of the year in the Tuamotus. Many passes near villages feature numerous fixed fish-trap structures, constructed with wire mesh wings to guide fish transiting the pass into the main section of the trap. These devices capture marbled grouper; giant, bluefin, and other trevally; bonefish; and other species of interest to anglers. These efforts, possibly in combination with subsistence inshore gillnetting activities, may occur in sufficient numbers to depress some potential lagoon and flats sportfisheries in specific locations. Many other atolls are sparsely inhabited or uninhabited, and have been little explored by anglers, despite the existence of bonefish (and appropriate flats for pursuing them), trevally, a small species of tarpon, and other prime light-tackle targets.

High-profile pelagic species, particularly blue marlin and swordfish, are essentially unfished by recreational anglers in the Tuamotus. A growing fleet of local longliners, based in Tahiti, has in recent years become more active in the archipelago, although a significant portion of their effort has been directed toward the capture of a deep-dwelling, ocean sunfishlike species called "salmon of the gods," for which there is a lucrative regional market.

Society Islands

The Society Islands are spread in a loose east-to-west array across 685 kilometers of ocean west of the Tuamotus, between latitudes 15° and 18° south. The five eastern members of the group form the Windward Society Islands, and the nine western entities, the Leeward Society Islands. The main Society Islands are typified by a geological stage intermediate between the Marquesas and the Tuamotus—high, central volcanic islands that have subsided enough to encourage the formation of encircling barrier reefs that create protected lagoons. This constitutes an environment ideal for human inhabitation, with ample rainfall, lush vegetation, mild climate, and numerous protected anchorages. As a result, the Society Islands have been the most heavily populated and developed of the territory, with much of the population centered around the capital of Papeete, Tahiti.

Implications for the recreational angler are a wide choice of accommodations and amenities and the availability of charter fishing boats, and an environment that experiences more fishing pressure than the out-islands, particularly inshore. Several outlying islands within the Societies still offer pristine shallow-water fishing conditions, including five lightly populated coral atolls, but angling visits have to be specially arranged. The traveling angler would be hard pressed to choose a more pleasant, spectacular backdrop.

The Society Islands, like the Tuamotus, lie just south of the equatorial upwelling zone. Lagoon waters are clear near the outer reef but turbid near stream and river mouths and deep bays closer to central island shorelines. Outside the lagoon, blue water is often available immediately adjacent to the reef wall, sometimes tinted green from runoff that forms productive tide lines and plumes as it exits passes on the outgoing tide.

Approximately 633 inshore fish species occur in this island group, lending considerable diversity to potential catches. Many shallow-water species

The lush backdrop scenery for inshore or offshore fishing in Tahiti, as seen here in Papeete, is among the best in the world.

caught by locals for food are in short supply around the main islands due to gillnetting and other subsistence fishing activities. Populations of bonefish, for example, have been depressed below levels necessary for a reasonable angling opportunity; the only easily accessible bonefishing possibilities may be visits by special arrangement to the privately owned atolls of either Tetiaroa or Tupai. Some lagoon action can be had with Pacific little tunny, several species of trevally, queenfish, and scattered reef dwellers like emperors, snapper, and grouper. Deep-water snapper and grouper are fished on the outer reef slopes. Within the Societies, the degree of inshore and reef action is noticeably related to distance from population centers.

Offshore angling prospects are more uniform throughout the group. The Society Islands have a small core of serious anglers, private boats, and charter boats, located mostly in Tahiti, Raiatea, and Bora Bora.

Surface schools of skipjack and yellowfin tuna, usually marked by terns and boobies, are prevalent year-round. Commercial bonito boats tracking these schools commonly encounter blue marlin that chase the small tuna under the boat, frequently signaled by panicky tuna getting hit by the propeller. Black marlin and swordfish are known to pass through the area. Pods of larger mahimahi (over 15 pounds) are fairly common, as are 40- to 60-pound wahoo in the winter months. Several Fish Attracting Devices (FADs) have been deployed in the area. Local sportfishing boats sometimes effectively target bigeye tuna and albacore with natural bait drifted as deep as 900 feet, often near FADs.

Blue marlin are the focus of much of the offshore angling effort in the Society Islands. The season runs from November through March and peaks during the last three months of this period. Significant flurries of blue marlin activity also occur in August, September, and October. Tahitians claim that black marlin also make a consistent annual appearance close to the outer reef slopes in November and December, although they receive little directed effort. Sailfish are a rarity.

Austral and Gambier Islands

The Austral Islands, a widely spaced group of seven isolated isles located just over 600 kilometers south of Tahiti, occupy a lonely 1,170-kilometer northwest-southeast swath of the South Pacific that straddles the Tropic of Capricorn. The Gambier Islands form a tight cluster of 10, protected by a barrier reef on three sides, just above this latitude, 1,100 kilometers to the east below the southernmost extension of the Tuamotu Archipelago. Both groups are isolated, lightly populated, have cooler climates and very little tourism, and are geologically most similar to the Society Islands.

Tubuai and Rurutu in the Australs, and Mangareva in the Gambiers, have air service. Until closure of the French nuclear testing site at nearby Mururoa in 1996, access to the Gambiers was restricted. Thus there are no tourist accommodations. In the Australs, limited facilities exist at Tubuai and Rurutu, and arrangements can be made for other islands, which are accessible only by boat. Rapa, at just below 27° south latitude, is the southernmost outpost of French Polynesia and one of the most isolated Pacific islands, with steep peaks, a narrow fringing reef, and a distinctly cool, misty climate.

Lagoon angling environments exist in the Gambier Islands, and at Tubuai and Raivavae in the Australs. Fringing reefs in various stages of development occur at other islands. Rapa is the most isolated in terms of fish colonization, with only 220 known inshore species. Significant tuna and billfish populations are known for these areas. In particular, striped marlin frequent both the Australs and Gambiers. Sailfish are caught occasionally. Foreign commercial longliners have fished this area intensively in the recent past. Any assisted sportfishing outing requires special arrangements with local Polynesian anglers and could probably be considered, to at least some degree, a pioneering effort.

FREESPOOL

The condition in which line is able to freely unwind from the spool of a fishing reel; the disengagement of gears. When the gears of a reel are disengaged to allow line to come off the spool, the reel is said to be "in freespool." The spool itself may or may not actually turn or rotate. In most spincasting reels and in spinning reels, the spool is stationary; in baitcasting, conventional, and big-game reels, the spool revolves. In most fly reels and in some specialty reels having a direct drive gear, the spool is always free to turn and it is not put into or taken out of freespool.

A spinning reel is put into freespool when the bail is lifted; other reels are put into freespool when a line-release button, trigger, lever, or knob is depressed or lifted. All such reels are then ready to be cast, or to otherwise let line flow from the spool.

The term "freespool" is something of a carry-over from the use of baitcasting, conventional, and big-game reels. In these types of tackle, the spool does revolve to release line, and freespool really does indicate that the spool is free to rotate in order to easily release line. With spinning and spincasting reels, in freespool the gears are engaged and the bail or pickup pin (respectively) has just been moved out of the way so that line can flow off the spool.

See: Baitcasting Tackle; Big-Game Tackle; Conventional Tackle; Spincasting Tackle; Spinning Tackle.

FREESTONE STREAM

A stream originating from rain runoff and small feeder streams. Freestone streams grow slowly from tiny trickles to broad streams or rivers. Some begin from smaller springs in sandstone bedrock where ridges and mountains have been formed. Freestone streams are more numerous than limestone streams (see) and vary more in chemical and biological makeup. They may have fewer insects than limestone streams, but a greater variety.

FRESH-RUN FISH

A fish that has recently entered a river for upstream migration; also known as a fresh fish. This term primarily applies to salmon and steelhead on their upstream spawning journey. They usually have a silvery sheen, may have sea lice on their bodies, and are very strong.

FRESHWATER

Water with less than 0.5 gram per liter of total dissolved mineral salts.

See: Brackish Water; Saltwater/Seawater.

FRONT

The line along which two air masses of different density and temperature meet, generally identified as either a warm front, cold front, or stationary front.

See: Weather.

FROSTBITE

See: First Aid.

FRY

Young fish, or a group of recently spawned small fish of the same species.

FURUNCULOSIS

See: Diseases and Parasites.

FYKE NET

A net with a long bag and hoops that is set in lakes and streams for catching eels.

GABON

Straddling the equator on the western coast of Africa, Gabon is known for its rich mineral and forest resources. In addition, because it faces the Gulf of Guinea in the Atlantic Ocean, it is strategically situated along the migratory route of many pelagic species, especially sailfish, blue marlin, bigeye tuna, and wahoo, as well as sharks—not to mention huge tarpon and other species inshore. Its rivers are virtually unexplored by anglers.

The long shoreline of Gabon is south of Equatorial Guinea and north of the Democratic Republic of the Congo. Much of the country is a flat plain covered by dense equatorial forest; the coastal lowland perimeter encompasses golden beaches and mangrove shores in the vicinity of Libreville, the capital and largest city, and Port Gentil, the easternmost point and estuary for the nation's most prominent watershed, the Ogooué River.

The presence of huge tarpon off Port Gentil was established in the late 1970s and early 1980s, when a number of fish over 200 pounds and up to 250 pounds were captured, some establishing records at the time. Nevertheless, tarpon are lightly fished here, as well as in the other numerous river systems and estuaries along the coast, especially to the south. Many of these waters have undiscovered fishing potential and are believed to hold huge tarpon as well as snapper, jacks, grouper, barracuda, and sharks. The Ogooué River and its numerous serpentine tributaries extend far inland, although its fisheries resources are uncertain.

Offshore, however, Gabon boasts excellent year-round blue marlin angling. During the two dry seasons, when migratory marlin are descending, strikes are more numerous, but the fish tend to be smaller, averaging 350 pounds. A brief dry season occurs from December through mid-January; a longer one runs from June through mid-September. In the wet season, from mid-September through June, blue marlin are in the 500-pound range.

The primary reason for the aggregation of billfish, tuna, and other species off the entire West African coast are the shifts in the frontal zone of the Canary Current and the Equatorial Countercurrent. This is especially significant to the Ekwata Fishing Center, Gabon's principal sportfishing site, situated about a half-hour by boat from the Libreville airport. There is a good five-boat charter fleet at Ekwata, and anglers can troll productive water 50 minutes after leaving the docks. The typical fishing day is a long one, about 11 hours, not because of a long run to fishing grounds, but because the captains are committed to covering as much ground as possible. The weather and sea conditions are usually good in the Gulf of Guinea, but waters can sometimes be rough during the dry seasons.

Arrangements to fish the area can be made through the Big Game Fishing Club of Libreville, and accommodations are available at Ekwata, where there is a comfortable lodge.

GAFF

A sharp hook attached to a pole, stick, or handle used for landing fish. Gaffs come in hand, stick, and flying versions. A hand gaff is short-handled and primarily used for lip-gaffing fish that are to be released unharmed, usually from small boats with low freeboard. A stick gaff features a 2- to 4-inch hook attached to a stick or pole and used for fish up to about 150 pounds; the stick may be aluminum, wood, stainless steel, or fiberglass and from 2 to 6 feet long. A flying gaff features a large hook attached to a pole that is up to 8 feet long and connected to a rope tied to the boat; when the hook enters the fish, it separates from the pole and remains tethered to the rope. The flying gaff is used for large fish of 150 pounds or more.

Gaff hooks are stainless steel and vary from 2 to 16 inches in gap, which is the distance from the point of the hook to the shaft. Gap size should conform to the fish (many offshore saltwater boaters carry several gaffs with different hook sizes and handle lengths). Points may be cone (tapering uniformly to a point) or cutting (sharp edges) style, and a few have a barb; the hook is parallel to the handle for most gaffs, but on some it opens away from the shaft.

Gaffing techniques are discussed in a separate entry *(see: landing fish)*.

GAFFING

See: Landing Fish; Catch-and-Release.

GAG *Mycteroperca microlepis*.

Other names—charcoal belly; French: *badèche baillou*; Portuguese: *badejo-da-areia*; Spanish: *cuna aguají*.

Gags belongs to the branch of the grouper family that is characterized by a long, compressed body and 11 to 14 rays in the anal fin. Gags have white,

Gag

flaky flesh that makes excellent eating, although, like other grouper, they have deeply embedded scales that are virtually impossible to remove.

Identification. Pale to dark gray or sometimes olive gray, the larger gag is darker than the smaller gag and has blotchy markings on its side and an overall indistinctly marbled appearance. The smaller gag is paler and has many dark brown or charcoal marks along its sides. The pelvic, anal, and caudal fins are blackish with blue or white edges. The gag is distinguished from the black grouper by its deeply notched preopercles, and is distinguished from the otherwise similar scamp by the absence of extended caudal rays.

Size/Age. The gag weighs less than 3 pounds on average but may reach a weight of 55 pounds (about 51 inches in length). It can live for at least 15 years.

Distribution. In the western Atlantic, gags are found from North Carolina (sometimes as far north as Massachusetts) to the Yucatán Peninsula, Mexico, although they are rare in Bermuda and absent from the Caribbean and the Bahamas; they are also reported along Brazil. They are the most common grouper on rocky ledges in the eastern Gulf of Mexico.

Habitat. Young gags inhabit estuaries and seagrass beds, whereas adults are usually found offshore around rocky ledges, undercuts, reefs, and occasionally inshore over rocky or grassy bottoms. Adults may be solitary or occur in groups of 5 to 50 individuals.

Spawning behavior. Gags reach sexual maturity when 27 to 30 inches long or five to six years of age, spawning off the Carolinas in February, and from January through March in the Gulf of Mexico. The female may lay more than a million pelagic eggs.

Food. Gags feed on such fish as sardines, porgies, snapper, and grunts, as well as crabs, shrimp, and squid; young that are less than 20 centimeters feed mainly on crustaceans found in shallow grassbeds.

Angling. Like other grouper, gags are primarily caught by fishing at the right depth over irregular bottoms.

See: Grouper; Inshore Fishing.

GALAPAGOS ISLANDS
See: Ecuador.

GALLEY
The kitchen area of a boat.

GAMEFISH
In fishing parlance, gamefish are freshwater and saltwater fish that are sought by recreational anglers and are valued for their fighting virtues and willingness to take a lure, fly, or natural bait. Many species of fish are not encountered by anglers because of habitat, feeding habits, or other reasons, but would put up vigorous resistance if they were and do not make anyone's list of gamefish. Most, though certainly not all, species considered gamefish are predatory and carnivorous, which makes them likely to strike at the offerings of anglers. Species with such highly esteemed traits as ability to jump, strength to make long runs, aggressiveness in taking a lure, and attainment of large size tend to be the most popular gamefish, especially if they are abundant. Edibility is not a factor in whether a fish is considered a gamefish, although many top predatory fish are excellent to eat.

In many places, certain species are designated by law as gamefish, which prevents them from being captured commercially and prohibits their sale by anglers. This is decided by respective governing agencies, however, and varies widely. Legal gamefish status generally confers protective and managerial oversight, and it is reserved for species that are not only popular and intensively sought, but viewed as having more desirable sporting virtues than nondesignated species, and also as being more vulnerable. Thus, catfish and most panfish species seldom have gamefish status, whereas bass, walleye, pike, and trout do.

See: Sportfishing.

GAR
Gar are a family (Lepisosteidae) of primitive fish that were once abundant and widely distributed. The few species in existence today are found mainly in eastern North America, ranging as far south as Central America and Cuba. They live in shallow, weedy freshwater, rarely entering brackish water. Like the bowfin, gar have a highly vascularized air bladder that serves as an auxiliary lung, enabling these fish to take in air at the surface and thus survive in water that has become too fouled or too stagnant for most fish to tolerate. Much of the gar's time is spent resting quietly near the bottom or basking at the surface, but they can swim swiftly for short distances to catch their prey.

Gar in general are cigar-shaped, and their tooth-filled snout is broad and flat in some species and slender in others. The single dorsal fin is located far back on the body, directly above the anal fin. The vertebrae resemble those of amphibians, that is, convex in front and concave at the rear, so that they fit together like ball-and-socket joints. In most fish, the vertebrae are concave at both ends. The ganoid (diamond-shaped) scales of the gar fit one against the other like bricks in a wall and are composed of ganoin, an extremely hard compound. Indians used the scales of large gar for arrowheads, and pioneer farmers covered their wooden plowshares with gar hides. The hides have been processed to make luggage and novelties.

The longnose gar *(see: gar, longnose)* is the most widely distributed member of the family, generally ranging from the St. Lawrence River westward through the Great Lakes and southward to Florida and Texas. It occurs most abundantly in the Mississippi River drainage system, usually living in shallow, weedy, quiet waters in the warmer parts of its range but seeming to prefer clearer streams and lakes the farther north it goes.

The shortnose gar *(see: gar, shortnose)* occurs only in weedy, silted streams of the Mississippi River drainage system, and is the smallest of the gar, rarely exceeding $2^1/_2$ feet in length. Sometimes found in the same habitat with the shortnose gar, but ranging farther north and west, is the larger spotted gar *(see: gar, spotted)*. In peninsular Florida, the spotted gar is replaced by the slightly smaller but numerous Florida gar *(see: gar, Florida)*.

The giant of this clan in North America is the alligator gar *(see: gar, alligator)*, which lives only in the large tributaries of the Gulf of Mexico. Sometimes, although rarely, it strays far up the Mississippi. Although it was once numerous, and capable of growing to 10 feet long and more than 300 pounds, this species has been greatly reduced; monster-size fish are rare and even 6- to 7-footers are uncommon today.

Gar are voracious feeders that primarily consume forage or rough fish species, especially shad and golden shiners. They are not classified as gamefish in most states where they occur, and although they are strong fighters on rod and reel, they have a very low following among anglers. They are occasionally caught incidentally on lures or on baits by anglers using bottom fishing rigs for catfish; focused angling efforts usually require the use of a wire leader to counter the needlelike teeth of these fish. They are pursued by a limited number of bow-and-arrow hunters.

GAR, ALLIGATOR *Lepisosteus spatula*.

Other names—garpike; French: *garpique alligator*; Spanish: *gaspar baba*.

The alligator gar is the largest member of the gar family, Lepisosteidae, and one of North America's largest inland fish. It is a primitive species, dating from the Mesozoic era, 65 to 230 million years ago. Fossil remains of gar are often found in limestone quarries throughout the southern United States. The tough, armorlike scales of this species were once used by Indians as arrowheads, and pioneer farmers covered their wooden plowshares with gar hides.

The gar is a resilient fish with an adaptable specialized air bladder that enables it to take in air at the surface, allowing it to survive in the poorest water conditions. Holding a strong resemblance to its namesake, the alligator gar is strong and voracious, and a tough fighter when hooked. It is capable of jumping spectacularly.

The alligator gar has been under siege for most of the twentieth century, eagerly sought and killed. Efforts to eradicate them existed in many of their natural habitats under the ill-advised notion of ridding the waters of gamefish-killing monsters. Many huge fish, including specimens from 100 pounds to more than 300 pounds, were removed by commercial netters, anglers using big-game tackle, and others using steel-tipped arrows while bowfishing. Although their numbers are drastically reduced today, alligator gar are not classified as gamefish by most state fisheries agencies and are not regulated as to size or manner of fishing. There is virtually no concerted sportfishing for this species today.

Alligator gar is edible, but not highly rated. It is used to a slight extent as food; a few are caught commercially and smoked. The alligator gar's green roe is poisonous to humans, animals, and birds, although not to other fish.

Identification. The alligator gar's body is long and cylindrical, covered with heavy, ganoid (diamond-shaped) scales. The snout is short and broad like an alligator's, and there are two rows of teeth on either side of the upper jaw (other gar have only one). It has a single dorsal fin that is far back on the body above the anal fin and just before the tail. The tail is rounded, and the pectoral, ventral, and anal fins are evenly spaced on the lower half of the body. Its

Alligator Gar

coloring is olive or greenish brown above, and lighter below. The sides are mottled with large black spots.

These and other gar are often mistaken for floating logs. The alligator gar can be distinguished from all other gar by the two rows of teeth in the upper jaw, its broader snout, and its large size when fully grown. The alligator gar most closely resembles members of the pike family in body shape and fin placement, although the tail of these fish is forked, not rounded.

Size. The alligator gar is the giant of the gar family. It still attains weights in excess of 100 pounds, although such fish are not common; larger fish are occasionally captured in commercial fishing nets. The maximum size of alligator gar is not certain, although the figure evidently exceeds 300 pounds, and the can reach more than 10 feet in length. The all-tackle rod-and-reel record is a 279-pound fish captured in the Rio Grande River in Texas in 1951. There are reports, however of larger fish, including a 356-pound alligator gar that was 8 feet, 5 inches long and taken in Arkansas' Horseshoe Lake in 1931. A 190-pounder caught in a net in Arkansas in 1997 was 7 feet, 11 inches long.

Distribution. The range of the alligator gar extends from the Mississippi River basin of southwestern Ohio and southern Illinois south to the Gulf of Mexico, and from the Enconfina River of the western Florida Panhandle west to Veracruz, Mexico. It has reportedly been taken from Lake Nicaragua, but this catch could have been confused with a large relative, *L. tristoechius,* taken from Cuban, Central American, and Mexican waters—a fish that rivals the alligator gar in size.

Habitat. Large lakes, bays, backwaters, bayous, and coastal delta waters along large Southern rivers are the preferred habitat of the alligator gar, although this fish is seldom found in brackish or marine waters. It favors shallow, weedy environs and the sluggish pools and backwaters of large rivers, and can survive in hot and stagnant waters. Alligator gar are often seen floating at the surface. They occasionally come to the surface layer to expel gases and to take air into their swim bladder.

Spawning behavior. Spawning occurs in spring and early summer in shallow bays and sloughs. The female lays dark green eggs that stick to vegetation and rocks until they hatch in six to eight days. The female is capable of producing as many as 77,000 eggs at once. The young are solitary and float at the surface like sticks.

Food. Although the alligator gar is infamous for eating almost anything, from dead animals to ducks and popular gamefish, studies have revealed that the vast majority of its diet comprises gizzard shad, threadfin shad, golden shiners, and rough or coarse fish species.
See: Gar.

GAR, FLORIDA *Lepisosteus platyrhincus.*
The Florida gar is a member of the Lepisosteidae family, an ancient group of predaceous fish once in abundance and widely distributed. Its specialized air bladder enables the gar to take in air at the surface, allowing it to survive in the poorest waters. Although edible, Florida gar are unpopular as food. They are caught by anglers, although not extensively pursued. The roe is highly toxic to humans, animals, and birds.

Identification. The body of the Florida gar is cigar-shaped, and it has a tooth-filled broad snout. The single dorsal fin is located directly above the anal fin. Its tough scales form a bricklike pattern. Like the spotted gar *(see: gar, spotted),* it has spots on top of the head as well as over the entire body and on all the fins. These spots sometimes run together to form stripes.

The Florida and spotted gar can be distinguished from each other mainly by the distance from the front of the eye to the back of the gill cover. In the Florida gar, it is less than two-thirds the length of the snout; in the spotted gar it is more than two-thirds the length of the snout. The Florida gar can be distinguished from the longnose gar *(see: gar, longnose)*—the only other gar occurring in the Florida's range—by the absence of spots on its head and by the elongated beak of the longnose.

Size. The average size rarely exceeds 2 feet. The all-tackle record is 21 pounds, 3 ounces.

Distribution. The Florida gar ranges throughout peninsular Florida and in the Panhandle as far as the Apalachicola River drainage, where there is evidence that it hybridizes with the spotted gar. The Florida gar also occurs throughout part of southern Georgia to the Savannah River drainage.

Florida Gar

Longnose Gar

Habitat. The Florida gar is common in medium to large lowland streams and lakes with mud or sand bottoms and an abundance of underwater vegetation. It is also abundant in canals. Gar can be found resting both on the bottom or at the surface. It lives in freshwater but can survive in stagnated water that is intolerable to most other fish.

Spawning behavior. The spawning season is from May through July in backwaters and sloughs. A female can lay up to 6,000 eggs at once. Florida gar often travel in groups of 2 to 10 or more.

Food. Forage and coarse fish make up much of the adult gar's diet, although it also consumes shrimp, insects, crayfish, and scuds.

See: Gar.

GAR, LONGNOSE *Lepisosteus osseus.*

Other names—French: *garpique longnez;* Spanish: *gaspar picudo.*

The longnose gar is the most common and widely distributed member of the gar family, Lepisosteidae, one of the few remaining ancient groups of predaceous fish once in abundance. Its long endurance is due to a specialized air bladder that enables the gar to take in air at the surface, allowing it to survive in the poorest waters.

Although some longnose gar are caught commercially in nets, this fish is of minor sportfishing interest, and some anglers view it as a nuisance, believing that it preys heavily on gamefish. The flesh is edible but not popular, and the roe is poisonous to humans, animals, and small birds, although not other fish.

Identification. The body of the longnose gar is long and slender. It has an extended narrow beak (18 to 20 times as long as it is wide at its narrowest point). The skeleton is part cartilage and part bone. Both upper and lower jaws are lined with strong, sharp teeth. The nostrils are located in a small, bulbous, fleshy growth at the very tip of the beak.

The body is covered with bony, ganoid (diamond-shaped) scales. The dorsal and anal fins are set far back. Its coloring is olive brown or deep green along the back and upper sides, with a silver white belly. There are numerous black spots on the body, although not on the head or jaws. The longnose gar can be distinguished from other gar by its elongated snout.

Size. The average fish is 2 to 3 feet in length, but occasionally reaches 5 feet. The all-tackle record is 50 pounds, 5 ounces.

Distribution. The longnose gar is the most common and widely distributed of all gar. It is primarily found throughout the eastern half of North America, within the Mississippi River system and other drainages. Its range generally encompasses an area from Minnesota and the Great Lakes to Quebec, southward to southern Florida and the Gulf States, and westward to the Rio Grande bordering Texas and Mexico. It may reach as far as Montana in the north and the Pecos River in New Mexico to the south. Large concentrations exist along the Atlantic coast.

Habitat. Longnose gar inhabit warm, quiet water, frequenting shallow weedy areas and the sluggish pools, backwaters, and oxbows of large and medium rivers and lakes. They occasionally enter brackish water and can tolerate murky and stagnated environments.

Life history/Behavior. Groups of adult gar often lie motionless at the surface, strongly resembling floating sticks. In summer, they will roll over and break the surface to gulp air (usually in extremely murky water) and release gases from their air bladder.

Males mature when they are three or four years old; females at six years old. The spawning season is in spring in shallow water. Females can release more than 35,000 eggs, which are fertilized by two or three males. The eggs attach to vegetation and rocks. The young use sucking discs at the front of the snout to attach to submerged objects.

Food and feeding habits. Longnose gar feed on shiners, sunfish, gizzard shad, catfish, and bullhead. They sometimes slowly stalk their prey but are generally known to lie in wait for it to come close.

See: Gar.

GAR, SHORTNOSE *Lepisosteus platostomus.*

The shortnose gar is the smallest member of an ancient family, Lepisosteidae, of predaceous fish. It is the most tolerant of all the gar, as it is capable of withstanding murky and brackish water with the help of its specialized air bladder. The bladder allows the gar to gulp in supplementary air and release gases.

Because large numbers of coarse fish and panfish exist in many waters inhabited by gar, the shortnose gar (as well as other gar) can be useful in controlling these populations. In some areas, however, it is considered a nuisance by anglers and sometimes even a problem because of its abundance.

Shortnose Gar

The shortnose gar has good sporting virtues but is not widely pursued. It is often caught incidentally by anglers pursuing other fish. It is not considered a good food fish, and its roe is toxic.

Identification. The body is long and cylindrical, covered with ganoid (diamond-shaped) scales. There is a single row of teeth in the upper jaw, compared with the alligator gar's *(see: gar, alligator)* two rows. It has a short, broad snout. Unlike its relatives the Florida gar *(see: gar, Florida)* and spotted gar *(see: gar, spotted)*, it has no spots on its head, but it does have spots on its dorsal, anal, and caudal fins.

Size. The shortnose gar rarely exceeds $2\frac{1}{2}$ feet in length. The all-tackle world record is a 5-pound, 12-ounce fish caught in 1995 in Illinois.

Distribution. The shortnose gar occurs from the Great Lakes south to the Gulf of Mexico but is essentially limited to the low-gradient portions of the Mississippi River basin. In the United States, it is found from northern Alabama to Oklahoma and down through Louisiana to the Gulf of Mexico. In the north, it has a broad range in the river systems that feed the Mississippi, from southern Ohio to Montana.

Habitat. This species is common in quiet water, including the pools and backwater areas of creeks and small to large rivers, and in swamps, lakes, and oxbows, often near vegetation. The alligator gar is even more tolerant of muddy water than other gar, and it prefers warm water.

Spawning behavior. Spawning occurs in the spring in shallow bays and sloughs. The eggs attach to weeds or other objects.

Food. The diet of the shortnose gar is similar to that of other gar; forage and rough fish comprise the bulk of its food.

See: Gar.

GAR, SPOTTED *Lepisosteus oculatus.*
Other names—French: *garpique tachetée;* Spanish: *gaspar pintado.*

The spotted gar is a member of an ancient family, Lepisosteidae, of predaceous fish. It is often confused with its close relative, the Florida gar *(see: gar, Florida)*. The spotted gar has good sporting virtues but is not widely pursued, and it is often caught incidental to other fishing activities. It is not considered a good food fish, and its roe is toxic to humans but not to other fish.

Identification. The body of the spotted gar is long and cylindrical, covered with hard, ganoid (diamond-shaped) scales. It has a single row of teeth in each jaw. The spotted and Florida gar are the only two gar that have spots on the top of the head as well as over the entire body and on the fins. The spots on other gar are limited to the fins and the posterior portion of the body, usually after the pelvic (ventral) fins. The two are generally distinguished by the distance between the front of the eye and the rear edge of the gill cover. If the distance is less than two-thirds the length of the snout, it is a Florida gar; if it is more than two-thirds the length of the snout, it is a spotted gar.

Size. The spotted gar rarely exceeds 3 feet and averages $2\frac{1}{2}$ feet. The all-tackle world record is a 9-pound, 12-ounce fish caught in Texas in 1994.

Distribution. The spotted gar ranges from the Great Lakes to the Gulf of Mexico and down through the Mississippi River drainage system. It occurs all along the gulf coast from central Texas to the western portion of the Florida Panhandle. East of the Apalachicola drainage, in the remainder of Florida, the spotted gar is replaced by the Florida gar. Both species occur in the Apalachicola drainage itself, where they are believed to hybridize to some

Spotted Gar

extent. In the north of its range, it occurs eastward to the north and south shores of Lake Erie in northern Ohio, Michigan, and Ontario, but it seldom occurs much west of Illinois.

Habitat. The spotted gar is common in the pools and backwaters of creeks and small to large rivers, and in swamps, lakes, and oxbows, often near vegetation. It occasionally enters brackish water and is highly tolerant of warm, stagnant water.

Life history/Behavior. Like other gar, this species is often observed basking on the surface on warm days, resembling a floating log. It occasionally breaks the surface and gulps air from its specialized bladder. Spawning occurs in the spring in grassy sloughs.

See: Gar.

GARFISH
See: Needlefish.

GARRICK *Lichia amia.*
Other names—leerfish; Afrikaans: *leervis;* Arabic: *crhelan, erian, serra;* French: *caranga, liche, liché amie;* Greek: *litsa;* Hebrew: *amit, arian;* Italian: *leccia, lizza;* Polish: *amia;* Serbo-Croat: *bilizma, bjelica, lica;* Spanish: *palometón;* Turkish: *akya baligi, iskender baligi.*

A popular gamefish in the Mediterranean and surrounding areas, the garrick is a large species of the Carangidae family and related to jacks and trevally. It is a fair table fish and has limited commercial food value, marketed mostly fresh.

Identification. A cross between a permit and a mackerel in overall shape, the garrick has an extended body and an unusually curvy lateral line, which arches high over the pectoral fins, dips to or below the pectoral fins, and rises back to the midline as it nears the tail. In many members of the Carangidae family, there is a prominent lobe at the beginning of the long second dorsal and anal fins; however, the garrick has short pectoral fins and no scutes. The first dorsal fin consists of eight very short, almost detached spines. The second dorsal fin has 1 spine and 19 to 21 rays. The anal fin has three spines, two of them separate, preceding the rest of the fin, and 17 to 21 rays. A silvery fish with a leathery, scaleless appearance, it is actually covered with minute embedded scales and is dusky to brown or blue gray, with a white belly. The fin lobes may be black or dusky tipped, and juveniles less than 4 inches long have orangish to brownish black bars on their sides.

Size. The garrick can reach a weight of 71 pounds, which is the South African angling record for the species. The official all-tackle world record is for a 51-pound, 3-ounce fish taken from Italian waters in 1991.

Distribution. In the eastern Atlantic Ocean, garrick occur from the southern Bay of Biscay to South Africa, including the Mediterranean. In the western Indian Ocean they occur from South Africa to Delagoa Bay, Mozambique. The Eastern Cape region of South Africa probably has the best garrick angling in the world.

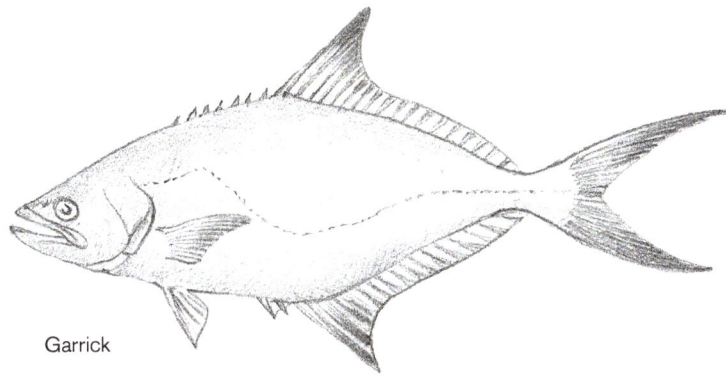
Garrick

Habitat. Found in coastal waters, garrick form small schools in estuaries and in the surf zone off beaches and rocky promontories. The garrick is seasonally migratory, some populations moving south to the cape in summer and north to Natal in winter, possibly following the sardine run occurring at those times.

Food. The young eat crustaceans, and adult garrick feed primarily on fish.

Angling. A highly rated sportfish, the garrick is pursued from rocks or from shore, as well as from boats. It takes both live baits, such as mullet and sardines, and lures with zeal. Bluefish (known as elf in South Africa) are one of its favorite foods when aggressively foraging along the coasts, and it is not uncommon to see garrick chasing mullet on the surface.

GEAR RATIO *(and Line Recovery)*
The heart of any reel is the gear set. The moment that the handle is turned, the gears engage and the reel begins to recover line, either for the purpose of retrieving a lure or bait, or for fighting a fish. The demands placed upon the gears vary with the manner of fishing and the species, and performance is influenced by certain mechanical factors and product properties.

Gear Basics
The gear set in a typical fishing reel consists of the drive gear, pinion gear, oscillation gear(s) or levelwind gear(s), and perhaps a transfer gear. Of these, the most important are the drive and pinion gears, which establish the speed or power found in any reel.

The drive gear is usually directly linked to the reel handle in a spinning reel and indirectly through a drag mechanism in a baitcasting reel or a conventional reel. The purpose of the gear is to set the retrieve of the reel. The pinion gear is normally smaller in diameter than the drive gear and connects to the rotor of the spinning reel or to the spool in revolving spool reels. The diametric difference between the drive and pinion gears constitutes the basic numerical ratio of any reel. The number of individual gear teeth machined into each gear is used to calculate the precise ratio.

In almost any simple gear set, one gear material is normally harder than the other. This both directs and controls the action of the two parts throughout their life and actually keeps the gears running smoothly for a longer period. Two hardened gears running together would amplify even the smallest machining imperfection or piece of grit on the gear teeth.

It is common in spinning reels for the pinion gear to be made of brass. This is hard material, and it allows for the more intricate machining required in this smaller part as well as absorbs the greater anticipated wear in this gear with its fewer teeth. The corresponding drive gear is most often made of aluminum in quality reels, and is sometimes made of easily die cast zinc, which tends to be somewhat harder than aluminum. In either case, the gear teeth should be machined as precisely as possible to ensure smooth operation and long life.

Baitcasting and conventional reels typically use brass for the drive gear and bronze for the pinion. Here, too, the hardness differential favors the smaller diameter pinion gear to provide longer life. The gears in these reels are generally smaller than those in spinning reels, and they require a still greater degree of precision and strength. The other gears in any reel will not face anywhere near the stresses and loads encountered by the drive and pinion and therefore do not need to be significantly harder.

Almost all reel gears in better-quality fishing reels are helically milled. This means that each gear tooth is curved, rather than straight, on the gear circumference. Helical milling results in greater strength, thicker cross section, and a high degree of inherent smoothness. The major benefit is that, unlike straight-milled gears where only a single gear tooth is fully engaged at one time, helical gears allow at least partial engagement of several gear teeth at all times, spreading the load and potential wear.

The best way to prolong the life and performance of reel gears is regular maintenance and lubrication. Heavily used reels should be cleaned and properly relubricated on at least an annual basis. A midseason lubricant check, and possibly a small addition, can also be helpful. Even the best-designed and best-produced gear set can eventually wear out or strip, regardless of regular maintenance or lubrication. Ordinary wear failure results from a weakening of the gear teeth through the removal of material over time. The typical warning of impending failure is that the gears seem to become rougher and "sloppy," with an increase in free play. The final failure results in the gear teeth skipping over one another, particularly in a small area of the handle rotation. Once this occurs, you should replace both the drive and the pinion gears.

Gear Ratio

The basic numerical ratio of the drive and pinion gears in any fishing reel merely establishes the number of revolutions made by the reel spool or rotor per turn of the reel handle. That number is determined by counting the gear teeth on the larger drive gear and dividing that by the tooth count of the smaller pinion gear.

In a gear set consisting of a 60-tooth drive gear and a 12-tooth pinion gear, the ratio would be calculated at 5:1 (read as "five to one"), since the pinion will turn five times for each full rotation of the drive gear. The drive gear is normally linked to the reel handle, and the pinion gear is engaged with the spool or rotor. Thus, in a 5:1 ratio reel, one turn of the handle will cause the spool or rotor to turn five times.

Typical low gear ratios are 3.5:1 or 4:1, and typical high gear ratios are 6:1, although they range both higher and lower. The average or all-around ratio for a spinning reel used in freshwater is 5.2:1. For a baitcasting reel, it is 5.1:1; and for a conventional (inshore trolling) reel, it is 3.8:1. These ratios are often referred to in terms of speed; for example, a high gear ratio reel is frequently called a high-speed reel, but in fact gear ratio does nothing more than designate the mechanical gear action of the reel, which is not the whole story about the true speed of any reel.

Line recovery. To determine the useful speed, the mechanical ratio must also be factored by the size of the reel spool, creating a geometric ratio that establishes how much line is wound onto the spool with each turn of the reel handle. The geometric ratio for every reel is determined by spool diameter, which is a key dimension for any reel and which sets the circumference of the line level on the spool and the amount of line wound onto the spool with each turn of the reel handle. What the geometric ratio really establishes is a more meaningful number than gear ratio: the *line recovery* ability of an individual reel, or the length of line placed back onto the spool per turn of the handle.

For example, a 4.4:1 gear ratio reel with a 2-inch-diameter spool will recover 13.8 inches of

This view of helical reel gears helps illustrate the way these objects relate to each other and how numerical ratio is determined by the number of teeth on the respective gears.

Line Recovery by Spool Diameter/Gear Ratio

Spool (line level) diameter (in inches)	Numerical gear ratio		
	4.4:1	5.1:1	6.2:1
1.25	5.39	6.25	7.60
1.50	7.77	9.01	10.95
1.75	10.58	12.26	14.91
2.00	13.82	16.01	19.47**
2.25	17.49	20.27	24.65*
2.50	21.59**	25.03*	30.42
2.75	26.13	30.28	36.82
3.00	31.09	36.04	43.82
3.25	36.498	42.30	51.42
3.50	42.33	49.06	59.65
3.75	48.59	56.32	68.47
4.00	55.29	64.08	77.90

* A quarter-inch of increased spool diameter makes an average gear ratio reel (5.1:1) faster than a high numerical ratio model (6.2:1).

** A half-inch of increased spool diameter makes a low gear ratio reel (4.4:1) faster than a high numerical ratio model (6.2:1).

line per turn of the handle. A 6.2:1 ratio reel with a 1.5-inch-diameter spool will recover less than 11 inches of line per handle turn. Therefore, it is the size of the spool in combination with gear ratio that most affects the recovery of the line. In the aforementioned example, the 6.2:1 reel would be considered a high-speed model based on its numerical gear ratio. But, by comparison, the "slower" 4.4:1 reel will move a lure through the water at a faster speed per turn of the reel handle. Of course, if that 6.2:1 gear ratio reel were equipped with a 2-inch-diameter spool, it would take up almost 19.5 inches of line per handle turn, which is much greater than the 4.4:1 reel.

The point is that you need to know how much line a reel will recover per turn of the handle in order to compare it to another reel; gear ratio alone does not provide enough comparison. Obviously, two reels with identical gear ratios but different spool circumferences will have different recovery rates.

The preceding table shows a line-recovery comparison of spool (line level) diameters by typical numerical gear ratios. These calculations have been simplified by using the maximum line level diameter at all times for the highest resulting linear value, but bear in mind that spools are not normally filled to their maximum possible capacity, and should not be, for practical fishing use. In normal fishing use, the line level will vary as line leaving the spool reduces the working circumference; differences in line thickness can further reduce the line level even when casting identical distances.

The dimensions used in this table are representative of a wide variety of spinning reels marketed for uses from ultralight freshwater through heavy saltwater applications. The same pattern holds for other types of reels, although the range of spool diameters is less broad. A typical baitcasting reel spool will have a diameter between 1.25 and 1.5 inches. Heavier-duty conventional casting and trolling reels can range to spool diameters of over 4 inches.

As shown by the numbers with single asterisks, a quarter-inch of increased spool diameter makes an average gear ratio reel (5.1:1) faster than a high numerical ratio model. An increase of a half-inch in diameter can make a "slow" numerical ratio reel (4.4:1) faster than the one that is generally accepted as high speed, as indicated by those examples with double asterisks.

Thus, selecting a reel for a particular technique, lure type, or species of fish involves not only considering numerical ratio, but also line recovery rate to get the best tackle advantage. But there are still other considerations.

Cranking Power

Although the line recovery rate of any reel affects how much line is wound onto the spool, the numerical ratio of a reel indicates the available cranking power of the gear set. This is similar to the operation of an automotive transmission, where the lower ratio of the first and second gears is much more powerful because these gears transmit greater torque to overcome inertia. Once the vehicle is moving, it is easy to step up in gears through second and third to fourth gear or higher. The low-ratio power gears aren't designed for speed, and the high-ratio speed gears aren't designed for power. Try to move a manual transmission car from dead-still in fourth gear and see what happens.

In a fishing reel, the ability to winch in a sizable fish—or any object with great resistance—is achieved only through a powerful, low-numerical-ratio gear set. "Pumping" a fish during the fight is recommended with any tackle, but it is almost mandatory with high-ratio reels. You have more ability to crank a fish toward you with a power ratio of 3.5:1 or 4.4:1. These ratios in a reel with a respectable spool diameter deliver a compromise of line recovery and gear power that is hard to beat.

Certain applications or situations demand a conscious choice of gear ratios. When using a

 One of the worst red tide events on record occurred in 1946–47 off Florida and is estimated to have killed 500 million fish.

highly water resistant lure, such as a deep-running crankbait with a large lip, the ideal choice would be a low-numerical-ratio reel. A 3.8:1 gear set can comfortably deliver the necessary power to drive this bait down and through the water with minimal wear and tear on the angler. A very high-speed reel can bind under the line load created by this lure's water resistance. Trying to fish high-speed lures with a slow 3.8:1 ratio would wear out most casters before lunch time. The effort required to turn the handle fast enough to work a truly high-speed lure would be exhausting.

It is more difficult and fatiguing to reel a slow-ratio gear set fast than to reel a high-ratio gear set slowly. A high-ratio reel can easily be used to retrieve slow-technique lures or bait as long as they do not create a great deal of water resistance. However, some anglers make the mistake of fishing too fast by virtue of using a high-speed reel when they really need to be fishing more slowly. For instance, when a lure or technique calls for a slow presentation or retrieve, anglers sometimes inadvertently retrieve too fast because of their reel; in such a situation, a slow-speed reel would be better if you cannot keep using a fast-speed reel slowly.

Some surf anglers will remember that an ideal choice for use with either high- or low-speed retrieve lures was the original Crack 300 spinning reel, an expensive imported reel that had a spool diameter of 3.75 inches and a power ratio of 3.2:1 and that was a forerunner for that market until production ceased in the 1980s. It provided anglers with a superb combination of line recovery and gear power, and was one of the most respected surf fishing reels ever made. The benefits of such a diameter and power ratio for that activity were such that other manufacturers later developed reels with similar attributes.

The simplest and most powerful reel ratio is 1:1. This is commonly found in almost all flycasting reels, which typically do not have gear sets but are direct drive. They are also typically slow, especially when the level of line is low, such as when a fish has stripped the fly line off the reel and gone down to the much-thinner diameter backing. A few of the more modern designs of saltwater flycasting reels achieve greater line recovery speed by increasing spool diameter. They are employing the geometry factor to achieve a line recovery advantage. The capacity of the reel, however, does not necessarily increase. This is because the central arbor area of the spool is also increased in diameter. This large arbor helps minimize line set, and it reduces the amount of backing required to properly fill the spool. One such 10-weight reel needs 27 percent fewer turns of the handle to retrieve a 90-foot line than a standard design reel. It recovers more line and puts less wear on the angler, and is still a powerful 1:1 reel, but it may not have the total capacity (fly line and backing) that some fishing circumstances warrant.

True big-game fishing reels start out with fairly powerful ratios (3.1:1 to 3.5:1) and large-diameter spools. These reels are expected and designed to deal with big, powerful fish. The large spool diameter allows for sufficient line capacity in a variety of line tests and for acceptable line recovery. Fishing for big game species requires power to control their movements and bring them to the boat as quickly as possible. Large-diameter spools on big-game reels can rapidly recover line when a speedy fish charges the boat or even when clearing lines from the trolling pattern upon hookup. The 3.1:1 ratio is, of course, mechanically powerful. Anglers can quickly wind significant amounts of line onto the spool and have the ability to winch in line against a large fish.

Two-Speed Reels
Sometimes even a powerful 3.1:1 gear ratio isn't enough to control big-game species. Controlling these fish can often require a reel with two separate gear ratios. In the case of the modern two-speed big-game reels, the ratio shifts from the typical 3.1:1 to the still lower and more powerful 1.3:1. The very largest two-speed big-game reels intended for use in fighting giant fish can offer ratios such as 4.0:1 and 1.7:1 or 4.5:1 and 2.0:1. In these cases, the reel delivers both the speed necessary to catch up to a charging gamefish and the power to exert control over its movements.

These reels change gear sets in different ways. Some demand that the angler physically relocate the reel handle to switch gears. Simpler designs require the push of a button to shift in one direction and the turn of a knob or movement of a lever to return to the original ratio. All of these operations have to be fast and easy to permit up and down shifting in the heat of battling a large, powerful fish. And, obviously, the gear sets have to be strong, precise, and durable to withstand the stresses applied.

Attempts at producing multiple-speed spinning reels have not been successful, although a few manufacturers have applied a good deal of time and effort to the project. Two-speed baitcasting reels have been introduced, and these unique tools provided both a higher speed ratio and a true power ratio in a single reel suited for most freshwater and some inshore saltwater applications. Some of these products even offer an automatic shifting design that downshifts as the load on the line increases (as upon hookup). When the load decreases, such as when a fish turns toward the angler, the reel automatically upshifts to permit rapid recovery of line with the higher-ratio gears and to catch up to the movements of the fish. This reel also allows the angler to adjust the amount of force needed to cause the gears to shift up or down. It's a very versatile item and ideal if the amount of tackle available to you is limited.

The first writing devoted to fishing, The Treatyse of Fysshynge with an Angle, appeared in The Boke of St. Alban's in 1496. Authorship was attributed to Dame Juliana Berners, although some historians dispute this.

Retrieval Considerations

Some of the important fishing considerations relative to this subject have already been noted, but it's worth recapping these to emphasize some of the advantages and disadvantages of different ratios and line recoveries.

Although recent trends favor high-ratio or so-called high-speed reels, and many people equate speed with fishing value, it is important to recognize that line recovery is the real issue, not speed. Reels with a technically low gear ratio, but a high line-recovery rate, are actually better in situations where large fish are encountered, powerful fish are played, and where hard-pulling lures are cranked. These reels simply have more power, are less likely to bind, are less likely to get stripped gears (assuming the gears are of strong material to start with), and require less effort to land tough fish.

One of the main reasons why high-speed reels are popular in freshwater is because most of the fish caught in freshwater are small on average (bass and walleye, in particular) or do not put up a long tackle-testing struggle. Anglers like the high-speed retrieves because, among other reasons, they feel that they can quickly catch up to fish that run toward them (as many bass do). This is only true when the spool diameter is large enough to permit a lot of line recovery with each turn of the handle, and if the fish is not so large as to be difficult to handle.

People who fish jigs and worms in freshwater are likely to be good candidates for a reel with a high gear ratio, since it lets them pick up a lot of slack with each turn of the handle. But fishing a large spinnerbait and especially a deep-diving plug will be wrist-punishing unless the reel has cranking power for the drive, meaning that a slow-speed reel is preferable there.

For many anglers who cast and retrieve lures, especially those using baitcasting tackle, a reel with 5.1:1 retrieve ratio is a good all-around choice for most fishing, especially if the line recovery is adequate.

See: Baitcasting Tackle; Big-Game Tackle; Conventional Tackle; Flycasting Tackle; Reel, Fishing; Spincasting Tackle; Spinning Tackle.

GEORGIA

Georgia gained what seems like everlasting fame in the freshwater fishing world when George Perry landed a 22-pound, 4-ounce largemouth bass in Lake Montgomery, an oxbow of the Ocmulgee River, in 1932. That fish became the most coveted of all world records and also one of the longest-standing ones.

Catching a fish like that today in Georgia is unlikely, but this in no way overshadows the abundant and high-quality resources existing in the Peach State. In fact, anglers still go to rivers like the Ocmulgee, where fishing is as good or better than ever, especially in the southern half of the state, where lakes are scarce.

Georgia's fishery has changed markedly in many respects. Today anglers can choose from nine huge U.S. Army Corps of Engineers reservoirs, totaling some 500,000 acres, that teem with native largemouth bass, catfish, and bream, plus such popular additions as pure-strain striped bass, spotted bass, and hybrid stripers. A superb trout management program thrives in north Georgia, taking in some 4,000 miles of mountain streams, as well as the Chattahoochee River down to Atlanta.

Not to be overlooked is Georgia's biggest secret asset: saltwater fishing. The 100-mile-long Georgia coast has the largest saltwater marsh in the eastern United States. This fertile estuary sustains a vast resource of inshore species, especially large populations of seatrout, redfish, and flounder, plus big tarpon.

Freshwater

The largest state east of the Mississippi River, Georgia has a varied landscape that is reflected in its resources and freshwater fishing opportunities. Rolling hills, coastal plains, the Appalachian Mountains, the Okefenokee Swamp, and the rivers that flow to the Atlantic Ocean or the Gulf of Mexico provide divergence. Although it has no large natural lakes, as the result of river impoundments Georgia does have big waters, some of which it shares with neighboring states. Several of these are among the most heavily used recreation sites in North America.

Mountain Waters

Lake Allatoona. Allatoona, a 11,860-acre Corps of Engineers reservoir on the Eltowah River, has a good combination of structure—deep and clear in the main body, and flats around rivers—that gives anglers a variety of fishing.

Striped bass are plentiful here, and have been caught up to 40 pounds. They are a favorite quarry in winter, although some anglers catch stripers in midsummer in the cool pockets of deeper water. Hybrid striped bass, which are nearly four times as abundant as pure-strain stripers, also provide excitement.

Crappie fishing is good year-round, although most anglers concentrate on the spring. The black bass population is about 80 percent spotted bass, which favor the mountainlike structure, and fishing is considered good. To have consistent success, however, an angler must spend some time learning the lake. Boat traffic can be a problem at Allatoona, which is less than an hour from Atlanta; the lake gets heavy use from boats of all sizes.

Lake Blue Ridge. Walleye, white bass, smallmouth bass, and bluegills are the most sought-after species in Lake Blue Ridge, a 3,290-acre Tennessee Valley Authority (TVA) reservoir in Fannon County. Walleye fishing is best in the spring and fall. The white bass run begins in early February, with a lot of activity centered on Toccoa River shoals at the head of the reservoir. Smallmouth fishing is good except during the annual November to February drawdown, when ramp access is limited. Fishing is also good for yellow perch, channel catfish, and flathead catfish, and the lake has been known for large bluegills (bream), especially around fish attractors in 15 to 20 feet of water.

Lake Burton. Lake Burton, a 2,775-acre power company reservoir in the northeast and west of Clayton, is noted for good spotted bass and largemouth bass angling. Trophy-size largemouths are caught in February and March, and fishing for spots peaks in May and November. Burton is also an excellent yellow perch fishery, and although the average perch are not jumbos, a $2^1/_2$-pound state record was caught here. Bream and catfish are also excellent during summer months. Large shellcrackers inhabit the Cherokee Cove area, and good-size channel cats come from Timpson, Wildcat, and Cherokee Coves.

Carters Lake. A popular 3,220-acre Corps of Engineers reservoir, Carters is between Calhoun and Ellijay on the Coosawattee River. With deep, clear water it is known for large spotted bass—many over 6 pounds—and a good population of striped bass, some of which have reached 20 pounds. Walleye, introduced in 1995, are growing into an excellent fishery; catches average 20 inches and 3 pounds, and are expected to do very well here thanks to ample gizzard and threadfin shad forage. Crappie fishing is fair and getting better as the forage fish base grows. The key to success with any species here is power generation. Carters is a pump-back operation, and when generation stops, the fish become inactive.

Lake Chatuge. Spotted bass dominate Lake Chatuge, a 7,050-acre TVA reservoir that straddles the Georgia–North Carolina border. Largemouth bass, which are heavier on average than spots, take a back seat to their cousins, and once-populous smallmouth (home of a 7-pound 2-ounce state record in 1973) continue to dwindle. White bass and walleye populations have been increasing, and hybrid stripers make for exciting catches at times. The state record hybrid, which weighed 25 pounds 8 ounces, was caught here, but most hybrids are in the 2- to 4-pound range. Chatuge also offers a good population of channel catfish.

Lake Hartwell. Georgia and South Carolina share Lake Hartwell, a deep, clear, 56,000-acre reservoir and the northernmost in a chain of Corps of Engineers dams on the Savannah River. Hartwell is distinguished for a number of reasons, perhaps the best being that it receives light fishing pressure when compared with other large Georgia impoundments. Another plus is that it offers the chance to catch spotted bass and largemouths on back-to-back casts, rather than in the usual order of three or more spots to one largemouth.

Although the lake has not been known for large black bass, it does provide a high average catch rate. Crappie fishing is also excellent, and there is always the chance of landing a hybrid or striped bass. White bass are here as well, and the Tugalo River provides notable action in April and May, when the spawning run for this species is underway. Because it is still underutilized, Hartwell provides the chance for a solitary fishing experience in a pristine, rustic setting.

Lake Lanier. Calling the 38,800-acre Lanier a mountain lake might seem improbable, but its qualities—depth and clarity—are those of a mountain lake, and it is in the foothills of north Georgia, even if it is only 45 minutes north of Atlanta. Although recreational boating traffic is heavy, the fishing is still excellent. The most popular species here are spotted bass—very few anglers fish for largemouth anymore—striped bass, and crappie.

Lanier is a championship striper lake. On a good day, catching six isn't unusual, and the average will be 11 to 12 pounds with some in the 25- to 30-pound range. Winter is best for stripers, but there's good fishing in late fall and early spring. The state record spotted bass, which weighed 8 pounds, 5 ounces, was caught at Lanier; and this is not an accident. Fishing for spots is good year-round. The spring white bass spawning run also makes for great action, and crappie fishing is excellent in the winter around major marinas.

Lake Nottely. Largemouth bass, spotted bass, striped bass, and crappie are the most popular species on Lake Nottely, a 4,180-acre TVA lake in Union County, but it also has smallmouth bass, walleye, and large yellow perch. Nottely has a reputation for producing big largemouth bass, which thrive here in greater numbers than do spotted bass. Stripers are plentiful, and many specimens are in the 8- to 15-pound range. Half-pound crappie are numerous. Walleye were stocked in the early 1990s.

Lake Russell. Impounded in 1984, Lake Russell is Georgia's newest Corps of Engineers project. It is a remote, almost pristine, 26,650-acre reservoir and is one of the best crappie lakes in Georgia because of the timber left standing in its depths. An impoundment of the Savannah River on the South Carolina border, Russell is downstream of Lake Hartwell. Largemouth bass average about $1^1/_2$ pounds, but some go to 10 pounds. There is a growing spotted bass population, and increasing numbers of stripers, which are arriving from other lakes in the system. Although walleye aren't stocked, an 11-pound, 6-ounce state record was caught at Russell in 1995, and most catches of this species come from the lower third of the lake.

Lake Weiss. Most of Lake Weiss is in Alabama, but a 2,000-acre portion is in Georgia. Weiss is noted nationwide for its springtime crappie fishing. Groups in convoys from as far away as 1,000 miles make the spring pilgrimage and go home with full creels. Overlooked, however, is the good fishing for largemouth bass, although most are in the $1^1/_2$- to 2-pound range. White bass fishing is excellent during the annual spring spawning run, and striped bass fishing is improving annually on the lower Coosa River.

Trout fishing. Georgia boasts approximately 4,000 miles of trout streams throughout the Chattahoochee National Forest in the north Georgia mountains. The Chattahoochee River, from the mountains down to Atlanta's city limits, is considered one of the top trout streams in the Southeast. Because soils are low in calcium, and trout streams are relatively unproductive in their natural state, most of the fishing is for stocked rainbow, brown, and brook trout. This is primarily an annual put-and-take fishery, but the occasional big brown or rainbow survives the initial stocking and lives two or more years, mainly on the Chattahoochee. More than 100,000 anglers buy trout stamps and enjoy this fishery, which is testimony to its quality and popularity.

On the Chattahoochee, anglers fish with fly rods, waders, and tubes, and cast flies into rushing rapids. They watch their offerings float toward a trout, suspended and waiting in an eddy downstream, in a mountainlike atmosphere—all while traffic roars overhead on an Interstate 285 bridge. Smaller mountain streams yield smaller fish but offer a more gentle ambiance. Many streams are seasonal (March through October), but others, including portions of the Chattahoochee, are open year-round.

Middle Georgia

Clarks Hill. Called Strom Thurmond Lake in neighboring South Carolina, 71,535-acre Clarks Hill is the largest Corps of Engineers reservoir in the Southeast. It might also be the best fishing lake in the state because of its balance of structure and fertility, and because its distance from metropolitan Atlanta enables it to remain relatively uncrowded.

Largemouth bass fishing here rates among the best in the state, and the angling is good year-round, especially at the flats near the confluence of the Savannah and Broad Rivers. Hybrid and striped bass fishing is particularly productive; catches average 3 to 7 pounds. Crappie fishing is excellent and especially good in the spring. Shellcrackers are big, many in the $^1\!/_2$- to $^3\!/_4$-pound range, and white perch are numerous and easy to catch. Clarks Hill also is home of the state record blue catfish, a 62-pounder.

Lake Jackson. Relatively small at 4,750 acres, and very old (impounded in 1910), Jackson could still possibly be the best big bass lake in Georgia. From October through February, this power company reservoir in Jasper, Butts, and Newton Counties yields many largemouth in the 5-pound-plus category. It produces big crappie, too, with some slabs reaching 2 pounds (the lake record is $3^1\!/_2$ pounds). Panfish fanciers will find that Jackson has some of the best and biggest bluegills, shellcrackers, and redbreast sunfish, and a huge population of white catfish.

Lakes Sinclair and Oconee. Some say that 14,750-acre Sinclair, and 19,050-acre Oconee, are among the best crappie fishing lakes in the state. Angling for these species is good year-round on both

West Point is one of Georgia's largest and most popular lakes.

lakes, but it's best from February through April.

Both are power company impoundments on the Ocmulgee River, but Sinclair is older. Extensive development around Sinclair's shores, and thousands of boat docks, compensate for the deterioration of its natural structure. While Oconee retains some natural structure, it is also loaded with boat docks, albeit upscale ones, because this is the hot lake property for metropolitan Atlanta, which is only 60 miles to the west. Largemouth bass fishing on Oconee is good, but mostly for smaller specimens; Sinclair has bigger, though unpublicized, bass. Both lakes have good fishing for hybrid stripers. Anglers also visit Oconee for white bass, and Sinclair for its excellent supply of channel catfish.

West Point. One of the state's most consistent producers of 5- to 7-pound largemouth bass, West Point is a 25,900-acre Corps of Engineers reservoir on the Chattahoochee River, along the Alabama border. The lake's natural fertility and 16-inch minimum size limit for largemouths produce superior fishing for this species year-round. Hybrid stripers have a glowing reputation as well; nearly 40 percent of this species is in the 15- to 20-inch category. Springtime crappie fishing is outstanding, but it runs good year-round. West Point is also the best channel catfish lake in middle Georgia, offering an abundant supply of these fish in the 12- to 14-inch range.

Bartlett's Ferry, Goat Rock, Oliver. These three lakes, forming a small chain, are older power company reservoirs on the Chattahoochee River, downstream of West Point Lake. Bartlett's Ferry, at 5,850 acres, has excellent fishing for largemouth bass and spotted bass; good fishing for white bass, hybrid stripers, and crappie; and good to excellent fishing for catfish. Goat Rock, at 940 acres, has good fishing for largemouth bass, shoal bass, spotted bass, and catfish; excellent fishing for bream; and a growing fishery for hybrid stripers. Oliver, at 2,150 acres and within the city limits of Columbus, is usually too busy with recreational boats during the summer but has good largemouth bass angling in the fall and winter, with some fish up to 10 pounds. Crappie are good in late winter and early spring, and bream are excellent as well.

South Georgia

Lake Walter F. George. Also known as Lake Eufaula, 45,180-acre Lake George is yet another Corps of Engineers reservoir on the Chattahoochee River. It is one of the best largemouth bass fishing lakes in the Southeast, and definitely the best summertime fishing lake in Georgia, for two reasons: It has great structure, which gives bass shelter, and it has a 16-inch minimum size limit that has produced largemouth averaging 3 to 4 pounds, along with trophies 10 pounds or better. The hottest period is from mid-March through May, but fishing is consistently good year-round. Crappie angling is excellent all year but starts heating up in February and March. The fish average 12 inches and can weigh upward of 2 pounds. The catfish population is dominated by channel catfish, but the population of blue catfish is on the rise. Angling is good for both species. White bass and hybrid stripers are abundant here, and striper fishing, with larger specimens providing excitement, has become more popular in recent years.

Lake Seminole. Formed at the junction of the Flint and Chattahoochee Rivers, Lake Seminole is a 37,500-acre Corps of Engineers reservoir in the southwest corner of the state on the Florida border. It is like no other lake in Georgia. Topography and wildlife not seen anywhere else—large concentrations of waterfowl, alligators, lily pads, and standing timber—give it a tropical appearance.

Many places claim to be year-round fisheries, but Seminole really is just that. Thousands of northern anglers plan winter fishing vacations to Seminole, where they have great success if they learn the key. Because this lake is covered with aquatic vegetation, anglers have to learn to fish weedbeds by casting worms, spinnerbaits, or topwater lures along the edges of these beds for Seminole's bass. The reward is an average small keeper of 12 to 14 inches, but bass weighing 5 pounds or more exist in the Flint and Chattahoochee arms.

Hybrid bass fishing is also excellent at Seminole. Fish averaging 2 to 3 pounds are caught in open water away from weeds. Crappie fishing is not a main attraction at Seminole, but this fishery is good in the spring and fall. Channel catfish generally provide excellent fishing in the main lake and in the Flint and Chattahoochee arms.

Lake Blackshear. When the dam broke, the flood of 1994 virtually made a new lake of this 7,000-acre reservoir west of Cordele on the Flint River. It may go through the "new lake" syndrome for a while, providing south Georgia with hot fishing. This is a shallow, stained body of water with lots of cypress knees, but most of the lake's structure is formed by docks from the many homes on the highly developed western side. Large populations of crappie provide excellent fishing, especially around 12 scattered fish attractors; the best time to fish is February and March. More than 65 percent of the lake's bream are 6 inches long and upward of $3/4$ pound. Fishing for these is most productive in May and June. Striped and hybrid bass fishing is good, with special regulations in effect for these species. Fishing is good for smaller channel catfish, especially in deeper water where creek and river channels meet.

Lake Chehaw. Partly inside the Albany city limits, Lake Chehaw—a 1,400-acre power company impoundment—is fed by the Flint River and creeks. Chehaw is not noted for big largemouth bass, although numbers of 1- to 3-pounders are caught in the backs of creeks in the spring and fall, and in the main lake during the summer. Hybrid bass fishing is also good in summer. Channel catfish averaging 2 pounds are plentiful in coves and on flats in the spring, and along main river and creek channels during the summer. Fishing is fair to good for crappie, bluegills, and redear sunfish (shellcrackers).

The Southeast Coastal Plain

This huge area, nearly half the state, is so flat that it is unsuitable for large impoundments, so anglers fish farm ponds, rivers, and creeks. Fortunately, much of Georgia's 12,000 miles of warmwater streams are in this area, and some of the more notable ones are noted here.

Altamaha River. The Chattahoochee might be the best known and longest river in Georgia, but the Altamaha is the biggest. It starts at the convergence of the Ocmulgee and Oconee near Lumber City and meanders more than 100 miles down to the Atlantic Ocean. The fishing is so good that the Altamaha hosts many largemouth bass tournaments each year, and catch rates are among the best. Although largemouths can be caught year-round, fishing peaks in the spring and again in late fall. A 44-pound, 12-ounce state record channel catfish and a 58-pound, 7-ounce state record flathead catfish were caught in the Altamaha, and even larger flatheads should be taken in the future. This fishery begins in early spring and continues through the summer. Crappie fishing is good, especially in the oxbow lakes between Georgia Highway 84 and the Seaboard Railroad. The redbreast sunfish have declined, but fishing is still good for bluegills and shellcrackers.

Ocmulgee River. The large, sluggish Ocmulgee

originates at Jackson Lake and flows 251 miles southward to converge with the Oconee River and form the Altamaha River. The fishery north of U.S. 280 differs from the fishery to the south. To the north, sportfish numbers are dominated by shoal bass, redeye bass, and redbreast sunfish in the shoals, and largemouth bass, bluegills, and redear sunfish (shellcrackers) in the slower stretches. Below U.S. 280, largemouth bass are numerous, but pressure is heavy and most are caught soon after they reach the 14-inch minimum size. Redbreast sunfish and shellcracker fishing is good; some shellcrackers weigh as much as 1 pound. The best action is in early spring. As on several other south Georgia rivers, flathead catfish, introduced illegally, are growing in number and have significantly impacted the sunfish population.

The lower Ocmulgee includes Lake Montgomery, home of the long-standing world record largemouth bass. Montgomery is accessible only at high water these days, but fish are still there. Today, however, nothing rivals the size of George Perry's 22-pound, 4-ounce specimen. A few anglers still fish for largemouth bass at this famous sloughlike site, but angling is becoming more difficult as the oxbow slowly fills with silt. Someday Montgomery will be gone but not forgotten; it is part of Horse Creek Wildlife Management Area, where an historical landmark commemorates North America's most famous fish.

Oconee River. With a stable, abundant, and healthy largemouth bass population, the Oconee could be a hotspot. Although it compares favorably with the Altamaha, the Oconee receives the least bass fishing pressure of any river here. During the summer months, fish in the 12- to 14-inch range are plentiful, and numerous lunker-size largemouth thrive here, too. During the winter and early spring, crappie fishing is very good. Fishing for flathead catfish is very good, but the redbreast sunfish population is down due to predation by catfish. Still, some larger redbreasts are caught, along with bluegills and redear sunfish.

Ogeechee River. The Ogeechee is a redbreast sunfish hotspot, and nearly a quarter of the redbreast caught range between 6 and 8 inches. The best opportunities come during spring and summer, when the river drops into the 3-foot range on the geological survey gauge at Eden. Fishing is also good in April and May, however, when water temperatures rise and water levels range from 5 to 7 feet. Other panfish include bluegills, redear sunfish, and spotted sunfish (called stump-knockers here). Scattered pockets of black crappie provide good cold weather fishing upstream of Midville.

Satilla River. The Satilla meanders eastward some 260 miles to the Atlantic Ocean and is considered one of the premier redbreast sunfish rivers in the Southeast. Anglers frequently catch fish 8 inches or longer and weighing a pound or more. Fishing is outstanding in April and May, until the water warms; then anglers turn to largemouth bass, crappie, and several species of catfish. Bass fishing peaks in late winter and early spring, when river levels are too high for panfish.

St. Mary's River. The river winds eastward from the Okefenokee Swamp to the Atlantic Ocean and is the southernmost point in Georgia. Although it doesn't rival the Satilla for trophy fish, the St. Mary's is one of the better redbreast sunfish rivers in southeast Georgia. The St. Mary's is also known for quality largemouth bass, especially in the lower section around King's Ferry.

Savannah River. North of Augusta, the Savannah is a series of reservoirs, but southward to the Atlantic Ocean it is an outstanding river angling resource. Largemouth bass average $1^1/_2$ to 5 pounds, and some people hook into bigger ones. Angling is good in most areas of the river, especially at the mouths of creeks and in oxbows, for redbreast and redear sunfish, bluegills, and channel catfish. The state of striped bass fishing is on hold indefinitely, because altered flow conditions in the lower Savannah caused a drastic decline in stripers. The natural flow has been restored, and biologists are waiting for the stripers to find their habitat again. Both pure-strain and hybrid stripers have populated this water, and the Savannah produced record-class hybrid stripers in the past. The flow rate is largely controlled by upstream water releases, and water levels can fluctuate weekly with hydropower demands. This is especially true in summer and can adversely affect fishing.

Suwannee River. The 33-mile portion of the Suwannee in Georgia offers an experience that differs from that provided by most other Georgia rivers, owing to the influence of the Okefenokee Swamp. The tea-stained waters of this flowage are excellent habitat for chain pickerel, warmouth, flier (shiners), and bullhead, but largemouth bass, bream, and other catfish aren't numerous because of the water's high acidity.

Saltwater

For years, northern anglers—and most Georgians as well—zipped down Interstate 95 through Georgia as fast as they could on the way to Florida, unknowingly bypassing some great inshore salt-water fishing that now even draws native Floridians. With more than 400,000 acres of rich salt marsh along its nearly 100 miles, and with a series of barrier islands—including Ossabaw, Sapelo, Cumberland (18 miles long and the site of Cumberland Island National Seashore), Jekyll, and Saint Simons—the Georgia coast is a rich but underutilized saltwater fishing resource. Inshore, there's outstanding angling for spotted seatrout and red drum (redfish), whiting, flounder, sheepshead, croaker, and tarpon, as well as opportunities for ladyfish, bluefish, sharks, and jack crevalle. Offshore are king mackerel, snapper, grouper, cobia, sharks, barracuda, and black sea bass.

Inshore fishing is best from mid-May through

> The largest gulf in the world is the Gulf of Mexico; it covers 596,000 square miles and has 3,100 miles of shoreline.

December for most species. September through December are peak months for spotted seatrout and red drum. Warmer months are better for sheepshead, black drum, and some fairly large tarpon, especially in the Altamaha River.

Tarpon are overlooked here, and although Georgia doesn't provide the type of flats action that occurs in other places, it does have plentiful fish around islands, creeks, and the many bays and streams feeding the Intracoastal Waterway, as well as within a few miles of the barrier island beaches, including fish from 100 to 150 pounds. Tarpon are available from sometime in June until mid-October; September is an excellent period, as these fish are feasting on migratory bait and on abundant forage flushed from coastal environs by storms.

The tremendous amount of food available in the vicinity of the southern barrier islands, known here as the Golden Isles, also draws other prominent species in the same warmer-month time frame. Red drum, in particular, some of which are in the 40- to 60-pound range, are caught in the holes of channels and creeks, and near sandbars, and may be caught concurrent with sharks or tarpon. Sea trout are caught from the beach, along dropoffs, around structures, and on the edges of grassbeds throughout the region.

The key to inshore fishing here, as elsewhere, is the tide. An outgoing tide pulls bait-rich water from the marshes, and all types of fish search the shallows for food. Fluctuations as high as 9 feet during full and new moons and 5 to 7 feet during the rest of the month can muddy the waters, but they can also be a strong influence on angling. Fishing isn't too good from four days before the full or new moon to four days after, as the water clears.

Tides are an element of catching kingfish, an activity pursued several miles off St. Simons in Brunswick Ship Channel, at Portuguese Slough, and in Doboy Channel at the D Buoy. High tide pushes good-colored water to within 3 miles or so of shore, whereas low tide pushes it several miles farther out.

Offshore from Georgia, the ocean bottom is flat, with little structure other than Gray's Reef. This situation is improving, however, as the state continues to add to its artificial reef program, using tires, cement, and even old Liberty ships. The artificial reefs are identified in various literature.

Gray's Reef, 17.5 nautical miles east of Sapelo Island, is a National Marine Sanctuary encompassing an area of approximately 17 square nautical miles. The reef is 55 to 65 feet deep and hosts a wide variety of species, some seasonally present. Those of sportfishing interest include assorted sharks, jacks, mackerel, bluefish, cobia, barracuda, flounder, sea bass, snapper, grouper, and dolphin. The reef is also a prime spot for divers.

Another hotspot is the Navy Tower, a navigation aid for the King's Bay submarine base near St. Mary's, which attracts huge numbers of fish.

A few Georgia anglers will go to the Gulf Stream for pelagic species, but the 98-mile one-way trip discourages many.

GERMANY

Spanning from the Alps to the Baltic and North Seas, and covering more than 137,000 square miles of landscape that includes mountains, forests, plains, and seacoast, the Federal Republic of Germany is a big country with diverse resources in the heart of Europe. Although it does not attract many visiting anglers, especially Westerners, several million Germans enjoy angling, and the country boasts more than a dozen popularly sought species as well as a wide variety of waters.

Bordering on nine European nations, Germany extends some 800 kilometers from south to north and 400 kilometers from west to east, covering an area similar in size to the state of Montana in the United States. The country is divided into 16 states, each with its own fishing governance and each different according to its particular environment, species, and population of fish.

Although a large country, Germany is highly urbanized; 86 percent of its 82 million inhabitants live in communities of at least 2,000 people. More than 1 million anglers are organized in roughly 10,000 clubs. More than 1.5 million people purchase German state fishing licenses annually, and it is believed that another million people who do not require licenses fish in private waters at home or on holiday in other countries.

Although more than 13 million tourists visit Germany annually, angling tourists number almost none; this may be largely due to the country's licensing structure, which requires that anglers pass a test before being granted a state license. For more on this topic, refer to the section "Legislation" below. The few non-Germans who angle here seldom fish on their own. They use all-inclusive packages offered by hotels and pensions (boarding houses), which usually have creek and brook fishing opportunities, or they employ the services of someone who can provide lake access, boats, and sometimes accommodations.

Very well equipped tackle dealers exist in almost every German city. English is commonly spoken, and it is easy for English-speaking visitors to approach the dealers. These people are the best source of advice on where and how to fish in a certain area for a certain species, as well as for advice on obtaining access to local waters.

Land, Climate, and Resources

The Alps are the southernmost border of the republic, and the Zugspitze (2,962 meters or 9,718 feet) is the highest mountain in Germany. Many creeks and rivers flow out of the Alps. These run in a northerly direction, with very high water in the spring and very low water in the fall. All waters enter the

Danube River, which flows eastward into Austria and eventually to the Black Sea, thereby forming a drainage area in Germany with a different ecology than one finds in the rest of the country.

In addition to the creeks and rivers in the south, most notable are the Voralpen lakes. The Bodensee is the biggest of these, encompassing 538 square kilometers and having depths up to 252 meters; it lies partly in Austria and Switzerland as well. Other large lakes are the Chiemsee, the Starnberger See, and the Ammersee. The majority of the southern region is in the state of Bayern (Bavaria); the westernmost part of this region is in the district of Baden-Württemberg.

The character of Germany's midlands is formed by many intermediate-size mountains with an average altitude of 500 meters. Deep, large forests cover the mountains. Numerous brooks and creeks run here; these exit the forests to fill water dams (reservoirs) and form or merge with rivers, which include the Danube, the Rhein, the Elbe, and the Weser, all of which flow into the North Sea; and the Oder, which, along with the smaller Neisse River, forms most of eastern Germany's border with Poland and discharges into the Baltic Sea. The Weser, Elbe, and Oder Rivers flow slowly over the lowlands to the north of the country—a wide, mountainless area with some spots below normal sea level, where water is drained by pumps. High dikes along hundreds of kilometers of coastline protect the land facing the fearful North Sea. Quite the contrary exists along the Baltic Sea coast, where a sandy, sometimes stony littoral is bordered by a steep shoreline that is 60 meters high in places.

Northern Germany is characterized by the wide lowlands of the northwest, where the Weser and Elbe Rivers flow into the North Sea and where very large forests cover wide, infertile sandy heather landscapes that include national parks (in the state of Niedersachsen). The Elbe winds from the Czechoslovakian border in the southeast up to the North Sea. The coast of the North Sea is formed by a large, muddy, and slimy dark substrate called the Wattenmeer (Wadden Sea), which undergoes full tidal drying and flooding. This area is also a national park, and known for its unique bird life.

Offshore from the mainland are many large, sandy, and green islands in a pearl-like string; most are inhabited and popular with summer visitors. Their fine, white sand beaches face open sea and are a surf caster's heaven. The most favored sea angling spot in Germany is the rocky island of Helgoland, situated in the middle of the Deutsche Bucht (German Bay). Sixty kilometers from the closest harbor, Helgoland is a rocky island that is 61 meters high and covers 2 square kilometers.

In northeastern Germany the states of Schleswig-Holstein and Mecklenburg-Vorpommern face the Baltic Sea. This large inland sea has natural connections with the North Sea. The littoral area was formed by glaciers, resulting in a sandy, sometimes stony shoreline. The water is crystal clear, and the salinity is only 2 percent (in the North Sea it is 3.5 percent). In cold winters, ice may keep fishing boats in port during January and February.

Germany's climate is determined by medium temperatures (day/night) in January of minus 4° to plus 3°C, and in July of plus 14° to plus 20°C. Rain falls all year long in short periods, mostly driven by western winds. The midlands and lowlands receive 500 to 700 millimeters of rain per year; the mountain areas are flooded by 1,300 millimeters of rain; and 2,000 millimeters of rain fall in the Alps. High winds or stormy weather usually do not last longer than two to three days, and very stormy conditions are restricted to late winter and late autumn.

Beginning late in the nineteenth century, pollution became a serious problem for many of Germany's creeks, rivers, and streams. Salmon, which were found by the hundreds of thousands in big streams in years past, became extinct. Other fish also succumbed to pollution. It was not until the 1970s that a nationwide campaign resulted in strong legislation, high penalties, and a steady improvement in water quality.

German anglers have done a lot to maintain and increase their revived fisheries resources. Management efforts and stocking activities have reintroduced fingerling fish into the watercourses year-round. Today, many brooks and creeks, as well as rivers, are full of brown trout; the lowland rivers have good stocks of sea trout; and Atlantic salmon restocking programs are progressing, supported by the government, with some angling for this species already available.

For the traveling angler, the most notable fishing regions are Fränkische Schweiz (Bavaria); Voralpenland (Bavaria); Schwarzwald (Baden-Württemberg); Sauerland and Rothaargebirge (Nordrhein-Westfalen); the Harz-Mountain area (Niedersachsen); and the lake district (Mecklenburg-Vorpommern).

Germany has a wide variety of fishing waters. These include deep slow-running streams and rivers; fast-running, well-oxygenated brooks; deep coldwater lakes; shallow, warm brown-water lakes; canals; reservoirs (water dams); and abundant small lakes and ponds. All kinds of European freshwater fish thrive in these waters, with a total of some 70 native species, as well as such introduced species as steelhead, lake trout, grass carp, and numerous subspecies. Largemouth and smallmouth bass have reportedly been introduced in some German waters, perhaps illegally, and are said to be a very rare catch.

The most popular species are *aal* (European eels); *äsche* (grayling); *bachforelle* (brown trout); *barsch* (yellow perch); *brassen* (bream); *döbel* (chub); *hecht* (northern pike); *karpfen* (common carp); *meerforelle* (sea-run brown trout); *regenbogenforelle* (rainbow trout); *schleie* (tench); *wels* (catfish); and *zander* (pike-perch).

Since late in the twentieth century, anyone in

The first officially weighed tuna (183 pounds) caught on sporting tackle was landed off Catalina Island, California, in 1898; however, a few unweighed tuna had been caught previously.

Germany who owns fishable waters is obliged to replace the catch and to preserve the fish, and restoration of fauna and flora in and alongside the watercourses is practiced. Owners take special interest in the most preferred species, such as brown trout, sea trout, grayling, eels, and carp, and in some waters also rainbow trout and pike.

In general, coarse fishing is good throughout the country; trout fishing is satisfactory in some areas; and perch and pike fishing is good in certain lakes, especially in autumn. In saltwater, angling is good for cod year-round, for tope in September, for herring in March and April, for garfish from May through July, and for mackerel in July and August.

Gamefishing

Brown trout are the most popular freshwater fish in Germany. They are caught in almost all cold, quick-running water that flows from the midland mountains. In bigger waters they grow from 5 to 10 pounds, but the normal size is 2 to 3 pounds, with the national record being 35.64 pounds.

Larger brown trout are rare in small brooks; they generally inhabit larger creeks or small rivers, and lowland waters fed by cold springs, such as those in the district of Lüneburger Heide in the state of Niedersachsen.

The best trout fishing opportunities are in the hands of private owners who typically operate hotels and pensions and sell fishing licenses only to their guests. Some waters are owned by clubs or communities, and they sell licenses, too. Most licenses are subject to strong rules regarding minimum size, bag limits, baits, and methods; fly fishing is the main method. The closed season traditionally falls between October 1 and March 31, but these dates may differ among states.

Waters with brown trout sometimes also hold rainbow trout, but anglers usually find them tougher to pinpoint because they roam widely through an entire watercourse. Rainbows do grow big in Germany; the record fish is a 42-pounder, and the average size is about 10 to 12 pounds. All rainbows are stocked, as they do not spawn naturally in Germany.

The best-known sites for trout fishing, listed from north to south by state, include the following:

Bayern (Bavaria). Brooks and creeks running from the Rhön Mountains to the river Fränkische Saale; waters coming from the Fichtelgebirge and Spessart Forests flowing to the Main River; and chalk streams in the Fränkische Schweiz area. The latter features Puttlach, Wiesent, Ailsbach, Leinleiter, and Trubach Creeks; these are famous chalk waters with very good trout and grayling fishing, and are a preferred destination for anglers from abroad, with many hotels accommodating anglers.

Other sites include the Loisach, Lauterbach, Schwarzach, and Zottbach watercourses in the Fränkische Alb area; these rivers flowing from the Alps: Amper, Glonn, Isar, Isen, Inn, Loisach, Mangfall, Ramsauer Ache, Salzach, Sempt, and Traun; the Allgäu district rivers like the Hopferauer Ache, Iller, Lech, Trauchgauer Ach, Trettach, Upper Donau, Vils, and Wertach; and such Schwäbische Alb rivers as the Breitach, Brenz, and Untere Argen.

Baden-Württemberg. In this wine-cultivating state, the Schwarzwald district (known to many as the Black Forest) is especially notable because of its great number of hotels and pensions with first-class trout waters. These are mostly brooks and creeks, and include such watercourses as the Alb, Elz, Gaubach, Grosse Enz, Gutach, Heimbach, Hundsbach, Kinzig, Langenbach, Lauter, Maisach, Murg, Nagold, Oos, Reichenbach, Rench, Schultach, Schutter, Steinbach, Waldach, Wehra, Wiese, and Wolfach.

Rheinland-Pfalz. Trout rivers include the Ahr, Irsen, Kyll, Nims, Our, Prüm, Rur, and Salmbach.

Nordrhein-Westfalen. The Agger, Bigge, Latropbach, Leune, Ruhr, Sieg, and Sorpe watercourses in the Sauerland region are among the area's notable trout rivers.

Hessen. Trout frequent the upper part of the rivers Diemel, Eder, Efze, and Schwalm.

Niedersachsen. All water dams in the mountain region of the Harz; and the rivers Böhme, Este, Ilmenau, Luhe, Ortze, Oste, and Seeve in the Lüneburger Heide region. The latter rivers are supported by massive plantings of trout fingerlings, particularly sea trout (which grow to 20 pounds or more), and some grayling. Most parts of these rivers are rented to clubs, where licenses are often obtained only through membership.

Schleswig-Holstein. The rivers Stör and Treene are famous for sea trout; these have been maintained by angler stocking, and many thousands of fingerlings are annually planted in the watercourses running into these rivers.

Other Salmonids

The sea trout is not only caught in the aforementioned inland rivers and creeks, but also in all creeks and rivers close to the sea, and in the Baltic Sea itself.

Atlantic salmon restoration has resulted in an ongoing, massive reintroduction in all big streams and rivers, but the results have been generally disappointing. Only one river, the Oste in Niedersachsen, has enough salmon to provide yearly sportfishing.

Huchen growing to 130 pounds still exist but are mainly restricted to the Danube River. Nowadays, big huchen are a rare catch, but some huchen are landed each year in other Bavarian rivers due to reintroduction by anglers. These include the Alz, Iller, Ilz, Isar, Lech, Schwarzer Regen, Tiroler Ache, Wertach, and Wurm Rivers. A tiny stock of natives exists in the river Mitternacher Ohe.

Native stocks of charr inhabit the cold, deep lakes close to the Bavarian Alps, and they are planted into some of the water dams in the Harz area of Niedersachsen. Many subspecies are reared in hatcheries and put into many creeks of the midlands, but they seldom reproduce naturally.

British needle manufacturers are said to have started making fishhooks in the mid-1500s; modern hook manufacturing started with the Mustad Company of Norway in 1832.

Coarse Fishing

Angling for coarse species is popular alongside the banks of slow-running rivers, streams, and channels, as well as in lakes. It is easy to land a large catch of roach and bream on a given day, and a total take weighing a ton is common when clubs fish in competitions.

There is also coarse fishing for such popular species as pike and carp. Large pike are numerous and widespread, but the biggest fish and best overall angling for this species occur in the lakes. German anglers are very fond of lake fishing for pike, and autumn is viewed as the best time.

Carp are second to pike in popularity, and some specimens to 65 pounds have been recorded. Because of their high food value, carp have been introduced to almost all brown-, warm-, shallow-water sites, even the smallest ponds. Although the carp is not an indigenous species, it may spawn successfully in especially warm summers. The great fighting ability of carp has led to the formation of Specimen Hunting Groups by German anglers, and these specialists pursue only big carp.

Eels are found everywhere in Germany, and some are caught up to 25 pounds. They favor slow-moving waters in the lowlands and are even in the smallest trenches. Smoked eels—a highly prized delicacy—are the most expensive freshwater fish product in Germany.

Zander inhabit all brown, warm waters, and some have been recorded to 40 pounds. They are a popular market fish and are common in many lakes and rivers, but they are not easily caught.

The wels catfish is the biggest freshwater fish in Germany; the national record is a 165-pounder. Native stocks inhabit the rivers Naab and Regen in Bavaria, the Oderbruch region alongside the river Oder, and the river Wakenitz in northern Germany. Because wels brought a good price in the market, they were introduced to many lakes in all regions of Germany. It is now possible when fishing for other species, like pike or eels, to have a monster wels take the bait. The fish is said to be rare, but its nocturnal and bottom-hugging habits are the true reason for its alleged rarity.

The best way to catch the aforementioned species is to find a professional fisherman; these locals have access to most of the best lakes and can sell licenses and provide rental boats.

Saltwater

Deep-sea angling. Ocean (referred to as deep-sea) angling in Germany from party boats has increased in popularity since the 1960s. In the Baltic Sea, nearly 50 party boats (called charter boats here) operate from German harbors daily, there are about two dozen of them in the North Sea. Most of the boats are former commercial fishing trawlers, but they now have many amenities on board, including a kitchen, small shops, and toilets. They can accommodate up to 50 anglers and travel from 5 to 20 miles offshore. A growing fleet of smaller boats is available for rent, and these carry four to eight anglers. To operate boats with more than a 5-horsepower motor, one must possess a motorboat driver's license *(Motorbootführerschein)*. Small boats for rent are available only along the Baltic.

Deep-sea angling takes place year-round in the Baltic Sea but is restricted to the spring-to-autumn season in the North Sea due to higher winds and waves. Cod are a predominant species here. The record fish is a 62-pounder, and the best season is in May and June, as well as in autumn. The most popular lure is a *pilker* (pirk, or heavy metal jigging lure) weighing 100 to 150 grams, combined with a soft plastic twist tail. Anglers use 20-pound conventional or spinning tackle in the Baltic; 30-pound gear for wreck fishing is favored in the North Sea.

Mackerel fishing is popular in the North Sea from June through the end of August. Herring are caught at a rate of a hundred per day from jetties in the harbors of the Baltic Sea. Anglers pursue the herring during a short peak period in March and April. Tope are caught around Helgoland Island in the North Sea in early autumn. Some professional fishermen offer their open 30-foot boats *(Börteboot)* for shark fishing a few miles off the island, using 30-pound tackle and mackerel for bait. The record weight for tope around the island is more than 200 pounds.

Surf casting. This sport became much more popular with the reintroduction of sea trout late in the twentieth century. Sea-run brown trout are reared in great numbers in hatcheries managed by anglers.

The entire shoreline of the Baltic is sea trout territory, particularly where gravel, stones, and plants are found. Many eager light tackle anglers wade and cast flies or spoons. The top season is from April through June, and fishing for trout is closed from August through the end of October. The fish average from 3 to 6 pounds but have been taken to 30 pounds.

Traditional surf casting methods are preferred for other species. Surf casters trying to catch cod, flatfish, and the occasional sea trout use rods that are 4 or more meters long, and weights up to 180 grams, to cast from 80 to 150 meters into the surf. Baitfish are available from every tackle dealer along the coast. Best catches are possible in the months of May and June, and again from September through November when the wind is blowing ashore. The Baltic Sea is a preferred surf casting area, second only to the outer islands of the North Sea, whose sandy shores face the open ocean.

Other Issues

Trolling. Trolling is new to German anglers, but it is gaining popularity as Germany's Scandinavian neighbors catch more and more fish annually with this method; trolling with downriggers, in particular, has become more popular. Most well-equipped

trolling boats are privately owned, however, and it is uncommon to find such boats for hire. Most trolling is practiced in the Baltic Sea, and in some large lakes for trout.

Put-and-take sites. In the area surrounding big cities there are many ponds and small lakes that provide put-and-take fishing. The quality differs, as do the amenities, but some have facilities, including toilets and shops, and some of these waters offer exceptionally large fish, mainly rainbow trout.

Legislation. As mentioned briefly in the opening paragraphs on angling in Germany, each of the 16 German states has its own fishery laws. With the exception of Niedersachsen in the north, all states require a state-issued license (*Jahresfischereischein*) for freshwater and saltwater angling.

Yearly or lifetime licenses exist, and these can be obtained only when the angler has passed an examination (*Sportfischerprüfung*), administered by the German Angling Federation and its district associations. The test is given only in German, and there are no lessons for preparation in the English language; however, if demand grows, this may change. The northernmost state, Schleswig-Holstein, is the only exception; it issues a 40-day license for holiday anglers without requiring an examination.

In addition to possessing a state fishing license, anglers must purchase a site-specific license issued by the owner of the water they wish to fish. Children under 12 do not need a license. Owners of fish waters can be clubs, communities, professional fishermen, or private landowners. Licenses for private waters are issued for a day, a weekend, a week, or a month and sometimes are accompanied by regulations regarding catch limits, size limits, catch-and-release, angling methods, baits, and the like. In Niedersachsen, which has no state license requirements, landowners often require proof that an angler has passed the national examination before they will grant a fishing license for most private waters.

State licenses cover sea angling also, except in the state of Mecklenburg-Vorpommern. A separate license for shore angling is necessary there and is available from tourist information offices.

In Germany it is illegal to fish with live bait, and the laws specify that a fish destined for consumption must be killed immediately and must not be wasted. It is also illegal to use nets to keep fish alive.

Information sources. All-inclusive angling tours for Germany are generally unavailable, and contacting the state or local boards of tourism is necessary to locate hotels, pensions, clubs, and professional fishermen who sell licenses, accommodations, and boats for hire. Contact the Central German Tourist Board to get the address of the official Tourist Board of the German state in question, then contact that state board to locate regional tourist offices.

It's a good idea to read advertisements in one of the big monthly German angling magazines. Fishing club addresses are available from the National German Angling Federation (VDSF) at Siemensstr. 13, D-63071 Offenbach (telephone: 069-8550068; fax: 069-873770), and the German Anglers Association (Deutscher Angler-Verband DAV), at Weissenseer Weg 110, D-10369 Berlin (telephone: 030-97104379; fax: 030-97104389).

GIARDIASIS
See: First Aid.

GIGGING
Taking fish with a handheld prong, harpoonlike device, or spear, any of which may also be known as a gig. These devices are meant to spear or impale fish by means of a pronged or barbed instrument, which is attached to a rigid object such as a pole. Also known in some places as spearing, gigging is primarily a freshwater activity and one that has been practiced traditionally to procure food. The legality today varies in freshwater and is regulated by fisheries agencies. Gigging usually requires a fishing license, is subject to seasons, and may be restricted to certain species. Where legal, gigging is considered a form of recreational fishing; it is not widely employed, however, and is not treated as sportfishing by the general angling community.

Gigging is sometimes confused with jigging and the use of jigs to catch fish by sporting means.
See: Spearing.

GILL
A breathing organ with much-divided thin-walled filaments for extracting oxygen from the water. In a living fish, the gills are bright red feathery organs that are located on bony arches and are prominent when the gill cover (*see*) of the fish is lifted.
See: Anatomy; Gill Rakers.

GILLIE
A fishing guide; also ghillie.

GILLNET
A commercial fishing net in which fish are caught as they swim into the mesh, where they are entangled by the gills. The net is suspended vertically by means of bottom weights and top floats, and the mesh is sized according to the species sought. Gillnets entangle anything larger than the net's mesh size, resulting in tremendous amounts of bycatch (*see*).
See: Commercial Fisherman.

GILL RAKERS
Toothlike extensions, located along the anterior margin of the gill arch, that project over the throat opening and strain water that is passed over the

gills. These protect the gill filaments and, in some fishes, are used to sieve out tiny food organisms. The number of gill rakers on the first gill arch is sometimes used as an aid in identifying or separating species that closely resemble one another.
See: Anatomy.

GIMBAL
A pivoting receptacle for fishing rods that may be located on a rod belt *(see)*, mounted on the front of a fighting chair *(see)*, or located in rod holders. It contains a receiver with locking mechanism to receive the rod butt, and it pivots when the rod is pumped while fighting a fish. A gimbal is customarily used in saltwater fishing with heavy tackle and large or powerful fish, although it may be used with lighter tackle as well.

GIN POLE
A tall pole with rope and blocks, found in older sportfishing boats and used to hoist large fish out of the water and into the cockpit. No longer prevalent on large sportfishing boats, these have been largely replaced by a transom door/gate *(see)*.
See: Sportfishing Boat.

GLOBAL POSITIONING SYSTEM
An electronic navigation method known by the acronym GPS.
See: GPS; Navigation.

GOLDEYE *Hiodon alosoides.*
Other names—Winnipeg goldeye, western goldeye, shad mooneye, toothed herring, yellow herring; French: *la queche, laquaiche aux yeux d'or.*

A member of the Hiodontidae family of mooneye, the goldeye is one of Canada's most celebrated freshwater fish from an Epicurean viewpoint. When smoke cured, it is sold as Winnipeg goldeye, commands a high price, and is well known among gourmets. The goldeye looks very much like the mooneye *(see)*, but only the goldeye is of commercial interest. Its bony flesh, when fresh, is soft and unpalatable, but it is a delicacy when smoked. In processing, the fish are gutted, lightly brined, dyed orange red, and then smoked over oak fires. It is marketed whole.

Although often called a herring or a shad, it is neither. The goldeye provides good sport for light tackle anglers, but it is not pursued in many parts of its range.

Identification. The goldeye is a small fish whose compressed body is deep in proportion to its length and is covered with large, loose scales. Dark blue to blue green over the back, it is silvery on the sides, tapering to white on the belly. It has a small head and a short, bluntly rounded snout with a small terminal mouth containing many sharp teeth on the jaws and tongue.

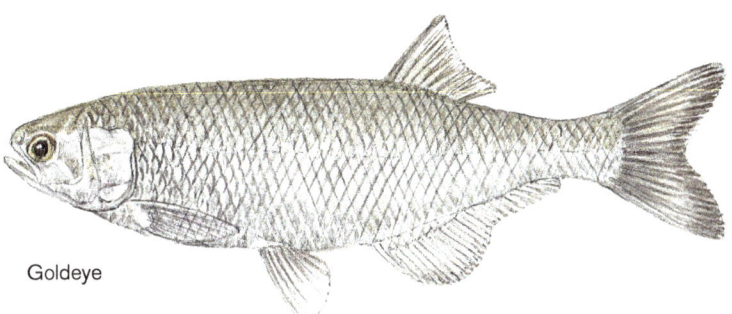
Goldeye

The color of its eyes and the position of its anal fin distinguish it from the mooneye. The iris of the large eyes are gold and reflect light. The goldeye's dorsal fin begins opposite or behind its anal fin (the mooneye's begins before the anal fin). The goldeye can be distinguished from the gizzard shad by the absence of a dorsal fin ray projection.

Size/Age. Adults average from 10 ounces to slightly more than a pound in weight, and seldom exceed 2 pounds in most waters. They can grow to 5 pounds. The Manitoba record is a 2.3-kilogram fish from the Nelson River. They reportedly can live for 14 years.

Distribution. Endemic to North America, goldeye are found in both Canadian and American waters. They occur from western Ontario to the Mackenzie River at Aklavik in the north, from below the Great Lakes south throughout the Ohio and Mississippi River drainages on the east, and from western Alberta throughout eastern Montana and Wyoming to Oklahoma on the west. Lake Winnipeg in Manitoba has historically been the largest commercial producer of these fish; its stocks were greatly depleted in the 1920s through overfishing, and took decades to recover.

Habitat. Throughout their geographical range, goldeye are most often found in warm, silty sections of large rivers and in the backwaters of shallow lakes connected to them.

Spawning behavior. In the spring, mature goldeye move into pools in rivers, or backwater lakes of rivers, to spawn when the water temperature is between 10° and 13°C.

Food and feeding habits. Goldeye feed on a variety of organisms, from microscopic plankton to insects and fish. They do most of their foraging on or near the surface, and predominantly on insects, although they will eat minnows and small frogs. Small goldeye serve as prey for large predators, including walleye, pike, and salmon.

Angling. Goldeye are caught on flies and on small hook baits, including worms and grasshoppers, suspended below a light float. Light spinning and fly tackle are the favored gear. Most angling for goldeye occurs in central Canadian waters, primarily to produce fish for home smoking. Elsewhere, they are seldom deliberately pursued on rod and

Wild Goldfish

reel, but they may be fished live or as cut bait by anglers pursuing other species, notably catfish.

GOLDFISH *Carassius auratus*.

A member of the large Cyprinidae family of freshwater fish, and a relative of carp *(see)*, goldfish are primarily known as aquarium species, but they do exist in the wild.

GOOSEFISH *Lophius americanus*.

Other names—American goosefish, anglerfish, monkfish, lotte, bellyfish, frogfish, sea devil, American angler; French: *baudroie d'Amerique*; Spanish: *rape americano*.

The goosefish has been described as mostly mouth with a tail attached, and reports of goosefish eating prey almost as big as themselves are common. A member of the Lophiidae family of deep-sea anglerfish, the goosefish is an ugly, bottom-dwelling species of temperate waters that attracts prey with a fleshy lure and then sucks it inside its huge mouth. It is not a targeted gamefish, but it is occasionally caught by deep-water bottom anglers. Goosefish and related species have been highly prized in European markets for a long time but have become prominent in North American markets and restaurants only since the mid-1980s, usually under the moniker "monkfish."

Before the mid 1980s, the American goosefish was harvested almost exclusively as a bycatch in groundfish trawl fisheries and the sea scallop dredge fishery, but it became increasingly targeted in response to dwindling supplies of traditional groundfish species and the development of new markets for goosefish parts (tails, whole fish, livers, cheeks, and belly flaps). Meat from the tail of the goosefish is firm, white, and excellent table fare; the liver is a delicacy in France and Japan.

More than two dozen species of anglerfish exist worldwide in tropical and temperature seas, and the American goosefish is the largest among them. Commercial landings of the American goosefish have so increased that the average fish is smaller and the species is overexploited.

Identification. The American goosefish is dark brown with a mottling of dark spots and blotches. It has almost armlike pectoral fins located about midway in its greatly flattened body. Small gill openings are just behind them. The head is extremely large for its body size, and the mouth is cavernous, filled with sharp, curved teeth and opening upward. Fleshy flaps of skin margin the head and lower jaw, and smaller flaps of flesh run along the sides of the scaleless body. The first three spines of the dorsal fin are thin and sharp, and they are widely separated from one another. On the tip of the first spine is a flap of flesh that serves as a lure for attracting small fish within grasping range of the mouth. If the prey comes close enough, the goosefish opens its big mouth and sucks its victim inside.

Size/Age. The growth rate is fairly rapid and similar for both sexes up to about age 4, when they are approximately 19 inches long. After this, females grow a bit more rapidly and seem to live longer, about 12 years, growing to slightly more than 39 inches. Males have not been found older than age 9, with a length of approximately 35 inches, and few grow older than age 6. Their maximum weight is 50 pounds, and the all-tackle world record is a Maine fish that weighed 49 pounds, 12 ounces.

Distribution. This species ranges from the Grand Banks and northern Gulf of St. Lawrence south to Cape Hatteras, North Carolina. A similar but smaller species, the blackfin goosefish *(L. gastrophysus)* occurs in deeper waters from North Carolina to the Gulf of Mexico and south to Argentina.

Habitat. Individuals are found from inshore areas to depths exceeding 435 fathoms. Highest concentrations occur between 38 and 55 fathoms, and in deeper water at about 100 fathoms. Seasonal migrations occur, apparently related to spawning and food availability.

Life history/Behavior. Sexual maturity occurs between ages 3 and 4. Spawning takes place from spring through early autumn, depending on latitude. Females lay a nonadhesive, buoyant mucoid egg raft, or veil, which can be as large as 39 feet long and 5 feet wide. Incubation ranges from 7 to 22 days, after which the larvae spend several months in a pelagic phase before settling to a benthic existence at a size of about 3 inches.

Goosefish

Food. The carnivorous and rapacious goosefish eats a wide array of fish, some nearly as large as itself, as well as assorted crustaceans and squid. It has been reported to consume diving ducks as well.

GPS

The satellite navigational mode commonly referred to simply as GPS is actually NAVSTAR GPS, which stands for *NAV*igation *S*ystem with *T*ime *A*nd *R*anging *G*lobal *P*ositioning *S*ystem. This system is divided into space and ground control segments. The space segment consists of a constellation of satellites in precise orbits 10,900 nautical miles out in space, arranged so that at least six satellites are always in view from any point on Earth. The ground control segment includes a master control station, a number of monitoring stations, and ground antennas located around the world, which work together to track and communicate with the satellites.

GPS obsolesced the older DECCA and Loran *(see)* navigational systems, which could be used only by receivers within range of their chains of land-based transmission towers. It also obsolesced the Transit System (sometimes called Sat-Nav) of navigation, which used low-orbit satellites so widely spaced that position fixes were infrequent.

GPS features extremely quick fixes and easy use; you simply turn the receiver on and start navigating. There are no calibrations to make, no chains of towers to select, no operational pitfalls like Loran's baseline extensions to worry about, and, unless you leave the planet, there are no fringe areas. Thanks to the high angle of the satellites and the very high frequency used to carry signals, GPS is immune to weather problems and highly resistant to localized interference, both of which were problems with Loran. It can be used 24 hours a day, in any weather, anywhere where there is an open view of the sky.

In a relatively short period of time, GPS has become a fixture for marine and inland navigation and an increasingly common part of both the sportfishing-by-boat scene and the backcountry travel scene. The first handheld GPS was introduced in 1988, and early handheld units retailed for about $3,000. A decade later, handheld models were available for $100, and they were far more sophisticated. From a fishing perspective, the major use today is on the water for both navigational and fish-locating purposes. Sportfishing boaters are using fixed-mount and handheld GPS to get to and from selected locations and to determine the exact location of important fishing grounds; in addition, they use GPS as an aid to actual fishing activities, especially when angling in wide-open waters for nomadic schools of fish or pelagic species or when fishing specific bottom structures.

How GPS Works

Principles. Each satellite constantly broadcasts the time and its position. Timing is all-important to accuracy, and the satellites are equipped with atomic clocks reputed to be accurate within one second every 70,000 years.

A GPS receiver calculates its distance from a satellite by measuring the time it takes for the satellite's signal to reach it. The receiver determines its two-dimensional position (latitude and longitude) by measuring its distance from three satellites. It finds its three-dimensional position (latitude, longitude, and altitude) by measuring its distance from a fourth satellite as well. The receiver knows the positions of the satellites overhead and automatically uses those that provide the best geometry for accuracy.

GPS receivers don't have a compass or any other mechanical direction-finding device built into them; they rely entirely on position fixes derived from satellite signals. Normally, they find your position about once every second, and they calculate speed, direction of travel, and distance by comparing where you are one second with where you are the next. You must be moving for GPS to determine your speed and direction of travel; you can't stand still and use the unit as a magnetic compass. It will work at slow trolling speeds, but the faster you travel, the easier and more accurately a receiver can track speed and direction.

Conventional accuracy. The satellites broadcast signals for two levels of service: Standard Positioning Service (SPS) for civilian use and an encrypted Precise Positioning Service for the military. Civilian SPS is accurate enough to get anglers within 25 meters or less of a target destination. However, the United States Department of Defense chooses to degrade SPS accuracy with Selective Availability (SA) interference for military security reasons. The government's accuracy specification for GPS is 100 meters (328 feet) horizontally and 150 meters (492 feet) vertically, 95 percent of the time. In other words, the position shown on a receiver could be up to 100 meters in any direction from your actual position, and your altitude could be plus or minus 150 meters from what is shown on the screen. Most users report seeing latitude/longitude accuracy of 15 to 50 meters on average, but for safety's sake all users need to remember that they could be 100 meters from where GPS says they are at any time.

GPS satellites are arranged in six separate orbital groups to ensure global coverage, and each satellite orbits the earth once every 12 hours. Since the satellites and anglers' boats are in constant motion, the geometry between them is in a state of perpetual change. The best accuracy is possible when a receiver can navigate with three satellites that are low on the horizon and spaced evenly (120 degrees) apart. Less than ideal satellite geometry results in less than ideal accuracy for position fixes, although these errors are negligible compared to SA.

GPS satellites transmit signals in a straight,

Tarpon is one species that rises periodically to the surface to breathe atmospheric air. Young tarpon do this about three times per hour.

line-of-sight path. When a receiver can't get a clear view of most of the sky, it may not be able to pick up signals from enough satellites to work properly. A bridge overhead or a high vertical cliff nearby can block necessary satellite signals. A receiver will warn you when it can't receive enough satellites for navigation, and all you should have to do is move clear of these obstructions for the unit to resume navigation.

When installing a GPS antenna on your boat, mount it where things like metal windshield frames, outboard motor power heads, and seated or standing passengers are least likely to block satellite signals. Never mount a GPS antenna in a radar antenna's transmission path, since the radar emissions can cook some of its delicate internal components.

DGPS accuracy. Accuracy better than 100 meters is required for commercial ships navigating coastal harbors, the Great Lakes, and major rivers, as well as for private and commercial airplane pilots. A system enhancement called Differential GPS (DGPS) was developed to increase accuracy to around 10 meters by countering the effects of SA, and anglers can take advantage of this improved accuracy. DGPS uses land-based receivers installed at surveyed locations. They compare their known location with their satellite-derived position and compute a correction. A DGPS station might, for instance, determine that it is really 100 feet northwest of where the satellites currently say it is and compute a correction. This correction is then broadcast on a special U.S. Coast Guard DGPS radio beacon frequency from a tower located at the same site. Different DGPS station locations use different frequencies, so a DGPS unit always knows which one it's receiving.

In order for a unit to use DGPS, it must contain special built-in circuitry to process the corrections and must be connected to a differential beacon receiver to acquire them. Most units require a separate beacon receiver, but some have them built-in. Units built to use the differential system are advertised as being DGPS-ready or DGPS-capable.

Unfortunately, the maximum broadcast range for a U.S. Coast Guard differential beacon tower is only about 200 miles. Therefore, freshwater anglers more than 200 miles from a saltwater coast, the Great Lakes, or a navigable river are probably out of range of the nearest tower and may not be able to use DGPS; through the phenomenon of skipping, some broadcasts have been received over much greater distances, but this is usually in unobstructed coastal areas rather than inland.

Also on the negative side, DGPS brings land-based towers and their much lower radio transmission frequencies back into the overall equation. Thunderstorms between your boat and the tower can kill reception just as they could with Loran. However, losing the beacon signal just causes a DGPS receiver to revert to normal GPS. You lose the extra accuracy, but you don't lose the ability to navigate as would happen with Loran.

Wide area augmentation accuracy. To overcome the range and tower deficiencies of DGPS, and to get maximum accuracy out of standard GPS for airplane pilots, the Federal Aviation Administration (FAA) is developing the Wide Area Augmentation Service (WAAS). This is a system enhancement signal emanating from very high orbit satellites (covering a wider area than the satellites producing GPS signals); the WAAS signals provide differential information that is collected directly by a GPS receiver, which automatically computes a correction to counter Selective Availability.

This will work in newer GPS products that have a 12-channel receiver, with one channel being preprogrammed by the manufacturer for dedication to WAAS. Older 12-channel products may or may not be retroprogrammed by the manufacturer. There is no need for a differential beacon receiver.

The benefits of WAAS are twofold: First, it works anywhere in North America and all the time because it doesn't rely on land-based towers to relay a differential correction signal; second, accuracy is improved to a range of 3 to 10 meters. Whether Selective Availability is being applied or not, a GPS unit that is WAAS-capable will provide the utmost in accurate position identification.

Types of Receivers

GPS receivers are available as handheld portables, as stand-alone bracket-mounted or in-dash models, and as "black boxes" integrated into sonar and other types of electronics. The actual receiver (sometimes called a GPS engine) has been miniaturized to fit on a small printed circuit board. The same board can be used in nearly any style of unit, which allows a manufacturer's tiniest handheld model to be as fast and accurate as the maker's largest panel-mount unit that incorporates the same board.

A receiver's level of performance depends more on its number of parallel channels and the software used to manage them than just its physical size. Early models had a single channel that could receive the signal from only one satellite at a time. In order to navigate with the three satellites necessary for determining latitude and longitude, it had to lock onto one satellite, get its information, and then unlock and go to the next one. This process was repeated constantly; when signals were lost or blocked, early units sometimes had trouble reacquiring them to start the process over again. The next generation of receivers had multiple channels (usually between 2 and 6) and could keep one channel locked onto each of the satellites it was using for navigation. They took less time to find a position when first switched on, and they were less bothered by temporary signal interruptions. Most newer receivers have 12 channels and deliver performance that, in comparison, is incredible. When first switched on, they find a position in seconds rather than minutes, and they suffer performance interruptions only when the receiver is blocked from the transmitting satellites or the power is disconnected (handheld units may be susceptible to blockage from dense foliage). They have enough channels to lock onto all the satellites in view and can switch instantly back and forth as necessary if signals are blocked.

Handheld portables. These pocket-size receivers have built-in antennas and self-contained power supplies and are the most versatile type of GPS unit. They are a good choice for anglers using canoes, inflatables, rental boats, and other craft without electrical systems, or when temporarily fishing from someone else's boat. They are also perfect for hike-in fishing on remote waters. Although they are a good compromise for anglers who use GPS for a variety of outdoor activities that require portability, they aren't the best choice for a permanent mounting in your boat. It can be more difficult to see their smaller screens and press their smaller keys while bouncing across the water than when using a full-sized, permanently mounted model.

The standard power source for handheld GPS units is AA batteries, and battery consumption varies greatly between models. The more power-hungry versions eat them up as fast as about six batteries every 3 hours, whereas the more conservative units can use as few as four batteries every 24 hours through internal power management systems. Some companies are taking advantage of advancements made in the portable computer industry and offer exotic rechargeable power cells that run units longer than a set of AAs and can be recharged hundreds of times. Manufacturers also usually offer accessory power cords that allow a handheld to run from a cigarette lighter receptacle when used temporarily in a boat, tow vehicle, or even an ice angler's snowmobile. Accessories like remote antennas and mounting brackets are available for many handhelds and make them easier to use in such cases.

Permanent mount units. These receivers are larger than handhelds and have bigger, easier-to-see displays. Most come as two separate assemblies: a head unit that mounts near the helm and contains the display and controls, and a compact antenna that mounts on a gunwale or console. These units are powered by the boat's electrical system. The head is generally designed to be mounted on a gimbaled bracket, but some can also be flush-mounted on a flat panel surface. Beware of flush-mounting any instruments having liquid crystal displays because they have a relatively narrow viewing angle. Once flush mounted, they can't be tilted or turned for better visibility.

The larger screens on permanent units have more room for multiple-window displays and more elaborate graphics than the small screens on handheld models. They can also be clearly read from farther away.

Combination models. GPS receivers are commonly available in combination with sonar units and as plug-in options for chart plotters, radars, and other electronics. Combination units are usually

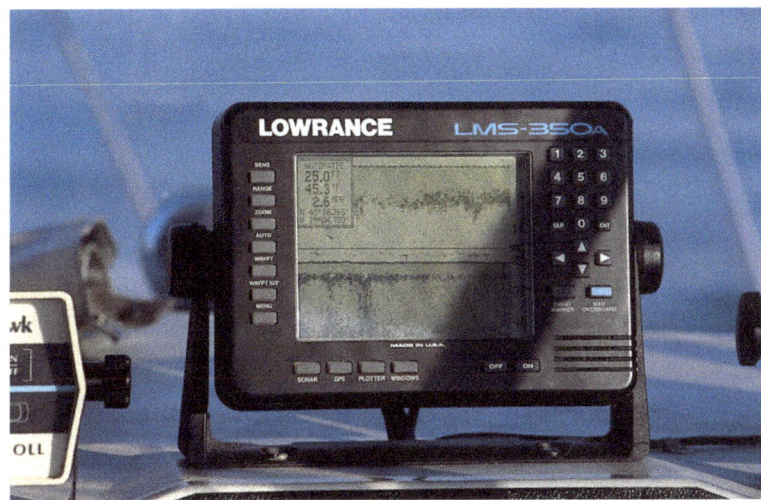

The GPS portion of this combined sonar-and-GPS unit allows an angler to assess speed and location at all times, as well as instantly preserve the location of something observed with the sonar.

less expensive than separate models and can help ease console crowding on boats where space is at a premium.

Sonar/GPS combinations are probably the most common. Anglers can show either sonar or GPS readings on the whole screen, or they can split the screen to show sonar displays on one side and GPS information on the other. Although this saves space and money, it also has disadvantages. If the sonar breaks, the GPS has to go with it to the service facility because it's in the same case. You may also find yourself in a serious fishing situation that requires precise navigation and maximum sonar detail, wishing that each function could be shown full-screen at the same time. Some professional guides, tournament competitors, charter boat captains, and big-water skippers use two sonar/GPS combo units in their quest for maximum redundancy. They use one as a sonar and the other as a GPS, and have an automatic double backup in case of trouble.

There are also combined GPS/communications units that have the ability to send wireless e-mail messages from any outside location. Battery-operated palm-size units can send and receive e-mail messages in wireless form by using orbiting satellites. The number of satellites capable of receiving and transmitting e-mail messages was originally limited but is increasing, so that 24-hour coverage can be provided.

General Use
Anglers can save important locations like favorite fishing spots, launching ramps, marinas, reefs, wrecks, and navigational aids or hazards in the electronic memory of a GPS receiver. Submerged open-water fishing hotspots that are out of sight of land can be almost impossible to find without electronic help. Even familiar launching ramps and marinas can be elusive in fog or darkness.

The locations saved in GPS receivers are called

waypoints. Once a location has been saved as a waypoint, an angler can return to it at any time. A waypoint is most commonly saved by pressing a button while the unit is located at the waypoint's position; the position can also be saved by entering its latitude and longitude coordinates through the keypad. These coordinates are important because with the lat/lon coordinates you can find a place that you have never been to; the coordinates can be given to you, or you can take them off a good navigational chart.

It's a good idea to record waypoint information in a logbook as a backup, in case the unit is lost, stolen, or breaks down. You can reenter the waypoints manually after fixing or replacing your unit or acquiring another. Integrating with a personal computer will allow you to store appropriate information as well as plan trips. Some manufacturers have software that allows you to share information with other users and to download, upload, store, and edit navigational data; this can include sorting waypoints, printing route lists and plots, calculating sunrise/sunset times and lunar phases, and determining the bearing and distance between waypoints.

A receiver guides you to a waypoint by providing the compass bearing from your present position to the waypoint's location. When you veer off course, it tells you which way to steer to get back on course, and it constantly provides digital readouts of your speed, direction of travel, remaining distance, and even how long it will take you to get there at the current speed. This information can be displayed in several ways.

Digital box display. The most basic way to display information is with digital boxes containing numbers and letters. Anglers most comfortable with this type of presentation need only pay attention to three of the boxes. The "Bearing" box shows the compass direction (in degrees) from the present position to the destination waypoint. The "Heading" or "Track" box shows the direction that you are actually traveling as you attempt to steer your boat on the proper course. Forces like wind and current can push a boat sideways as you steer on your bearing and move it in a slightly different direction than your compass reads. The closer the bearing and heading readings are to the same number, the more accurately you are navigating. The third important box is labeled "Distance To Go." You simply steer on the correct compass bearing until the distance-to-go reading counts down to zero.

Some units also have a simple "Direction to Steer" screen that provides navigational information as compass bearing numbers or simply as a directional arrow.

Road/highway display. Some anglers find pictures easier to use than numbers. Some types of displays show a road or highway on the screen with an icon (a graphic symbol) representing your boat traveling down it. You simply steer the boat so that its icon stays in the middle of the road. As you approach your destination waypoint, the waypoint appears as a symbol ahead of you. When your boat icon reaches the waypoint symbol, you're there. The same digital readings found on the first type of display are usually shown somewhere on this screen to let you check your progress.

Track plotter. This display method is often preferred by anglers used to navigating by the seat of their pants. It shows a bird's-eye view of your boat and the surrounding area. The amount of area shown on the screen is adjustable from a fraction of a mile to hundreds or even thousands of miles. The screen shows an icon representing your boat connected by a dotted line to another symbol representing your destination waypoint. The screen will also show symbols for any other waypoints in the area, and some units can show "event markers" that you can place on the screen at will. They are typically used to mark where fish are caught or hazards are identified. These markers appear whenever you are in the area, but they don't take up any of your valuable waypoint memory.

Anglers maintain the best screen resolution by adjusting the plotter range to show the smallest amount of area large enough to contain both the boat icon and the destination waypoint symbol. As you move, the boat icon leaves a solid line on the screen, marking its track. You simply steer the boat so that the solid track line of the boat icon covers up the dotted line.

Track plotter screens can usually be set for either a north-up or course-up orientation. This means that either the direction "north" or your present direction of travel will always be at the top of the screen. Anglers who like to view maps in the same orientation as they are usually printed (with the direction north at the top) prefer the north-up setting. Those who like to turn the map so that the direction in which they're going is at the top prefer the course-up setting. Either way, when the boat icon covers the destination waypoint symbol, you're there.

Routing. A routing feature lets you list several waypoints in the order that you wish to visit them and then save the list as a "route" in memory. This is most useful for blazing a safe trail from a launching ramp to a fishing spot, or even from a marina deep within a harbor out through an inlet. Routing lets you overcome problems caused by the fact that GPS navigates in straight-line legs.

When you tell a GPS unit to take you to a waypoint, it plots a straight line from where you are at that moment to where you want to go. It considers that straight line your course, and it guides you along it. If your destination is 2 miles away and there are points of land, islands, or rock bars between you and your destination, GPS will guide you right into them. You can blaze a safe trail by saving a waypoint each time such obstacles force you to make a turn and then listing the waypoints, in order, as a route that leads you around hazards in short, straight-line legs.

Tooth loss is a natural and regular occurrence in the well-dentured tigerfish; dozens of teeth were found on the floor of a tank after eight large tigerfish were held in captivity for one month.

When building a safe route, anglers should keep the worst-case accuracy for GPS in mind and strive to stay at least 100 meters from the closest hazard when saving waypoints. If the local geography doesn't offer you that much room on certain legs of a route, be extra careful when traveling them. When running a route, anglers can start at any of the route's waypoints and run the route forward or backward.

Other features and terms. GPS units employ a number of symbols that all users become familiar with. Icons are used to identify specific positions on the screen and may be used together to delineate a certain area; when placed within a route, they may become waypoints, which are stored in memory as a specific set of lat/lon coordinates. The number of icons and the type of graphic symbols offered varies.

When you wish to note the occurrence of something on the screen, you may be able to place a mark there; this may be numbered, and a specific symbol may be used for it. An event could simply be a strike while trolling, the location of a net buoy, or something that is unique. The feature that permits this marking may be called an event marker. In a similar vein, some fixed-mount units have a specific function allocated to emergencies, called a man overboard (MOB) feature. When the appropriate button is pressed, the unit instantly records the boat's position and charts a course to that spot. Of obvious use to sailors and boaters in rough seas, it can also be employed when some object has inadvertently fallen out of your boat (like that lucky fishing hat).

Three terms used with regard to obtaining position are acquisition time, cold start, and warm start. Acquisition time is simply the amount of time required for a GPS unit to lock onto the appropriate number of satellites and obtain a position fix. When a GPS unit is started for the first time, and when it has been moved a long distance from where it was last used, the receiver has no idea where to look for satellites and will take a long time, perhaps up to 20 minutes, to find its current position. This is called cold start. Every time that the GPS unit is turned on, the receiver assumes that it is in the same position as it was when previously operating. If it is in, or relatively near, that position, it will rely on the data stored in memory and locate the appropriate satellites fairly quickly. This is called warm start.

When a GPS unit is used in relatively the same area, it should be able to lock onto satellites fast. Speed of acquisition is less of a concern in fixed-mount versions, which are connected to a 12-volt battery and left on all day. It is much more of a concern in handheld units, which are commonly turned on and off periodically. On a warm start, the better handheld units can be fully functional in less than a minute.

Common sense and sonar. Keep in mind that the bearing indicated to reach a desired location is always depicted in a straight-line mode. The receiver does not take into account that an island, another vessel, or any obstruction might be in the path of travel. Thus, following a GPS bearing must be done with the understanding that it is not always possible to follow a straight course and that even when there are no obvious above-water impediments to following a straight course, underwater obstructions such as a shoal, reef, or other object may require altering your heading. As you alter heading, the receiver repositions you and recomputes the direction and time to your destination. Nevertheless, in the same way that using a compass (see) is not a substitute for applying common sense, nor is operating a GPS, and it is generally advisable to employ GPS, as well as any other navigational instrument, in conjunction with sonar.

Also keep in mind that these are electronic navigational aids, and they will not be useful if there is an electronic malfunction within the unit or if the power supply is cut off or exhausted. Handheld units that work on battery power are especially susceptible to power depletion, and most have a low-battery warning. Spare batteries will really be appreciated at such a time.

Finally, there are times when a receiver is unable to function properly even though the unit has sufficient power. This is usually when an impenetrable object obstructs the receiver's line of sight to the sky. The biggest problem is with handheld units operated in places where there is a full canopy of cover overhead; handheld units rarely can keep a fix under leafy cover. Most people who fish from a boat and use fixed-mount units do not experience this problem unless they have mounted the receiver in a location that is sometimes obstructed. A person standing in front of a receiver, or an object placed near it, could temporarily block the receiver.

Chart Plotters/Mapping Units

Many anglers find navigating with digital, on-screen

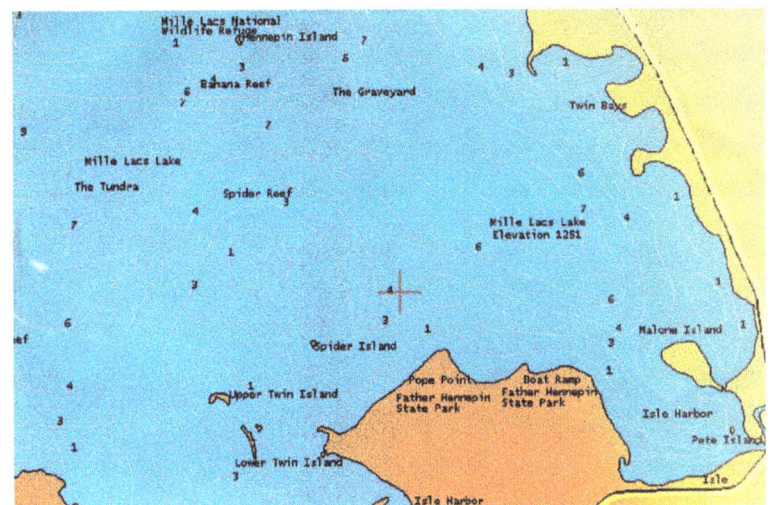

Chartlike details, such as this view of a section of Mille Lacs Lake, Minnesota, are provided in devices that combine charting with GPS navigation.

maps easier than finding their way with just numbers, virtual highway graphics, or track plotters. Accessories that feature map- or chartlike detail in electronic cartographic form are called chart plotters or mapping units, and the usage of fixed-mount versions in marine environments is referred to as electronic charting. The word "map" is generally used with handheld models, mainly those that are intended for diverse usage, especially inland; the word "chart" is used with fixed-mount units destined for marine applications. Chart plotting and mapping are available on stand-alone devices but may be incorporated into other products, including radar and sonar instruments. Stand-alone versions may be interfaced with these other devices, as well as others, including autopilots.

The highly detailed information for a given area is contained on cartridges that plug into the body of the unit. The topographic information displayed on-screen looks much like a road map, whereas the hydrographic information displayed looks like a navigational chart and displays detailed information on harbors, marinas, ship channels, and navigational aids. The detailed nautical information is, in fact, derived from navigational charts; thus, these electronic products are only as accurate as the paper government-agency charts from which they are obtained.

The quality of the detailed information in these units will depend on the scale that was used when digitizing the information. The larger the scale, the more detail that will be provided. Some chart plotters show the same information even when the zoom feature is used, which means that the same level of detail is provided on large and close views. Others provide a new set of more detailed information when you zoom in, which means that the more detailed zoom view has come from a different, and larger scale, chart. Naturally, more detailed information requires more memory storage, so it may result in a cartridge that covers a smaller area than one that does not have as much detail. However, this is an important difference between chart plotters. Fewer cartridges to cover a given geographic area may mean that you can view more overall area per cartridge, but you will not necessarily see more specific detail.

Another area of difference between older and newer chart plotters is whether they're "seamless." Older models redrew the chart screen when they jumped from the edge of one chart to the edge of the next; newer versions scroll from one to the other in an uninterrupted fashion.

Like a track plotter, chart plotters show a bird's-eye view of a boat icon and an adjustable amount of the surrounding area, including the locations of waypoints and event markers. Instead of being on a blank screen, however, these objects are shown on a detailed, on-screen chart or map of a lake, river, or coastline that shows a boat's movement in relation to shoreline or coastal features, local towns, highways, etc. This gives boaters the best possible feel for where they are at any given time and where they're going. In all chart plotters, the boat's position is displayed as an icon. In some, the icon moves to the edge of the screen, and then the chart area depicted changes and the icon is returned to the center of the new screen; in others, the icon always remains in the center of the screen and the chart moves beneath it. The former is known as true motion and the latter relative motion.

The most sophisticated contemporary cartridges do more than display depths as lines; they depict the depths in colored shades and even interactively compare the boat's draft with the water depth of the area and sound a warning. Some also depict spot soundings.

Such a high level of detail requires the storage of a lot of memory, so most manufacturers use plug-in cartridges of local areas to do the job. Some cartridges are no larger than a postage stamp. Some GPS manufacturers have developed their own information on their own cartridges, and some have used cartridges from established electronic charting companies; certain GPS units are capable of accepting both. Digital map/chart cartridges vary in the amount of area covered, level of map detail, and price. Some systems require the purchase of several cartridges to cover the entire area of large states or provinces, or large coastal areas, and even people who will use GPS in a relatively small area may need to have two cartridges if the dividing point for coverage happens to be in the area they navigate most frequently. Cartridge-capable GPS units for mapping or charting are available in both handheld and fixed-mount models, and they will become increasingly sophisticated and a greater part of everyday boating electronics.

Fishing with GPS
The navigational value of GPS is obvious. The additional value to anglers is in pinpointing places to fish, schools of fish, or significant underwater structures, and being able to return to them unerringly. In some instances, there is great value to pinpointing the specific part of an area to fish, such as the riprap near a submerged wreck. Trollers, in particular, who spend a lot of time searching for fish on the move (salmon and walleye, for example, in freshwater, or billfish, dolphin, or tuna in saltwater), may get a lot of benefit out of track plotters for returning to schools of fish; it is easy to lose your position when you are trolling at a fast speed or have no nearby visual landmarks. Drift anglers likewise may get a lot of value out of using the plotter and icons to identify places for focusing their efforts rather than covering a lot of unproductive water.

Marking structure. A GPS plotter can be of great use when simultaneously employed in conjunction with sonar to define the edge of any structure, whether that is a canyon in offshore water, a deepwater dropoff in a reservoir, the perimeter of a

---

In 1739, Massachusetts parson Joseph Seccombe gave a sermon defending the recreation of angling and described it as "necessary for the better support of the body and soul."

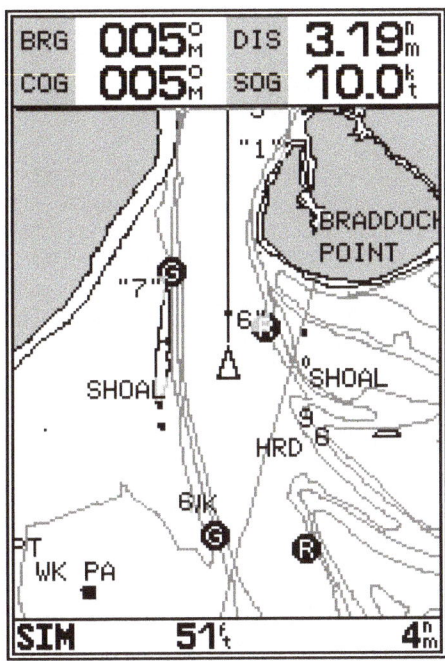
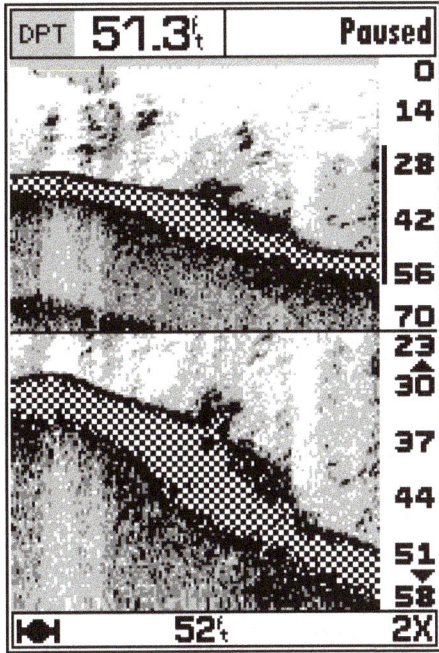

This screen view from a Garmin combined GPS and sonar device provides digital navigational details (left), water depth (right), and chartlike information with a track plotter; the boat is represented by an icon at dead center.

reef or shoal, or any specific underwater contour. If you have not been to a particular place before, you might want to scout the area first without fishing it; this will help familiarize you with the outline of that structure. The fact that you can visualize on a screen exactly where you have been and where you are heading will make fishing the area much easier.

Generally, the track plotter function of a GPS unit does not provide very precise information when the boat is traveling at slow speeds, as it is when slow-trolling or drifting, because of the effect of Selective Availability. If you are going fast enough to get good plotter detail, then zipping around the edges of the structure that you want to define will create a plot trail that you can reference when you actually fish the area, whether by trolling, drifting, or casting.

When you follow the edge of a structure, place an icon on the screen when there are significant changes; these might be a turn, an intersection with some other structure, or the ends or corners of the structure. When the sonar indicates that you're passing over a significant group of fish or a large individual fish, place an icon there; this might be a place to target your angling effort. When you have completed the scouting of an area, it will be fully defined on the plotter; then you can start to fish the most likely places based upon the depth, species sought, and whatever wind or current might be of influence. To make sense of your information when using icons, allocate specific icons to specific usage; for example, pick one icon to use for corners and prominent edge locations; pick another to use just for schools of fish or for baitfish; pick a third to use for big fish. Learn to manage the information to keep from being confused.

Do you have to use a plotter in this way for fishing? No. But it sure is easier. Without a plotter to provide a visual image of the structure, you can accomplish the same thing by using sonar alone and dropping marker buoys at specific locations; obviously this is an inferior method of defining an area in terms of the time it takes and the numbers of marker buoys (which have to be retrieved). Before sonar, this was done with weighted drop lines and trial-and-error probing.

Trolling. On the track plotter screen, you can see your course and direction of travel while trolling; when you locate or hook a fish, you can identify that specific locale by pressing the event marker function or by placing an icon on the plotter screen. After trolling onward or after fighting and landing a fish, you can use the plotter screen to show exactly how to get back to the place you identified.

This function is important when you're locating moving schools of baitfish or such wandering species as striped bass, salmon, and steelhead, or when you are out in the middle of a big body of water and come upon a feeding school of fish. Some anglers regularly use the plotter and event marker functions to help relocate fast and frequently moving schools of fish like striped bass, even when they are in locations (a large river or near a coastal shoreline) where they can clearly see where they are and how to get from one place to another. But if the targeted fish move about quickly because of tide, current, and baitfish activity, you have to stay with them and keep relocating them to stand a good chance of catching them.

In offshore big-game fishing, working the edge of structures or dropoffs can be very important, and many trollers follow a zigzag or S-curve pattern of boat maneuvering while fishing so that they can follow and stay with the contours below as defined on their sonar. If you are doing this, you can place an icon on the screen every time you go over the edge. Later, a series of icons will precisely show the edge so that you can then troll in a straight path from icon to icon. When you hook a fish or if you have a looker come into the baits, mark the spot with a different icon.

When trolling, use different icons to indicate different things; for example, use a fish icon for a school of baitfish and an anchor icon for big, individual fish. Some units have icons that represent schools of fish or large individual fish, so what you use depends on what the machine provides.

If fish are moving and you're retracing your travel, the plotter trail will build up and you may want to erase it; on the other hand, if the fish are stationary, then let the plotter trail build up. It may not be helpful to reduce the plotter screen to the smallest range possible (.10 mile in some units); it's better to get a larger view, perhaps by using the .5-mile range. When trolling, you can set the plotter to update infrequently (say every 30 seconds) instead of using an instant update mode, so the plot trails will last on the screen for a couple of days; if you will be returning to the same places for the same fish, then keeping information available could be very helpful. If you want the plotter trail to last for just the day, then use a 10-second update. For the most detail, use the quickest update frequency possible, although on most units the quickest update will clear out the plotter trail in a few hours.

Some combined sonar/GPS units allow you to construct windows so that half the screen is a sonar view, one-quarter of it is plotter, and the other is a digital depth readout. When not using the plotter, you may want to use full-screen sonar with the following displayed digitally in the upper left corner: depth, speed, surface temperature, and distance traveled.

Drifting and wreck fishing. Drifting across large expanses of water, like a bay or flat, is common for many types of fishing, especially when seeking bottom-feeding fish. The GPS can be used to close in on likely areas for fish or to identify specific places that are producing fish. You thus can maximize your time in productive places and eliminate fishing across unproductive expanses.

Initially, you may have to make a long drift in a particular area. Use the plotter screen to see where you've been and to identify places where fish were caught (by placing an icon there at the time of hookup). Naturally, any drift that is taken without the occasional use of an electric motor for positioning is subject to the direction of wind, current, and tide. These factors may change during a day, and a glance at the track plotter will reveal whether you need to reposition yourself to drift over the proper place because of changing conditions.

Finding wrecks is one of the most important uses for GPS. Keep in mind that simply knowing where a wreck is doesn't mean that you are right on it when the GPS says you have arrived. The waypoint for the wreck may coincide with your position, but the actual underwater wreck is just approximately in this spot. You'll still need to move around to precisely pinpoint it (and in many cases you want to pinpoint the rubble near a wreck). You can then run an east-west or north-south travel pattern to find it with your sonar, using the track plotter to set the trail and sonar to find the object. Do not just drive in circles looking for it.
See: Maps; Navigation; Sonar.

GRABBLING
See: Noodling.

GRAND SLAM
Although borrowed from a baseball term—a bases-clearing home run—this expression is used in angling to signify a broad array of feats. A grand slam is commonly associated with tropical water fishing and the capture of billfish or highly prized inshore or flats species, but the expression has been adopted for any combination of species that are highly valued and require a reasonable level of difficulty to catch. Guides, charter boat captains, and tourism promoters have varying spins to put on what constitutes a grand slam, as befits either the most notable or glamorous species in their areas, or the techniques they use.

A grand slam is usually associated with catching these species in a single day of fishing, but this, too, is variable. It may be associated with catching certain species over extended periods of time, since those species are usually not available in a single day (such as catching all billfish species in a year). A grand slam may also refer to accomplishments with certain types of tackle.

In the Atlantic Ocean off North America, for example, catching a blue marlin, white marlin, and sailfish in a single day is a grand slam; adding a swordfish or a spearfish would make it a super grand slam. Varying this in different combinations is possible.

Tarpon, bonefish, and permit are the traditional grand slam of the flats, and in some areas a snook might be added to make this a super grand slam. In backcountry areas, a grand slam might be a redfish, snook, and seatrout, with a tarpon making it a super grand slam.

Obviously a grand slam can be configured any way that makes sense. In the Northwest, a grand slam might be a salmon, halibut, and rockfish, or three major salmon species. In the mid-Atlantic, it might be a red drum, black drum, and cobia. Offshore it might be a variety of different big-game species.

These slams are generally unrecognized by official bodies, although the International Game Fish

---

Fishing in Japan dates back at least to 200 a.d., and Japanese interest in angling has continued through the centuries; Ebisu is a Japanese god of angling.

Association does have four grand slam clubs to honor saltwater catches. These are called Offshore or Inshore Grand and Super Grand Slams, and they recognize accomplishments by a single angler in a single day. They include blue marlin, black marlin, sailfish, swordfish, and spearfish in the offshore categories; catching any three constitutes a grand and any four a super grand. The inshore species include tarpon, bonefish, permit, and snook; catching any three is a grand and all four is a super grand. In both cases, the fish do not have to be landed or weighed (they can be released in the water at boatside, for example) to qualify and receive certificate recognition.

GRAPHITE

A synthetic material, also known as carbon fiber, used as a prominent material in fishing rod construction and in certain components of fishing reels.
See: Baitcasting Tackle; Conventional Tackle; Flycasting Tackle; Graphite Rod; Rod, Fishing; Spinning Tackle.

GRAPHITE ROD

A fishing rod that uses graphite material in the construction of the blank. Graphite is the most important material used in rod construction today, and rods made with graphite or a mix of graphite and other materials, primarily fiberglass and secondarily boron, dominate the marketplace.

Graphite came into fishing rod production from aerospace applications at a time when the majority of fishing rods were made of fiberglass. It took a while for manufacturing and design problems to be resolved (with a lot of early breakage and other problems as a result of using fiberglass rod manufacturing technology for graphite, which did not work), but better weights of this material and improved production technologies delivered products that made good on the hallmark characteristics of the graphite: lighter weight, greater strength, and better sensitivity.

The tensile modulus of graphite runs from four to eight times that of fiberglass. Thus, a graphite rod intended for the same type of fishing as one made of fiberglass can have thinner walls and a more slender configuration. The net result in properly designed products is a significant savings in the weight of the finished rod, an improvement in strength, and an improved ability to feel lures or bait working and to detect strikes.

Some confusion has arisen over the modulus (a measure of how effectively a material resists deformation) of graphite available, the generations of graphite that have evolved, and the content of graphite in some fishing rods. However, the most important issue is not so much the material as it is the design of the fishing rod. Even with graphite material, only a well-designed rod can achieve the performance that is necessary for specific angling applications. That performance entails obtaining accuracy, achieving distance, and having maximum sensitivity—all of this with the least amount of effort by the angler. Graphite rods can do this better than any other when properly designed.
See: Rod, Fishing.

GRAPH RECORDER
See: Sonar.

GRASS
See: Aquatic Plants; Seagrass.

ARCTIC GRAYLING *Thymallus arcticus.*
EUROPEAN GRAYLING *Thymallus thymallus.*
Other names for the Arctic grayling—American grayling, arctic trout, Back's grayling, bluefish, grayling, sailfin arctic grayling; French: *ombre artique, poisson bleu.*
Other names for the European grayling—grayling; Danish: *stalling;* Dutch: *vlagzalm;* Finnish: *harjus;* French: *ombre commun;* German: *asch;* Italian: *temolo;* Norwegian and Swedish: *harr;* Russian: *kharius.*

Grayling belong to the Salmonidae family and are

Arctic Grayling

Grayling, Arctic and European

European Grayling

related to trout and whitefish. They are distinctive-looking fish with a sail-like dorsal fin, and a superb sportfish known primarily in the cool- and coldwater northern regions of North America and Europe. Their firm, white flesh is good table fare, although it is not on a par with that of the wild trout and charr that inhabit similar ranges. Grayling are excellent when smoked, however.

Identification. With their graceful lines, large fin, and dramatic coloration, grayling are striking fish. Most striking is their large purple to black dorsal fin, which extends backward and fans out into a trailing lobe, speckled with rows of spots. This fin may look bluish when the fish is in the water. Grayish silver overall, grayling usually have shades or highlights of gold and/or lavender, as well as many dark spots that may be shaped like an X or a V on some fish.

Young arctic grayling can be distinguished from similar-looking young whitefish by narrow vertical parr marks (whitefish have round parr marks, if any). When the arctic grayling is taken from the water, a resemblance to the whitefish is especially apparent, as the beautiful colors fade to a dull gray. It has a small, narrow mouth with numerous small teeth in both jaws. The arctic grayling also has a forked caudal fin and relatively large, stiff scales.

Size. A small fish, with maximum lengths to 30 inches, grayling can reach a maximum weight of about 6 pounds. The all-tackle world record for arctic grayling is a 5-pound, 15-ounce fish from the Northwest Territories in Canada, but any arctic grayling exceeding 3 pounds is considered large, and a 4-pounder is a trophy. European grayling tend to run smaller.

Distribution. Arctic grayling are widespread in arctic drainages from Hudson Bay to Alaska and throughout central Alberta and British Colombia, as well as in the upper Missouri River drainage in Montana. Previously known to inhabit some of the rivers feeding Lakes Huron, Michigan, and Superior in northern Michigan, arctic grayling have been considered extinct there since 1936. They have been widely introduced elsewhere, especially in the western United States.

European grayling occur in northern Europe from England and France to the Ural Mountains in northwest Russia.

Habitat. Grayling prefer the clear, cold, well-oxygenated waters of medium to large rivers and lakes. They are most commonly found in rivers, especially in eddies, and the head of runs and pools; in lakes they prefer river mouths and rocky shorelines. They commonly seek refuge among small rocks on the streambed or lake bottom.

Life history/Behavior. Adult grayling spawn from April through June in rocky creeks; fish from lakes enter tributaries to spawn. Instead of making nests, they scatter their eggs over gravel and rely on the action of the water to cover the eggs with a protective coating. The eggs hatch in 13 to 18 days. Grayling are gregarious and flourish in schools of moderate numbers of their own kind. Arctic grayling of northern Canada may be especially abundant in selected areas of rivers.

Food and feeding habits. Young grayling initially feed on zooplankton and become mainly insectivorous as adults, although they also eat small fish, fish eggs, and, less often, lemmings and planktonic crustaceans.

Angling. European grayling are a bit more accessible than their North American counterparts, which primarily inhabit remote and difficult-to-access areas; for this reason, arctic grayling are not known to many North American anglers and are seldom the primary quarry of distant traveling anglers. They do serve as a desirable secondary attraction to anglers primarily seeking lake trout, walleye, northern pike, or charr. Arctic grayling, however, have saved the day for more than one traveling angler who found the main quarry unavailable or uncooperative. Outfitted with a light spinning rod or a fly rod, these anglers could take advantage of the 1- to 2-pound feisty grayling that were available, more likely than not feeding in the evening on the surface.

Most grayling are in the 1- to $1\frac{1}{2}$-pound class, although some waters are noted for fish that are larger in average size than elsewhere. They are routinely found in groups and feed heavily on aquatic insects in all stages of development. Grayling are most commonly observed in flowages while dimpling the water and feeding on surface insects,

A tall, spotted dorsal fin is characteristic of grayling.

which in North America are usually mosquitoes; they often do this very daintily, but occasionally feed dramatically by clearing the surface and coming down on the insect.

Primarily caught by fly anglers, grayling provide challenge and thrill. Dry fly fishing with 5- to 7-weight lines is the preferred method. When not rising freely to insects, grayling may be better pursued with a wet fly or nymph. A floating fly line is best most of the time, but a sink-tip line may be necessary. Grayling can be leader shy, and they pursue flies and often strike at the end of a drift, so attention to detail can be important. Fly size ranges from No. 12 through 18, and the favored offering is skimpy and dark. Exact representations aren't usually critical, but using a black or brown pattern is important.

The grayling is an excellent catch on light or ultralight spinning tackle, too, using 2- through 6-pound-test line. Small spinners and spoons are popular, but the best artificial is a small, dark jig. Black or brown marabou or $1/16$- to $1/8$-ounce soft plastic jigs produce especially well in flowing and stillwater.

Although most grayling are caught in the slick water of rivers and streams, and sometimes where it flows quite fast, they are also found in lakes near river inlets, usually along shores studded with small rocks. There, in calm water, they cruise along inhaling surface insects, and are taken on flies, jigs, or spinners.

Grayling have small mouths, so many fish that strike are lost. These are scrappy, feisty fish that jump and fight to the end, but they must be handled gently, as they die quickly when held out of the water or if mishandled. Grayling bleed easily and profusely, and unfortunately squirm and wiggle all the time, making it difficult to unhook them in the water and even harder to grasp them. Barbless hooks are especially useful for grayling fishing, not only for unhooking them easily, but also because these fish are sometimes caught with great abundance in areas where they are active.

GRAYSBY *Cephalopholis cruentata*.
Other names—Spanish: *enjambre, cherna enjambre, cuna cabrilla*.

A member of the grouper/seabass family, the graysby is a small, secretive reef fish. Graysby are commonly caught on hook and line but their small sides precludes them from being particularly sought after.

Identification. Varying from pale gray to dark brown, the graysby has many darker orangish, red brown spots on its body, fins, and chin. There are three to five distinctive marks, like pale or dark spots, that run along the base of the dorsal fin. A white line runs between the eyes from the nape to the lower lip. The spots change color, either growing pale or darkening in contrast with the body. The tail of the graysby is more rounded than it is in similar species. There are 9 spines and 14 rays in the soft dorsal fin, compared to 15 to 17 rays in the closely related coney.

Graysby

Size. The graysby generally grows to a length of 6 to 10 inches and can reach a maximum of 1 foot.

Distribution. Graysby range from North Carolina to the northern Gulf of Mexico and south to Brazil. They are common in southern Florida, the Bahamas, and the Caribbean and are also found in Bermuda.

Habitat. Small ledges and caves in coral beds and reefs are the preferred haunts of graysby, where they blend with the surroundings at depths between 10 and 60 feet.

Food. Graysby are nocturnal predators, feeding mainly on fish.

GREASED-LINE FISHING
Fishing a wet fly close to the surface and at a uniform swim speed diagonally down and across fast water in a stream. The term was used early in the twentieth century and is derived from the fat that was applied to the line to help float it in the pre-silicone era. Mending *(see)* the line is necessary to achieve the right presentation, especially if there are conflicting current speeds, and a high-floating fly line helps achieve this.

GREAT BRITAIN
See: England; Scotland; Wales.

GREEN FISH
A fish brought to the angler so quickly that it is very vigorous, often thrashing about wildly as the angler attempts to land it. Although it is advantageous to unhook and free fish that will not be kept for personal use, landing some fish, because of their nature or size, before they are tired out can be harmful to the fish, and also dangerous to the angler or other person landing it.
See: Catch-and-Release.

GREENLAND
The largest island in the world, Greenland lies northeast of North America and is a self-governing part of Denmark situated between the North

Atlantic and Arctic Oceans. Most of this country's nearly 2.2 million square kilometers is north of the Arctic Circle, and 85 percent—the interior plateau—is permanently covered with ice. This plateau is drained by ice fiords, which contribute to the numerous icebergs along its coast. Although reached by air from international locations, Greenland itself has no interior road network and thus requires domestic transport by air and boat. Its population of 55,000, mostly Inuit, has long been dependent on fishing, particularly for shrimp, salmon, charr, halibut, and cod.

In freshwater, sea-run and resident arctic charr are found in lakes, rivers, and streams on both coasts. Inland, because natives net fish, the size of charr increases as distance from settlements increases. Most fish range up to 1.5 kilograms. In remote rivers, 2- to 5-kilogram charr occur. Some of the largest fish inhabit Greenland's glacial rivers, and among these one of the best is the Robinson River. Arctic charr also favor river mouths and coastal waters.

Only one Greenland river, the Kapisigdlit, which runs through the bottom of Nuuk Fiord, has a temperature suited for Atlantic salmon. It features small fish that range from 2 to 4 kilograms. The waters off Greenland, however, are critical grounds for salmon that migrate here from their natal North American and European waters. As late as 1956 the first tagged salmon—a smolt marked in Scotland—was captured in a net off west Greenland; only then was it understood where Atlantic salmon migrated after leaving the rivers of their birth. Both commercial and subsistence netting for salmon in Greenland waters, by Greenlanders as well as non-Greenlanders, partially contributed to the collapse of Atlantic salmon populations. By the late 1990s, fishing quotas (established by international agreement) were the lowest they had ever been. Thus, although there is no sportfishery here for Atlantic salmon, the waters off Greenland are critical to the fishery, not only in terms of population but also for salmon fishing opportunities elsewhere.

Relatively unexplored but good potential for sharks, cod, skate, wolffish, and halibut exists offshore, although these species are not likely to attract visiting anglers. The adventurous and hardy have pursued fish from the ocean ice, the most extreme catch being large specimens of Greenland sharks caught on big-game tackle.

GRILSE
A salmon, usually male, that returns to freshwater rivers after one year at sea. These are small fish, generally weighing from 2 to 4 pounds.
See: Salmon, Atlantic.

GRIP
The part or parts of a fishing rod held by the angler and a major component of the handle. The grip consists of a foregrip, which is not found on some rods (usually light models) but is situated ahead of the reel and used for gripping the rod with the hand that is not turning the reel handle, and the rear grip, which is the section usually held by the angler and which incorporates the reel seat.
See: Rod, Fishing.

GROIN
A man-made structure, usually of concrete or stone, projecting into the water from the shore to protect a sandy beach from erosion. Groins usually exist in a series of parallel structures along a beach and are commonly referred to as jetties *(see)*. They may be constructed of wood and stone, or all stone, and form a perpendicular wall-like extension into the water. They are primarily found in saltwater along the coasts and are intended to prevent erosion by stabilizing the sand in the immediate vicinity. Groins do not usually have navigational aids, but they may be common beach fishing locations.
See: Jetty Fishing; Surf Fishing.

GROUNDBAIT
A chumming preparation made from crushed bread crumbs or stale bread that is soaked, mixed into a paste, and stiffened with bran or cornmeal. These items are made into balls and tossed into the water, clouding and flavoring it. "Groundbait" is a European term and an innovation primarily used in carp fishing.
See: Carp; Chumming.

GROUNDFISH
A species or group of fish that lives most of its life on or near the seabed. The term may be used synonymously with demersal. Groundfish refers to Atlantic cod, haddock, pollock, American plaice, white hake, redfish, and various flounders.

GROUPER
Grouper are members of the Serranidae family of sea bass *(see)*. Most are nonschooling species that generally congregate in the same area. Dozens of species inhabit all warm seas, preferring rocky shores and deep reefs. Grouper in general are good to eat and are a frequent catch of anglers.
See: Coney; Gag; Graysby; Grouper, Black; Grouper, Nassau; Grouper, Red; Grouper, Spotted Coral; Grouper, Warsaw; Grouper, Yellowfin; Hind, Red; Hind, Rock; Jewfish; Wreckfish.

GROUPER, BLACK *Mycteroperca bonaci*.
Other names—rockfish; Portuguese: *badejo-ferro, badejo-quadrado;* Spanish: *bonaci, cuna bonaci, cuna guarei*.

Black Grouper

The black grouper is a fairly large and hard-fighting member of the Serranidae family. It is an excellent food fish, although the flesh is occasionally toxic and can cause ciguatera *(see)*.

Identification. Depending on location, the black grouper may be olive, gray, or reddish brown to black. It has black, almost rectangular blotches and brassy spots. It can pale or darken until its markings are hardly noticeable. It has a thin, pale border on its pectoral fins, a wide black edge and a thin white margin on its tail, and sometimes a narrow orangish edge to the pectoral fin; the tips of the tail and the soft dorsal and anal fins are bluish or black. The black grouper has a squared-off tail and a gently rounded gill cover.

Size. Regularly reaching 40 pounds, black grouper can grow to more than 100 pounds; the all-tackle world record is shared by two 114-pound fish, one from Texas and the other from Florida. The average length of the black grouper is 1½ to 3 feet; the maximum is 4 feet.

Distribution. Black grouper occur from Bermuda and Massachusetts to southern Brazil, including the southern Gulf of Mexico, and occur commonly to occasionally in the Florida Keys, the Bahamas, Cuba, and throughout the Caribbean. Adults are unknown on the northeastern coast of the United States.

Habitat. Black grouper are found away from shore near rocky and coral reefs and dropoff walls in water more than 60 feet deep. Although black grouper typically drift just above the bottom, young fish may inhabit shallow water inshore, and adults occasionally frequent open water far above reefs.

Life history/Behavior. Black grouper spawn between May and August. As in many species of grouper, the young start out predominantly female, transforming into males as they grow larger.

Food and feeding habits. Adult black grouper feed mainly on fish and sometimes squid, and juveniles feed mainly on crustaceans.

Angling. Like other grouper, the black grouper is primarily caught by fishing at the right depth over an irregular bottom.

See: Grouper; Inshore Fishing.

GROUPER, NASSAU *Epinephelus striatus*.
Other names—hamlet; Creole: *negue*; French: *mérou rayé*; Spanish: *cherna criolla, mero gallina*.

The most important commercial grouper in the West Indies and a member of the Serranidae family, the Nassau grouper has been very heavily fished and is continually vulnerable to overfishing, especially during its spawning and migrating seasons.

Identification. Although its color pattern varies, the Nassau grouper usually has a light background with a wide, dark brown stripe running from the tip of the snout through the eye to the start of the dorsal fin, as well as four to five irregular dark bars running vertically along the sides. Two distinctive features are the black dots always present around the eye, and a large black saddle on the caudal peduncle, also always present no matter what color the fish is. The third spine of the dorsal fin is longer than the second, the pelvic fins are shorter than the pectoral fins, and the dorsal fin is notched between the spines. It has the ability to change color, from pale to almost black.

Size. The Nassau grouper is usually 1 to 2 feet in length, reaching a maximum of 4 feet and about 55 pounds, although most catches are under 10 pounds. The all-tackle world record is a 38-pound, 8-ounce Bahamian fish.

Nassau Grouper

Distribution. In the western Atlantic, Nassau grouper are found in Bermuda, Florida, the Bahamas, the Yucatán Peninsula, and throughout the Caribbean to southern Brazil. They are absent from the Gulf of Mexico, except at Campeche Back off the coast of Yucatán, at Tortugas, and off Key West. Once abundant throughout their range, their numbers have been greatly reduced by spearfishing.

Habitat. Found in depths of 20 to 100 feet, although almost always dwelling in less than 90 feet of water, Nassau grouper prefer caves and shallow to midrange coral reefs. Smaller fish are usually closer to shore and common in seagrass beds, whereas adults are usually farther offshore on rocky reefs. Nassau grouper tend to rest on the bottom, blending with their surroundings. They are usually solitary and diurnal but occasionally form schools, as they do when spawning.

Spawning behavior. Spawning around the new moon, Nassau grouper come together in large masses of up to 30,000, making them highly vulnerable to overharvesting.

Food. Nassau grouper feed mainly on fish and crabs and to a lesser degree on other crustaceans and mollusks.

Angling. Like other grouper, the Nassau grouper is primarily caught by fishing at the right depth over an irregular bottom.

See: Grouper; Inshore Fishing.

GROUPER, RED *Epinephelus morio.*

Other names—grouper; Portuguese: *garoupa de Sao Tomé;* Spanish: *cherna americana, cherna de vivero, mero americano, mero paracamo.*

The red grouper was one of the most abundant grouper in the Caribbean and surrounding waters until spearfishing and general overfishing depleted its numbers. This member of the Serranidae family has firm, white meat and is marketed fresh and frozen, although it is susceptible to toxins.

Identification. Of varying coloration, the red grouper is usually dark brownish red, especially around the mouth, and may have dark bars and blotches similar to those on the Nassau grouper, as well as a few, small whitish blotches scattered in an irregular pattern. It is distinguished from the Nassau grouper by its lack of a saddle spot and its smooth, straight front dorsal fin. On the Nassau grouper the dorsal fin is notched. It has a blackish tinge to the soft dorsal, anal, and tail fins; pale bluish margins on the rear dorsal, anal, and tail fins; and small black spots around the eye. The lining of the mouth is scarlet to orange. The second spine of the dorsal fin is longer than the others, the pectoral fins are longer than the pelvic fins, and the tail is distinctively squared off. The red grouper pales or darkens in accordance with its surroundings.

Size/Age. The red grouper is commonly 1 to 2 feet long and weighs up to 15 pounds, although it can reach $3^1/_2$ feet and 50 pounds. The male red grouper lives longer than the female and has been known to live for 25 years.

Distribution. In the western Atlantic, red grouper range from North Carolina to southern Brazil, including the Gulf of Mexico, the Caribbean, and Bermuda; some fish stray as far as Massachusetts. They are found only occasionally in Florida and the Bahamas and rarely in the Caribbean, a result of the large reduction in their population.

Habitat. Red grouper are a bottom-dwelling fish, occurring over rocky and muddy bottoms, at the margins of seagrass beds, and in ledges, crevices, and caverns of rocky limestone reefs; they are uncommon around coral reefs, where they have been replaced for the most part by Nassau grouper. They prefer depths of 6 to 400 feet, although they more commonly hold between 80 and 400 feet. Younger fish (from one to six years old) usually stay closer to shore than do older juveniles and adults. Red grouper are usually solitary, resting on the bottom and blending with their surroundings.

Life history/Behavior. Like many other grouper, red grouper undergo a sex reversal: The females transform into males, in this case between ages 7 and 14, or when they are 18 to 26 inches long. Although some females can reproduce for the first time as early as age 4, all fish can reproduce by age 7. Spawning takes place from March through July, with a flurry of activity in April and May, in water temperatures ranging from 63° to 77°F and in depths between 80 and 300 feet. The eggs are pelagic and can number 300,000 to 5.7 million, depending on the size of the fish; larvae settle to the bottom after remaining on the surface for 30 to 40 days.

Food and feeding habits. Red grouper feed on a wide variety of fish, invertebrates, and crustaceans, including squid, crabs, shrimp, lobsters, and octopus. They usually ambush their prey and swallow it whole.

Angling. Like other grouper, the red is primarily caught by fishing at the right depth over an irregular bottom.

See: Grouper; Inshore Fishing.

GROUPER, SPOTTED CORAL *Plectropomus maculatus.*

Other names—coral trout (widely used in Australia),

Red Grouper

coastal trout, island trout, bar-cheeked trout, bluespot trout, common coral trout, coral cod, leopard trout; Arabic: *hamour;* Japanese: *siji-hata;* Malay: *jin hou, kerapu.*

A very beautiful fish and a member of the Serranidae family of grouper, the spotted coral grouper is also a superb table fish that is eagerly sought by anglers and fished for commercially. Large specimens (exceeding 7 to 8 kilograms) are suspected of harboring the toxin ciguatera *(see).* Smaller (4 to 5 kilograms) members appear not to carry this toxin.

Identification. The spotted coral grouper is strikingly colored and has a remarkable range of coloration. Deep-water specimens are a bright scarlet with round, bright-blue circular spots on the head and body. This coloration can change to pink with blue spots in fish that inhabit shallower waters, or the fish can be grayish, and barred or blotched.

This grouper has a strong, solid, compressed body with a slightly concave caudal fin, a large mouth, large teeth, and a spinous dorsal fin with 8 spines and 11 soft rays. The preoperculum carries three large spines on its lower edge.

Size. Although known to grow to 21 kilograms, the average fish taken by Australian anglers weighs between 2 and 5 kilograms; an Australian record stands at 11 kilograms.

Distribution. The spotted coral grouper occurs in the western Pacific in Thailand, Singapore, the Philippines, Indonesia, Papua New Guinea, the Arafura Sea, the Solomon Islands, and Australia. Known as coral trout in Australia, this fish and other related grouper inhabit semitropical and tropical waters from central Western Australia to central Queensland.

Habitat. Inhabiting both inshore and offshore reefs, these fish usually prefer shallow water to a depth of 100 meters. Within the reef environment, they dwell in caves and roam from reef to reef to forage.

Life history/Behavior. Spawning takes place during the spring and summer, coinciding with the new moon and a water temperature of 25° to 26°C. The eggs float just below the surface, and when the larvae hatch out they grow rapidly until about three years of age. Individual adults are hermaphroditic, starting off as females and then becoming males.

Food and feeding habits. Adults live mainly on fish such as herring and anchovies; juveniles feed on small fish, crustaceans, and squid. They will take pieces of tuna, mackerel, and mullet, as well as squid and prawns.

Angling. Most angling for spotted coral grouper is a daytime project. Because fish dwell mainly in reef habitat, anglers use heavy tackle. Whether your preference is bait or lure fishing, and spinning or conventional tackle, the minimum line requirements begin at 7 kilograms and range up to 15 kilograms. Rods are built to match. Handlines, which are popular, are even heavier (to 40 kilograms).

Natural bait anglers fishing from anchored boats use 6/0 to 8/0 extra-strong hooks. These are fished just above the bottom and require only the weight sufficient to take the baits down to that level. Jigging the bait will also attract the fish and encourage strikes. The spotted coral grouper is a strong fish that tries to return to the sanctuary of the reef when hooked. The angler must prevent this with a tough initial response; once the fish has been wrestled to a higher plane in the water column, it can then be played more gently until brought to the boat.

Anglers also use surface poppers, minnow-type lures, leadhead jigs, and spoons, which they either cast or troll. Because lure loss can be high due to the strength of the fish and the coral reefs in which they live, many anglers make their own and find them just as effective as expensive commercially produced lures.

Trollers usually work along the edges of the reefs, offering spoons or saltwater flies. Heavy lines to 40-kilogram strength are necessary so that the hooked fish's instant diving response can be checked, thus avoiding cutoff on the reef.

See: Grouper; Inshore Fishing.

GROUPER, WARSAW *Epinephelus nigritus.*
Other names—Spanish: *mero de lo alto, mero negro.*

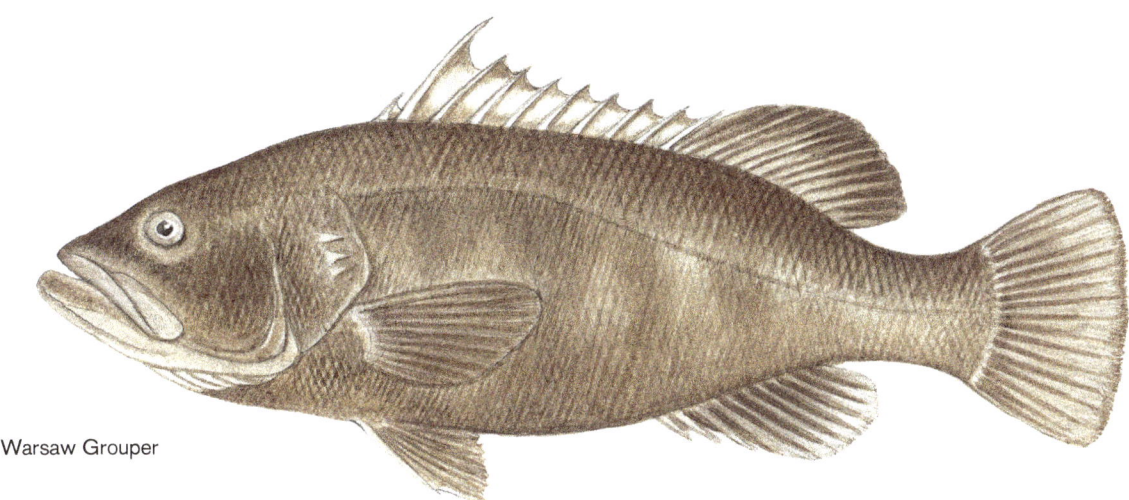

Warsaw Grouper

The warsaw grouper is one of the largest members of the Serranidae family of grouper and sea bass, second only to the jewfish *(see)* in size. It has white, flaky meat that is marketed fresh. It is more widespread than the jewfish and caught more frequently.

Identification. The warsaw grouper has a gray brown or dark red brown body, occasionally irregularly spotted with several small, white blotches on the sides and the dorsal fins, although these are indiscernible in death. The young warsaw has a yellow tail and a dark saddle on the caudal peduncle. The warsaw is distinctive as the only grouper with 10 dorsal spines, the second of which is much longer than the third. It also has a squared-off tail. In contrast to the jewfish, the rays of the first dorsal fin on the warsaw grouper are much higher and the head is much larger.

Size/Age. The average weight of the warsaw grouper is roughly 20 pounds or less, although 100-pound fish are not uncommon. It can reach a length of $6^{1}/_{2}$ feet and can weigh up to 580 pounds. The all-tackle world record is a 436-pound, 12-ounce Florida fish. The warsaw grouper grows slowly and can live as long as 25 to 30 years.

Distribution. In the western Atlantic, warsaw grouper range from Massachusetts to the Gulf of Mexico, and south to Río de Janeiro in Brazil, although they are rare in Cuba, Haiti, and Trinidad. They are otherwise fairly common along both coasts of Florida.

Habitat. Usually found over rough, rocky bottom, deep rocky ledges, and dropoffs, warsaw grouper prefer depths of 300 to 1,000 feet. Young warsaw grouper are occasionally seen or caught near jetties and shallow-water reefs.

Spawning behavior. The eggs and larvae of the warsaw grouper are thought to be pelagic, although little else is known about spawning and other behavior.

Food and feeding habits. Warsaw grouper feed on crabs, shrimp, lobsters, and fish, swallowing prey whole after ambushing it or after a short chase.

Angling. Heavy tackle is necessary when deep fishing for this species, not only because of the size of the fish but also because they have a habit of taking bait into rocky hideaways and the angler needs to muscle them away. Wire leaders are essential. Preferred baits are whole squid, cut amberjack, or a live red porgy or vermilion snapper. Warsaw grouper usually bite a free-spooled or slack line best. Like other grouper, the warsaw is primarily caught by fishing at the right depth over an irregular bottom.
See: Grouper; Inshore Fishing.

GROUPER, YELLOWFIN
Mycteroperca venenosa.
Other names—princess rockfish, red rockfish; Spanish: *arigua, bonaci cardenal, cuna cucaracha, cuna de piedra.*

The scientific name of this member of the Serranidae family means "venomous," a reference to the yellowfin grouper's association with ciguatera poisoning. Despite this, its flesh is good to eat and is usually considered safe for commercial sale.

Identification. The yellowfin grouper has highly variable coloring, usually with a pale background and horizontal rows of darker, rectangular blotches covering the entire fish; the ends of these blotches are rounded, and they can be black, gray, brown, olive green, or red. There are also small dark spots running across the body, which grow smaller toward the belly and usually appear bright red. The outer third of the pectoral fins are bright yellow, whereas the tail has a thin, dark, irregular edge. An overall reddish cast is present in fish from deep water, and the yellowfin grouper has the ability to change color dramatically, or to pale or darken.

Size. The yellowfin grouper is common to 20 pounds in weight and 3 feet in length; the all-tackle world record is a 40-pound, 12-ounce Texas fish caught in 1995.

Distribution. Found in the western Atlantic, the yellowfin grouper is most common in Bermuda, Florida, and the southern Gulf of Mexico, and ranges to Brazil.

Habitat. Young yellowfin grouper prefer shallow turtlegrass beds, and adults occur on offshore rocky and coral reefs. They also hold over mud bottoms in the northern Gulf of Mexico.

Life history. As with other grouper, the yellowfin undergoes a sex reversal, transforming from female to male in the latter part of life.

Food. Yellowfin grouper feed mostly on coral reef species of fish and squid.

Angling. Like other grouper, the yellowfin is primarily caught by bottom fishing at the right depth over irregular structure, although some anglers land it by surface trolling.
See: Grouper; Inshore Fishing.

GRUB
The larva of an insect, especially a beetle, used to tip the hook of a small ice fishing jig or placed on a small-bait hook; also, a term for a small- to medium-size soft body on a jig hook.
See: Jig; Maggot.

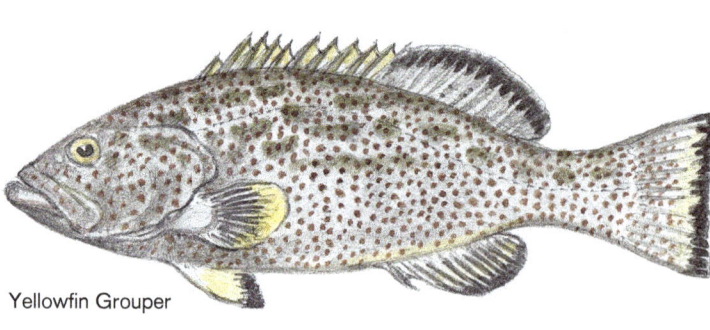
Yellowfin Grouper

GRUNION, CALIFORNIA *Leuresthes tenuis.*
Other names—smelt, little smelt, grunion, lease smelt.

The California grunion is a member of the Atherinidae family of fish known as silversides *(see)*. It is an important forage species for predator fish; in season, large numbers of anglers gather on the beaches to fill buckets with grunion undergoing a remarkable spawning ritual in the sand.

Identification. The California grunion has an elongate body and head that are more or less compressed. The mouth is small, and the scales are small, smooth, and firm. Its coloration is bluish green above and silvery below; a bright silvery band tinged with blue and bordered above with violet extends the length of the body.

Size/Age. The maximum known size of grunion is $7^1/_2$ inches; a 7-inch female full of eggs weighed less than 2 ounces. The life span is usually three years, with some individuals surviving four years.

Distribution. The California grunion occurs from Magdalena Bay, Baja California, to San Francisco; however, the principal range is between Point Abreojos, Baja California, and Point Conception, California. A similar species, the gulf grunion *(L. sardina)*, is restricted to the Gulf of California.

Habitat. California grunion are nonmigratory and are most often found in schools a short distance from shore in water 15 to 40 feet deep.

Life history/Behavior. The most rapid growth takes place during the first year, at the end of which they are 5 inches long and capable of spawning. The spawning behavior of grunion is one of the more unusual among all marine fish. They are the only California fish known to strand themselves on the beach to deposit their reproductive products in the moist sand.

Females, accompanied by one to eight males, swim onto the beach with an incoming wave, dig themselves into the sand up to their pectoral fins, and lay their eggs. The males wrap themselves around the female and fertilize the eggs. With the next wave, the fish return to the sea. Thus, the spawning process is effected in the short period of time between waves. During spawning activities, grunion may make a faint squeaking noise. Most females spawn from four to eight times a year, producing up to 3,000 eggs every two weeks, and thousands of the fish may be along the beach at a time.

Spawning takes place from early March through September, and then only for three or four nights following the full moon, during the one to four hours immediately after high tide.

Food. The feeding habits of this species are not well known; however, they subsist on small crustaceans and fish eggs.

Angling. California grunion may be taken only by hand. No gear of any kind may be used, and no holes may be dug in the beach. The season is closed in April and May, although these are good months to observe spawning activities.

White Margate

GRUNT

Several hundred species of grunt exist in warm seas throughout the world. The name "grunt" is derived from the grunting noises these fish make by grinding their pharyngeal teeth, the sounds amplified by the taut swim bladder that serves as a resonator. Their pharyngeal teeth are well developed; the jaw teeth are weak. This dentition distinguishes them from snapper, which they resemble in body form.

Most grunts are deep-bodied fish that range from 6 to 10 inches in length, although a few grow larger. They typically travel in schools. Many grunts have the habit of "kissing" others of their kind, the fish coming face to face, pressing their open mouths together, and then pushing against each other.

Grunts are bottom feeders and are viewed as saltwater panfish. Anglers catch them on light tackle, using shrimp, cut pieces of fish, or other natural baits, or, occasionally, artificials like small jigs and flies. They are typically caught around reefs, where they travel in small or extensive schools, and provide important forage for larger predators. Divers frequently encounter grunts on tropical reefs.

Most of these fish are sensitive to the feel of a line and may also bite lightly, so bait rigs are generally prepared with lead weights that carry the bait or lure to the bottom but permit the line to run freely through the weight. Anglers typically jerk the bait or lure to give it a slight motion, which attracts the fish. Most grunts are good to eat, but they may be ignored by anglers because of their small size; no concerted sportfishing effort is directed at these fish.

Common grunt species encountered by anglers include French grunt *(see: grunt, French)*, white grunt *(see: grunt, white)*, bluestriped grunt *(see: grunt, bluestriped)*, pigfish *(see)*, tomtate *(see)*, and sargo *(see)*.

Other species that may be caught occasionally are various margates. The white margate *(Haemulon album)* is pearl gray, with two or three black bands running the length of its body. The most prominent of these extends from the snout through the eye to the tail. Although most individuals weigh less than a pound, the white margate can grow quite large, and may be found farther offshore than are

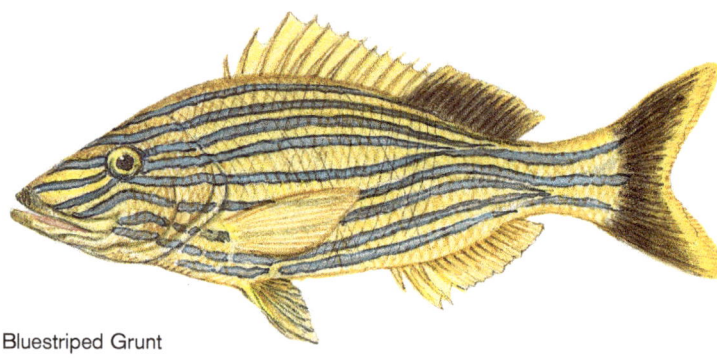

Bluestriped Grunt

other grunts. The all-tackle world record for the species is a fish that was caught in Belize in 1996 and weighed 15 pounds, 12 ounces.

One of the most striking of all grunts is the black margate *(Anisotremus surinamensis)*, which averages only about a pound but can grow much larger. A deep-bodied fish with a small mouth and thick lips, it is silvery gray, the fins bordered or edged with black. A broad light band extends obliquely up the body behind the pectoral fins. The inside of the mouth is white.

The closely related Atlantic porkfish *(Anisotremus virginicus)* is a common inshore species that attains a weight of 2 pounds but averages only 4 ounces. It is distinguished by two black bars on the front of the body, one from the top of the head through the eye to the rear angle of the upper jaw and the other from the base of the spiny dorsal to the base of the pectoral fin. Behind this bar, the body is striped horizontally with blue and yellow. Its Pacific cousin is the Panamic porkfish *(Anisotremus taeniatus)*, which ranges from Baja California to Ecuador and is especially common off Cabo San Lucas. It is extremely similar in appearance to the Atlantic porkfish but grows to just 12 inches.

GRUNT, BLUESTRIPED *Haemulon sciurus.*
Other names—Spanish: *ronco catire*.

Frequently used as an aquarium fish when young because of its magnificent coloring, the bluestriped grunt is also considered an excellent table fish and is easily caught on natural baits.

Identification. The bluestriped grunt is distinguished from all other grunts by its color pattern of continuous blue horizontal stripes over a yellow gold body. The tail and dorsal fins are dark and dusky with a yellow tinge. Other fins are yellow. The inside of its mouth is blood red. It has 12 dorsal spines, 16 to 17 dorsal rays, and 9 anal rays.

Size. Its average length is up to 1 foot, but it can reach as much as 18 inches in length.

Distribution. It is common from southern Florida through the Caribbean to the West Indies and southward along the Gulf of Mexico and along the coast of Central and South America to Brazil.

Habitat. The bluestriped grunt drifts along reefs, especially near the deep edges. It remains relatively close to the shore in shallow water from 12 to 50 feet deep. Juveniles are found in seagrass beds in bays, lagoons, and coastal waters.

Behavior. A schooling fish, the bluestriped grunt gathers in medium-size groups along reefs during the day. Scaring easily, the grunt will swim away quickly when slightly startled.

Feeding habits. Adults feed on the bottom at night over open sandy, muddy, or grassy areas, primarily foraging on crustaceans. They also consume bivalves and occasionally small fish.

Angling. See: Grunt.

GRUNT, FRENCH *Haemulon flavolineatum.*
Other names—Spanish: *ronco amarillo*.

The French grunt is one of the most abundant panfish in southern Florida. These and other grunts often make up the largest biomass on reefs in continental shelf areas. Although it is too small to be of commercial value, the French grunt is an excellent panfish. It is also a common aquarium fish.

Identification. Its coloring is white to bluish or yellowish with bright-yellow stripes. The stripes set below the lateral line are diagonal. There are yellow spots on the bottom of the head. The fins are yellow, and the inside of the mouth is blood red. It has 14 to 15 dorsal rays, 8 anal rays, and 16 to 17 pectoral rays.

Size. The average length is 6 to 10 inches, although this fish can reach 12 inches.

Distribution. The French grunt is abundant in Florida, the Bahamas, and the Caribbean. It also inhabits the waters of South Carolina, Bermuda, and the Gulf of Mexico, and south to Brazil.

Habitat. Preferring shallower water close to shore, the French grunt inhabits coastlines and deeper coral reefs in depths from 12 to 60 feet. Grunt populations are less prominent around islands lacking large expanses of grassbeds and sand flats.

Behavior. The French grunt is a schooling fish, drifting in small to large groups that can number in the thousands. The schools travel in shadows during the day. Juveniles hide in grassbeds in bays, lagoons, and coastal waters.

Feeding habits. French grunts are nocturnal bottom feeders that scavenge sand flats and grass-

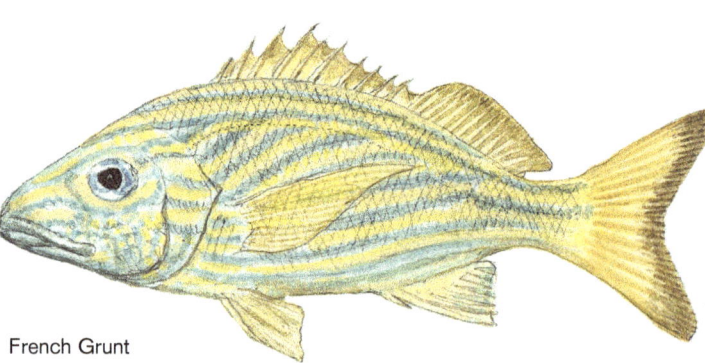

French Grunt

beds near reefs for crustaceans.

Angling. The French grunt is easily caught on the lightest of tackle. It takes natural baits, such as pilchards, cut mullet, and dead shrimp.
See: Grunt.

GRUNT, WHITE *Haemulon plumieri*.
Other names—redmouth; Spanish: *ronco margariteño*.

The white grunt is a wide-ranging and abundant fish. This and other grunts often make up the largest biomass on reefs in continental shelf areas. The white grunt has some commercial value, as it grows to larger sizes than do most other grunts, and it is a tasty panfish that is also commonly used in aquariums.

Identification. One of the more colorful grunts, this fish has a silver gray body with moderate yellow body striping and numerous blue and yellow stripes on its head. The scales may be tipped with bronze and produce a checkered pattern. The inside of the mouth is red. It has 12 dorsal spines and 15 to 17 dorsal rays, 8 to 9 anal rays, and 17 pectoral rays.

Age/Size. The average length and weight is 8 to 14 inches and about a pound, although they can reach 25 inches and weigh 8 pounds. White grunts are reported to live up to 13 years.

Distribution. The white grunt exists in the western Atlantic, from the Chesapeake Bay throughout the Caribbean and Gulf of Mexico south to Brazil. It was reportedly introduced unsuccessfully to Bermuda.

Habitat. White grunts prefer shallower water from nearshore to outer reef areas.

Life history/Behavior. Like other grunts, this species is a schooling fish often found in large groups. Schools travel in shadows during the day and are often located along the edges of reefs and at the base of coral formations. Fish are sexually mature at about 10 inches, and spawning takes place in the southeastern United States in late spring and summer.

Food and feeding habits. White grunts are bottom feeders that root in the sand and bottom matter near reefs. They feed on worms, shrimp, crabs, mollusks, and small fish.

Angling. See: Grunt.

GRUNTER, SOOTY *Hephaestus fuliginosus*.
Other names—black bream, sooty, blubberlips, khaki bream, purple grunter.

A member of the Teraponidae family of grunter and tigerperch, the sooty grunter is a favorite freshwater sportfish among tropical anglers, and, from a recreational fishing viewpoint, is one of the most important of a number of freshwater grunter found in Australia. Despite its poor reputation as a table fish, it is eagerly sought by anglers, who find it a

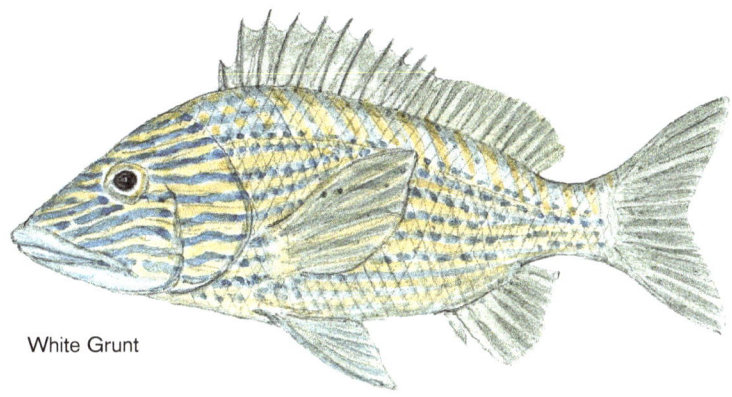
White Grunt

challenge on light tackle. Juveniles are sometimes held in large home aquariums where they will grow rapidly if enough food is available. Dedicated sooty grunter anglers, for study purposes, sometimes keep small specimens in an aquarium environment where their enormous appetite and aggressive nature make them suitable only for the one-species tank. A hardy fish, it is often transported long distances to other streams for stocking purposes. Impoundment stocking is possible, although it will not breed in this situation, nor in aquariums.

Identification. The sooty grunter can be a difficult fish to identify because its members can vary in shape, size, color, and lip size, hence the name "blubberlips." The body is deep and compressed, and color variations appear to be the result of water color. Adults are usually dark brown to blackish purple, but some are a golden color or blotched with patches of brown and gray, or gold on brown, giving the fish a diseased appearance. The single dorsal fin is unnotched, the pectoral fins are gray or gold, and the caudal fin is lightly forked and almost concave. The dorsal fin and height of spine webbing can also differ among specimens.

Size. This species is known to reach a weight of 4 kilograms and a length of 500 millimeters; the average size taken by anglers is about 0.5 kilogram and 250 millimeters. A record specimen of 4.96 kilograms was taken on a lure from Tinaroo Dam in North Queensland.

Distribution. Sooty grunter extend across the tropical north of Australia, from Queensland across the Gulf of Carpentaria to Western Australia. Within these areas they range from tidal freshwa-

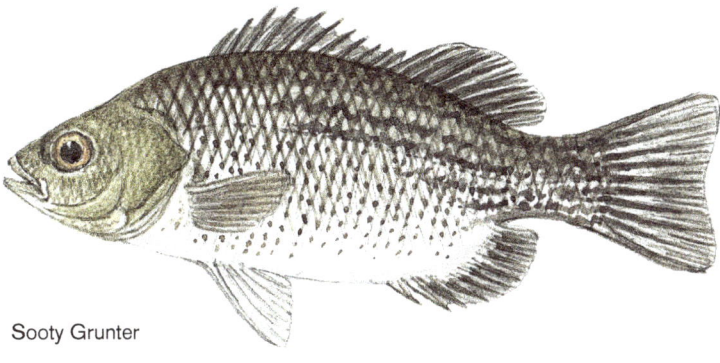
Sooty Grunter

ter to upstream areas, where natural obstructions such as waterfalls prevent their moving farther. Some have been introduced into streams in central Queensland, and they are known to survive in impoundments. They have also been reported in southern Papua New Guinea.

Habitat. Able to survive within a temperature range of 12° to 34°C, the sooty flourishes in clear or turbid streams, whether flowing or nearly still. It tends to live in and close to streamside cover, under the branches of overhanging trees (especially those that drop berries into the water), and can be found among submerged tree branches and other obstructions, as well as around the mouths of creeks flowing into the main stream.

Life history/Behavior. Sooty grunter breed only in streams during the summer months (December through March) when the water temperature exceeds 25°C and there is a stimulating rise in water levels. This usually takes place in or near areas where current flows. The process usually occurs in the afternoon and takes several hours. More than 100,000 eggs may be produced at one time. Carried by the current, they are nonadhesive and sink to the bottom, where they are lodged in gravel crevices. The eggs hatch out after two days, and the juveniles start to feed after four days. Group spawning appears to occur. They are a hardy and aggressive fish, and anglers have found it easy to transport them above waterfalls into areas they could not otherwise reach. Queensland hatcheries have successfully induced spawning with hormone injections.

Food and feeding habits. This species is omnivorous and will feed on shrimp, frogs, small fish, worms, aquatic and terrestrial insects, plant roots, berries that fall from overhanging trees, and algae growing on the bottom of pools. They have an enormous appetite and will eat almost anything, including bread crust, cheese, and red meat.

Angling. Most anglers pursue these fish from canoes or small aluminum dinghies, or, where possible, from the banks of the stream. When fishing from boats in fast-flowing streams, anglers take turns at fishing and maintaining position. On some streams, the angler wades up the middle while casting to cover on either bank. The most popular technique is casting lures with light spinning or baitcasting tackle. Lures range from diving bass plugs to spinners and surface poppers to soft plastics, and are usually worked slowly at a speed that will just bring out the lure's action. Many of these lures are homemade. This strong, aggressive fish attacks a lure with much the same enthusiasm as does the Australian bass (see: bass, Australian), and is a tenacious fighter.

Lures are cast into waters overhung by the branches of trees like the palm tree; the sooty grunter takes the berries readily when they fall into the water. These trees serve to identify likely sooty grunter territories. Lures are also cast to visible underwater structure, and in the vicinity of the mouths of in-flowing tributaries. So eager are sooty grunter to fill their stomachs that two have been known to be taken on one lure.

The fly angler, using a No. 5 or 6 outfit, will find that the sooty grunter eagerly takes Matuka flies, Muddler Minnows, other streamers, fly-rod poppers, and nymphs and dry flies. Bait fishing is sometimes practiced, but it is not as popular. The sooty grunter is not a good table fish, and most are released upon capture—often as many as 40 to 50 a day.

GUAGUANCHE *Sphyraena guachancho*.
Other names—guachanche barracuda; Spanish: *picuda guaguanche;* French: *bécune guachanche*.

A member of the barracuda family, the guaguanche is a long, slender, silvery fish often mistaken for a young great barracuda (see: barracuda, great). There is no concerted sportfishing effort for the species, but they are occasionally caught by anglers.

Identification. Silvery olive brown above, the guaguanche has silvery sides with a yellow to golden stripe running along the middle of its body. Like other members of the barracuda family, it has an elongated body and large canine and shearing teeth. Its caudal fin is large, forked, and blackish, and it has widely separated dorsal fins. The pelvic fin begins below a point just in front of the first dorsal fin, which distinguishes it from the similar-looking sennet. On the young guaguanche, there are three broad bars at the rear of the body that are often interrupted in the middle of the side.

Size. The guaguanche can grow to 2 feet, although it more commonly measures 6 to 14 inches.

Distribution. Found occasionally in Florida, the Bahamas, and the Caribbean, guaguanche occur from Massachusetts to the northern Gulf of Mexico and south to Brazil. In the eastern Atlantic, they exist in Senegal, Guinea, Sierra Leone, Côte d'Ivoire, Ghana, Togo, Benin, Nigeria, Cape Verde, Angola, and the Canary Islands.

Habitat. Guaguanche inhabit shallow and generally turbid coastal waters, including sand flats, grassbeds, mud bottoms, bays, and estuaries, although they are rare around reefs. They are a schooling species, forming schools at depths from 3 to 40 feet, and can be found near the surface at night.

Food. Guaguanche feed on fish and shrimp.

GUAM
An unincorporated territory of the United States, Guam is the largest and southernmost of the 15-island Mariana archipelago in the North Pacific

Guaguanche

Ocean. Roughly 1,500 miles from Japan and the Philippines, and 1,100 miles from New Guinea, this 30-mile-long island was formed millions of years ago when a pair of volcanoes sank beneath the ocean, leaving only their twin peaks above sea level. Nearby is the Mariana Trench, the deepest ocean trench in the world; there, Mount Humuyong Manglo, the highest mountain in the world, rises more than 7 miles from the ocean floor to the highest point on Guam. A majority of the island is surrounded by a coral table reef with deep-water channels. The coastline is characterized by sandy beaches, rocky cliffs, and mangroves.

Sportfishing action heats up in June and July, and peaks in late July or early August, when blue marlin and yellowfin tuna are most abundant. In season, five or six marlin were raised per day on average in the mid-1990s. Skipjack tuna, mahimahi (dolphin), and wahoo are also among the catch. Mahimahi appear in January and peak in late February or March. Wahoo have spring and fall surges but are more closely tied to the full moon. Skipjack tuna are abundant and can be caught all year but peak in summer months.

Boats cruise into 100-fathom water shortly after leaving the harbor at Agaña, the capital city, in search of area banks and seamounts that produce upwellings attractive to baitfish and gamefish. Pelagic species congregate within $1/4$ mile of the shoreline, and the deep water close to shore attracts fish to the lee of the island. This is convenient when winds prevent travel farther offshore. Most big-game fishing occurs north of Orote Point.

This is not a virgin fishery, and it has been affected by commercial fishing from Asian fleets. Blue marlin are not large on average, ranging from 100 to 200 pounds in summer, which makes this a good light tackle location. A 967-pound fish was reportedly caught in 1991, however, and in 1969 the island produced a former all-tackle world record 1,173-pound blue. The catch rate is fairly high even if fish size generally is not.

Reefs around and near Guam offer a variety of jacks, snapper, and grouper. Some anglers here combine casting on reef flats at remote island groups near Guam with offshore trolling near Guam. Twelve fish aggregating devices are located nearby.

Tourism at Guam is popular, particularly for diving; Guam is renowned for its vivid turquoise lagoons and water clarity (up to 150 feet between December and May), and features undersea observatories and one of the world's few swim-through aquariums. A fleet of well-equipped charter boats specializing in offshore fishing is based in Apra Harbor, a busy recreational and commercial port.

On a par with Nicaragua and Manila at 13° north of the equator, Guam has a tropical humid climate with an average annual temperature of 81° F. The dry season is from January through May, and the rainy season from July through November. Easterly trade winds prevail throughout the year, and typhoons, some of which caused great damage in the 1990s, occur.

A guapote from the Parismina River, Costa Rica.

GUAPOTE

Guapote (pronounced "wha-poe-tay") are members of the huge, worldwide Cichlidae family of mostly tropical freshwater fish. The *Cichlasoma* genus of guapote is characterized by a moderately deep and compressed body, sometimes with distinctive markings. They are good-fighting but generally small fish and are caught on small surface and diving plugs, usually along the covered banks of rivers and lakes.

The guapote (*C. dovii*), also known as *guapote blanco*, is found in Honduras and Costa Rica; its ultimate length and weight are unknown, but the all-tackle world record is a Costa Rican fish that weighed 12 pounds, 9 ounces. *C. friedrichsthalii*, also known as the yellowjacket cichlid, occurs from Mexico to Guatemala and Belize; the tiger, or jaguar, guapote (*C. managuense*) occurs from Honduras to Costa Rica; and the green guapote (*C. beani*), also known as the Sinaloan cichlid, is found on the Pacific slope of mainland Mexico.

GUATEMALA

The most western and most densely populated of the Central American nations, Guatemala is a rugged country with mountains and rain forest, volcanoes and swamps, a few lakes and various rivers, and coastline on both the Caribbean and the Pacific. The most significant sportfishing opportunity presently is on the Pacific coast, which has experienced some of the world's best sailfishing in the latter 1990s. Tarpon run in the rivers, snook and permit exist on the flats, and the rivers and brackish lakes contain tarpon and snook, but there have been few attempts at organized fishing in all areas of the country through the latter decades. With two-thirds of Guatemala's interior mountainous, and minimum infrastructure to facilitate travel, what little angling occurred was done by intrepid solo adventurers.

Guatemala possesses roughly 250 miles of Pacific coastline, all washed by favorable currents and adjacent to the Middle America Trench. As of the late 1990s, organized sportfishing was concentrated at the small town of Iztapa, about a quarter of the way up the coast from Guatemala's southern border with El Salvador. At least two camps and more than a half-dozen sportfishing boats were operating year-round and enjoying sailfish action supreme.

The confluence of currents here and an abundance of baitfish over deep water (600 to 1,500 feet) have provided sailfishing in all months. Winter offers exceptional action, and calm seas that make it highly conducive to light tackle use. Most of this activity occurs from 15 to 30 miles offshore, but some occurs out to 50 miles. An hour's run by a fast, modern sportfishing boat is standard, but that hour is one of few during which little is happening.

The sailfish are so numerous that they are readily coaxed with hookless teasers to the boat wake, and, once excited, pounce on nearly any fly or lure or bait tossed their way. Raising less than 15 to 20 sails (many in the 75-pound class, and some 100 pounds or better) in a single day, per boat, is considered abnormal, and some anglers have more than doubled these figures, which is so outstanding that it is hard to believe. In December of 1997 one boat actually caught and released 166 sailfish in three days—a truly staggering feat. Cold snaps and other weather aberrations can produce poor days, but even the poor days here are akin to good ones in many other locations.

Although the sails are caught year-round, the prime period for greatest action has been from mid-October through May, a season of little or no wind and rain. As if all these sailfish weren't enough, yellowfin tuna are prominent from October through November, dolphin are plentiful, and blue and striped marlin are occasionally caught in winter. At least one grand slam of blue marlin, striped marlin, and sailfish was caught on a three-day charter.

Anglers fly to Guatemala City and then travel by ground transport to Iztapa. The commercial fishery here has been described as casual, and mainly focused on sharks and inshore species; it is illegal to fish commercially for sailfish or to bring a sailfish ashore, and there is no billfish consumption—policies that, if continued, will ensure the health of this fishery.

With everyone's attention focused offshore, little is pursued inshore, although snook have been reported in the Iztapa area. Nearly a dozen small and mostly fast-flowing rivers empty into the ocean along this coast. Roosterfish and jack crevalle have also been reported along this coast.

Over on the short Caribbean coast, no organized sportfishing operation existed in the late 1990s, but speculation about this possibility was intense. This is an area to watch in the future when travel conditions and services improve. The nearby keys and flats, some in the waters of Belize, hold permit and bonefish and should offer similar opportunities in Guatemala; it is possible that these fish are plentiful. Sailfish and white marlin reportedly frequent the offshore environs, but there has been no effort to fish for them.

Tarpon and snook are definitely in the cards here, as seems reasonable, because they are found to the east in Honduras. Respectively called *robalo* and *sabalo,* they should be along the whole coast, especially in the vicinity of the mouths of the two most prominent rivers—the Motagua and the Dulce. The Motagua drains the eastern highlands, and its lower reaches form the eastern border with Honduras. The Dulce is a short, navigable river that flows out of Lake Izabal and into El Golfete Lake before entering Amatique Bay at the town of Livingston. Another coastal river, although smaller than the others, is the Sarstún, which forms a partial boundary with Belize.

Tarpon and snook are reportedly in Lake Izabal, and by extension in Golfete as well as Amatique Bay. In the late 1980s they reportedly entered the Dulce River in large numbers from March through June. Commercial or subsistence fishing efforts here are unknown, and equally uncertain is the availability of a suitable local fishing boat or guide, although it seems possible to find such along the Dulce. That river, and Lakes Izabal and Golfete, cover a wide area (Izabal alone some 300 square miles), and would seem to offer considerable potential.

Tarpon have been reported inland in other Guatemalan lakes that presumably are not brackish environments like Izabal and Golfete. In the early 1980s, Lake Petexbatún in the northern Petén rain forest region had numerous tarpon, including fish well over 100 pounds, mainly in the high-water season of July and August. Snook and peacock bass were supposedly here, but are unverified. This is the heart of ancient Mayan country, with Tikal National Park nearby. Tikal was once a jungle community of 55,000 people in the ninth century.

Guatemala's other interior lakes and rivers have not been known for sportfishing opportunity. Famous Lake Atitlán, about 40 miles west of Guatemala City, reportedly had largemouth bass and crappie. The bass reputedly reached 20 pounds in the 1970s and were the object of extensive spearfishing; their current status is unknown, but stocking has clearly decimated native fish popula-

In the salmon grounds of Nakwato Rapids of Slingsby Channel, British Columbia, the water flow may reach a rate of 16 knots.

tions and bird life. Atitlán and Amatitlán, south of Guatemala City, also contain mojarra and a variety of small cichlids. At more than 5,000 feet above sea level and with depths exceeding 1,000 feet, Lake Atitlán is a popular attraction known for its mountain beauty and three nearby volcanoes.

Volcanic eruptions elsewhere in Guatemala, as well as earthquakes, have often caused disasters, and hurricanes and tropical storms occasionally strike the coast. The coastal regions are hot and humid, with an annual average temperature of about 82°F. May through October is generally the rainy season.

GUIDE
See: Fishing Guide.

GUIDE BOAT
A generic term that broadly refers to a boat in the 15- to 20-foot class operated by a fishing guide and hired on a daily basis. In earlier times, a guide boat was one that was rowed and was large enough to take one or two passengers in addition to the operator. Today, almost all guide boats are motorized, and they take from one to three passengers aboard, depending on the size of the boat and type of fishing to be done.

A guide boat might be an 18- to 20-foot flats boat (see) used for shallow saltwater fishing, a 16- to 20-foot bass boat (see) used for freshwater bass fishing, or a variety of less-shallow draft boats. Those few that are rowed include river-fishing drift boats (see) and the occasional skiff, although some guides at lodges in the Campbell River area of British Columbia offer row-trolling for salmon as a means of joining the traditional Tyee Club (membership requires catching a large salmon from a boat that is rowed).

The term "guide boat" may be loosely applied to any boat operated by a fishing guide, although practically the term is meant to be more limited, distinguishing this vessel from a charter boat (see), which is bigger, usually capable of taking more passengers, and built for large waters where seas can become heavy.

Operators of a guide boat may or may not have much formal training or licensing, depending on the locale. In some places, the requirements for guiding are virtually nonexistent and may not even include any permit or license. In other places, more formal training, testing, and certification are required. Any person who takes people for hire onto navigable waterways that are under the jurisdiction of the United States Coast Guard must have a captain's license and pass a rigorous examination. Even if that person operates a boat only on a bay, near-shore flats, or tidal river, and may be called a "fishing guide," the person must still obtain a captain's license.

Generally, you hire a guide as opposed to hiring a guide boat; some guides have more than one boat (especially in saltwater), switching as fishing circumstances warrant. Many guides are booked in advance by reservation and deposit, although in places where guides are numerous it may be possible to hire a guide for a day (through a lodge, hotel, or booking service) without prior reservation.
See: Fishing Guide.

GUIDE, ROD
The component of a fishing rod that is attached to the exterior of the blank and that aids in dispensing and retrieving line, absorbing stress from the exertion of a strong fish, and keeping the line from contacting the rod blank.

Nearly all fishing rods have guides, the exception being the relatively few line-through-blank rods; this includes a tip-top guide and a variable number of intermediate guides along the length of the blank. Other than the blank itself, guides are the single most significant factor affecting rod performance.

Guides are situated above or below the axis of the rod, depending upon the style and fishing application of the finished rod, and they vary in style, size, number, spacing, placement, and materials of the guide rings (the surface that contacts the fishing line).
See: Rod, Fishing.

GUINEA-BISSAU
Facing the Atlantic Ocean in northwestern Africa, Guinea-Bissau is sandwiched between Senegal on the north and Guinea on the south. Much of this small country is a low, swampy coastal plain, and it includes about 60 offshore islands, among which is the 18-island Bijagós archipelago. Numerous rivers form wide estuaries here, and a virtually infinite number of small atolls, banks, and sandbars exist along the coast, most surrounded by mangroves and other swampy vegetation.

Due to the presence of four great rivers, the local flora and fauna can count on a great supply of food. Birds, mammals, and fish are particularly abundant in the Bijagós, and after the archipelagos were discovered by French anglers in the early 1980s, the Acaja Fishing Club was established there in 1983.

Situated on large Rubane Island just in front of the Geba River, the club is about 45 miles south of the capital city of Bissau, with a stunning pan-

Atlantic Guitarfish

orama across the clear waters of the Atlantic. Acaja guests can take club boats to the nearby sandbanks and reefs, where they enjoy light tackle trolling and casting with lures and flies around exotic and private sand islands. Inshore and river fishing are also offered.

The major fish of the area are courbine (meagre) and tiger sharks. Up to 150 tiger sharks are taken annually, with an average weight of 400 pounds. Other species regularly caught include bluefish, cobia, barracuda, king mackerel, African pompano, skipjacks, spotted sea bass, garrick, snapper, guitarfish, hammerhead sharks, bull sharks, tope, and various jacks. About 40 percent of these fish are caught by anglers surf-casting from the beach, and the remainder are caught by trolling and light tackle drifting. Bottom fishing and casting are the favored methods for landing red and gray sea bream and grouper. The season is year-round, with a light increase from October through May.

Normally, 400 angling tourists from Europe pass through the Acaja Fishing Club each year, most arriving from Paris via Dakar, Senegal.

GUITARFISH, ATLANTIC
Rhinobatos lentiginosus.
Other names—French: *poisson-guitarre tacheté*; Italian: *pesce violino*; Spanish: *guitarra*.

A cross between a skate and a shark in appearance, the Atlantic guitarfish is a member of the Rajiformes family, along with skate and ray. It is occasionally encountered by anglers but is not a targeted species.

Identification. The head and pectoral fins of the Atlantic guitarfish form a triangular disk at the front of the body. The rear of the body is thick and tapered like a shark's, and it has two large dorsal fins and a well-developed caudal fin. The Atlantic guitarfish varies in color from gray to brown, with several pale spots on its body.

Size. This species is normally 1 to 2 feet long and can attain a maximum length of $2^1/_2$ feet. Females are somewhat larger than males.

Distribution. Atlantic guitarfish extend from North Carolina to the Gulf of Mexico, although they are not reported in the Bahamas or the Caribbean and are uncommon in Florida and the Yucatán. The Brazilian guitarfish *(R. horkeli)* and the southern guitarfish *(R. percellens)* are two closely related species that range from the West Indies to Brazil.

Habitat. Inhabiting sandy and weedy bottoms, Atlantic guitarfish are found near small reefs, usually buried in seagrass, sand, or mud at depths of 1 to 45 feet.

Life history. Atlantic guitarfish are ovoviviparous, which means they bear live young, with up to six in a litter. At birth they are 20 centimeters long.

Food. Small mollusks and crustaceans form the diet of the guitarfish.

> The largemouth bass record of 22 pounds 4 ounces has stood since 1932; however, naturalist William Bartram, exploring Florida's St. Johns River in 1773, reported catching a 30-pound bass on a deer-hair jiggerbob (presumably a bass bug).

GULF STREAM
The Gulf Stream is the northern and western swing of the North Atlantic Current and one of the strongest currents *(see)* in the North Atlantic Ocean. It separates the warm, salty Sargasso Sea from the cold, less saline inshore water, moving northerly at between 4 and 5 knots per hour, with a passage that courses off North America through the Florida Straits off Key West, Florida, along the coast to about Cape Hatteras, then away from the coast to the Grand Banks off Newfoundland, after which it joins the North Atlantic Current flowing toward Europe.

The Gulf Stream is normally about 75 miles from Jacksonville, Florida. Anglers who make the long run here and elsewhere fish the edge of the Stream, where different bodies of water meet, especially for pelagic species.

GUNWALE
Pronounced "gunnel" (rhymes with "tunnel"), the gunwale is the upper edge of the side of a boat. Gunwales vary in width, thickness, curvature, and strength. They are often used in fishing for supporting various accessories, especially rod holders, and may be designed to provide underneath storage, especially for unused rods in a horizontal position. Gunwales usually project above any platforms or decks, but in some specialized craft gunwales may be flush with them, especially a foredeck.
See: Boat.

GURNARD, FLYING *Dactylopterus volitans.*
Other names—Spanish: *alón, chichara*; French: *poule de mer.*

A member of the Dactylopteridae family, the flying gurnard is a minor commercial species that is occasionally caught incidentally by anglers.

Identification. The flying gurnard may be shades of gray or yellow brown with white spots. It has large, fanlike pectoral fins that extend almost to the tail; these "wings" are used as gliding surfaces for the occasional excursion to the surface. The flying gurnard also has stiff-spined pelvic fins that are directed downward and enable the fish to "walk" along the bottom.

Size. This species ranges from 6 to 14 inches in length; it is usually smaller than 12 inches and can reach a maximum of 18 inches. A 4-pounder caught in Florida is listed as an all-tackle world record.

Distribution. In the eastern Atlantic, the flying gurnard is found from the English Channel south to Angola, including Madeira, the Azores, and the Mediterranean, with the exception of the Black Sea. In the western Atlantic, it is ranges from the Gulf of Mexico north to Massachusetts and south to Argentina.

Habitat. Inhabiting subtropical or tropical seas, the flying gurnard is found in depths of 1 to 35 feet in sandy or seagrass areas, over rocks or coral rubble, and among fringe reefs.

Food and feeding habits. Flying gurnard feed on clams, crabs, and small fish. When foraging, they "walk" along the bottom and turn over rubble with their ventral fins.

GUYANA

Formerly known as British Guiana, this small country in northern South America is bordered by Suriname on the east, Brazil on the south, Venezuela on the west, and the Atlantic Ocean on the north.

The coastline extends for about 270 miles, but coastal fisheries are unreported. The continental shelf is far from shore, and the coastal landmass is low lying, much of it protected by dams and dikes. Several major rivers converge at a substantial bay near Bartica.

Some rivers in the highlands are reported to have lots of peacock bass, payara, pirarucu, catfish, and piranhas, but no infrastructure for sportfishing exists and there are no outfitters in most of the remote, upper watershed rivers.

The Essequibo River and its major tributary, the Rupununi, are sandy-bottomed black-water rivers *(see: Brazil)* that begin in the Guyana Highlands along Guyana's borders with Brazil and Venezuela. Near the Brazilian state of Roraima, the Rupununi meanders through savannas where several large, natural black-water lakes provide excellent peacock bass fishing. The peacocks average 4 to 6 pounds, but some in the 12- to 15-pound class are taken; the action overall can be fast. The river itself produces peacock bass as well as piranhas, catfish, and the occasional pirarucu. A few ranches in the area provide very rustic guest facilities, meals, boats, motors, and native guides, all at reasonable prices.

The Essequibo and tributaries like the Rewa also have peacock bass, catfish, and pirarucu, plus big piranhas and excellent fishing for payara, with 20- to 25-pounders possible. There are also pacu, bicuda, surubim, matrinxa, and other species. One outfitter offers a motorized float trip with primitive tent camping on both these rivers.

Since the Essequibo and Rewa have very few lakes and lagoons, fishing is primarily done in the main rivers, especially below numerous rapids and small falls, through which native guides easily portage boats. The upper tributaries contain only a few small native villages, and the scenery and wildlife viewing can be spectacular.

GYOTAKU

A Japanese art form in which ink prints are made of fish. The process involves the application of ink to one side of a whole fish; an impression is obtained by pressing different types of paper or cloth over the inked body of the fish.

HABITABLE ZONES

The various areas that marine organisms occupy in the ocean environment. Life is concentrated in only about 4 percent of the total water area of the world's oceans, primarily because sunlight is needed to permit photosynthesis for plankton, which is the basis of the marine food chain. The greatest abundance of ocean life is found in the open ocean from the lowest tide line to the outer edge of the continental shelf.

HABITAT

In a broad sense, the area or space in which an organism or group of organisms live; an estuary, a pond, a marsh, etc., can be construed as habitat for fish as well as numerous other animals. In a narrow sense, habitat is the specific place occupied by an individual. Anglers often speak of habitat in both senses, but when seeking fish they usually focus on the most definitive aspects of the habitat, especially the specific cover or structure that holds or attracts fish, even if temporarily.

HACKLE

Bird feather of fly-tying quality, which is wound around the hook in constructing an artificial fly.
See: Fly.

HADDOCK *Melanogrammus aeglefinus.*

Other names—haddie, scrod; French: *eglefin;* Italian: *asinello;* Norwegian: *kolje;* Portuguese: *arinca, bacalhau;* Spanish: *eglefino.*

Closely related to the genus *Gadus*, the haddock is often considered a member of the Gadidae, or codfish, family. Haddock have long been important commercially and are an even more highly valued food fish than Atlantic cod, although stocks of haddock have declined rapidly since the 1960s due to overfishing. Sportfishing for haddock is minor, in part due to current historically low levels of this fish.

Commercial fishing for haddock is principally conducted with otter trawls. Today, the commercial catch of haddock is far below historical levels, and haddock are generally in a collapsed or near-collapsed condition, having been overexploited by commercial fishing. This crisis has occurred in the face of commercial and recreational management of cod fisheries under the New England Fishery Management Council's Multispecies Fishery Management Plan. The 1980s and 1990s experienced record low commercial catches, and haddock abundance and recruitment have been at all-time lows. With spawning stock biomass at unprecedented depressed levels, there is enormous concern for the future of this species.

Identification. Characteristic of a cod, the haddock has three dorsal fins and two anal fins, and the first dorsal fin is high and pointed. The small chin barbel is sometimes hidden. Its coloring is purplish gray on the back and sides, fading to pinkish reflections and a white belly. There is a black lateral line along the side and a black shoulder blotch commonly called the "Devil's thumb print," or "St. Peter's mark."

The dark lateral line and shoulder blotch can distinguish it from its close relatives in the cod family. The three dorsal fins distinguish the haddock from its relative the silver hake *(see: hake, silver).*

Size/Age. The average haddock is 1 to 2 feet long and weighs 1 to 5 pounds. The all-tackle record is 11 pounds, 3 ounces, but they have been reported to attain $16\frac{1}{2}$ pounds. Haddock can live for 14 years. The growth rate of haddock has changed substantially over the past 30 to 40 years, possibly in response to changes in abundance. Prior to 1960, when haddock were considerably more abundant than at present, the average length of a four-year-old fish was approximately 19 to 20 inches. Presently, growth is more rapid, with haddock reaching this size at three years. Changes in sexual maturation have also been observed. In recent years, the maturation schedule has shifted downward by about one year; currently, nearly all haddock at age 3, and three-quarters of age 2 female haddock, are mature. Although the presence of early-maturing fish increases spawning stock biomass, it is uncertain if these younger fish are spawning successfully or producing eggs of sufficient quality to contribute strongly to the reproductive success of the population.

Haddock

Distribution. The haddock is found on both sides of the Atlantic, from the North Sea and Iceland to Newfoundland and Nova Scotia, and southward to southern New Jersey. It occasionally inhabits the deep water to Cape Hatteras. The highest concentrations off the U.S. coast occur on the northern and eastern section of Georges Bank and in the southwestern Gulf of Maine. Two stocks occur in U.S. waters: the Gulf of Maine stock and the Georges Bank stock.

Habitat. Preferring deeper water than do cod, haddock inhabit depths of 25 to 75 fathoms. Although generally a coldwater species, preferring temperatures of 36° to 50°F, they are commonly found in warm water over bottoms of sand, pebbles, or broken shells.

Life history/Behavior. The spawning season is between January and June, and activity peaks during late March and early April, when large congregations form in depths of 20 to 100 fathoms. For several months, the young live at the surface until they settle to the bottom. Individual females can produce up to 3 million eggs, but a 22-inch specimen produces approximately 850,000 eggs. Major spawning concentrations occur on eastern Georges Bank, although some spawning also occurs to the east of Nantucket Shoals and along the Maine coast.

Haddock swim in large schools, and there is some seasonal migration to the north in spring, and south again in the fall. Adult haddock on Georges Bank appear to be relatively sedentary, but seasonal coastal movements occur in the western Gulf of Maine. There are extensive migrations in the Barents Sea and off Iceland.

Food and feeding habits. Primarily consuming crabs, snails, worms, clams, and sea urchins, the haddock seldom feeds actively on fish.

Angling. There is virtually no current sportfishing for haddock, although techniques are similar to those for Atlantic cod *(see: cod, Atlantic)*.
See: Cod and Hake.

HAGFISH
Hagfish are one of two groups of jawless fish (the other being lampreys), which are the most primitive true vertebrates. They are members of the Petromyzontidae family. Fishlike vertebrates, jawless fish are similar to eels in form, with a cartilaginous or fibrous skeleton that has no bones. They have no paired limbs and no developed jaws or bony teeth. Their extremely slimy skin lacks scales.

The repulsive-looking hag is the most primitive of all living fish, resembling an outsize, slimy worm. The hag is exclusively marine, and only one family, Myxinidae, is known. The hag has the ability to discharge slime from its mucous sacs, which are far out of proportion to its size.

Their habit of feeding primarily on dead or disabled fish makes hagfish doubly unattractive. Commercial fishermen consider them a great nuisance because they penetrate the bodies of hooked or gillnetted fish, eating out first the intestines and then the meat, leaving nothing but skin and bones. The hagfish bores into the cavity of its victim by means of a rasplike tongue. Unlike many lampreys *(see)*, it is not a parasite. Hags' eyes are not visible externally, and they are considered blind. Food is apparently detected by scent, and large numbers of hags are often taken in deep-set eel pots baited with dead fish.

The hag can be differentiated from its close relative, the lamprey, by the following characteristics: The hag has prominent barbels on its snout, no separate dorsal fin, eyes that are not visible externally, a nasal opening at the tip of the snout, and a mouth that is not funnel-shaped or disklike. The largest hags are 2 feet or more in length. They range the cold, deep waters, and at least one specimen was recorded at a depth of 1,335 meters.

HAIR BUG
A deer-hair bug style of artificial fly.
See: Fly.

HAIR RIG
A European bait rig for light-striking fish.
See: Carp.

HAIRTAIL *Trichiurus savala.*
Other names—hairy, smallhead hairtail, savalani hairtail, spiny hairtail, smallheaded ribbonfish; Malay: *langgai, puchuk, timah.*

Often mistaken for the pike eel *(Muraenesox bagio)* and a related tropical inshore species, the frost fish *(Lepidotus caudatus)*, the hairtail is a rather mysterious fish that is much sought after by anglers along the East Coast of Australia. Although there is no commercial fishery for this species, anglers regard it as very good table fare, provided it is not overcooked.

Identification. The hairtail has an extremely elongated, deeply compressed, scaleless body that is bright silver along its entire length. The single dorsal fin extends the full length of the body, which tapers to a slender threadlike tail. This fine tail readily distinguishes it from the frost fish, whose tail is small but forked, and from the pike eel, whose tail is rounded and much broader. Its pectoral fins are small. The arrow-shaped head has large eyes and an undershot jaw that contains sharp teeth and three or four huge, barbed fangs under the snout.

Size. This fish is known to exceed 2 meters in length and reach a weight of 5 kilograms. An Australian record stands at 4.25 kilograms.

Atlantic Hagfish

Distribution. Hairtail occur in Indo-Pacific waters from India and Sri Lanka to Southeast Asia and north to China and south to New Guinea and Australia. In Australian waters, hairtail are mainly confined to New South Wales waters, particularly the Sydney region. Elsewhere they have been reported from Western Australia, South Australia, and as far north as Townsville in northern Queensland.

Habitat. Hairtail seem to prefer the deep waters of marine inlets and bays, where small yellowtail (scad) and mullet are available.

Life history/Behavior. Little if any serious research has been carried out on the habits of the hairtail. Enigmatic creatures, they are well known for their sudden appearances and disappearances in a waterway. It is not known if they spawn in Australian waters. Small specimens are frequently seen in the fish markets of Asia.

Food and feeding habits. Anglers' experiences show that hairtail feed at any time of the day or night but are most active after dark. They appear to move in schools and will circle a bay as they feed. Hairtail eat small fish such as yellowtail, mullet, pilchards, and garfish, and readily take a bait of king prawn or fish fillet.

Angling. Hairtail fishing is usually carried out from a boat, although occasional captures are made from rocky shores that drop off into deep water. Short boat rods and a reel spooled with at least 5-kilogram (preferably 7-kilogram) line are the norm. Handlines to 10 kilograms are also popular.

When using ganged hooks with garfish or pilchard baits, no wire leader is necessary, but single or double hooks demand the use of wire because of the razor-sharp nature of the hairtail's fangs. A favorite rigging technique is to secure a 15-centimeter wire leader to a curtain ring, the latter offering a secure finger hold when the fish is brought to the surface. Hook sizes vary from 5/0 to 7/0. Small sinkers, riding on the hook eye, are sometimes used when it's necessary to get the bait down quickly to where the hairtail are feeding; when speed is not an issue, the bait is allowed to sink under its own weight.

The last two hours of a rising tide that peaks at around 10 P.M., and for a short time after the peak, are regarded as the best times to fish for hairtail. Boats anchor in a selected area, and chum (usually fish scraps) is fed into the water. Rigged baits are allowed to sink a couple of rod lengths to where the fish are thought to be. Two or more anglers in a boat will vary the depth of their baits. Although some anglers fish during the day, fishing after dark generally produces better results.

Despite its formidable appearance, the hairtail signals its presence by a gentle movement of the line, and the angler's strike is empirical. On many nights, anglers rely on the phosphorescence given off by minute organisms to indicate when the fish has taken the bait; when the fish strikes, the line straightens and disturbs these organisms, causing them to glow.

The fish's strength is considerable, as its length gives it great purchase in the water. When the fish is drawn to the surface, the angler slips a finger into the curtain ring, and the flailing fish is pulled inboard. At this stage, great care is essential in avoiding the impressive teeth of the hairtail.

Lure anglers have found that hairtail respond to metal jigs of various patterns, jigged up and down near the bottom. This method is used during daylight hours.

HAIRWING

A term for a bucktail-style streamer fly, tied with hair or other fur.
See: Fly.

HAKE

See: Cod and Hake; Hake, Pacific; Hake, Silver.

HAKE, PACIFIC *Merluccius productus.*

Other names—Pacific whiting, whitefish, haddock, butterfish, California hake, popeye, silver hake, ocean whitefish; French: *merlu du Pacifique nord;* Spanish: *merluza del Pacífico norte.*

A member of the Merlucciidae family, the Pacific hake is sometimes classified as a member of the Gadidae family and thus included with codfish. It is the only representative of the hake family in the Pacific. Common in commercial and sport catches because of its abundance, the Pacific hake is not generally sought for its food value, but it is made into fish meal. Because it does not remain fresh very long, once caught, it must be immediately chilled or the flesh becomes soft and undesirable.

Many Pacific hake are caught incidentally by anglers fishing for salmon or bottom fish, and are generally discarded. They are also considered a nuisance because they raid salmon nests for eggs.

Identification. The body of the Pacific hake is elongate, slender, and moderately compressed. The head is elongate and the mouth large with strong, sharp teeth. The thin scales fall off readily. Its coloring is gray to dusky brown, with brassy overtones and black speckles on the back.

The elongated shape, notched second dorsal and anal fin, and coloration separate the Pacific hake from other similar fish in its family.

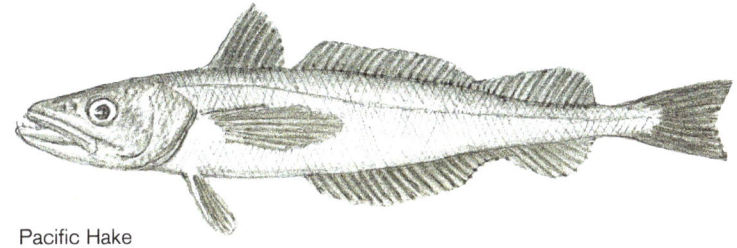

Pacific Hake

Size/Age. The Pacific hake can grow to 3 feet in length. The all-tackle record is 2 pounds, 2 ounces.

Distribution. This fish occurs in the Gulf of California (isolated population) and from Magdalena Bay, Baja California, to Alaska. It has been reported along the Asiatic coast.

Habitat. The Pacific hake prefers a deep, sandy environment, and has been reported in depths exceeding 2,900 feet.

Life history/Behavior. Spawning occurs in the winter or from February through April, beginning at three to four years of age, off Southern California and Baja California, Mexico. After spawning, the adults migrate northward to Oregon, Washington, and Canada and return to their spawning areas in the fall. This species is classified as demersal, but is largely pelagic in oceanic and coastal areas. Adults exist in large schools in waters overlying the continental shelf, except during the spawning season, when they are several hundred miles seaward.

Food. The Pacific hake feeds on a variety of small fish, shrimp, and squid.

Angling. Pacific hake are an occasional, incidental catch and not a targeted species for anglers. They are usually caught on squid, herring, and anchovy baits.

See: Cod and Hake; Hake, Silver.

HAKE, RED *Urophycis chuss.*

Other names—squirrel hake, ling; French: *merluche éureuil;* Spanish: *locha roja.*

Red hake are somewhat of an incidental catch for deep-water anglers and have become less significant to commercial trawlers. Although not considered overexploited, red hake are now caught commercially at much lower levels than previously.

Identification. The body of the red hake is elongate with two dorsal fins—the second one long—and one long anal fin. Its coloration is variable, but the sides are usually reddish and often dark or mottled. The fins are not dark-edged, as they are in some other hake, and the pelvic fin rays are shorter than those of other hake.

Size/Age. The maximum length reached by red hake is approximately 50 centimeters, or about $19^{1}/_{2}$ inches. Their maximum age is reported to be about 12 years, but few fish survive beyond 8 years of age. The all-tackle world record is 7 pounds, 15 ounces, which is their known maximum size; the common size is roughly 2 pounds.

Distribution. Red hake are found from the Gulf of St. Lawrence to North Carolina but are most abundant between Georges Bank and New Jersey. Research from bottom-trawl surveys indicate that red hake have a broad geographic and depth distribution throughout the year, undergoing extensive seasonal migrations. Two stocks have been assumed, divided north and south in the central Georges Bank region.

Habitat. These fish generally occupy deep water over soft or sandy bottoms. Although juvenile fish may frequent shallow water along the coast, adults typically migrate to deeper water, generally between 300 and 400 feet deep, although reports indicate that they exist at depths greater than 1,650 feet.

Life history/Behavior. Red hake winter in the deep waters of the Gulf of Maine and along the outer continental shelf and slope south and southwest of Georges Bank. Spawning occurs from May through November, and significant spawning areas are located on the southwest part of Georges Bank and in Southern New England south of Montauk Point, Long Island.

Food and feeding habits. Red hake feed primarily on crustaceans, but adult red hake also feed extensively on fish.

Angling. There is no significant recreational fishing effort for red hake.

See: Cod and Hake.

HAKE, SILVER *Merluccius bilinearis.*

Other names—Atlantic hake, whiting, frostfish; French: *merlu argenté;* Spanish: *merluza norteamericana.*

A member of the Merlucciidae family, the silver hake is primarily known as whiting. An aggressive fish and a swift swimmer, it is a good species for sportfishing. Whiting are a common fish for party boat anglers, especially in the winter and early spring, and are sometimes an early-season surf catch.

Whiting have been a significant commercial fish, particularly with the demise of groundfish species like cod and haddock. They are primarily caught in otter trawls in the winter and spring. However, the stock abundance of these fish has been low in recent times, there are few older fish, and the pressure on young fish has intensified, resulting in an overexploited fishery. Most of the commercial catch is frozen and sold in packaged form, especially as fish sticks and fish cakes.

Identification. The body of the whiting is long and slender, with a flattened head, a large mouth, and strong, sharp teeth. The second dorsal fin and anal fin are deeply indented, giving the fin a divided appearance. The first fin is short and high. Its coloring is dark gray above, with iridescent purple hues that fade to silvery white on the belly.

The whiting, or silver hake, can be distinguished from the cod (see), pollack (see), tomcod (see), and haddock (see) by the presence of only two dorsal

Red Hake

fins and one anal fin. It also lacks the chin barbel characteristic of cod and haddock.

Size/Age. The whiting can reach $2\frac{1}{2}$ feet in length and a weight of 8 pounds, although the average catch is a fish of less than 14 inches; fish exceeding 4 pounds are rare. Ages up to 15 years have been reported, but few fish older than age 6 have been observed in recent years.

Distribution. Found from the Newfoundland banks southward to the vicinity of South Carolina, the whiting is encountered in large numbers between Cape Sable and New York. Closely related forms are taken in the southern parts of the United States and in the Gulf of Mexico. In U.S. waters, two stocks have been identified based on morphological differences; one extends from the Gulf of Maine to northern Georges Bank, and the second occurs from southern Georges Bank to the mid-Atlantic area. Whiting undertake extensive migrations; in winter, the northern stock travels to the deeper waters of the Gulf of Maine, and the southern stock moves along the outer continental shelf and slope.

Habitat. Whiting primarily inhabit the cool, deep waters of the continental shelf, although they often visit shallower waters in pursuit of prey. Adults stay in deep water offshore, whereas juveniles are generally stay in shallow water closer to shore. They make seasonal onshore-offshore migrations; the range of their location, however, extends from near the surface to 600 feet deep, and they have been reported much deeper. They prefer sand and pebble bottoms, and temperatures between 36° and 52°F. Whiting move toward shallow water in the spring, spawn, and return to the wintering areas in autumn.

Spawning behavior. Spawning occurs in late spring and early summer, when whiting release their buoyant eggs at the surface, allowing them to drift with the current. Future stocks depend on the weather; if the wind blows the eggs away from inshore, very few will survive, having nothing to feed on. More than 50 percent of fish at age 2 (8 to 12 inches), and nearly all fish at age 3 (10 to 14 inches), are sexually mature.

Peak spawning occurs earlier in the southern stock (May and June) than in the northern stock (July and August). Important spawning areas include the coastal region of the Gulf of Maine from Cape Cod to Grand Manan Island, southern and southeastern Georges Bank, and southern New England south of Martha's Vineyard.

Food and feeding habits. Whiting feed aggressively in large groups on herring, silversides, menhaden, young mackerel, and on squid and other invertebrates. They have been known to strand themselves on shoals and in shallow waters during the height of their feeding activity after spawning.

Angling. Because whiting are normally present close to shore in the winter and early spring, they are one of few species available to saltwater anglers at that time. The fish are pursued primarily from

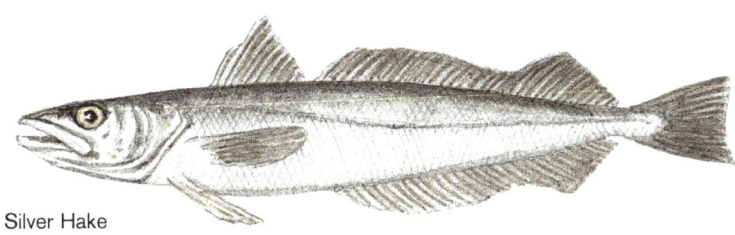
Silver Hake

party boats, but private boaters may catch them as well, and surf anglers can score if the fish are near the beach.

See: Cod and Hake.

HAKE, WHITE *Merluccius bilinearis.*
See: Cod and Hake.

HALFBEAKS AND BALAO
Other names—French: *demi-bec;* Spanish: *aguja, agujeta, saltador.*

Halfbeaks are closely related to flyingfish *(see)* and needlefish *(see).* These sparkling, silvery fish travel in schools and are abundant in warm seas. They are important food fish for pelagic species, especially billfish, and are used as rigged trolling bait for marlin, dolphin, and other big-game fish encountered in blue water. Although live halfbeaks are seldom available to anglers, frozen packs of halfbeaks (mainly balao or ballyhoo) are sold at most coastal marinas and tackle shops, and individuals are defrosted and rigged for offshore fishing *(see).*

A halfbeak's body is elongated, rounded, and flattened from side to side only in the tail region. The dorsal and anal fins are located far to the rear and directly opposite each other. In halfbeaks, only the lower jaw is long; the upper jaw is of normal length. They stay mainly close to shore, commonly leaping or scooting rapidly across the surface with only their tail in the water. The tail is vibrated rapidly to propel them. Most species lay their eggs in the open sea; a few are ovoviviparous, retaining their eggs in their body until they hatch and then "giving birth" to young.

The wrestling halfbeak *(Dermogenys pusillus)* of southeastern Asia is one of the few halfbeaks kept in aquariums. An ovoviviparous species, the females carry the eggs for about a month, sometimes longer, before giving birth to the young, usually 20 or more. At birth, the fry are less than a half inch long, and they do not have an extended lower jaw. When mature, about $2\frac{1}{2}$ months later, the females are nearly 3 inches long. The males are slightly shorter, and their anal fin is modified as a sexual organ for internal fertilization of the female. These little halfbeaks feed on insects and other live foods, which they capture as they swim along at the surface. Their long lower jaw serves as a scoop of sorts, and the open upper jaw is clamped shut to hold the animals.

Male wrestling halfbeaks are pugnacious, circling each other belligerently with their mouths

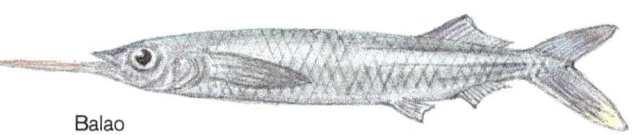
Balao

open and their gill covers lifted. Their battles are mainly sparring bluffs, however, and they usually make no physical contact with each other.

The balao (*Hemiramphus balao*) is a halfbeak that inhabits tropical and warm-temperate waters nearly worldwide. In the western Atlantic, it ranges from New York to the Gulf of Mexico and southward to Brazil, including the Caribbean; in the eastern Atlantic, it is found around the Canary Islands and in the Gulf of Guinea from Victoria, Nigeria, to Luanda, Angola. Its pectoral fin is long, the lower jaw and caudal fin have orange red tips, and the sides and belly are silvery. It averages 8 to 10 inches in length and can grow to 16 inches.

The ballyhoo (*Hemiramphus brasiliensis*) is a halfbeak that is common off the Florida coast and in the Caribbean, traveling northward along the eastern coast and occasionally as far north as Massachusetts in summer. It ranges as far south as Brazil, and is also found in the eastern Atlantic, from the Cape Verde Islands and Dakar in Senegal to Angola. Three black stripes extend the full length of the greenish back. The sides and belly are silvery, and the caudal fin is yellowish orange. Ballyhoo average 6 to 10 inches in length, rarely longer. They are netted, often by attracting them to lights at night, and are the most common halfbeak used as bait for pelagic species in North America. The last ray in the ballyhoo's dorsal fin is elongated, much longer than in most halfbeaks. The closely related longfin halfbeak (*H. saltator*) of the Pacific also has a long ray in its dorsal fin. An Indo-Pacific species, *H. far,* is one of the largest, reaching a length of 2 feet. In Japan, the sayori (*H. sajori),* which can attain a length of 16 inches, is commonly harvested for food.

The halfbeak (*Hyporhamphus unifasciatus*), which attains 12 inches in length, lives in the same geographical area of the Atlantic as the ballyhoo but occurs also in the Pacific from Point Conception southward to Peru, including the Galápagos Islands. It has a single grayish stripe down each side of its body and three dark lines down the middle of the back. The tip of the long lower jaw is red, and the body is less deep in profile and more rounded than that of the ballyhoo or balao. The halfbeak is used for bait; it makes good eating itself, although it is seldom caught specifically for this purpose. The related California halfbeak (*H. rosae*), is smaller, rarely more than 6 inches long. The Indo-Pacific *H. dussumieri* is sometimes 18 inches long.

Included among the Pacific halfbeaks off the coast of North America is the ribbon halfbeak (*Euleptorhamphus viridis),* which grows to as much as 18 inches and has long pectoral fins. The smaller flying halfbeak (*E. velox*), which lives on both sides of the Atlantic and ranges from the Gulf of Mexico to Brazil in the western Atlantic, is so named because of its habit of leaping and skittering over the surface and sometimes gliding for short distances, much as flyingfish do; it can grow to 20 inches in length but seldom enters coastal waters.

HALF-STEPPING
See: Walking the Dog.

HALIBUT, ATLANTIC *Hippoglossus hippoglossus.*
Other names—common halibut, giant halibut, right-eyed flounder, chicken halibut (under 20 pounds); Dutch: *heilbot;* Finnish: *ruijanpallas;* French: *flétan de l'Atlantique;* Icelandic: *heilagfiski;* Japanese: *ohyô;* Norwegian: *kveite;* Portuguese: *alabote;* Spanish: *flétan del Atlántico, hipogloso;* Swedish: *hälleflundra, helgeflundra.*

The Atlantic halibut is among the largest bony fish in the world and a member of the Pleuronectidae family of right-eyed flounder. Flounder have a unique type of maturation from larvae to adult stage in which one eye migrates to the opposite side of the head.

The Atlantic halibut is a highly prized table fish, with white, tender flesh that has a mild flavor and is often likened to chicken; it has been marketed fresh, dried/salted, smoked, and frozen. It is an excellent fighter, but it is a deep-dwelling fish that is seldom deliberately pursued by anglers. It may be caught incidentally by anglers fishing for other deep ocean dwellers. It has historically been an extremely important market species, but it has been greatly overfished by commercial interests, who primarily catch it by bottom longlining.

Identification. The body is wide and somewhat flattened, rimmed by long dorsal and anal fins. The lateral line, which has a scale count of about 160, arches strongly above the pectoral fin. The dorsal fin has 98 to 106 rays and the anal fin has 73 to 80 rays. The teeth are equally well equipped in both sides of the jaw. Its coloring is usually pearly white and featureless on the blind side. Some specimens, nicknamed "cherry-bellies," have a reddish tint on the blind side.

Size. Atlantic halibut weighing between 300 and 700 pounds have been reported, although the all-tackle rod-and-reel record is 255 pounds.

Distribution. The Atlantic halibut occurs in North Atlantic waters, including the Barents Sea and off Iceland and Greenland; it ranges from Labrador to Virginia in the western Atlantic, and from the Barents Sea to southwest Ireland in the eastern Atlantic. This species does not occur in

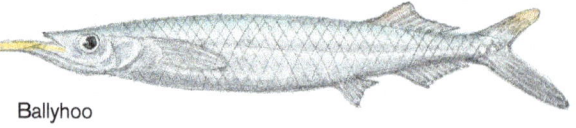
Ballyhoo

Atlantic Halibut

near-freezing polar waters as many people believe; there, it is replaced by the Greenland halibut (Reinhardtius hippoglossoides).

Habitat. A deep-water species, the Atlantic halibut seldom enters water shallower than about 200 feet and is commonly found to 3,000 feet. It inhabits cold (40° to 50°F) water over sand, gravel, or clay bottoms.

Spawning behavior. Spawning occurs from late winter through early spring in deep water. The eastern Atlantic fish spawn from March through May. Females can release up to 2,000,000 eggs, and the fish move shallower after spawning.

Within a few days of hatching, these and other halibut begin to lean to one side. The eye on the underside migrates upward and across the head so that both eyes are on top of the body. As the eye migrates, the baby fish's skull twists and, in many cases, the mouth does also. In this way, the halibut transforms into a flatfish.

Food and feeding habits. The Atlantic halibut is a voracious feeder, pursuing its prey in the open water. It forages primarily on fish, including cod and their relatives—ocean perch, herring, skate, mackerel, and other flounder. It also eats crabs, mussels, lobsters, and clams.

Angling. As noted, there is a minor, concentrated rod-and-reel effort for these fish, owing to their extraordinarily deep-dwelling nature and low population. They are caught in the western Atlantic on banks in 100 to 500 feet of water. Anglers drifting bait rigs or heavy metal jigs on the bottom often catch Atlantic halibut while fishing for such other bottom dwellers as Atlantic cod (see: cod, Atlantic). Although natural baits may differ, techniques are similar to those used in fishing for Pacific halibut (see: halibut, Pacific).

HALIBUT, CALIFORNIA
Paralichthys californicus.
Other names—flatty, flattie, fly swatter (small), barn door (large), alabato, Monterey halibut, chicken halibut, southern halibut, California flounder, bastard halibut, portsider; Spanish: *lenguado de California.*

The California halibut is a large flatfish and a member of the Bothidae family, or left-eyed flounder. It is the largest and most abundant flatfish within its range, although it is greatly smaller than the more northerly Pacific halibut (see: halibut, Pacific). It is an important commercial quarry and sportfish, one that is often deliberately sought by anglers and valued for its excellent firm white flesh.

California halibut were routinely caught to 20 and 30 pounds, often even larger, in California waters in the 1940s, but both numbers and size have dwindled over the decades. However, a minimum length limit (22 inches in California), elimination of gillnetting for this species, improved water quality, and other factors contributed to a resurgence in the population in the mid- to late 1990s.

Identification. The body of the California halibut is oblong and compressed. The head is small and the mouth large. Although a member of the left-eyed flounder family, about 40 percent of California halibut have their eyes on the right side. The color is dark brown to black on the eyed side and white on the blind side. Rare specimens may be either brown or white on both sides or have partial coloration on both sides. The gill rakers are slender and numerous, totaling about 29 on the first arch. Their numerous teeth, very large mouth, and a high arch in the middle of the "top" side above the pectoral fin make them easily distinguishable from other flatfish.

Size. The largest California halibut recorded was 5 feet long and weighed 72 pounds. The all-tackle rod-and-reel record weighed 53 pounds, 4 ounces. Females grow larger, live longer, and are more numerous than males. In California, these fish average between 8 and 20 pounds; 20-pounders are considered large, and fish exceeding 30 pounds are trophies.

Distribution. This species occurs from Magdalena Bay, Baja California, Mexico, to the Quillayute River, British Columbia. A separate population exists in the Gulf of California in Mexico.

Habitat. Found mostly over sandy bottoms, California halibut appear beyond the surf line and in bays and estuaries. They range from near shore to 600 feet deep but are most commonly caught in 60 to 120 feet of water. They are not known to make extensive migrations.

Spawning behavior. Males first mature when two or three years old, but females do not mature

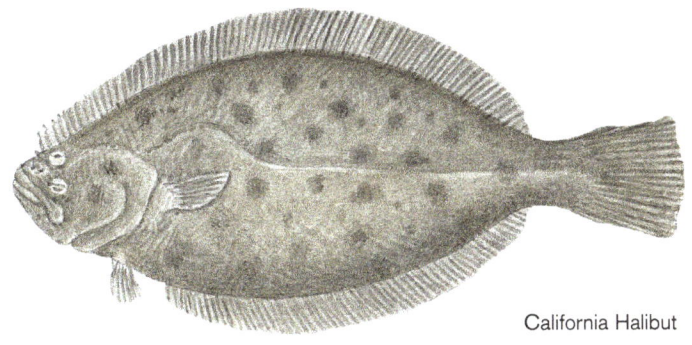

California Halibut

until age 4 or 5. A 5-year-old fish may be anywhere from 11 to 17 inches long. Spawning takes place in relatively shallow water from April through July, and spawning fish feed actively.

Food and feeding habits. These halibut feed primarily on anchovies and similar small fish, often well off the bottom and during the day, although they also consume squid, crustaceans, and mollusks. At times they are observed jumping clear of the water as they make passes at anchovy schools near the surface.

Angling. California halibut are relatively aggressive fish, and offer variety in terms of technique and location. Although drift fishing with bait on sandy flats is almost synonymous with fishing for this species, trolling with lures and bait, fishing in shallow water, and fishing on deep structure are also productive.

Live anchovies are popular natural bait, and the primary method of fishing these is by drifting along the bottom. Most anglers keep their conventional reel in freespool with a thumb on the line to maintain control, and watch the rod tip, waiting for a sharp tap. When a fish strikes, they yield a little line, then engage the gears and set the hook.

Although this method catches fish of all sizes, it is often less productive for larger halibut, perhaps because many smaller ones are more aggressive. Some anglers have had more success on larger fish not by drifting but by concentrating on gravel and shale bottoms, wrecks, breakwalls, rockpiles, and other structure. They anchor instead of drift, and use a sliding sinker while bottom-fishing with live bait, preferring sardines, queenfish, and squid over anchovies. Leadhead jigs adorned with soft-plastic bodies also work, and both bait and jigs are twitched and moved along the bottom.

When the fish are shallow, trolling with mid- to deep-running minnow-style plugs produces halibut; fly fishing also produces fish at this time. Trolling with wire line is favored when the fish are in deeper water with swift current; plastic squid or hoochies on a multiple-lure bottom rig with a heavy (1- to 3-pound) sinker get down to the fish in the 30- to 100-foot depths.

Fifteen- to 20-pound line is used for most halibut fishing, although wire line trolling is an exception. A stronger leader may be employed to prevent breakoffs caused by the teeth of large specimens. For live bait and shallow plug trolling, a 7-foot rod with a fast tip, and a conventional star drag reel, do fine; line capacity is not a significant issue.

These halibut need to be played with firm, steady pressure, and not with aggressive pumping, which sends them on a getaway run.

HALIBUT, PACIFIC *Hippoglossus stenolepis.*
Other names—giant halibut, northern halibut, hali (Canada), barn door; Japanese: *ohyô;* Portuguese: *alabote do Pacifico;* Spanish: *fletán del Pacifico.*

The Pacific halibut is the largest flatfish found in Pacific Ocean waters, and one of the world's largest bony fish. It is a member of the family Pleuronectidae, or right-eyed flounder. A strong fighter that grows to impressive size, the Pacific halibut has long been a favorite among Pacific Northwest anglers. That popularity has soared since the mid-1980s, when halibut populations boomed and large numbers of mostly young fish started to provide excellent fishing from Oregon to Alaska. Pacific halibut populations remain generally healthy, thanks to close monitoring of the sport and commercial longline fisheries, but halibut bycatch *(see)* by commercial trawlers remains a threat.

Table quality. The firm, white flesh of the Pacific halibut is prized by anglers and fish connoisseurs alike. Dryer and with a more delicate flavor than most, the worst thing a gourmet can do is overcook halibut. Otherwise, it provides excellent table fare whether baked, grilled, or poached. For the table, smaller, "chicken" halibut of 50 pounds

Pacific Halibut

or less are generally favored over larger fish. Any halibut killed for the table should be bled upon capture to ensure the highest quality and flavor.

Identification. The halibut usually is dextral; that is, both eyes are on the right side of the head. Its coloration varies from olive to dark brown or black with lighter, irregular blotches. More elongate than other flatfish, the average width of the Pacific halibut's body is about one-third its length. The mouth is large, extending to the lower eye. The small, smooth scales are well buried in the skin, and the lateral line has a pronounced arch above the pectoral fin. The tail is crescent-shaped, longer at the tips than in the middle, which distinguishes it from most other flatfish.

Size. A typical sport-caught Pacific halibut is a fish of 28 to 50 inches, weighing 10 to perhaps 60 pounds, but the species grows much larger. Rod-and-reel records include several halibut in excess of 400 pounds (the all-tackle record is 459 pounds), and 500-pounders have been caught commercially. Reports of Pacific halibut measuring 9 feet and weighing more than 700 pounds are unverified, but within the realm of possibility. Most Pacific Northwest anglers consider a halibut of 100 pounds or more a trophy. These largest halibut all are females, as males of the species seldom top 90 pounds.

Distribution. Pacific halibut are found on the continental shelf of the North Pacific Ocean and have been recorded along the North American coast from central California to Nome, Alaska. They are also found along the Asiatic coast from the Sea of Japan to the Bering Sea. They live on or near the bottom and have been taken as deep as 3,600 feet, although most are caught during the summer, when they are at depths of 75 to 750 feet. They generally move back into deeper water in fall and winter.

Life history. Spawning occurs in the North Pacific Ocean and Bering Sea during winter, with each female distributing 500,000 to 4 million eggs, which are fertilized externally and hatch after roughly 15 days. The eggs and larvae float freely in the ocean current for six months, during which time they are transformed from "normal" fish to flattened creatures with both eyes on one side and become perfectly adapted to life on the ocean bottom. Settling to the bottom in shallow, inshore waters, they continue the counterclockwise migration through the Pacific that is common to the species. Juvenile halibut show a tendency to migrate back toward the place where they were spawned, reaching that destination by adulthood and repeating the life cycle.

Habitat and feeding habits. Preferring cool water (3° to 8°C), halibut are most commonly found where the bottom is composed of cobble, gravel, and sand, especially near the edges of underwater plateaus and breaklines. Here they wait for tidal currents to wash food within striking range. Halibut are strong swimmers, however, and will leave bottom to feed on pelagic fish such as herring and sand lance. They will also inhabit virtually any kind of habitat if crabs, squid, octopus, cod, pollack, sablefish, or other sources of food are abundant.

Angling. Its impressive size, relative abundance, and brute strength make the Pacific halibut a popular target of anglers' efforts from the southern Oregon coast to the Bering Sea. Younger, smaller halibut of under 50 pounds constitute most of the sport catch along the Oregon, Washington, and southern British Columbia coasts, and fish in these areas tend to congregate in specific areas where food is abundant. Farther north, off the northern British Columbia coast and Alaska, halibut are more widely dispersed and large fish are more common.

Oregon's top halibut fishing spots are Heceta Bank, Stonewall Bank, and Nelson Island, all within about two hours by boat from Newport. Halibut fisheries also occur out of the Oregon coastal ports of Charleston, Depoe Bay, and Garibaldi. Washington's top halibut producers are Swiftsure Bank and an underwater hump known as Blue Dot, both of which are fished by anglers departing Neah Bay. There are also halibut fisheries out of Ilwaco and Westport, and, on the "inside" waters of the Strait of Juan de Fuca, such places as Sekiu, Twin Rivers, Freshwater Bay, Green Point, Hein Bank, and Middle Bank all support worthwhile halibut fisheries.

Working north up the coast of British Columbia, halibut can be found as far south as Race Rocks and Pedder Bay, near the south end of Vancouver Island. A long bank that runs along the southwest corner of Vancouver Island provides good fishing for anglers out of Bamfield, Ucleulet, and Tofino. Several islands and submerged banks between Telegraph Cove and Port Hardy are good bets around the northeast corner of Vancouver Island. The west side and north end of the Queen Charlotte Islands offer perhaps the best halibut fishing in the entire province but require significant travel from the mainland. Productive fisheries around Dundas Island, Chatham Sound, and Edye Pass make Prince Rupert another popular destination of halibut anglers.

Without question, Alaska offers the best fishing for Pacific halibut. There are rich halibut grounds within easy reach of the Southeast Alaska towns of Ketchikan, Wrangell, Petersburg, Sitka, Juneau, and Yakutat. Farther up the vast Alaskan coast, Kodiak Island and several spots along the east side of Cook Inlet offer both large numbers of halibut and good opportunities for a trophy fish. Best known among these is Homer, the so-called Halibut Capital of the World, and the Deep Creek/ Ninilchik area, where halibut anglers launch in the surf to reach the halibut grounds. The Alaska Peninsula also is a halibut angler's dream, and in recent years the peninsula's Unalaska Island has been the focal point of a growing halibut sport-

An unusual fly-caught halibut from Seward, Alaska.

fishery. Waters around Unalaska have produced numerous halibut exceeding 300 pounds, including record-class fish of 395, 440, and 459 pounds.

Basic halibut fishing techniques apply wherever the fish are found; the key is to get a bait or lure down to them and keep it there long enough for a fish to find it. Most anglers prefer to fish with bait, and large herring are the most popular choice. Squid, octopus, belly skin off halibut or salmon, and whole cod, greenling, or other small bottom fish also are effective baits. Bait is usually fished on a wire spreader or a sliding-sinker rig, with sinker size ranging from 4 ounces to 4 pounds, depending on depth, current, size of the bait, and line diameter. Bait hooks range from size 5/0 to 12/0, depending on size of the bait and the size of the quarry; some anglers prefer traditional J-style hooks, whereas others like commercial circle hooks. Halibut use their eyes, nose, and lateral line to locate a meal, so anglers often lift the bait well off the bottom to increase visibility and then drop it quickly to create a thumping vibration.

This same "bottom-banging" strategy also works for anglers using artificials. Favorite lures are large, metal slab-type jigs or homemade versions constructed of tubing or small-diameter pipe filled with lead. Both imitate herring and other small fish on which halibut feed. Leadhead jigs also take halibut, especially if adorned with large plastic grub bodies, pork rind, or strips of white belly skin off another halibut.

Rods, reels, and line vary in size depending on fishing conditions. For deep water (more than 200 feet), a 7-foot boat rod with a stiff action, equipped with 4/0 conventional reel, is standard. Such tackle not only helps to level the playing field in the event a monster fish is hooked, but also makes it possible to fish the 2-pound jigs or sinkers required to reach bottom in deep-water halibut spots. For shallow-water fishing, though, some anglers fish much lighter tackle, down to and including bass-action flipping rods or freshwater spinning outfits.

Deep-water halibut anglers use line in the 80- to 130-pound range, whereas light-tackle anglers may prefer line of 15- to 50-pound test. Most serious halibut anglers prefer the low stretch and sensitivity of the modern, high-tech braided lines.

Because of their size and strength, halibut demand respect when they're brought to the boat; many anglers have been injured, or have had equipment destroyed, by fish that weren't controlled quickly or properly. Halibut over about 50 pounds are commonly shot in the head or harpooned rather than simply gaffed or netted, although both activities disqualify fish for International Game Fish Association (IGFA) record consideration. A team effort by everyone on board often is the difference between success and failure when landing a big halibut. Securing a strong line through the jaw and another around the base of the tail will allow a big fish to be controlled without bringing it aboard, a method commonly practiced by small-boat anglers. Once a tough halibut is under control, it should be dispatched with several raps behind the eyes from a heavy club, severing two or three gill arches, or both.

HANDLE

The component of a fishing rod that is usually held by the angler and that incorporates the reel seat and gripping area. Although some rods, primarily those used in big-game fishing, are held by the foregrip while the angler is fighting a fish, most rods, especially those used for casting, are held by the rear grip section, so comfort and ability to control the rod are important elements of the handle.

Handle materials, largely decided by application, primarily include cork and foamed polymers, and are found in varying lengths and styles.
See: Rod, Fishing.

HANDLINE

A line with a weight and a baited hook, which is dispensed and retrieved by hand. In a sense, this is the most basic fishing tackle; it has obvious deficiencies for casting, retrieving line, and playing and landing a strong fish, but a possible advantage in detecting a strike.

Handlines today are primarily used in underdeveloped regions, sometimes with a (baited or unbaited) jig or jigging spoon, and predominately as a means of procuring food rather than providing sport; they may also be used in commercial fishing. Using a handline is the way most people fished throughout history for subsistence purposes.

HANDLING FISH
How fish are handled once they are caught depends on whether they are going to be kept for consumption or whether they will be released.
See: Fish Preparation—Care; Catch-and-Release.

HARBOR
A secure refuge for boats, protected from storms, usually for docking and mooring. Harbors are often associated with inlets *(see)*, jetties *(see)*, piers *(see)*, and tidal marshes *(see)*, and have a variety of features that may be attractive to fish.

HARDWARE
Artificial lures other than flies.
See: Lures.

HARLING
A term for trolling with flies and flycasting tackle for Atlantic salmon in large rivers. Particularly practiced in parts of Europe, especially Scandinavia, harling involves row trolling with a long length of fly line in the water, with the oarsman manipulating the boat in order to maneuver the fly for presentation. This may also be done with bait or lures, and is largely employed in waters that are impossible to cast and wade effectively. Although the length of line is longer in harling, the technique is essentially identical to backtrolling *(see)* in rivers.

HARNESS, BAIT
A device that secures a live or dead bait for trolling. Among these are plastic bridles for whole or headless minnows or small baitfish, and two-hook spinner rigs for nightcrawlers; plastic bridles are used in salmon trolling and the two-hook spinner rigs in walleye trolling. Nightcrawler harnesses are more common to freshwater anglers and are complete rigs that feature a Colorado or Indiana spinner, five or six plastic beads, and two short-shanked snelled bait hooks that are embedded in a whole live nightcrawler.

HARNESS, FIGHTING
Also known as a kidney harness in smaller sizes, this device is worn around the shoulders and upper back, and is connected to a reel; the harness provides back support, arm relief, and reel security. A fighting harness is worn like a vest, may be padded, and is usually made from nylon, canvas, or nylon webbing. Heavy-tackle versions are incorporated into, or used with, a rod belt *(see)* and may be used in conjunction with a fighting chair *(see)* when fishing.

Some harnesses are difficult to get into or do not fit comfortably on the spur of the moment (the decision to wear one may not come until after a fish is hooked and known to be sufficiently large). It is important that the harness fit properly, and offshore regulars usually have their own to avoid the adjustments that must be made to loaned or borrowed harnesses.

Ideally a harness should take pressure off the back, evenly distributing it instead over the hips and thighs. In use, a harness-wearing angler with rod butt in the belt gimbal leans back against the pull of the fish, making the knees, rather than waist or back, the pivot point.

To prevent an angler from possibly being pulled overboard by a fish (if the reel seizes, for example) while the angler is strapped to the heavy tackle, some harnesses are equipped with a quick safety release, and sometimes a safety strap is attached to the harness.
See: Big-Game Fishing; Standup Fishing.

HATCH
The occasion when aquatic insects emerge from the water, shed a skin or case, mate, and deposit eggs on the water. Single species often all hatch into a terrestrial stage in a very short time, and huge numbers may be observed emerging from the stream or as a swirling mass above it.

HATCHERY
A place for the hatching of fish eggs and the growing of fish for stocking or for food. Fish hatcheries may be public or private. Publicly owned hatcheries rear fish for stocking, usually exclusively into public waters, either to create fishing opportunity, sustain existing fisheries populations, and provide prey for predator fish populations, or to restore depleted fisheries. Most publicly operated hatcheries belong to state natural resource and fisheries agencies; some hatcheries are operated by federal agencies. Privately owned hatcheries, some of which are also called fish farms, supply fish to food processors and consumers, to organizations and individuals for stocking in private or public waters (often with a government-issued permit), and on rare occasions to state agencies in times of need to supplement government programs.
See: Fisheries Management.

HATTERAS HEAVER
A heavy-action rod and large reel combination for surf casting.
See: Surf Fishing.

HAWAII
The Hawaiian Islands stretch for 1,523 miles across the north-central Pacific, intercepting the

migration routes of marlin, tuna, sharks, and other gamefish that grow to world-record sizes and are highly prized by sport anglers. The archipelago consists of 132 islands, reefs, and shoals, from the southernmost point of the United States (Ka Lae on Hawaii Island) to Kure Atoll, west of Midway Island. Eight main islands (Hawaii, Maui, Oahu, Kauai, Molokai, Lanai, Niihau, and Kahoolawe, from largest to smallest) make up 99 percent of the 6,425 square miles of land area. The six largest provide sportfishing access, and the remaining two have accessible fishing waters.

Hawaiian Island waters are home to more than 700 species of fish, most of which are known throughout the Indo-Pacific. Approximately 30 of these, from billfish to bonefish, are important to sport anglers (fishing is the sixth most popular recreational activity among local residents). Saltwater fishing is paramount because few natural bodies of freshwater exist.

Hawaii was a Polynesian kingdom until 1893, a republic until 1898, and annexed by the U.S. as a territory in 1900. It became the 50th state on May 21, 1959. The earliest settlers arrived at Ka Lae (South Point) in A.D. 124, more than a thousand years before Captain James Cook sailed into Kealekekua Bay in 1778. The 200,000 to 300,000 residents of Cook's time depended greatly on fishing for subsistence and developed many effective fishing techniques that survive today.

Offshore fishing in Hawaii gains most of the world's attention because inshore fishing opportunities are limited. The islands are near the northern limits of coral reef development. Fringing reefs are narrow even on the oldest (westernmost) islands, and nonexistent on the youngest (to the southeast).

Northeast trade winds dominate the weather, generate the dominant wave patterns, and drive surface currents ranging from 0.4 to 0.6 knot. These currents are modified by the shapes of islands, which causes them to create large eddies important to the development of sea life, from baitfish to gamefish. Tides are modest, with less than 3 feet of change everywhere throughout the islands. Two main seasons mark the year. Trade winds (10 to 20 miles per hour) prevail from May through October, which is considered "summer," and winds are more variable (gusting to 30 miles per hour at times, then switching to the south to southwest at others) from November through April, when the weather is a bit cooler and wetter. At sea and on land, August and September are the warmest months, with air temperatures in the 80s to 90s and sea temperatures above 80°F. January and February are the coldest months, with many days in the low 70s, and sea temperatures ranging from 72° to 76°F.

Hawaii's most important offshore species are marlin (blue, black, and striped), tuna (yellowfin, bigeye, skipjack, and albacore), spearfish, sailfish, *mahimahi, kawakawa,* amberjack, and barracuda. Big-game anglers also catch tiger sharks (even tonners), makos (over a half ton), and other types. Deep-sea bottom anglers plumb the depths for red snapper (four or five different species) and grouper. Shore anglers catch jacks (roughly a dozen species, topped off by giant trevally and bluefin trevally), bonefish, barracuda, and ladyfish (the biggest in the world at 24 pounds plus). The giant trevally "slide bait" method of angling, described later, is unique to Hawaii. Assorted panfish are also caught at night.

Hawaii offers limited freshwater angling opportunities. The only native freshwater fish in Hawaii are four gobies and an eleotrid. Streams on the leeward slopes of the major islands are mostly intermittent; on the windward slopes, where there are cliffs and valleys and high annual rainfall, many of the streams are perennial. Throughout the Hawaiian Islands are more than 260 freshwater reservoirs ranging up to 400 acres. Most reservoirs, stream banks, and streambeds in Hawaii are privately owned, however, and require permission from the landowner for access.

Kauai's Waimea River, which runs about 20 miles, is the longest stream. The largest natural lakes are Halalii (1.3 square miles) on Niihau, Kola Reservoir (0.6 square mile) on Kauai, and Salt Lake (0.4 square mile) on Oahu. Various man-made impoundments serving irrigation needs have been stocked with largemouth and smallmouth bass, tucunare (peacock bass), pongee, Chinese and channel catfish, bluegills, oscars, jewel cichlids, and other exotic species. A limited fishery for rainbow trout exists on Kauai. Despite the limited opportunities, more than 5,000 freshwater anglers hold licenses on Oahu alone.

Thanks to deep water nearby, trolling within sight of the islands is a common part of offshore fishing in Hawaii.

Established Saltwater Fisheries
Billfish. Blue marlin and striped marlin are the main billfish targets. A significant sportfishery also exists for Pacific shortbill spearfish. A few black

marlin and sailfish are hooked each year but are only an incidental catch.

Most big Hawaii marlin are caught within a few miles of shore. The 100-fathom line curves in as close as 1/4 mile from the beach in places like the Kona coast, and the 1,000-fathom line is only a few more miles away. Substantial island lee eddies help pull bait and big fish back into the protection of the shoreline, creating a boon for anglers.

The biggest fish are usually caught on lures trolled at 8 to 12 knots. That is fitting because Hawaii anglers pioneered lure trolling for billfish back in the 1950s and 1960s, long before the method caught on elsewhere.

Big-game fleets operate out of Kona on the Big Island, Lahaina on Maui, Kewalo Basin in Honolulu, and Lihue on Kauai. A few boats can be chartered in other spots, notably Hilo Harbor on the Big Island.

Blues are caught every week of every month of the year. In a typical year, more are caught in June, July, August, and early September than in other months. In about three of every five years, however, October and early November are just as good as the summer months. Granders can show up at any time. One year, the only grander caught was boated in November. Another, the only two granders caught were landed in July and December. And in still another year, all of the granders were caught in January and February. Hawaii's blues rank high on the all-time list of largest blue marlin caught anywhere in the world and include a 1,805-pounder, the largest on record anywhere.

Summer combines Hawaii's calmest seas, gentlest breezes, and best runs of blue marlin. Warm sea conditions bring huge female marlin (1,000-pounders are caught nearly every summer) to spawn, escorted by eager males. The males are smaller (rarely exceeding 300 pounds) and quicker, getting to bait and lures faster than their more ponderous mates. As a result, the summer marlin catch is dominated by aggressive, quick-hitting, high-jumping billfish of 150 to 200 pounds. Although the males match perfectly with light tackle of 20- to 50-pound class, expect to use heavier gear or lose the chance to boat the occasional big marlin.

Island anglers troll for billfish with locally made plastic high-speed big-game plugs that are run at 8 to 12 knots, or they slow-tow live bait (skipjack tuna) around baitfish schools. For billfish, the burst of skipjack *(aku)* activity each summer is a major part of Hawaii's attraction. Averaging 3 to 10 pounds, *aku* are big-game snacks and a reliable supply of energy for the vigorous effort of spawning.

The big challenge for visiting anglers may be finding the charter boat of their choice during the busy summer season. Offshore fishing tournaments crowd the summer calendar, and many of the best-known boats are booked as much as a year in advance.

Striped marlin are a winter-to-spring catch, most abundant from December through June. Blue marlin techniques produce most of the stripers, although trollers switch to smaller lures rigged with smaller hooks when the 50- to 100-pound stripers are swarming in the wake.

Spearfish are the target of dedicated light-tackle anglers, and Hawaii may be the best place to set a world record for this species. Most abundant in January through May, they are caught by trollers who drag hookless teasers to attract the fish. When a spearfish follows a teaser, the angler assesses its size, picks a suitable rod from several ready to cast, and tosses the spearfish a prerigged bait.

Yellowfin tuna. As regular as spring itself, hordes of yellowfin tuna, known as *ahi,* churn into Hawaiian waters at the start of June and remain through September. At times the tuna attack anything in sight, but just as often you can troll through acres of big yellowfins busting around you or breezing by without showing the slightest interest in whatever is trailing behind the boat.

Hawaiian anglers have perfected methods that regularly produce when tuna turn up their noses and clamp their jaws tight. Their successes have produced record catches (Hawaiian waters have rewarded record hunters with dozens of International Game Fish Association [IGFA] yellowfin tuna marks over the years), steady daily catches throughout the summer season, and occasional surprises year-round.

Central Pacific anglers are uniquely situated to learn, develop, and pass on tuna fishing techniques. Their methods combine new ideas fresh from the Orient with traditional ideas from early Polynesian cultures dependent on fishing for survival. Look at a modern arsenal of tuna fishing weapons—birds, jetheads, octopus skirts, bulb squid, shell lures (lures made with pearl-shell inserts), tuna circle hooks, *ika-shibi* gear (using light to attract squid and tuna at night), to name a few—and you'll see ideas that originated somewhere in the Pacific, were introduced and developed in Hawaii, and are now being used successfully around the world.

Central Pacific tuna schools seem to migrate from west to east, which means the first catches are reported from boats berthed at Port Allen, Nawiliwili, and Hanalei Bay on Kauai. The news spreads only slightly faster than the fish. Within two weeks Oahu boats begin bringing *ahi* back to Haleiwa Harbor, Pokai Bay, and Kewalo Basin. Look for them off Maui a few days later, and then almost immediately off the Kona and Hilo coasts of the Big Island.

Some years, sporadic bursts of tuna pop up unexpectedly throughout the islands as early as March. Even so, dependable schools don't usually settle in everywhere until nearly June. Action for *ahi* usually continues throughout the island chain until the end of July, tapers off during August, and disappears by the end of September.

Tuna anglers have learned to suffer sporadic lean

seasons. Each year's early arrivals generate hopeful predictions for a return to the hot action common in the best years of the past. Hawaii's yellowfins average 100 to 200 pounds, not heavyweight statistics by standards of the eastern Pacific, where only 300-pound fish set records. Local commercial anglers have talked about 300-pound Hawaiian tuna, but the only 300-plus-pounder on record was caught in July 1990, on a catamaran sailing off Lanai. This state-record claimant registered 325 pounds.

At their most aggressive, *ahi* attack in packs. Then, they'll hit every lure in a trolled spread of four or five. Boats in the thick of early action check in with a dozen or more big fish and a crew of exhausted anglers.

Tuna specialists use streamlined jet-style lures skirted with plastic tails. Skirt colors are mixed to match forage. The most popular combinations are "angry squid" (a mix of pink, yellow, and brown) and *"opelu"* (a type of mackerel scad showing silver, green, blue, and yellow). Tuna are sharp-eyed, requiring lures rigged with nylon rather than wire and armed with a single tuna-bend hook to catch the jaw hinge. Such lures are designed for the fast trolling speeds (10 to 12 knots) pioneered on Hawaiian water.

It's not always possible to match the hatch because every year something different happens. One year, it was a filefish hatch that turned *ahi* on and off. Every tuna belly was loaded with the remains of 4- or 5-inch filefish. The following year, action was dominated by huge swarms of little anchovies with schools of bait 2 and 3 miles across and showing 10 to 60 fathoms deep on sonar. Around the anchovies were clouds of skipjack tuna, and below them were large schools of *ahi*.

Some years, live-baiting with skipjacks is the single best way to catch an *ahi*. Other years, the *ahi* won't touch them. You just have to be prepared for anything, then wait and see what weird thing they're doing this year.

Ahi anglers must be ready to change and adapt. When *ahi* aren't showing or are traveling with *mahimahi* schools, boats troll fast with streamlined, skirted lures from 8 to 12 inches long in an assortment of colors. Others tow bait around fish aggregation devices (FADs). They use a downrigger to present a bridled skipjack tuna at depths of 150 to 200 feet, and swim another skipjack at the surface for tuna coming up to feed.

Minnow-style swimming plugs attract smaller yellowfins at the FADs. Chugging a popping plug from a slow-moving boat has taken FAD tuna up to 200 pounds. If tuna show down deep on sonar but not at the surface, stand-up anglers drop a diamond jig down below them and jig it up, alternating each sweep with a drop-and-reel motion.

Spreader rigs and daisy chains are effective in the late afternoon. Spreaders with 16 to 22 small squid in amber or yellow, trolled in clusters of two or three, draw up tuna from considerable depths. *Ahi* gather near inshore bottom features known locally as *ahikoa*. Once located on sonar, they are baited with fillets of mackerel scad dropped down 150 to 250 feet in a modern duplication of Hawaii's traditional "stone drop" method, which early Hawaiians invented to catch *ahi* from dugout canoes. Hawaii's yellowfins spend most of their time in the cooler waters 25 to 50 fathoms down, and gather at the same sites from year to year. Early Hawaiians reached them with a handline carried into the depths by a stone the size of a brick but rounded like a potato. They baited a hook with a fillet of *opelu*, placed it on the stone with a *ti* leaf and some pieces of chum, then wrapped a few turns of leader around the package. With additional wraps, they added more chum, then secured the package with a slipknot. After lowering the baited stone to a predetermined depth marked on the line, they jerked the line to release the knot. The stone fell away to the bottom, the chum dispersed to attract tuna, and the baited hook emerged to flutter in the current. A striking tuna can pull a line across a canoe gunwale so fast, the wood burns and smokes; this is why Hawaiians named this fish *ahi*, or "fire."

Other tuna. Albacore (*tonbo ahi* or *ahi palaha*) may be the most seasonal offshore gamefish in Hawaii. The highly migratory longfins usually begin to show up in late July and are gone by the end of October. During daylight hours, they stay in the cooler waters at great depths (60 fathoms or more), rising to feed at night when they are greeted by drift anglers, who attract them with lights and chum. Most albacore fishing is commercial, but anglers willing to fish overnight can hook record-size longfins. Hawaii's *tonbo* average 40 to 50 pounds and range up to 80 or more pounds.

Skipjack tuna *(aku)* are here year-round but are most abundant from June through August. Schools of 3- to 5-pounders are common and can cover acres. Mostly sought as baitfish for marlin and *ahi*, they are also great sport on light tackle. They hit small jigs, spoons, and plastic worms rigged on very light leaders. Big skipjacks *(otadu)* range up to 35 pounds in Hawaii waters and will sometimes attack the biggest lures in a marlin troller's spread.

Bigeye tuna *(po'onui)* are most often caught when gathered around FADs, flotsam, and jetsam. These "floater" fish range from 1 pound to more than 100 pounds. During the winter months, a few larger bigeyes are caught trolling with lures. Such catches are rare because bigeyes seldom venture up into the warmer surface waters.

Kawakawa, which are closely related to skipjack tuna, are present year-round but are seldom abundant. The Hawaiian name for this tuna species is also the IGFA standard. They average 5 to 15 pounds and grow to 25 in Hawaii waters. Aggressive feeders, they are caught by trolling, jigging, and baiting (whatever you're doing when a *kawakawa* swims by will usually work).

American fishing rods were made of wood through most of the nineteenth century; in the 1860s, Hiram Leonard improved bamboo rod construction by using six, instead of four, strips.

Mahimahi. Known in many locales as dolphin or dorado, but as *mahimahi* in Hawaii, these exciting fish are found in island waters year-round but are seasonal in abundance, with annual peaks in April and May and again in October and November. Then, catches can be outstanding, especially off the windward coast of Oahu and in the triangle formed by Maui, Lanai, and Kahoolawe. Fishing is incredible at times, especially when huge schools of fish gather near drifting objects. Catches of 20 to 100 fish totaling up to a ton are not unheard of. Windward coastlines are especially blessed because drifting debris shows up there first. Often, trailered boats are able to reach hot action first because few large craft harbor on the blustery northeast sides of the islands.

Hawaii's biggest *mahimahi* are usually caught on blind strikes by anglers dragging lures for bigger game. The most electrifying technique for hooking *mahimahi* is chugging popping plugs on casting gear. To succeed, the first requirement is finding fish, since blind casting over open water is arm-numbingly tedious. As a result, the normal chugging targets are *mahimahi* gathered around a FAD or flotsam and jetsam. You can also keep a chugging rod rigged and ready for times when you hook a *mahimahi* while blind trolling. The fighting fish often bring in followers, which trail their partner to the transom, excited and ready to pounce on a well-presented surface disturber.

Hawaiian *mahimahi* seem to like a buoyant, level-riding plug with a scooped face cut with very little angle. Although some anglers make their own from wood, the most popular models are produced from surfboard materials. Several local craftsmen have their own versions, but all of these plugs gain their buoyancy from a core of surfboard foam with wire-through rigging for strength and a body envelope molded of plastic casting resin to create shape, action, and casting weight.

Standard practice among FAD anglers is to postpone plugging until after they have hooked a live bait and rigged it for slow trolling from an outrigger. This bait is usually a small skipjack tuna, yellowfin tuna, or *kawakawa*, sewn to a hook with a head bridle. These small tuna gather at FADs by the thousands and attract marlin, *mahimahi*, big yellowfins, and wahoo. *Mahimahi* can't resist the 1-pounders and will even eat the 5-pounders when feeling particularly arrogant.

Live baits are usually tuna or bonito caught right on the scene. The best baits are small slim fish of a pound or less. *Mahimahi* snatch them, turn them headfirst, and swallow them whole, all within a greedy few seconds. Give them a lot of time to get the bait down, as much as 30 seconds or more. The test of strike time is the second run. A *mahimahi* usually grabs the bait in a rush, slows to swallow, then heads back to join its partners. That's the time to hit the brakes and set the hook.

Live baits are usually better than dead baits, but the latter will often do. Rig a dead scad with a stinger hook, drawing a short leader up through the body with a bait needle so the hook is in the hind third. Rigged this way, the scad is trolled very slowly on an outfit with the drag set at strike. The usual dead-bait strike is the sudden appearance of a lit-up *mahimahi* a few feet under the water behind the bait, which then disappears as the reel screams and empty water erases the vivid image.

Although scads are inviting bait, they aren't as durable as ballyhoo. These long, silver halfbeaks are found in Hawaii but can be hard to land. During the early spring, they are caught at night in harbors, where they gather under lights to feed on small organisms drawn to the lights. With ballyhoo, the favored rig is a leader drawn up through the body with the hook positioned behind the vent. Tie the leader to the beak and then sew the hook to the backbone.

Ono. The wahoo *(ono)* catch triples in June, July, and August. Most are caught by patient trollers working jet lures, leadhead jigs, and skirted plastic lures along the near-shore ledges (40- and 50-fathom depths are reachable within $1/4$ mile of the surf line). Here, the wahoo average 20 to 40 pounds, with fish over 60 pounds uncommon. Rig with wire and keep hooks sharp.

Deep sea. Amberjack *(kahala)*, trevally *(ulua, kagami,* and *omilu)*, snapper *(uku, opakapaka, ehu, lehi,* and *ula ula)*, barracuda *(kaku)*, and grouper *(hapu'u pu'u)* inhabit the deep waters around all islands. Amberjack and trevally (some well over 100 pounds) and barracuda (including 50- to 80-pounders) generate great sport for stand-up anglers dropping jigs or whole bait down 70 to 100 fathoms. Snapper (from 2 to 30 pounds) and grouper (usually 5 to 40 pounds, but some monsters exceed 500 pounds) take hooks baited with strips of squid, *aku,* or *opelu* in depths of 40 to 150 fathoms; this is lots of work whether you catch them or not. The best action occurs over bottom structure in the path of moderate to strong currents.

Shore fishing. Shore anglers separate their sport into whipping, dunking, and slide-baiting. Whippers cast jigs, spoons, and surface plugs on light to moderate spinning gear (2- to 20-pound test) to catch bluefin trevally *(omilu)*, giant trevally *(ulua)*, barracuda *(kaku)*, Pacific threadfin *(moi)*, and ladyfish *(awa aua)*. Whipping is best at dawn or dusk, when the fish feed most actively and beach goers are out of the water. Dunkers cast bait (squid, shrimp, and strips of octopus) on hook-and-sinker rigs and wait for bonefish *('o'io)* and trevally. Dunking spots are usually sandy-bottomed bays and channels. Coral-reefed bottoms are avoided because of snags and bait-stealing reef fish.

Slide-baiting is a specialized form of big-game surf casting unique to Hawaii. It makes use of very heavy tackle (stiff 12- to 14-foot rods and trolling reels of 6/0 to 9/0 are common) cast from rockcliff shorelines where deep water (100 feet or more) comes within reach of a 60- to 100-yard cast. An unbaited line is cast with a heavy sinker armed with wire hooks to tangle in the bottom. Once the sinker is secured in the coral, a large bait (perhaps a whole octopus, moray eel, or baitfish) on a specialized hook and leader is attached to the line with a slide buckle, which allows it to slide freely down the line until it comes to rest against a stop in the line several feet above the sinker. The quarry, usually a giant trevally, takes the bait and either releases the sinker from the bottom or breaks the sinker line. The best slide-bait fishing for *ulua* is at night along remote coastlines of all islands.

While waiting for the big strike, shore casters fill the time and coolers with some of the prettiest and tastiest panfish ever hooked. The experts use specially designed rods (light, flexible rods up to 14 feet long), but standard spinning gear works, and visiting anglers should feel free to bring their own and get in on the action. The panfish are caught on small hooks baited with luminescent strips or worms, or weighted flies trimmed with luminescent materials. Tackle shops provide advice and a look at gear custom-designed for these unique fishing styles.

Island Details

The Big Island. The southernmost and largest Hawaiian island bears the name "Hawaii." To avoid confusing the island name with the name of the 50th state, local residents just call this the "Big Island." Roughly the size of Connecticut, it is formed by three large volcanoes, two of which are dormant. The geology is important, because that's what makes it such a great fishing area.

The predominant trade winds blow from the east, driving currents with them. These rivers of water squeeze between the islands and whirl in eddies on the western sides. The lee side of the Big Island is the Kona and Kohala coastlines. The currents in these calm, protected eddies push up against the undersea shelves formed by great masses of volcanic rock. The upwellings churn with baitfish, which are preyed on by marlin, tuna, sharks, *mahimahi,* wahoo, jacks, barracuda, and most other kinds of tropical Pacific gamefish. Kona is served by daily flights from the U.S. mainland (about 2,500 miles away) and by more frequent flights from the largest Hawaii city, Honolulu (about 150 miles away).

Kona is the top choice of veteran and novice big-game anglers from around the world because of its special combination of remarkable conditions. Big fish are caught in calm water near shore. The Kona coast sits in a calm lee; the normal trade winds of 10 to 20 knots are blocked by the looming mass of the volcanoes. The deep blue 100-fathom-depth water needed to attract blue marlin is no more than a $1/2$ mile offshore in many places.

At the north end of the Kona coast, the port of Kawaihae is home to a small charter fleet and provides facilities for an active fleet of small boat owners who troll the coastline for *mahimahi* and wahoo. On the east side of the island, Hilo Harbor provides access to the windward coast for recreational and commercial anglers, and Hilo Bay attracts shore casters who dunk for *ulua* and *'o'io.*

Oahu. Oahu is the most populated island, and its major city, Honolulu, is the seat of state government. Kewalo Basin, near downtown Honolulu, is home to Hawaii's second (to Kona) largest recreational fleet. Boats leaving from Kewalo can head across the Molokai Channel to fish Penguin Bank in the productive Molokai lee, troll the shipping lanes along the south coast, turn east around Diamond Head to fish the windward coast, or head west to the Waia'nae coast. The latter coast, which produced the 1,805-pound all-time record blue marlin, is most easily accessible by boats fishing out of Poka'i Bay. Boats leaving from Poka'i are usually the first to greet the spring *ähi* run.

Freshwater anglers have three good opportunities on Oahu. The best known is Lake Wilson (Wahiawa Reservoir), a hairpin-shaped streambed flooded to create an irrigation impoundment. It holds largemouth and smallmouth bass (over 4 pounds), tucunare, pongee, oscars, tilapia, bluegills, and feral aquarium fish (jewel cichlids and red devils). Fishing quality varies with water level, which fluctuates considerably depending on rainfall and draw-down for irrigation. Wilson sees 20,000 to 30,000 trips per year, and tilapia is a main target.

Feeding activity on Lake Wilson is highest during the first few hours after dawn and the last few hours of evening, when fish are most active on the surface. Tucunare can be so aggressive, they will grab any lure and will gang-attack lures; jerkbaits are particularly effective. At such times, this action stirs up the competitive instincts of bass, who join the melee. By midday, surface waters warm, fish go deeper, and anglers switch to standard bass tactics used in bass waters everywhere. Lures may be the most fun for tucunare, but live bait (mosquitofish, cichlids, and tilapia) are preferred here. Rig a live bait on a bobber, cast it a few feet offshore of the targeted spot, and then let it swim in to danger.

Tucunare spawn from May through June, when they frequent the shallows, guarding their nests. Although they will attack anything nearby while spawning, conservation-minded anglers leave them alone. February is the peak spawning time, and the off-season, for largemouths.

Nu'uanu Reservoir provides limited and restricted fishing for channel cats and convict cichlids. Ho'omaluhia Reservoir (32 acres) in Kane'ohe has channel cats, tilapia, and cobalt/orange cichlids. Both are popular with bank anglers (especially kids with cane poles) because they are easily fished from shore. Baits include bread, chicken liver, squid, tuna belly strips, and worms.

A Canadian study of pike feeding habits determined that pike ate 10 percent of the local duck hatch each year; experiments showed it took 10 days to digest one duckling.

Maui. Offshore anglers are served by two Maui ports, Lahaina and Ma'alaea Harbors. Both are in the lee and send boats to fish the triangle between Lanai and Kahoolawe. Maui fleets see exceptional fishing for *mahimahi* and *ono* but do not get as much credit for their marlin catch, which can be outstanding at times (the Lahaina Jackpot Tournament has produced granders on several occasions).

Kauai. The westernmost of the main islands, Kauai sees the first tuna of the spring run. The major fleet operates out of Nawiliwili on the east coast, but others fish out of Port Allen to the south, and Hanalei to the north.

Unique in Hawaii, and to Kauai, is the chance to catch rainbow trout. There is little natural propagation of rainbow trout because streams are not cold enough to support natural reproduction. The single exception is Koaie Stream, and anglers determined enough to fight their way through underbrush to its headwaters are sometimes rewarded by wild rainbows. Rainbows were first stocked on Kauai in the 1920s; the program was intensified in the 1970s and then limited in the 1990s. Eggs are imported from California, hatched at a state facility on Oahu, and transported to Kauai, where they are kept at Pu'u Lua Reservoir. Stocking in streams was discontinued in 1991, and trout stocking is now limited to the reservoir.

Private impoundments on Kauai also hold bass and tucunare, the state records for which (both over 9 pounds) came from Kauai reservoirs. These are not open to the public, but fishing can usually be arranged through private guide services.

Molokai. A rural, agricultural island with few resort accommodations, Molokai is best known for the shore fishing opportunities available to dunkers on its west coast beaches and to skiff anglers on its south coast flats. Whippers cast from skiffs along the outside of the fringing reefs to stir up explosive strikes from *ulua*. Boats operating out of Kaunakakai Harbor have quick and protected access to productive Penguin Banks, an undersea extension of the island pointing to the southwest.

Lanai. Small, rural, and sparsely populated, Lanai has two small-boat harbors. Manele Bay and Kaumalapau offer limited services for anglers trolling the short length of lee coast. When the trade winds ease, Lanai anglers expand their opportunities toward Molokai to the north and Kahoolawe to the southeast.

HAYWIRE TWIST

A method of forming a loop in single-strand wire or Monel wire, the Haywire Twist is primarily used in saltwater fishing to prevent wraps from coming loose under severe pressure.

To form the Haywire Twist, start by making a loop and crossing the strands (1). Hold the loop tightly with one hand or pliers, and with your free hand press down at point A (the upper strand) with forefinger and up at point B (the lower strand) with thumb; then twist the tag end around the main stem. Check to see that the twist looks as illustrated in step 2, and make four more twists in the same manner. Then wrap (not twist) the tag end of the wire as snugly as possible several times around the main strand (90 degrees to the main stem) to keep the entire rig from unwrapping (3). Bend the end of the tag wire to form a crank (3); holding the loop tightly in one hand, crank the tag wire in a circle in the same direction as the wrap and parallel to the main strand until the wire neatly parts where the last wrap was made. A neat cut is necessary because this wire is likely to be handled, but it is not accomplished by cutting, since cutters cannot cut the wire close enough to avoid a sharp end.

Haywire Twist

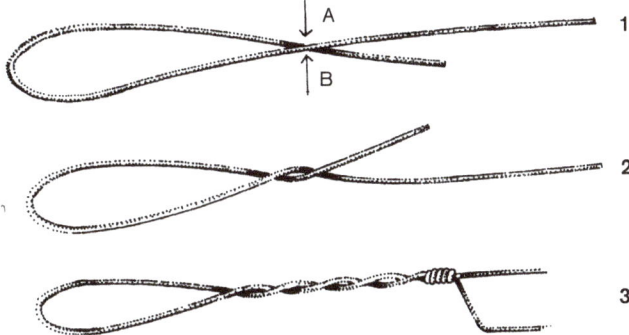

HEAD BOAT

A sportfishing boat that takes anglers out for a per-person fee. Most commonly referred to as a party boat, it is different from a charter boat in that people on a head boat pay individual fees as opposed to one flat fee for renting the boat.
See: Charter Boat; Party Boat.

HEAD SEA

Waves coming toward the bow of a boat and from the direction in which a boat is headed.
See: Waves.

HEADWATERS

The origins of streams and rivers.
See: Basin; Watershed.

HELLGRAMMITE

See: Dobsonflies, Fishflies, and Alderflies.

HELM

The wheel, tiller, stick, or other steering device on a boat.

HEN

A female fish in spawning mode; this term is usually applied to anadromous *(see)* spawners.

HERRING

Herring and their relatives are among the most important of commercial fish worldwide. They are also extremely important as forage fish for a wide variety of predatory fish, sea birds, seals, and other carnivores. In the past, some countries depended entirely on the herring (or related species) fishery for their economic survival. Wars have been waged over the rights to particularly productive herring grounds, which are found in all seas except the very cold waters of the Arctic and the Antarctic.

Large herring are eaten fresh, but many are processed for human consumption by pickling, smoking, or salting. Smaller herring are generally canned and sold as "sardines." They are also used for fish meal, fertilizer, fish oils, and other products. The roe of some herring is a valuable delicacy in certain countries. Many herring species have been depleted through commercial fishing, however.

Most members of the herring family are strictly marine. Some are anadromous and spawn in freshwater, and a few species (those of freshwater origin) never go to sea. Herring typically travel in extensive schools; in the ocean, such schools may extend for miles, which makes harvesting possible in great quantities.

Herring are plankton feeders, screening their food through numerous gill rakers. As such, and because they are generally small, herring are seldom a deliberate quarry of recreational anglers (American and hickory shad are notable exceptions). They are primarily used as bait, either in pieces or whole, by freshwater and saltwater anglers for various game species.

Prominent species with the herring name include Atlantic herring *(see: herring, Atlantic)*, Pacific herring *(see: herring, Pacific)*, blueback herring, and skipjack herring. At least two members of the herring family, alewife *(see)* and blueback herring, are collectively referred to as river herring.

There is minor angling effort for some species, such as blueback and skipjack herring, when they ascend coastal rivers en masse to spawn; this fishery is generally geared more toward procuring food or bait than to pure angling sport. They may, however, be caught on light spoons and small jigs or flies. When massed, they are also taken by snagging (where legal), and also in cast nets. Coastal herring are sometimes also caught, snagged, or taken by a cast net, mainly for use as bait.

See: Menhaden, Atlantic; Sardine, Pacific; Shad, American; Shad, Gizzard; Shad, Hickory; Shad, Threadfin.

HERRING, ATLANTIC *Clupea harengus*.

Other names—herring; Danish: *Atlantisk sild, sild;* Finnish: *silakka, silli;* French: *hareng de l'Atlantique;* German: *allec, hering;* Norwegian: *sild;* Polish: *sledz;* Spanish: *arenque del Atlántico.*

A member of the Clupeidae family of herring, the Atlantic herring is in the *Guinness Book of World Records* as the world's most numerous fish and is certainly one of the world's most valuable fish. It is used fresh, smoked, salted, and pickled, and is often packed as "sardines," also being shipped frozen as bait and used in the manufacture of oils, fish meal, and fertilizer, and in the pearl-essence industry. Herring are extremely important as forage for predator species; Atlantic herring may be used as bait by anglers but are not a sportfishing target, although they may be caught (or snagged) by coastal anglers who seek to use fresh specimens as live bait.

Atlantic herring inhabit both the eastern and western Atlantic Ocean. Important commercial fisheries for juvenile Atlantic herring (ages 1 to 3) have existed since the last century along the coasts of Maine and New Brunswick. Development of large-scale fisheries for adult herring is comparatively recent, primarily occurring in the western Gulf of Maine, on Georges Bank, and on the Scotian Shelf. Herring stocks have been seriously depleted from commercial overfishing, and some stocks collapsed as long ago as the 1970s; in the late 1990s there were signs of an increase in populations.

A related and similar species in the western Atlantic Ocean is the blueback herring *(Alosa aestivalis)*, which ranges from Nova Scotia to Florida and reaches a maximum length of roughly 13 inches. The skipjack herring *(A. chrysochloris)* occurs in the Gulf of Mexico from Texas to the Florida Panhandle, and ascends the Mississippi River and some of its tributaries, including the Ohio River, and is also found in some impoundments; also known as skipjack shad and golden shad, it reaches

Members of the herring family have a wide lower jaw that curves, a short upper jaw that reaches only to below the middle of the eye, and a cheek that is longer than it is deep.

Atlantic Herring

a length of 19 inches.

Identification. The Atlantic herring is silvery with a bluish or greenish blue back and elongated body. The dorsal fin begins at about the middle of body, and there are 39 to 47 weakly developed ventral scutes. At the midline of the belly are scales which form a sharp-edged ridge. Teeth on the roof of the mouth distinguish the Atlantic herring from the similar alewife.

Size. Ordinarily less than a foot long, the Atlantic herring can grow to 18 inches. The all-tackle world record is a 1-pound, 1-ounce fish taken off Long Beach, New York; a 3-pound, 12-ounce record stands for the skipjack herring.

Distribution. Atlantic herring are the most abundant pelagic fish in cool, northern Atlantic waters. In the eastern Atlantic Ocean, they extend from the northern Bay of Biscay north to Iceland and south to Greenland, eastward to Spitsbergen and Novaya Zemlaya, including the Baltic Sea. In the western Atlantic Ocean, they are widely distributed in continental shelf waters from Labrador to Cape Hatteras, and have been separated by biologists into Gulf of Maine and Georges Bank stocks.

Habitat. This species schools in coastal waters and has been recorded in temperatures of 1° to 18°C.

Life history/Behavior. Atlantic herring usually spawn in the fall, although in any particular month of the year there is at least one group of Atlantic herring that moves into shallow coastal waters to spawn. (Blueback and skipjack herring, which are anadromous, spawn in coastal rivers in the spring.)

Spawning in the Gulf of Maine occurs from late August into October, beginning in northern locations and progressing southward. The female lays between 25,000 and 40,000 eggs, which are demersal and typically deposited on rock or gravel substrates, hatching in less than two weeks. Larvae grow by late spring into juvenile brit herring that may form large aggregations in coastal waters during summer.

Almost 5 inches long by the end of their first year, Atlantic herring nearly double their length in two years and reach maturity at age 4 or 5. Schools of herring may contain billions of individuals. In the western Atlantic, herring migrate from feeding grounds along the Maine coast during autumn to the southern New England–Mid-Atlantic region during winter, with larger individuals tending to migrate greater distances.

Food. The Atlantic herring feeds on small planktonic copepods in its first year, graduating to mainly copepods.
See: Herring.

HERRING, LAKE
See: Cisco.

HERRING, PACIFIC *Clupea pallasii*.
Other names—herring, north Pacific herring; French: *hareng Pacifique;* Japanese: *nishin;* Spanish: *arenque del Pacifico.*

A member of the Clupeidae family of herring, an important food for many predatory fish, and the principal food of salmon, the Pacific herring also has many uses for human consumption. Sold fresh, dried/salted, smoked, canned, and frozen, the Pacific herring is commercially caught in the eastern Pacific for its roe; it is marketed in Asia as an extremely expensive delicacy called *kazunokokombu,* in which the roe are salted and sold on beds of kelp. Pacific herring may be used as bait by anglers, but are not a sportfishing target, although they may be caught (or snagged) by coastal anglers who seek to use fresh specimens as live bait.

Identification. Similar to the Atlantic herring *(see: herring, Atlantic),* the Pacific herring is silvery with a bluish or greenish blue back and elongated body.

Size. The Pacific herring can grow to 18 inches in length.

Distribution. In the western Pacific Ocean, Pacific herring are found from Anadyr Bay and the eastern coasts of Kamchatka, including possibly the Aleutian Islands, southward to Japan and the west coast of Korea. In the eastern Pacific Ocean, they are found from Kent Peninsula and the Beaufort Sea southward to northern Baja California.

Habitat. Pacific herring inhabit coastal waters, and during the summer of their first year, the young appear in schools on the surface. In the fall, schools disappear as the young move to deep water, in depths of up to 475 meters, to stay there for the next two to three years.

Life history/Behavior. Depending on latitude, mature adults migrate inshore from December through July, entering estuaries to breed. These herring do not show strong north-south migrations, with populations being localized. Like other herring, they school in great numbers.

Food and feeding habits. Pacific herring lar-

Pacific Herring

vae feed on planktonic foods, including ostracods, small copepods, small fish larvae, euphausids, and diatoms. Juveniles feed on crustaceans as well as on small fish, marine worms, and larval clams. Adults feed on larger crustaceans and small fish.
See: Herring.

HERRING, RIVER
A term applied collectively to alewives (*Alosa pseudoharengus; see: alewife*), blueback herring (*Alosa aestivalis*), and skipjack herring (*Alosa chrysochloris*).
See: Herring; Herring, Atlantic.

HIGHLINE
A line that is fished far behind a trolling boat.
See: Flatlining; Trolling.

HI-LO RIG
A saltwater term for a two-hook bottom fishing bait rig. Featuring a bank sinker, two three-way swivels, and hooked leaders extending from the swivels, which are 2 to 3 feet apart, a hi-lo rig permits fishing one low bait on the bottom and another higher, as well as allows presentation of two different baits.

HIND, RED *Epinephelus guttatus.*
Other names—strawberry grouper, speckled hind; French: *mérou couronné*; Spanish: *mero colorado, tofia.*

A grouper of the Serranidae family, the red hind is an important fish in the Caribbean, where large numbers are caught every year. It has excellent white, flaky meat that is usually marketed fresh.

Identification. As with all grouper, the red hind has a stout body and a large mouth. It is very similar to the rock hind *(see: hind, rock)* in appearance, although the red hind is slightly more reddish brown in color with dark red brown spots above and pure red spots below over a whitish background. It differs from the rock hind in having no spots on the tail or dorsal fin, and no dark splotches on the back or tail. The outer edges of the soft dorsal, caudal, and anal fins are blackish and are sometimes also edged in white. It can pale or darken to blend with surroundings.

Size/Age. The red hind can grow to 2 feet, although it is usually less than 15 inches long; most 12-inch and larger fish are males. Although it can reach 10 pounds, the red hind is rarely larger than 4 pounds in weight; the all-tackle world record is for a 6-pound, 1-ounce fish taken off Florida. The red hind can live for 17 years or longer.

Distribution. In the western Atlantic, red hind occur from North Carolina and Bermuda south to the Bahamas, the southern Gulf of Mexico, and to Brazil. They are common in the Caribbean, occasional in the Bahamas and Florida, and rare north of Florida.

Habitat. Red hind are one of the most common grouper in the West Indies, inhabiting shallow inshore reefs and rocky bottoms at depths of 10 to 160 feet. In Florida and the Bahamas they are usually found in quieter, deeper waters. Red hind are solitary and territorial fish, often found drifting or lying motionless along the bottom, camouflaged by their surroundings.

Spawning behavior. Spawning takes place from March through July in 68° to 82°F waters at depths of 100 to 130 feet. At this time, mature fish of age 3 and older form large clusters over rugged bottoms. They lay pelagic eggs in numbers between 90,000 and more than 3 million. Some fish undergo sexual inversion.

Food and feeding habits. Red hind feed on various bottom animals, such as crabs, crustaceans, fish, and octopus; they hide in holes and crevices and capture prey by ambush or after a short chase.

Angling. As with other grouper, bottom fishing is the best method to catch red hind, using cut fish or squid as bait. Fishing is best inshore over irregular bottom in water 80 to 180 feet deep, and along the shelf break where the depth ranges from 240 to 350 feet. Sturdy boat rods and reels with heavy line are primarily used. Terminal tackle usually consists of a heavy sinker and two 4/0 to 6/0 hooks baited with squid or cut fish rigged on a very heavy monofilament leader.
See: Grouper; Inshore Fishing.

HIND, ROCK *Epinephelus adscensionis.*
Other names—grouper, jack, rock cod; French: *mérou oualioua*; Portuguese: *garoupa-pintada*; Spanish: *mero cabrilla.*

A grouper in the Serranidae family, the rock hind is found in the same range as the red hind *(see: hind, red)* and is also good table fare. Divers can often distinguish the two species by their behavior alone, as the rock hind is reclusive and shies away from humans.

Identification. The rock hind has an overall tan to olive brown cast, with many large, reddish to dark dots covering the entire body and fins. Similar in appearance to the red hind, it has one to four distinctive pale or dark splotches along its back,

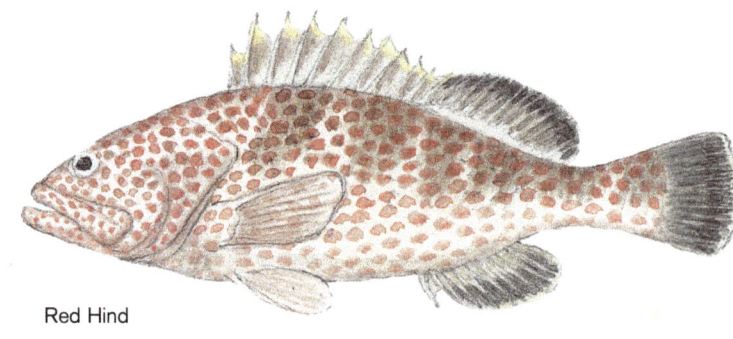
Red Hind

Rock Hind

appearing below the middle of the dorsal fin, behind the dorsal fin on the caudal peduncle, and below the spinous and soft parts of the dorsal fin. The tail and anal fins have a broad, whitish outer edge but lack the additional blackish margins found on the dorsal, caudal, and anal fins of the red hind. It can pale or darken dramatically.

Size. The rock hind can reach 2 feet in length; the all-tackle world-record fish is a 9-pounder.

Distribution. In the western Atlantic, rock hind occur from Massachusetts to southeastern Brazil, including Bermuda, the Bahamas, the eastern Caribbean, and the northern Gulf of Mexico; they are rare north of Florida. Rock hind are also found in the eastern Atlantic around the Ascension and St. Helena Islands.

Habitat. Solitary fish, rock hind inhabit rocky or rough inshore regions in shallow waters, although they occasionally inhabit deep reefs. They are often found drifting near the bottom.

Food and feeding habits. Ordinarily feeding on crabs and fish, rock hind are said to feed on juvenile triggerfish and young sea turtles at Ascension Island.

Angling. Like other grouper, rock hind are primarily caught by fishing at the right depth over an irregular bottom.

See: Grouper; Inshore Fishing.

HIP BOOTS (Hippers)
See: Waders.

HIRE BOAT
A small boat available for rent on a daily, multiday, or weekly basis, operated by the person who rents it, and not accompanied by a fishing guide or boat captain. This is essentially an Australian term for a self-guided rental boat, not to be confused with a guide boat *(see)* or charter boat *(see)*.

HOGSUCKER, NORTHERN
Hypentelium nigricans.
Other names—sucker, hog sucker.

This is a widespread and distinctive-looking member of the sucker family.

Identification. Northern hogsuckers get their name from their piglike appearance, particularly their head. They have a very steep forehead and long, protruding lips, bearing a strong likeness to a pig's snout. Their head also has a concave depression between the eyes, a trait distinctive among suckers. The body is conical, with the head region much thicker than the caudal peduncle. The body is marked with four lateral bars that come together on the fish's back to form saddles. Northern hogsuckers are generally darkly pigmented on the back and lightly pigmented on the belly.

Range. The northern hogsucker is widely distributed across central and eastern North America, occurring in the Great Lakes, Mississippi, Ohio, and some Atlantic drainages.

Habitat. The northern hogsucker inhabits primarily large streams and small rivers. It is usually found in areas with high water quality and clean substrate, free of heavy siltation. It is well-suited to a benthic lifestyle, remaining close to the bottom in areas of various depth and flow velocities. Adults may inhabit deep pools and runs, as they are too large to be preyed upon by bass and other predators. The young and subadults live in faster water and in the stream margins.

Food. Like most suckers, the northern hogsucker preys upon many varieties of benthic

Northern Hogsucker

organisms, the most common of which are insect larvae, small crustaceans, detritus, and algae. It feeds by disturbing the stream bottom with its large snout and sucking up organisms that it dislodges. It can often be seen with its body angled upward, tail high, nearly perpendicular to the stream bottom as it forages around larger rocks. Its small air bladder and large pectoral fins help support it in the current while feeding.

Size/Age. The northern hogsucker is a medium-size sucker, reaching up to 12 to 14 inches in length. Sexual maturity is reached between two and three years old, although most fish do not spawn until age 4. The northern hogsucker may live for eight years.

Spawning behavior. Northern hogsuckers spawn in mid- to late spring as the water begins to warm. They do not make long upstream migrations as many suckers do, but spawn in pool tails, riffles, and stream margins near where they reside. Like most suckers, northern hogsuckers require clean gravel substrate for successful reproduction. They have a reproductive behavior unique among suckers. One female spawns with a group of three or more males that follow her around when she enters the reproductive areas. They will move around each other and move alongside the female, but spawning does not occur until the female begins to quiver.

Angling. The northern hogsucker is not considered a desired game or commercial fish because of its soft flesh. It is taken by snagging and jigging where legal. It is also not frequently used as bait, although it is likely of value as food for large gamefish.
See: Suckers.

HOLDING

An expression for the position of a fish, usually in a stream or where there is current; this is similar to a lie *(see)*. An example might be, "The shad are holding in the channel at the tail of the pool."

HOLDOVER FISH

Stocked fish, usually trout, that survive through at least one winter in the wild; also known as carryover fish.

HOLE

Angling jargon, primarily used in freshwater fishing, with several related meanings. In the simplest sense, a hole is a place to fish or a place where fish may be congregated and where a person has good success ("My favorite fishing hole is at the first bend of the river"). Generally the term "hole" is used to refer to a deep spot in a river, stream, or creek, which is more widely known as a pool *(see)*. River holes or pools, because of their depth and darkness, and perhaps cooler temperature, are places where some species of fish are especially likely to be found. In a lake or reservoir, the term "hole" refers to a place that produces a good catch of fish at a given time, or repeatedly over time; such a place might be notable for its depth, structural elements, or other features that cause fish to congregate there.

An angler who is "sitting on a hole" is one who stays in a certain productive spot. A person who has "got a hole" is one who has a somewhat confined location (usually on a big body of water) that may not be known to others and that produces good catches of fish.

HONDURAS

The largely mountainous country of Honduras in Central America is bordered by Nicaragua on the south, Guatemala on the west, and El Salvador on the southeast. A small portion of southeastern Honduras fronts on the Pacific Ocean at the Gulf of Fonseca, but it is not known for sportfishing opportunity. The northern and eastern regions abut the Caribbean, however, and offer more than 400 miles of coastline. Here there are numerous rivers, large estuaries and lagoons, many small islands, and a few offshore islands.

Most of Honduras' rivers flow to the Caribbean, the most prominent being the Ulúa, which drains the western third of the country and empties into the Gulf of Honduras. In these west-central mountains, Lake Yojoa was a hot largemouth bass lake for a brief period in the late 1970s and early 1980s but has fallen off the radar screen in ensuing years. Bass up to 18 pounds were once caught at the clear 13-mile-long, 8-mile-wide Yojoa, mostly by fishing excruciatingly deep, but netting took its toll on the fishery.

In the far east, a great watercourse, the Patuca, originates deep in the eastern highlands and flows through the Mosquito Coast to the sea, just east of Patana National Park; the nearby Coco River does likewise, forming the boundary with Nicaragua. Along the coast and sandwiched between these two systems is a vast network of swampy mangroves collectively known as Laguna de Caratasca, which includes numerous lakes, inflows, and backwater areas that stretch for more than 45 miles. These are difficult to access but are loaded with promise for snook, tarpon, and snapper, and likely other species.

This enormous area is not known to be fished; however, east of the Patuca River mouth by about 30 miles is the entrance to Brus Lagoon, where a lodge set up operations at Cannon Island in the mid-1990s. This location has tremendous fishing for snook and tarpon, including large specimens of both species. Tarpon in the 200-pound class, and snook up to 46 pounds, have been caught here.

The relatively short Sigre River enters the lagoon, and nearby is the Patána River, which flows directly into the sea. Many smaller rivers flow into Brus Lagoon, however, and each is a lush tropical wonder, with dense brush and good fishing at various times. The lagoon mouth is deep and wide and provides excellent angling opportunities. The main river mouth and vicinity have big tarpon, larger apparently than are found farther down in the Caribbean near the mouths of Costa Rican rivers. Snook are caught at the Brus River mouth as well, and along the beach.

This area is still being explored, and its angling opportunities are still evolving. Erratic weather patterns hindered its early development. From September through March snook and tarpon are abundant, as are cubera snapper (including a 78-pound line-class record caught in 1995). September and October, and January through April, are the best times for snook activity. November and December usually bring heavy rains, which greatly swell the area and flush so much muddy water through the lagoon and into the Caribbean that the fishing turns off. Trolling outside the river mouths is the main method for locating tarpon when the water gets muddy.

This area has become an ecological protection zone, and netting is supposedly prohibited in critical areas. If these regulations hold, a good fishery is ensured. Legal and illegal netting activities in areas like this have adversely affected numerous good coastal and inland sportfisheries in Mexico, Central America, and South America.

A number of small keys exist out in the Caribbean, east and north of this coast. These reportedly harbor bonefish and permit, but their distance offshore—roughly 40 to 60 miles from Laguna de Caratasca and much farther from Brus Lagoon—makes them an unknown entity, an area likely to be explored only by long-distance cruisers.

To the west, however, Roatán and Guanaja Islands lie offshore northeast of La Ceiba and are accessible by plane from San Pedro Sula. Guanaja has an established camp that attracts avid reef divers and is known for an abundance of small bonefish and permit on shallow grassy flats. Roatán, a larger island west of Guanaja, has extensive flats, but they are not known to have the bonefish and permit that exist at Guanaja.

HOOK

A recurved piece of metal wire, one end of which tapers to a sharp point, used to impale and capture fish.

Also known as a fishhook, a hook is truly an indispensable piece of sportfishing equipment. Tens of millions of hooks are manufactured daily around the world for use in both sportfishing and commercial fishing, and some manufacturers have tens of thousands of individual hook models. For sportfishing use, hooks are stand-alone equipment used as is with various types of natural or processed bait; they are attached as is or with dressing to an extremely diverse range of hard and soft artificial lures; they are dressed with various materials to become artificial flies; and they are used in molds for the construction of lead and hard-metal lures.

The hook originated long before any other fishing equipment, having been used in some form with spearing instruments in prehistoric time. It is speculated that the oldest fishhooks were made out of wood during the Stone Age, possibly evolving at the same time as gorges. A tree with branches that stick out at acute angles can be the source of a hook strong enough for angling, but the deterioration of wood precludes finding ancient evidence of this.

It is known, however, that gorges were used to capture fish during the Stone Age. These were straight, tapered shafts made of bone, stone, shell, wood, etc., that were placed inside a natural bait to lodge in the stomach or mouth of a fish. Hooks made of bone were used during the latter period of the Stone Age. When used for hooks, bone had a tendency to break, although it withstood hard use, even in saltwater. Historians report that processing bone hooks took patience, but Stone Age people had implements good enough to make extra-fine hooks from this material. Old bone hooks have been unearthed in many places, including Europe, Egypt, and Palestine. The oldest bone hook found in Palestine is reportedly 9,000 years old. Although there was a lot of diversity to the oldest bone hooks, they were not made with barbs, which developed much later.

Hook material evolved over thousands of years from bone to copper to bronze and then iron. The genesis of modern hooks was during the Middle Ages. It is not known exactly when fine hooks for sportfishing were fashioned from steel needles, but the use of steel hooks was noted in print for the first time by Dame Juliana Berners in her 1496 essay *Treatyse of Fysshynge With an Angle;* this essay was included in the second edition of *The Boke of Saint Albans,* the first known manual of sportfishing. Dame Berners recommended using the finest darning needles for small fish, embroidery needles for larger fish, and tailor's or shoemaker's needles for the biggest fish, and she also detailed how to make the steel pliable, fashion a barb, and shape and temper the steel.

Hooks were being manufactured as a business in the seventeenth century, when Izaak Walton recommended buying hooks from London's Charles Kirby, whom he described in *The Compleat Angler* as "the most exact and best Hook-maker this nation affords." Kirby is credited with the advancement of the modern fishhook—through his metal tempering and hardening processes—and the invention of the kirbed offset, which is still in use today.

Hooks were largely made by hand until mechanization took over in the middle of the nineteenth century. For a time, England was the hook-making center of the world (the town of Redditch in particular), and this still accounts for the names that were given to many of the popular patterns that have stayed throughout the years.

> Zane Grey had his membership from the Catalina Tuna Club revoked in 1921 when a woman caught a 426-pound broadbill, larger than his own 418-pound catch, and he accused her of having assistance in the catch.

Today hook manufacture is widely dispersed around the globe, and there is an astounding array of hooks in production—many quite similar and many vastly different—and the number of patterns and sizes is impressive and confusing. The array of hooks is due to fishing methods, the differing mouths of fish, and the lures and bait used to attract them.

Characteristics

The majority of fishhooks are made from high carbon steel; a good number are made from stainless steel, and some are made from alloys. The physical parts of a hook include the eye, shank, bend, point, gap, and throat, as depicted in the accompanying illustration. The point may have a barb, and the eye may actually be flattened solid instead of having an eyelike opening. All of these parts have notable features and variations.

In the most basic evaluation of a hook, there are three commonly accepted types described according to the number of points. These are characterized as single, double, or treble hooks; quadruple hooks (four points) have been produced but are not currently in sportfishing use.

Single hooks are the most common hook and the overwhelming favorite for fishing with most types of bait; they are used on all but a tiny percentage of artificial flies and are attached to many types of lures. Double hooks are by far the least common type; they are mainly used in tying artificial flies, but some are employed in baitfishing, and some are fastened to weedless lures. Treble hooks are very popular on a wide range of lures, which are prerigged by lure manufacturers; they are almost never used in fly tying and are only occasionally fished with bait.

Eye. The eye is the portion of the hook to which the line is attached, and it probably should be called the butt or line connector because it is not always shaped like an eye. The most popular eye style is the ball, which is also known as a ring eye and has a straight-cut end that meets flush with the stem of the eye. A similar but more expensive-to-produce version is the tapered eye, which has a taper-cut end that meets the stem. In both of these,

Hook Features

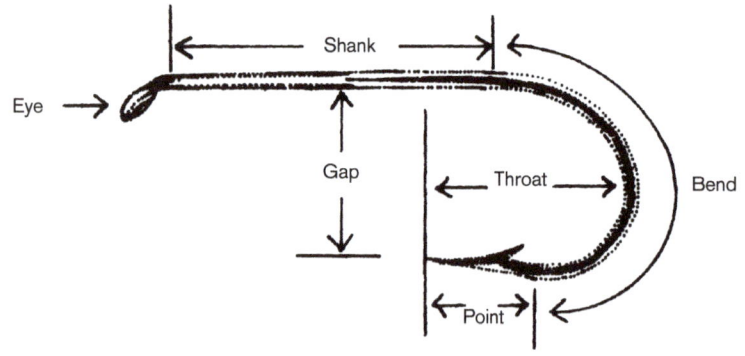

Hook Eyes

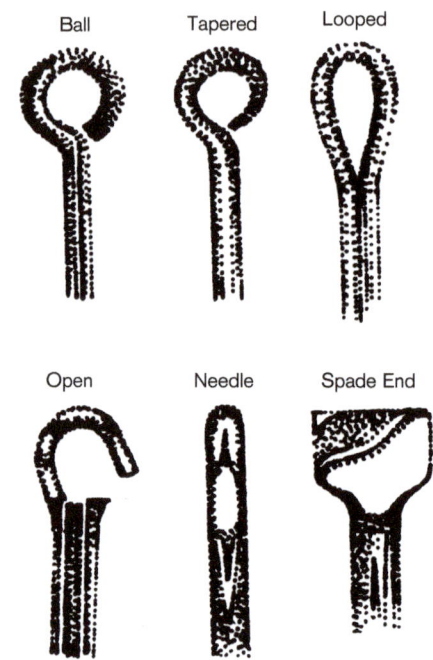

there should be no gap that fishing line can slip through; if a gap exists, the hook is poorly made and you should discard it.

Other eye styles include the oval and needle, which are common on treble hooks, and the looped, which is a traditional style for salmon and steelhead flies. Several versions of open eyes exist; these have a ringlike end. Open eyes are intended for easy changing on lures where hooks are prerigged to lure bodies without split rings; they are subject to loss if the eye isn't fully closed (you need very good pliers) and also to weakening if they are opened and closed a few times.

In addition to being characterized according to shape, an eye can be typecast according to position. Eyes may be straight (in line with the hook), turned up, or turned down; turned-up eyes are preferred on short-shanked heavily dressed flies, and turned-down eyes are preferred by some people for their line of hook penetration. Angled eyes are often snelled to the line when used with bait.

Eyeless hooks are those in which the line is snelled to the shank, since there is no ring or loop to fasten a knot to. The ends of the eyeless hooks are flattened, often to a spadelike form or a knob. These hooks are popular in Europe for coarse and match fishing, especially with very fine-diameter lines and small bait.

Shank. The shank is that part of the hook between the eye and the bend. Hook patterns have a normal or standard length, but they come several sizes larger and smaller in shank length. A short or long shank designation means that the length of the shank of that item is equal to that of the next smaller or larger regular-shank hook of the same pattern.

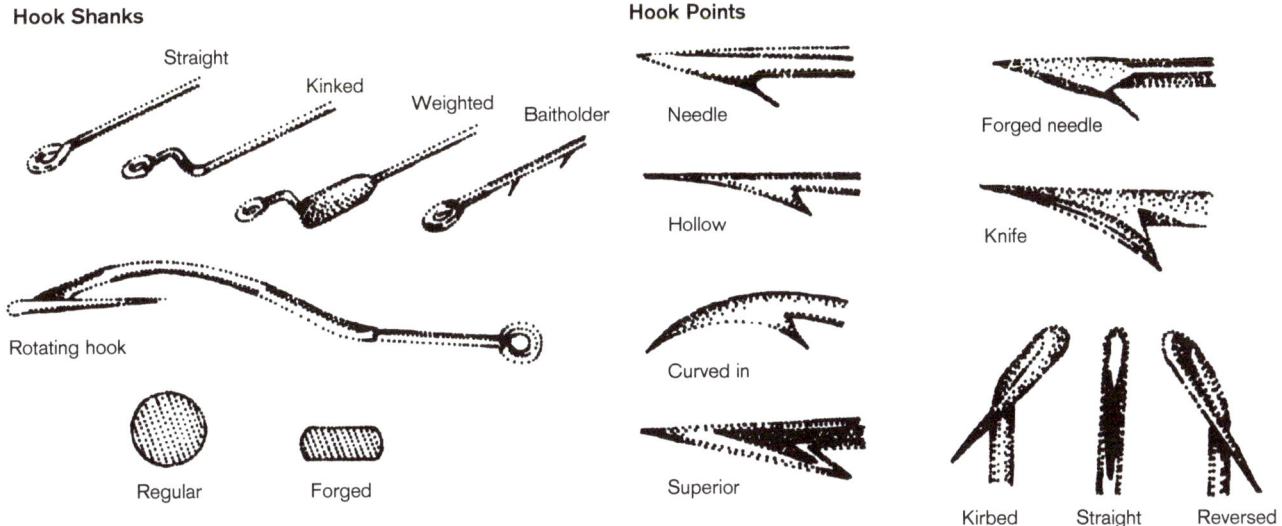

Variations of more than one step are denoted by the letter *X* or the word "extra." A short-shanked 2X hook, for example, is equal in shank length to a regular-shank hook of the same pattern that is two sizes smaller.

Shanks are straight, bent, curved, humped, and contorted in various ways. Certain styles are favored for their hooking efficiency or for their appearance when dressed with various materials. A keel or humped shank, for example, is popularly used with Texas-rigged soft worms and also for tying some streamer flies. Some shanks have multiple curves for rotating into the fish's mouth, although these may not be as strong as other models. Most shanks are smooth, but some have multiple slices on the upper and lower portions. These are like mini-barbs and are meant for holding bait or soft-bodied lures; hooks with this feature are usually called baitholders. Some shanks also sport a small weight on the shank, either near the bend or just behind the eye; these are mainly used with soft lures that are rigged Texas style without a slip sinker.

Point. The point is the tapered sharp business end of the hook. It may or may not incorporate a barb, which is the sharp projection behind the point that impedes the hook's backward movement when it has impaled a fish (or clothing, skin, etc.).

Hook points have many configurations. The more common ones in sportfishing hooks are needle or conical, hollow, curved or rolled, knife, and spear or superior. Penetration and holding power are the critical elements of a point. Especially noted for their penetration are the needle point, which is conical in shape, and the knife point, which has triangulated sharp edges. The curved point, which rolls inward toward the shank, has an inward line of pull that helps to keep the hook driving in under sustained pressure.

It is arguable whether long or short points penetrate better, and this is a matter of the sharpness of the hook, the point style, the fish species, and the hooksetting abilities of the angler, as well as the size of the barb in some cases. If a point is long but slender, it should penetrate as well as one that is short but thicker, although points that are too long are weaker.

As a result of improved manufacturing processes, the sharpness of hooks has progressed significantly in recent years. This is an important advancement because sharpness is the one hook property that anglers readily see the value of. Although most new hooks can still be improved by sharpening *(see: hook sharpening)*, many of the new chemically sharpened hooks are very sharp when fresh. This chemical operation incorporates a series of dips and rinses in extremely potent acids that shave off a tiny layer of the surface of the steel. The result is a perfect shape and superb sharpness.

Hook points primarily lie parallel to the shank when viewed from a straight-on position. However, the point, and sometimes part of the bend, may be offset to one side, in theory for better hooking. If viewed from a straight-on position, a point is

Magnified view of a conical-style hook point.

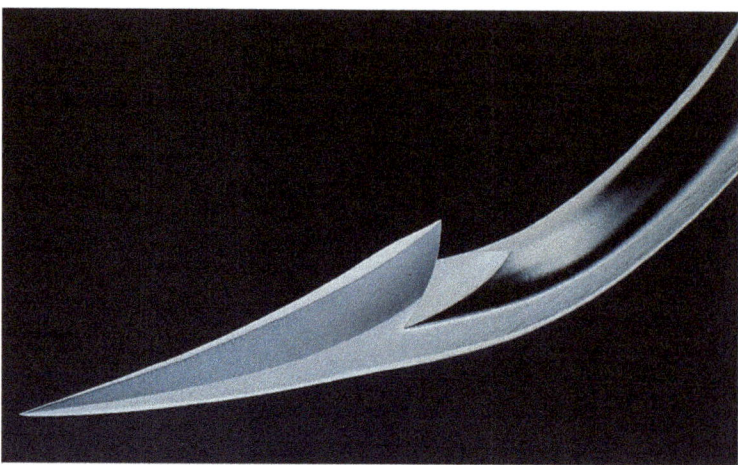

Magnified view of a knife-style hook; note triangulation.

called kirbed (after Charles Kirby) when the point is angled to the left of the perpendicular plane; it is called reversed when it is angled to the right. These are more likely to be used in bottom fishing situations with bait than in circumstances where an actively moving hook can drag in the water and cause spinning.

The points of some hooks may also have a wire or nylon guard. Hooks so equipped are called weedless, and the guard extends from the hook eye to the point.

Barb. Barbs exist on the majority of manufactured hooks. Those without them are labeled barbless. Many anglers pinch or file a barb down to make a hook barbless. Some hooks have a slight, smooth bump along the lower point in lieu of a barb. The purpose of the barb is to hold the hook in the fish. A large barb is not necessarily helpful in this regard and may actually make it harder to attain full penetration of the point, not to mention create a large entry hole that can cause the hook to slip out when you don't want it to. Barbless hooks facilitate hook removal and may be mandated in some waters to minimize injury to fish that are released.

Barbs

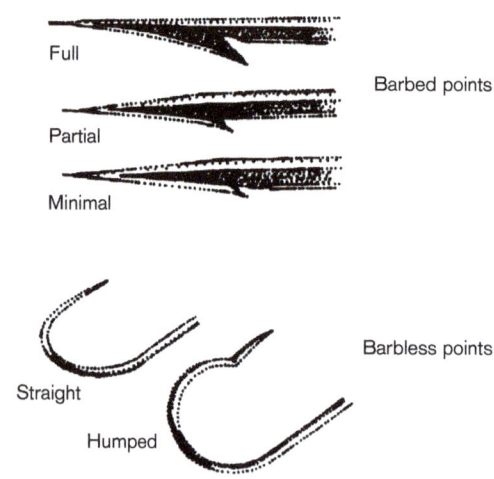

The role of a barb in keeping fish on the hook is greatly overrated; many anglers have little or no loss of fish on barbless hooks provided that good fish-playing measures are employed (see: catch-and-release). Nevertheless, it is often hard to find barbless hooks in the range of styles and sizes that you may want.

You can make your own hooks barbless by filing off the barb or by pinching it down. Filing works best with small fine-diameter wire hooks. To pinch the barb down, use a pair of good-quality pliers, place the blunt end over the barb, and squeeze tightly to flatten the barb. Sharpen the point well afterward. Remember to maintain a constant tight line on a fish when using barbless hooks, because the hooks can easily become dislodged if there is even momentary slack in the line.

Bend/pattern. The name by which a style of hook is known is called a pattern, and this is a function of its bend, which is the curved section between the point and the shank. The bend has a lot to do with the strength of the hook. Ideally a hook should resist bending up to a stage where the hook almost would break, preferably bending instead of breaking. Resistance to direct-pull pressure is influenced by hook style and size, is substantially aided by forging, and is related to the bite and gap. The gap is the distance between the tip of the point and the shank. The distance from the peak of the bend to the gap is known as the bite or throat. Most hooks have a deep or relatively deep bite and a fairly wide gap, both of which keep hooked fish more secure than a shallow bite or narrow gap.

Most hooks avoid having a sharp angle to the bend and are formed such that the initial stage of the bend is gradual and the final stage of the bend is pronounced. This design is actually less easily bent than a symmetrically round one.

Popular patterns and attributes include:

Sproat	Straight point; popular with flies and lures.
Kirby	Point offset helps prevent hook from slipping out; good for baitfishing.
O'Shaughnessy	Outward bend to the tip of the point; heavy wire; many applications.
Aberdeen	Light wire, round bend good for use with minnows; will bend before breaking.
Carlisle	Stronger than Aberdeen; used with bait; long shank prevents fish from swallowing the hook.
Siwash	Heavy wire; extra-long point offers good retention; used for big, active fish.
Salmon Egg	Short shank; concealed by small bait.

Claw or Beak	Point is offset and curved inward to aid penetration; used often with bait.
Limerick	Long shank, wide bend provides extra hooking space.

There are many more patterns, of course, and many with very specialized applications. Freshwater bass anglers, for example, have such an affinity for fishing with soft lures, especially worms, that there is a whole genre of so-called worm hooks (which should not be confused with fishing with natural worms) having various humps and bends to the shanks, as well as different bends and worm-rigging enhancements. One of the more specialized saltwater hooks is a circle hook, which has become very popular in baitfishing, especially for tuna, but also other species. The circle hook has a wide bend and long inward point that at first glance makes you wonder how it could ever stick a fish, but not only does it stick the fish, it also doesn't pull out very easily under fishing rod pressure, so a greater number of fish hooked are landed.

Size/gauge/temper. No matter what the pattern, hooks are all designated according to size, which in principle is the width of the gap. This is just a relative designation, however, instead of an absolute one. Gap width may differ between families of hooks, and there is no consistency between manufacturers in sizing, so the matter of size designation is relative to individual manufacturers and specific patterns.

Sizes are specified in whole numbers at the smaller end of the spectrum and as "aught" fractions as they get larger. The smallest hooks, depending on manufacturer, are No. 32, 30, or 28; the largest

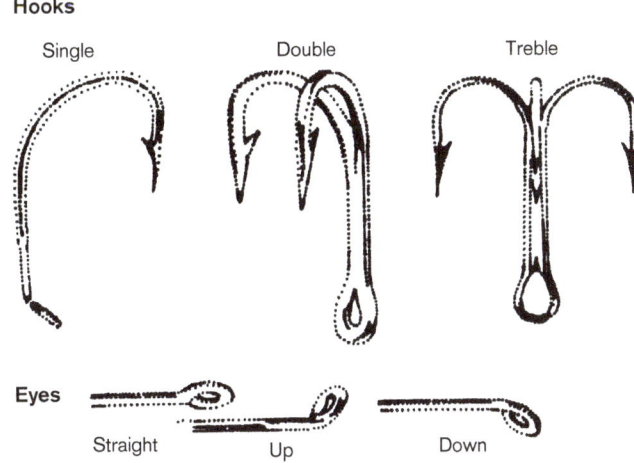

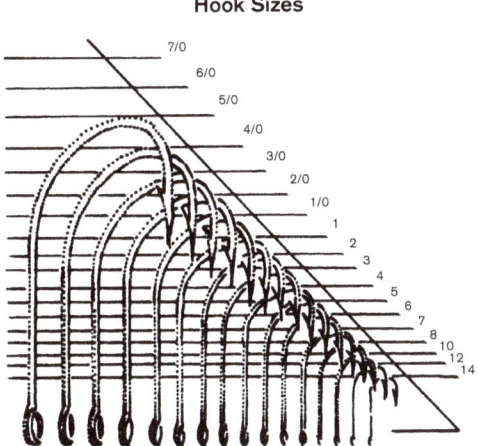

Hook Sizes

The distance between the point and the inside of the shank, known as the gap, determines hook size. Large hooks (1/0 to 7/0) increase in size as the number increases. Small hooks (1 to 14 and beyond) decrease in size as the number increases, and come in many smaller sizes than are depicted here. This illustration is drawn to actual scale and based on a standard, popular American bait hook, the rolled-point, offset, forged Eagle Claw No. 084.

hooks range from 14/0 up to 19/0.

Although not reflected in size designations, the diameter of the wire used to make the hook has a bearing on its performance and its proper use. This diameter is reached in manufacturing by taking steel wire rods and reducing them to the wire gauge that is necessary for a particular pattern. The wire is pulled through a series of ever-narrowing orifices, which reduce the gauge, sometimes by as much as 90 percent.

There are fine, medium, and heavy wire gauges corresponding to relative diameter. Heavy wire is used in making hooks for the strongest applications and for situations where it is beneficial for a hook to sink fast (large wet flies, for example, or big-game baitfishing); fine wire is used in making hooks for light-line fishing, angling with small and delicate bait, and in slow-sinking or floating uses; and medium wire is used for general-purpose hooks.

In the manufacturing process, the drawn wire is machined into shape and then heat-tempered. Tempering is the hardening process that gives the material its strength within that shape. It is a critical operation, because overtempering results in soft hooks that don't adequately resist bending and undertempering results in hard hooks with no flexibility. The ideal is a strong hook that will flex moderately; if the hook has no flex under load, the hook will snap at less of a load. (Incidentally, with the exception of some light-wire hooks, like Aberdeen patterns, when a hook bends out of its original shape and does not spring back, it is permanently deformed and should be discarded.) Some hooks are also given extra strengthening by forging, which is stamping the sides flat. Although this increases resistance to bending on a straight pull, it does not help resist side torque and is often not found on hooks with offset points for this reason, since offset points do not resist side pressure as well as straight points.

Finish/corrosion resistance. In the manufacturing process, different finishes are applied to hooks to provide either cosmetic value (appealing to the angler or, in a few cases, to the fish) or corrosion resistance. Some carbon steel hooks are given color varnishes or lacquers; these are mainly blue, black, bronze, green, and red, but fluorescent and luminescent colors are also applied. Tin, cadmium, nickel, black nickel, gold, and chrome/zinc platings are applied to other carbon steel hooks. Most stainless steel hooks receive no finishing after being polished.

Of the tinted varnishes, bronze is most common and also the most basic one for freshwater use, though it (and the other varnishes) has low corrosion resistance. Gold finishing may involve plating 24 karat gold in better hooks or lacquering lesser-quality products with brass; these are strictly used in freshwater because of low corrosion resistance, and mainly with Aberdeen and salmon egg hooks. Nickel is also a prevalent freshwater finish; it results from electroplating, provides a shiny silver appearance, and has better corrosion resistance than bronze.

An advanced version of nickel plating, called electroless nickel, has an improved corrosion resistance and sharper hooks than standard nickel-plated hooks. A related new multiple-layer finish is nickel Teflon, which is a durable hook with a fast hooksetting property due to the slick Teflon exterior. Black nickel, which is not well known to many anglers, is a newer multiple-layer (zinc oxide over nickel) finish that has a silvery black appearance; it has more corrosion resistance than all of the aforementioned finishes.

Electroplated tin is a standard saltwater finish for carbon steel hooks; this is a step up the corrosion-resistance scale from the aforementioned finishes and is itself exceeded by cadmium-tin plating and chrome-zinc plating, which are finishes that receive different trademark names with different manufacturers. Cadmium is a substance with adverse environmental implications, so manufacturers who use chrome-zinc plating point out the additional safety value of chrome-zinc. These finishes rank with or actually exceed stainless steel in corrosion-resistant properties.

Obviously the ability of hooks to withstand corrosion varies, particularly in saltwater, and is an important aspect of selection. No finish is completely rustproof. As a material, carbon steel is significantly less resistant to corrosion than stainless steel or cadmium-tin and chrome-zinc. Freshwater anglers seldom use the latter three finishes in ordinary fishing activities. In any environment, however, if a hook sits in a wet tray for a long period of time, it will corrode; however, the most important aspect of corrosion applies to hooks purposely left in fish that are to be released (a common occurrence, especially when using bait) or to hooks inadvertently stuck in escaped fish.

Some tests have shown that varnished hooks (bronze, blue, etc.) and nickel or gold hooks, which are most common in freshwater, will break down (defined as being well corroded, brittle, and unusable though not totally decomposed) in two to three weeks of freshwater immersion, compared with 48 to 54 hours in saltwater. Thus, saltwater anglers should not regularly use varnished, plain nickel, and gold hooks unless they release a lot of fish with hooks in them. Stainless steel and cadmium-tin hooks take an indeterminate time to break down in freshwater. In saltwater, stainless steel hooks may take several months to break down, and still longer to decompose entirely. Cadmium-tin takes even longer. Thus, freshwater anglers have virtually no need to use highly corrosion-resistant finishes in freshwater.

The more that a hook is used—meaning that it is sharpened and comes into contact with rocks, sand, and even the teeth of fish—the less resistance it has to corrosion, since the finish becomes partly removed and the underlying carbon steel is exposed.

See Bait; Fly; Hook Sharpening; Lure.

HOOKBAIT

A European term for a bait with a hook in it, used to distinguish this item from a similar or identical unhooked bait that has been distributed for chumming.

See: Carp; Chumming; Float.

HOOK EXTRACTOR

A tool for removing a hook from a fish. This may be needle-nosed pliers, forceps, a long slender pinching device, or other objects that allow a person to avoid teeth and/or reach into the mouth of a fish to remove a hook without injuring the fish or its captor.

See: Catch-and-Release.

HOOK PULLER

A tool used to release fish without having to touch them; a hook puller is primarily used in saltwater by anglers fishing with fairly heavy line or leader. Commercial and homemade models look similar to an old ice block hauling tool, except that the business end is hooked and is used to grab around the bend of a hook when a fish is lifted up with the heavy line or leader.

See: Catch-and-Release.

HOOK REMOVAL

See: First Aid.

HOOKSETTING

Some angling situations and techniques cause a fish to hook itself when it strikes bait or lure; all you have to do is keep tension on the line to keep the hook point from slipping free. Most of the time,

The strongest ebb current on the West Coast: 7 knots at Chatham Strait, Alaska; strongest ebb on the East Coast: 5.2 knots at St. Johns River, Florida.

and nearly always when casting and retrieving hard and soft artificial lures, an angler must react to a strike by setting the hook. This seems rather obvious and easy to accomplish: You just jerk back. Not quite.

Setting the hook on some fish is harder than on others, and there are enough variables—whether the fish is swimming away from or toward you, whether you are sitting or standing, whether you are using a stiff or limber rod, etc.—to make a nonstudious appraisal very risky. Indeed, few anglers have an accurate notion of how much force they generate when they set the hook to the best of their ability. Actually, the average angler is quite inefficient when punching home the hook, as tests using instruments that gauge the amount of force applied have demonstrated.

Consider that you may not set the hook as efficiently as desired each and every time, especially when caught unaware by a strike or hampered by a bony-mouthed or strong-jawed fish. Other factors (such as a bow in the line while river fishing or a striking fish that runs toward you) will also impede your efforts. Thus, you can see that it is imperative to do your best to execute the best possible hookset time after time.

Hooksetting starts with proper technique. Its effectiveness has little to do with physical stature or with brute strength. If you doubt this, tie a barrel swivel to the line on any fishing rod and have a friend stand 40 feet away from you, holding the swivel clenched between thumb and forefinger. Raise the rod slowly and apply all the pressure you can to try to pull that swivel out of your friend's hand. If you don't jerk back violently, you can't pull it out.

Effective hooksetting depends on timing and hook point penetration. Pulling back on the rod with steady pressure after you detect a strike is not how you should set the hook, although many anglers mistakenly react to a strike this way.

There are two recognized and effective techniques in hooksetting, one with a no-slack approach and the other with a slight, controlled amount of slack.

With a no-slack hookset, you lean toward the fish, reel up slack until the line is taut, and then punch the hook home. This is accomplished in the blink of an eye, and it is crucial that you reel up slack only until the line is taut but not pulling on the fish. If you tighten the line so much that the fish feels tension, it may quickly expel your offering; this is especially true with bait and with soft-bodied lures. This technique takes timing, which is acquired through experience.

With a controlled slack-line set, the line is not reeled taut to the fish, but nearly so; and the hook is punched home quickly to provide shock penetration. The theory here is that you get better hook point penetration from a snappy shock force than from a tight-line pull. With the head of a hammer,

Proper hooksetting begins with the rod low and pointed toward the fish (top) and concludes with the rod butt held chest high (bottom), where power is delivered and control is maintained.

try to push a nail into a wall, and then use the hammer to strike the nail sharply; you'll see the difference and appreciate how it applies to hooksetting.

Of course, many times a fish strikes without warning; the angler feels tension immediately and reacts by bringing the rod back sharply. Sometimes, that is all it takes, but unfortunately the more typical outcome is that the hook never becomes firmly embedded in the fish. Just reacting and raising back the rod is often not enough, and a second or third hookset may be warranted.

A principal reason why many anglers are ineffective at hooksetting is not their inability to respond quickly and generate rod tip speed, but the way they use their bodies and contort themselves while doing so. Hooksetting is not a whole-body maneuver, but an exercise of wrists and arms. Back and legs have little to do with it. Someone thin and short might deliver more hooksetting force and better hook penetration than a larger, more powerful individual.

Preparing yourself for what is about to happen before it happens is important. Start by keeping your rod tip down during the retrieve (although in some instances this is not the best position for accomplishing a proper retrieve or for detecting a strike). With the tip down, you're in the best position to respond quickly to a strike, even if, as often happens, your attention is elsewhere when the strike actually occurs. If there is little or no slack in the line, you can make a forceful sweep up or back when you set the hook and then be in immediate control of the fish to begin playing it. When working certain lures, however, you need to keep the rod tip up to work the lure properly and to readily detect a strike. When setting the hook, you can compensate for a high rod position by bowing the rod slightly toward the fish while reeling up slack; this action enables you to get a full backward sweep and be in the proper position for the beginning of the fight.

Where possible, you should be reeling and striking all in one motion, keeping the pressure on constantly and not yielding unless the fish is strong enough to pull line off the drag. Good hooksetting technique is never more important than when long distances are involved, and the same is true for fish-playing tactics. Fish a long distance off are harder to control than those up close. Keeping a strong fish away from an obstruction is more difficult when it is 125 feet from you than when it is 40. When fishing from a boat, you may have to maneuver the boat in order to change the angle of pull on a large fish and steer the fish away from obstructions. You have to anticipate and react quickly, however, because often a fish is fairly close to some type of obstruction when it first gets hooked. How you handle the situation from the outset—especially if the fish is a powerful one or if you're using light tackle—can greatly influence the outcome.

Hooksetting should be a quickly accomplished maneuver. When a fish strikes, you should react reflexively, bringing your rod back and up sharply while holding the reel handle and reeling the instant you feel the fish. The position of the rod is important. The butt is jammed into the stomach or midchest area, and the full arc and power of the rod is brought into play, without having hands or arms jerk wildly over your head. In order to countermand line stretch, you must reel hard and fast the moment you set the hook.

Nylon monofilament lines on average have a stretch factor of up to 30 percent when wet, which in part explains why you can deliver more force with a short nylon monofilament line than with a long one (also with a dry line versus a wet one). By comparison, a low-stretch braided Dacron line or a microfilament line, if it had other desirable fish line qualities, would be better for hooksetting over all distances, though you would still generate more force on short lengths. Because of line stretch, an angler is more effective at setting the hook at short and midrange distances than at long distances. If you have a long length of line out, it is harder to counter the effect of stretch when setting the hook. Thus, you can generate more force and be more efficient at setting the hook at short distances than at long distances.

Good hooksetting procedure, however, doesn't end once you have reacted and you feel the fish. Like a golf swing, hooksetting requires follow-through, and that action is sometimes critical. The line must remain tight; bringing the rod tip back behind your head or raising your arms up high often puts some momentary slack into the line when you bring the rod back down in front of yourself. Not having to do this is the advantage of keeping the rod in front of you, and it is also the advantage of reeling continuously until the fish is firmly hooked and offering some resistance. Once you have the fish firmly hooked and everything under control, you can change the angle of pull as conditions warrant; changing the angle usually means applying sideways pressure rather than upward pressure.

The type of rod you use can aid or impede hooksetting efforts. Generally speaking, limber rods decrease your ability to generate hooksetting force and stiff rods increase it. The soft and somewhat spongy response of a limber rod does, however, make it harder to break the line and to cast light lures, so there are functional trade-offs in tackle used. A stiff rod can aid strike detection, but it could lead to breaking light lines if the hook is set particularly hard. Is there a difference in hooksetting effectiveness between types of rods? Not as much as anglers like to think. The difference is really one of rod action.

Light lines can pose hooksetting problems, especially for those who are accustomed to heavier tackle and jaw-breaking hooksets. Again, the problem is usually a rod that is too stiff for the line. Where light line is used, you need a rod with some cushioning effect. With a medium- or light-action rod that is used with light line, and with the appropriate drag setting, it's almost impossible to break the line when setting the hook. You can prove this to yourself when you're hung up on some obstruction while using such tackle; try setting the hook to break the line, and you'll find that it is extremely difficult to do so.

If your line has a belly or bow in it (as it might when river fishing or when a fish takes your offering and runs laterally with it), you may not have time to take out all or most of the slack or to reel up the line for a direct shot, without alerting the fish, when you set the hook. In this situation, you might execute a slack-line snap, being sure to keep the line tight after the hookup. Fly anglers using light tippets and fishing in current don't want to muster much force anyway, so they'll use this method. Most of the time when fly fishing, especially when using light-wire hooks on small flies and thin tippets, you just need to snap the tip up and keep the line taut to set the hook (although the bonier the mouth of the fish, the larger the hook needed, and the heavier the tippet or shock leader, the more you need to "reef" it to the fish).

A line that is impeded by some obstruction presents another problem, since your hooksetting force is directed more at that impediment than at the fish beyond. You can't do much about this situation (which often happens with big fish that take

---

The award for longest fish name goes to Hawaii's humuhumunukunukuapuaa. That's the queen triggerfish, and the English translation means "the trigger fish that grunts like a pig."

bait and run a short distance) except to realize the problem, fish with heavy line in thick cover, and regularly check your line for damaged spots.

Drag slippage can also impede hooksetting. Some anglers who use baitcasting tackle put a thumb on the reel spool when setting the hook so that they can prevent slippage. However, the better solution is to have the drag *(see)* set precisely for the line strength so you don't have to do this.

One way to deliver better-than-average hooksetting force is to strike with both hands on the rod, one on the handle around the reel and one on the foregrip. Most anglers set the hook with one hand on the rod handle and the other on the reel handle. Usually this is adequate. Certain circumstances, however, may necessitate using two hands to reef the hooks home. Occasionally it is desirable to set the hook two or three times in rapid succession.

What about when trolling? The fish already has the lure when you pull the rod out of its holder. Should you set the hook then? It depends on the situation and the fish. When the quarry is large and hard-mouthed, yes. When using very light line or angling for soft-mouthed fish, no, because you run the risk of pulling out the lure. In either case, you will still have to concentrate on keeping pressure on the fish and on playing it mistake-free.

In big-game fishing and offshore trolling, heavy-duty reels are adjusted with greater drag for setting the hook (called a strike drag) the drag is relaxed to a lighter tension once the fish is on. The heavier drag allows a lot more force to be applied and counters the effect of stretch.

Paying attention to these matters will help you be more efficient at setting the hook. To get the most benefit from this information, however, be sure to sharpen new and used hooks. A super-sharp hook can make all the difference in landing or losing a fish. Most fish are lost because the hook slipped out or was thrown when the fish jumped. A super-sharp hook penetrates easier and increases your chances of landing a fish. The primary advantage of having a sharp hook is to gain penetrating effectiveness. Maximum penetration translates into optimum hooksetting efficiency and better hook retention, which ultimately means more fish hooked and landed.

See: Hook Sharpening; Line.

HOOK SHARPENING

It is certainly true that if anglers paid more attention to the sharpness of their hooks, they would catch more fish. The fact that manufacturers of hook (and knife) sharpeners annually spend more time at consumer shows teaching people why and how to sharpen their hooks than about the products used to sharpen them bears this out. Freshwater anglers in general are less attentive to hook sharpening needs than saltwater anglers, but everyone can benefit from tending to this detail. Even though modern hooks, especially smaller and finer-diameter wire hooks, are factory sharpened to better levels today than they ever were, hooks quickly lose sharpness through use, especially from impacts.

If you were to look at a standard fish hook under a powerful microscope, you'd see that it has many rough spots. This is especially true of hooks that have been used and have been in a tackle box for a while. Some will also have a bent point (a sure way to lose fish), or have burrs on the barb (which will impair penetration). Sharpening new and previously used hooks smooths out the rough spots and facilitates getting the point and barb deep enough in the fish to keep it on your line.

You can improve the sharpness of a hook by grinding the point and barb over a sharpening stone or file. The best way to sharpen bigger, hardened thick-bodied hooks, including those of cadmium and stainless steel, and hooks that are forged (flattened around the bend on both sides) is with a file. The file cuts only on the forward stroke, so keep this in mind as you sharpen. Start by sharpening the barb and the inside cutting edges that lead toward the point, as shown in the accompanying illustration; use same angle as the factory-made cutting edge (if there is one). Do both sides; then move the file forward and do the same thing to the imme-

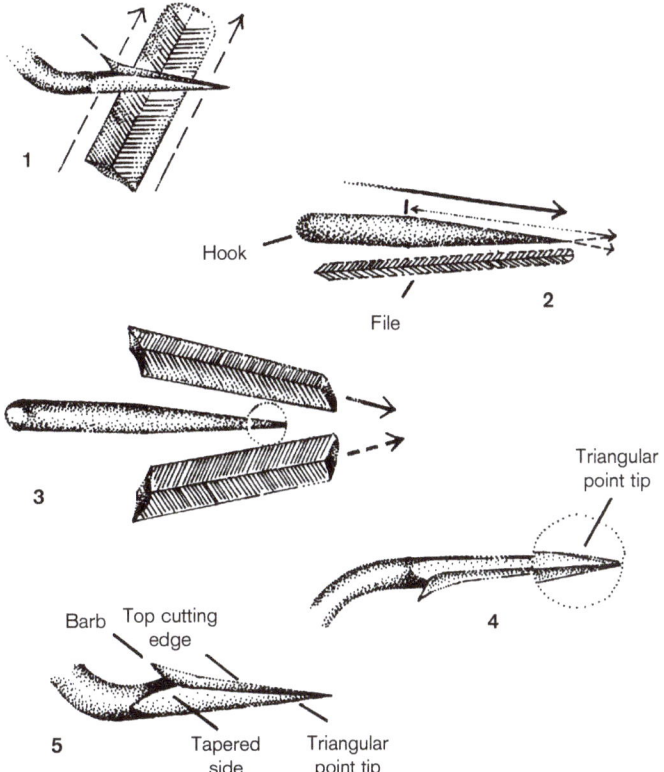

When using a file to sharpen a hook, effect a triangulated cutting area by filing across the inside or top cutting edge, including the barb (1), and by filing along both sides of the hook point (2). With this accomplished, focus on filing the extreme point area (3), creating a mini-triangulated point tip (4). The final result is a well-sharpened barb, top, sides, and point tip (5).

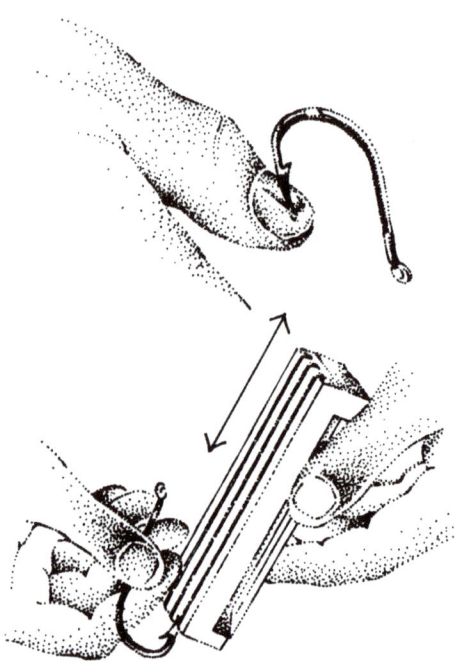

When using a channeled stone, move the hook point back and forth in a channel, changing the angle; then turn the stone crosswise and run it across the barb and sides. The point is sharp enough when it digs into your thumbnail when you drag it across the nail.

diate point area, filing repeatedly toward the point on both sides. It's a good idea to put a mini-cutting edge on the very tip of the point opposite the barb; this little edge really facilitates penetration.

For smaller hooks—the kinds used on most inland waters and nearly all freshwater fish—use a medium-grit honing stone with some type of channel in it. If a file is all you have, use it to the best of your ability. The key to sharpening is not the shape of the sharpening device or its cost, but the fact that it is abrasive and that you use it to put a triangulated shape on the hook. Honing stones (generally in the form of a stick) should be sized to the hook being sharpened, since large models do not adequately reach all parts of a smaller hook.

Sharpening stones can be run forward and backward and should be used in the same manner as a file, first grinding on the inside of the point and then on the left and right sides and the very tip. If you use the channel or groove in a sharpening stone, be sure to rotate the hook so that all parts of the point are affected. Hold the stone and hook firmly to avoid pricking or hooking yourself with the point, and make smooth, deliberate motions.

To test for sharpness: Take a hook, rest the point on your thumbnail, and lightly drag the point across the nail. If the hook is sharp enough, it will catch on the nail; if not sharp enough, it will slide across. Just be careful.

Finally, be wary of oversharpening. If the tapered wedge of the point becomes too short (through excessive sharpening), it may not penetrate as well. If it is ground too thin, it may be susceptible to bending or breaking.
See: Hook.

HOOP STRENGTH
The ability of a hollow tubular structure to resist oval deformation, which leads to the inward collapse of its walls. This is a critical property of fishing rods.
See: Rod, Fishing.

HOTSHOTTING
See: Backtrolling.

HOUNDFISH
See: Needlefish.

HUCHEN *Hucho hucho.*
Other names—Danube salmon, Danube trout; French: *huchon;* German: *sibirischer huchen;* Hungarian: *dunai galóca;* Polish: *glowacka;* Romanian: *lostrita;* Yugoslavian: *mladica.*

A member of the Salmonidae family, which includes salmon and trout, huchen are closely related to *Hucho hucho taimen,* the taimen *(see).* The huchen is one of evidently four species in the same genus. The huchen and the taimen cannot be separated by conventional scientific analyses but are distinguished by virtue of Asian versus European geographical location and separation.

Other species within the *Hucho* genus include *H. perryi* and *H. ishikawae.* Little is known about both. *H. ishikawae* is found in the upper reaches of the Yalu River in North Korea. *H. perryi* is known as Japanese huchen or stringfish *(itô)* and is a sea-run species that occurs in the Sea of Japan from southern Kuril Island and Primorskii Krai, Russia, to Hokkaido, and in streams on eastern Hokkaido.

Because the huchen is relatively rare, it is not a common food fish, nor is it as highly valued as other salmonids. It is edible and of good quality, however. Huchen populations have diminished rapidly with overexploitation, pollution, and habitat deterioration.

Identification. Within Europe, the huchen is not confused with any species except the brown trout or the Atlantic salmon, and can be identified by counting the scales along the lateral line. It has by far the smallest scales, numbering 180 to 200, as compared to 110 to 120 in brown trout and 120 to 130 in Atlantic salmon. The huchen is completely covered with minute black speckles, but never has the red spots that may be present on brown trout and Atlantic salmon.

Size. The huchen grows to at least 114 pounds, making it one of the largest salmonids. The all-tackle world record is a 76-pound, 11-ounce

Huchen

Austrian fish.

Distribution. This species is endemic to Europe, where it is restricted to the Danube River and its tributaries, and occasionally to lakes within the Danube basin. It also occurs in the basin of the Prut River and was introduced into other European rivers, including the Thames, in the nineteenth and early twentieth centuries, although unsuccessfully. It stays in river systems and does not migrate to sea.

Habitat. The habitat of huchen is primarily the deeper regions of fast-flowing rivers and streams with oxygen-rich water.

HULL

The structural frame or body of a boat. Hull style is often the most important element of a boat, and for comfort and safety the hull style should depend on the size of the body of water you fish. Generally, there are displacement and planing categories of hulls.
See: Boat.

HUMP

A moderately elevated and generally isolated portion of an otherwise flat lakebed or seabed. Humps vary in size and characteristic, but they do not rise close to the surface as a freshwater reef *(see)* does, nor do they rise as profoundly as an ocean seamount *(see)*. Because they are an irregular feature of the bottom and may be influenced by current and have objects (stumps, rocks, etc.) on them, they can be good places for catching certain species of fish. In saltwater, this would include many different bottom dwellers. In freshwater, it would include striped bass and largemouth bass, provided the water is not too deep. Humps may hold fish at all times or only sporadically. They are fished with deep natural bait, various jigs, plastic worms, and jigging spoons, and by drifting, vertical jigging, and occasionally trolling.

HUMPY

Short for humpbacked, and a term for pink salmon *(see)*.

HUNGARY

Hungary is home to more than 300,000 anglers, and the majority of sportfishing occurs in small bodies of water, primarily canals, lakes, and backwaters connected to rivers. Carp, pike-perch (zander), catfish, pike, bream, eels, and different species of whitefish thrive almost everywhere, but distribution of trout is limited.

Although Hungary has the Danube, its principal river, the landscape is fairly flat and lacks plentiful water reserves. Only 5 percent of Hungary's surface water originates within its borders, and 66 percent of the water used for human consumption originates in the Danube. Pollution, especially from agricultural runoff, has been a problem, as has eutrophication of lakes.

The temperature of the standing water in Hungary is 13° to 15°C at the beginning of April, 18° to 20°C in May, and 20° to 25°C in summer. Temperatures drop back in September and October to 12°C, but this is when really big carp and catfish are caught.

Eastern Region

Bács-Kiskun County. The Main Canal at Kiskunság is the most popular and productive water in the area. About 730 acres in area, it begins at the Ráckeve Danube Branch over the lock of Tass and joins the Danube Valley Main Canal at the border of Akasztó. The water is standing or slow moving, and great amounts of reeds are present. Species include common carp, grass carp, whitefish, tench, pike, pike-perch, and catfish.

Other waters of note include the Canal of Füzvölgy at Kiskunság, the Dead Tisza at Szikra, and Lake Szelidi. The latter is narrow and 5 kilometers long, and has many carp and pike-perch, as well as big catfish.

Jász-Nagykun-Szolnok County. The Dead Tisza of Alcsi Island is a good backwater near Szolnok that has carp, pike, pike-perch, catfish, bream, and whitefish, with potential for record specimens.

Tisza Lake is a large impoundment that spans Szolnok and Heves Counties not far from Budapest. Fishing activities are based in the communities of Porozló, Tiszafüred, Tiszaderzs, and Abádszalók, where accommodations, tackle shops, and guide services available, as well as boats.

The lake impounded the old Tisza riverbed and produced many small bays and coves; it requires some big-water knowledge to fish properly. In winter the water level is particularly low, and in the spring it is very high, covering nearly 25,000 acres when full. Big carp inhabit these waters, as do catfish, pike-perch, pike, bream, tench, and whitefish. Many anglers also pursue fish in the river below the dam.

Csongrád County. Noteworthy waters in Csongrád include the Backwater of Atka, a small but remote and scenic impoundment with a variety of species; the Dead Tisza of Mártély, which is on the road to Mindszent; and the Matyér Lake, located near Szeged. At less than 90 acres, the latter impoundment is small, but it was the site of a world match fishing championship and is known for common carp, grass carp, pike-perch, catfish, and whitefish.

Hajdú-Bihar and Békés Counties. Látókép Lake in Hajdú-Bihar is about 13 kilometers from Debrecen and is known for pike, pike-perch, and carp. The Körös River and its tributaries in Békés County provide a variety of opportunity. The best place on the river is near the dam at Békésszentandrás, where three flows converge; below there are pike-perch, carp, bream, catfish, and whitefish. The backwaters at Kákafog are especially popular. These also contain pike.

Szabolcs-Szatmár-Bereg County. The major fishery in this area is the winding, blind arm of the Szamos River near Tunyogmatolcs, which is similar in species composition to the Tisza River. Camping and accommodation facilities are available practically everywhere here.

Northern Region

Budapest area. Fishing opportunities are somewhat limited near Budapest, although the Danube flows southerly through the city. The Danube itself can provide good angling at times and in certain places, but it is a big water. Pike, pike-perch, whitefish, barbel, and bream are the available species.

A good smaller local site, however, is Stonemine Lake in the Csepel District, at the southern end of the city. Carp, pike, and pike-perch are here, as well as other established area species. Szilas Lake in the 16th District of Budapest at Mátyásföld is also notable for the whole gamut of locally established species.

The Rackleve Branch of the Danube is a large watercourse that flows behind Csepel Island. It is influenced by two locks here, with water flowing southerly toward Tass. Its depth is 2 to 3 meters at the upper section, and 4 to 5 meters at the lower section. The uppermost portion is in the capital. Grass and reed lines grow alongshore in many places. Common carp, grass carp, whitefish, pike-perch, catfish, pike, and bream are available; and the area is stocked with pike-perch. Some large specimens exist, and record catches are possible.

Below the Tass lock is a small bay that forms before the remaining water from the Rackleve Branch merges with the Danube. This water is always at the same level as the Danube, and splits into a flowing section noted for pike-perch and bream, and a standing section noted for pike along the banks. Carp, catfish, and whitefish are everywhere between the lock and the mouth of the Danube.

Borsod-Abaúj-Zemplén County. Notable waters here include Rakaca Lake at Szalona, Lake Monok in the village of Monok, the Stonemine Lake of Csorbatelep near Miskolc, and Hámori Lake near Eger. Hámori is a small, beautiful mountain lake with trout and pike-perch; the others hold pike-perch, pike, and carp.

Heves and Nógrád Counties. Lake Egerszalók in Neves and the Ipoly River in Nógrád are noted for the usual coarse species as well as pike. The Ipoly is Hungary's northern border water, and at 18 to 60 meters wide, it is a pleasant river to fish.

Western Region

Lake Balaton. By surface area, Balaton is the largest lake not only in Hungary, but also in central and western Europe. About 77 kilometers long, it is a shallow lake with an average depth of just 3 meters. The deepest area—more than 12 meters—is near the tip of the Tihany Peninsula.

Pike-perch, pike, common carp, grass carp, wels catfish, asp, eels, and several species of bream are present, with huge specimens of some reported. The lake has produced a 30.5-kilogram carp, a 91.5-kilogram catfish, and a 9.6-kilogram asp. Coarse fishing is very popular from piers and along the shoreline, and especially along weedlines in bays for carp and bream.

Balaton can be reached from Budapest via Route M7, which also passes the southern shore of the lake; Route 17 follows the northern shore. A fishing license can be obtained in nearby tackle shops, at post offices, and at tourist offices.

Győr-Moson-Sopron County. The best fishing opportunities in the county include the backwater of the Danube River at Moson, in the city of Győr, and the Zátony Branch of the Danube in the village of Halászi.

Tolna County. The Fadd-Dombori Backwater in the villages of Fadd and Tolna is well known for big catfish and has significant numbers of carp and pike-perch. Lake Szálka, an impoundment situated in a beautiful valley surrounded by forest, is small but very popular for coarse species.

Baranya County. Carp, whitefish, catfish, pike-perch, and pike are the main species at Lake of Pécs, which is known for extremely big carp and catfish. Nearby Orfü and Kovácsszénája Lakes are also worth visiting.

Komárom-Esztergom County. The main angling waters in Komárom-Esztergom County, all of which hold similar species, include Danube Bay at Pilismarót, the cooling power plant lake at Bánhida; and the power plant lake of Oroszlány at Bokod.

Somogy and Vas Counties. In Somogy, Deseda Lake is known for its record fish potential; species include carp, whitefish, catfish, pike-perch, and pike. The Rába River is the main fishing water of Vas County; also notable are the impoundment of Gébart, located near Zalaegerszeg, and Lake Nagykanizsa, in the village of the same name.

Fejér and Veszprém Counties. Lake Velence is the second largest natural lake in Hungary and is located about 40 kilometers from Budapest. Just 2 meters deep, it is a shallow lake, but it

---

The largest known sport-caught fish, a 3,427-pound great white shark, was landed in 1988 at Montauk, New York. It was denied record status because the angler chummed with meat from a dead whale.

covers more than 5,400 acres and is loaded with reeds. Velence is one of the best pike-perch waters in Europe, and here float fishing methods predominate. Anglers can rent boats in many places, and fishing is good from the shore on the southern end of the lake. Also of note in Fejér County are the Cikola Lakes near Adony, and Lake Fehérvárcsurgó near Mór. In Veszprém County, picturesque Inner Lake of Tihany is noted for carp, pike-perch, pike, eels, and whitefish between mid-April and mid-October.

Regulations
Anglers must have a state (national) angling ticket and a regional permit to fish. The latter is specific to the body of water to be fished. With few exceptions, the state angling ticket and the regional permit can be obtained at the same place; county angling associations can provide information. The state angling ticket is valid for the calendar year, and you can apply for any number of regional permits in the year of issue by presenting your state angling ticket. Regional permits, however, are valid only for a specific day or a set period.

Regulations regarding seasons are in effect for some species, as are length restrictions, and these may vary with the authority issuing permissions. There may also be total catch restrictions by weight in some waters. It is necessary to obtain regulations for each site before one begins fishing. For information contact the Hungarian National Angling Association, 1124 Budapest, Korompai út 17.

HYBRID
The offspring of two individuals of different species. The offspring of two individuals belonging to different subspecies of the same species are not hybrids.

Hybridization may occur in the wild or under artificial conditions. Some species that have been known to crossbreed naturally, although not frequently, include lake trout and brook trout (splake), northern pike and muskellunge (tiger muskie), and walleye and sauger (saugeye). Hybrid fish have been cultivated in hatcheries by fisheries managers for stocking purposes; hybrid striped bass (known as whiterock bass, wiper, and sunshine bass), which result from a cross of pure-strain striped bass and white bass, have been extremely popular for stocking and are widely spread in freshwater lakes and reservoirs. Most hybrid fish are sterile (although some, like whiterock bass, are not), so the stocking of these fish is attractive because they can be controlled fairly well; if the initial stocking experiment does not achieve the desired results, the population of hybrids can be extinguished by discontinuing stocking.
See: Bass, Whiterock; Muskellunge; Saugeye; Splake.

HYDROFOIL
A winglike device that attaches to the antiventilation plate on an outboard or stern-drive motor to provide lift when getting on plane. These are available in single- and double-fin versions, which are bolted onto the plate. A hydrofoil is best suited to boats that are underpowered, stern heavy, or with deep-V hulls. Their benefit is getting a boat on plane quickly and increasing visibility; when a boat plows onto plane with the bow thrust up, the driver's visibility may be impaired for a short time. This device also aids fore-and-aft running attitude, somewhat like trim tabs, but cannot control side-to-side attitude. It can improve riding comfort by keeping a boat on plane at lower speeds, but it does not significantly improve top overall speed or fuel economy.
See: Boat.

HYDROGRAPHIC MAP
A map depicting underwater features.
See: Maps.

HYPOLIMNION
The lower and colder layer of water in a lake or pond that is stratified; the layer of water below the thermocline *(see)*.
See: Stratification.

HYPOTHERMIA
See: First Aid.

ICE FISHING

Fishing through the ice is a traditional activity in northern locations where the ice is thick enough for people to safely venture onto frozen lakes and ponds. In some places, a winter community develops, and ice houses, also known as shacks, shanties, and bobhouses, dot the surface.

The roots of fishing through the ice extend back to the era before modern reels and line. North American natives speared fish through holes chopped in the ice. They used decoys to attract fish to their holes, or they simply waited for the fish to pass underneath. Lying on top of the holes, wrapped in skins and blankets, kept them warm and blocked out light so they could see into the water.

Spearing is still practiced in some places today, and the use of decoys and spears has some passionate followers. Most decoys are still handmade and designed to behave like a wounded fish. They vary in size, ranging up to 30 inches long for wooden or metal models; the larger decoys are used for sturgeon. However, this is a limited activity and a controversial one.

General Hardware

The only thing that today's ice anglers have in common with those early spear-wielding anglers is the hole in the ice. Making the hole generally requires an auger or spud. Augers can be manual or gas-powered, and they create holes that are 7 to 10 inches in diameter. Larger holes are necessary for landing outsized fish, and the drill bit needs to be sharp. A spud or chisel can also be used to make holes and widen existing holes; these tools are generally used for cutting through in places where the ice isn't very thick, or for testing the thickness of relatively new ice (since a lot of chiseling is needed to get through 2 to 3 feet of ice).

Where the ice is thick, a long-bladed chainsaw can be used to cut large rectangular holes. The large hole allows for plenty of angler movement and for easy landing of any size fish. A chainsaw is also useful for creating a holding pool for the caught fish. The angler cuts a large shallow depression in the ice and pokes a hole through to flood the depression.

A scoop is another necessary item. It is used to clear the hole of ice fragments and may be a wide perforated metal ladle with a long handle or a shallow perforated plastic bucket. A Styrofoam-insulated minnow bucket is also important, especially in very cold and windy weather. The Styrofoam helps keep the bucket water from freezing. A plastic minnow scoop is handy for retrieving bait. Not a necessity but highly valued and important to many ice anglers is a portable sonar unit. A long-handled gaff is useful for large fish, like trout; obviously it is used only on fish that will be kept.

Portable or permanent shelters are used in some locales, although many ice anglers like to be mobile and move from place to place to fish and to search for schools of fish. Permanent shacks, which look like large outhouses, may need to be registered and will require setup and removal, but they provide protection from the elements and are great for serious and regular fishing if they are located in a good spot. Some houses are heated and equipped with various amenities, greatly increasing the comfort level; the most deluxe versions are mini-palaces, with color television, propane cookstove, and beds. Obviously these ice houses are not easy to move, and in most places they must by law be removed from the ice by a certain date (for safety reasons and also to keep debris from falling into the water as the ice weakens).

Mobile anglers need a means of toting their equipment, and some have devised boxes that are dragged on sleds over the ice or are towed behind a snowmobile. (Anglers on foot, incidentally, may need cleated boots for traction on sheer ice.) Likewise, portable tentlike shelters are ferried across the ice. Complete sled-based mobile systems, some with a covered retractable top, are a more deluxe option. The systems are made to be easily pulled so that anglers can keep up with fish that are on the move;

In lakes where the ice gets very thick, chainsaws are used to cut large holes; some anglers use delicate tip-ups for fishing.

When the fishing's good, some frozen lakes draw a lot of activity, although a telephoto lens has exaggerated the clustering in this scene.

these also store tackle and give protection from the wind. Small heaters can be used with them.

Tip-ups. An essential element of ice fishing, especially with live bait, is a tip-up. This device sports a spool filled with line, to which a baited hook is attached, and sprouts a highly visible flag that stands up when the bait has been struck. Fish are retrieved by handlining. The frame of the tip-up is wooden or plastic, and it sits on top of the ice.

Tip-ups come in many different styles, sizes, and materials, with varied bite-indicating systems. There are basically two types of tip-ups. In wind-assisted tip-ups, the arm moves up and down and jigs the bait with any kind of breeze. The extent of movement can be adjusted. When there's a bite, the spool rotates, which releases a bite-indicating flag. This type of tip-up can freeze up under bad conditions, although retrieving wet line onto the ice can help prevent spool freeze-up.

The more common type of tip-up is a simple line-filled spool placed under the water to prevent freezing up. There is no wind assist or jigging action with this type, and movement of the spool trips a flag to indicate a bite. Both versions are mainly used for larger predators rather than for panfish, and live or dead bait can be fished at any level. Complete outfits ready to fish are found in most tackle stores in areas where there is ice fishing.

Rods/sticks/line. Short jigging rods and sticks in the 18- to 48-inch range are used for jigging through the ice with assorted jigs and special ice-jigging lures, some tipped with bait. Jigging sticks come in a variety of materials and handle styles and feature 20 to 50 feet of line wrapped around a loop that is in or on the handle.

The angler adjusts the line to the depth selected, lowers the bait into the hole by hand, sets the hook with the stick, plays the fish by hand, and lifts the fish out of the hole with the line. You can use a balsa float (not the old-style round bobber) or spring bobber (a thin strip of flat or round wire attached to the tip) with the stick.

Rod and reel combinations are plentiful. Rod and reel must be matched, and the action of the rod must be soft enough to keep from breaking the line being used. Like sticks, rods should be short, and they usually have few guides, which are large to help minimize ice buildup. Reels are often light spinning or spincasting models.

The line used for ice fishing on rods or sticks varies with the application. A guideline is 2- to 4-pound line for panfish; 4- to 8-pound line for pickerel, walleye, and smaller trout; 10- to 20-pound line for pike and large trout; and 15- to 30-pound line for big flathead catfish. Wire leaders are needed for some species. The golden rule in line choice is to go heavy if the fish are aggressive. You can use heavier line and lighten up the last 10 to 20 feet by using a lighter leader.

Thin-diameter lines are obviously helpful for clear water and for fishing with small baits and tiny jigs. A line that stays limp and doesn't stiffen in the cold is important. Microfilament line is helpful here, since it doesn't change characteristics and is very sensitive. A monofilament leader may be advisable when fishing with heavier microfilament lines, and a softer rod may also be useful for absorbing shock, since this type of line has no stretch. Some anglers like a fluorescent line for its visibility, and it can easily be watched in a dark ice house.

Lures/Bait

Minnows are the favorite live bait of ice anglers, especially when fished on a bait hook below a tip-up. They are most often hooked through the lips, which is the strongest location, and then behind the dorsal fin. They are also popularly fished on a jig hook. Bait anglers who use tip-ups also need an assortment of hooks, split shot weights, floats, and other terminal tackle, as well as small baits like maggots and grubs.

There are loads of jigs and jigging spoons suitable for ice fishing, depending on the target species, as well as some specialty ice fishing lures. Each behaves differently in the water, and the action is also influenced by the addition of bait. Generally, however, any jigging lure should be worked in a subtle manner for panfish and more dramatically for larger predators.

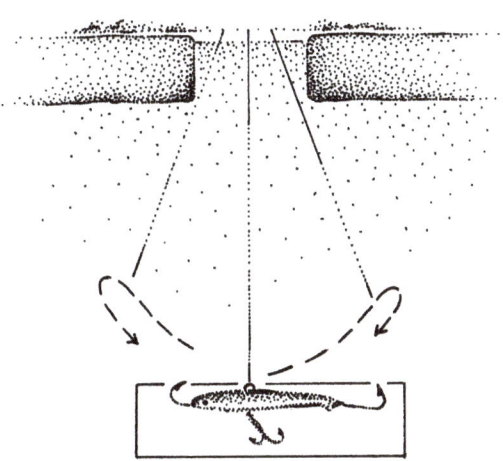

A balanced ice fishing jig has a unique darting, swimming action, moving up and out to the sides as shown by the arrow paths.

Different shapes of small ice jigs are used, as are different types of jigging spoons, most of which weigh from $1/8$ to $1/12$ ounce. Another choice is small leadhead jigs, which are dressed with soft lure bodies or tipped with bait. Balanced jigging lures, which lie horizontally and have a hook at each end as well as under the belly, swim in a unique manner due to a tail fin, and these lures are popular in different sizes for various fish.

Methods

Like open water angling, ice fishing encompasses both passionate devotees and anglers who fish only occasionally. The most serious ice anglers work hard at trying to catch fish and learn new methods; other anglers enjoy just being outside in the winter and aren't concerned with success. Many people, of course, fall in between.

Ice fishing involves a range of approaches for successfully attracting and landing fish. The best ice anglers know they can't make the fish do what they want them to do, so they try to adjust to the fish and avoid being locked into fixed ideas about lures, baits, and locations. If you assume that, in general, fish are aggressive only 10 percent of the time, in a negative mood 60 percent of the time, and in a neutral mood for the remainder of the time, then your best approach is to finesse the situation, being a bit crafty and cautious and assuming that the fish are in a negative mood. This approach will not alarm fish no matter what their disposition is. On the other hand, an aggressive approach, such as jigging a large spoon for perch, will probably scare or turn off most fish. Thus, beginning with a tiny jig baited with a single maggot should bring better results.

When you're starting out, a companion who is an experienced ice angler is a great advantage. Ask questions and try to learn the basics. For catching panfish, you can start very simply with a jigging rod and a thin, small float (see) about $1^1/_2$ inches long and $3/_{16}$ inch wide. The float is held in place on a light line (4-pound test is good) with two silicone tubes (now found in most tackle shops). Use two BB lead split shots (each of which is $1/_{64}$ ounce) to balance your float, placed about $2^1/_2$ inches above a No. 12 or 14 hook (switch to a smaller hook and lighter line if the fish are hard to catch). Carefully place one or two maggots or waxworms on the hook.

This approach will be effective during the first three to five weeks of the ice fishing season when panfish are normally close to the shore in shallow water that is 18 inches to 4 feet deep. Carefully lower your hooked bait in the hole, and watch for any movement of the float up, down, or sideways.

The float can fly down on a strike or move very slowly just an eighth of an inch. This is why a float is best if you are a beginner; you can see the entire range of bites and get accustomed to them. Sometimesit's better to jig without a float, but if you have had success seeing bites, you can easily learn straight jigging and you can imagine how the bites feel (see: jigging).

This approach just described is a good way to get started on ice fishing for bluegills, crappie, or perch. By using a finesse approach, you can readily adapt to those easier times when fish are aggressive.

To be aggressive about catching fish you need to locate them; in ice fishing, using portable sonar and keeping on the move are important elements for locating fish. Make sure your sonar unit can shoot through the ice and can depict both the fish and the weeds where some species may be holding. You can facilitate the effectiveness of the sonar by squirting nontoxic antifreeze on the ice and then placing the

A lake trout like this is a superb catch for any ice angler; this specimen was caught at Lake Simcoe, Ontario.

transducer on the wet spot. Ice has to be fairly clear for this, but thickness is no problem. In heavily marbled ice or snow-saturated ice, make a hole and place the transducer in the hole.

Using sonar allows you to keep moving. When fish appear on the sonar screen, drill a hole and then carefully watch the fish on the screen as you jig. You can often see how the fish respond to your bait or lure (and also to its color) and to the jigging action; you can even watch the fish take the bait. You'll need to jig at various levels for good coverage, just as you would in open-water fishing.

Safety

Never take ice for granted and assume it is safe. Invisible underwater currents, springs, and heat-attracting debris in or on the ice can weaken it dramatically. Some well-frozen lakes develop pressure ridges that you should stay away from. As a rule, always fish with a companion, and test ice thickness before you travel on it.

Right after freeze-up, ice toward the middle of the lake is thinner than that along the shoreline. River ice and lake ice can vary in thickness throughout the winter and in different parts of the river or lake. Do not assume uniform thickness.

The thickness of the ice is not always an accurate measure of its strength. Cracking and sudden temperature drops can severely weaken ice. Heavy snow cover insulates ice, drastically reducing its growth; the snow may cause water to overflow around the edges, thus weakening the ice there.

If you drive on the ice with a vehicle, especially a heavy one, be aware that sudden braking or driving over a bump increases the effective weight of the vehicle and can cause ice failure. Driving fast over thin ice may create an under-ice wave similar to a boat wake; this force can crack the ice ahead of the vehicle under the right conditions. Therefore, it's best to drive carefully and slowly.

As a guideline, the minimum ice thickness for certain loads is as follows: 4 inches for a person walking; 6 inches for a snowmobile; 8 inches for a vehicle weighing 3,500 pounds; and 12 inches for a vehicle weighing 8,000 pounds.

If you're fishing by yourself (which may not be wise) early in the season when the ice is thin, consider hanging ice picks around your neck (two 6-inch nails tied to 15 to 20 inches of nylon cord and covered with a super glue). Cover the points with tissue paper that is taped in place, and hang the whole rig around your neck. If you fall into the water, you'll have something with which you can grab onto the ice and pull yourself out. Carrying extra clothes—even if you leave them in your vehicle on shore—is a good idea, though you'll probably never need them if you're careful.

Always dress properly for ice fishing. The danger of developing hypothermia or frostbite is obvious. Fortunately, excellent clothing and footwear exist to help prevent this.

See: First Aid; Float.

ICELAND

Lying roughly 300 kilometers east of Greenland in the North Atlantic Ocean, Iceland is a mysterious and beautiful island with volcanoes, thermal springs, rolling hills, more than 120 glaciers, and numerous small lakes and swift-flowing rivers. Its northern extremity barely touches the Arctic Circle, and although Iceland has a relatively mild climate, the country features a mixture of nature's extremes, including summer temperatures ranging from 7° to 14°C.

Although Iceland encompasses 103,000 square kilometers and has nearly 6,000 kilometers of coastline, it is sparsely populated with some 260,000 inhabitants. Most have settled along the coastline and in the southwest, and half of these live in the capital city of Reykjavik. The infrastructure is generally good, with plenty of roads and regular domestic flights to most larger towns. Visitors are surprised to find that this lightly populated country has a good road network; with a rented four-wheel-drive vehicle, a lot of waters can be reached. Iceland's Keflavik Airport has excellent connections to several cities in North America and Europe.

Iceland's Atlantic salmon fishery is the main attraction for visitors and is regarded as one of the best in the world, despite the poor state of this species across its range. In Iceland, the standard is crystal clear waters in an unpolluted environment, and salmon fishing has a significant place in the tourism industry. Local newspapers carry daily reports on river conditions and on the number of fish passing by fish counters. The salmon are well looked after in Iceland; coastal netting in the sea has been prohibited since 1932.

Approximately 100 rivers have salmon runs, and from the mid-1970s to the mid-1990s the top

20 had average catches of between 450 and almost 2,000 salmon a year. Over this long period, the best ones were the Laxá i Adaldal, Thverá, Nordurá, and Laxá i Kjos.

In general, Icelandic salmon run 3 to 6 kilograms; a fish over 10 kilograms is unusual. The fishing season is between May 20 and September 20, with variations according to location. Often the fishing takes place in two passes a day, one from 7 A.M. to 1 P.M., and another from 4 P.M. to 10 P.M. On the more expensive rivers it is not unusual for two anglers to share a beat and to fish in shifts. Some of the less well-known rivers may provide good sport at a fair price, along with opportunities to catch charr and sea trout.

The opportunities to pursue freshwater and sea-run trout and charr are equally excellent and more economical. Compared with the Scandinavian countries, only a few districts in northern Norway offer the same quality of fishing for brown trout as does Iceland, and only the rivers in Greenland offer arctic charr fishing of the same caliber. One river, the Laxá i Husavik, offers world-class brown trout fishing from Sog to Myvatn, which is above the falls that prevent salmon from moving upriver. Only fly fishing is permitted on this 30-kilometer stretch of river, and only a certain number of rods per day are allowed.

Anglers catch lots of trout every year in this beautiful river, which flows out of Lake Myrvatn. The upper river courses steadily, with minor falls; then it is forked by islands, and farther downstream it quickens. On the lowest part it flows more gently again. Large streamers and locally productive patterns are favored. The best fishing is from mid-June through July. In August, when the water is low and clear, fishing is more difficult, and nymphs and dry flies are productive. The trout range up to 2 kilograms in the upper river and are a bit larger on average in the lower and more difficult section. Both trout and charr inhabit Lake Myrvatn.

Falls on the Laxá i Husavik prevent salmon from migrating upstream, where there is superb brown trout fishing.

Iceland has much more freshwater fishing to offer, mostly on the northern and northeastern coasts. On the Melrakke flat north of Kopasker, several good coastal lakes with both sea-run and freshwater charr beckon. West of Olafsfjordur near Hraun are more fine coastal lakes and lagoons. The sea-run charr normally enter from mid-July through the end of the season. In Saenautavatn and Anarvatn, between Myvatn and Seidisfjordur, there are fine charr in the 3- to 4-kilogram range.

Nice-size but shy trout hold in the shallow and weedy lakes north and east of Egilstadir. Sea-run charr enter the side rivers of Jokulsás north of Seidisfjordur. The river Svartá and Lakes Isholtvatn and Svartarkotsvatn, 50 kilometers southwest of Myrvatn, are known to harbor large trout.

A particularly good spot is on the south coast near Lake Pórisvatn's adjacent lakes; these are not far from road access. In northwestern Iceland, Anarvatnsheidi is another large lake district. It can be reached with four-wheel-drive vehicles or via horseback, and by snowmobiles in the winter for ice fishing. East of Blónduos in the northwest are several coastal lakes with very good populations of both sea-run and resident charr.

Literally thousands of other small ponds, lakes, and lagoons hold little-known populations of fish. Some waters might produce only smaller fish, others 1- to 2-kilogram fish; and odd lakes have big fish that range from 3 to 6 kilograms. Sea trout enter a number of rivers, especially on the south, east, and west coasts; these fish are normally from 1 to 2 kilograms.

Iceland's economy depends heavily on the rich fish populations in the surrounding sea: fishing and fish processing are the country's most important industries. Cod, sharks, haddock, coalfish, halibut, capelin, crustaceans, and herring are the mainstays, but there is no real charter fishing industry, because anyone with a seaworthy vessel is fishing commercially. Finding a boat to go sportfishing may nevertheless be possible. The Breidafjordur Fiord has a good reputation for halibut between 10 and 25 kilograms, but it also produces some from 80 to 100 kilograms.

ICE OUT

That time when enough ice melts on a lake to make open water fishing possible. Complete ice out may take many days or more than a week on some cold, deep, large, and northerly waters, and the amount of open water will gradually increase over that time.

The legal angling season for some species, especially salmonids, on many northern lakes, usually commences on a certain date, which, in a practical sense, is subject to ice out—the lake is all or partially unfrozen. Fishing for trout and salmon in particular is deemed very good immediately following ice out, because the upper water layers are cold and fish will usually be shallow and more accessible.

ICHTHYOLOGIST

A person who studies fish. This is different from a fishery biologist *(see)*, who studies and manages fisheries, although ichthyologists are frequently referred to as biologists.

IDAHO

Idaho excels in both the variety and quality of its fishing. It has, for example, produced the biggest rainbow trout taken in freshwater by a sporting angler in the United States—a 37-pound Kamloops-strain specimen from Lake Pend Oreille that has survived more than 50 years atop the record books. And an 8-pound, $1/2$-ounce smallmouth bass, taken from Dworshak Reservoir near Orofino, would win bragging rights in nearly any state that has this species.

Size isn't the only measure of successful fishing, of course. The Henry's Fork of the Snake River in southeastern Idaho is holy water for trout lovers from around the nation, who come to test their skills against the wariest of trout. The river is as clear as liquid crystal, and its mayfly hatches draw hordes of anglers in early summer. The lucid waters of Silver Creek just south of legendary Sun Valley have been fished by the famous for decades; but the trout aren't impressed by screen credits or anything short of a perfect presentation.

As if year-round resident fish weren't enough, Idaho also boasts sizable runs of steelhead, the mighty rainbow trout that migrate to the Pacific Ocean and back—a journey of at least 1,000 miles from their natal water. If valiant efforts to save chinook salmon succeed, the state may yet reclaim its glory days when the summers marked the return of the kings. In the meantime, Lake Coeur d'Alene holds landlocked chinook nearly as big as their oceangoing cousins.

In addition to its healthy salmonids, Idaho offers respectable largemouth bass fishing, northern pike a few meals shy of 40 pounds, and one of the biggest fish in freshwater—the white sturgeon. The biggest Idaho sturgeon landed with rod and reel and officially recorded was a 394-pound bruiser landed in 1956, when it was still possible to keep a sturgeon landed in Idaho waters. Since then, the Snake River in Hells Canyon has yielded a heavier 12-foot-long sturgeon that was revived and released.

A slogan popular in some quarters proclaims "Idaho is what America was" and reflects the beauty of the state. Indeed, Idaho's lakes and streams are still remarkably pure. Its backcountry remains as rugged and remote as when prospector Elias D. Pierce led the first party that found "color" in the Clearwater River country in 1860.

Idaho possesses 4 million acres of federally designated wilderness, including the massive Frank Church River of No Return Wilderness, which sprawls across 2.4 million acres, or 3,750 square miles, along the Salmon River. Idaho angling may be at its best here. The 78-mile run, from Corn Creek near North Fork at the eastern edge of the wilderness and downstream to Vinegar Creek at its western margin near Riggins, offers scenic solitude normally found only in the wildest parts of the globe. Passage is by brawny welded-aluminum jet boats, or by more quiet craft like kayaks, rubber rafts, or whitewater dories. The exclusive domain of float boats, the Salmon's middle fork offers excellent fishing for west-slope cutthroat.

Trout

In one form or another, Idaho *is* trout fishing. When Ernest Hemingway moved for the last time, it was the allure of Idaho and its trout that caught his eye. At least a part of Hemingway's relocation to Idaho was spurred by the fine trout streams near Ketchum. This included the Wood River and its tributaries, among them Silver Creek, the home of very large and educated trout that demand precision fishing. But also notable is the Snake River to the south, where Billingsley Creek is perhaps less famous but still capable of growing trout as big as those in Silver Creek. To the west is the Boise River and its tributaries, also hallowed waters for trout aficionados. Bear Lake, the turquoise wonder of the state's southeastern corner, produced Idaho's record cutthroat. An ounce shy of 19 pounds, the record held up for nearly three decades.

The focus of trout fishing in America, or at least the West, is the Henry's Fork of the Snake, hard by Yellowstone National Park. The province of flycasters from around the world, the Henry's Fork hits its peak in early summer, when massive mayfly hatches boil off the water. Henry's Lake at the river's headwaters not far upstream produces massive rainbow-cutthroat hybrids and world-class brook trout from its prodigious underwater forest of weedy growth. The Millionaire's Hole in Harriman State Park is a shrine to big trout that demand expertise.

The South Fork of the Snake, the mighty river's other main headwaters tributary, spills over from Wyoming and Jackson Hole. The South Fork is famed for both cutthroats and rainbows. But the biggest trout in the river are browns; specimens weighing in the teens are caught regularly, and monsters in the 20s are rare but possible.

Mountain trout. Reliable fisheries for west-slope cutthroat trout, a fish of the purest mountain streams, attract most of the summertime attention in the upper Clearwater drainage. Kelly Creek, the upper North Fork, and the Lochsa River, which is paralleled by U.S. Highway 12, are recognized nationally as blue-ribbon trout streams. Catch-and-release fishing is the rule for most of these waters because the beautiful cutthroat would be too gullible to survive otherwise.

The neighboring Selway River is also a popular destination in its lower reaches. Its upper waters are tucked away in the Selway Bitterroot Wilderness and accessible only by foot trail or boat. The Upper

Clearwater appears much as it did when the Lewis and Clark expedition faced its most serious challenges here in 1805 and 1806, as it struggled across the Bitterroot and Clearwater Mountains. Today, while camped along Kelly Creek or the Lochsa River, it is possible to hear the song of the wolf and experience a taste of the pioneer days.

More than two-thirds of Idaho remains in federal ownership and much of that, nearly 20 million acres, is overseen by the U.S. Forest Service as national forest land. Here, Idaho's mountainous heart holds some 2,000 lakes tucked into glacial nooks and crannies. Some, like a few in the Sawtooth National Recreation Area near Ketchum, or Seven Devils Lake southwest of Riggins, are relatively accessible by road during the summer months. Others require a major hike to reach, or, better yet, a pack trip with horses to carry the load. The Bighorn Crags west of Salmon and high above the Salmon River's Middle Fork offer a sparkling necklace of high lakes that reward exertion with exceptional fishing and scenes that approach the sublime.

A midsummer adventure to the high country offers mountain lake fishing and a chance to see the heart of Idaho's wilderness from a primitive gravel road. The Magruder Road scratches its way across the Nez Perce and Bitterroot National Forests from east of Elk City, Idaho, to Darby, Montana. The road was pioneered by the Civilian Conservation Corps during the 1930s and has been changed relatively little since. A vehicle with high clearance, preferably with four-wheel drive, is the best bet during late July and August, when conditions are most favorable.

Because the high country reaches elevations of 8,000 feet, even August can bring snow here, and adventurers are advised to take all wilderness precautions. Rain gear, cold-weather clothes, extra food, and means for fire and shelter are all requisites. The Sheep Hill lakes along the corridor provide a spectacular reward to adventuresome anglers up for the task.

Snake River

In Idaho, big waters hold big fish. The Snake River itself reaches more than 1,000 miles from its headwaters to its confluence with the Columbia River, and most of the river's length is in Idaho. With much of its terrain receiving less than 20 inches of precipitation a year, Idaho is like a desert. The state depends heavily on its rivers to irrigate its famous potatoes and other crops that take root in the fertile soils along the wide arc of the Snake River Plain across the south. The reservoirs that catch the Snake's spring runoff so it can be metered out through the long, dry summers or converted into hydroelectricity harbor sizable fish populations.

American Falls Reservoir downstream from the Snake is famed for its trout fishing. Farther downstream, C. J. Strike Reservoir near Mountain Home is noted more for its bass and crappie. At Salmon Falls Creek Reservoir nearby, anglers have a chance to catch walleye, a rare opportunity because proposals to establish them widely were jettisoned by fears they could become serious predators of the state's tiny salmon and steelhead heading to the ocean. Near Boise, waters like Lake Lowell—an irrigation impoundment off the Boise River—provide notable opportunities for panfish and bass.

Brownlee Reservoir, along the Snake to the northwest of the capital, ranks as one of Idaho's most heavily fished impoundments. Smallmouth bass and crappie are the main prizes here, but the lake's rich waters also produce sizable numbers of big flathead and channel catfish. One of the state's largest impoundments, Brownlee is the Idaho Power Company's largest storage reservoir and the keystone of its three Hells Canyon dams. Its water levels fluctuate throughout the year.

After Hells Canyon Dam, the Snake begins its 100-mile whitewater rush out of Idaho. Although what purists would call Hells Canyon now lies under the waters backed up by the dam, popular thinking and official acts say otherwise. The U.S. Forest Service administers the Hells Canyon National Recreation Area along more than 70 miles of the Snake. The river here is a stronghold for the white sturgeon, the largest freshwater fish in North America. Around the turn of the century, a monster estimated at 1,500 pounds was captured from near the mouth of the Weiser River, now at the headwaters of Brownlee Reservoir. But the free-flowing river below the dam complex is the best place left in Idaho to pursue monster sturgeon. In the 1980s, a fishing guide and his crew landed and released a behemoth that stretched the tape at 12 feet long and weighed an estimated 500 to 600 pounds.

In Idaho, sturgeon must be released immediately after they're landed and cannot be removed from the water. Although hearty fish, changes in the rivers caused by dams, and the sturgeon's slow growth rate, make their future tenuous. With strict catch-and-release rules, however, sturgeon are the focus of a sizable community of anglers who both zealously pursue and protect them.

As a result of these regulations, Idaho's two sturgeon records appear unbreakable. The biggest sturgeon officially recorded from Idaho waters was a 675-pounder caught from the Snake with a setline in 1908; the angling record is a 394-pounder caught in 1956. Lewiston, which is downstream along the Snake at its confluence with the Clearwater, is home to a thriving tour boat and guiding industry that includes several outfitters who offer sturgeon fishing.

The Hells Canyon stretch of the Snake, widely known as one of the deepest and most rugged gorges in North America, can also hold large numbers of rainbow trout and crappie, depending on water conditions. When high runoff occurs, rainbows become scarce and are overshadowed by a crappie boom from fish washed out of Brownlee Reservoir

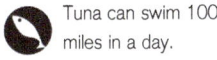

Tuna can swim 100 miles in a day.

upstream. When spring and summer flows are low, the trout prosper. Channel catfish are also present in the canyon, although their numbers have fluctuated widely as well. A more reliable pursuit for anglers is smallmouth bass. Good numbers of bass populate the river, with a few each year approaching 5 pounds. Early spring, when the water temperatures approach 50°F and before the rivers rise and grow murky with runoff, is the most productive time for catching big smallmouths from the lower reaches of the Snake in Idaho waters.

Steelhead and Salmon

The Snake from Hells Canyon Dam downstream, and its largest tributaries—the Salmon and Clearwater Rivers—are also revered by Idaho anglers and others as the home of noteworthy runs of steelhead (sea-run rainbow trout). Classified as summer steelhead because they begin their migration out of the Pacific Ocean about June, the fish begin surging past Lower Granite Dam, 34 miles downstream from Lewiston, as early as August. Located in neighboring southeastern Washington, Lower Granite serves as the last fish-counting station before Idaho waters.

Since the 1970s, a boom in federal hatchery construction to mitigate for lost fish habitat caused by dams has sparked a steelhead renaissance in Idaho waters. The 1980s produced the largest steelhead counts on record, peaking at more than 135,000 fish across Lower Granite, and anglers reaped record harvests of steelhead ranging from 4 to more than 20 pounds.

All this success, of course, demands the tempering of a historical perspective. Idaho's rivers once produced the bulk of the Columbia River's chinook salmon runs. During the 1890s, at least half of the 3 million spring and summer chinook salmon that returned to the mighty Columbia each year migrated upstream to their spawning beds in the Snake and its tributaries. The river's chinook runs now cling tenuously to an uncertain future.

The late 1990s produced seasons with more widespread salmon fishing in Idaho waters than in the prior two decades, a hopeful sign. But salmon numbers have fluctuated widely because of ocean conditions unfriendly to salmon and steelhead and due to the extensive development of hydroelectric dams on the Snake and Columbia. Hatchery production of salmon has proved a hit-or-miss proposition, largely because of the complexities of environmental conditions. The Snake's wild-spawning chinook runs are listed as threatened with extinction under the Endangered Species Act. A massive effort to restore the salmon runs has been underway since the early 1990s, when the fish were first protected by the National Marine Fisheries Service.

In more dire straits than the chinook, Idaho's sockeye salmon are classified as an endangered species. The number of sockeyes making the 900-mile migration home to their last spawning refuge at Redfish Lake near Stanley could be counted on one hand during the 1990s.

Happily for anglers, steelhead have proven themselves tougher than their larger chinook cousins. Although catch-and-release fishing starts in August in Idaho waters, anglers can't take home a fish until September, and the bulk of the run typically doesn't arrive until October. A remarkable aspect of the steelhead's life cycle is that they stop eating once they enter freshwater. They live off the reserves they've built up in their rich ocean pastures until they spawn in the spring. Unlike chinook and other Pacific salmon, steelhead can survive spawning, although the rigors of the process typically claim more than 95 percent of the run.

The Clearwater harbors exceptionally large steelhead. These fish, most of them produced by Dworshak National Fish Hatchery at Ahsahka, average 12 to 14 pounds. Typically each year, several fish topping 20 pounds are landed along the Clearwater or from the nearby Snake. The steelhead that begin their migration in the summer won't spawn until the following spring. That cycle gives anglers nearly six months of fishing most years.

The Clearwater from Ahsahka downstream is a popular winter destination for both Idahoans and Montanans. It remains ice free in all but the coldest weather because of releases from Dworshak Dam across the river's North Fork.

The Salmon River, because of its sizable runs of steelhead, which typically average 6 to 11 pounds apiece, is popular in both fall and spring. Winter along the Salmon, one of the nation's longest undammed streams as well as one of the longest originating and ending in one state, is generally the quiet season. The river becomes icebound in most years sometime in December, and remains so until February.

The lower reaches of the Salmon near White Bird and Riggins offer the best fall fishing. Crowds begin gathering along the upper reaches of the Salmon from Salmon City upstream to Stanley as soon as the ice goes out and the water warms enough to reawaken the fishes' migratory urge to return to their spawning streams.

Idaho's statewide steelhead regulations typically allow anglers to pursue the fish until April, although the anglers' interest typically begins to wane in late March or so. The condition of the fish usually deteriorates quickly as the spring advances and they channel their energy into spawning.

Although the Clearwater River draws much attention for its big steelhead, it offers other notable angling as well. Dworshak Reservoir, which backs up 54 miles of the North Fork, has become the likeliest place to land the next state record smallmouth bass. It boasts two fish that have carried that distinction, including the current record, weighing just over 8 pounds and caught in 1955. Dworshak also has offered a popular kokanee (landlocked sockeye salmon) fishery in past years, although it was in a rebuilding phase in the late 1990s.

The Big Lakes

The Panhandle's Lake Pend Oreille, home of big Kamloops rainbows, is still untainted by development and, at 180 square miles covering 115,000 acres, offers plenty of room to roam. Slightly smaller Lake Coeur d'Alene to the south is richer in nutrients and produces more fish, but it bears some scars, namely elevated levels of heavy metals from a long and storied history of mining in the Coeur d'Alenes to the east. Shallower and more productive are Hauser, Hayden, Spirit, and Twin Lakes. In addition to producing some big largemouth bass, Hauser also produced a 19-pound rainbow that was the state record for more than 50 years. Priest Lake, the least developed and purest of the Panhandle's big lakes, produced a 57-pound, 8-ounce lake trout in 1971.

The big lakes are home to Idaho's largest fish. Record bull trout and a cutthroat-rainbow hybrid have come from Pend Oreille Lake. Although Sandpoint may be the best-known community along the big lake's shoreline, Hope and Bayview serve as fishing centers where charter boats can be found.

IGFA

Acronym for the International Game Fish Association *(see)*.

ILLINOIS

It was not too long ago that serious anglers rarely thought of fishing in Illinois. Farm pond bluegills and silty river catfish were the extent of Illinois' sportfishery. Although a few largemouth bass lived in southern lakes, the fish were small. Northern lakes—especially near densely populated Chicago—were overfished to the point of exhaustion. And the rivers were so putrid and polluted that the fish commonly bore cancerous lesions.

Even southern Lake Michigan was denuded of its bread-and-butter commercial lake trout and herring fishery. By the 1960s, it had become choked with exotic alewives from the St. Lawrence Seaway. Smelly piles of these oily little ocean fish had to be bulldozed from beaches.

If you liked carp and bullhead, Illinois was your place. You went to Wisconsin for walleye, pike, and muskies; to Michigan and Minnesota for smallmouth bass; to Kentucky, Missouri, and farther south for crappie and largemouth bass.

The fishery changed dramatically in the 1980s with the Clean Water Act, which revived the rivers. Today, smallmouth bass richly populate streams in the upper third of Illinois. Walleye and sauger, kick-started by mitigative stocking programs, dominate sportfishing on rivers like the Mississippi, Illinois, and Rock. Catch-and-release ethics nurtured a citizen-driven stocking program on a dozen lakes that now produce steady trophy muskie fishing. Big largemouth—for Illinois (6- to 8-pounders)—thrive throughout the state. And large hybrid stripers, walleye, catfish, and all kinds of bass populate many power plant cooling lakes.

Size and strength make chinook salmon the premier fish of Lake Michigan.

The breakthrough for Illinois arrived with the Jake Wolf Hatchery in 1983, which added a stocking capacity of 60 million fish, spread among 15 to 20 species, to the production of two older, smaller hatcheries. Another hatchery opened at LaSalle Lake, to service cooling ponds and the Illinois River.

Tourism-driven state fisheries management programs were instituted to lure visitors and stop Illinois anglers from flocking out of state. Programs evolved for every type of fishery, augmented by state funds and increased license fees.

The eye-opener was the successful turnaround of Lake Michigan as a salmon and trout fishery, a process that actually began in the 1960s. Illinois joined Michigan, Indiana, and Wisconsin in a bold cooperative stocking program that introduced coho salmon, chinook salmon, steelhead, lake trout, and brown trout, which foraged on the lake's alewives, creating a new shoreline and deep-water sportfishery.

By the late 1960s, derbies and tournaments took place around the lake, broadcasting huge catches of giant fish. A charter boat fishing industry that works all but the coldest winter months blossomed as a result. Marinas proliferated, serving thousands of pleasure boats. Each spring, shoreline anglers and small-craft boaters enjoy a coho run through harbors and along piers and jetties. They typically long-cast spoons and flies for 3- to 7-pound fish that grow larger through the summer.

As these salmon and trout reduced the overabundance of alewives, perch and rainbow smelt proliferated, but those species endured a tailspin in the 1990s. Whether this is cyclical or due to predation or the straining of nutrients by newer, undesirable, exotic species (the zebra mussel, the spiny water flea, the round goby) has not been determined.

One particularly positive result has been the rebirth of smallmouth bass along riprap sea walls and breakwaters from mid-Chicago into Indiana.

Anglers using spinners and crankbaits can have 50-fish days, including the occasional 4-pounder.

Water clarification by mussels, as well as a ban on phosphorus, enables anglers to see fish life as deep as 40 feet on calm days, and Lake Michigan's protected harbors have become virtual aquariums. Deeper sunlight penetration has improved aquatic vegetative cover, causing largemouth bass and panfish—not to mention the occasional northern pike—to enjoy a resurgence in harbors.

These achievements are only part of the Illinois story. Vast improvements have occurred in every region.

Northeast

Fishing pressure can overwhelm the Chicago area. With three-fourths of Illinois' 11 million people living in six Chicago metropolitan counties, local anglers historically traveled far to find productive fishing.

But not anymore. Even the former sewer of the Chicago River and its system of sanitary canals is a viable, reproducing fishery. Anglers have seen a resurgence of bass—smallmouth in the inner harbor of Lake Michigan and largemouth downstream through the industrial belt below the Loop. Following several successful years of European-style carp fishing tournaments in the midst of Chicago's Downtown, anglers now plan other competitions in the revived Chicago River.

Cleaner water and an abundance of wood and rocky bass structure in a thicket of old and rarely used barge slips have contributed to the recovery of Chicago's fishery. Similarly good bass fishing exists in the South Side Calumet River and Lake Calumet and down through industrial CalSag Channel—a canal that joins the historic Chicago Sanitary & Ship Canal in suburban Lemont. Both of these once-dead waterways now host bass and panfish chiefly around massive aeration stations built by the Metropolitan Water Reclamation District.

City anglers' appetites have been whetted by a strong urban fishing program conducted by the Illinois Department of Natural Resources (DNR) and the Chicago Park District in Chicago park lagoons, plus continually improved fisheries management at more than 20 Cook County forest preserve lakes. Walleye as big as 10 pounds have been seen in prolific Tampier Lake on the Southwest Side, and bass up to 5 pounds are pulled from Busse and Maple Lakes, as well as Saganashkee Slough. Rehabilitated Skokie Lagoons has become a major destination for largemouth bass and catfish.

State-managed Wolf Lake on the industrial Illinois-Indiana border has a vastly improved bass program thanks to better aquatic vegetation, as well as a burgeoning smallmouth bass population in its northwest section. Anglers must have licenses from both states to fish the entire lake.

The Des Plaines River—another former sewer coursing from the Wisconsin border through several western suburbs—has seen a spectacular smallmouth bass and pike recovery in its restored northern wetland reaches as well as in the long, rocky stretch below Hoffman Dam in southwest suburban Lyons. The Des Plaines has recovered through its merger with the Sanitary Canal above Joliet and, farther downstream, through its merger with the Kankakee River near Wilmington to form the Illinois.

The Kankakee, Fox, and DuPage Rivers also have become substantial near-urban fisheries, largely due to cleaner water and careful regulations. All three support specific catch-and-release areas for trophy smallmouth bass, demanded by anglers after such regulations were successfully implemented downstate on the Rock River.

Besides smallmouth bass, the Kankakee can yield walleye above 10 pounds in deep holes before the spring spawning run. It also has good fishing for pike and panfish in its upper wetlands and farm runoff ditches.

The Fox sees good walleye action below its numerous dams, as well as smallmouth bass, panfish, and some creditable muskies at creek mouths that drain lakes and reservoirs. In places along the Fox, versatile anglers can work creek mouths for muskies, wade to channel dropoffs for walleye, and then wade toward a nearby riffle for smallmouth bass.

The leafy DuPage was one of Chicago's first suburban streams to develop a recovering smallmouth fishery, now augmented by the state. Protected by several forest preserves, it yields steady catches of respectable bass and catfish.

Major Rivers

More than half of Illinois' borders are rivers—the Mississippi on the west, the Ohio on its southern rim, and the Wabash along southern and central Indiana. The DNR estimates that most of Illinois' fish harvests occur in the substantial backwaters, channels, and dam holes of the Mississippi, which indicates the volume of fishable shoreline along that prolific body of water. The Mississippi's 580 river miles along Illinois have two parts: the pooled reach above St. Louis, with 15 dams creating effective lakes, and the unpooled deeper channel below St. Louis.

These sections are essentially separate rivers with respect to fishing. The pooled stretches offer year-round walleye and sauger fishing. The deep cuts below the dams are productive from fall through early spring; the submerged artificial wing dams, particularly on outer bends, are good in summer. Depending on current speed, anglers use $1/4$- to 1-ounce jigs and minnows on three-way rigs below the dams, and jigs, spinners, and crankbaits cast above or alongside the wing dams.

Channel cats and smallmouth and largemouth bass abound in the upper Mississippi, whereas flathead catfish and a strong, recovering population of blue cats proliferate along with largemouth bass in the lower river. Flatheads and blues frequently top 40 and 50 pounds.

It has been speculated that a fisherman from the Bay of Biscay north of Spain informed Christopher Columbus of the existence of Newfoundland before the explorer undertook his journeys.

Significant tributaries that feed the Mississippi include the smallmouth-rich Apple, Plum, Green, and Rock Rivers—the latter boasting its own substantial walleye population below dams. In fact, the walleye harvest on the Rock quadruples that of the larger Illinois River, which drains half the counties in the state.

Along with walleye, sauger, white bass, and smallmouths in its reaches above Peoria, the Illinois offers good largemouth fishing from Peoria downstream, especially in the labyrinthine backwaters of Bath Chute and Snicarte Slough below Havana. Many duck clubs and managers of waterfowl areas, such as Anderson and Sanganois Lakes, control backwater levels and thereby contribute to the fishery.

Other feeders include the Kaskaskia River, with logjams, root wads, brush piles, undercut banks, oxbow channels, and shoreline riprap that produce substantial numbers of bass and catfish, especially below Fayetteville and above New Athens.

The Ohio River is famed for its maze of backwater creeks in Smithland Pool, 70 miles from the mouth of the Wabash to Smithland Dam below Golconda. Largemouth and Kentucky spotted bass average 12 to 15 inches, with some reaching 21 inches. Crappie and catfish also abound in waters that deeply penetrate the Shawnee National Forest.

The Wabash River is widely known for catfish and largemouth bass, the latter improving measurably in recent years.

The Rock River's trip through northern Illinois dispenses not only substantial walleye below its dams in Oregon, Dixon, Sterling, and Rock Falls, but also a magnificent 9-mile catch-and-release smallmouth area between Oregon and Grand Detour. Large catches of good eating–size channel cats occur in rocky currents. The Rock feeds 96-mile-long Hennepin Canal—a well-stocked panfish and catfish area of many pools between locks (anglers "troll" for fish by walking briskly along the towpath)—and offers deep holes for 30- to 50-pound flatheads between Grand Detour and Dixon.

Other substantial streams include the Mackinaw, Vermilion, Iroquois, Kishwaukee, Pecatonica, and Mazon for smallmouth bass, and the poetically famous Spoon, Embarras, Muddy, LaMoine, and Sangamon for catfish.

Reservoirs and Cooling Lakes

Three main Army Corps of Engineers flood-control reservoirs serve Illinois anglers. Lake Shelbyville, covering 11,100 acres near Mattoon, has developed an excellent largemouth bass and muskie fishery. Many bass are in the 2.2-pound range, and some exceed 5 pounds. Muskies proliferate here, drawing anglers from several states, especially in the weeks before fall turnover. Crappie fishing is another staple.

Carlyle Lake, which spans 24,580 acres east of St. Louis, has largemouth bass up to 6 pounds, and decent crappie, white bass, bluegill, and channel cat numbers, especially in the cover-laden waterfowling areas on its periphery. Rend Lake's 18,900 acres between Mt. Vernon and Benton, has numerous largemouth bass in the $1^1/_2$- to $4^1/_2$-pound range, and so many catfish that jug fishermen routinely lay in a winter's supply.

Illinois' array of power plant cooling lakes draws huge numbers of anglers to catfish factories like LaSalle, which also feature smallmouth, hybrid, and striped bass. Decent walleye and bass frequent Heidecke Lake, and Braidwood harbors bass, panfish, and catfish. Powerton's submerged drainage ditches and rocky riprap yield large numbers of 1-pound-plus catfish and flurries of excellent smallmouth in March, April, and early October along rocky ledges and levees in the coolest available water. Newton, Coffeen, and SangChris have good numbers of bass and panfish.

Northern Lakes

The Fox Chain O'Lakes in Lake and McHenry Counties has recovered substantially, although heavy boat traffic remains a pain to anglers on weekends. Muskies proliferate in Lake Marie and other northern reaches, especially on offshore weed beds near channels. Speed trollers have up to eight-fish days in early summer by running shallow-diving shadlike crankbaits no more than 8 to 20 feet from the boat. One lure should be in the prop wash, held down by an 8-ounce weight.

Shabbona Lake was built to field pressure from Chicago, offering trophy muskies, walleye, and bass as well as steady panfish. Four state record muskies have been produced at Shabbona.

Other popular destinations are Pierce Lake near Rockford, and George, Otter, Decatur, Springfield, Spring, Banner Marsh, and Snakeden Hollow Lakes in central and western Illinois. Snakeden Hollow and Mazonia Lakes near Joliet represent an array of bass and panfish challenges, each involving more than 100 flooded strip-mine lakes. Carlton, a tiny lake with numerous shallow bays, routinely yields the highest catch rates of muskies, as well as excellent largemouth bass.

Southern Lakes

Kinkade Lake near Carbondale has achieved premier stature for its large population of 45-plus-inch muskies, as well as excellent numbers of largemouth bass in a wildly beautiful setting. Lake-of-Egypt, and Horseshoe, Crab Orchard, Cedar, and Little Grassy Lakes offer excellent angling for bass and panfish, including occasionally nice crappie. Shawnee National Forest has an abundance of ponds and smaller lakes that yield a variety of action. Also worth checking are numerous county- and city-park lakes with creative management programs.

IMPROVED CLINCH KNOT

A fishing knot for terminal connections.
See: Knots, Fishing.

INBOARD BOAT
A boat powered by an inboard motor.
See: Boat; Sportfishing Boat.

INBOARD/OUTBOARD BOAT
A boat powered by an inboard/outboard motor.
See: Boat; Sportfishing Boat.

INCONNU *Stenodus leucichthys*.
Other names—sheefish, connie, Eskimo tarpon; Russian: *beloribitsa*.

A member of the Salmonidae family, and a relative of whitefish and cisco, the inconnu is a species with limited northern range. It is poorly known to most anglers, in keeping with the meaning of its French name: unknown. In North America, most anglers know this exotic species as the sheefish. The only predatory member of the whitefish group in North America, it is highly favored by anglers as an exciting and large sportfish, but it is perhaps the least caught of North American and Asian gamefish. Its silvery coloring and tendency to leap high out of the water when hooked have earned it the nickname "Eskimo tarpon." Inconnu also have minor commercial importance, especially when smoked, although it is endangered in some portions of its eastern range.

Identification. The general body shape of inconnu is very similar to that of char or whitefish, but the head is relatively long, pointed, and depressed on the top. Its mouth is large, and the lower jaw clearly projects outward beyond the upper jaw. The maxillary, or upper jaw bone, extends back at least as far as the middle of the eye. Small, fine teeth are found on the anterior part of the lower jaw, and on the tongue, premaxillaries, the head of the maxillaries, the vomer, and the palatines (bones of the roof of the mouth). The tail is distinctly forked. Sheefish have large scales and a dark lateral line, and, like all salmonids, an adipose fin.

Size/Age. Inconnu are said to grow to 60 pounds. The all tackle world record is a 53-pounder from Alaska. Like many arctic and subarctic fish, they are long-lived, which makes large fish vulnerable to exploitation; the largest fish may be between 25 and 35 years old.

Distribution. In North America, inconnu are found in Alaska, from the Kuskokwim River (Bering Sea drainage) north, throughout the Yukon River in Canada, in the Mackenzie River, in Great Bear and Great Slave Lakes in Canada's Northwest Territories as far as the Anderson River near Cape Bathurst, and in isolated areas of extreme northern British Columbia. The largest North American fish occur in the vicinity of Selawik to Kotzebue, where tributaries enter into Hotham Inlet and Kotzebue Sound. In Asia, inconnu occur westward as far as the White Sea, and an isolated population inhabits the Caspian Sea and its drainage.

Habitat. Although generally viewed as a freshwater species, the inconnu occurs in strictly freshwater lakes and rivers and also in anadromous sea-run forms that winter in brackish deltas, bays, and tidewater areas and ascend coastal tributaries to spawn. It evidently evolved from purely freshwater fish to estuarine-anadromous fish.

Life history/Behavior. Spawning takes place in late summer and early fall, when inconnu ascend freshwater tributaries. Inland inconnu leave lakes and run up tributaries as well. In coastal regions, inconnu migrate from estuaries to river mouths after ice out, then ascend freshwater tributaries; this migration may last a few weeks in short-length rivers, or months in longer ones, such as the Yukon River. After spawning, they do not die, but quickly migrate downstream.

Food and feeding habits. This species feeds mostly on small fish. Salmon smolts, cisco, smelt, and whitefish are among the common forage, and in coastal areas large schools of inconnu will fatten on baitfish prior to their spawning migration, making it possible to spot fish by looking for bird activity.

Angling. Inconnu are aggressive fish, but they can also be spooked by activity. Spoons, spinners, and streamer flies are the common lures, employed mostly in casting. Heavy-bodied spoons are often necessary for casting in windy situations and to get down in the current. Large, weighted flies are likewise usually better for larger fish. Inconnu are caught from boats and by wading anglers, and large coastal fish have the ability to make long runs and take a lot of line. They will leap out of the water when caught and have hard bony mouths that make it necessary to put muscle into the hook-setting motion. Most sport-caught inconnu are released.

INDIA

The Indian subcontinent is a vast country with rich aquatic resources. It offers a variety of fishing opportunities—little known outside its borders—in both its freshwater and brackish water environments.

As the seventh largest country in the world, India stretches 3,200 kilometers from north to south and 2,700 kilometers from east to west. Its territory is one-third the size of the United States but encompasses 25 states, more than 32 million square kilometers of land, more than 50,000 kilometers of rivers and streams, and more than 3,000 kilometers of coastline bordering the Arabian Sea, the Indian Ocean, and the Bay of Bengal.

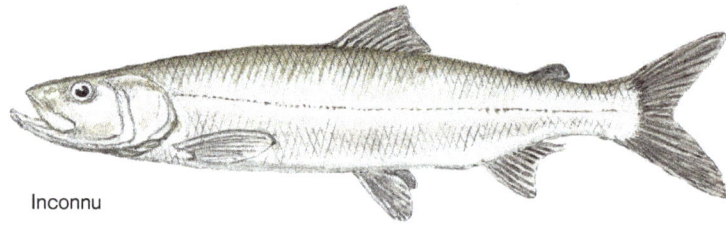

Inconnu

Two major rivers in the north run through the 2,400-kilometer-long Himalayan mountain range, and both are lifelines for the local population. One of these is the Ganga (Ganges), which is 2,512 kilometers long, stretching from its headwaters at Gaumukh in the Himalayas to the Bay of Bengal. It actually has a combined length of 8,047 kilometers when all of its significant tributaries are included. The other is the Brahmaputra, which is 4,023 kilometers long. Important rivers draining peninsular India are the Mahanadi, Godavari, Krishna, and Cauvery, with a total length of 6,437 kilometers. The Western Ghats are drained by the Tapti and Narmada Rivers, and flow all of 3,380 kilometers.

India's population of 950 million is the second largest in the world (after China), and a significant portion of the country's citizens are poor, spending most of their time trying to make ends meet. Three-quarters of the population lives in rural villages. Fishing as a hobby or recreational pursuit is a luxury, and far less than 1 percent of the population partakes in sportfishing. The poor and lower middle-income groups of Indian society fish only for subsistence. Among those who do fish as a hobby, very few appear to practice catch-and-release. Invariably, fish taken by sporting methods end up in the kitchen.

At present, India lures few foreign anglers, primarily because scant outfitting services cater to sportfishing, and detailed information has been lacking; those who visit must be adventurous and adaptable. Access to fishing sites on noteworthy rivers is easy because all major cities and villages are located on their banks, if not within a short distance. For specialized fishing, and especially far northern mountain trout angling, resourceful anglers travel long distances.

Sportfishing for pleasure alone, as practiced in North America and Europe, was virtually unknown in India until the middle of the twentieth century. Prior to that, Indians ranked fishing below hunting for wild animals. For many centuries India was divided into 560 small kingly states ruled by feudal heads and kings who were interested in hunting wild animals. The inclination to hunt wild game permeated to the general population from the nobility, whom they were supposed to help in this pursuit.

Recent American and European influences have spurred interest in recreational angling in India. Because of this trend, sportfishing is likely to grow in economic significance and might provide leverage for tourism.

Various changes and improvements in facilities are necessary, however, to accommodate any growth in recreational angling. There is, for example, an urgent need to build publicly accessible fishing piers in numerous locations. To popularize angling, India must launch an extensive publicity and advertising campaign, and clinics must be organized to teach sportfishing methods to young people as well as adults. These will likely have to be arranged and conducted by the Departments of Fisheries in the Indian states on a regular basis.

Nevertheless, India has opportunities to offer anglers. Sportfisheries exist in the cold waters flowing out of the of the Himalayan, Satpuras, and Aravallis Ranges (respectively in the north, central, and northwestern region) and the hills of southern India; warmwater fishing exists in the great plains, and brackish water fishing can be enjoyed along the extensive coasts of the eastern and western edges of peninsular (south) India. Fishing sites along all the rivers and streams are generally accessible through rail and road connections; however, a certain amount of walking is required to reach some places. Very few people fish from boats; they invariably approach fishing sites by road, and fish from the banks of the rivers or lakes.

There are 31 freshwater fish species in India that are of interest to anglers. Local names of fish differ according to region, but there is, as yet, no listing of standardized local fish names. The species pursued by local anglers are cyprinids (family: Cyprinidae); catfish (families: Siluridae, Bagridae, Pangasiidae, Schilbeidae, Sisoridae); murrel (family: Channidae); and trout (family: Salmonidae). All but trout, which were introduced from Europe around the beginning of the twentieth century, are endemic.

With sportfishing in India gaining strength, in 1982 Raj Tilak and Uma Sharma published their English-language book, *Gamefishes of India and Angling,* as an aid to eager anglers. Tilak and Sharma give an illustrated account of 31 species of freshwater gamefish in India, with keys to their identification, methods of angling, use of lures, and so forth. Through the late 1990s, theirs remains the only book on this topic.

Finding and catching these species is complicated by several factors. The food and feeding habits of some Indian fish are not known to many native or visiting anglers. Also, the complement of gamefish varies regionally, and it is not well known which species inhabit which regions or specific waters, although Indian tourism agencies have been working to make specific details available.

The following information is a general guide to finding and catching fish in Indian waters. Bear in mind that at any given time climatic conditions vary widely in different parts of India. Hence, dry and wet seasons are not necessarily the same from region to region. In the Himalayas, for example, September and October are comparatively dry months with moderate temperatures, allowing access to almost all important fishing sites in the region.

North India

In northern India, the best sportfishing opportunities are available along the base of the Himalayas and the Shiwaliks, and in the plains. The Shiwaliks are low-hill ranges running parallel to the Himalayan mountain region, all along its length on the southern edge.

In the hilly sections of the rivers, the king among Indian sportfish is the mahseer, the largest member of the minnow and carp clan and belonging to the Cyprinidae family. These include the putitor, or yellow-finned, mahseer *(Tor putitora);* the tor, or red-finned, mahseer *(Tor tor);* and the mosal, or copper, mahseer *(Tor mosal).* The putitor mahseer grows to a length of 2.7 meters; the male may reach an astounding 1.9 quintal (190 kilograms, or 418 pounds), and the female can grow to 2.2 quintal (220 kilograms, or 484 pounds). The tor mahseer can reach a length of 1.7 meters and a weight of 100 kilograms (220 pounds). The mosal mahseer does not grow longer than 1 meter.

These fish are omnivorous and accept any kind of natural food, but a paste bait works especially well. Various spoons are also effective. Light to heavy tackle is preferred, depending on the size of the fish targeted. The best fishing is in August and September. Another cyprinid, the chaguni *(Chagunius chagunio),* which does not grow bigger than 450 millimeters (about 17 inches), offers good sport on a small hook.

In Himalayan streams, the schizothoracids, such as the alwan *(Schizothorax richardsonii),* which is a column feeder, and the chhiruh *(Schizothoraichthys esocinus)* and dinnawah *(Schizothoraichthys progastus),* which are bottom feeders, are good sportfishes. These are cyprinids, too, but are found in hilly streams at higher altitudes than are mahseer. They take well on paste baits and are prized table fare. The best time to fish in these regions is September and October.

In the northern Indian plains, a large number of sporty cyprinids and catfish are loved by anglers along such noted rivers as the Ganga and the Yamuna, as well as in many small rivers and streams. Prominent cyprinids here are the katla *(Catla catla),* which attains a recorded size of 1.83 meters; the rohu *(Labeo rohita)* and kalbose *(Labeo calbasu),* which grow to 1 meter; the mirgal *(Cirrhinus mrigala),* which grows to less than 1 meter; and the bola *(Barilius bola),* which grows to 300 millimeters. Most of these are stocked in ponds and reservoirs and form a major part of the fisheries of northern India. They take well on paste and worm baits, and provide a good fight. Among these cyprinids, the rohu is a prized fish and fetches a higher price in the commercial markets than that of all other cyprinids.

Catfish are also loved by Indian anglers. They are carnivorous and destructive to other species, but their size, fighting quality, and tasty boneless flesh make them a favorite quarry. Locals generally catch them using small fish, worms, frogs, and some lures.

The important species of catfish for sport are the aar *(Mystus aor),* growing to 1.8 meters and 68 kilograms; the seenghari *(Mystus seenghala),* growing to 400 millimeters; the boali, or mulley *(Wallago attu),* growing to 1.8 meters and 45 kilograms; the khagga *(Rita rita),* growing to 1.3 meters; the pungas *(Pangasius pangasius),* growing to 1.5 meters and 55 kilograms; the silond *(Silonia silondia),* growing to 2 meters and 45 kilograms; the bachwa vacha *(Eutropiichthys vacha),* growing to 350 millimeters; the garua bachcha, or gaurchcha *(Clupisoma garua),* growing to 1 meter; and the goonch *(Bagarius bagarius),* growing to 2 meters and 135 kilograms (297 pounds).

Also available and pursued here is the murrel *(Channa marulius),* a long-bodied fish characterized as a "snakehead" by some, which grows to 1.2 meters and takes live baits, particularly frogs.

Anglers avoid the rainy season (summer monsoons), which varies according to the region, and extremely cold days.

Peninsular India

In peninsular India, the Mahanadi, Krishna, Godavary, and Cauvery Rivers, as well as other rivers and streams, provide angling for different species. Prominent sportfish include the khudchee *(Tor khudree),* which grows to 450 millimeters and 22.6 kilograms; the mussullah, or high-backed, mahseer *(Tor mussullah),* which grows to 1.5 meters and nearly 90 kilograms; the wulnus, or purree *(Silonia childreni),* which grows to 460 millimeters; and the white carp *(Cirrhinus cirrhosus),* which grows to 450 millimeters. The wulnus takes both live and dead baits employed with a small hook. The white carp strikes like the rohu and can be taken on a small hook with paste or a worm.

With the exception of the rainy season, which starts in June here, anglers pursue fish throughout the year.

East India

The two important sportfishes of the Brahmaputra River and small streams in this region are *Tor progenius,* known as jhungha in Assam and growing to 1 meter, and *Acrossocheilus hexagonolepis,* which attains a length of 0.6 meter and a weight of 9.5 kilograms. This fish is known as bokar in Assam, and as katli among the Nepali-speaking people of Assam and North Bengal.

Trout

In addition to the endemic sportfish of India, two exotic species are well established in hilly sections of northern, eastern, and peninsular India: brown trout and rainbow trout. The browns were introduced in India around the turn of the century; rainbow trout came later. Brown trout are widespread in the wild, whereas rainbows are restricted only to experimental ponds. Trout grow to large sizes in big rivers and lakes—up to 7.5 kilograms in some high-altitude lakes in Himachal Pradesh—and attract foreign tourists. Brown trout are caught here on dry and wet flies and small spoons.

Coastal Regions

India's long coast is flanked by the Arabian Sea on the west, the Indian Ocean on the south, and the

---

It is said that sailfish can sustain a speed of close to 70 mph, salmon 30 mph, and bonefish 22 mph. A human's top speed is 20 mph, and we don't have to do it through water.

Bay of Bengal on the east. The common marine sportfish targeted by anglers are tuna, marlin, sailfish, mackerel, sea bass, snapper, jacks, croaker, snook, perch, sharks, and tripletail. Some large specimens of these fish have been landed in Indian waters; snook, for example, have been registered as large as 914 millimeters. For brackish water and marine fishes, anglers use heavy tackle and a variety of live and artificial baits. Comparatively, brackish water and marine anglers are much fewer in number in India than those in freshwater.

Fishing in the estuaries and the coastal regions is possible only with the help of boats, of which there are few specifically designated for angling. One can hire boats for any purpose at all seaports in India, but hardly any system for hiring charter boats for fishing exists. There are no fishing guides or charter captains either. Contacting local anglers, or the Department of Fisheries of the coastal state, may lead to information about the availability of boats.

Significant ports along the western coast of India include Kandla (Maharashtra), Bombay (Maharashtra), Nhava Sheva (Maharashtra), Marmagao (Karnataka), New Mangalore (Karnataka), and Kochi (earlier called Cochin in Kerala). On the eastern coast they include Calcutta-Haldia (West Bengal), Paradip (West Bengal), Vishakhapatnam (Andhra Pradesh), Madras (Tamil Nadu), and Tuticorin (Tamil Nadu).

Gamefish Management/Fish Sanctuaries

The fish stocks in various Indian waters have suffered greatly in recent times, both in quality and quantity as a result of harmful direct or indirect human activities. The effect on fisheries resources has been more severe in some places than others.

Radical changes in the occurrence and abundance of fish in certain important river systems is generally related to recent human activities in the area. Technological development, including the construction of dams and hydroelectric power–generation projects, have modified the ecology of rivers by slowing down the flow, increasing the depth, and altering the course. In addition, overfishing, illegal fishing activities, introduction of exotic fast-breeding species, expanded state programs of maximum exploitation of fishery resources, pollution through urban/agricultural/ industrial wastes and effluents, and so forth have added to the problem. The construction of vehicular roads, the gradual extension of urban areas, and certain socioeconomic changes appear to have aided the decline. The chain effect of these activities has profoundly influenced fish populations in India, as well as species diversity in the streams and rivers. These influences have led to a pronounced impoverishment or even total disappearance of some important species.

Fisheries agencies of the Indian states are aware of these problems and are attempting to remedy some of them. Good laws to protect fisheries exist in India, but implementation is poor. Although India has not yet achieved total exploitation of its fisheries resources, far-reaching deteriorating effects on fish fauna are strongly manifest. Thus, although angling opportunities are available, they are not as good as they were in the past, nor are they as good as they could be with proper care.

Among the food fish of India, the major carp—such as the katla, rohu, kalbose, and mirgal—form the backbone of fish propagation in northern India, although katla and mirgal have been successfully transplanted into the rivers of peninsular India. Among the major gamefish, the putitor, or yellow-finned, mahseer; the mosal, or copper, mahseer; and the tor, or red-finned, mahseer are distributed by authorities in the waterways of the lesser Himalayas in the north. The khudchee and the mussullah, or high-backed, mahseer are likewise distributed in the rivers in peninsular India.

Hatchery rearing techniques have been perfected for important carp species, and fish are stocked as necessary where natural reproduction is not sustaining fish populations. The natural breeding of important carp and mahseer species has suffered greatly, and as a result the natural production of these fish has substantially declined. Due to a continuing depreciation of fish fauna and reduced natural production, the role of fish sanctuaries has increased as a means of improving the fish stock.

Fish sanctuaries have been in existence in India partly because of the religious beliefs of the people, which require that they protect natural resources, and partly because of legislation introduced by the departments of fisheries or forests in various states. Many such fish sanctuaries exist in India, and they preserve the gene pool of important fish species by providing seed for further propagation of those species. The idea of creating fish sanctuaries is catching on and may become a vital means of maintaining and/or restoring fish stocks.

Angling and Tourism

Tourism ranks sixth among the major industries in India, although it ranks much higher in many other nations. Adequate attention has not been paid to this lucrative trade in India, and much could be done to attract foreign tourists and enhance foreign exchange. The national Department of Tourism is working to provide tourists with incentives to visit various places of interest in the country. Apart from a large number of historic monuments, religious sites, national parks and biosphere reserves, and other rare attractions, India's gamefish and angling sites—if properly managed—could lure many more foreign as well as domestic tourists. Its large carp would interest many Europeans, and the mahseer and trout would entice Europeans and non-Europeans alike. To date, most anglers visiting India are interested in angling for trout.

Among the various efforts undertaken by tourism agencies of the national government and the different states is the circulation of brochures that provide details on India's important gamefish and beautiful angling sites. These have been dispatched to Indian diplomatic missions in other countries. Also available are leaflets describing routes to angling spots, modes of transportation and communication, seasonal weather patterns, campgrounds and lodging, and similar necessities. Tourist information centers provide specifics on current fishing laws and where to obtain fishing licenses.

In addition, some states have constructed fishing lodges and huts at preferred angling sites, making it easier for visiting anglers to enjoy them. Transportation is improving due to better road connections. At some tourist offices, personnel can provide information and plan an itinerary for anglers. Licenses indicate the closed seasons for fishing (mostly the breeding season of important species), but inquire in advance, to spare yourself unnecessary expense and disappointment.
See: Sri Lanka.

INDIANA

Sandwiched between Lake Michigan to the northwest and the Ohio River to the south, and with 21,000 miles of rivers and streams, 452 natural lakes, 580 man-made impoundments, thousands of farm ponds, and gravel pits to its credit, Indiana has water and fishing opportunities that belie its status as the 38th largest state. With this diversity in venues comes a plethora of species, in part the result of naturally occurring features and in part due to the successful introduction of highly desirable gamefish.

For many years, fishing in Indiana meant angling strictly for largemouth and smallmouth bass, bluegills, crappie, and catfish. Today, the largemouth bass is still the most-sought species, the bluegill is still the most caught species, and catfish and crappie are not far behind in popularity. Traditional fisheries for walleye and northern pike, not to mention assorted panfish and such rough fish as carp and sucker, also exist.

The modern Hoosier angler, however, has choices that were not possible in earlier decades, including Skamania steelhead, several species of salmon, purebred striped bass, hybrid stripers, and purebred muskies, thanks to aggressive stocking programs that are not necessarily meant to engender natural reproduction. The Division of Fish and Wildlife (DFW) has also stocked saugeye and tiger muskies, but these programs are being phased out.

Indiana's geographic location, length (300 miles), and weather patterns have a special influence on angling. There are at least three weather zones in Indiana. Like prevailing winds, they run from southwest to northeast, and this often means different weather conditions for the northern, central, and southern regions on a daily basis and over longer periods.

The northern region is the area north of the imaginary line that runs from east to west through the cities of Bluffton, Peru, and Monticello; this is roughly the northern third of the state. The central region is the area from that line south to Indiana Highway 46, an east-west road that runs through Greensburg, Columbus, and Bloomington. The southern region is the area south of that highway.

Anglers in the northern tier counties (the first three or four rows of counties south of the Michigan-Indiana state line) almost always have safe ice for fishing by Christmas. Those in the central part of the state think in terms of safe ice by mid-January or early February, and those of the southern third never know when surface waters will ice up, if at all. Larger waters in southern Indiana seldom have safe ice.

An interesting facet of the influence of geographic location and weather is the difference in growth rates of gamefish, especially largemouth bass, in these regions. In general, it takes longer for bass to attain a certain size in smaller, northerly waters than it does in larger, southerly ones; and there is a difference between growth of bass in natural lakes (smaller) versus impoundments.

Thus, minimum size limits on bass vary greatly from one end of the state to the other and even within the regions. Moreover, they are subject to change. On most standing waters the minimum size limit on bass is 12 or 14 inches. Some standing waters, however, have minimum limits between 15 and 20 inches. Others have 12- to 15-inch slot limits, and still others have no minimum size limit.

Skamania-strain steelhead have been a big success for Indiana's Lake Michigan anglers.

A good thing to remember when seeking hotspots for black bass, bluegills, and other members of the sunfish family is that the DFW occasionally renovates and restocks man-made lakes when imbalances of these species occur and the body of water in question is being lowered for some other reason. Growth rates of all species often are phenomenal a year or so after the renovation, and the good fishing can prevail for several years.

Northern Region

The north is well known for its trout and salmon fishing in Lake Michigan, in the big lake's two tributaries at Michigan City, and in the St. Joseph River. These fisheries are discussed separately later.

Trout and salmon notwithstanding, largemouth bass are by far the most important species to anglers in this region. The effects of the Ice Age are evident in the northern region of Indiana, especially the northeast, which was the southern extremity of glacial activity many thousands of years ago. As a result, the northern-tier counties offer several hundred natural "kettle" lakes that provide especially good angling for bass, several other members of the sunfish family, and numerous other species. However, some very good bass fishing is available in the northwest as well.

Nevertheless, at 3,410 acres, Lake Wawasee is the largest of the state's natural lakes and the undisputed best largemouth lake of the northern region. This Kosciusko County lake is one of those rare Indiana waters that also hosts smallmouth in good numbers. Likewise, the 454-acre West Lakes Chain, a series of four lakes in Noble County, offers very good fishing for both largemouths and smallmouths. Steuben County's 509-acre Hamilton Lake is another top largemouth spot in the region.

Other well-known largemouth bass lakes of more than 300 surface acres include Lake Manitou in Fulton County; Dewart and Syracuse (connected to Wawasee on the north) in Kosciusko County; the Indian Chain in Lagrange County; Koontz, Maxinkuckee, and Lake-of-the-Woods in Marshall County; J. C. Murphey at Willow Slough State Fish and Wildlife Area in Newton County; Worster Lake at Potato Creek State Park in St. Joseph County; and Bass, Crooked, James, and George Lakes in Steuben County.

Robinson Lake covers only 59 acres in Whitley County, but it has big bass in good numbers. It was acquired by the state and is operated as a trophy fishery.

Bluegills, redear sunfish, crappie, and some other sunfish are present in nearly all of the natural lakes of the north, and these species offer both food and exciting action. The smaller kettle lakes are better for the smaller sunfish species than are larger lakes, especially those that do not have shad populations. Biologists say the smaller sunfish species are boosted by a lack of competition for food with shad. However, crappie do well in shad-infested lakes because they feed heavily on this unwanted species. Lakes at Tri-County (Kosciusko County) and Willow Slough (Newton County) State Fish and Wildlife Areas, and Chain O' Lakes State Park, offer very good fishing for these species.

The best smallmouth fishing of this region is in rivers and streams. The St. Joseph River in St. Joseph and Elkhart Counties has been one of Indiana's best smallmouth sites for many years. Bringing salmonids into this river has not changed the smallmouth fishery. Another very good smallmouth site is the Tippecanoe River all the way downstream from Tippecanoe Lake to the town of Buffalo at the upper end of Lake Shafer in White County.

The best lakes for northern pike are Manitou (Fulton County), Chapman and Wawasee (Kosciusko), the Indian Lakes Chain (Lagrange), Fish Lake (LaPorte), West Lake (Noble), and Lakes Hamilton and James (Steuben). The Iroquois River through Jasper County; the Tippecanoe River through Kosciusko, Marshall, and Pulaski Counties; and the Kankakee River in Newton County are also good bets for pike.

Catfish inhabit all the rivers of the northern region. Channel cats are the main species, but there are some flatheads and blues. Thanks to an ongoing stocking program, most northern lakes offer good fishing for channel catfish.

Central Region

Few of the largemouth bass waters of the central part of Indiana compare favorably with those of the north and south. Still, this region offers very good fishing, especially for smallmouth bass.

Among the most notable bass waters are the West Fork of the White River through Hamilton County and the northern part of Marion County (Indianapolis); the headwaters of the East Fork of the White River through Henry, Rush, Shelby, and Johnson Counties east of the capitol city; and such Wabash River tributaries as Sugar, Walnut, and Raccoon Creeks to the west. The headwaters of the Wabash River through Huntington, Wabash, and Miami Counties produce some big bronzebacks.

The West Fork of the White River is as good for smallmouths as any river in the state, and maybe the best, from the 146th Street Bridge south of Noblesville through Lake Indy, a wide, slow-moving stretch on the southwest side of Indianapolis. Below Lake Indy occasional sewage spills lessen the value of this water as a smallmouth fishery, but the river overcomes this handicap by the time it reaches Martinsville. From there downstream to its confluence with the Wabash River at East Mt. Carmel in Illinois, it offers good angling for a wide variety of fish, including largemouth bass, some smallmouth bass, big catfish (channels, flatheads, and blues), and many nongame species.

Smallmouths and the other species mentioned inhabit the White upstream from Noblesville, but the fishing is not as good on most stretches upstream from Muncie. It is not as productive from there up to its rise north of Lynn in Randolph County, near the Ohio border. The headwaters of the Big Blue River and Sugar Creek rise east of Indianapolis in Henry and Shelby Counties respectively, and join at the southeastern corner of Johnson County to become Driftwood River as it flows southward to Columbus in Bartholomew County. At a dam on the south side of Columbus the Driftwood becomes the East Fork of the White. The main stem of the White—from the confluence of East and West Forks at the southeast corner of Knox County to the Wabash River—is the best water for large flathead and blue catfish in the state. It is also good for channel cats.

Several other streams of this vast East Fork drainage area also produce good smallmouth fishing. The East Fork of the White is better known for large catfish, however.

The best combined largemouth-smallmouth fisheries in the central part of the state are Freeman and Shafer Lakes and Brookville Reservoir on the Ohio border in Union and Franklin Counties. Smallmouths dominate at Brookville, but the opposite is true at Freeman and Shafer.

Morse Reservoir in Hamilton County, and Geist and Eagle Creek Reservoirs in Marion County, are surprisingly good for largemouth bass. Cataract Lake on the Owen-Putnam County line offers good largemouth fishing, with some bronzebacks.

The best crappie fishing in the central part of the state may be in Mississinewa and Salamonie Reservoirs in Miami and Wabash Counties respectively. All of the reservoirs previously mentioned, however, and Raccoon Reservoir in Parke County, have good crappie populations. Fish of 10 to 12 inches are fairly common, and they get bigger.

The best bluegill and redear fishing is at Summit Lake in Summit Lake State Park in Henry County, and at Glenn Flint Lake northwest of Greencastle in Putnam County. However, all of the farm ponds, gravel pits, and small watershed lakes host bluegill in both good numbers and size. A 6- or 7-inch bluegill or redear sunfish is considered a good catch, but in some waters fish of 8 to 10 inches are fairly common.

All of the reservoirs and rivers have good populations of channel catfish. Flatheads and blues show up less frequently but are present.

Southern Region

Monroe Reservoir not only claims the best largemouth bass fishing Indiana has ever known, but it has maintained that reputation since it was impounded in 1964. This 10,750-acre man-made lake is the largest "inland" body of water in the state, and its bass population is the result of a highly successful stocking that same year.

Monroe is the most likely place to produce a largemouth greater than the existing 14-pound, 12-ounce state record; it still gives up bass that average more than 2 pounds in tournaments. Fish in the 6- to 8-pound range are not uncommon, and a few 9- and 10-pounders are logged there every year.

No less exciting at Monroe is the fishing for crappie, bluegills, and channel catfish. Blue and flathead catfish are also present.

The second best largemouth fishery in this region is Patoka Reservoir, an 8,880-acre multipurpose reservoir in Orange and Crawford Counties. Patoka was a great largemouth fishery for several years after being impounded; then it experienced stunted fish and was subsequently put under slot limit regulations and then a 15-inch minimum size limit. Bass fishing here has been improving.

Patoka also offers particularly good fishing for slab-size bluegills, redear sunfish, and crappie. Excellent fishing for these species is also found at West Boggs Lake in Martin County, and Dogwood Lake at Glendale State Fish and Wildlife Area in Daviess County.

Other top largemouth bass fisheries are the Indiana holdings of the Ohio River. In 1985 the U.S. Supreme Court ruled for Indiana in a suit contending that the navigational dams on the Ohio had raised the river and given Kentucky control of countless acres of Indiana land.

The decision made Indiana a part owner of the Ohio and led to reciprocal agreements between the two states on fishing rights. Now Hoosiers can use their Indiana fishing licenses on all of the Ohio and all of the stream and river embayments on the Indiana side. To fish Kentucky embayments, however, Hoosiers must have a license from that state.

From the southeast corner of Indiana, the pools are Markland, which includes 40 miles of Indiana shoreline; McAlpine, 74 miles; Cannelton, 116 miles; Newburgh, 55 miles; Uniontown, 70 miles; and Smithland, 2 miles. Add to this the waters of the many embayments of Indiana tributaries of the Ohio, and the enormity of this bass fishery becomes apparent. All of the embayments of larger rivers and even smaller creeks and ditches are potential largemouth hangouts.

A few of the larger tributaries of the Ohio are Hogan, Laughery, Grant, and Bryant's Creeks on the Markland Pool; Big Blue River, Little Blue River, and Oil Creek on the Cannelton Pool; and Anderson River and Little Pigeon Creek on the Newburgh Pool. The main stem of the Wabash River flows into the Ohio at the southwestern corner of Indiana, and it offers some angling for bass and other species, especially catfish.

Strip-mined lands and farm ponds in this region offer good bass fishing, but much of this is on private land. These waters are also especially good for bluegills and crappie.

Another outstanding largemouth fishery is Turtle Creek Reservoir, a 1,500-acre man-made hydropower impoundment in Sullivan County. The lake is used for cooling water. It produces good numbers of big bass, and special regulations exist to make it a trophy fishery. Turtle Creek also hosts big crappie and bluegills.

Hardy Lake, a 741-acre reservoir on the Scott-Jefferson County line, is also a good lake for largemouth bass.

Introduced Fisheries

Trout and salmon. The first, and oldest, salmon fishery on Indiana waters is centered on the state's 234 square miles of Lake Michigan and the big lake's two tributaries between the Indiana-Michigan state line and the Twin Branch Dam east of Mishawaka.

Development of trout and salmon stocking programs date back to 1960, when rehabilitation of Lake Michigan's lake trout fishery was begun by the state of Michigan. This work included the introduction of coho and chinook salmon, brown trout, and steelhead. Although the stocking of lake trout was aimed at bolstering this population, the work with the other species was designed to create put-grow-and-take fisheries and to cut an overabundance of alewives, which were depleting food sources for the alewives themselves and other species.

Indiana has been stocking salmon and trout in Lake Michigan, Trail Creek, and Burns Ditch since the late 1960s, and was the first state to stock the enormously popular Skamania strain of steelhead.

As a result, Indiana's salmonid fishery on its share of Lake Michigan, Trail Creek, and Burns Ditch produces very good angling for coho salmon in the late winter and early spring, for chinook salmon from spring through fall, and for both summer- and winter-run steelhead.

A coho bonus occurs for Hoosiers in the spring, when fish from the stocking of other states congregate on the southernmost shores of Lake Michigan where alewives are spawning. Close-in fishing—even in the harbors and along the shorelines—produces especially good coho action.

The St. Joseph River, which exits Indiana and courses through Michigan on its way to Lake Michigan, is a significant component of the Hoosier State's trout and salmon opportunities, especially since completion of an Interstate Anadromous Fish Project to allow fish passage to its upper reaches. The $15 million project involved natural resources agencies in both Indiana and Michigan and the U.S. Fish and Wildlife Service; it took nearly 15 years to finish. But when the five fish ladders were completed on dams at Berrien Springs, Buchanan, and Niles in Michigan, and at South Bend and Mishawaka in Indiana, trout and salmon could make spawning runs of 65 miles upstream on the St. Joe.

Now Hoosiers can try their luck for salmon in the fall, and for Skamania-strain steelhead from mid-July or August, when this summer-run species starts thinking of spawning, through the fall and winter months. The St. Joe offers good steelhead angling into the late winter and early spring. A fish hatchery was constructed by Indiana at Twin Branch, upriver from Mishawaka.

Muskellunge. The stocking of purebred muskies at Brookville Reservoir in Franklin County in 1974 was the state's first effort at augmenting the few native fish found in tributaries of the Ohio River, and it has been a successful one. Although Brookville has never been a great muskie fishery, it has given up some good fish. More importantly, the work at Brookville did inspire state biologists to stock other waters, and that led to 774-acre Lake Webster in Kosciusko County becoming the centerpiece of the state's muskie fishery. In a national competition in 1997, 80 muskie anglers from around the country caught 27 legal-size fish in three days and encountered 60 others.

Some other good bets for the spreading muskellunge fishery are Ball Lake in Steuben County, Skinner Lake in Noble County, Loon Lake in Whitley, Plover Lake in the Atterbury State Fish and Wildlife Area, and Hardy Lake in Scott County.

Striped bass. Brookville Reservoir in Franklin County, and the Ohio River, have been the only Hoosier waters where purebred striped bass were taken for a number of years, but this species has more recently been introduced at Raccoon Reservoir in Parke County and has been doing well there.

Hybrid striped bass, also known as wipers, also thrive in Indiana. Monroe Reservoir now sports the best hybrid striper action in the state; anglers focus on the big water section just above the dam. Night fishing off the face of the dam is very good in October on full-moon nights and a day or two after a rain.

Some other good bets for hybrids are Lake Freeman, the Tippecanoe River below the Lake Freeman impoundment, and Cataract Lake.

Walleye. Walleye have been stocked in some Indiana waters since the late 1800s, but modern management efforts by the state go back only to 1970. Brookville Reservoir now offers the best walleye fishing in Indiana, but Clear Lake in Steuben County is very good. Monroe and Mississinewa Reservoirs produce sizable walleye in good numbers.

When Mississinewa, Salamonie, Brookville, and Monroe Reservoirs are releasing more than normal amounts of water in the spring, their tailwaters offer very good walleye fishing.

INDIVIDUAL TRANSFERABLE QUOTA

A saltwater commercial fisheries management allotment that grants certain private property rights to commercial fishermen by assigning a fixed share of the total allowable catch *(see)*. An individual transferable quota (ITQ) is a form of management in which entry to an overharvested fishery is limited to help rebuild depleted stocks.

Fossils of ancient fish have been used to shed light on the nature and association of landmasses hundreds of millions of years ago.

INDONESIA

Located south and east of mainland Asia and north and west of Australia, the Republic of Indonesia extends 5,100 kilometers from west to east, comprising most of the Malay Archipelago and nearly 13,700 islands. About half of these are inhabited, and in total Indonesia has the fourth largest population in the world.

The major islands of Sumatra and Java, in the western and southern regions, are very densely populated. The primary entry points to this part of the country are the capital city of Jakarta on Java; Medan on Sumatra; and the popular tourist island of Bali. The eastern and northern regions of Indonesia are remote, more inaccessible, and less populated. Major entry points to these regions are Balikpapan on Kalimantan (Borneo), Ujung Pandang and Manado on Sulewasi (Celebes), Ambon in the Moluccas, and Biak on Irian Jaya (the western half of New Guinea).

Indonesia straddles the equator and is surrounded on the north by the South China Sea, the Celebes Sea, and the Pacific Ocean, and on the south and west by the Indian Ocean. It has some 55,000 kilometers of coastline.

Sportfishing is a relatively new activity in Indonesia; consequently, its angling opportunities are little explored. Because of the imbalance between land and sea area, together with the dense population in the west, saltwater fishing is generally more popular than freshwater fishing. There are, however, an increasing number of "managed" freshwater fisheries.

Indonesia has deep blue water where it is bounded to the west and south by the Indian Ocean; there is deep blue water throughout eastern Indonesia. Much of western and southern Indonesia is cultivated, and mangrove swamps have been replaced by cultivated land. Rivers are muddy, and freshwater fishing opportunities are restricted to man-made ponds and lakes. Eastern and northern Indonesia are rugged and forested with clear jungle streams draining into extensive mangrove systems that have hardly seen a rod and line.

The climate throughout Indonesia is tropically humid. Daily temperatures range from the mid-20s to the mid-30s Celsius, and the humidity hovers between 70 and 90 percent. There are two seasons or "monsoons." The southeasterly monsoon, or dry season, runs from April through October. It is hot and humid during this time, but rains are infrequent. Near coastal areas, a constant sea breeze makes the climate balmy. The westerly monsoon, or wet season, runs from November through March. During this season, the weather is often oppressively humid, and there are frequent tropical downpours with associated brief heavy winds.

Throughout Indonesia anglers can find boats for hire. These are usually wooden and slow, or they are local fiberglass designs with outboard motors (known as longboats), with crews who

This fly-rod-caught narrowbarred mackerel exemplifies the nearshore opportunities available in Indonesia.

have no experience at sportfishing. Angling can be a difficult experience on such boats. Sometimes the crew is accustomed to taking anglers. These operations, while safer and faster, are only a little better in terms of their sportfishing experience and equipment. Professional, well-equipped sportfishing charter boats are mainly restricted to areas in and around Jakarta, although new operations are springing up all the time.

All the usual tropical sportfishing species inhabit Indonesia waters, but some areas are better known for certain species than others. Although fishing takes place year-round, it is best just before and just after the rainy season.

Billfish thrive throughout Indonesia; these include black marlin, blue marlin, striped marlin, and sailfish, often in huge numbers. Swordfish are not caught by angling, but they are the most common billfish caught by local handliners! Black marlin are generally small throughout Indonesia; 20- to 25-kilogram fish are common. The current Indonesian record is a 169-kilogram black from Pelabuhan Ratu, and a similar-size fish was caught at Ujung Kulon. Commercially caught black marlin that would push the 450-kilogram mark have been reported from the fish market. Sailfish average 25 to 30 kilograms, but some up to 60 kilograms have been caught.

Several varieties are available, including yellowfin tuna, dogtooth tuna, skipjack tuna, mackerel tuna, frigate mackerel, and occasionally bonito. Yellowfins are big; a 73-kilogram fish was caught at Pelabuhan Ratu and a 71-kilogram tuna at Ujung Kulon. Ambon and Banda have produced bigger ones that remain undocumented and unclaimed, but these locations may hold some specimens over 90 kilograms. Dogtooth tuna run to 36 kilograms.

Wahoo, narrowbarred mackerel *(tenggiri)*, and barracuda are common; barracuda are known to reach at least 20 kilograms, whereas the others have been caught to 32 kilograms and may be larger in eastern Indonesia. Giant trevally are huge and plentiful. Several species of sharks are available. Mahimahi (dolphin) are a common catch. Smaller species include rainbow runner, bluefin trevally, bigeye trevally, and a variety of bottom fish.

Western and Southern Islands

Sumatra. Sumatra is bounded to the west by the Indian Ocean and to the east by the shallower waters of the Java Sea and the Malacca Straits. Northern Sumatra juts into the Andaman Sea. Off the west coast is an archipelago chain, of which the largest and most accessible island is Pulau Nias.

Charter operations consisting of longboats exist in some of the more popular tourist destinations. Pulau Nias is one of these, as it is quite famous for excellent surfing. Sumatra has numerous regional airports; the international facility at Medan is the biggest.

Lake Toba in the Barisian Mountains is a popular and prominent tourist destination about 180 kilometers south of Medan. Covering 1,145 square kilometers, Toba is the largest lake in Indonesia; it features steep mountain cliffs, sandy beaches, and large Samosir Island. The freshwater angling potential here and throughout this island is poorly documented, but its numerous ponds and lakes contain the ubiquitous carp and catfish.

Blue water sportfishing is confined to the west and north of Sumatra, where there is deep water close inshore. Black marlin and sailfish have been recorded in many parts, and yellowfin tuna, dogtooth tuna, wahoo, narrowbarred mackerel, giant trevally, mahimahi, and barracuda, together with a host of smaller species, can all be expected. Fishing is best in October, November, April, and May, before and after the rainy season.

Eastern Sumatra has much shallower water and extensive mangroves and tidal inlets. Mangrove jacks, queenfish, barramundi, threadfin salmon, and various species of trevally are present in these waterways, but they are heavily fished, trapped, and netted, as Sumatra is heavily populated. Because the banks are largely inaccessible, casting lures from small boats is the only way to gain access to much of this fishing.

Java. Java is the population center of Indonesia and consequently the most accessible and most explored of the islands. Facilities here are good, and there is a thriving sportfishing community. Jakarta has good tackle shops, and most equipment is readily available.

Freshwater fishing opportunities are limited to managed ponds and lakes where carp and catfish are stocked, although Java does have several rivers.

Saltwater fishing, however, has a strong following. The local marinas have their share of modern yachts, but not many are rigged for sportfishing and none are available for charter. Limited sportfishing centers exist here, but some of these do have sportfishing fly-bridge cruisers—with twin diesel engines, full electronics, and good tackle—for charter. Elsewhere, the common and cheap outboard-powered longboat is the standard for Indonesian charter operations.

Carita, on the west coast of Java, is probably the best equipped of these centers, and charter operations here fish the waters around the remote and beautiful Ujung Kulon Peninsula. Carita is an easy two-hour drive from Jakarta and is consequently very popular with visitors and residents alike.

Ujung Kulon is situated on the southwestern tip of Java. To the south lie the waters of the Indian Ocean, to the northwest is Sumatra, and between Ujung Kulon and Sumatra lie the waters of the Sunda Strait. This is a major seaway leading north to Jakarta and Singapore, and it is here one finds the famous Krakatau volcano. Ujung Kulon Peninsula, a national park and world heritage site, is one of the last strongholds of the Javan rhino.

Ujung Kulon offers an almost endless variety of terrain and angling opportunity. The waters are virtually untapped and have tremendous light tackle potential. The Indian Ocean is very deep close to shore, with steep underwater dropoffs down to the Java Trench. These are some of the deepest and least explored waters in the world. The coastline varies from steep cliffs and rocky headlands with deep water very close in, to sandy beaches with big rolling surf, coral reef fringes, sheltered bays and flats, and mangrove swamps.

Many tropical sportfishing species inhabit Ujung Kulon. Techniques for catching these fish are wide ranging and include trolling with artificials, dead baits, and live baits; trolling with downriggers; kite fishing; casting poppers; jigging; drift fishing with live and dead baits; and bottom fishing. The best time to fish is just before and just after the rainy season, but angling remains good throughout the year—there isn't an off-season per se.

On the south coast, Pelabuhan Ratu, another prime Indonesian sportfishing location, is also a reasonably short drive from Jakarta. Pelabuhan

Fishing the rugged coast of Ujung Kulon.

Fishing tackle manufacturer Zebco used to be known as the Zero Hour Bait Company when it made electric time bombs for drilling oil wells.

Ratu is still serviced primarily by longboat operations, and you generally have to bring your own tackle. Boats launch from the beach, as the area lacks a good marina.

The same species are available here as in Ujung Kulon, but Pelabuhan Ratu carries a reputation for yellowfin tuna, which are both large and plentiful. Traditionally, these are caught after the rainy season in April and May, but they are available throughout the year. Like Ujung Kulon, Pelabuhan Ratu doesn't really have an off-season.

Bali. Bali is the main tourist center in Indonesia, and one of its main attractions is diving. Surprisingly, sportfishing is not well advanced, and few truly professional sportfishing operations exist. Charter boats are few as well. Commercial longline operations catch black, blue, and striped marlin from well offshore. Yellowfin tuna are also plentiful, again with the best time being before and after the rains in April, May, October, and November. The high and rocky coastline of southern Bali is home to some outsize giant trevally, which are caught by trolling or by casting big popper-style lures up to the rocks.

Lombok, Komodo, Flores, Sumba, and Sumbawa. The southern islands of Lombok, Komodo, Flores, Sumba, and Sumbawa are little known and little fished, but all have magnificent diving and varying standard accommodations. Sportfishing of any sort is not well documented, although those who have arranged for local boats and taken all their own gear with them say the fishery is excellent. Deep water lies close inshore, and some of these islands also have extensive bays, estuaries, and mangrove systems. The freshwater potential is unknown.

Eastern and Northern Islands

Timor. Timor is accessible through the city of Kupang, but it's a long and arduous flight. Although facilities are limited, guest houses and other accommodations are available. Timor even has limited "transient" charter operations in Kupang, but travelers are advised to expect nothing and carry everything they need. The fishing has been documented as excellent by pioneering Indonesian anglers, and marlin are reportedly common. Boats equipped to catch them, however, are generally nonexistent.

Kalimantan. Kalimantan is yet another little-known, little-fished Indonesian site. Access to the island is through Balikpapan on the east coast. Kalimantan boasts Indonesia's largest rivers, which include the Mahakam, Martapura, and Barito, which originate in the mountains and course through extensive swampy lowlands along the coast. The eastern coastline is dominated by the Mahakam Delta, a huge tidal deltaic complex northeast of Balikpapan. The freshwater and estuary fishing potential is undocumented, but rumor has it that numerous sailfish frequent the waters offshore of the delta mouth.

Farther north, deep blue water predominates, and the fishing consists of marlin, sailfish, wahoo, dogtooth tuna, yellowfin tuna, narrowbarred mackerel, barracuda, sharks, and giant trevally. Access to these waters is difficult due to the lack of suitable boats for charter.

The rest of Kalimantan is unexplored by anglers; however Brunei, which is north of Kalimantan and surrounded by the Malaysian portion of the island, is rapidly establishing a reputation as a superb light tackle fishery for small black marlin. Anglers are just beginning to explore the potential of the South China Sea and the Natuna Sea. Early reports are that the fishing looks good.

Sulewasi (Celebes). Sulewasi can be reached via Ujung Pandang in the south and Manado in the north. Ujung Pandang is relatively commercial, so transfer flights are available to many places in Eastern Indonesia, as are flights to the international airports at Jakarta and Bali.

Manado is tourist oriented and offers excellent facilities catering mainly to divers who come for the superb wall-diving and famed 150-foot underwater visibility. Manado also has a thriving tuna industry based around the yellowfin tuna, which is commercially harvested from a large number of simple fish aggregation devices (FADs) installed by the fishermen themselves. Sportfishing is unexplored.

Ambon. Ambon is famous for its big yellowfin tuna. Deep water is close wherever you fish, and dropoffs and canyons are within a stone's throw of shore. Commercial operations are numerous, and the locals traditionally handline for tuna.

Sportfishing is largely confined to trolling large floating and diving minnow-style plugs for yellowfin tuna, but also available are dogtooth tuna, giant trevally, narrowbarred mackerel, and wahoo. Big black marlin and blue marlin must surely be available, but only a few charter operations exist, and these are restricted to longboats with outboard motors for strictly inshore work.

Although anglers fishing takes place year-round, the catch is likely to be best in October, November, April, and May—before and after the rainy season.

Banda. A small cluster of volcanic islands jutting out from very deep water in the Banda Sea, the Banda Islands are reached by a short flight from Ambon. The waters around Banda hold monster-size yellowfin tuna, which are caught by visiting anglers trolling mainly with big minnow plugs. Other fish are also available, and there must be huge marlin following the bait schools.

The water is extremely deep close to shore, and the wall diving is justifiably world famous. Resorts are of varying standards, and boats are few and cater mainly to divers. There are no sportfishing charter operations in the Banda Islands. The tuna fishing is best from October through December, when large numbers are present. They are normally accompanied by vast schools of spinner dolphin—a dead giveaway for the tuna. The locals fish for them with live baits and handlines. For deep-feeding fish, they use an ingenious system of wrapping a rock in a banana leaf hooked onto the bait. When the bait has reached the desired depth, a sharp jerk on the line releases the leaf and suspends a free-lined bait.

Irian Jaya. Irian Jaya is the Indonesian half of New Guinea and adjoins Papua New Guinea. It faces the Pacific Ocean on its northern side, with deep water and precipitous dropoffs very close to shore; the southern side faces the Arafura Sea and is shallower water, with bays, estuaries, and extensive mangrove swamps. Inland are jungle highlands with clear fast-flowing streams. Some 30 rivers course through Irian Jaya from the central mountains, including the 400-kilometer-long Baliem, which flows to the Arafura and along which live various native tribes.

This area is largely unexplored by anglers, but the superb salt- and freshwater fishing known to exist in Papua New Guinea is hardly likely to stop at the border. Although the potential of Irian Jaya is therefore enormous, the area is inaccessible and has no infrastructure. No guided services or charter boats operate here and, of course, with the exception of Jakarta, there are no tackle shops.

Species to expect in the west of Irian Jaya include blue and black marlin, sailfish, yellowfin tuna, bigeye tuna, dogtooth tuna, skipjack tuna, wahoo, narrowbarred mackerel, giant trevally, barracuda, mahimahi, and various sharks. To the east in the bays and estuaries are narrowbarred mackerel, cobia, giant trevally, golden trevally, queenfish, barracuda, and various inshore sharks. In the mangroves, species include barramundi and mangrove jacks, together with possibly Niugini bass. In the unknown waters of the rivers, Niugini bass and spot-tail bass are likely residents.

INFLATABLE BOAT

A modest amount of fishing, usually in remote locations, is done from inflatable boats, which are lightweight collapsible craft with inflatable pontoon-like sides and bow, powered by a small-horsepower outboard motor. Inflatable boats are usually in the 10- or 12-foot range and are quiet, seaworthy, and durable. They are lacking in stability for most anglers; standing and casting in an inflatable boat without a deck or floor is akin to standing on a waterbed. This can be improved if the boat is outfitted with a full-frame marine-grade plywood floor or deck, but this increases the weight and thwarts portability. Inflatable boats have a shallow draft, but a flat bottom makes them pound in rough water and all gear inside is subjected to open storage. Some inflatable boats have been equipped by manufacturers with rod racks, a bow electric motor bracket, and other accessories, and creative anglers have outfitted them even more elaborately. Though rugged, they are not highly favored by avid anglers.
See: Boat.

INLET

A tributary mouth to a lake or the sea, primarily the latter; an entry point to the sea from a bay, harbor, or estuary. An inlet is primarily the area that connects a safe harbor to a large bay or the open ocean. It often has one or more jetties *(see)* at the mouth; may have been dredged to allow passage of large ocean-going vessels; and has many characteristics of harbors *(see)*, estuaries *(see)*, and marshes *(see)* or wetlands *(see)*.

Inlets are strongly influenced by current, primarily tides in saltwater, and usually receive the outflow of marshes. Bars, channels, cuts between channels or creeks, deep holes, and jetties are prime fishing locations, especially jetties, which have a significant amount of usually channelized flow when the tide is moving. Breakwalls, bridges, piers, docks, and power plant discharge areas are all man-made structures that may provide good fishing as well.
See: Jetty Fishing.

IN-LINE SPINNER
See: Spinner.

INSECT REPELLENT
See: First Aid.

INSECTS

Insects are among the most numerous of all animals and have very diverse forms and habitat. As a food source for trout species, aquatic and terrestrial insects are considered paramount, although they are also a very important food source for the adults and the juveniles, in particular, of many other freshwater species.
See: Aquatic Insects; Terrestrial Insects.

INSHORE

The waters from the shallower part of the continental shelf toward shore. In saltwater fishing parlance, inshore is a loose and variable term referring to that portion of the water from which land is visible or is nearly visible, usually on the shoreward side of major currents or shelves, and populated by nonpelagic species. This term is seldom used by freshwater lake anglers.
See: Inshore Fishing; Nearshore.

INSHORE BOAT
See: Sportfishing Boat.

INSHORE FISHING
Fishing Coastal Estuaries, Rivers, Bays, and Nearshore Ocean Waters

The term "inshore" is a generic one used by anglers to refer to coastal marine areas. Although the spot where inshore ends and offshore *(see)* begins is not strictly defined, in general inshore fishing refers to angling from a boat for resident and migratory species in estuaries, rivers, bays, and nearshore ocean waters, whereas offshore fishing refers to blue-water fishing for pelagic species.

Inshore environs may be fished from a variety of craft: cartop boats and canoes, outboard-powered rental rowboats and skiffs, a wide array of medium-size runabouts, center console and walk-around cuddy cabin boats, and even cruisers and large sportfishing boats. Anglers also have the option of inshore fishing from party boats *(see)*, which sail daily to pursue a wide variety of species.

Inshore waters are popular for many reasons. Chief among these is the limited travel time required to reach the fishing grounds, which makes short outings feasible and facilitates a swift return to port for any reason, particularly stormy weather.

Of course, another reason is that inshore waters hold a variety of popular gamefish and bottom feeders. Coastal estuaries, generally identified as the area where the tide line meets the river current, are the spawning grounds and, in turn, the nursery areas for many species. Estuarine environs provide a delicate balance of water conditions favored by many marine species, and they are also suitable for a few freshwater species that are comfortable living in water of nominal salinity.

Some anglers travel great distances in pursuit of their favorite gamefish and bottom feeders while overlooking fine inshore fishing close to home. Inshore waters often hold an abundance and variety of species to satisfy the most discriminating angler with a fine catch.

Tackle. Inshore fishing is suitable to a variety of angling methods. Even though drift and bottom fishing with bait may be the most popular methods overall, inshore anglers have opportunities to cast and jig for various species, troll for some species, and, in certain cases, stalk and sight-fish for their quarry. This wide variety opens up the game for many different types of equipment and approaches.

Generally, however, inshore fishing is well suited to light tackle. The waters are protected and usually not very deep, and inshore species for the most part are relatively small, although heavyweight specimens of such species as striped bass, bluefish, snook, tarpon, redfish, salmon, and halibut can test the angler's tackle and skill.

For maximum enjoyment, the choice of tackle should be appropriate to the species sought, so that the angler isn't handicapped by tackle that is too light or too heavy. Those fishing out of private boats have more latitude in gear selection and more opportunities to use lighter equipment than those fishing out of party boats, where maneuverability is less and where more people of differing skill levels have to be accommodated.

Conventional tackle is popular with many inshore anglers; a light- or medium-weight casting or popping rod, $5^1/_2$ to 6 feet long and coupled with a levelwind reel loaded with 150 yards of 10- to 15-pound-test line, is ideal for this type of fishing in most locations. It's well suited to casting artificials, drifting natural baits, chumming, and bottom fishing.

Spinning tackle has some following, although less than conventional tackle, and is more likely to be used for shallow water situations, for casting activities, and for smaller species. Lighter outfits, as opposed to the heavy ones employed in surf fishing *(see)*, are best for most applications. Rods that are $5^1/_2$ to $6^1/_2$ feet long, capable of handling lures or rigs ranging from a half ounce through $1^1/_2$ ounces, are ideal for most inshore fishing, coupled with a reel that holds at least 150 yards of 8- to 15-pound-test line. For some inshore fishing, like casting light jigs and small plugs or soft plastics, you can use a lighter weight outfit, like a $6^1/_2$- to 7-foot rod and a reel that holds 6- to 10-pound line.

In saltwater inshore fishing, it's usually better to use a line that is on the heavier side rather than one on the lighter side to reduce the attrition rate of lures and terminal rigs, which often become snagged while drifting or casting. Within reason, line diameter (which often correlates to strength) is not a major factor in most inshore fishing, except in shallow, clear water situations where a lighter, thinner line is less likely to spook the fish and call attention to the lures or bait.

Though less common than either conventional or spinning gear, flycasting tackle is effective on the inshore scene for some species and in certain environs (it is good, for example, for shallow water striped bass but not for deep bottom feeders). Eight-, 9-, and 10-weight outfits are used depending on the species (lighter for bonefish and redfish, for example, and heavier for striped bass and tarpon). The reel needs ample backing for those fish that are likely to make serious runs, and a variety of fly patterns, mainly large streamers, are used in bays, rivers, and the open ocean.

Primary Species and Tactics

The following briefly reviews the primary inshore species and the most popular methods of fishing for them along the Atlantic, Gulf, and Pacific coasts of North America. Not all fishing tactics and opportunities can be mentioned here; nevertheless, the traveling angler far from familiar waters will often find conditions very close to those in home environs and will be able to use favorite tackle to enjoy good sport as well as some fine-eating fish.

Northeastern flounder. The rock-studded coastline of Maine offers hundreds of rivers and bays that empty into the Atlantic. Many have mud, sand, or pebble bottom where winter flounder take up residence. By anchoring on mud flats or along channel edges and chumming with a mixture of ground clams or crushed mussels sent to the bottom in a chum pot, these tasty flatfish are quickly attracted within range.

Small No. 8 or 9 Chestertown or Wide Gap hooks baited with sandworms or bloodworms readily bring strikes from flounder, and sometimes harbor pollock or small codfish are caught on the same rigs, although most are immature fish that should be immediately released.

Much the same scene is repeated along the Massachusetts, Connecticut, Long Island, and New Jersey coasts. The difference is, instead of a rock-studded coastline, many barrier islands, with broad bays separating them from the mainland, provide an abundance of winter flounder for fine action each spring and again in the fall.

Atlantic mackerel. The Atlantic mackerel summers in the inshore waters of Maine, often traveling in schools that number in the tens of thousands. While mostly found in the close-to-shore ocean waters, they'll often invade large coastal bays as they search for food. These provide fine light tackle sport and will strike tiny diamond jigs, bucktails, or tube teasers. Flies worked with a sinking line will often draw strikes until the angler's arm is weary.

These same mackerel, averaging three-quarters of a pound to 3 pounds, usually winter off the Virginia Capes and provide boat anglers with fine action as they move north to the Maritime Provinces for the summer and then return again in early winter. They're fun to catch and especially well suited to newcomers and youngsters; when you get into a school, the action is often fast and furious, and a great deal of skill isn't required.

East Coast stripers and bluefish. It would be difficult to determine whether striped bass or bluefish are the most popular inshore gamefish along the Middle and North Atlantic coasts. Both species frequent the same inshore waters and are regularly targeted by anglers casting or trolling artificials, chumming, bottom fishing, drifting, and jigging.

Most of the stripers and blues that migrate north to New England have achieved respectable size. Many smaller fish are encountered along their midrange of Long Island and south to New Jersey and through the Chesapeake Bay area. Many of the youngsters of both clans spend their first few seasons in the bays, rivers, and creeks near where they were hatched. The inshore nursery grounds have an abundance of grass shrimp, spearing, sand launce, and other forage to satisfy their ravenous appetites.

Some of the fish are small but provide fine catch-and-release sport for anglers armed with light outfits. Both species are readily caught on plugs, plastic-tailed and bucktail-dressed leadheads, metal jigs, and streamer flies.

Inshore party boat fishing for both stripers and blues is popular throughout their range, because it enables anglers to catch trophy fish with minimal cost. The most popular technique for catching bass and blues is using a diamond or slab-sided chromed jig, with a plastic or feather teaser 18 to 24 inches ahead of it. The schools are often mixed, with stripers on or near the bottom and bluefish closer to the surface.

Party boats use their sonar to locate the schools and then drift over them. Jigging is accomplished by lowering the rig to the bottom and retrieving to the surface. As a rule, a slow retrieve concentrated near the bottom gets strikes from the stripers and a fast, jigging retrieve gets action from the blues near the surface.

Tautog, sea bass, and porgies. Bottom feeders like tautog, black sea bass, and porgies are plentiful in inshore waters along the Middle Atlantic. They're found around most broken, irregular bottom, particularly rock ledges and artificial fishing reefs, and frequent these areas because of abundant food and sanctuary from predatory species.

The most popular technique for catching all three of these bottom dwellers is to use a high-low rig, employing a pair of hooks snelled to 12- to 18-inch leader. Virginia, Sproat, Claw, or Beak style hooks are most popular. Use a No. 8 or 10 hook for porgies, which often average from less than a pound to over 2 pounds, and a No. 4 or 6 hook for the generally larger sea bass. With tautog it's a matter of where you're fishing; in open ocean waters where they range in weight from 3 to 6 pounds or more, Nos. 2, 1, and even 1/0 hooks are preferred.

Small pieces of conch, clam, squid, or seaworm are preferred baits for porgies and sea bass, while tautog prefer green crabs and fiddler crabs, although they'll take the aforementioned baits as well.

This is relaxing fishing; simply find some structure, such as artificial reefs or rockpiles or mussel beds in bays and the open ocean, and anchor your boat so it is positioned directly above the structure. All three species stick very close to the structure; if you're positioned even just a few feet away from the structure over sand bottom, you're apt to not catch a thing.

Once anchored, bait up, using sufficient sinker weight on your rig to hold bottom, lowering the rig

Inshore waters that provide good fishing opportunity include estuary environs such as this marsh area in Chesapeake Bay, Virginia.

to the bottom and waiting for strikes. All three have notorious reputations as bait stealers, so be alert and lift back smartly with your rod tip at the first tug on the bait.

Weakfish and seatrout. The weakfish is a darling of inshore anglers when plentiful because it grows to over 10 pounds, provides a variety of angling opportunities, and is excellent table fare. Caught from New England through the Chesapeake Bay area, the species is also found in numbers through the Carolinas. From Virginia south, the spotted weakfish, locally called trout or seatrout, becomes more prevalent and is found throughout the inshore waters of Georgia and Florida, and up the Gulf Coast of Florida and across through Texas. The only major difference in appearance is the large black spots that are prominent on the backs of the spotted weaks.

The techniques, habitat, and feeding patterns of these species are very similar, and in some places you may catch both in a day's outing. Both are creatures of habit and tend to be lazy when seeking a meal. As a result, they're easily attracted to a chum line of their favorite food, which includes the tiny grass shrimp so plentiful in coastal bays and rivers, as well as the larger shrimp that are targeted as table fare.

The technique of chumming *(see)* for weakfish and seatrout doesn't vary much along the many miles of Atlantic and Gulf Coasts that weakfish and seatrout frequent. They spend much of their time in the shallow reaches of bays and rivers, moving across eelgrass and weedbeds where forage is abundant. Often the water on the shallow flats ranges from 3 to 6 feet deep.

Armed with 3 or 4 quarts of live grass shrimp or their larger culinary counterparts, you can easily seek out promising water and double anchor—to keep your boat steady and prevent it from swinging in the wind—and begin chumming.

Dribble only a few shrimp over the side at a time, allowing them to be carried away with the tide over the weedbeds. For larger shrimp, cut them into dime-size pieces and sparingly distribute them to establish a chum line that attracts the weakfish, but don't provide so much food that they hang well back to feed. You want to get them moving toward the source of the food.

Once the chum line is established, it's time to bait up. Tie a No. 1 or 2 Claw or Beak style hook with a bait-holder shank directly to the end of your nylon monofilament line. Bait up with three or four tiny grass shrimp, or use a small piece of a larger shrimp. Ease the baited hook into the water, and permit the current to carry it along, much the same as the current is carrying your chum. Once the bait has drifted off 40 to 60 feet, even more at times, simply reel in and repeat the procedure. Often the strikes will come from as close as a rod's length from the boat on out to the end of your drift. The key is keeping the bait moving naturally with the chum line.

If you're chumming in very shallow water and the weed growth is heavy, the baited hook may sink to the bottom and not drift properly, especially if there's little current. At such times an effective strategy is to add a float to the line so that your bait is suspended just above the level of the weeds. A small split shot or rubber-core sinker may be added to the line between the float and the hook, thus ensuring that it drifts along perpendicularly to the bottom.

Although plastic floats are popular, veteran weakfish anglers have found that a cork or plastic float with a scooped-out head, which emits a popping or gurgling sound as it is pulled through the water, attracts the attention of the fish more readily than an ordinary plastic or cork float.

You can also catch weakfish by working a tiny, quarter-ounce bucktail jig or soft-tailed jig through the chum line. Small swimming plugs work, too.

Drifting across open bottom often brings strikes on an ebbing tide when the weakfish vacate the shallows. At such times a high-low bottom rig with a pair of hooks snelled to a 12- to 18- inch leader works fine. Use a bank or dipsey style sinker of sufficient weight to effortlessly glide along the bottom. Shrimp, strips of squid, spearing, and live killies are effective baits.

Both species of weakfish often migrate as seasons change, and they do so by vacating the protected waters of estuaries, bays, and rivers and moving into the open reaches of the Atlantic Ocean and the Gulf. They travel in huge schools, often mov-

A small weakfish comes aboard within sight of a New Jersey beach.

ing close to the bottom and feeding on baitfish. On these occasions they offer exciting opportunities to catch them on diamond jigs and teasers, bucktails, or natural baits drifted along the bottom.

Trolling with small plugs, bucktail jigs, or spoons takes many of both species, as the small-boat angler can cover a lot of water. Once a school is located, the troller can continue trolling the area or shut down the motor and drift and jig over the fish.

Southern flatfish. Although weakfish are the darlings of many anglers along a really long stretch of coastline, the summer flounder and its cousin the southern flounder are two of the most popular species sought in much the same range.

Both summer and southern flounder spend a lot of time in the shallow environs of bays and estuaries, and they inhabit open reaches of the Atlantic and Gulf, generally close to shore. However, they often frequent humps or high bottom locations several miles from shore, especially when forage species are plentiful at these sites.

Unlike sea bass, porgies, and tautog, which stick close to structure, summer and southern flounder move about while searching for a meal and are aggressive bottom feeders. They typically forage over sandy bottom, where their backs take on the color of the bottom over which they're traveling. This chameleon-like characteristic is very pronounced, with light sandy color when frequenting light bottom, with mottled or spotted brown and beige tones when over gravel or pebbly bottom, and with dark chocolate brown when feeding over mud bottom.

When resting, flounder usually lie on the bottom and use their fins to partially cover themselves with sand or mud. If a cold snap develops, which is not to their liking, they will lie on the bottom for days without moving about or feeding. At such times the mud will actually stick to their undersides; if you catch one shortly after it emerges from the mud, it will still carry a light covering of the mud on its otherwise snow white bottom.

As flounder rest on the bottom, their eyes extend upward, always alert for an unsuspecting baitfish, shrimp, or crab that happens by. They're extremely fast and will engulf the prey in an instant. As a result of this trait, successful flounder anglers find drifting to be the most successful fishing technique. Although chumming does produce strikes from flounder, as does fishing at anchor, you'll catch more flatfish if you leave the boat unanchored and cover known flounder grounds while drifting at the mercy of the current or wind.

Light tackle is ideal when seeking flounder inshore; however, in more open waters, where you may fish in 25- to 50-foot depths, somewhat heavier gear is appropriate.

The most popular flatfish rig is a simple setup with a small three-way swivel. Tie one end of the swivel directly to your line. To another end tie a 30- to 36-inch leader of 20-pound test, and then snell a No. 1/0 through 3/0 Carlisle, Beak, Claw, or Wide Gap hook to that. To the remaining end of the swivel, tie a 6- to 8-inch piece of monofilament line with a loop in the end of it; slip a dipsey or bank style sinker of sufficient weight to hold the bottom onto the loop.

The summer flounder, popularly called fluke through much of its range, feeds on a wide variety of forage species, including sand eels, spearing, crabs, shrimp, squid, and the young of almost every species in residence. All of these may be used as hook baits. Perhaps the most popular bait is the saltwater killie, or mummichog; it is quickly taken by the hungry flatfish when it is fished live and hooked through the lips and drifted along the bottom.

Redfish. Channel bass, often called redfish, are a formidable target of anglers fishing inshore waters from the Virginia Capes south through Florida and across the Gulf Coast. Often called the southern counterpart to the striped bass, they frequent much the same waters and have very similar habits.

Perhaps the most exciting method of catching redfish is to sight-cast to them as they travel in schools just beyond the surf line off the Atlantic coast during spring. This is also done in Gulf waters and in the backcountry, where schools of a hundred or more redfish may be encountered.

A hammered stainless-steel jig is one of the most popular lures for enticing strikes when the fish are on the move. Schools present themselves in different ways. In open ocean waters, they often appear as a huge dark shadow or dark area while they cruise along, whereas in the shallows of bays and estuaries, their movement often disturbs the surface as the tightly packed schools mill about.

The key is positioning your boat upcurrent from the school and permitting wind or current to move you within casting range. Don't approach too closely while motoring in because you may spook the school. Once positioned, place your cast so it goes beyond and ahead of the fish; then work the lure back toward the school. Properly presented, the spoon draws quick strikes. Bucktail jigs and their plastic-tailed counterparts, swimming plugs, and small spoons all prove effective in this exciting inshore sport.

Not to be overlooked are opportunities to catch redfish on live shrimp, spot, pinfish, or grunts, or to troll for them using spoons. Much fishing for reds is done by seeking and casting to small groups or individuals in the shallows of bays, where they are feeding. These fish are often caught by stalking and making presentations to individual fish, especially with soft-tailed jigs. When the wind is blowing and the water is too deep to spot fish, blind casting can be effective with the same lures, with shallow-running plugs, and with shrimp bait.

Bonefish, tarpon, and permit. Bonefish, tarpon, and permit are among the most prized fish of inshore environs. Although they are usually associated with flats fishing (see) and sight-casting activities, they may also be caught in the bays and in the deeper holes of near-shore waters by using methods suited to fishing for nonvisible fish. All three of these species are caught by a variety of techniques, including live baitfishing at anchor, drift fishing, and in some cases deep jigging.

Unquestionably the most challenging, exciting, and popular technique is to pole across the shallow flats and sight-cast to the fish as they move through water barely deep enough to cover their backs. All flats travelers are spooky, and care must be exercised to avoid approaching too closely. This entails poling until a fish is sighted and then positioning yourself and waiting until the fish moves within range. In some cases, mainly for bonefish on the shallowest flats, you can wade into position and cast to a fish slowly feeding across a flat.

Bonefish are fairly plentiful and, though generally traveling alone, they do sometimes gather in small pods and even schools. Many anglers employ a single live shrimp on a 1/0 Beak style hook and cast just ahead of the cruising fish. Tiny jigs also bring strikes, and fly fishing has become more popular. Permit are sometimes encountered on the flats, and they present a formidable challenge because of their wariness, greater size, and fast speed. Permit are also caught on shrimp; they can be taken on flies, although fly fishing for permit is more difficult than it is for bonefish. The most common offering is a small, live crab.

Tarpon are a particularly good fly fishing species when they cruise the flats; they, too, may take shrimp and crab baits. In the channels between flats and islands, they are popularly caught on live mullet or pinfish. Fishing for big tarpon in such renowned areas as Key West and Boca Grande Pass in Florida, and the many passes emptying into the Gulf of Mexico all the way to Texas, is usually a baitfishing proposition. Live crabs, pinfish, grunts, mullet, squirrel fish, and other small species are drifted through the area frequented by the tarpon, which move with the tides searching for a meal. Frequently, large pods of feeding tarpon are encountered on the surface and may be caught by casting a live bait to the cruising fish.

Grouper and snapper. Many species of grouper and snapper are popular with inshore anglers from the Carolinas to Texas. They're found on nearly every patch of rock bottom, on myriad coral reefs, and around every shipwreck and ledge where food is abundant.

Inshore small boat anglers fishing these various structures employ a variety of techniques for snapper and grouper. Anchoring and chumming adjacent to and above the structure is very effective for yellowtail snapper and porgies. Fishing live baits in the depths is also productive, particularly with big black grouper, red grouper, mutton snapper, and red snapper. Bottom fishing with a high-low rig produces all bottom dwellers.

An especially enjoyable method of catching all of these species is to drift and deep-jig the reef with bucktail jigs or plastic-bodied leadheads. When there is deep water and swift current or strong wind, you may need to use jigs weighing from 1 to 4 ounces in order to reach the bottom; then keep the jig perpendicular to the bottom as you retrieve.

Schools of grouper and snapper are located by cruising the reef areas and employing sonar. Once fish are located, simply position the boat so that the current or wind will carry you over the fish and away from the reef. In this way, as fish are hooked you'll be drifting to deeper water or away from obstructions.

All grouper and snapper are fast. Make no mistake about it. As a result, an effective method of working your jig is to let it settle to the bottom, then quickly lift your rod tip so that the jig darts toward the surface, and continue reeling and jigging until it reaches the surface. If a strike isn't received, drop it back down and continue jigging and retrieving.

This strategy requires tackle rated at 20 pounds or heavier. Fish that weigh 15 to 50 pounds or more will often break free with little effort if you're using light line. Fish a firm drag; as soon as a fish is hooked, lift back smartly and work hard to get the fish up and away from the bottom. Once a grouper turns back to the coral, it can rip line from your reel and instantly cut you off.

Bonus inshore catches are possible when you're deep-jigging the reefs. This includes species like jack crevalle, king mackerel, wahoo, Spanish and cero mackerel, dolphin, barracuda, and little tunny.

Cobia. Cobia are still another great inshore gamefish that provide sterling action. Found in nominal quantities along the Atlantic coast from the Carolinas south, they really come into their own along the Gulf Coast, where they're apt to be found cruising around channel markers, buoys, docks, and anchored boats.

Although cobia are found out in the open Gulf where they cruise among the anchored shrimp boats culling their catch, the greatest numbers are inshore residents and found in most every bay and pass. One of the two most popular methods of catching them is anchoring in a pass and using a sliding-egg sinker rig on the bottom with a live pinfish or grunt as bait. The second, more exciting, approach is to cruise the passes, visiting buoys, channel markers, and dock areas; once a cobia is spotted, cast to it. Bucktail jigs and swimming plugs all bring strikes, but a live baitfish hooked just beneath the dorsal fin and cast within range of a hungry cobia will quickly bring an exciting surface strike. Many cobia top the 30-pound mark along the Gulf Coast, so here you need heavier gear than what is customarily used for inshore fishing, with 20-pound-class spinning or casting tackle preferred.

Pacific kelp fishing. The Southern California coast has a great variety of gamefish and bottom feeders that are a challenge to catch and a welcome addition to the dinner table. Some of the most enjoyable inshore action is had while fishing waters

England's King Henry I died on December 1, 1135, in Lyons, France, reportedly after a wanton banquet during which his highness gorged on lamprey eels.

adjoining the kelp beds. The kelp can best be described as a giant tree growing up from the bottom, its big, thick willowy branches adorned with huge leaves. Unlike green seaweed of the Atlantic coast, which is carried along by the current, the Pacific coast kelp, which is a brown seaweed, grows in huge beds and is stationary for the most part. The limbs of the kelp are often as thick as a man's arm, and the leaves are several feet long by a foot or more in width. This mass of kelp provides sanctuary for anchovies, sardines, and a host of small fish and the fry of others, all of which often satisfy the appetites of bigger game.

Chumming is a popular method of fishing the kelp beds. After leaving dockside, boats stop at a bait barge located in most coastal harbors and take aboard a supply of several scoops of anchovies, sardines, or mackerel to be employed both as chum and hook baits. Private and charter boats generally anchor just off from the kelp beds, positioning the boat so that anglers are sufficiently close to cast their baits near to the kelp, or to permit the current to carry the lively baits along the edge of the kelp.

Because tiny anchovies and other small baitfish are the favored bait, anglers prefer a rod with a delicate tip action, one that can softly cast a bait weighing a fraction of an ounce a fair distance from the boat. Correspondingly light lines are used, often only 12- to 15-pound test, with either a conventional or a spinning reel.

The most popular technique is to swim a tiny anchovy bait, hooked lightly through the gill collar or lips with a small No. 1 or 2 fine wire hook, tied directly to the monofilament line. As the bait swims along, often swiftly heading for the sanctuary of the kelp, other anchovies are tossed out sparingly to attract but not feed the fish.

The key is to have the reel in freespool or the bail open and let the bait keep moving. It struggles to get into the kelp, thus attracting the fish that are cruising along the perimeter searching for a meal.

There is no mistaking a strike; in fact, you know it's coming. As a big fish approaches, the tiny baitfish senses the predator and furiously tries to avoid capture. When you feel the bait get excited, you know that in an instant you'll receive a runoff as the bigger fish inhales the helpless anchovy. Here it's important to keep your rod tip in a lowered position, with the tip pointed in the direction the line is moving. In the instant that the line moves off quickly, engage your gear or close the bail, and lift back smartly to set the hook. With the fine wire hook, which is necessary because of the delicate baits, you just set the hook once, as repeated strikes may rip the hook free or spring it open.

You must maintain sufficient pressure on the fish so that it can't reach the kelp. If it does, the line often becomes fouled and you won't be able to work the fish back to the boat. Usually the combination of the line becoming fouled and the fish pulling on it strongly will break the line.

In this kind of fishing, you never know which species will take your bait, because there is variety galore cruising along the kelp searching for a meal. Pacific barracuda and Pacific bonito are two of the most popular, although somewhat smaller, of the targeted species. Pacific yellowtail and white seabass also call this habitat home and are among the prized catches. Kelp bass readily inhale a lively anchovy fished tight to the kelp.

Bottom fishing along the kelp also brings results. Although chumming usually entices strikes from fish that move through the midrange and surface layers, you can often score down on the bottom, too. When the other species mentioned aren't cooperating, many anglers add a weight to their lines, sending the bait right down to the bottom for sand bass, California corbina, or Pacific halibut.

Silver and king salmon. Inshore anglers have opportunities for silver salmon and king salmon off Northern California, where the time-proven technique of using cannonball sinkers to get anchovy baits down to the fish proves most popular. Most of the party boats use cast-iron breakaway cannonballs, often weighing up to 3 pounds. However, many small boats employ downriggers to send their attractors and anchovy- or herring-baited hooks down to the level of the salmon.

This angling takes place in open waters not far from shore, and finding fish is of tantamount importance. At times, slow trolling for the big salmon is fast and furious. Frequently, though, you have to put in the time, searching with sonar for schools of baitfish and, once they're located, systematically slow-trolling the area until the bigger signals, indicating salmon, show up on the screen. When the season gets underway, the fish are usually concentrated, with the professional party and charter boats communicating daily and zeroing in on the fish, and smaller boaters working the same areas.

Rockfish and lingcod. The many species of rockfish that inhabit the cold Pacific waters from the Golden Gate north to Oregon and Washington are among the tastiest fish these waters have to offer, and are regularly sought by inshore bottom anglers. While they are caught well offshore in deep habitats, sufficient numbers are found inshore wherever the bottom is broken and with irregular rocks. Drifting chunk baits using a basic high-low rig with sufficient weight to hold bottom results in fast action when you locate a piece of choice underwater terrain. Small boat anglers will often drop a marker buoy once a productive area is located, and they will repeatedly drift over it. Another option, of course, is anchoring right above the productive spot.

Many consider lingcod to be the Pacific's finest eating species, and they are a favored target of small boat and party boat anglers in Oregon and Washington waters. Although lingcod are the favorite here, literally dozens of species of rockfish are also caught as a bonus, and live baits are favored for these. In fact, anglers who catch a small fish on the lingcod grounds will often bait up with it or will use live anchovies or sardines, with live baits usually providing best results.

Slack tides usually afford the best opportunity to hook lingcod, because it's easiest then to work a bait or lure straight down to the rocky, snaggy bottoms where this big predator is found; too much current or wind results in a flat line angle and constant hookups on the rocky bottom.

Metal slab jigs that imitate smaller fish work well, as do big leadhead jigs with soft plastic bodies or pork rind strips. Many bait anglers use herring, and live baits work much better than dead ones. The ultimate lingcod bait, though, is a live greenling, about 10 inches long, fished with a large, single hook through both lips to pin its mouth shut. Live bait anglers must use a sinker large enough to take the offering down but must exercise care in keeping it just off bottom, or the bait will dodge into a hole and become snagged before a lingcod finds it.

Lingcod also have a habit of diving for a rocky crevice when hooked, so anglers should try to turn them toward the surface and reel them as far off the bottom as possible after setting the hook. For this reason, many anglers use rather stout tackle for lingcod, including stiff boat rods; large, conventional reels; and low-stretch braided line of 40- to 80-pound test. A tough monofilament leader of 50-pound test or larger also helps avoid abrasions and breakoffs.

West Coast stripers. The waters of the San Francisco Bay delta are home to striped bass of all sizes. The original stock came from New Jersey over a century ago and prospered; then the population was depleted, but it has rebounded to a point where Bay anglers now enjoy superb sport. Enjoyable striper fishing here occurs with light casting or spinning tackle, using plugs and bucktails along the many miles of marsh that border undeveloped areas of the bay. Increasing in popularity is fly fishing from small boats for predominately school stripers in the 2- to 10-pound class.

The world-renowned San Francisco Bay Bridge offers exciting striped bass action. The bridge's supporting tower in the water causes currents to swirl about it, often trapping baitfish and in turn attracting striped bass. The bridge is productive for small boat anglers, since the fish take up a feeding station there and become targets for casting bucktail jigs and deep-running plugs. Position your boat on the downcurrent side of the tower, and cast up into the swirling maelstrom of back eddies that are formed as the tide rushes along. Also try fishing the upcurrent area, where moving water is separated by the tower, resulting in a dead spot of minimal current where the stripers take up station to wait for food to be swept their way.

Northwest salmon and halibut. Oregon and Washington anglers who fish the inshore grounds have a choice of seeking silver salmon or king salmon on the inshore grounds, or they can send their rigs down to the bottom for Pacific halibut.

Inshore trolling at the river mouths is very popular for catching all salmon species. This is very seasonal sport, with the runs of each species taking place at different times. Deep, fast water at river mouths and turbulent currents result in anglers having to employ conventional outfits rated for 20- to 30-pound line. Trolling whole herring baits has for years been a proven method of scoring with these great gamefish. Depending on tidal flow and water depth, the baits are run into the depths with the aid of heavy trolling sinkers or via downriggers. Using sonar both to locate fish and to ascertain the proper depth to troll is essential.

Its impressive size, relative abundance, and brute strength make the Pacific halibut, which is the largest member of the flatfish clan, a popular quarry from the southern Oregon coast northward. Younger, smaller halibut under 50 pounds comprise most of the sport catch along the Oregon, Washington, and southern British Columbia coasts, and fish in these areas tend to congregate in specific areas where food is abundant, especially near islands and over banks and humps. The large fish are farther north off northern British Columbia and especially Alaska.

The key to fishing halibut successfully is to get a bait or lure down to them and keep it there long enough for a fish to find it. Most anglers prefer to fish with bait, especially large herring. Squid, octopus, and belly skin off halibut or salmon, as well as whole cod, greenling, or other small bottom fish, also are effective baits. Bait is usually fished on a wire spreader or a sliding-sinker rig, with sinker size ranging from 4 ounces to 4 pounds, depending on depth, current, size of the bait, and line diameter. Bait hooks range from size 5/0 to 12/0, depending on size of the bait and size of the quarry; some anglers prefer traditional J style hooks, and others like commercial circle hooks. Halibut use their eyes, nose, and lateral line to locate a meal, so anglers often lift the bait well off the bottom to increase visibility and then drop it quickly to create a thumping vibration.

Heavy tackle is generally preferred for halibut fishing because of the weight of the objects fished, the depth, and the size of the fish possible. A 7-foot boat rod with a stiff action, equipped with 4/0 conventional reel, is standard. For shallow-water fishing, though, some anglers fish much lighter tackle, and deep monster chasers may go heavier. Light-tackle halibut anglers use line in the 15- to 50-pound-test range, but deep-water anglers go heavier.

See: *Individual states and provinces; individual species; Drift Fishing; Jigging.*

INTERMEDIATE LINE
A slow-sinking fly line.
See: *Flycasting Tackle.*

INTERNATIONAL GAME FISH ASSOCIATION

Known by the acronym IGFA, this nonprofit membership association was founded in 1939 primarily to establish ethical angling regulations and to serve as a central processing center for saltwater world record catch data. Today, it verifies and designates all freshwater and saltwater world record fish catches; creates and maintains the ethical standards and rules used in most fishing tournaments and for world record consideration; serves as an information source for the media, governments, scientists, and the general public; maintains an historical museum documenting the sport of fishing; has the world's largest, and most current, collection of angling literature; and is a leader in fisheries conservation issues.

The IGFA has more than 300 international representatives around the world. In 1999, it opened a stunning Hall of Fame and Fishing Museum complex and headquarters in Dania, Florida (near Ft. Lauderdale Airport), which houses its staff, historical collections, library, and other information; the center is open to the public and is especially notable for its interactive displays. Its E. K. Harry Library of Fishes, open to the public, has 13,000 books on angling, fish, and related subjects; thousands of past and current outdoor and fishing periodicals, films, and videos; the largest collection of historical fishing photographs in the world; and an array of historical artifacts. It publishes its own newsletter and an annual book, *World Record Game Fishes,* which, among other things, lists all current world records in every category and for every species for which records are maintained.

See: Records.

INTERTIDAL ZONE

The shallow area along shore and in an estuary between high- and low-water marks that is exposed at low tide and covered at high tide; also known as the littoral zone.

I/O

Acronym for Inboard/Outboard Motor and a boat powered with such motor.

See: Boat; Sportfishing Boat.

IOWA

When it comes to angling, this mostly agricultural state is sometimes overshadowed by its Minnesota and Wisconsin neighbors. Yet Iowa has some good fishing that is often overlooked. The fertile soils that grow Iowa's bountiful crops of corn and soybeans also help produce lunker walleye, chunky smallmouths, slab-sided panfish, scrappy trout, and some of the biggest muskies on the continent, not to mention the staple species: channel catfish, largemouth bass, bluegills, and crappie. Improved farming practices and environmental programs—such as the federal Conservation Reserve Program that began in the 1980s—have reduced soil erosion, improved water quality, and boosted fishing.

Replicas of world record fish float in the air in the hall between galleries at the IGFA Hall of Fame and Fishing Museum.

Close-to-home angling opportunities, with lakes, rivers, and ponds within easy reach of nearly every resident, also make fishing a popular family recreation activity throughout Iowa. One in three Iowans fishes. But they're not elitists; they like action, and they like to eat what they catch.

Thus, channel catfish—prized for both action and table fare—are the most sought-after quarry in Iowa's rivers and lakes. Bass fishing is also extremely popular in Iowa, and the feisty largemouth bass ranks a close second in angler preference. Yet, as in many other states, Iowans take home more bluegills and crappie than any other species, proving their appreciation for a delectable skillet of panfish fillets, even if they don't land a wall hanger.

Natural Lakes

The glaciers that shaped Iowa's prime farmland also scooped out more than 30 natural lakes, totaling 33,000 acres, in northwest Iowa. Residents boast that these waters offer some of the state's best fishing. One of these is 5,700-acre Spirit Lake, the largest natural lake in the state. Spirit owns the Iowa muskie record of more than 45 pounds. Muskie anglers regularly catch and release 50-inch fish around Spirit's weedbeds.

In nearby West Okoboji, biologists confirm bass anglers' beliefs that this deep, clear lake is one of the best in the country for smallmouths. Probing the rock piles with live baits in the fall, smallmouth specialists take plenty of fish over 5 pounds, and most of the bass are released.

Spirit, West Okoboji, and East Okoboji Lakes produce a ton of walleye, too. Some walleye fanciers wade the shoreline on spring and fall nights, casting crankbaits. Others troll with live baits or diving lures along weedlines in the summer. Ice anglers sometimes hit the jackpot with jigging spoons or minnows.

Clear, Storm, Black Hawk, and Lost Island Lakes, all of which are natural lakes in the northwest quadrant of Iowa, share walleye honors. In winter, aerators installed by the Department of Natural Resources (DNR) replenish oxygen in the shallow waters, reducing fish losses and boosting productivity. The aerators have expanded fishing success in lakes that formerly could not sustain gamefish through Iowa's snowy, cold winters.

Even with all the limelight on bass, walleye, and muskies, many vacationers visit Iowa's natural lakes primarily to catch lots of perch, bluegills, crappie, and bullhead. These species may be less sophisticated, but they subsidize many bait shops and resorts. Spring spawning may be the best time for both bullhead and bluegills, but summer anglers also catch big bluegills in the cool shade of boat docks. Try perch in the fall, or through the ice.

Border Rivers

Mississippi River. If you want an argument, just try to persuade a Mississippi River rat that there's any place better to fish. The "Father of Waters" flows 300 fishable miles along the state's eastern border. It's a 190,000-acre maze of backwaters, chutes, islands, running sloughs, and channels. The scenic, wooded bluffs and array of wildlife add aesthetic appeal to a Mississippi River fishing trip.

Although the Mississippi's locks and dams, built in the 1930s, cater to heavy barge traffic, the pools above the dams, and the tailwaters below them—combined with wing dams and rock levees—provide diverse fishing habitat.

Bass, bluegill, and crappie anglers seek the lily pads and submerged vegetation of lakelike shallows. Stump-field remnants—reminders of the forests that once covered the river valley—often hold bass. Some of the biggest panfish come in early winter, when bluegill and crappie anglers swarm to honey holes in the deeper backwaters.

Eddies and current breaks around submerged wing dams can be action-packed in the summer. For variety, a wing dam is the place to be. An angler can fish with a nightcrawler, leech, jig, or crankbait, and may catch walleye, smallmouth bass, white bass, catfish, bluegills, and freshwater drum.

In the spring and fall, walleye and sauger school in swift water near dams, or around gravel bars. Eager anglers may be elbow to elbow on rock riprap or commercial fishing barges. Boats get in line to troll or drift downstream from the churning tailwaters. Heavy rigs—either large jigs or sinkers on a three-way swivel—are a must.

Tournament anglers have discovered the Mississippi, and the river hosts dozens of walleye and bass contests throughout the season. Veteran river anglers usually have the inside track, as it can take a lifetime to learn the subtleties of the ever-changing currents, sandbars, and channels.

Missouri River. Iowa may be "The Land Between Two Rivers," but the Missouri River, which forms most of Iowa's western border, is a mere ghost of the once wild and productive stream that pioneers knew. Channelization destroyed countless pools, cutbanks, sandbars, and oxbows, along with many of the fish. Its waters now are squeezed into a rock canal, rushing past wing dikes—but the resilient Missouri still holds good numbers of big flathead and channel catfish, along with occasional sauger. Anglers who can overcome the limited access and swift current can expect to be rewarded well for their trouble.

Big Sioux River. Iowa's "other" border river, the Big Sioux, winds 130 miles from the Minnesota line to its confluence with the Missouri north of Sioux City. Wooded bends, gravel bars, and occasional rocks make it one of the state's better catfish waters, with a scattering of walleye and smallmouths. For seclusion, try canoeing and fishing the narrow upper stretches.

Interior Rivers

The 19,000 miles of fishable tributaries to the big border rivers bring catfish, walleye, or smallmouth bass within minutes of most Iowans. In the rolling farm country of southwest Iowa, the channel catfish is king. In northeast Iowa's wooded limestone bluffs, smallmouths dominate. Walleye fishing is surprisingly good in many streams wherever there are rocky reaches.

The Des Moines River, which first ambles through Minnesota before cutting 400 miles across the heart of Iowa, typifies river fishing opportunities. Channel catfish love its snags, pools, and gravel bars. Walleye may show up almost anywhere, especially near a couple of big Army Corps of Engineers flood-control impoundments—Red Rock and Saylorville—in Central Iowa.

Veteran anglers always knew where to find pockets of smallmouths in Iowa rivers, but now the secret is out. Length limits on fish caught in all rivers, coupled with catch-and-release mandates on several, have led to a smallmouth boom in most streams with suitable rocky habitat. The best waters are in the northeastern half of Iowa. Favorites include the Upper Iowa, Yellow, Turkey, Maquoketa, Cedar, Winnebago, Middle Raccoon, Iowa, and Boone Rivers. Canoeists can catch some smallmouths, but specialists prefer to wade, casting spinners, leadhead jigs, or crankbaits. Crawdads and minnows can be deadly.

Channel catfish also may grab a bass lure, but serious cat anglers choose live baits or commercial "stink" baits. Savvy cat seekers select their baits by the food that's available. Fishing starts in the spring with sour (rotten) shad or carp for bait. When hot-weather doldrums hit, odoriferous prepared baits are used to get the fish's attention. In late summer, they may feed on grasshoppers, turning to frogs and then minnows in the fall feeding frenzy. Drop the bait where the current can carry it to cats lying in wait under snags or cut banks. But don't pass up pools, riffles, or rocks. A jonboat with a small motor will take a river catfish angler anywhere, but bank or wading anglers catch their share, too.

Biologists fondly call Iowa's prairie streams "catfish factories." Indeed, channel catfish are everywhere, with the possible exception of the coolest, rockiest upper reaches of some creeks. Favorite channel cat rivers include the Boone, Cedar, Chariton, Des Moines, English, Grand, Iowa, Little Sioux, Middle, Nishnabotna, Raccoon, Skunk, and Wapsipinicon.

And don't forget walleye. Anglers who think only of big lakes or the Mississippi River are missing a walleye bonanza in Iowa. Thanks partly to an aggressive state stocking program, many interior rivers hold 10-plus-pound lunkers. Fishing action focuses on low-head dams in the spring, but the walleye don't vanish the rest of the year. Seek them out around rocks and snags in the cleanest, coolest water. The Cedar, Des Moines, Iowa, Raccoon, and Wapsipinicon Rivers rank among the best walleye sites.

Reservoirs

Conservationists still debate the merits of flood-control reservoirs on major rivers, but water regulation issues notwithstanding, four such reservoirs in Iowa offer a variety of fishing opportunities.

Lake Rathbun, an 11,000-acre pool on the Chariton River near Centerville, leads the pack. Rathbun has earned a national reputation as a crappie lake, and regular competitions are held here. The impoundment also produces enough lunker walleye to supply the state's high-tech fish hatchery there, and to draw trophy anglers from all over the region.

Biologists rate Rathbun's catfishing as exceptional. Anglers catch channel cats of all sizes, from pan-size to lunkers pushing 20 pounds. The fastest action typically comes as the shallows begin to warm just after ice out, and the fish devour winter-killed shad and other baitfish. Anglers hold their noses, bait up with evil-smelling cut fish, and hang onto their bucking rods.

White bass add spice to Rathbun's fishing, too. Anglers who find late-summer schools may catch dozens by casting lures or drifting with minnows.

Lake Red Rock, on the Des Moines River downstream from Des Moines, never has drawn as many anglers or produced as many fish as Rathbun. Its fishing goes in spurts, affected primarily by wide fluctuations in water levels, but diehards often find good channel catfish, white bass, or crappie fishing in Red Rock. The tailwaters of the dam also attract hardy winter and early-spring anglers to try for northern pike and walleye.

Saylorville Lake, upstream from Des Moines, is Red Rock's younger and prettier sister. The 5,400-acre reservoir can be crowded with recreationists, but protected shorelines harbor good crappie and channel catfishing, along with largemouth bass and walleye. Hybrid striped bass, called "wiper" here, also provide wild action for fish that may reach 20 pounds.

Coralville Reservoir, built on the Iowa River near Iowa City in the 1950s, may be getting old, but don't count it out for top-notch channel catfishing. The lake grows lots of big flathead catfish, with 10- to 30-pounders common. Coralville also has good numbers of walleye, crappie, and saugeye.

Artificial Lakes

More than 200 artificial lakes, ranging from a few acres to nearly 1,000 acres, put flat-water fishing close to most Iowans. To many anglers, easy access—perhaps near a campground or playground in a county or state park or recreation area—may be more important than a full stringer or livewell. Consider it a bonus that these convenient lakes provide some of Iowa's best largemouth bass, channel catfish, bluegill, and crappie fishing. A few are stocked with walleye or saugeye, too.

The fishing season starts on the ice, when anglers score heavily on bluegills and crappie. The most successful anglers use the lightest tackle, and keep moving until they find the schools.

Come spring, people start catfishing when the ice goes out and the fish feast on winter-killed baitfish. For some of the best results, anglers zero in on lakes where fingerling channel cats are raised in cages on commercial feed before they're allowed to swim free.

Schools of spawning crappie take tiny jigs or minnows around brushpiles or other structure in early May. The bluegill bonanza follows, when the fish move onto their shallow-water, panlike spawning beds.

Bass anglers may cast rocky shorelines, flooded timber, and weedlines all year. As winter approaches, anglers may find the least competition, and the best chance for a lunker largemouth. Nine-hundred-acre Big Creek Lake near Des Moines, one of the state's biggest artificial lakes, has consistently good fishing; but size is only part of the story. Dozens of smaller impoundments fill a real need for close-to-home fishing.

Some favorite artificial lakes in southwest Iowa include Anita, Little River, Twelve Mile, and Green Valley. In southeast Iowa, try Pleasant Creek, Macbride, Sugema, and Geode.

Trout Streams

Tucked away in nine northeastern Iowa counties, 266 miles of spring-fed trout streams provide a sharp contrast to the rest of the state's farm-country rivers and warmwater lakes. But regular stocking of most, along with restrictive regulations on some, have transformed these streams into surprisingly good trout waters. The region's

Flyingfish leap out of the water at an estimated speed of 40 mph, then expand their broad spineless pectoral fins to glide above the surface of the sea.

nickname "Little Switzerland" fits the scene of a fly angler working a clear, rocky pool beside a wooded limestone bluff.

Native brook trout survive in a few sites where they're carefully protected by no-kill rules. Rainbows and browns offer decent put-and-take fishing in many streams. Catchable-size trout are stocked by the DNR in dozens of streams; three-quarters of these are rainbow trout, and the remainder are browns and a few brookies. Not all of these are caught immediately, and some holdovers grow large in secluded pools. Hundreds of brood fish are released in these waters annually as well. A small number of streams are managed as special trout fisheries and are subject to special regulations regarding methods, size, and release requirements. In addition there are 28 streams managed as put-and-grow fisheries where fingerling trout—primarily browns—are stocked.

Farm Ponds

Iowa has 90,000 private ponds, and although public access is restricted, farmers often allow fishing. Most of these ponds average about an acre, although some are substantially larger. With landowner permission, a pond angler may have the best chance of catching a real trophy largemouth bass or bluegill. Most people fish from shore, but a small boat helps when working the edges of aquatic vegetation, where the big fish may lurk.

IRELAND

The westernmost island in the British Isles, the enchanted land of Ireland is recognized as a top angling destination in Europe. Atlantic salmon are the favorite attraction for anglers from across the Atlantic, followed by brown trout and sea trout; however, the country is also known for its excellent numbers and size of coarse species, which attract many European visitors, and also for northern pike. Irish anglers are especially fond of salmon and trout fishing, and they also enjoy saltwater angling for a host of species ranging from shark to cod and bass to pollack.

Situated in the North Atlantic Ocean, Ireland is approximately 500 kilometers long and 300 kilometers wide, with a very high ratio of water to land (1 part water to 35 parts land). There are virtually thousands of lakes and 14,000 kilometers of fish-bearing rivers, plus lengthy canal systems.

The main rivers are the Erne and Shannon, which are actually chains of lakes (loughs) connected by sections of river. The Erne and Shannon respectively drain the northern and central portions of the Midlands; the Shannon is longer and enters the Atlantic via a lengthy estuary.

The Irish climate favors most anglers; prevailing warm, moist winds from the Atlantic produce a temperate climate with moderate summers, mild winters, and adequate rainfall throughout the year. With the warm waters of the North Atlantic Drift lapping the south and west coasts, the climate is milder than Ireland's geographical location would indicate.

With salmon and trout the mainstays, few Irish anglers fish for pike and coarse species, which here mean anything other than species of salmon and trout. Thus, excellent populations of pike, bream, tench, roach, rudd, and eels are largely left to the visiting angler, as is the sea angling, particularly along the south and west coasts.

Established Fisheries Boards operate a continuing research and development program for all fresh and marine waters. Lakes, rivers, and coastal stretches are surveyed and mapped, and fisheries are managed and stocked as appropriate, with banks and access routes to the freshwater's edge developed for direct and easy access.

Most Irish angling opportunities are recognized and organized; well-developed angling centers exist and cater to angling tourists. Hundreds of rivers, streams, and loughs are serviced by hotels, lodges, and gillies (guides). Salmon and trout fisheries are usually the property of an individual, club, organization, or the state, and permission (including a permit) is generally required except in the case of some state lakes, such as the great western loughs and those of Killarney. Some waters, however, are seldom fished.

Gamefishing

The quality of Ireland's gamefishing (trout and salmon) is very good, with many opportunities to angle for wild salmon and trout in natural, undisturbed habitat. The main species here are Atlantic salmon, sea trout, and nonmigratory brown trout, but there are some rainbow trout as well.

Trout. Brown trout are available in almost every stretch of freshwater in Ireland. The average size and coloration vary; limestone rivers and lakes produce the larger fish, which can range from all silver to gold with numerous black and red spots.

Resident anglers tend to concentrate on the loughs for their brown trout fishing, although they never completely ignore the rivers. The great western lakes of Corrib, Mask, Carra, and Conn have long been the main brown trout attractions because of their natural wild fish populations. Developed lakes like Owel and Sheelin in the Midlands are also important. Lough trout tend to average 1 to 2 pounds and are primarily caught by standard fly fishing means or by dapping natural insects on the surface, using a long (14 feet or more) pole and fine monofilament line.

Loughs Corrib, Mask, and Leane have a population of very large browns called "Ferox" trout, which can reach 20 pounds or more; fish in excess of 10 pounds are quite common. They are normally taken by trolling.

In Ireland's thousands of mountain lakes and streams, an exploring angler is likely to catch a number of free-rising and beautifully speckled brown trout that have seldom been covered by a fly. The fish in these less fertile sites may be small, but they provide terrific sport.

In areas with a shortage of readily available trout fishing, the local Fisheries Boards operate regulated fisheries. These are maintained at a very high standard by regular stocking with brown or rainbow trout (rainbows exist only in managed fisheries); opening and closing dates vary, but all are open during the summer.

The Irish records for brown trout are 26 pounds, 2 ounces for a lake fish and 20 pounds for a river fish; trophy, or specimen, fish are those that exceed 10 pounds in lakes and 5 pounds in rivers. Spinning tackle and lures or baits are employed successfully in many locations. Permits are required on very few Irish trout fisheries, but the visitor should inquire. Brown trout fisheries open between mid-February and March 1; most close on September 30, but a few close between mid-September and mid-October.

Salmon and sea trout. Most Irish rivers get a run of salmon. Some may produce only a few salmon to the rod each year, whereas on others many thousands are caught. Most of the better fisheries are privately or club owned and permit costs vary depending on their exclusivity and productivity. No permits are required for the "free" fisheries of Loughs Corrib, Mask, Conn, Leane, and Currane. Gillies and boatmen are available on the more organized fisheries.

Some rivers get an early run of "spring" salmon (from 5 to 10 kilograms) and open to fishing on January 1. "Springers," as they are known, are available in many salmon rivers, although they are notas numerous as grilse; this fishing lasts through April but can extend into May. June sees the beginning of the prolific grilse run. These fish usually weigh less than 3.5 kilograms, and the run extends from June through September. The Irish record for salmon is 57 pounds, and a specimen catch is a 20-pounder.

Visitors should check to make sure that the season is open for any particular salmon water. A small number of salmon and sea trout fisheries open on January 1 each year; others open on various dates up to March 1. Most salmon fisheries close on September 30, although a few close between the end of August and the middle of October.

Some of the country's better known salmon waters are the Rivers Liffey, Drowes, Erriff, Moy, Ballinahinch, Corrib, and Owenea. The Drowes, in northwestern Ireland, is just 6 miles long and drains salmon-holding Lough Melvin. It and the Liffey gather several hundred anglers apiece for January 1 opening-day competition, and the Drowes produces about 1,000 salmon per season, with peak results for large fish in March and for grilse in August and September. The first mile of the Drowes is channeled and flanked by fishing platforms, with lies easy to cast to; the remainder courses through fields and woods.

Many more fish are produced by the Moy, which has become one of Europe's top salmon fisheries since commercial netting and trapping operations were bought out by the Irish government. Fishing rods and angling tourists have replaced the nets and traps, and some of the better pools (Ridge and Cathedral) produce a couple thousand salmon apiece each season.

Some salmon fisheries permit only fly fishing, whereas others allow various methods. Many of the smaller rivers, particularly in western Ireland, require a fresh flood to induce the fish to take freely. When in condition, these spate rivers offer tremendous sport, and six or seven fish to a rod is not uncommon. Although catch-and-release angling for salmon (and trout) is gaining in Ireland, angling for both here is predominantly a catch-and-keep fishery, except for private waters with restrictions that exceed those of the state. This ethic is increasing, however, and with a greater effort at environmental protection and fisheries restoration efforts, there could be a good future, for salmon fisheries in particular.

For salmon fly angling, double-handed 13- to 15-foot rods for a 10- or 11-weight fly line are employed locally, although single-handed 10- to 12-foot rods for 8- or 9-weight lines are used for summer grilse fishing. Bring various densities of line to cope with circumstances. Chest waders are essential for much of the spring and some summer angling.

The main run of sea trout is from June through August, but it can last into September. These fish seem to favor the shorter river systems. Both species can be fished in the rivers or on loughs from boats. Many sea trout fisheries close on September 30, but some close between the end of August and mid-October—like the salmon fishery. A 16-pound, 6-ounce fish holds the Irish record, and a trophy is considered one of 6 pounds or more.

Coarse and Pike Fishing

Although there is some fishing for pike by Irish

Salmon anglers work the River Mourne in Northern Ireland.

anglers, to a large extent both pike and coarse fishing are very much the domain of the tourist angler. There are thousands of rivers and lakes, and miles of clean canals, packed with well-conditioned bream, rudd, roach, tench, hybrids species, and pike, and these all offer good fishing in tranquil and idyllic rural surroundings. Ireland is known for its superior coarse fishing opportunities throughout Europe, and it attracts dedicated coarse anglers.

The Tourism Board, together with national and local groups, develops coarse fisheries for visiting anglers, and in many places they have provided access points, including footbridges and platforms, to facilitate shore fishing. Charts of developed sites are available locally and from the Fisheries Boards.

Coarse angling is largely focused around fishing centers in towns and villages where experienced providers specialize in servicing angling tourists. There may be many lakes and rivers within reach of a center, and local information is always available. Baits for coarse angling are widely available from tackle shops and bait suppliers in the majority of angling centers, but prior notice is always advisable. Visiting anglers are advised to order in advance.

There is no closed season for coarse angling in Ireland, but there are best periods for the various species. Bream and rudd feed mostly from mid-April through October. Roach are at their best during the colder winter months but are available for much of the year. Tench fishing is best in May and June. Unlike salmon and trout, Irish anglers return all coarse fish alive.

Pike fishing is good throughout the year, but it is at its best during the cooler fall months. Specimen pike (30 pounds in lakes and 20 pounds in rivers) can be taken at any time; Irish pike records are a lake fish of 42 pounds and a river fish of 38 pounds, 2 ounces.

Sea Fishing

Beach, estuary, nearshore, and deep-sea angling opportunities exist along the 3,000 miles of Irish coastline. This includes steep and shingle beaches in the lightly indented east; quiet backwaters and estuaries as well as snug harbors in the south; and massive cliff faces, roaring storm beaches, and hundreds of small islands on the west and northwest.

The most commonly encountered species along the Irish coasts are sharks, tope, ray, skate, monkfish, pollack, coalfish, cod, ling, conger, and various dogfish, flatfish, and gurnard. Angling launches (small party boats up to 45 feet long) are located at harbors all around the coast and generally accommodate up to 10 anglers, with gear on board for rent. Some specialize in fishing over submerged wrecks for large ling, conger, and pollack. Along the east coast and in sheltered bays and estuaries of the south and west, fishing from small dory-type boats is increasing in popularity, and excellent catches are being recorded.

The piers, beaches, and rocky ledges of Ireland's shoreline produce an incredible range of fish. Most of the species already mentioned (including sharks) are also available. Tope, ray, cod, bass, flounder, turbot, conger, wrasses, coalfish, pollack, and dogfish make up the bulk of the catch. Much of this fishing requires little experience, and maps guiding visitors to local hotspots are available from the Central Fisheries Board.

Especially favored fish include mackerel, which are common and sometimes numerous on all coasts; European bass, which primarily inhabit estuaries and beaches south of Galway on the west and south of Dublin on the east, although their numbers have decreased substantially in recent times; pollack, which are taken from both boat and shore on all coasts; and cod, which are also caught off all coasts and are most common in May and June from boats, and in December and January from shore.

Regulations

Fisheries in Ireland are managed by the Central Fisheries Board (in Dublin) and seven regional Fisheries Boards. These were established to protect, develop, and promote all forms of sportfishing; they are not profit-making, and their income is devoted to fisheries management and conservation. For sea angling, the boards update and issue maps and guides of shore, small-boat, and deep-sea angling opportunities. They have developed hundreds of coarse angling lakes, especially catchments at Shannon and Erne, and prepared many watercourses for angling. They manage 150,000 acres of lakes and more than 1,000 miles of rivers and streams for trout fishing. They also manage and control many quality salmon waters, including the Erriff in Connemara, the Galway Weir Fishery, the Lower Lee in Cork, the Owenea in Donegal, and the Glenamoy Bunowen and Carrowinskey in May. Details on these activities are available directly from the boards.

A state (national) angling license is required to fish for salmon and sea trout on private and public waters. This license is available from the Fisheries Boards and from larger tackle shops and angling outfitters. A permit is also required from the owner or manager of a private fishery, and regulations at such a location may differ from those established by the state. Few regulations exist for pike, coarse, and inland trout fisheries, although this is changing under the establishment of local fisheries cooperatives, which may issue permits for regional fishing.

The Central Fisheries Board has provided a general guide to sportfishing in Ireland, and the Irish Tourist Board has general information as well.

ISRAEL

A small country of just 21,596 square kilometers, with a short rainy season, chronic water shortage, and a few rivers that are largely dried up, Israel would not seem to offer much in the way of sportfishing opportunity. Indeed, although there are reports of some freshwater angling in this narrow 420-kilometer-long country, and although Israel has 195 kilometers of western and largely unindented coastline bordering the Mediterranean Sea, it is the narrow tip of southern Israel bordering the Red Sea that is known to provide opportunities for pelagic species, in a location with generally calm waters protected by the Sinai Mountains.

The port of Eilat affords access to the Gulf of Aqaba, a narrow arm of the Red Sea bordered mostly by Saudi Arabia and Egypt, with a small northern portion bordered by Jordan and a comparatively tiny section bordered by Israel. Eilat is a bustling site, with luxury hotels, a fishing center, and a marina that houses a number of charter boats.

This portion of the Red Sea is known for crystal clear waters and has attracted divers for decades. Offshore game species include sailfish, swordfish, yellowfin tuna, bonito, dolphin, barracuda, amberjack, mako sharks, and blue sharks.

The area close to Eilat in the northern part of the Gulf of Aqaba offers some fishing, but considerable pleasure-boat activity, much of it stemming from adjoining Jordan, is intrusive. Ras Borka, 40 miles south of Eilat, is a popular site. The Straits of Tiran are also notable; this passage to the deep waters of the Red Sea is more than 150 kilometers from Eilat, and beyond it lie numerous islands and the tip of the Sinai Peninsula at Egypt's Sharm el-Sheik. In the past, overnight and multiday trips have been made to this region, where the fishing is reportedly outstanding. Nevertheless, security concerns are ever-present in this region and may restrict boat travel.

ITALY

One of the most geographically varied countries on the European continent, Italy comprises territory that ranges from the rolling, fertile plains of the Piemonte and Tuscany hills to the southern Calabrian bushes, and from the wide-open croplands of the Central Emilia to the peaks of the Alps and the Dolomite Mountains in the north. And although all of Italy's diverse regions amply address most cultural interests, outdoor travelers can easily look to Italy's sportfishery alone for a satisfying visit.

Surrounded on most of its borders by the Mediterranean Sea, Italy offers excellent saltwater sportfishing, especially for tuna, billfish, and numerous inshore and bottom species. In addition to possessing two of the Mediterranean's most prolific seas, the Adriatic and the Thyrrenian, the country contains literally hundreds of rivers, lakes, natural and artificial drains, dams, gravel pits, streams, marshes, and river mouths. Excellent road and rail systems, an abundance of top-rated accommodations, and appealing amenities allow anglers to pursue their passion in comfort. Furthermore, many world-renowned sites, such as Venice, Florence, Rome, Milan, and Naples, are only a few miles from the best fishing hotspots, whether the focus is giant bluefin tuna or trout.

Although Italy's climate has considerable regional variations, temperatures remain uniformly pleasant throughout the year. The best time for saltwater fishing is March through November, and for freshwater fishing from mid-February through December.

Freshwater

Sportfishing practices in Italy are varied, as befits the country's geographic, ethnic, sociological, and even political diversity. Such dissimilar locales as Sicily and Piemonte, Calabria and Veneto, Puglie and Sardinia, and their wide range of water types, provide a little something for everyone.

Freshwater stocks in Italy include about 80 species, although only a handful are avidly pursued by anglers. Their presence and distribution has been shaped by many factors, predominantly climate.

The most important angling species in the northern and central regions are rainbow trout, lake trout, brown trout, grayling, whitefish, barbel, catfish, pike, perch, tench, carp, chub, dace, bream, and roach. In the southern regions anglers primarily target rainbow and brown trout, carp, chub, dace, bream, and roach. The following species, imported and introduced into Italy essentially at the end of the nineteenth century, came from the United States, Canada, and Russia: largemouth bass, smallmouth bass, lake trout, zander, sunfish, catfish, wels, brook trout, and rainbow trout.

Recreational fishing in Italy has been practiced since at least the beginning of the eighteenth century, when rods, lines, and live baits were used for barbel, perch, tench, grayling, brown trout, carp, chub, dace, bream, and roach. Since the 1980s, increased use of spinning and fly tackle has revolutionized fishing in both freshwater and saltwater, but especially the former.

The majority of Italian anglers fish with floats, primarily seeking coarse species belonging to the cyprinid family. The most common freshwater technique is ledgering *(see)*, also known as *pesca all'inglese* and *roubaisienne,* because it was imported respectively from the United Kingdom and France.

Coarse fishing is highly specialized here, as elsewhere in Europe, and competitive fishing has a strong following. Italy is the most passionate and intense match fishing nation in the world (England is not far behind), and Italian match anglers are eager to learn new methods to increase their success. They have excelled in international championship match fishing events and won numerous world titles.

Italy's climate and geography influence the main coarse fishing techniques, making them different from those in western Europe. All beginners and professionals use telescopic rods, and the preferred quarry is *arborella* (bleak), a species similar to the emerald shiner *(see)* and very abundant across the country. Italians have mastered the art of catching these small fish at high speed in a three-hour com-

 Forty-five American states have officially designated state fish; top recipients: brook trout (8), cutthroat trout (7); only 3 states have freshwater and saltwater designees.

petition (most of the top match anglers can catch 1,500 of these quick silver fish in this time span).

A unique method of coarse fishing, called *bolognese,* developed on the Po River around Bologna. It incorporates a telescopic rod with a reel and allows the angler to fish with a fixed float at depths up to 28 feet. Anglers can cast these rigs 50 yards and present their baits perfectly, even in fast flows.

Italians are developing an interest in casting with lures for appropriate species in private lakes and gravel pits. This interest is met to some extent by the development of put-and-take lakes in all regions of the country. In these waters, which are mostly small, the endemic species have often been eliminated by rotenone poisoning, and restocking has included rainbow trout, carp, and largemouth bass, with the trout and bass being of interest to those casting lures.

Interest in angling for cyprinids (carp and chub, among others), generically referred to as carp fishing, is on the rise. Among members of fishing clubs, carp and related species are often the objects of specimen hunting—the focused pursuit of large or trophy fish; this type of angling has become more popular, and cyprinids are also the principal target of fishing competitions in open waters.

Most freshwater anglers in Italy use baits and apply various technical methods locally referred to as *bolognese, inglese, canna fissa, roubaisienne,* and *al tocco,* either with spinning or fly tackle. Anglers are organized by the Italian Sport Fishing Association (FIPSAS), which has more than 350,000 members.

Italy is divided into many fishing districts that have adopted different regulations and seasons. A national license is required. Detailed information on regulations, as well as maps, brochures, and guides, can be obtained by contacting the local FIPSAS office.

Species

For Italians, the most important family of fish is the cyprinids, due not only to the relatively large number of species they represent (approximately 25), but also to their traditional significance in Europe. More than two-thirds of anglers here are pole fishermen (bank anglers using poles from 7 to 18 meters long) who catch roach, bream, chub, tench, and common carp.

In most of the larger streams that flow through the plains, cyprinids are the species best equipped to resist pollution, even benefiting from some of its environmental effects. These species have increased rather significantly since the 1960s; at the same time, however, their natural predators (perch, zander, and pike) have suffered declines.

Salmonids are the second most important family of fish. Brown trout, which are native to Italy, and the introduced rainbow trout and lake trout (actually a charr), are the mainstays, the latter especially in the northern regions. Brown trout average 2^1/$_2$ pounds in the northern and central regions and 1^1/$_2$ pounds elsewhere. European grayling are still rather strongly represented in the northern regions of Piemonte, Veneto, Lombardia, Friuli-Venezia Giulia, and Trentino-Alto Adige. Brook trout are found in the north as well, and can be caught in the streams, lakes, and ponds of Veneto, Lombardia, Piemonte, Liguria, and Trentino-Alto Adige.

Most of these species are pursued by dedicated specialists, especially fly anglers.

Perch, zander, and pike are of interest to Italian anglers. Zander have spread throughout northern and central Italy by migrating among waterways and also through direct importation. Zander represent the second major carnivorous species (wels being first), and where it has prospered it has done so at the expense of northern pike. Pike are prized in Italy, as they are throughout Europe, and large pike are in the dreams of every Italian freshwater angler, although the average size is close to 8 pounds. Pike are fairly numerous in major rivers and lakes in the northern and central regions, and less prominent in the south due to the scarcity of large rivers and lakes.

Other species with constituencies include eels, which are popular throughout the country but especially in the Veneto region (Comacchio Valleys); the Twaite shad, which attracts spinning tackle users in the river mouths of the central regions; and the wels catfish, locally known as *siluro,* which can exceed 500 pounds and has become common in the Po, Italy's greatest river.

Largemouth bass have been introduced throughout northern and central Italy and are prominent in ponds as well as impoundments. Fishing for them became more popular in the 1990s. The fish average 3 pounds and are normally caught on light spinning tackle. Smallmouths have also been introduced into similar waters and in private ponds. Some can be caught in Chiusi Lake in Tuscany, near Florence. A complete list of waters with bass can be obtained from any regional FIPSAS agency. Various sea bass and mullet inhabit the country's numerous river mouths and are popular among anglers who also fish in freshwater.

Northern Region

In the mountainous far north, numerous rivers and streams flow down from the Alps and the Dolomite Mountains into long, narrow, and lush river valleys that resemble linear oases and form beautiful lakes. Due to their isolation, most of these spectacular rivers receive low resident pressure, so the quality of fishing is generally very good.

Within easy driving distance from the cities of Milan, Turin, Verona, Udine, and Venice are a numerous sportfishing spots and many reservoirs locally known as *laghetti a pagamento.* The best of them is Naviglio Langosco, which lies in the Lombardia region.

Rivers and streams in northern Italy offer good fishing to both lure and fly anglers, especially for trout and grayling. Small streams fish well with dry flies, whereas larger rivers are productive with nymphs. The best time to fish these waters for trout and grayling is between March and September. Fishing for carp and chub is very good year-round, but summertime is the peak season.

Northern Italy is also famous for its good lake fishing. The most well-known lakes are the Garda, the Maggiore, Como, d'Iseo, Mezzola, and Varese. In these lakes, the major angling interests are brown trout, lake trout, perch, whitefish, and some cyprinids; various methods are permitted, including trolling (locally called *traina a tirlindana*) and casting with lures.

In the central portion of this region, the huge water systems of the Po basin (the 405-mile-long Po is Italy's longest river, navigable for 300 miles, and has numerous tributaries) have contributed much to Italy's reputation as a top European angling spot. In fact, this area is one of the most prolific for chub and wels anywhere in Europe. Chub are generally caught with specific pole techniques that require chumming with a natural chum mix. Bottom fishing from a boat or from a riverbank is the most successful method of catching the huge wels, which are abundant in the Po watershed. Fish over 150 pounds are regularly caught, especially during spring and summer.

The most important rivers for sportfishing in northern Italy are the Po, Ticino, Adige, Tagliamento, Brenta, Sarca, Sesia, Tanaro, Mincio, Adda, Piave, Reno, Dora Baltea, Dora Riparia, Panaro, Taro, Trebbia, and Bormida.

Central Region

The Apennine Mountains are intrinsic to all sections of the central region, especially Emilia-Romagna, Tuscany, Lazio, Marche, Umbria, and Abruzzi. As in the northernmost portion of Italy, numerous rivers and streams flow down from the mountains into long, narrow, and lush river valleys that resemble linear oases and form beautiful lakes and many productive estuaries. Tuscany (Arno River) and Emilia-Romagna are the sources of Italy's long-established sportfishing and hunting traditions, and all important national sportfishing magazines have their headquarters in Florence, the capital of Tuscany.

Sportfishing here is conducted using traditional techniques. Various trout, pike, chub, and other cyprinids are the locally favored species. The most important rivers include the Tevere, Sieve, Tronto, Secchia, Arno, Ombrone, Marecchia, Metauro, Esino, Chienti, and Nera.

Central Italy is also famous for its good lake fishing. The best-known lakes are the Trasimeno, Bolsena, Corbara, Chiusi, Massaciuccoli, Montepulciano, Bracciano, Occhito, Lesina, Piediluco, and Vico. In these lakes, the major interests for anglers are brown trout, perch, pike, and some cyprinids; various methods are permitted, including trolling, fly fishing, and casting with lures.

Southern Region

Southern Italy has numerous rivers and streams with stocked trout and coarse species. On the two major islands, Sicily and Sardinia, freshwater is restricted to a few rivers and lakes due to the warm climate. Several streams and ponds in the interior of these areas are accessible by a series of both paved and woods roads, and offer good fishing for chub and brown trout.

The most important rivers and streams for sportfishing in southern Italy are the Sangro, Liri, Biferno, Volturno, Sele, Calore, Ofanto, Bradano, Fortore, Carapelle, Basento, Agri, Crati, Neto, Simeto, Belice, Platani, and Salso. Most of these rivers are beautiful and, due to their isolation, receive low resident angling pressure, so the quality of the fishing is generally very good

Brown trout, perch, pike, chub, barbel, and other cyprinids are the main species.

Pole fishing with natural baits (worms or insects), and casting artificials with spinning and fly tackle, are prevalent techniques here.

Saltwater

Italy is comprised of three geographically separate and distinct saltwater sportfishing areas: the Adriatic coast, the Thyrrenian coast, and the territory around the Big Islands. The latter includes Sicily and Sardinia; two smaller and isolated deep south-oriented islands, Lampedusa and Pantelleria; and numerous small archipelagos. Each area boasts distinct but varied saltwater sportfishing opportunities.

A terrific brown trout from one of northern Italy's rivers.

Adriatic Sea

The Adriatic Sea can be compared to the Sea of Cortez in Baja California, Mexico, as it is enclosed between the Italian peninsula and the former country of Yugoslavia. This 430-mile-long basin consists of two main fishing territories: the North Adriatic, from Venice to Porto San Giorgio, which has a long, narrow, sandy-gold shoreline; and the Central Adriatic, from Porto San Giorgio to Santa Maria di Leuca, which has a rocky shoreline with some short white-sand beaches.

The major angling interest in the Adriatic is the giant bluefin tuna, although considerable enthusiasm is devoted to blue and thresher sharks, albacore, mackerel, and sea bass.

The bluefin tuna was likely the first big-game species encountered by fishermen in this region. They were subsistence fishermen, however, and far removed from the sophisticated population inhabiting Italy today. History suggests that the earliest meetings between tuna and man occurred in the Mediterranean Sea. The northern bluefin began its trek toward exploitation well before the birth of Christ. More than 4,000 years ago, the Phoenicians used the first rudimentary net traps in the Mediterranean to catch this species. The design of nets to catch these formidable fish has been handed down through the centuries, and today two remaining descendants of the practice, called *tonnare,* are still in operation out of Sicily—living legends and the last keepers of an old way of life on the sea.

It was not until the 1970s, however, that the first giant bluefin tuna was caught with rod and reel by trolling a dead mackerel just off the mouth of the Po River in the Adriatic Sea. This discovery became a catalyst for many inshore anglers, who decided to outfit their boats for tuna. The true impetus behind Italy's bluefin sportfishery, however, was importation from the United States and France of drift-and-chum fishing tactics.

Schools of tuna of all sizes were spotted practically all along the peninsula in every region of the country. By the 1980s and early 1990s, hundreds of giants had been caught under International Gamefish Association (IGFA) rules and Italian law. (Italy allows only one bluefin tuna boated per day per boat, except during sanctioned tournaments.) The anglers observed that each size of bluefin—small (up to 70 pounds), medium (70 to 200 pounds), and giant (up to 900 pounds)—did not intermingle and engaged in different seasonal movements. It was eventually learned that small bluefin frequent the southern Adriatic, Ionian, and Ligurian Seas; medium-size bluefin run all along the Thyrrenian, Ligurian, and central Adriatic Seas; and giant bluefin prefer the Sardinian and Sicilian water, and the northern and central Adriatic Sea.

In late spring, after having spawned in the cool waters of the Ionian and Aegean Seas, hungry bluefin scatter in two main directions to pursue huge schools of bait. One moves toward the Adriatic Sea, the other passes through the Sicilian and Sardinian Channels to enter the Thyrrenian and Sardinian Seas.

In this erratic period, the bluefin that have gone the Adriatic way will follow the warm northward surface current that passes close to the Yugoslavian coast, arriving at their final destination in the northern Adriatic in early summer. Some schools of tuna are turned westward in the central Adriatic by a frontal eddy formed around Gargano's Promontory, so the first giants arrive in the southern Adriatic in late spring.

The majority of giant bluefin remain in the shallow waters of the northern Adriatic until early fall, when they return to the eastern Mediterranean, following the hot southward surface current that passes close to the Italian peninsula. They return to the central Adriatic in late autumn.

In essence, the giant bluefin tuna season in the northern Adriatic runs from June through November; July, August, and September are the peak months. In the central Adriatic, giants run from April through December; May, August, September, and October are the peak months. The medium and small bluefin frequent the deeper waters off the central and southern Adriatic year-round. Fishing opportunities for medium tuna peak in spring and winter, and for small tuna in autumn.

At the beginning of the fishing season in the northern Adriatic Sea, giants feed more than 30 miles offshore from Chioggia, Albarella, Porto Garibaldi, Porto Barricata, Rimini, and Pesaro. All of the northern Adriatic Sea is characterized by shallow depths (maximum of 90 feet) and by an extremely variable demarcation line between the inshore and offshore waters. For these reasons the local sportfishing boats, which are small but fast, mount their fighting chair on the bow, so the skipper can chase the big tuna during their long, shallow runs.

The central Adriatic has a longer fishing season, and giants are landed from modern marinas at Pesaro, Porto San Giorgio, Numana, San Benedetto del Tronto, Pescara, and Termoli. It is possible at these sites to charter well-equipped sportfishing boats with experienced skippers and mates who have countless giants to their credit.

Incidental catches while drifting for bluefin tuna include thresher sharks, blue sharks, and swordfish. During the off-season for bluefins, however, anglers can count on a lot of sharks, particularly blues (February through May) and threshers (year-round), together with green mackerel sharks (November through May), and sea bass (year-round). These fish are regularly caught on light drifting tackle.

Thyrrenian and Ligurian Seas

In the early 1980s, the good news concerning the bluefin tuna boom in the Adriatic encouraged anglers in western Italy to give it a try. The bottom

---

The earliest, nearly complete fish fossils were discovered in sandstone near Alice Springs in central Australia in the mid-1960s and have been dated at 470 million years old.

structure of the Thyrrenian and Ligurian Seas differs greatly from that of the Adriatic. These have deeper waters, and current patterns are particularly influenced by the winds. The western fleets must operate in harder conditions than their Adriatic counterparts, so they tend to mount the fighting chair on the stern and back down while fighting big bluefins.

The tuna fishing operations in the Thyrrenian Sea start in May and June, when the giants invade northwestern Sicily and southwestern Sardinia, passing through the Sicilian and Sardinian Channels. The so-called Sicilian giants move northward in early July, reaching the central Thyrrenian area in August and September, and the northern Thyrrenian and the Ligurian Seas in September and October. The Sardinian schools move northward toward France in July and August, joining the Sicilian groups in September and October. In the southern Ionian Sea, the giants run plentiful in July and August.

The average weight for giants in the Thyrrenian Sea is around 250 pounds, about 180 pounds less than the Adriatic standard. Small and medium bluefins can be caught here in late spring and autumn all along the coasts, about 25 miles offshore.

Through the 1990s, Thyrrenian anglers documented many zones where giant and medium bluefins were most frequently caught by drifting. They vary somewhat from year to year, and each bluefin tuna port has its own prime areas. Many of the best tuna zones are along the 60-fathom curve, between 10 and 40 miles off the coast.

Big concentrations of giants are reported in late spring off Palermo and the Egadi and Eolie Islands in Sicily, and off Portoscuso in Sardinia; summer hotspots are the along the west coast of Sardinia, the Pontine Islands, San Felice Circeo, Anzio, and Civitavecchia. In late summer, prime hotspots include Livorno, Marina di Cecina, Piombino, and Siracusa.

As a result of the country's productive angling, the Italian coasts are dotted with giant bluefin ports that offer good marina facilities and excellent accommodations. Among the most notable are Pesaro in the Adriatic Sea, and Livorno, Palermo, and Siracusa in the Thyrrenian Sea. These latter three ports have excellent restaurants, hotels, marinas, and the best skippers and boats in Italy. During the height of the tuna fishing season, it may be hard to find space, so it is a good idea to make reservations well in advance for accommodations, charter boats, and flights.

In the same months, anglers can troll or drift with live baits and light tackle in inshore waters and catch other gamefish, including amberjack, snapper, grouper, bluefish, and garrick.

Fishing in the estuaries of central Italy is very popular, and species pursued include chub, garrick, sea bass, snapper, jacks, drum, bream, mullet, flatfish, and rays.

In virtually all the estuaries, once the water level drops, big gutters appear along the muddy banks. Casting shallow-running or surface lures or live mullet into the head of the gutter is a locally proven method for catching these species. The best prospects for shore angling are from the end of May until September.

The Big Islands

The territory of the Big Islands includes Sicily and Sardinia, the smaller and southerly Lampedusa and Pantelleria Islands, and such small archipelagos as the Egadi, Eolie, Pontine, Tremiti, and Tuscany Islands. Each island boasts various sportfishing opportunities whether one is angling from shore or boat.

Surf casting and rockfishing all along the wide beaches and rocky shorelines of western Sardinia and northern Sicily provide the best possibilities for barracuda, jacks, sharks, snapper, drum, grouper, rays, and sea bass. These species are also available in the estuaries, as are garrick, which are plentiful in the murky waters.

The species regularly caught around the islands by surf casting and rockfishing include bluefish, bonito, sea bass in great quantities, garrick, snapper, bream, croaker, amberjack, and various other jacks.

Many red and gray sea bream and grouper are caught by bottom fishing and light tackle casting; amberjack, garrick, tuna, sea bass, and snapper can be caught by light-tackle trolling in inshore waters. The season is year-round, with increased activity from September through November.

Fantastic action for spearfish and broadbill swordfish is available around all these islands; some big spearfish cruise these waters. Local anglers show a lot of interest in these species, and in giant bluefin tuna in the same areas and the same seasons.

Most bluefins landed by anglers succumb to drifting dead sardines. In certain areas, such as Siracusa and Marina di Ragusa in Sicily, some anglers pursue bluefins by trolling small feather jigs in October and November, catching up to five fish per day in the 15- to 70-pound range.

Others use the same tease-and-bait methods for spearfish that are applied elsewhere for sailfish, resulting in record-size specimens. The biggest Mediterranean spearfish run in the Straits of Messina from August through November, when fish in excess of 100 pounds are common.

The 60-fathom curve, and the numerous banks off all these islands, produce a good number of broadbill swordfish. Local charter boats assure good swordfish action from April through December, with May through July the peak months. These efforts sometimes produce up to four strikes per night, although the fish rarely exceed 100 pounds.

In Italian waters, swordfish are taken in one of two ways: the classic sight fishing, which consists of seeking, spotting, and presenting a dead and/or live natural bait to the finning fish in daylight conditions; and night fishing by drifting a dead or live squid over canyons, banks, and submerged sea mountains. The latter is the more modern and successful method, and it is most popular with Italian anglers because it can be applied year-round with practically the same chance of success (daylight swordfishing is effective only during their spawning season around the islands from March through May), and because there are fewer swords finning due to severe commercial overfishing. Each method, however, requires skill, preparation, hard work, vigilance, and concentration.

Fishing for broadbills, especially at night, requires increased sophistication in boats, tackle, and crews. This results in additional costs to those chartering a boat to seek this species.

IVORY COAST

Côte d'Ivoire, or the Ivory Coast, is situated about 5° to 10° above the equator on the western coast of Africa. Its southern boundary and coastal region face the Atlantic Ocean and the Gulf of Guinea; to the east lies Ghana, which has the greatest commercial fishing fleet in all of Africa. The Ivory Coast is a leading country of the African continent, serving as both an international crossroads for commerce and a vacation favorite, and it is widely known for its hospitality.

Much of the Ivory Coast is a flat, forest-covered plain; it has golden beaches and a number of mangrove lagoons to the east in the regions of Abidjan and Assinie, and to the extreme east in the regions of Tabou and Grand Bereby. The several rivers here are navigable for short distances and are subject to low water during the dry season. The climate along the southern region is tropical—hot and humid. The wet season, which brings periods of heavy rain, runs from May through October.

The Ivory Coast boasts some of the best blue marlin fishing in the eastern Atlantic, especially during the two peak seasons of November/December (descending migration) and March/April (ascending migration). It is one of the few spots where one can rely on two distinct annual blue marlin migrations, but—depending on a combination of such factors such as wind, current, and water temperature changes—both migrations could be year-round events.

The main reason for the aggregation of billfish, tuna, wahoo, and other species off the entire coast of West Africa is the shifting frontal zone of the Canary Current and the Equatorial Countercurrent, which particularly affects the Ivory Coast ports of Abidjan and San Pedro.

Known as the "Pearl of Lagoons," the city of Abidjan hosts one of the oldest sportfishing centers in Africa, the Marlin Club. Sportfishing and accommodation arrangements are handled by the Mobaya Club (18 BP 347, Abidjan, Côte d'Ivoire; phone: 225-326532; fax: 225-331064), which hosts a good five-boat offshore charter service.

Oversize blue marlin, yellowfin tuna, and wahoo are caught just 45 minutes from the docks of the Mobaya Club Marina. Fifteen miles offshore is a large underwater valley called "The Boulevard," an area between two oil-drilling platforms. The Boulevard is an east-west-oriented rectangle, 30 miles long and 3 miles wide, with a depth that varies from 360 to 760 feet. Inside its perimeter are two fishing zones named "Jacqueville" and "Belier," where blue marlin hunt down tuna and wahoo.

Since 1988, another port on the Ivory Coast, San Pedro, has gained notoriety for large blue marlin. Two hundred miles west of Abidjan, it is the main city of the Ivory Coast's southwest region, and its nearby waters have gained international attention. Despite its reputation, however, San Pedro remains relatively undiscovered, and only a few professional charter boats are available at Club Nautique, where the local sportfishing boats are moored.

The blue marlin fishing zone in front of San Pedro is an ample one. The continental shelf is just 10 miles from port, parallel to the African perimeter. The bottom gradually drops from 180 to 420 feet, then plunges thousands of feet in a span of only 4 miles. All along this passage, constant trade winds and powerful currents create numerous upwellings and provide good concentrations of baitfish.

The typical fishing day here is long—about 11 hours—because the captains are committed to covering as much ground as possible during the day. The boats usually leave the dock at 8 A.M. and, after a 30-minute run, begin trolling in 240 feet of water, where blue marlin frequently chase baitfish into inshore waters. According to local anglers, marlin change direction in midmorning, turning toward the dropoff to find cooler water. The boats troll the dropoff until 3 P.M., then resume inshore trolling for several hours. The weekend captains sometimes work an enormous seamount, 35 miles from the coast, which rises from 3,000 to 900 feet.

The weather and sea conditions are usually good in the Gulf of Guinea, which partly explains the small- and medium-size charter boats found there. Arrangements for anglers fishing out of Club Nautique are handled at the four-star Balmer Hotel, 2 miles from San Pedro and a 10-minute car ride from the airport and marina.

The Ivory Coast also has untapped inshore and estuary fishing potential due to the presence of four large rivers that are navigable for short distances and have related estuaries. These are the Cavally and Sassandra Rivers near San Pedro, and the Bandama and the Comoé Rivers near Abidjan. All hold huge tarpon, snapper, jacks, grouper, barracuda, and sharks. Arrangements to fish these areas can be made through the Mobaya Club and the Hotel Balmer.

Conversion Charts

THE SYSTEM OF WEIGHTS AND MEASURES USED IN MOST COUNTRIES AND IN ALL SCIENTIFIC work is the International System of Units (SI), which is commonly referred to as the metric system. A notable and influential exception to this is the United States, where the general public, and non-scientific publications, use the U.S., or U.S. customary, system of weights and measures. Throughout the *Ken Schultz's Fishing Encyclopedia & Worldwide Angling Guide*, there is a liberal use of both metric and U.S. customary weights and measures without parenthetical conversions to equivalent weights or measures. Some anglers, especially those who travel widely and those who pay close attention to world-record fish weights and fishing line classifications, are accustomed to both systems, which are often found mixed at boat docks, fish camps, and tackle shops throughout the world. The following information is provided to help the reader make the conversion from one system to another.

U.S. To Metric Conversion Formulas

When You Know...	Multiply By...	To Determine...
Inches (in)	25.4	Millimeters (mm)
Inches (in)	2.54	Centimeters (cm)
Inches (in)	0.0254	Meters (m)
Square Inches (sq in)	645.0	Square Millimeters (sq mm)
Square Inches (sq in)	6.45	Square Centimeters (sq cm)
Square Inches (sq in)	0.00064	Square Meters (sq m)
Feet (ft)	30.5	Centimeters (cm)
Feet (ft)	0.305	Meters (m)
Feet (ft)	0.0003	Kilometers (km)
Square Feet (sq ft)	0.093	Square Meters (sq m)
Fathoms (fath)	1.827	Meters (m)
Fathoms (fath)	0.0018	Kilometers (km)
Yards (yd)	0.914	Meters (m)
Square Yards (sq yd)	0.836	Square Meters (sq m)
Statute Miles (mi) (5,280 ft)	1.61	Kilometers (km)
Nautical Miles (n mi) (6,020 ft)	1.852	Kilometers (km)
Square Miles (sq mi)	2.56	Square Kilometers (sq km)
Miles per hour (mph)	1.61	Kilometers per hour (kph)
Knots per hour	1.84	Kilometers per hour (kph)
Acres	0.405	Hectares
Ounces of Weight (oz)	28.3	Grams (g)
Ounces of Weight (oz)	0.0283	Kilograms (kg)
Ounces of Fluid (fl oz)	29.6	Milliliters (mL)
Pounds (lb)	454.0	Grams (g)
Pounds (lb)	0.454	Kilograms (kg)
Pints (pt)—U.S.	0.473	Liters (L)
Pints (pt)—Imperial	0.568	Liters (L)
Quarts (qt)—U.S.	0.946	Liters (L)
Quarts (qt)—Imperial	1.14	Liters (L)
Gallons (gal)—U.S.	3.79	Liters (L)
Gallons (gal)—Imperial	4.55	Liters (L)
degrees Fahrenheit (°F)	0.555 (after subtracting 32)	degrees Celsius (°C)

Metric To U.S. Conversion Formulas

When You Know...	Multiply By...	To Determine...
Millimeters (mm)	0.039	Inches (in)
Centimeters (cm)	0.394	Inches (in)
Centimeters (cm)	0.0328	Feet (ft)
Square Centimeters (sq cm)	0.155	Square Inches (sq in)
Meters (m)	39.37	Inches (in)
Meters (m)	3.281	Feet (ft)
Meters (m)	1.09	Yards (yd)
Meters (m)	0.547	Fathoms (fath)
Square Meters (sq m)	1.2	Square Yards (sq yd)
Kilometers (km)	3,279.0	Feet (ft)
Kilometers (km)	1,093.0	Yards (yd)
Kilometers (km)	546.0	Fathoms (fath)
Kilometers (km)	0.621	Statute Miles (mi)
Kilometers (km)	0.545	Nautical Miles (n mi)
Square Kilometers (sq km)	0.386	Square Miles (sq mi)
Kilometers per hour (kph)	0.621	Miles per hour (mph)
Kilometers per hour (kph)	0.545	Knots per hour
Hectares	2.47	Acres
Grams (g)	0.035	Ounces of Weight (oz)
Grams (g)	0.002	Pounds (lb)
Kilograms (kg)	35.2736	Ounces (oz)
Kilograms (kg)	2.2	Pounds (lb)
Milliliter (mL)	0.034	Fluid Ounces (oz)
Liters (L)	2.11	Pints (pt)—U.S.
Liters (L)	1.76	Pints (pt)—Imperial
Liters (L)	1.06	Quarts (qt)—U.S.
Liters (L)	0.880	Quarts (qt)—Imperial
Liters (L)	0.264	Gallons (gal)—U.S.
Liters (L)	0.22	Gallons (gal)—Imperial
degrees Celsius (°C)	1.8 (and add 32)	degrees Fahrenheit (°F)

Table Of Metric and U.S. Equivalent Line Strengths

Metric	U.S. Customary	Metric	U.S. Customary
1 kg	2.2 lb	10 kg	22.0 lb
2 kg	4.4 lb	15 kg	33.0 lb
3 kg	6.6 lb	24 kg	52.8 lb
4 kg	8.8 lb	37 kg	81.4 lb
6 kg	13.2 lb	60 kg	132.0 lb
8 kg	17.6 lb		

Table of Fish Weights

Metric	U.S. Customary	Metric	U.S. Customary
1 kg	2.2 lb	60 kg	132.0 lb
2 kg	4.4 lb	70 kg	154.0 lb
3 kg	6.6 lb	80 kg	176.0 lb
4 kg	8.8 lb	90 kg	198.0 lb
5 kg	11.0 lb	100 kg	220.0 lb
6 kg	13.2 lb	200 kg	440.0 lb
7 kg	15.4 lb	300 kg	660.0 lb
8 kg	17.6 lb	400 kg	880.0 lb
9 kg	19.8 lb	500 kg	1,100.0 lb
10 kg	22.0 lb	600 kg	1,320.0 lb
20 kg	44.0 lb	700 kg	1,540.0 lb
30 kg	66.0 lb	800 kg	1,760.0 lb
40 kg	88.0 lb	900 kg	1,980.0 lb
50 kg	110.0 lb	1,000 kg	2,200.0 lb

www.ingramcontent.com/pod-product-compliance
Lightning Source LLC
Chambersburg PA
CBHW040933240426
43673CB00054B/1966